A Comprehensive Guide to
Child Psychotherapy and Counseling

THIRD EDITION

Christiane Brems

University of Alaska Anchorage

WAVELAND

PRESS, INC.

Long Grove, Illinois

This book is dedicated to Jan Strubel
and his graceful transition to adulthood.

For information about this book, contact:
Waveland Press, Inc.
4180 IL Route 83, Suite 101
Long Grove, IL 60047-9580
(847) 634-0081
info@waveland.com
www.waveland.com

Contents

Preface   vii

PART I: PRELIMINARY ISSUES   1

1   Markers of Effective Child Clinicians   3
Educational Needs and Backgrounds of Child Clinicians   3
Positive Personal Traits of Child Clinicians   6
Common Reactions of Child Clinicians   14
Common Vulnerabilities of Child Clinicians   19
Themes Surrounding Parents and Relationship Issues   22
Challenges in Working with Parents   26
Working with the Special Needs of Children   29
Summary and Concluding Thoughts   33

2   Cultural Sensitivity in Child Therapy and Counseling   34
Ethnic and Cultural Diversity of the United States   36
Becoming a Culturally Sensitive Child Clinician   38
Process Issues in Culturally Sensitive Work with Children   53
Summary and Concluding Thoughts   58

3   A Developmental Context for Child Therapy and Counseling   60
Development: Definition, Influences, and Types   61
Development Made Relevant to Child Clinicians   63
Summary and Concluding Thoughts   75

4   Environments and Materials for Child Therapy and Counseling   84
Physical Layout and Design of the Clinic   85
Features of the Playroom   91
Toys and Materials to Support the Work   97
Summary and Concluding Thoughts   107

5   Legal and Ethical Issues in Child Therapy and Counseling   **108**

Laws and Ethics Codes   110
Informed Consent   111
Confidentiality   113
Limits to Confidentiality: Duties to Warn, Protect, and Report   115
Miscellaneous Other Legal and Ethical Issues   122
Summary and Concluding Thoughts   123

PART II: ASSESSMENT 129

6   The Intake Interview   **131**

Preliminary Data Collection   132
Necessary Information to Be Derived from the Intake Interview   133
Structure of the Intake Interview   140
Intake Interview with the Family   145
Intake Interview with the Parents   151
Intake Interview with the Siblings   156
Intake Interview with the Identified Child   157
Feedback and Recommendations Section of the Intake Interview   164
Summary and Concluding Thoughts   168

7   Supplementary Assessment Strategies   **170**

School Records   170
Previous Treatment Records   173
Referral Sources and Consultation   173
Psychological Assessment   175
Summary and Concluding Thoughts   206

8   Conceptualization and Treatment Planning   **207**

Preparing for Conceptualization: Diagnosis   208
Conceptualization: Understanding Case Dynamics   222
Treatment Planning   230
Summary and Concluding Thoughts   235

PART III: TREATMENT 237

9   A Framework for Child Therapy and Counseling   **239**

Goals for the Therapy and Counseling Process   239
Phases of Child Therapy and Counseling   241
Catalysts for Change   247
Challenges to the Therapy or Counseling Process   266
Summary and Concluding Thoughts   275

10   Using Play in Child Therapy and Counseling   276
Conceptual Background   276
Application to Child Therapy and Counseling   280
Variations on the Technique   282
Practical Implementation   287
Case Example   289
Summary and Concluding Thoughts   299

11   Storytelling in Child Therapy and Counseling   300
Conceptual Background   300
Application to Child Therapy and Counseling   303
Variations on the Technique   310
Practical Implementation   312
Case Example   317
Summary and Concluding Thoughts   322

12   Graphic and Sculpting Art in Child Therapy and Counseling   324
Conceptual Background   325
Application to Child Therapy and Counseling   328
Variations on the Technique   336
Practical Implementation   337
Case Example   339
Summary and Concluding Thoughts   344

13   Behavioral Techniques in Child Therapy and Counseling   346
Conceptual Background   346
Application to Child Therapy and Counseling   353
Variations on the Technique   355
Practical Implementation   364
Case Example   366
Summary and Concluding Thoughts   370

PART IV: TERMINATION 375

14   Creating Thoughtful Endings   377
Types of Endings   378
Natural Termination   379
Preparation for Natural Termination   383
Process of Natural Termination   385
Premature Termination   393
Summary and Concluding Thoughts   396

Bibliography   397
Name Index   419
Subject Index   424

Preface

Welcome to the third edition of *A Comprehensive Guide to Child Psychotherapy and Counseling.* If you are holding this book in your hands to decide whether to buy it, please read on; the information in this preface should help you make up your mind. If you have already purchased it, thank you and enjoy! The preparation of this text was a pleasure, and I hope that the readers of the book not only will learn but will also discover within themselves an enthusiasm for the work described that will translate into a happy and fulfilling career.

Why I Wrote This Book

This book represents the culmination of my personal experiences as a clinician for children, as a supervisor of individuals who wish to learn this skill, and as a teacher who has introduced graduate students to the principles and concepts of conducting child psychotherapy and counseling. It presents a comprehensive metatheoretical approach to working with children age 3 years to approximately 12 years. Its discussions of treatment are geared to both novices and advanced professionals in the mental health field; thus, it provides thorough introductions, definitions of key concepts, and outlines to clarify material.

A Comprehensive Guide to Child Psychotherapy and Counseling addresses several concerns I had developed over the years about existing books written about child therapy.

- The book differs from others in its pragmatic approach to working with children. It is a down-to-earth reference that can be helpful not only to students but also to seasoned professionals. It does not get lost in the intricate details of research but is nevertheless research-based. It provides tables and figures that succinctly summarize material that is important enough to be at a clinician's fingertips.

- The book differs from others in its applied nature. It was written as a companion to the actual process of treatment with children. The sequencing of chapters mirrors the sequence of events in an actual treatment situation, making it possible for clinicians to read along in the book as the treatment of a child unfolds.

- The book differs from others in its theoretical complexity. It does not push any single approach to psychotherapy or counseling. Instead, it provides a thorough metatheoretical foundation for assessment and conceptualization that is conducive to tailored and individualized treatment that is not specific to the clinician, but rather to the child who is being treated.

- The book differs from others in its diversity of presented techniques. Because it is not founded in a single theoretical system or based on a single therapeutic approach, the book offers a broad and creative presentation of techniques, illuminating the great variety of possibilities that can be explored to help children and their families grow in treatment.

- The book differs from others in its ease of presentation. Given that it was conceived as a reference for novices and experts alike, the writing style is clear and jargon-free, which makes concepts easy to read and understand. There are no pretensions, and all aspects of the book were developed to make learning as easy as possible.

For Whom I Wrote This Book

The book is written for students and professionals alike. It has a certain level of sophistication that requires some prior exposure to mental health training. Thus, in an academic setting, it is geared more to graduate students (rather than undergraduate students) who have already taken courses in basic psychotherapy or counseling skills. Despite its advanced nature, the text makes ample use of features that facilitate learning; case examples bring the material alive and help readers better understand the more complex points that are being made in the text.

The book targets any professional or budding professional in a mental health discipline that concerns itself with the mental health of children and their families. Thus, students and practitioners in the following fields should find the *Comprehensive Guide* useful:

- Clinical or counseling psychology
- Counseling or counselor education
- Clinical social work
- Marriage and family counseling
- Child psychiatry
- Psychiatric nursing

What I Cover in the Book

The book, written as a companion to actual treatment with children, is laid out in such a way as to reflect the normal sequencing of events that a clinician encounters over the course of treatment, walking readers through all preliminary and crucial steps of therapy or counseling in four distinct sections of the text:

- The first section prepares clinicians to explore their own personal traits that may facilitate or hinder the work with children, providing thorough overviews of relevant issues in ethics, development, and multicultural psychotherapy and counseling.
- The second section walks child therapists and counselors through the initial stages of intake, assessment, and conceptualization before moving on to therapeutic issues.
- The third section focuses on the therapeutic process and specific techniques in the middle stages of counseling and psychotherapy.
- The fourth section presents a thorough discussion of termination issues.

The conceptual system underlying the book is both theoretical and applied, drawing heavily on developmental, interpersonal, family systems, and self-psychological schools of thought. It integrates the core components of all of these approaches in a clear and concise manner that results in a conceptualization for child treatment that is both complex and practical. Not surprisingly, the book emphasizes the need for intensive assessment to precede conceptualization and treatment planning, which leads to the use of a variety of techniques as dictated by the needs of each individual child and family. The techniques covered in include everything from simple play to storytelling, art, and behavior modification.

Although combining strategies of these diverse approaches may sound incompatible, this approach is a preferable way of conducting work with children. Literature exists that is supportive of psychodynamic and behavioral approaches, and clinical experience has demonstrated that a combination of the two schools of thought is highly successful in creating change in children. Specifically, a comprehensive and integral approach avoids the mistake of disregarding important features in a child's life. Strict adherence to one approach of looking at children is simplistic and disregards the realities of modern life. Children rarely grow up in the vacuum of a nuclear family, and the family is not a simplistic or an easily understood system. Children are profoundly affected by their larger environments and culture, and all of these factors must be considered by clinicians. Similarly, children are not merely the product of cause-and-effect or reinforcement contingencies. Human interactions are much more complex than such a strict behavioral approach would suggest. Nevertheless, behavioral strategies are an important aspect of treatment for children.

What I Chose Not to Do

This book is not to be mistaken as a text on research about child psychotherapy or counseling. It does not cover specifics about matching diagnoses with treatment

approaches. Although such considerations are beginning to appear in the child literature and are no doubt important and valuable, they are beyond the scope of this book.
Here, readers are introduced to the basic and practical principles of direct clinical
work with children. Once these basic principles have been mastered, clinicians are
encouraged to move on to research-focused texts that cover specific findings with
regard to evaluating the appropriateness of various family or child interventions in
relation to specific presenting concerns or diagnoses.

Old and New Features of the Third Edition

It is as important to talk about what is the same in the third edition of *A Comprehensive Guide to Child Psychotherapy and Counseling* as it is to talk about what has
changed. The third edition has not changed the format of the book; it continues to
speak to both the student and the practicing professional; it is still an excellent companion over the course of therapy or counseling for children; it still has many tables
and figures for easy reference; and it still remains theoretically complex, suggesting an
individualized approach to the treatment of each child with whom a clinician works.
Thus, all the features that made the first and second editions of the *Comprehensive
Guide* popular among its readers have been maintained.

To address the fact that the *Comprehensive Guide* was aging rapidly at a time of
many changes and advances in the field, revisions for the third edition were chosen
carefully to bring the book into the new millennium. As such, the following primary
modifications were accomplished:

- A new opening chapter creates an opportunity for readers to explore personal
experiences and features that may support or hinder their work with children.
This new chapter provides a better context for child work and challenges readers to develop self-awareness that can counteract misalignments in the relationships with children and their families.

- Several chapters were reorganized to follow more logically the development of
clinicians as they embark on their work with children. This new order mirrors
the natural flow of work with children from self-exploration to new learning
about special aspects of children (such as diversity and development), to awareness about the special needs and demands of children as related to environmental, legal, and ethical issues.

- The section on assessment instruments was revised thoroughly to bring it up to
date. If revisions had been made to an instrument, this information was added;
if new instruments emerged that met one of the purposes deemed essential to
child treatment, they were included; if tests had become obsolete or outdated,
they were deleted; and Web sites for publishing companies were added.

- One chapter that appeared in prior editions of the book was deleted, namely,
the chapter on parent education. The chapter has never fit well into the flow
and purpose of the book; there are much superior primary resources for materials related to parent education and the treatment of the topic within this text
could not do it justice.

- Throughout all chapters, references were updated as relevant and needed. New editions of books previously cited were incorporated and referenced, new research findings as gleaned from professional journals were perused and presented as appropriate and obsolete material was deleted.

- "Counseling" has been added to the title because so much of therapeutic work with children is done not exclusively by psychologists but also by individuals from a variety of helping professions.

I hope these changes please instructors, students, and professionals who have been loyal to the first and second editions of the *Comprehensive Guide* and serve to entice those who have never seen the book before to pick it up and read it. I would love to hear from you, both good and bad, as it is my goal to make this book better and better as it grows and evolves over the years. The book has now moved from its childhood to its adolescence—a happy evolution indeed, with hopes for an even more sophisticated adulthood in the future.

Happy reading!

Acknowledgments

I wish to express my gratitude

- to my life partner, best friend, and valued colleague, Mark Johnson, who not only contributed valuable chapters to this book but also patiently endured my preoccupations and busy schedule and lovingly supported my every effort as I wrote this text;

- to my students who were willing to read portions of this book as it was being developed, who listened to and expressed appreciation about my lectures, and who challenged me with their cases as I supervised their work;

- to my small clients, who often opened new worlds for me in my attempts to help them, who trusted me and allowed me into their lives, and who helped me crystallize many of the ideas expressed in this volume;

- to my own teachers and supervisors over the years who have contributed to my growth, my love for my profession, and my enthusiasm about my work;

- to my parents, Rosemarie and Bernherd Brems, who provided a nurturing and safe home for me in which to grow and mature, build the self-confidence to become a psychologist, and form the strengths to become a teacher;

- to my sister and her family, Gabriele, Floh, and Jan Strubel, who have lent support and nurturance over the years;

- and to Jeni Ogilvie at Waveland Press, whose confidence and trust has inspired and helped birth the third edition of the *Comprehensive Guide*.

Thank you all.

PART I

Preliminary Issues

1

Markers of Effective Child Clinicians

> *In all actions concerning children, whether undertaken by public or private social welfare institutions, courts of law, administrative authorities or legislative bodies, the best interests of the child shall be a primary consideration.*
>
> —Article 3.1 of the UN Convention on the Rights of the Child

The decision to work with children is difficult and has many implications. Children are unique and different from adults in a variety of challenging ways. They are at a different developmental level; take different approaches to problem solving, living, and setting priorities; their language, cognition, emotional expression, and perception are still evolving; and they are still far more comfortable with nonverbal ways of self-expression and communication than adults are. Special sensitivities are necessary, and verbal interchanges are not primary in the treatment process, often a significant challenge to adults, especially bright and highly educated adults who have been taught for many years that talking is the way to solve most problems. Not surprisingly, it is extremely important for clinicians interested in working with children to consider a number of important factors before leaping into the work.

Educational Needs and Backgrounds of Child Clinicians

Many professions prepare child clinicians, including psychology, psychiatry, and social work. Many different job titles encompass child clinicians, and across them vast differences exist in training, experience, and approach. It is impossible to determine which profession best prepares its members to work with children, as most prepare generalists, that is, counselors who supposedly are able to work with any type of client. Being trained as a generalist often means that the bulk of the clinician's training experiences has centered on adult clients and adult interventions. Although various systems of psychotherapy or counseling are generally included in training mental health professionals, strategies are all too often only applied to adult examples and tried out for the first time with adult clients. This leaves many clinicians unprepared for work with children. Any clinician trained only with adults needs to receive intensive and specialized supervision for the first child case, regardless of training background. A summary of professionals qualified to provide children's mental health services is provided in Table 1.1 on page 5.

Training Qualifications for the Child Therapist

Many avenues are available to those who want to provide clinical services to children. The specific qualifications required for each of these avenues vary depending on the professional path that is chosen. Each profession or discipline determines its own requirements for licensure and/or certification and these requirements vary somewhat from state to state. Additionally, some disciplines provide the opportunity for advanced certification with a specialization in children and adolescents. For example, the National Association for Social Workers offers a path for individuals to become Certified Children, Youth, and Family Social Workers. This certification requires degree, licensure, and documented clinical work with children. Similarly, the American Board of Professional Psychology offers certification in child and adolescent psychology for doctoral-level psychologists.

Regardless of the professional path chosen, increasingly training programs are recognizing the special needs of this population and have made curricular adjustments to prepare clinicians more optimally for intervention with children. Specializations in child clinical work are available at many universities offering doctoral-level training and numerous internship sites. In reviewing curricula of child-sensitive programs and observing child clinical practice, a few minimum requirements emerge that appear necessary for students who plan to engage in child clinical work. These requirements include course work, practical experience, and supervision.

Recommended Course Work

Relevant course work includes graduate training in a number of academic fields. Additionally, child clinicians need formal course work in child development, focused not only on traditional theories of development that deal with specific developmental aspects such as cognition, psychosocial and psychosexual stages, motor and language development, or morality (e.g., Bjorklund, 2004; Erikson, 1950; Freud, 1952; Kagan and Lamb, 1990; Owens, 2008; Piaget, 1967), but also nontraditional developmental theories that consider self-development and the interpersonal context during the growing-up years (e.g., Altman, et al., 2002; Brandell and Ringel, 2007; Brems, 1998a; Stern, 1977, 1985, 1989; Wimbarti and Self, 1992).

Formal course work in child psychopathology is indicated, as disorders manifest differently at different ages. Further, several disorders occur only in childhood and are typically not covered sufficiently in general psychopathology courses. It is also necessary to take at least one assessment course specifically focused on children, without being primarily about intellectual or cognitive testing. The latter aspects are adequately covered in general individual assessment courses. However, personality assessment courses need to be focused very differently depending on whether the intended clientele is over or under 18.

A specific course in child therapy or counseling is helpful in enlightening trainees about outcome literature in child treatment and types of interventions that are successful with children. Such a course can also focus attention on specific skills relevant in a child intervention. However, optimally, the research-focused and clinically focused materials are taught in two separate courses, each covering the separate subject matter in some depth. Child clinicians also need knowledge about family violence and child abuse and neglect; they should also have a basic understanding of assessment, treatment, and ethical or legal implications. Ethical and legal issues not only arise in the context of interpersonal violence but also more generally. Hence, child clinicians need to receive training in legal issues and ethics specific to children, including information about informed consent, search and seizure, release of information, and duties to warn, protect, and report.

All clinicians working with children have to confront the parents of their young clients. Parents are often in need of therapeutic support and parenting-skills training. Hence, course work in parent education and consultation is very helpful to child clinicians. Further, more and more child mental health specialists recognize openly the embeddedness of the child in the family matrix. Not all children referred for individual therapy are ultimately most likely to benefit from this approach, and family therapy may be a better intervention. Optimally, skilled child clinicians are trained in family interventions. Even if child clinicians have no special expertise in family therapy or counseling, they benefit from having course work in family assessment, as most child clinicians use an intake model that involves the entire family.

Table 1.1   Training Backgrounds of Child Clinicians

Career Path	Degree	Common Title
Psychology		
Counseling Psychology	Ph.D. or Psy.D.	Psychologist
Clinical Psychology	Ph.D. or Psy.D.	Psychologist
Child Psychology	Ph.D. or Psy.D.	Psychologist
School Psychology	Ph.D. or Ed.D.	School Psychologist
Developmental Psychology	Ph.D.	Developmental Psychologist
Counseling Psychology	M.A. or M.S. or M.Ed.	Counselor or Psychological Associate
Clinical Psychology	M.A. or M.S.	Psychological Associate
Counseling		
Counseling	Ph.D. or Ed.D.	Counselor
Counselor Education	Ph.D. or Ed.D.	Counselor or Counselor Educator
School Counseling	M.S., M.A., M.Ed.	School Counselor
Social Work		
Clinical Social Work	M.S.W.	Clinical Social Worker
Social Work	B.S.W.	Social Worker
Medicine		
Psychiatry	M.D.	Psychiatrist
Child Psychiatry	M.D.	Child Psychiatrist
Pediatric Psychiatry	M.D.	Pediatric Psychiatrist
Others		
Child Development	M.S., M.A., M.Ed.	Child Development Specialist
Marriage and Family	M.S., M.A.	Marriage and Family Counselor

Practical Experience

It is obvious that becoming a child clinician requires a number of specially focused courses. Additionally, child clinicians need special clinical opportunities. Child therapy or counseling cases must be part of practicum and internship caseloads. Most optimally, child clinicians have had at least one semester-long practicum or internship entirely focused on children. Although the obvious reason for a child-focused practicum or internship is the exposure to working with children, another advantage is the fact that it is during this time in a person's career when supervision is freely and generously available. All child clinicians must have supervised experience in working with children. Even clinicians who have long graduated and later in their career decide to incorporate children into their caseload need to seek out supervision or intensive consultations as they embark on this venture. Merely having enrolled in a few additional courses is not sufficient in training a provider for the special demands of work with children.

Positive Personal Traits of Child Clinicians

There are many personal attributes that are either conducive or counterproductive to work with children, and child clinicians must take the responsibility to evaluate themselves on these markers of effectiveness. Although it may be challenging and time-consuming to engage in this self-evaluation, it is a worthwhile endeavor, and it can be helpful to engage in specific exercise to enhance these skills (Courtney, 2007). Looking at the traits that are discussed here and summarized below is crucial and never to be omitted, regardless of how tempting it might be.

Summary of Positive Personal Traits

- acceptance that not all children are "lovable"
- lack of fear of children
- self-respect and self-esteem
- self-awareness and willingness for self-exploration
- open-mindedness about values, behaviors, and approaches to life
- restraint from imposing own values, standards, or beliefs
- cultural and gender sensitivity
- awareness of the impact and manifestation of prejudice
- use of nonoffensive, nonsexist, and nonracist language
- respect for child's needs and wishes
- respect for child's privacy and confidentiality
- acceptance of child's definition of what is important
- awareness of child's cognitive level and limitations
- adaptability to child's level and style of functioning
- knowledge and understanding of symbolism and metaphor

- empathy and willingness to listen
- tolerance for ambiguity and tentativeness
- truthfulness to one's self
- awareness of personal style
- compatibility of personal style with chosen therapeutic style
- awareness of dress and other aspects of appearance
- appropriate clothing to prevent injury or offense
- respect for and acceptance of child's parents
- willingness to seek consultation

Self-Respect and Self-Esteem

Child clinicians need a healthy dose of self-respect and self-esteem. Early interactions with difficult children are often taxing for the clinician's self-esteem, as all empathic and reflective skills that tend to work even with the most difficult adults may be ineffective with challenging children (if not only because these skills rely very heavily on verbal communication, an avenue not always usable in the work with children). Even when faced with such a potential failure or difficulty, the therapist must be able to maintain a sense of self-respect and esteem to remain efficient and capable. Self-esteem and self-respect are crucial even in the work with children who have less challenging symptoms. Deficits in counselors' self-confidence result in their need to have a child perform in a specific manner to validate that they are good at what he or she does. Deviation from the "good-client" role by the child is perceived as a threat to counselors' professional self-esteem and may result in inappropriate interventions. Basically, self-esteem and self-respect are crucial to not using the child to satisfy personal psychological needs.

For instance, one trainee was distraught after his second session with a child. This trainee had previously experienced some difficulty with his adult clients, showing some limits in empathic potential and often feeling the need to convince his clients that they were already doing much better than when they entered treatment. The trainee had been made aware by his supervisor that there was a likely connection between his need to perceive progress and his significant doubts about his own competence. However, this connection became even clearer after his first two sessions with his child client.

The child, being referred for oppositional behavior, had consistently refused to listen to directives (the appropriateness of which certainly was also in question) given by the therapist. It became clear upon viewing the tape of the session that the trainee became more and more exasperated and finally no longer knew what to do. At that time he literally begged the child to behave, as otherwise he (the therapist) would not receive a good grade in his practicum. Clearly, not all examples of low self-esteem will end up surfacing in a manner quite this obvious. But self-doubts have a way of showing themselves in treatment with children, if only in subtle ways that communicate to the child that the clinician is not really resourceful or in control.

Self-Awareness

Child clinicians need a high level of self-awareness and maturity, otherwise all sorts of confounding feelings and attitudes may enter the treatment process. Self-awareness is a therapist trait that is important in the work with all clients regardless of age (Brems, 2001; Stern, Hyman, and Martin, 2006), but is of particular importance in the work with children because this interaction often pulls for countertransferences that stem from very early life (Metcalf, 2002). The younger the child, the more deeply buried the material that is evoked in the clinician (Altman et al., 2002). Lack of awareness of early-life desires or needs can result in feelings of being startled, overwhelmed, or confused.

Children tend to be experienced by clinicians as much more vulnerable than adults. Thus, therapists who have a caretaker stance may be able to control this trait in their work with adults but not in their work with children. Further, children are even more likely than adults to ask for direct advice or guidance, making it more difficult for counselors not to fall into the trap of becoming advice givers or teachers (Siegel, 1990). This is a common problem for new clinicians anyhow, as they tend to think that they should have answers for clients—that they should be able to deliver an obvious service or product. For example, one trainee who was working under supervision was upset after the third week of work with a child because, according to her, nothing was happening in the treatment of this 12 year old. In exploring the clinician's last session with this girl, it became very obvious to the supervisor that the child was beginning to experience a significant level of trust in the clinician and was beginning to open up and to "work on" several important therapeutic family issues. The clinician had not been able to see this progress because the child did not complete a project begun during the session, failed to engage in much verbal interchange (despite her advanced age), and indicated that she was getting bored. The client's expression of boredom occurred, however, after she had spontaneously begun drawing a picture of her family. In this picture, her father was an imposing and very large figure in the middle of the page, her brother was next to him, also quite large, and the client herself was in a corner of the drawing, very small and without elaboration. While drawing, the client indicated that her brother tended to get all the attention since the parental divorce because her mother was afraid that he was not receiving sufficient male role-modeling because the male parent was no longer living with the family. In an attempt to make this up to the brother, the mother had been focusing many of her energies on this child, leaving her two daughters to their own devices.

The child never previously had indicated that she felt affected by her parents' divorce; instead she indicated that she felt quite relieved by it. This was the first sign that she indeed was affected significantly and was ready to share this with her therapist. However, she abandoned the drawing at this point, turned to her therapist and claimed she was bored. The therapist, concerned about her inability to keep the client engaged, perceived this session as a failure because it did not result in the product she had expected. Once she was able to recognize that her own needs for tangibles had interfered in her ability to make a realistic assessment of her session, she felt much more comfortable about her next session.

Open-Mindedness

Self-awareness is an important trait and it often brings with it another important characteristic of child therapists, namely, open-mindedness. Open-minded counselors welcome children who have values that differ from their own and do not force personal values on their child clients. This is especially important if children grew up in an environment that was significantly different from that of the clinician. Differences in background are likely to have forged different sets of values and priorities for child and clinician, differences that do not threaten treatment as long as the clinician can keep an open mind and can see the child's world from the child's unique perspective. What the therapist may need to understand is that some of the child's behaviors that would have been considered maladaptive or questionable in the therapist's background may have great adaptive value in the child's environment.

For instance, one trainee had grown up in a family in which expression of emotion was very desirable and in which the parents encouraged their children to speak about feelings even if they were negative. Subsequently, this counselor endorsed free communication of affect as an important therapeutic goal in his work. However, as he came to recognize very painfully, this standard could not be realistically upheld with several of his child clients. In one case in particular, the free expression of affect by the child subsequent to one session that had utilized storytelling as a primary intervention strategy, almost led to physical abuse of the child by the mother. This child's family was not ready to incorporate the counselor's value system about free affective expression or honesty. This example also clarifies that children are embedded in an interpersonal matrix that may not always change along with the child, regardless of the strides made in individual treatment. It is important for clinicians to proceed cautiously and be respectful of family values and standards.

Finally, therapists must never assume that they know what is right or wrong for a given family. They must explore their ability to adapt their values and beliefs, given their unique environment and history and that of their clients. Therapy or counseling is no place for value judgment. Rather, it is a place for flexibility and willingness to see things in a manner that maximizes options and choices, while ascertaining that they are adaptive and useful for the psychological growth and safety of the child (Holowiak-Urquhart and Taylor, 2005). Clearly, neither science nor art (and counseling is generally considered to contain both) can be entirely free of values and value judgments. However, clinicians are encouraged to be as flexible and open-minded as possible and to recognize personal values and how they may collide with values of clients.

Cultural and Gender Sensitivity

Open-mindedness about values and standards is also implied in the therapist's need for sensitivity to ethnic differences. Children come from a variety of ethnic backgrounds, all of which differ slightly in their interpersonal emphasis, affective expression, understanding of human life, priorities for living, and other aspects of being human (Gibbs and Huang, 2003). Clinicians must be willing to explore children's background to understand fully from where they are coming and to where they return after a session is over or treatment is complete. Knowledge about, awareness of, and sensitivity to culture and ethnicity are so crucially important to work with children that this topic receives an entire chapter of its own and hence is not covered in detail here.

Respect for the Child

An attitude of respect toward children is by some considered to be as or more important than technique in the work with children (Wustinger, 2006). Related to open-mindedness and sensitivity, respect takes many shapes. It includes honoring a child's sense of what is and is not important. In his now dated but still relevant book, Coppolillo (1987) provides a beautiful example of scheduling his treatment around a child client's favorite TV show. Another therapist challenged Coppolillo's action, but as he points out, a child's play is a child's work. Clinicians rarely require an adult client to cancel a business appointment if it can easily be avoided by scheduling sessions at a different time. Why not extend this courtesy to children? Children have lives of their own, important preferences, and a clear understanding of what they want and do not want. Forcing children to come to treatment at a certain time or to engage in specific behaviors without considering their preferences lacks respect and opens the door for unnecessary resistances.

Respect for children also includes respecting their privacy and confidentiality. Clinicians do not even have to be warned about the many ways in which they violate children's confidentiality when they are dealing with adult clients. It would be rare and impolite for a therapist who is expecting an adult client to enter the waiting area, and ask "Are you Mary Simmons?" Yet, numerous therapists violate this easily avoidable breach of confidentiality with children. How many counselors would tell an adult client's curious mother what the client said about her in the last session? How many therapists of an adult client (even with a release-of-information) would divulge specifics about a client's treatment to a concerned father? Yet all of these behaviors are displayed by clinicians of children. They violate children's rights and disrespect children's confidentiality in ways that can easily undermine treatment.

Respect also means honoring a child's preferences, being conscious of the child's health, understanding the child within her or his developmental level, and communicating with the child through metaphor. Children, especially young children, have vastly different ways of thinking than adults. Their cognitive processes are less flexible and logical and their reasoning is relatively concrete. Clinicians must be willing to use language and explanations that make sense to the child at the child's developmental level. Given the importance of this issue it is further addressed in a subsequent chapter in great detail.

Empathy and Willingness to Listen

It is crucial for child clinicians to have the ability to look at life from the unique perspective of the child. It is not sufficient that they understand how they would feel or would have felt if they were in the child's shoes. Instead, they must understand how the child feels in a given situation, given that child's specific and unique experiences, history, and background (cf., Kohut, 1984). Empathy, thus defined, requires therapists to listen carefully and hear or see not only overt content of what is being expressed either verbally or behaviorally but also the latent message contained within the child's expression. Such empathy is not a warm, fuzzy feeling of caring, but rather is an artful and scientific approach to better understanding (Brems, 2001).

Empathy is also incomplete if entails just the clinician's internal or private understanding of the child. For empathy to serve a positive purpose, clinicians need to communicate their understanding back to the child. In other words, once therapists have listened carefully and believe they have empathically understood the child, they need to respond to the child. Only when the child receives a message of understanding and feels the counselor's empathic concern is the interpersonal cycle of empathy considered to be complete (Brems, 1989a, 2001). Communicating empathy to a child, however, does not necessary mean giving verbal feedback, and it hardly ever means making an interpretation. Empathy is most easily communicated to children through nonverbal media; for instance, by joining a child's play or by matching one's affect to the child's (cf., Stern, 1985). It may be as simple as joining in a child's laughter, sharing a child's delight, or recognizing a child's fears and providing support. Or it may be a complex process of interaction that involves thorough understanding of child, therapeutic medium, and metaphor.

An example of a sophisticated empathic cycle is provided by this brief vignette of a child–counselor interaction. A 10-year-old girl was referred for treatment of night terrors that had been increasing in frequency over the past four months. She was engaged in a successful counseling with a clinician with considerable experience in her work with children. Toward the middle phase of treatment, this child told the following story:

> Once there was a little house. This little house had many many rooms and a big attic and a basement. The house liked all its room but was very afraid of going in the basement because down there lived a big ugly looking monster animal. The monster animal was always awake because it could not sleep. The house didn't like the monster animal so it didn't go to the basement. One day it had to go down there because it needed potatoes to eat. And the big ugly monster came out and roared at the little house. The house ran as far away as it could but it never forgot the monster animal—after that it made sure never that it never goes to the basement.

The counselor listened to the story and given what she knew about the girl understood her communication. The girl had often sought to receive more nurturance from her parents who were rather rigid and strict people who showed little emotion and caring. One time, after the girl had felt particularly lonely and frightened after a nightmare, she had crawled into her parents' bed. Rather than comforting the child and asking why she had come into their bedroom, both parents responded with anger. After that time, the little girl never returned to her parents' bedroom and had apparently given up seeking emotional (or other types of) help from them. Understanding the girl's communication, the counselor responded as follows:

> The little house got so scared because all it wanted was some potatoes. It did not mean to upset the basement or the monster animal—it's just that it was so hungry. Now the little house is so scared of the monster animal that is doesn't even want to come close to it. The problem is that that's where the potatoes are. So now the little house is all confused and scared! What was it going to do now?

The little girl began to cry and it was clear that the counselor had communicated her understanding correctly. The two began to problem-solve about what the little house could do to be fed without the fear of being hurt by the monster. This example clarifies the power of empathy, as well as the power of remaining within the child's metaphor, rather than communicating understanding concretely. In other words, the counselor's empathic understanding would not have been nearly as successful, had she tried to make the latent content (i.e., the metaphor) manifest.

Flexibility and Tolerance of Ambiguity

Respect and empathy for children as well as sensitivity to their gender or ethnic background imply that therapists must not treat all children alike or treat the same child always the same way. Children change; so do their systems and presenting concerns. To remain ever aware of these changes requires tolerance and flexibility (Blom, 2004; Chused, 2000). New information constantly emerges as work progresses, resulting in revisions of treatment plans and conceptualizations and requiring adaptability of treatment strategies in a meaningful and plan-oriented manner. Not all human beings are capable of functioning in such an environment of ambiguity and tentativeness. Not a few will attempt to make the therapy or counseling fit a rigid model, forcing the understanding of the child into a mold. This dangerous lack of flexibility can cause stagnation at best, iatrogenesis at worst. No child, no family, no treatment fits a mold. The entire therapeutic process relies on change, upheaval, tentativeness, and not uncommonly, ambiguity.

Counselors have to be able to deal with unknowns and willing to take risks and explore new ground. All child therapists have to be capable of "epistemological feeling" (Knobel, 1990, p. 61), that is, they must have the ability to listen empathically and alter their assessments of a situation flexibly and appropriately to changing contexts. Unwillingness to follow intuitions can result in leaving facets of the child undiscovered that may prove crucial to growth and change. Certainly, risk taking has to be weighed against possible consequences of making a mistake. However, it is rare that one failed or inappropriate treatment intervention derails the entire therapeutic process. In fact, some clinicians believe that the occasional empathic failure of the clinician is crucial to successful treatment (Kohut, 1984). It is often much more preferable for the therapist to risk a new intervention than to adhere rigidly to one that is clearly unsuccessful. Repeated failures are likely to have more negative impact than one unfortunate choice of wording or behavior.

Being True to One's Self

In intervening with a child, it is important that the clinician's personal self comes through authentically (Knobel, 1990). It is generally impossible for clinicians to deny who they really are outside of the playroom. Personality can neither be hidden nor should it be camouflaged (Rowan and Jacobs, 2002). Yet, authenticity does not imply that the therapist engages in self-disclosure. Treatment is focused on the child, not the counselor. However, all clinicians have a personality and an interpersonal style (so one would hope, at least). Some are extroverted and active, others introverted and observing. This general pattern shows through. For example, it is unreasonable for the active, extroverted therapist to expect to engage in the type of play therapy that Virginia Axline (1947) conducts and that requires the therapist to sit back rather passively, simply observing the child while commenting on the child's behavior, but never physically interacting with the child. Extroverted, active clinicians would find themselves denying who they really are—such clinicians are much better suited for more interactive models of play therapy.

Thus, as therapists search for their way of working with children, their own personality needs to be considered, accepted, and used to their advantage. Trying to deny who one is never works for any length of time. Only if their work style fits clinicians' humanity will they be able to muster the day-to-day commitment and enthusiasm so crucial to the treatment of any client. A bored or inauthentic therapist is indeed a difficult one to picture as successful in instilling a sense of enthusiasm and challenge in the child.

A note of caution is necessary here. While being true to one's self is important, there are some personality traits that are counterproductive. Such traits include excessive formality, rigidity, intolerance of getting dirty or messy, arrogance vis-à-vis children, selfishness, lack of awareness of safety limits, and similar characteristics. Any and all of these traits are not appropriate if expressed in play therapy. Their presence makes it questionable whether the individual should be a child clinician at all.

Awareness of Dress

Regardless of personal style, there are some cautions about dress. An old rule of thumb in the work with children is to wear neither a tuxedo nor clothing that is entirely outside the cultural norms of the society within which the clinician practices (Ginott, 1964). This leaves plenty of leeway in terms of choices, but a few more cautions seem helpful. For instance, there is some agreement that overly formal dress can impede the establishment of rapport (Barker, 1990). Further, children show affection spontaneously without regard to whether their fingers are clean or dirty. Thus, wearing clothes that cannot be easily washed is a set-up for anger or hostility on the part of the clinician in response to what was meant to be a positive interaction by the child. In other words, clinicians have to be willing to let their clothes get dirty. This does not imply that there are no rules in the playroom. Indeed there are; however, harmless and occasional violations, accidents, or spontaneous shows of affection should not become problems in the child–clinician relationship. Aside from clothing, counselors also need to use common sense about jewelry, scarves, neckties, high-heeled shoes, and similar accessories that can be used to hurt, either purposefully or accidentally. Women need to decide whether wearing a skirt makes them uncomfortable in situation where they may have to sit on the floor, climb on a chair, or engage in similar activities that may result in potential embarrassment, lack of comfort, preoccupation with one's clothing, or even injury. Clearly, therapeutic style affects choice of clothing.

The clientele's socioeconomic background also affects choice of dress and jewelry. Some clinical settings are in neighborhoods or catchment areas of lower socioeconomic status than the clinician's. Before putting on expensive clothing or obvious jewelry, counselors need to consider the impact of this behavior on their clients. A child who may not always be adequately nourished may have significant difficulty trusting a therapist who wears clothing or jewelry that looks expensive. From this child's perspective, this type of appearance conveys someone who cannot possibly understand the child's very basic physical concern.

Respect for the Parents

Tolerance and understanding for the child have already been stressed and the same basic attitudes and feelings must be extended to the child's parents (Chused, 2000). Clinicians need the ability to keep track of parents' perspectives as well as those of children. It is very easy to forget that parents too are in pain, even if they are abusing or neglecting their child. It is important to muster empathy even for the most inappropriate parent, as one reason this parent behaves so dismally toward the child may be that she or he also has significant psychological or emotional deficits, unmet needs, or concerns. Often the parents of abused children were abused themselves and are in dire need of treatment (Crosson-Tower, 2008). Regardless of the overt resistance they may show, their pain, however deeply buried, needs to be kept in mind by clinicians to assure adequate empathy and understanding (Brems, Baldwin, and Baxter, 1993). Angry or hostile confrontations only alienate parents, which may lead to premature termination of services for their children. It is not uncommon for clinicians to have strong negative feelings, sometimes even disgust, about abusive parents. Such an attitude does not help the treatment process.

Sometimes the best way to address negative countertransference toward parents is through being assigned as the clinician for one of the parents, not the child. This gives clinicians a chance to look at the parent's background and childhood history and often brings home the tragedy of the parent's life that led to being abusive. Trainees so repelled by abusive parents as to not be able to work with them are strongly advised to seek supervision or consultation. No child therapist can work with children without encountering abusive or neglectful parents. Inability to establish rapport or a positive interaction with such parents only gets in the way of successful treatment for the child. Parents are crucial to the work with children; they bring them, they control when a child comes and how often a child comes, they are responsible for payment, and they decide whether treatment is effective and worthwhile. Alienating them can short-circuit the chance of positively influencing a child's life altogether.

Common Reactions of Child Clinicians

Emotional reactions and countertransferences on the part of clinicians working with children are unavoidable and deserve to be worked through to assure effective treatment of children (Gil and Rubin, 2005). Surprisingly, this topic has received relatively scant attention in the child treatment literature compared to the frequency with which countertransference issues are discussed in the clinical literature pertaining to adult work. Nevertheless, a number of reactions result in the work with children ranging from traditionally defined countertransference to inappropriate attachment to unhealthy identification. Although discussion of these processes perhaps appeals most to clinicians who favor psychodynamic or psychoanalytic traditions, it is truly important for all child clinicians to have some understanding of them. Nobody, not even the most symptom-focused clinician, can escape feelings and reactions altogether. Human beings respond to the plight of others, identify with them, react to them, and perhaps even dislike them. In fact, "few clinicians would deny the obvious fact that they bring personal needs and expectations to their work, but therapists often 'forget' this when they should most keep it in mind, while they are doing their work" (Schowalter, 1985, p. 41). Having an awareness that emotional and irrational reactions are possible before, after, and during treatment helps child clinicians maintain a therapeutic stance.

Countertransferences

Countertransference is most traditionally defined as a response to a client that is based on the unconscious in general and on unconscious anxieties and conflicts in particular (cf., Freud, 1959). However, this definition is global and does not differentiate several possibilities contained within it. Further definition clarifies four types of countertransference that can occur in the treatment of children. The first three may be disruptive to treatment; the fourth can serve a positive purpose.

Issue-Specific Countertransference.   This type of countertransference results from stimulation of a clinician's unconscious material in response to specific behaviors, feelings, and needs expressed by the child. In other words, a therapist's reaction to a child's issues is flavored by the therapist's own unconscious material. For instance, a therapist who has anxieties about sexuality may be particularly threatened and may respond negatively to the discussion of sexual abuse by a young client, especially if the child has learned and incorporated seductive behaviors. Another therapist who is free of unconscious sexual conflicts may respond to the same child in an entirely different manner. The crux of this countertransference is the coincidental and unfortunate coming together of clinician and client issues (or transferences) that are incompatible, too similar, or too threatening.

Stimulus-Specific Countertransference.   A second type of countertransference is independent of the child's needs, feelings, or behaviors but rather occurs in response to an external, treatment-irrelevant stimulus of the child. For instance, a counselor with yet to be explored issues around sibling rivalry with a younger brother may respond inappropriately to young male children who remind her or him of this brother. The reaction is not specific to the child's expressed treatment issues but would occur in the interaction with any such child, whether a client or not. The crux of this countertransference is the therapist's unconscious and immediate reaction to an external stimulus that is independent of the child's treatment needs.

Trait-Specific Countertransference.   Yet another countertransference reaction is even more global and has previously been labeled the clinician's "habitual modes of relating" (Sandler, 1975, p. 415, as quoted in Bernstein and Glenn, 1988, p. 226) or "expression of character traits" (Lilleskov, 1971, p. 404, as quoted in Bernstein and Glenn, 1988, p. 226). Here, clinicians respond to the child as they would respond to anyone and any time in their life. For instance, a therapist with rigid morals who tends to be condescending and judgmental in general, brings this attitude into the treatment room. It influences the work with a given child client, regardless of the issues presented. Another therapist, who may detest aggression, may be unable to allow children to act out their angry feelings, however justified they may be. The crux of this countertransference is the clinician's habit-driven manner of relating in all contexts, including in therapy or counseling.

Child-Specific Countertransference.   Finally, the fourth type of countertransference is a reaction to the child that is solicited in most, if not all, adults with whom the child interacts. For instance, a very oppositional and demanding child with poor self-esteem and strong attention-seeking behavior may overwhelm and alienate adults after even the shortest contact. Clinicians may experience the same frustration others do when they encounter the child. This reaction is not specific to the clinician but rather to the child. The crux of this countertransference is a child's solicitation of a consistent (e.g., negative, protective) response from the environment.

Child-specific countertransference, unlike the other three, provides aware clinicians with added insight about the child and added empathy for the adults in the child's life. It provides information about a child and excellent feedback about a child's impact on the environment. It provides insight regarding target behaviors that need to be modified quickly to help the child become more acceptable to the potentially helpful adults in her or his life. Lanyado (1989) long ago referred to this reaction as an "in loco parentis counter-transference" (p. 99), suggesting that it provides an excellent means of creating empathy with a child's parent by being put in a situation that simulates the relationship between parent and child.

Identifications

Not unlike countertransferences, identifications can have negative or positive effects on treatment, depending on whether they are processes emanating from the clinician and expressed without awareness or whether they are processes emanating from the child and used consciously by the clinician. There are two broad settings within which identifications can occur that are unique to work with children. Specifically, only in work with children can clinicians have a number of different identification reactions with two separate sets of players—namely, the child and the parent(s). In both contexts, two possible types of identification can occur. With the child, the clinician may experience identification or projective identification; with parents, the clinician may experience identification or reactive identification.

Identification with the Child.   Identification with the child implies that the clinician has become so uniquely interested in and empathic with the child's situation that she or he identifies with it completely. The therapist feels for the child and understands the child from her or his unique perspective. So far, this definition is strikingly similar to the definition provided for empathy. However, identification takes the process of empathy one (unhealthy) step further. In their identification with the child, clinicians begin to relate to the child's environment as the child would. In other words, they begin to relate to the child's parents through their identification with the child, not as separate and objective observers. Clinicians develop transferences and feelings for parents that reflect those of the child, hence they are likely to be biased and immature. They fail to see parents' perspectives and are likely to judge them harshly, subjectively, and unrealistically. Through the identification with the child, clinicians lose their empathic stance with the parents.

Identification with the child can also result in regressive behavior and affect on the clinician's part (Bernstein and Glenn, 1988). Clinicians not only respond toward others as the child would, but they become like the child in sessions. They are no longer guiding adults but are themselves a child, unable to respond or deal with a given situation maturely. They may experience certain affects as overwhelming, much like the child, and their problem-solving skills become poorly defined and targeted. Clearly, this is not a helpful stance and it must be dealt with through supervision and consultation.

Projective Identification.   In this scenario, a child attempts to get rid of an unacceptable or frightening affect or self-aspect by projecting it onto the clinician. Depending on the level of awareness about the process by the clinician, projective identification can be positive or negative in its effects on treatment. If the projection is successful, it helps calm and soothe the child because it keeps disturbing aspects of the self out of the child's awareness. The projection of the child is met by the clinician with acceptance or understanding, which means the clinician *experiences* the feeling projected by the child. If clinicians are aware that their current affect has its origin in the child (not in the self), they are capable of tolerating it and often can alter it. Once altered, the affect is accepted by the child as her or his own and reintegrated into the self. This process of reintrojection is crucial to the therapeutic success of projective identification, as without it, no change in the child can occur (van Beekum, 2005).

Without reintrojection, projective identification merely would have served as a defense in the same manner as pure projection. Without the alteration of the projected affect by the clinician, reintrojection is not possible in a therapeutic manner. The affect, unaltered, remains overwhelming for the child, cannot be reintegrated into the self, and continues to be rejected by the child. However, if the clinician is successful and accepting, recognizing and altering the affect, it becomes acceptable to the child and can be incorporated successfully.

Although this process sounds technical and abstract, it is actually a very experience-near procedure and always deepens the affective involvement between child and clinician. However, it is this very affective involvement that occasionally causes the cycle to derail and end unsuccessfully. If clinicians "receive" the affect but do not recognize it as the child's, but rather perceive it as their own, a projective counteridentification is set in motion. Clinicians then feel overwhelmed or disturbed by the affect, cannot contain or alter it, and the therapeutic cycle cannot be closed. Clinicians are left with feelings identical to those in the child and without recognizing that they originated in the child. They accept or perceive the feelings as their own and are unable to deal with them.

Clearly, projective identification can be a helpful experience for the child or can stifle the therapeutic process. The process of evoking feelings in adults via projective identification is a nonverbal means of communication for children (Altman et al., 2002) and is a nonverbal process used in normal human development by infants to communicate affects to parents to have needs met (Klein, 1955). Child clinicians must be particularly aware of such nonverbal expressions of affect by children, as lack of awareness hinders therapeutic resolution of feelings and needs. For more detailed discussions of the projective identification cycle, both positive and negative, the reader is referred to primary sources. The concept as applied therapeutically with children is presented by Brems (1989b), whereas application with adults is presented by Ogden (1993).

Identification with the Parents.   If clinicians experience identification with parents, on the other hand, the same process occurs, but in reverse. Now clinicians so indiscriminately empathize with the parent(s) that they lose empathic track of the child. They are essentially in cahoots with the parent(s) and can no longer function as effective advocates for the child. Their alliances are with the adult(s) and the child is left out of the process. This type of identification is dangerous in that it can result in the retraumatization of the child who in treatment is subjected to the same attitudes and behaviors experienced in day-to-day life from the parents.

Reactive Identification.   Also destructive is clinicians' reactive identification with a child's parents. In this case, clinicians disagree with parents and, because of this disagreement, attempt to be different from them (Bernstein and Glenn, 1988). Clinicians may become rigid and controlling if parents are perceived as too permissive or incapable of setting appropriate boundaries, or clinicians may become overly permissive and tolerant of the child if they perceive parents as controlling and emotionally abusive. Either way, interactions between child and clinician are no longer determined by the child's needs and the clinician's therapeutic stance but rather by a reaction to parental behavior. Such an approach cannot be successful as it provides neither therapeutic contact with a caring adult nor a corrective emotional experience in a growth-promoting therapeutic atmosphere.

Attachment

Most, if not all, children stimulate attachment from their clinician; children with traumatic histories of abuse or other types of suffering often evoke very strong attachment reactions from their clinicians (Edgeson, 2007). Strong attachments are not bad in and of themselves. In fact, at times they are the only thing that preserves treatment under adverse circumstances, as especially children with abuse histories can be difficult to treat. Their behaviors may be out of control or they may present significant emotional challenges to their clinicians. Having formed strong attachment to such children early in treatment facilitates clinicians' ability to tolerate and endure negative interactions (including hostility, anger, and hatred) later in treatment, preventing premature terminations (Lanyado, 1989).

At times, however, overly strong attachments may interfere with treatment, especially if clinicians become so attached to their child clients that the emotional tie overrides clinical judgment. Therapists begin to respond from an emotional level, not a cognitive one, and relate to children no longer as clients but as love objects. Intense attachments can lead to violations of healthy therapeutic boundaries as counselors may follow the urge to help children in settings other than therapy or counseling and may make unhealthy decisions about interventions in academic, home, or other settings.

An additional danger of attachment gone too far is the possibility of a child becoming a "narcissistic extension" of the clinician (Bernstein and Glenn, 1988). Clinicians, like some parents, use a child's reactions as a means of judging their own competence. If children behave or feel well, therapy or counseling is viewed as progressing and clinicians feel positive about their role in the child's treatment; if children behave or feel poorly, progress is assessed negatively and clinicians' self-esteem and self-confidence falters. This degree of attachment oversteps healthful boundaries of the child–clinician relationship and fails to facilitate treatment progress.

Common Vulnerabilities of Child Clinicians

Many clinicians have chosen to work with children because of a special affinity they feel for them. This affinity can have many reasons, healthy and unhealthy. It can have many outcomes, again healthy and unhealthy. Awareness of motivations for having chosen to become a child clinician and insight into one's personal level of functioning are crucial to avoiding less than therapeutic reactions in the work with children. So far, this chapter has presented general processes and definitions of reactions in clinicians that can derail or facilitate the therapeutic or counseling process. These processes come alive in very specific ways in the treatment of children with some predictable and unique patterns. Having some knowledge of common clinician reactions in the work with children can prevent therapeutic mistakes and misalliances. Thus, the themes that follow are not included to frighten clinicians about working with children. Instead, they are presented to help clinicians become aware of internal forces and overt behaviors that may otherwise remain undiscovered. If clinicians look for these patterns, they can be prevented from careening out of control and entering treatment in an unchecked and nontherapeutic manner.

Desire to Be a Child Again

All adults, regardless of their level of satisfaction with adulthood, at one time or another muse about what it would be like to be a child again. This wish, however infrequently it normally occurs in a person's life, is often mobilized in work with children. Childhood is viewed as an enjoyable time of life, and clinicians who may not have experienced childhood to its fullest or had to undertake parenting roles as children may experience an urge to become children again. This urge is not negative if realized outside the treatment setting. Thus, child clinicians not uncommonly find themselves loosening up in their lives outside the playroom. If the desire is brought into therapy, however, it can prove counterproductive. The play in which children and clinicians engage together can be pleasure producing for both. The interaction, especially if engaged in freely and happily, can provide an excellent backdrop for appropriate empathy and communication. Such an ability to "regress in the service of therapy" (Bernstein and Glenn, 1988, p. 231) is helpful and adaptive. However, if the clinician's behavior turns into a means of gratifying personal wishes and needs, the process becomes counterproductive as objectivity is lost. Play still takes place, but work is no longer on the agenda. At best, the child is having a fun hour; at worst, the child becomes a source of gratification for the clinician.

Fear of Being a Child Again

Quite to the contrary of the previous theme, some clinicians become frightened by the playfulness and emotional flavor of work with children. They become frightened of their own behavior, and more so of their own enjoyment of the activities in which they engage in the playroom. This fear is usually fueled by a strong fear of regression that signals the possibility of vulnerability. This vulnerability generally stems from the belief that play equals regression which in turn equals loss of control. Such loss of control is perceived by the clinician as the harbinger of poor coping and fragility of self-esteem.

Undoing Personal Harm

The wish to undo harm that was experienced by the clinician as a child is another common counterproductive theme. Clinicians express the desire, similar to new parents, to do something for their child clients that no one has ever done for them and to make sure that they are safe. Therapists most vulnerable to this type of reaction entered the profession in an attempt to have their personal needs cared for. Thus, assumptions are made about what children may need or desire based on the therapist's own needs and desires. Interventions are patterned according to this understanding, regardless of whether it reflects the child's or counselor's reality. Many blind spots enter into the treatment process. Because of the clinician's needs and the commitment to have them met once and for all, she or he becomes very committed to a positive treatment outcome. Much more hinges on the success of the treatment than the growth of and health of the child; the therapist's personal improvement is at stake. No wonder objectivity is lost and failure becomes overwhelming as it signals failure for the clinician at a very personal level.

Reemergence of Personal Trauma

Some clinicians did not choose the profession to deal with personal trauma, but instead repressed or denied the presence of trauma in their own childhood or believed to have resolved it (Joshi, Daniolos, and Salpekar, 2004). For these clinicians, certain child cases may suddenly trigger a painful reemergence of personal childhood trauma. Given that such clinicians were not prepared for a reemergence of the trauma, it leaves them stunned and in need of careful supervision or consultation. Reemergence is best dealt with swiftly for the sake of the clinician and the child. Reemergence can certainly also occur in the treatment of adults. However, the identification with a child (as opposed to an adult) makes clinicians more vulnerable, taking clinicians back to the developmental age of the client and leaving them with the affects, needs, desires, and resources they had at that age. Reemergence results in feelings of being overwhelmed, frightened, startled—feelings not easily dealt with by the clinician alone.

Clinicians may also react strongly to a child's parents, especially if abuse or neglect is part of the presenting picture. Not only is reexperience a definite danger in this case, but so is the emergence of affects against the child's parents reflective of the therapist's affects against her or his own parents in childhood. Interactions with parents may become strained and confounded by personal experience. As a positive relationship with a child client's parents is generally crucial to the continuation of the child's treatment, this reaction can be particularly destructive if it leads to a breach in the relationship between counselor and parents.

Caretaking and Protection

Children also not uncommonly evoke in the clinician the desire to be a caretaker or protector (Thompson and Kennedy, 1987), as children may be viewed as vulnerable or powerless. This perspective leads to the wish to safeguard and protect the child and provide as much nurturance and protection during sessions as possible. One therapist, who was working with a three-year-old child who was experiencing a particularly difficult divorce of her biological parents, was overcome with the desire to nurture the girl in treatment. She often emphasized the safety of the room and the therapeutic relationship and provided a very warm and cozy atmosphere for the child. The girl did appear to need this nurturance very much and certainly responded extremely well to it during the sessions. However, the approach failed to help the child face the difficult parental situation in the home and provided her no new resources with which to protect herself once she left the therapy room. When the girl began to struggle more and more against ending her sessions, the therapist painfully recognized her role in the girl's refusal to leave and recognized that she herself often wished the session could continue. The therapist was then able to move on to employ several additional therapeutic strategies, such as mutual story-telling, to help the child build resources that could be carried beyond the walls of the therapy room.

Another danger of the protective role is the tendency to avoid talking about or otherwise processing trauma. Clinicians may harbor the mistaken belief that children cannot tolerate reliving the trauma and may, overtly or subtly, keep them from processing what has occurred. Often this is a false protection, meeting the needs of the clinician more so than the needs of the child. Children need to process trauma they have experienced. This is not to be mistaken for the child's need to talk about the trauma or to discuss it verbally. Instead, children may simply need permission to express and lay to rest traumatic experience through play.

Being the Rescuer

Working with children and their families often places clinicians in situations in which a number of people look toward them to be wise, tolerant, and a rescuer. These kinds of expectations that some families and children have of clinicians can lead to their becoming the rescuer. As many therapists enter the mental health field with the motivation to help others, the rescuer role is easy to accept. However, as positive as the role may appear, it has many inherent dangers. First, despite the fact that it may have been elicited by transferences of the child and family toward the clinician, actual acceptance of the role as rescuer only reinforces for the child and her or his family that they are helpless and out of control. It suggests that the child and family are incompetent and may lead to feelings of humiliation and even rage (Webb, 1989). Further, the rescuer role gives clinicians a false sense of control and power that is likely to translate into self-righteous, condescending behaviors and attitudes that get in the way of empathic, caring, and respectful treatment. Finally, being the rescuer can result in negative feelings toward the therapist by the family and tends to stifle the work with the child. It places a tremendous burden on the counselor who now feels that she or he has to meet all of the child's needs and has to help make up for past hurts perpetrated within the family (Webb, 1989). Such a heavy burden leads to resentment and premature termination as the clinician begins to feel that nobody else is sharing the workload.

Themes Surrounding Parents and Relationship Issues

Several other themes are related to dealing with parents. Some clinicians are prone to engaging in competitions with the child's parents, believing that they are better for the child than the parents, a stance that can lead to contempt for the parent (McElroy and McElroy, 1991). This attitude interferes with the establishment of a positive working relationship with the parents, who often feel very vulnerable or defensive when their children are referred for therapy anyway. This defensiveness heightens their sensitivity to rejection, judgment, and contempt. If it is met by that very attitude on the part of the clinician, the relationship is doomed to failure.

Not only does competition with the parents affect the clinician–parent relationship it also may influence the clinician–child relationship and therapeutic process. Children identify with their parents and often get very attached to their therapists. If these two groups of people do not get along, children get confused. Further, if clinicians give subtle messages about their negativity toward the parents, children, feeling very much part of their parents, are likely to perceive this as personal criticism. Children must be able to idealize their parents to derive the full benefit of the child–parent relationship. Messages from clinicians that parents are somehow bad or inadequate undermine the possibility of a positive child–parent attachment.

Another reaction that tends to arise strictly because of interfacing with parents is the expectation that parents interfere with therapy. Mild transgressions of boundaries (e.g., bringing the child with food because there was no time to eat at home), coincidental violations of limits (e.g., being late because of a snowstorm) are interpreted as treatment resistance and used as proof that the parent is not supportive of the child's counseling. The counselor inadvertently or overtly expresses resentment to this parent, who in turn, picking up the counselor's frustration and anger, is likely to feel guilty or to respond with hostility and anger in kind. Either way, a negative interpersonal cycle has been set in motion because of a clinician's habitual expectation that parents hinder their children's treatment.

Occasionally, clinicians develop reactions to parents that are not negative but instead are idealizing. The parents are seen as perfect human beings who have the sorrow and burden of dealing with a child who is identified as a "problem." Such an idealizing relationship with parents is as harmful as a negative one. Although it may facilitate a bond between therapist and parent, it interferes with the establishment of a therapeutic bond with the child. When there are two parents who are not in the same home, it is possible that splitting occurs, which involves the idealization of one parent and the perception of the other parent as deserving all the blame and responsibility for the child's problems. This can have grave consequences for treatment, especially if the child is attached to both parents.

Emotions in Relation to the Victim

Working with traumatized children is difficult and presents many challenges that can result in strong countertransference reactions (Powell, 2006). Not surprisingly, clinicians often feel a sense of inadequacy and helplessness as they cannot generally alter the family environment for the child. Helplessness may lead to advice giving and placating, superficial interactions that present an escape from the stifling feeling that comes from not knowing how to protect the child (McElroy and McElroy, 1991). Clinicians may express sympathy rather than empathy in the attempt to protect children from reexperiencing the trauma. However, a sympathetic, as opposed to empathic, response on the part of the clinician results in insufficient exploration and processing of the child's trauma. It merely falsely protects child and therapist from the painful and useful investigation of traumatic events (Reynolds-Mejia and Levitan, 1990). Rather than protecting out of a sense of helplessness and inadequacy, it is much more therapeutic for child and clinician to deal with the suffering. The rescuer fantasy discussed above is also a common reaction to abused children.

Emotions in Relation to the Perpetrator

Clinicians' responses to parents of victimized children are often directly related to their responses to the child. If the child is idealized, viewed as innocent and in need of protection, it is likely that clinicians develop a nonempathic relationship with perpetrators. They exhibit a lack of sensitivity to the perpetrator's needs and historical context that might help explain (if not justify) her or his action (Reynolds-Mejia and Levitan, 1990). Parents may be rejected or condemned and are not given a chance to vent and explore why they developed abusive behaviors in the first place (Friedrich and Leiper, 2006).

Quite to the contrary, some clinicians who have a stronger alliance with adults may end up being very hesitant to believe in the guilt of a parent or may have strong hesitations about confronting other adults about their behavior. However, and unfortunately for the child, such a stance revictimizes the child and perpetuates unhealthy interactional patterns. Clearly, given the consequences of both attitudes toward perpetrators, it is best if clinicians can be empathic *and* confrontational with both child and parent, intervening to protect when necessary and supporting when appropriate (McElroy and McElroy, 1991).

A final word of caution is necessary about the relationship of clinicians with adult partners of perpetrators. Care needs to be taken not to make quick assumptions about nonprotective parents. It is easy to make a judgment that a partner knew about the abuse and failed to protect the child; however, there are some clinicians who argue that perhaps the parent was indeed innocently ignorant of what was going on (Crosson-Tower, 2008). This caution serves to reinforce a general point: clinicians cannot allow themselves to respond to anyone out of a habitual set of values. Instead, each individual child and family member must be assessed carefully to assure that the understanding of them is based in reality not countertransference.

Common Relational Patterns

In addition to the themes and reactions outlined above, many years ago Paul Adams (1982) identified and labeled six specific relational patterns that are common among child therapists. Although written over 25 years ago, this work deserves continued attention as it is as relevant today as it was then. Although the six types (the True-Faith Healer, the Me Adult/You Child, the Good Enough Parent, the Big Sibling, the Babysitter, and the Cop) overlap somewhat with the above patterns, they deserve separate mention. It is important to note that all of these patterns contain within them behaviors and attitudes that are appropriate to some degree and not problematic in and of themselves. If clinicians recognize some of these traits in themselves, there is no need to panic, as use in moderation may be quite useful (much like a child-specific countertransference). They become counterproductive only if adhered to rigidly or applied unconsciously.

True-Faith Healer.   The True-Faith Healer holds the belief that there is one and only one appropriate therapeutic model and rigidly adheres to it regardless of how it meshes with the child's personality and presenting problem. This rigid approach forces the child's problem to fit into a preconceived mold, rather than exploring the child and her or his symptoms from a unique and individualized perspective. As pointed out previously, rigidity is not a desirable trait in child clinicians, as therapists and counselors must be able to adapt treatment strategies to the unique presentation of each child and family. However, this is not to imply that clinicians must not follow a preferred theoretical system. Indeed, it is quite helpful for clinicians to have a preferred style or treatment approach. Flexibility comes from being capable to use a large number of strategies within and compatible with that approach. Thus, even psychodynamically oriented clinicians do not shun other strategies if they are compatible with particular treatment goals and may use reinforcers and extinction consciously and purposefully. However, the basic understanding of the child is derived through a theoretical system. Clinicians must avoid the problem verbalized so eloquently by Maslow when he said, "To those whose only tool is a hammer, every problem looks like a nail."

Me Adult/You Child.   In the Me Adult/You Child Countertransference emphasis is placed on adult–child differences through which the child is disadvantaged because of less experience, less knowledge, and less power. In such a relationship, the development of trust is easily thwarted, and a relationship in which the child can be understood from her or his perspective is not given a chance. Instead, children are viewed through a lens that colors them helpless and dependent. This approach frequently implies that the adult in the relationship felt this way as a child and has learned to overcome or hide feelings of powerlessness and helplessness through identification with the aggressor, that is, with adults in the childhood environment. Thus, the clinician's own adult behavior is driven not by mature adult feelings but by the attempt to cover insecurity through firm, even aggressive, attitudes. In the therapy or counseling relationship, this type of adult–child relationship is counterproductive and fails to allow for adequate rapport.

Good-Enough Parent.   The Good-Enough Parent Countertransference is based on the mistaken idea that therapy or counseling is like being a parent—the clinician uses parenting skills to effect change. However, therapy and counseling are in no way equivalent to parenting. Parenting is done on a daily basis; it envelops the child in a way treatment can never do. Yes, some parenting skills translate into the treatment environment, but they are crucial neither to building rapport nor to understanding the child. Clinicians who are parents are particularly prone to misusing this relational pattern as it is easy to fall back on the familiar when in a new or challenging situation. In fact, more problems are encountered by therapists or counselors who have children and identify with their parenting role than by those who are not. For instance, one trainee who had four (very well-adjusted) children of her own frequently found herself cleaning up after her clients, teaching, caretaking, and otherwise taking a mothering role. She was painfully aware of this tendency and had great difficulty ridding herself of habits that become ingrained over 20 years of parenting. She initially thought that her experience as a parent would enhance her therapeutic interaction with children, but she quickly realized that, more often than not, it got in the way. This is not to say that all parents will have difficulty being child clinicians. They may simply need to watch this particular countertransference more cautiously.

Big Sibling. The Big Sibling Countertransference refers to clinicians who take the approach that they are to become the big sister or brother for the child. In this approach, the clinician avoids real issues and provides guidance in a cautious manner. Clinicians are reluctant to confront and challenge for fear that this may be painful for the child. Focus is on play with the intent to provide a supportive holding environment in which the child can feel safe and somewhat intellectually stimulated. Thus, the child may be introduced to new games, new ways of dealing with stressful situations, new manners of playing with toys, even new problem-solving strategies, but process issues and history issues are not adequately addressed. This treatment, while often engaging for the child, remains superficial and fails to explore problems in sufficient depth to create lasting change.

Babysitter. Very similar to the Sibling Countertransference, the Babysitter Countertransference is focused on teaching and playing. In this approach, clinicians feel responsible for the child's welfare and change, as well as for all interactions in the playroom. Children are seen as having been placed in the care of the clinician who watches over them with a protective eye, but not necessarily with an eye that promotes self-awareness, psychological growth, change, or problem solving. This relational pattern is particularly common among clinicians who are not yet clear themselves about the purpose of therapy or counseling and who have not been able to identify process in treatment. It results in a fun-filled session for clinician and child after which the clinician cannot help but ask what has really been accomplished beyond keeping the child entertained and satisfied. Clearly, this is not the purpose of treatment, and such patterns must be addressed as they arise.

Teacher. The Teacher Countertransference is similarly nontherapeutic in that it focuses on didactic, rational, and instructional purposes. Although some instruction does and should occur in treatment, it is never the sole therapeutic strategy. Children cannot help but learn in treatment, and often rationality is an important aspect of intervention. However, there are many other components in the child–clinician relationship that are not present in the child–teacher relationship. For instance, the therapy or counseling relationship is focused not on new knowledge acquisition per se but rather on self-awareness and growth. Strong emotions are allowed to develop and difficult aspects of a child's life are faced and dealt with. Material about a child's life, to which a teacher would not routinely be privy, is shared with the clinician. Additionally, a teacher knows only limited parts of the child's life, whereas clinicians must keep abreast of as complete a picture as possible. The teacher-therapist focuses so much on cognitive material that other human aspects are neglected. The expression of affect, the voicing of needs, and the sharing of desires may fail to take place. Intellectualization, rationalization, and isolation of affect may be encouraged, and, in turn, further decrease expressed emotion in the child.

One trainee who had developed this type of countertransference frequently found himself helping the child with certain tasks the child had chosen for herself in the course of a session. For instance, one time, the young girl picked a floor puzzle that was in the playroom for assessment purposes. The child attempted to put the puzzle together, but frequently looked at the counselor to invite help. The counselor would respond to these looks by making suggestions about turning a particular puzzle piece or about trying a different place in the puzzle. When he was queried in supervision about the purpose of his behavior, he indicated he wanted to teach the child in a manner that would increase her cognitive complexity. Although a noble goal indeed, it is not the therapeutic issue that could have been followed up on in this context. For example, the counselor could have explored why the girl looked at him. Rather than reacting to the assumption she was openly asking for help, he could have continued to observe to see how she handled her frustration about being unable to complete the puzzle, or he could have addressed the idealizing transference that was developing. A wealth of truly therapeutic information and opportunity for intervention was lost through didactics. The Teacher Countertransference is an easy one for clinicians to fall into as it is easily understood and implemented by the intellectualizing, bright adult that therapists often are. However, if the counselors find themselves teaching and lecturing the child exclusively, they must take a thorough look at the appropriateness of the overall treatment process.

Cop.   The Cop Countertransference reveals clinicians to be preoccupied with power issues, commanding children and taking a shape-up attitude toward them. Cops spell out consequences and contingencies for behavior all the time at the exclusion of other therapeutic interventions. Again, in moderation this type of intervention is appropriate, but never as the only counseling strategy. Further, the preoccupation with power tends to get in the way of building trust, and the spelling out of contingencies and consequences makes it unnecessary for children to try to figure these out on their own, or even ever to have to experience them. Sometimes trial-and-error learning can be quite therapeutic for children and preventing this process is not always helpful. The Cop also tends to be quite distanced and aloof, failing to allow children to build a warm relationship with an adult in which they can safely experiment with new behaviors and affects. The aloofness of the counselor tends to squelch the expression of emotion and gives implicit messages about the inappropriateness of emotionality.

Challenges in Working with Parents

The term parent here is used in a wider sense of the word than usual. Specifically, it refers to any primary caretaker in a child's life, regardless of biological relationships.

As such, parents are any adults who serve in a parenting role with a child, including stepparents, adoptive parents, foster parents, surrogate parents, and so on. Given this definition of the term parent, anytime a clinician begins work with a child, the initial contact is made with a parent. A parent is in charge of bringing the child to treatment; a parent is in charge of payment; a parent is usually at least peripherally involved in the child's treatment. Given this reality, there are certain aspects of counseling children that arise specifically due to this involvement of a third party in the treatment. In adult therapy or counseling, there is rarely a third party whose involvement must be considered. Hence, child clinicians must be concerned about the impact of parental involvement on children's treatment.

Child as Identified Client

Treatment of children presents many challenges not routinely encountered in the work with adult clients. Most importantly, children rarely come to therapy or counseling of their own volition. Most commonly they are brought by a parent because of concerns of the parent about the child, or on the recommendation of a teacher or school counselor. These reasons for seeking treatment can create unique resistances for various reasons. First of all, children may perceive clinicians as being in cahoots with parents or teachers. Second, children may perceive clinicians as intrusive and frightening because of their understanding of what the referral is all about. Not uncommonly clinicians encounter children who were threatened with counseling by a parent. This leaves children with the expectation that counselors are somehow going to punish the child, require fast change, or side with parents. If referrals were prompted by delinquency or acting out, children may be quite suspicious. Children's preconceived notions about counseling and counselors may impede the development of therapeutic rapport and of therapeutic transferences and, therefore, must be addressed quickly by the clinician.

Children's and Parents' Expectations about Treatment

Related to the reality that they are rarely, if ever, the initiators of treatment, children often do not understand why they are taken to see a clinician, and they do not usually know what therapy or counseling is all about. They may have all sorts of misconceived notions about what will happen to them and about the process in general. In fact, one child who was seen in treatment was told that he was going to see a doctor because of his bad grades. He was convinced that he would receive "shots" (having had a previous negative experience with inoculations), and was extremely frightened. Even though this fear was allayed immediately, he remained hesitant during the intake interview and had great difficulty separating from his father for the individual child interview. Because of children's lack of knowledge about treatment, it behooves clinicians to talk about the reasons for and the process of treatment early in the intake interview. In fact, parents should be strongly urged to discuss the decision to come to counseling or therapy with their children prior to attending the very first session.

Asking parents to prepare children, however, is often difficult because often parents themselves do not quite know what to expect from treatment, much less how to prepare their child. For this reason, the first telephone contact is best made by a clinician so that this issue can be discussed. Clinicians can take this opportunity to inquire about parents' expectations about what counseling is like and how it is hoped to help the child, as well as to tell the parents what therapy involves regarding time commitments, expenses, and length of treatment. Soliciting and providing information allows clinicians to clear up misconceptions before the initial contact and lays the groundwork for helping parents prepare the child.

It is good practice to ask parents how they plan to prepare a child for the first session. If the parents have no such plan, suggestions about what the child may need to be told can be made. Such suggestions may include, but are not limited to, the introduction of the problem for which help is being sought, discussions of the difference between a counselor or therapist and a physician, the focus on talking and playing versus intrusive procedures such as inoculations or physical exams, the caring and nurturing position of the clinician as opposed to the punishing or challenging interaction that may be expected, the clinician's neutrality versus expected alliance with parents, the initial focus on the family rather than the individual child, and the idea that the child will be asked to meet with this adult alone. Recommendations about and provision of references for preparatory books can be made at that time.

Parental Abuse or Neglect of a Child

The many possible countertransference reactions a clinician might have because of parental abuse or neglect of a child was covered in detail previously. In addition to the stimulation of countertransference, however, parental abuse also brings with it unique challenges to the treatment of the child. These challenges are legal and therapeutic in nature. The legal aspects of child abuse are very clear-cut with regard to their definition and required action by law, but less clear-cut with regard to their effect on the therapeutic relationships. Although laws in almost all fifty states in the U.S. clearly require that any suspicion of child abuse or neglect must be reported to the appropriate government agency, therapeutic implications of such action have resulted in violations of the law by large numbers of clinicians (Horton and Cruise, 2001; Kalichman, Craig, and Follingstad, 1990; Kenny, 2001). Some clinicians have argued that once a family is in treatment, therapeutic progress may be hindered, not facilitated, by current reporting laws (Renninger, Veach, and Bagdade, 2002). Although this point is arguable, the law is clear. Suspicion of abuse must be reported. Given the importance of this issue, it is covered in detail in the chapter on ethics.

Parent Consultation about a Child's Treatment

Parents have a right to be informed about treatment progress and process of their children, if only because they generally provide payment and transportation. Treatment updates are done carefully, as they are necessary to keep parents informed, but must honor the confidentiality of the child. There is a fine line between divulging personal issues of the child versus providing evidence for movement and progress in treatment to the parents. It is generally best to focus update-sessions with parents on their perception of the child's behavior change and on process, as opposed to content, issues in the child's therapy.

Meetings with and involvement of parents may also affect the interaction of the clinician with the child. One 12-year-old boy was quite uncommonly hostile in a session that immediately followed a meeting between his mother and therapist. When the therapist commented on this, the boy disclosed that he was very upset about the meeting of the two women, as he was sure that they were talking negatively about him. This example demonstrates that the therapist must be sensitive to a child's suspicions and concerns about meetings with parents and best discuss the occurrence of such a consultation with the child before and after it has occurred. If the child is old enough, and the parents sufficiently reasonable, it might be best not to meet with the parents separately but to have a family meeting instead. This demonstrates to the child that the counselor has nothing to hide from the child and honors the child's confidentiality.

Coordinating Multiple Sets of Parents

Even more challenging is the coordination of treatment and consultation when more than one set of parents is actively involved with the child. It is preferable to have conjoint sessions with all concerned adults; however, this is not always possible as the adults involved may not always be on speaking terms. Such a situation necessitates separate meetings with different sets of parents, and not uncommonly results in parents' attempts to communicate with the other set of parents through the clinician. Such triangulation is to be avoided but at times may be necessary to ascertain optimal exchange of information among parents for the child's sake. Counselors must be very cautious about these issues and aware of the hidden demands placed on them by the child's parents. The more communication can be facilitated among various sets of parents, the better for the child. Finally, it would be a grave mistake if therapists ignored a set of parents who expresses the desire to be involved.

Cooperation of Parents in the Treatment of Their Child

One final challenge is the level of cooperativeness of parents. Children cannot generally bring themselves to treatment; they depend on the adults in their lives to do so. This fact often presents a great challenge for the child clinicians because it leaves an important aspect of treatment under the control of a third party. Absences and tardiness cannot be interpreted in the same manner as with an adult client. Absences and lateness cannot be challenged with the child directly, and can be hurtful for the child and frustrating for the therapist. However, the worst of all decisions that parents can make in this regard is related to the timing of terminations. Often treatment goals have not been entirely reached when parents decide that either enough progress was made to end treatment, or not enough progress has been achieved to date to warrant the hassles and expenses involved for the parent. Terminations under these circumstances are not only obviously premature, but often painful and frustrating for both child and counselor.

Working with the Special Needs of Children

Aside from special issues that arise because of parental involvement, there are also aspects of child therapy or counseling that are unique because of the special needs and features of children. Children have different ways of expressing themselves than adults, using verbal media significantly less often. Their developmental level is vastly different from that of the clinician and may present a unique challenge. Because of these differences, as well as because of children's uniqueness with regard to affective self-expression, clinicians must be prepared to have more intense feelings in their work with children. This requires preparation to respond appropriately and therapeutically.

The Use of Metaphor in Communication

Children communicate through metaphor and play, thus requiring clinicians to have some awareness and knowledge of symbolism. Often, children communicate through comments or questions that, on the surface, appear unrelated to their present-ing complaint—clinicians need to learn to decipher their metacommunication. For example, one girl, who was seen in treatment because of psychotic symptomatology and a very deprived background, once asked the therapist in the course of play whether the cow she was using was going to have enough milk. The therapist, know-ing the child's history, immediately understood her concern, which was twofold. First, the child was asking if the therapist (whom she saw leave the play therapy room prior to her session with another child) would have enough caring and understanding to give for her as well as other children. Second, she was asking if her own parents were able to provide adequate nurturing and support for her. The therapist, with this understanding in mind, indicated that the cow indeed would have sufficient milk, though occasionally it may appear as though there was not enough to go around. When this concern returned at a later point in this child's therapy, the child learned through mutual story-telling what the calf could do for herself when the cow runs out of milk.

This example demonstrates not only the importance of understanding a meta-phor, but also the need for counselors to respond within the metaphor. Responding to the latent content by making it manifest (e.g., in this example by saying that the mother and father, or the therapist, will indeed attempt to provide for the child as best they can) can be much too threatening. After all, there is usually a reason why a child chooses a metaphor, and generally it has to do with an attempt at keeping fear under control by addressing issues indirectly or unconsciously. It is important to remain with the child's choice of metaphor or language, that is, not to introduce the clinician's own metaphor. The child may have difficulty understanding it, or may feel misunderstood. Although the novice may feel overwhelmed by the prospect of having to understand symbols and metaphors, this process is generally much easier than it sounds. After all, therapists never enter treatment blindly but rather have in-depth knowledge about a child's dynamics and family situation. Having this context provides sufficient infor-mation to understand a child's symbolism. Further, children rarely use important symbols or metaphors only once. Thus, even if it is not understood the first time, there is usually another chance.

It is important to keep in mind that each child uses symbols and metaphors in unique ways. Thus, what may mean one thing to one child may have a totally and uniquely different meaning to another. The clinician should never assume that meta-phors translate across children. Studying symbolism (such as found in dictionary-type references that discuss the meanings of various story contents or objects) is generally not useful. It is much more productive to listen to a child's communication with an open mind and to place the play or verbalization in the context of the child's background and presenting concern. The same holds true for nonverbal communication, including body language. Behaviors or gestures are unique to each child and have specific meaning. For one child, lying down on the floor may indicate that she or he is beginning to trust the counselor, whereas for another child the same behavior may be a sign of resistance or avoidance.

Sensitivity to the Child's Developmental Level

Understanding a child's language and means of communication also fits into the larger context of adapting to the child's developmental level. Clinicians make efforts to be constantly aware of children's cognitive levels, and have the ability to adapt to children's ways of processing information and self-expression. This assumes that (as discussed previously with regard to educational background) clinicians have knowledge of developmental theory, as well as sensitivity to the special needs of children that arise from this developmental context. To prepare clinicians for this task, the clinician's previous education must have addressed child development in detail. Sensitivity to children's overall developmental levels is the key to successful treatment and is therefore covered in a full chapter later in this book. A few common cautions are discussed here.

Language and Reasoning.   Most importantly, clinicians need to learn to adjust language to the child's capabilities. Vocabulary may need to be scaled down, adjusted to specific regional variations, and expanded to include the language of the child's specific developmental stage (the latter is most relevant with adolescents). Communicating at a child's maturity level is crucial. It is important to not over- or underexplain concepts. In other words, clinicians must take care to use language and reasoning skills that are neither too advanced nor too basic. The latter is often forgotten in an attempt to downscale vocabulary or logic. However, treating all children at the same level of communication, whether they are three or ten is insensitive and can even be condescending to the older child who has more sophisticated logic and language.

Motor Development.   Clinicians have to adjust motor involvement to children's needs. It is unrealistic to expect a young child to sit still for a long time. Children need to move around as they explore their environment and express themselves. Hence, anyone considering doing child therapy must consider personal willingness to be physically active and engage in physically challenging interchanges with the child. Even if not a lot of gross motor movement is involved, fine motor activities are highly likely. Finally, any child counselor must expect to sit on the floor, at least on occasion.

Emotional Differentiation.   Young children do not yet have the skills of verbalizing emotions with regard to varying intensity and qualitative differentiation. For them, feelings are global phenomena that change rapidly. Child clinicians cannot expect an answer to questions that require the child to explain emotional experiences with regard to their subtleties. Children cannot tie more than one affect at a time to a given situation; they cannot explain nuances of affects felt in slightly different situations; they cannot recognize the simultaneousness of conflicting emotions. Not being sensitive to such developmental realities can lead to inappropriate lines of questioning that are frustrating to both child and counselor.

Sense of Time.   The clinician working with children must be aware that children's sense of time differs from that of adults. Young children do not think in terms of yesterday and tomorrow and may have difficulty with concepts that suggest that learning from behaviors and events in the past is valuable to preventing difficulties in the future. Children's experiences are much more bound to the present, and for them this type of argument has little value. Additionally, for very young children, concepts of minutes and hours are vague. Thus, they are not served by statements that use these variables. For instance, if a three-year-old child asks how much longer a session will last, the therapist would not respond by giving a concrete time frame in minutes (e.g., we have 12 minutes) but rather would respond with a process statement that responds to the child's question (e.g., we have enough time left to finish what we are doing).

Environment and Equipment.   A final developmental consideration is related to the size of the office used and the equipment and furniture contained within it. A child playroom cannot simply be an adult office modified for an hour a week to accommodate work with children. It must be responsive to children's smaller size, developmental needs for exploration, and reality that they need to move a round and want to touch things. A thorough discussion about child-appropriate therapy environments is presented in a later chapter.

The Child's Fluctuations in Affect

Children who present for treatment are also often observed to have wide fluctuations in affect and behavior during their sessions (Bornstein, 1948). These may range from severe acting out to significant expressions of depression. These quick fluctuations can be unnerving for clinicians who fail to consider that children's realities are much more momentary and situation-bound than those of adults. The younger the child, the more likely that large fluctuations and strong expressions of situational affects occur. This is particularly true for the expression of negative affects, which may be very intense at one moment and completely denied the next. Therapists must learn to understand these fluctuations from a child's developmental perspective, which will help alleviate unnecessary frustration. Counselors must also learn to live with a degree of unpredictability that arises from these wide fluctuations in children's affects and needs states.

Children tend to express significant needs for dependency on their environment and the adults within it. Thus, they may make requests for help or support that tempt clinicians to provide for them. They may express significant needs that counselors know are not met by parents. These situations are taxing for therapists, often leaving them feeling helpless and uncaring. For instance, one counselor who was working with a four-year-old child who had to leave her family for the summer and was very distraught by this fact, found himself feeling both angry and very helpless. He began to doubt the value of the treatment and became the victim of his own sense of not being able to help and to let the child depend on him for help. He had to come to terms with his own helplessness before he could help this child master hers. Once he came to grips with his frustration, he could help her ready herself for the summer without her family by using imagery and other visualization strategies that she could use to gain a sense of permanence of the existence of her psychological parents.

The Therapist's Evoked Feelings

Children, in addition to expressing affect more intensely and with more variability than adult clients, also tend to arouse more emotion in their clinicians than do adult clients. These feelings can range from aggression to protectiveness to fear to tension and to out-of-control feelings. Unless counselors are prepared for this affect they may easily be overwhelmed by it. Dealing with a child with a horrendous abuse history is taxing and draining and requires good mental preparation on the therapist's part. In fact, some children are best seen with no appointment scheduled immediately after the session because of the emotional impact the session can have on the clinician. This might appear like quite an unaffordable luxury; however, it may prove to be a necessity in terms of ascertaining that the next client being seen receives the full benefit of a well-functioning clinician. If schedule flexibility cannot be arranged, this child should be the last client seen on that particular day. Fortunately, not many children are so taxing that this is necessary.

Summary and Concluding Thoughts

There is multitude of issues about which a clinician needs to be knowledgeable and skilled before entering into treatment with a child. The type of relationship adults tend to forge with children, the special circumstances children bring to treatment, and the unique process issues that are intrinsic to the work with them present extraordinary challenges in child treatment. However, with self-awareness and the willingness to maintain an open mind and seek consultation, the work with children can indeed be one of the most gratifying experiences for a clinician.

Once clinicians have mastered the art of self-reflection and have explored the issues presented in this chapter, they are ready to decide whether they want to work with children. If they are ready to move on to the actual work with children, a few additional preparatory issues are best considered, especially as related to the impact of culture and ethnicity of children and their families on the therapeutic work, the ethics unique to work with children, and the environment in which children are seen. The next three chapters address these preliminary issues before moving into the actual details of assessing and then treating children and their families.

2

Cultural Sensitivity in Child Therapy and Counseling

By Mark E. Johnson*

> *In those States in which ethnic, religious or linguistic minorities or persons of indigenous origin exist, a child belonging to such a minority or who is indigenous shall not be denied the right, in community with other members of his or her group, to enjoy his or her own culture, to profess and practise his or her own religion, or to use his or her own language.*
>
> —Article 30 of the UN Convention on the Rights of the Child

Once clinicians have engaged in self-exploration to determine their readiness to work with children, the next logical step is to explore readiness to work with children from diverse backgrounds. It is virtually inevitable that child mental health care providers will work with clients who have racial, ethnic, or cultural backgrounds different from their own. This is true whether therapists or counselors are of African, Hispanic, Asian, European, or Native American descent and whether they are working in private practices, community mental health centers, or hospital settings. Gaining the skills and knowledge necessary to deal with racially, ethnically, and culturally diverse child clienteles is as important as gaining the basic skills and knowledge of child therapy and counseling themselves.

Before a discussion of culturally sensitive treatment approaches to mental health work with children can commence, a clear understanding of several central terms has to be developed. Specifically, *race*, *ethnicity*, and *culture* are often mentioned in the literature that concerns cross-cultural therapy and counseling approaches and need to be defined briefly. The term race refers to a biological classification based on physical and genetic characteristics, with only three primary races identified: Caucasoid, Mongoloid, and Negroid. Ethnicity, by contrast, refers to a classification based on shared

*Dr. Johnson is Professor of Psychology at the University of Alaska Anchorage.

social and cultural heritage, such as, for example, Native or Asian American. Finally, culture refers to learned behavior that is shared and transmitted within a group across generations or with new members, for instance, as occurs in gay and lesbian cultures. To elaborate further, although members of the Jewish ethnic group have a shared social, cultural, and religious heritage, they do not constitute a race. Similarly, within the White ethnic group in the United States, there are a number of cultures, such as Irish Americans, Italian Americans, and German Americans, each of which has a learned set of values, attitudes, beliefs, and behaviors.

In other words, race breaks down further to ethnicity, which, in turn, may cross racial boundaries (e.g., a Native American individual who has a biological race combining Mongoloid and Negroid). Similarly, ethnicity breaks down further into cultures, which in turn may cross ethnic boundaries (e.g., a gay individual who has an African American and Alaska Native ethnic identification). Individuals can belong to several cultural groups at once (e.g., may be upper middle class, Caribbean African American, and physically challenged), they may have varied ethnic backgrounds and identify with more than one ethnic group (e.g., may be Italian American and Navajo, identifying primarily with their Navajo upbringing but also incorporating Italian American values), and they may be biologically racially mixed (e.g., may have one Caucasoid and one Negroid parent). In fact, in modern society, most clients have multiple identifications and diverse backgrounds. Clearly, race, ethnicity, and culture are not identifiable by a person's appearance or even by easily observed behaviors, an assumption that is often made in day-to-day life. To understand a client's racial, ethnic, and cultural identity, careful questioning is needed to assess that person's self-identification and perception. The group with which the client identifies most (in which the client claims heritage) becomes that individual's reference group and has the strongest impact with regard to having shaped behaviors, attitudes, and values (Phinney, 1990, 1996).

In addition to differences accounted for by ethnic or cultural backgrounds of children, there are differences based on minority status. Although ethnic or cultural status often overlaps with minority status of a group of people, this is not always so. A comprehensive approach to multigroup or multicultural sensitivity therefore encompasses not only ethnicity and culture, but also minority status. Minority status as relevant in the treatment context has nothing to do with actual number of people within a specific group. Instead, a minority group has long been and remains best defined as

> a group of people who, because of physical or cultural characteristics, are singled out from others in the society in which they live for differential and unequal treatment, and who therefore regard themselves as objects of collective discrimination. . . . Minority status carries with it the exclusion from full participation in the life of the society. (Wirth, 1945, p. 347)

Given this definition, it is evident that the term *minority* characterizes a number of groups in American society that experience oppression and, as a result, are not able to participate fully in society as a whole. This definition makes the conceptual identification of a minority separate from the numerical concept. For example, in the United States, as in most countries, women have suffered oppression at the hands of males, rendering them a cultural minority, despite being a numerical majority. Using this definition, other minorities include, but certainly are not limited to, individuals with physical disabilities, the elderly, gays and lesbians, and individuals who are economically disadvantaged. Clearly, the child counselor in a culturally diverse society works with individuals who vary not only in terms of ethnic or cultural background but also in terms of various avenues of oppression. Given these definitions, this chapter focuses on work with children of different ethnic groups, whose cultural backgrounds are not mainstream, and who may be a member of a minority group.

Ethnic and Cultural Diversity of the United States

Throughout its history, the United States has been a pluralistic society. Even in the centuries before the European conquest of the continent, there were scores of different Native American tribes, each with its own unique heritage and culture. Since the mass immigration of Europeans, the North America has attracted individuals of various ethnicities and from different cultures around the world. Some of these peoples were brought here as slaves to serve the white settlers; some flocked to the new country to avoid economic and religious persecution; others came in hopes of attaining a new life. Over the years, immigration to the United States of America has continued and resulted in a society that is defined largely by its cultural diversity.

In the United States, this diverse society is often referred to as a "melting pot," implying that the U.S. is a conglomeration of different elements that leaves the final product different from the parts that constitute it. One adverse implication of this term is that by using a concept of merging cultures, it is implied that as different cultures are integrated into mainstream society, they lose their unique identity. This further implies that to become part of society, individuals from different cultural backgrounds must forsake their unique cultural heritage and background to be accepted or "melted" into the mainstream. A more accurate and realistic depiction of the United States would be as a "pluralistic quilt." In this characterization, the uniqueness of each culture is recognized and each culture adds to and strengthens society as a whole. Members of diverse groups maintain their cultural background and are embraced by and functioning within society as a whole. It is within the framework of a pluralistic quilt that underlies this chapter and defines the therapeutic work of a sensitive care provider.

The nature and extent of the pluralistic quilt that is the United States become evident when demographic data of its population are examined. In 1980, approximately 80 percent of the population was White (non-Hispanic) and 20 percent was non-White, primarily of African, Asian, Hispanic, and Native American descent (U.S. Census Bureau, 1980). By 1990, the White population comprised 75.6 percent of the total population, and by 2000, 69.4 percent. In contrast, the Hispanic population grew to 9 percent in 1990 and 12.6 percent in 2000; the African American population grew to 11.7 percent in 1990 and 12.7 percent in 2000; and the Asian American population grew to 2.7 percent in 1990 and 3.8 percent in 2000; the Native populations (including Native Americans, Alaska Natives, and Native Hawaiians) remained at less than 1 percent of the total population throughout this time period (U.S. Census Bureau, 2001). By 2050, it is estimated that the White (non-Hispanic) population will comprise a bare majority (50.1%) in United States. By contrast, Hispanics will make up 24.4 percent, African Americans 14.6 percent, and Asian Americans 8.0 percent. Foreshadowing these population estimates, in 2003, the U.S. Census Bureau estimated that the majority of the residents in three states and the District of Columbia were non-White (Hawaii, 77%; DC 72%; New Mexico, 56%; and California, 54%).

Breaking down these population numbers by age further reinforces the need for child clinicians in particular to be culturally sensitive and prepared to deal with culturally diverse children and families (Hinman, 2003). In 2000, approximately 24 percent of White residents in the United States were under the age of 18 years. This percentage contrasts with the approximately 33 percent of who were African American, 33 percent Hispanic, 27 percent Asian American, and 34 percent Native American under the age of 18 years. Given the higher birth rate among non-White families in the United States, the differences in number of members under the age of 18 years between White and non-White residents will continue to grow throughout this century, resulting in an increasingly non-White child clientele. Indeed, according to the U.S. Census Bureau, as of 2003, 45 percent of children under the age of five years were non-White. Nowhere is this trend toward the increasing presence of non-White children in the general population more evident than in the public school system, in which 42% of elementary and high school students are non-White. Further, in the 100 largest school districts in the United States, 69% of students are non-White, non-Hispanic (Sable and Hoffman, 2005). Clearly, the need for increased cultural sensitivity is not a fad or trend that will dissipate with time; rather it is a realistic and necessary movement for care providers who work with children and their families.

In recognition of the diversity inside and outside of the United States and the need to adequately and appropriately provide mental health services to all ethnic, cultural, and minority members of a given society, the American Psychological Association (APA), the American Counseling Association (ACA), the National Association for Social Workers (NASW), and other professional mental health organizations have expressed strong support of the need for mental health care providers to be culturally sensitive and for training programs to help meet this need. For example, the APA's ethical guidelines clearly state that "psychologists are aware of and respect cultural, individual, and role differences, including those based on age, gender, gender identity, race, ethnicity, culture, national origin, religion, sexual orientation, disability, language, and socioeconomic status and consider these factors with working with members of such groups" (American Psychological Association, 2002, p. 1063). Similarly, the ACA Code of Ethics states that counselors "actively attempt to understand the diverse cultural background of the clients they serve. Counselors also explore their own cultural identities and how these affect their values and beliefs about the counseling process" (American Counseling Association, 2005, p. 4). The need for inclusion of cultural issues in all therapists' training was advanced by the National Conference on Graduate Education in Psychology (American Psychological Association, 1987a) when this committee stated that "psychologists must be educated to realize that all training, practice, and research in psychology are profoundly affected by the cultural, subcultural, and national contexts within which they occur" (p. 1079). Obviously, then, there is a growing press from professional organizations, as well as from individual practitioners, for therapists to become culturally sensitive to meet the needs of a culturally diverse population and clientele (Lee, 2005; Ponterotto, Casas, Suzuki, and Alexander, 2001). The challenge presented by these statistics, definitions, and ethical dictates is one of becoming culturally sensitive to the wide diversity of clientele that may present for treatment. Following, practical guidelines are provided that counselors and therapists can use to become more culturally sensitive; general issues that may arise in cross-cultural treatment situations are reviewed.

Becoming a Culturally Sensitive Child Clinician

Although becoming a truly culturally sensitive child clinician can be a difficult, arduous, and challenging task, it is well worth the effort, both on a professional and a personal level. A large aspect of the difficulty some individuals have in becoming culturally sensitive is due to the fact that growing up in the United States has exposed them to a long history fraught with biases, stereotypes, and prejudices. Although it may be argued that prejudices have lessened considerably over the years and now exist only in isolated situations, it can also be asserted that prejudice is as pervasive as ever, though more covert than before. Regardless of the position taken, it is difficult to deny the presence of prejudice in our society toward many minority groups. The presence of prejudice in the United States is exemplified by the growing incidence of racially inspired violence on college campuses, increasing membership in and visibility of White supremacist groups, heightened debate over gay and lesbian rights, and relatively low numbers of women and other minority members on corporate boards and in elected positions.

More damaging than overt prejudice is the pervasive presence of covert discrimination and prejudice. This form of prejudice can be most damaging because it is insidious and difficult to recognize and challenge immediately. Over the years, covert discrimination has been perpetuated by the media through negative depictions of minority group members, such as by casting Americans of African, Hispanic, or Asian descent as criminals or in some other demeaning role or by reporting only the negative—and not the positive—activities of minority groups. Although the media have become more sensitive to these issues in recent years and have made considerable progress in eliminating stereotypic roles, pervasive subtle (and at times not so subtle) prejudice remains.

Another very covert manner in which prejudice is maintained and propagated in the United States is through the language that is used to describe various situations. A few very obvious examples are phrases such as "jew one down" to depict bargaining over a price or "Indian giver" to illustrate someone who gives something only to take it back later. Obviously, once examined, these examples emerge as clearly and overtly prejudicial and yet they are commonly used. Less overt, but equally prejudicial are depictions of goodness, purity, and virginity as white and evil and corruption as black. Other subtle linguistic examples of prejudice are contained in terms such as chairman, serviceman, and councilman, words that seem to exclude women from holding these positions. Similar damage is done by referring to all people with masculine pronouns (he, his, or him) and the generic use of the word "man," as in mankind instead of humankind.

Covert prejudice is also expressed in daily life, often completely unrecognized by the individual perpetrating it. For example, one adolescent revealed a memory of lasting impact that occurred when he arrived at his newly assigned special classroom for gifted children. When he entered the room, the teacher asked him if he was in the wrong class without even asking his name, implying that he could not possibly be in the right place (the gifted classroom). The teacher's judgment of the student's intelligence was attributed to the student because of his skin color and overt Filipino background. Another child recalled her agony and shame at being praised in her classroom for having artistic skills that she did not actually have but that were attributed to her simply by virtue of her Alaska Native background. This is a good example of how prejudice can hurt even when the ascription is—on the face of it—quite positive.

Growing up amidst overt and covert prejudices invariably has an impact on every child, leaving lasting impressions that, without some intervention, may carry forward into adulthood. This can be particularly difficult for minority children who are not able to find positive role models in public media and may begin to hold stereotypic prejudices toward (or against) their own people. Thus, people who grew up in a racist, sexist, and heterosexist society are responsible for casting out as many personal remnants of prejudice as possible. Eliminating prejudices is not always an easy task, but it is a critical step in the journey toward becoming a culturally sensitive child therapist.

Cultural sensitivity and competence are developed through introspective work and require a great deal of self-exploration and personal openness on the part of the developing professional (Fouad and Arrendondo, 2007a; Hogan, 2007). The effort is not only worthwhile, but also meets the spirit of contemporary professional ethical codes and is best applied toward the development of cultural competence with three major components: cultural awareness, cultural knowledge, and cultural skills (Pedersen, 2000). Simply put, cultural awareness is gained through self-reflection and respect for others, as well as through the strong recognition of and belief in the notion that difference does not equal deviance (Davis, 2006; Fouad and Arrendondo, 2007b; Namyniuk, 1996). Cultural knowledge can be accumulated via familiarization with cultural, anthropological, historical, and related events involving or affecting all cultural and ethnic groups with whom a clinician anticipates working (Ponterotto, Casas, Suzuki, and Alexander, 2001); cultural skill is developed through learning alternative approaches to intervention, reduction in prejudicial or stereotyped use of language, and political activism (Canino and Spurlock, 2000; Lee, 2006). Clinicians who strive to be culturally sensitive and competent need to be able to claim that all three of these traits are a part of their repertoire of skills and beliefs. Entire books have been written to assist mental health care providers develop these sensitivities (e.g., Fouad and Arrendondo, 2007a; Hogan, 2007; Pedersen, 2000; Roysircar, Sandhu, and Bibbins, 2003). Each of the three categories deserves further exploration, and an overview is provided in the Table 2.1. After a discussion of each area, information is provided on self-monitoring to maintain and enhance cultural sensitivity.

Awareness

Cultural awareness refers to the process of recognizing personal biases, prejudicial beliefs, and stereotypic attitudes or reactions. Gaining awareness has to precede

Table 2.1   Characteristics of Culturally Sensitive Child Clinicians

Awareness	• Is aware of and sensitive to own cultural heritage • Is aware of personal reactions to and behaviors with members of differing cultures • Is conscious and embracing of all minority groups of which she or he is a member • Values and respects cultural differences • Seeks out experiences involving members of differing cultural backgrounds • Is aware of own values and biases and their effect on therapy • Is sensitive to neither overemphasizing nor underemphasizing clinician–child cultural differences • Is aware of personal language use • Is aware of personal cultural identity and level of acculturation • Is comfortable with cultural differences between self and client • Is sensitive to situations that may require referral of a minority client to a member of the same cultural heritage • Is aware of within-group differences and respects individuality of all people
Knowledge	• Understands how the sociopolitical system in the United States treats minorities • Is knowledgeable about the presence of racism, sexism, and heterosexism and their effects on minorities • Is familiar with U.S. history, especially as relevant to various cultural groups • Knows about history of mental health treatment for minorities and potential biases of traditional psychotherapy theories • Knows cultural definitions of mental illness and perspectives on mental health services • Is knowledgeable about cultural and minority groups in the United States • Is knowledgeable about political, social, and economic pressures that come to bear on various cultural groups • Possesses specific knowledge about particular groups with whom she or he is working • Has clear and explicit knowledge and understanding of the generic characteristics of therapy and counseling • Is familiar with cross-cultural applications of therapy and counseling skills • Recognizes potential biases inherent in traditional therapy and counseling theories • Is knowledgeable about clients' native language • Is aware of effects that therapy and counseling setting and office can have on minority clients • Is knowledgeable about institutional barriers that prevent minorities from using mental health services
Skills	• Adjusts communication and therapeutic style to match individual clients' needs • Pays appropriate amounts of attention to role of culture • Makes appropriate use of nonverbal communication and silence • Manages not to categorize individuals • Shows flexibility in providing services to meet needs of clients • Demonstrates, when appropriate, institutional intervention skills • Selects and implements treatment strategies as appropriate for a given client • Acts as a social change agent to help reduce or eliminate racism, sexism, and heterosexism • Uses language that is devoid of prejudice and bias

modification of behavior and attitudes and can be a painful effort as clinicians begin to recognize that they are not free of recalcitrant prejudicial behaviors and beliefs.

A good first step toward gaining awareness involves the novice child therapist examining personal cultural background, assumptions, and stereotypes. This is best begun by taking a look at the cultures and minority groups of which the counselor is a member. Using the definition provided above—that a minority is a group that is a victim of oppression—clinicians-in-training need to consider whether they have been subject to oppression. Beginning with their own cultural heritage, counselors take into account aspects such as country of origin, language, skin color, and cultural practices. In so doing, therapists need to keep in mind that, although there have been some consistent recipients of oppression over the years, the focus of prejudice has shifted from culture to culture. Further, the degree of bias against a given culture may have waxed and waned but has always remained present in one form or another. There are numerous other considerations in identifying the minority groups of which new therapists may have been, or may currently be, a member. Gender is a consideration; despite being a numerical majority in the United States, women have experienced considerable oppression. Physical limitations are to be considered; individuals with physical disabilities have been the target of much bias. Another possible minority group is based on sexual orientation; gays, lesbians, and bisexuals have been the focus of much prejudice. As trainees begin to identify the groups of which they are members, they must contemplate their experiences that were the result of being members in that group.

Once the identification of personal background has taken place, attention shifts to assessing day-to-day reactions to different situations and different people to determine personal biases and prejudices. As trainees go through their day, they may start to become aware of personal reactions to people from different cultures and minority groups. Most people do not routinely assess such reactions. However, it is an important process on the road to becoming culturally aware. There are various ways in which therapists may be able to work on issues regarding other cultures. Internal reactions to ethnic jokes, for example, may provide valuable information to help the counselor develop self-awareness. Behavior while interacting with someone who is culturally different oneself can be attended to with new awareness. Many new clinicians recognize for the first time that they truly react differently with people from other ethnic, cultural, or minority groups, a realization that can cause concern or embarrassment. However, feeling shameful is not the point of assessing daily reactions. Rather, the point is to realize that everyone, even the most open-minded individual, has been influenced by societal and familial training. It is highly unlikely that anyone exists who is completely free of biases and differential reactions. It can be helpful to be aware of undue generalizations—applying negative attributes of one member of a group to all members of that group; to take stock of the cultural heritage or ethnic backgrounds of people with whom the clinician spends personal time; and to evaluate honestly whether friends and acquaintances are primarily of the same culture, and, if so, how this pattern came about.

The next step in developing increasing awareness involves seeking out experiences with different cultural, ethnic, or minority groups and identifying stereotypic beliefs and biases. In so doing, it is helpful to keep in mind that stereotypes can be both positive and negative but that both can be equally destructive because they move the counselor away from interacting with a client as an individual. Once stereotypes have been identified, they must be evaluated for accuracy, because for some stereotypes, there is a kernel of truth that renders them quite compelling. Testing stereotypes can be particularly difficult because it is always possible to think of at least one example to verify a preconceived notion. Therefore, it is important to look at the bigger picture of reality in evaluating stereotypes. For example, there is a prevalent stereotype held by many conservative Americans that non-White minority members exploit the welfare system in the United States. Although some minority members may do this, the reality is that the majority of welfare recipients are White, as are the majority of individuals who commit welfare fraud.

As a therapist striving to become culturally sensitive begins to monitor personal reactions to different situations and people, awareness of personal language adds an important component to self-exploration. Words are representative of thought processes used in communication and must be chosen carefully. At the extreme end, it is inappropriate to use blatant ethnic epithets, but attention must also be paid to the use of more subtle indicators of bias and prejudice (Sharma and Lucero-Miller, 1998). For instance, does the therapist use terms to describe an occupation that imply that women are incapable of holding the position, such as chairman, journeyman, or congressman? When referring generically to any professional, does the counselor use the word "he"? Is the assumption made when referring to clients that they are female whereas care providers are male? Are phrases used in which there is an ethnic bias present, for example, "being gypped," "welsh on a deal," or "Irish temper"? The use of racist and sexist terms is not permissible in the treatment setting even if the child and family themselves use the terms. That is, if a child uses offensive language, the therapist may reflect the child's feelings, but substitutes an appropriate term; the child's use of words such as Jap, nigger, or wetback *never* justifies the use of such expressions by the counselor.

Although some of these examples might seem subtle and innocuous, it is important to consider their potential negative effects. For example by using words that incorporate 'man' as the generic designation for both women and men, the clinician runs the risk of offending the adult women in a family and possibly the men and also sends subtle messages to the children. That is, if a therapist is working with a young girl who is quite withdrawn or unsure of herself, use of sexist language by the therapist no doubt contributes to the girl's view of herself as passive, as unable to reach many goals in life because they are reserved for men, and as not in control of her own destiny. Such sexism is not limited to the words that the counselor selects but may also be contained in actions. For example, sexism can occur in the choice of activities, toys, or rules set in the playroom. The culturally sensitive counselor recognizes personal stereotypes about what is deemed appropriate for girls versus boys. In actuality, every activity available in the room, every rule made in treatment, and every statement uttered by the clinician is best applicable to girls and boys alike. Even the subtlest influences over the child's behavior that are sex-role stereotyped can have long-lasting effects.

Another common prejudicial form of communication that is commonly used is to refer to members of a culture different from one's own as "they" or "them." This depersonalizes and segregates members of that culture, further perpetuating a separation of groups. As clinicians gain awareness of linguistic choices that reveal prejudice or bias (intentional or inadvertent), they are ready to select alternatives and to eliminate language that conveys prejudice and bias, no matter how subtle. As health care providers, counselors and therapists are looked up to and serve as a role model for children and their parents. Their behavior is scrutinized and even subtle and covert prejudice may be modeled and perpetuated. Thus, it is crucial that child clinicians present themselves as nonbiased professionals. As providers become conscious of their own behavior and work to increase their culturally sensitivity, therapy becomes considerably more valuable for children of any ethnic or cultural heritage (Ponterotto, Utsey, and Pedersen, 2006).

Given the focus on general respect for individuals, regardless of cultural or ethnic background, it is important for the child clinician to become aware that there are great differences among people within the same culture or ethnic group. Such differences within a group are often greater than those between cultures. One major within-group difference is the level of cultural identity development attained by an individual and the relative importance placed on an individual's own culture versus other cultures. Cultural identity development requires each individual to go through a process involving a number of stages. There are several models that describe this developmental process, including the Minority Identity Model (Atkinson, Morten, and Sue, 2003), the Black Identity Development Model (Jackson, 1975), and Negro-to-Black Conversion Experience (Cross, 1971). As an example, Cross's (1971) model views the development of an African American's cultural identity as passing through four stages: preencounter, encounter, immersion, and internalization. In the preencounter stage, the individual holds disdain and hatred for being Black; in the encounter stage, the person begins to value herself or himself for being Black; in the immersion stage, the individual rejects and hates all who are not Black; and in the internalization stage, the person gains a sense of self-confidence and security in who she or he is and is able to embrace all cultures. Although all models have been developed to describe the process encountered by minority group members, there are parallels to these models in White ethnic identity development (Carter and Helms, 1993; Helms and Carter, 1993). Further, this process does not hold true only for clients, but is present also among therapists. In recognition of this, to become culturally sensitive, child therapists must explore their own level of cultural identity. To do so, they need to examine deeply the sentiments that are held about their own and other cultures.

Related to the issue of cultural identity development, the child clinician needs to be aware that individuals within a culture vary considerably with regard to level of acculturation. Acculturation is defined as the degree to which an individual adopts the dominant society's social and cultural norms to the exclusion of her or his own culture's social and cultural norms (Pedersen, Draguns, Lonner, and Trimble, 2008). Acculturation is typically not a matter of endorsing one set of cultural norms versus another, but rather refers to the degree of incorporation of values or attitudes derived from both cultures. There are many factors that may affect a child's or family's level of acculturation, including socioeconomic status, number of generations that have been in the United States, educational and employment opportunities, and geographical location.

Gauging a person's level of acculturation is an important part of getting to know her or him and involves an evaluation of several factors, including the degree to which traditional cultural practices are followed and the native language that is used in thinking and speaking (Gibbs and Huang, 2003). A child's level of acculturation affects interactions with members of both cultures and may have an influence on choice of therapeutic approach. For example, if a Native American client appears very committed to Native culture, therapy might make more use of storytelling, a commonly used technique in Native culture, to resolve problems. It is important for child therapists on a path to cultural sensitivity to examine their own levels of acculturation and to further clarify their own cultural identity.

The previous paragraphs have presented but a few steps toward increasing clinicians' awareness on the road toward cultural sensitivity. In most major communities, workshops and courses are offered that aid and enhance this process of self-discovery and awareness. Further, there are a number of valuable books that may help counselors increase their cultural sensitivity (e.g., Fouad and Arrendondo, 2007b; Pedersen, 2000). Novice therapists are encouraged to take advantage of as many of these opportunities and resources as possible.

Knowledge

While awareness is being established, the clinician also strives to become more knowledgeable about cultural issues (Hinman, 2003). Courses, workshops, and seminars are obvious avenues for gaining accurate knowledge about the many issues related to culture. A number of additional possibilities are presented below. Cultural knowledge is essential for many reasons, including the fact that accurate information may help dissolve stereotypes and can lead to better appreciation and understanding of different cultures. In general, if used appropriately, knowledge assists counselors to interact effectively with members of other cultures. However, caution must be exercised so that newly acquired knowledge is not represented as the truth about *all* members of any given group. Such stereotypic or overgeneralized use of knowledge can be destructive and can get in the way of being truly effective and empathic (Namyniuk, 1996).

Knowledge gathered from books is best not limited to one discipline and optimally starts with a firm and accurate understanding of the history of the United States in general and the history of different ethnic and cultural groups within the United States in particular (e.g., Duran, 2006; Tataki, 1993; Zinn, 2003). This acquisition of knowledge may include an investigation of the history of immigration; the introduction, role, and history of slavery; and the conquest of the continent and historical trauma for Native Americans (Brave Heart-Yellowhorse, 2000, 2003). It is important to remember that history books can be very biased and selective in their reporting. As a result, it is often difficult to find books that provide a balanced perspective of historical events, making it important to read a variety of books and accounts written by numerous authors. Reading book reviews and descriptions (such as those on Amazon.com) can help clinicians identify and choose books written from an objective point of view. Through this reading, the therapist gains a better appreciation of what certain groups had to endure over the years and a better understanding of the contemporary issues they face.

Although it is important to have a historical perspective on the role of racism (and other prejudicial beliefs) in the United States, this knowledge would be incomplete without the information about the role of racism, sexism, and heterosexism in society today. In this context, the therapist must learn about the role of racism, sexism, and heterosexism in the development of minority children's self-identity. Counselors need to become knowledgeable about the processes of internalization and the adverse effects it can have on minority members who adopt biases about their own group, as well as other groups within society. Skilled therapists use this knowledge to help clients deal with prejudice and historical trauma in such a way that it does not adversely affect self-esteem and self-definition (Duran, 2006). Integrating this information with current statistics and data on poverty may provide added insights into the lives of many members of minority groups. Further, much has been written about political pressures that come to bear on minorities within the United States. Gaining this knowledge helps put many aspects of child clients' behavior into a more comprehensive and sensitive perspective.

The path toward cultural sensitivity includes reading books within the discipline of psychology, not just psychotherapy, and also on such topics as the psychology of racism. These readings also must include a review of empirical information about cross-cultural differences within the United States. However, a word of caution about much of this literature is in order. Some of this research, particularly projects that were completed before the 1980s, focused on comparing different cultural groups with European Americans, implicitly establishing White Americans as the cultural norm against which other cultures have to be compared to identify differences and similarities. Consequently, the results are frequently (mis)interpreted within a context of Whites as the ideal norm. Clearly, this is an inherent bias against cultural groups other than Whites that must be considered and compensated for when reading such research reports. Readers interested in more information about cultural biases in research are referred to Matsumoto (2000).

More specific to the field of child therapy, the road to cultural sensitivity must include a perusal of various books written on cross-cultural therapies. There are a number of books that offer specific information about providing therapy to members of various cultures. Of particular interest to child therapists are *Children of Color*, edited by Gibbs and Huang (2003), and *Ethnicity and Family Therapy*, edited by McGoldrick, Giordano, and Pearce (2005). Other books that provide separate chapters on providing therapy to members of various cultural groups (but not necessarily with a child-related focus) include those written by Atkinson, Morten, and Sue (2003), Lee (2005), Pedersen, Lonner, Draguns, and Trimble (2008), Ponterotto, Casas, Suzuki, and Alexander (2001), and Sue and Sue (2007). In reading these texts, novice child clinicians must remember that within-group differences are often greater than between-group differences, which are the primary foci of these texts. Therefore, the information provided in these books should be considered as general guidelines or possibilities rather than established facts that hold true for every individual member of a given ethnic group or culture. That is, counselors are encouraged to read these materials but to remain aware that not every member of a given culture fits the information that is provided.

Further, child therapists need to become knowledgeable about the often nonflattering history of mental health treatment for minorities. For instance, much has been written about the inherent biases that exist in many of the assessment tools (especially intelligence tests) that are commonly used in therapy settings (Geisinger, 2003; Samuda, 1998; Suzuki, Meller, and Ponterotto, 2007). Most of these instruments were normed on a primarily White population that did not include many, if any, individuals from other cultures. These instruments have been used historically in a very discriminatory manner. For example, Hispanic and African American children were often placed in special education classes solely on the basis of their scores on intelligence tests that were normed on White children. These placement decisions led to a disproportionate number of minority children in special education classes, ultimately resulting in a number of successful lawsuits ostensibly intended to eliminate this practice. Similarly, because of biases in norms, many tests tend to overpathologize members of cultures that are different from the White culture for which the instrument was standardized. With this knowledge, it is important that the culturally sensitive child therapist select assessment tools that have the most culturally appropriate norms and, if available, local norms. Even with these norms, well-trained care providers remain cautious in making clinical judgments based solely on assessment tools and consider the possible role of a child's culture in making interpretations and decisions.

In the process of becoming culturally sensitive, clinicians learn that the dominant theories of therapy in the United States were developed by White Europeans (predominantly male) and might not have universal application. Traditional personality theories as they are currently taught in most mental health programs emphasize values and worldviews that are ethnocentric in nature; specifically, they tend to be Eurocentric, reflecting European cultural heritage of majority culture. Personality theories were developed to provide a context in which to explore individuals with regard to their behaviors, values, beliefs, attitudes, language, relationship, and so forth. All of these aspects of what it means to be human are entirely culture-bound (Armour-Thomas and Gopaul-McNicol, 1998; Swanson et al., 2003). To look at these variables in clients or oneself without knowing the cultural context in which they developed is likely to distort what is expressed.

For instance, most primary personality theories focus on the individual and state as a basic premise that it is important for a child to individuate and separate from her or his family. From this perspective, indicators for a child's progress toward health would be lessened reliance on family and others along with increased independence. Continued dependence or reliance would be viewed as a sign of pathology and perhaps resistance to therapy. Such a viewpoint is not compatible with cultures that emphasize the importance of the family or clan and the role of the individual within it (French, 2002; Leong, Ebreo, Kinoshita, Inman, and Yang, 2007), such some Asian American, Hispanic, or Native American cultures, Culturally sensitive counselors know that the application of any therapeutic approach must be achieved within each client's own family, cultural, and social world. They do not try to impose a standard therapeutic or theoretical approach to all children, regardless of their cultural heritage.

It is important to become aware that there is no single universally accepted definition of "normal" and that 'normality' varies from culture to culture (Lum, 2007; Miranda and Fraser, 2002). Clinicians need to learn not to rigidly apply a single standard or definition of mental health to all children. Cultures vary greatly in what they consider a problem or an appropriate strategy for coping within a given situation (Dana, 1993; Dragus and Tanaka-Matsumi, 2003; Iijima Hall, 1997; Kinzie, 2001). What constitutes abnormality in one culture may be acceptable, if not mainstream behavior, in another. Different cultures may also express the same type of problem in different ways, choosing different idioms to describe an essentially identical emotional level and type of pain (Matsumoto, 2000). For example, depression among mainstream White clients may conform to the criteria outlined in the DSM-IV, whereas depression among the Chinese may manifest itself through a different set of highly somatized symptoms, such as constipation, loss of appetite, and fatigue, with little expressed dysphoric affect (Kirmayer and Groleau, 2003; Moore et al., 2001). Some disorders seem to be culture-bound, appearing only (or predominantly) in some but not all cultures (Lopez-Ibor, 2003; Suzuki, Meller, and Ponterotto, 2007). This latter phenomenon may be explained by the observation that different cultures reinforce different traits and behaviors. As any trait or behavior taken to an extreme may result in pathology, different cultural groups have different manifestations of pathology based on the types of traits it emphasizes in its healthy population (Dinnel, Kleinknecht, and Tanaka-Matsumi, 2002; Iijima Hall, 1997; Marsella and Kaplan, 2003).

It is important for child therapists to realize that mental health services are not universally held in high regard. Some cultures place greater emphasis on seeking assistance from family members or community elders; other cultures see any sign of mental illness as a disgrace to the family that must be hidden from all (Suzuki, Meller, and Ponterotto, 2007; Waldram, 2004). Some minority members view mental health services either as irrelevant to their everyday struggle for survival or as yet another tool for the White majority to pacify and control minorities.

Counselors need to become knowledgeable about the institutional barriers that may prevent minorities from seeking and using mental health services. They must learn that, for many reasons, minorities tend to underutilize mental health services (Manson, 2004; Pedersen, 2008). Reasons for this pattern include the possible perception by clients that mental health service providers are insensitive to diverse needs and may try to impose personal values on clients, the hours and days of operation, and the amount of charges for services. Therapists need to be aware that minorities are disproportionately represented in lower socioeconomic strata and take this into consideration when setting hours and fees. In further recognition of this reality, therapists might consider providing pro bono or reduced fee therapy as often as fiscally possible.

It is particularly vital to gain extensive knowledge about the primary minority group or groups with whom therapists anticipate the bulk of their work. For example, if a counselor were to conduct child treatment in rural Alaska, it would be in the best interest of the counselor and the children for the counselor to learn about Alaska Native cultures and rural population characteristics (Mishler and Simeone, 2004). Therapists working in a city with a predominantly Hispanic population, such as El Paso, Texas, serve their clients' best interest by learning about Hispanic culture and, if at all possible, to speak Spanish. Not only does such knowledge enable clinicians to be more effective in their work with children and families from these cultures, but it grants them greater credibility. Therapists also may not want to overlook one important source for learning about a child's culture: the child and family themselves. They are an especially valuable source of information, as they can give the care provider their own personal perspective of their culture, information that may prove invaluable in assessment, case conceptualization, and development of a treatment strategy (Brems, 1998b).

If at all possible, counselors are encouraged to learn the native language of the children with whom they will be working. Although this can be a difficult task, it pays considerable rewards in the increased rapport and respect gained from clients, both children and parents. Certainly, learning a language is a difficult process, and a therapist may never be completely comfortable conducting therapy in her or his second language. However, as a bare minimum, the counselor can begin the process by learning a few common words of greeting and farewell, as well as commonly used terms or phrases. If nothing else, trying to learn a second language gives the clinician a better appreciation of and empathy for those clients who are themselves learning a second language, namely, English.

Beyond reading and taking classes or workshops, one of the most important avenues to gaining knowledge about different cultures is through firsthand experience (Lum, 2007), such as attending various cultural events. These might include dances, plays, movies, and lectures. A word of caution here is to remember that these are merely pieces of the culture, not complete reflections of the entire cultural process and heritage. These cultural events often highlight the artistic or romantic aspects of the culture to the exclusion of other, perhaps less attractive, aspects. If these were therapists' only contacts with a given culture, they would indeed derive a highly distorted understanding of the culture.

Another avenue to gaining specific information about a culture is to seek out opportunities for interaction with its members, preferably including both professional and personal involvements. For instance, professionally speaking, there may be opportunities to volunteer at a community mental health center that offers special programs for members of a specific culture or that is located in a neighborhood that is predominantly made up of minority members. On a personal level, attending church services or doing volunteer work at a library or other community organization opens up opportunities for interaction with members of other cultures on a social level. All professional and personal efforts to learn more about a cultural or ethnic group with whose members' treatment is anticipated leads to more knowledge and experience and also increases recognition and respect for people in that group.

It is presumed that all contemporary graduate programs in the mental health professions teach cultural competence and sensitivity. Courses and curriculum infusion of these topics can be further enhanced through practica and internships that involve a culturally diverse clientele. If this cannot be achieved solely through careful selection of practicum or internship sites while in graduate school, seeking additional volunteer experiences can augment graduate training, as can supervised employment attained upon graduation. Counselors need to take responsibility to encourage their supervisors to challenge them with a culturally diverse clientele, given the limitations and parameters of a specific clinical site. If the choice is available to trainees, they can select a practicum or internship site that is located within a culturally diverse neighborhood or city. Throughout all of these experiences, culturally sensitive supervision is a crucial component of sensitive training (Allen, 2007). Within supervision, focus should be placed, as appropriate, on counselors' experiences with different types of clients. Through this use of supervision to monitor reactions to culturally different clients, therapists learn to avoid repeating previously learned biases and stereotypes.

Skills

Clinicians' awareness and knowledge of cultural issues have to be translated into skills; otherwise they are of no use to their clients. The process of becoming culturally sensitive therefore must include both the acquisition of new skills and the possible adaptation of existing skills. Perhaps most important, in recognition of the fact that there are cultural differences in the emphasis placed on different forms of communication, it is important for therapists to become adept at adjusting communication styles to meet the needs of each individual child (Hays, 2001).

Using language skillfully helps counselors adapt to differences between cultures with regard to emphases in communication. Some individuals are most concerned about the clarity of their message, some about the relationship between speaker and listener, some about the evaluation they receive on the basis of their expression, some about the impositions made by their remarks, and some about the effectiveness of their communication (Hays, 2001). Clinicians must learn to recognize their clients' and their own personal preferences in communication and adjust accordingly. For example, a client who tends to express issues in treatment in a manner that is mostly concerned with how the clinician responds to the client (i.e., is most concerned with being evaluated) may have a tendency to withhold facts that are perceived as potentially leading to negative evaluation. Another client, who is mainly concerned with not hurting the clinician's feelings, might not self-disclose information that is perceived as potentially critical of the clinician. Concern for relationship in communication tends to be correlated with cultures that are more collectivistic; concern for communication of facts and effectiveness correlate with cultures that are more individualistic (Hays, 2001).

Relatedly, therapists learn that some cultures may place greater emphasis on non-verbal communication and that members of these cultures are less likely to view talking therapies as ideal therapeutic modalities. Among these members, silence may need to be understood as a sign of respect, not resistance. Children from such a culture may be even less inclined to verbalize their feelings than children from other cultures, but instead demonstrate them in nonverbal ways.

Knowing that different groups of human beings have different preferences for diverse therapeutic modalities (Sue and Sue, 2007), culturally competent clinicians have to acquire the skills to identify and carry out the techniques that are most effective with any given client. Rather than approaching each and every child in the same manner, counselors modify their counseling approach based on the needs of the individual client (Ponterotto, Casas, Suzuki, and Alexander, 2001). With increased sensitivity to the differences in how children from different cultures may communicate, therapists do not pathologize a child on the basis of these differences (Achenbach and Rescorla, 2007; Canino and Spurlock, 2000). However, clinicians are also aware that there are marked differences within any given culture and are careful not to make broad generalizations of the types of treatments that work for all members of that culture. Thus, care providers are flexible in their therapeutic approach and use this flexibility in a competent and appropriate manner when dealing with children from different cultures.

Along with having flexibility in the use and choice of intervention techniques, in becoming culturally sensitive, child clinicians increase their awareness of the many issues that emerge concerning communication between them and the child. First, therapists become cognizant of possible language difficulties children may experience. Care is taken to determine children's native language and degree of proficiency in the predominant language. If therapists are not fluent in the child's native tongue, they take into consideration any language problems and adapt their interactions and exchanges accordingly, including making appropriate referrals if necessary.

As was mentioned above, counselors need to have awareness that different cultures may have preferred modes of communication. This means counselors not only become aware of how to "hear" clients, but also become aware of how clients "hear" them. Therapists know that children may be anxious initially and that this may be further compounded by the recognition that the therapist is culturally different. Given these factors, counselors work hard to develop rapport and communication with the child. One important avenue to facilitate this process is to choose a style of communication that matches the child's as closely as possible. For example, in many cultures, indirect communication is valued. If a child from such a culture holds many traditional cultural values, the care provider might want to deemphasize direct communication and instead focus on using stories or art to communicate. Conversely, some cultures value direct communication, and for children from such cultures, art or metaphors may be less effective.

Giving the appropriate amount of attention to the role of culture in therapy means neither overemphasizing nor underemphasizing its importance with a given child or family. Therefore, the skills to evaluate a situation effectively are crucial and assure that no prejudgment is made. Counselors remain aware that stereotyping and generalizing are destructive; within any given culture, members have varying degrees of commitment to traditional cultural values and behaviors. Skilled clinicians recognize that differences among the members of a given culture vary greatly; indeed, these differences may vary as much as or even more than the differences between members of that culture and another. Figure 2.1 provides a graphic representation of this concept. In this figure, two cultures are represented by two normal curves. By using the concept of overlapping normal curves, it is evident that the differences within each culture (dashed line arrows) are greater than the differences between the two cultures (solid line arrows). Finally, the commonalities between the two groups (shaded area) are larger than the differences (white areas). It becomes clear from this representation that

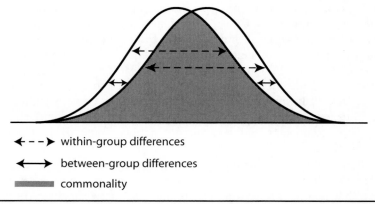

←- -► within-group differences

◄——► between-group differences

▬▬▬ commonality

Figure 2.1   Depiction of Within-Group and Between-Group Differences and Commonality

the similarities between any of the two cultures can outweigh their differences. Culturally sensitive clinicians recognize that there are great similarities and are aware that there are likely to be some differences. Adaptation of style is therefore important at an individual child level. Making assumptions about a child based on the child's ethnic or cultural identification is as destructive as ignoring this aspect of the child altogether.

One example of a misguided attempt at being culturally sensitive is that of a child therapist who based his treatment planning on a generalization about a specific culture. After a lengthy intake, this therapist presented the child's case at a staffing. In concluding his presentation, he indicated that this family was completely run and organized by the child's mother, adding that this was to be expected because the child was African American. Several clinicians who had listened to his presentation were quite surprised by his conclusions, as in actuality it was the father who had brought the family to treatment, the father who was caring for the children (he was unemployed, the mother worked), and the father whom the children sought out for problem solving. In the therapist's attempt to be culturally sensitive, he imposed his own stereotypes about African American culture onto this family to such a degree that he let it override the evidence that had been presented to him by the family. Thus, culturally sensitive therapists must juggle their desire to know as much as possible about each ethnic group in general with the need to be open-minded and enter each intake interview without preconceived notions.

Commensurate with the information reflected in Figure 2.1, child therapists need to have the skill not to categorize individuals according to their ethnic or cultural background, that is, not to treat all members of any given group as identical (Fouad and Arrendondo, 2007a). To help novice therapists gain an appreciation of the inherent problems associated with categorizing individuals into groups, the demographic information provided earlier in this chapter should be considered. In presenting these data, the population was categorized into five major groups: Whites, African Americans, Hispanic Americans, Asian Americans, and Native Americans. However, within each of these broad categories, a number of subcategories exist. For example, within the broad category of Asian Americans, there are a number of smaller groupings, each with its own unique cultural background and heritage. The group includes individuals whose cultural backgrounds lie in very diverse countries, including China, Japan, Samoa, North and South Korea, Vietnam, and Guam. Further complicating this issue is the fact that even within each of these country-based subgroups, there are further subgroups. For example, within Vietnam, there is a significant proportion of ethnic Chinese who have, over the years, maintained great autonomy. Further, even within the Chinese-Vietnamese group, there may be major differences such as rural versus urban, rich versus poor, gay versus straight, and Buddhist versus Christian. This example clarifies that broad categorization of individuals ignores the numerous differences that exist within this larger grouping. The same obviously holds true for other ethnic groups. For instance, among Whites, there are individuals from countries such as Ireland, Germany, or France, or who differ according to many other variables such as sexual orientation, physical abilities, socioeconomic status, religion, and age.

With the recognition that some institutional barriers exist that may prevent minorities from utilizing mental health services, flexibility in the provision of services becomes crucial (Manson, 2004; Namyniuk, Brems, and Clarson, 1997). Some problems reside outside the client and nontraditional steps may need to be taken to help resolve the situation. For example, if a minority child presents for therapy because of feelings of inadequacy or depression, the intake interview may reveal that the child is the only culturally different student in a predominantly White student body and that the White students have been making racist comments. The child, who is unable to make friends at the new school and is subjected to ongoing derogation, soon begins to incorporate many of these negative perceptions into her or his self-concept. In this situation, there is an outside force (racism at school) that has had a direct and adverse impact on the child. Hence, focusing on children in an attempt to improve their self-concept most likely is not the most effective intervention. Instead, the intervention is most effective if a three-pronged approach is adopted that involves the child, the family, and the school. By including interventions in the school setting, the clinician may be able to have an impact on the child's environment, which in turn, it is hoped, has a positive effect on the child's self-esteem.

In becoming culturally sensitive, another important set of skills to cultivate is that of being a social change agent (Hogan, 2007; Monges, 1998). Care providers need to learn how to eliminate discrimination, including that based on ethnicity, sexual preference, age, mental or physical limitations, religion, or gender, and ensure that everyone has access to services and resources as needed. In so doing, clinicians take a proactive advocacy stance to help victims of discrimination. Trainees need to recognize that as therapists or counselors, they are granted a great deal of power by child clients, their parents, and other community members. They must recognize their responsibility to use this power to help eliminate discrimination in society at large, both directly and indirectly. Indirectly, they come to serve as examples of nonbias. They learn to use words and actions that convey equality of all persons and respect for individuals from all walks of life. They recognize that people, particularly impressionable children, model their behavior after theirs. With this recognition, therapists and counselors learn to eschew interpersonal interactions that might convey prejudice or bias, even of the most subtle kind (Ponterotto, Utsey, and Pedersen, 2006).

When necessary and appropriate, mental health care providers learn ways in which to take direct actions to prevent or eliminate discrimination. This direct action can range from not condoning racist or sexist jokes told in their company to using political systems to create positive changes in society. In becoming culturally sensitive, therapists recognize that the primary purpose of treatment is to help enhance the quality of clients' lives and that it is equally important to complement this individual approach to improving life with a more general approach to enhancing the quality of our society. Thus, counselors do everything possible to help create a society that is more respectful and humane in its treatment of all individuals.

Self-Monitoring

Becoming culturally sensitive is not a final goal; it is an ongoing process. There is no single point at which therapists or counselors have gained all the awareness, knowledge, and skills to finish or complete their quest for cultural sensitivity. Instead, becoming culturally sensitive is a continual process in which clinicians not only remain open and responsive to further knowledge and experience but also actively seek it out. While gaining additional knowledge and experience, they continue to assess their reactions to different situations and people in a continuous quest for personal growth. They look for personal residues of stereotypes or biases that may affect perceptions and seek out challenges that broaden their cultural horizons. A major aspect of the journey toward growing cultural sensitivity is the role of consultation and supervision. It is important to realize that bias and prejudice are insidious attributes that are often beyond the awareness of the individual. Therapists who were brought up in a racist or sexist family or society may have many racist or sexist attitudes without being aware of them. Often, such attitudes are so subtle that they are very difficult to identify, let alone eliminate. Although self-exploration is a necessary and crucial approach to identifying personal biases and prejudices, there is a limit to the growth it can provide. Often, it is necessary to help promote self-awareness through the presence of an outsider who is interested in the well-being and growth of the clinician and can foster it through ongoing supervision and consultation. Such consultation gives the counselor an objective viewpoint about counseling skills and cultural sensitivity. Thus, in addition to focusing on general counseling or therapy skills, supervision or consultation should pay attention to clinicians' level of cultural sensitivity (Allen, 2007), and although it can be difficult to do so, it is important for clinicians to remain open and responsive to supervisory feedback. Feedback can be particularly difficult to accept when it involves the identification of biases and prejudices, as these are not commonly considered professional, but rather personal, attributes. Hence, it is important for supervisees to remember that supervisors or consultants have their and their clients' best interest in mind, as this perspective may enhance receptivity to feedback.

Selecting a supervisor or consultant to help the care provider who is in the process of enhancing cultural sensitivity is an important consideration. The selection of an individual who is culturally insensitive does not help in such a quest. Considering that supervision often evokes the presence of parallel process in which the supervisee and supervisor reenact the treatment process that is occurring between the supervisee and client, it may be desirable to have a supervisor or consultant who is culturally different from the clinician. This may enable the clinician to explore cultural issues that might not otherwise be present in supervision or consultation were it done with someone of the same culture. Short of this, it would be valuable to receive supervision or consultation from someone who has considerable experience, both personal and professional, with different cultures. This need for supervision and consultation is predicated on the fact that, as was mentioned previously, attaining cultural sensitivity is a process, rather than an end state.

Process Issues in Culturally Sensitive Work with Children

Under the best of circumstances, therapy and counseling are complex and complicated processes, with no two clinical relationships ever being exactly alike. A major contributing factor to this complexity are the numerous and often considerably divergent personal factors clinicians and clients bring to the room. These factors include personal characteristics such as cognitive styles, self-perceptions, life experiences, behavioral styles, modes of learning, coping strategies, ways of perceiving, family characteristics, social skills, and so forth. They also include the expectations children and families bring to treatment about clients' and care providers' roles, preferences for different clinician characteristics, attitudes toward the therapy or counseling process, and personal perceptions of reasons for presenting for treatment, as well as professional aspects of the clinician, including theoretical orientation, level of competence, and intervention style. Even without considering culture, the therapy or counseling process is a rich and complex situation. When a therapist's and a client's cultures are added as a consideration, the process becomes even more complicated (Canino and Spurlock, 2000). Some cultural factors that may affect process include therapists' and clients' ethnicity, minority status, degree of acculturation, and level of minority identity development, as well as each person's degree of cultural awareness and sensitivity. These cultural factors not only may further complicate counseling, but also can make the process more rewarding for both individuals. Figure 2.2 identifies just a few of these personal, professional, and cultural factors that affect the development and maintenance of a relationship, as well as the outcome of treatment.

Following is a description of several important, though certainly not all, process issues that are likely to arise in cross-cultural treatment situations. The influence of ethnicity or culture on the therapy and counseling process can begin at the moment the clinician meets a child and family. The manner in which the provider greets the family, the counselor's physical appearance, and therapy or counseling setting are but a few factors that can affect processes and relationships from the outset. Many of these events can occur without the clinician's awareness and may leave her or him wondering what happened. One such event may be the manner in which a therapist chooses to address the child client. Therapists must be careful never to anglicize children's names automatically. For example, a client named Jose or Yosaf should never automatically be called "Joe," even if this practice would be easier and more familiar for the English-speaking therapist, as it would show considerable disrespect for the individual's culture. The counselor should also be aware that different cultures have different uses of names. For example, in Vietnam, an individual typically has three names, such as Nguyen Duy San. In this case, Nguyen is the family name (similar to Smith or Jones), Duy a middle name, and San the given name (similar to Jim or Jane). For Vietnamese, because the family name is rarely used, this individual would be referred to with the given name, Mr. San, or San for close friends. Thus, being on a first-name basis with someone from this culture may have an entirely different connotation than it does with someone from a European heritage. The safest and most respectful approach in both of these situations is to pay attention to how clients identify themselves and to follow suit. Alternatively, or if clients do not reveal their preferred address, children can be asked what they would like to be called. The main issue is to be aware not to apply presuppositions across the board to everyone. Failure to take this sensitive and sensible approach may lead to the treatment getting off on the wrong foot.

Conversely, what clinicians expect to be called has important potential cultural implications as well. Many cultures vary with regard to the level of respect given to professionals. For some cultures (e.g., Hispanic), the professional is seen as deserving of great respect and reverence. For the therapist to insist prematurely that a child from such a culture call her or him by the first name may provoke undue and unnecessary discomfort for the child. This speaks again to a level of cultural sensitivity and understanding on the child therapist's part. Perhaps the safest guideline is for the counselor to refer to herself or himself, at least initially, with a formal title, such as Dr., Ms., or Mr. As the relationship with the client develops and more information is gained about the client's cultural identity, decisions may be made about allowing the child and family to call the counselor by a first name. Another issue that may arise in conducting cross-cultural work is the potentially divergent meaning of nonverbal communication.

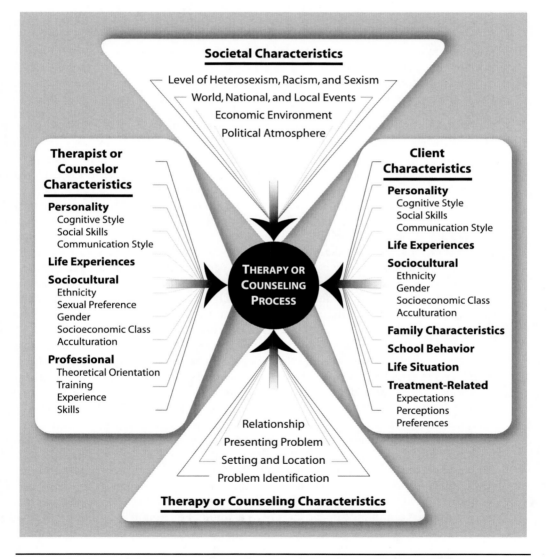

Figure 2.2   Personal, Therapy, and Cultural Contributions of Child and Clinician

That is, although there are some universal nonverbal communications, such as a smile, there are considerable differences across cultures for many other nonverbals. For example, cultures can vary considerably in regard to the amount of personal space that is required to feel comfortable in the presence of another person. Members of some cultures (e.g., Western European) keep considerable distance from one another, whereas members of other cultures (e.g., many Asian cultures) stay quite close to one another, often continually touching. This difference in personal space can lead to misunderstandings and miscommunications and may also be present in the child therapy or counseling setting.

Similarly, cultures often vary in the amount and type of acceptable touching between people. Members of some cultures (e.g., many Middle Eastern cultures) have no reticence in touching other members of the same gender without any sexual connotation. In other cultures (e.g., White Americans), however, this type of touching is deemed unacceptable and inappropriate. (There are some exceptions, such as when same-sex members of a sports team hug each other, bump their chests together, or pat each other on the back or derriere when a good play has been made.) Similarly, eye contact may be emphasized by some cultures (e.g., dominant United States society) and viewed as demonstrative of honesty and self-confidence. Other cultures (e.g., Native American cultures) place less emphasis on eye contact and, in fact, may consider it inappropriate in certain situations, such as between male and female strangers. Further, there are cultural differences in the amount of eye contact that is considered acceptable with someone in a position of authority. For example, some cultures (e.g., Hispanic) encourage their members to avoid eye contact with teachers, doctors, or bosses, as it is considered a sign of disrespect. Children from these cultures are often encouraged to be deferential and avoid eye contact with adults, particularly professionals. For those cultures that do not have these mandates, such behavior would be interpreted in a considerably different manner, perhaps as disinterest or extreme shyness. Failure to understand these possible connotations may lead to misinterpretations on the clinician's part. For example, it is foreseeable that a culturally insensitive White child therapist might automatically assume that a culturally different child has low self-esteem because the child does not make eye contact.

Another serious danger in cross-cultural therapy situations is the inappropriate imposition of the therapist's or counselor's values and attitudes on the client. Although the threat of a clinician imposing values on clients is present in all treatment situations, it is of particular concern when the clinician and the client differ in terms of cultural heritage. As has been mentioned previously, there are few universally accepted values; cultures vary relative to the importance and presence of different values. It is crucial that care providers take these differences into consideration in the treatment situation. One example of differing values is the relative importance different cultures place on the role of the individual versus the group. Whereas traditional psychotherapy places greater emphasis on an individual's independence, many cultures place greater emphasis on the individual's role in the larger group, whether it is the family, the community, or the culture as a whole. For example, traditional Native Americans emphasize the collective interdependence of tribal members, with complex relationships among extended family members. In working with a child who grew up in a community that holds such an interdependent perspective, it would be a travesty to attempt to impose automatically the value of independence. This is but one example of many in which cultures differ relative to values. Some other examples include level of self-disclosure, importance of material belongings and success, emotional expressiveness, degree of competitiveness, and importance of education.

As in all treatment situations, another major issue that emerges in cross-cultural work is the presence of transference and countertransference. In cross-cultural situations, these processes may be motivated by cultural differences between the client and the clinician. The child might demonstrate transference by reacting to a therapist in the same way that she or he reacts to other members of the therapist's cultural background. These reactions may be based on prior experiences or on expectations the child has incorporated from her or his parents, family members, or friends. Although this transference might have occurred regardless of the therapist's cultural heritage, it may be particularly strong if the therapist is from the dominant culture (which in most cases means "White"). This is likely because the minority child is more likely to have had negative experiences of oppression at the hands of Whites than members of any other ethnic or cultural group and therefore may transfer anger onto the therapist. As with all forms of transference, cultural transference needs to be attended to and resolved. Of course, transference is not always negative, and there may be instances of positive cultural transference that actually facilitate the treatment process.

Cultural countertransference is also a strong possibility in cross-cultural situations. Counselors might react to children of different cultural heritage the same way they would respond to other members of that culture. It is in this type of situation that counselors' own biases and stereotypes, both positive and negative, begin to interfere with the counseling process. Countertransferences can be based on previous experiences with members of another ethnic or cultural group or from public media representations of that culture. The problem that arises from cultural countertransferences is that counseling might focus on the stereotypes the counselor has projected onto the family, rather than on the child's presenting issues. These problems exist whether the stereotype is positive or negative because the counselor fails to recognize the child as she or he really is. It is a therapist's responsibility to maintain awareness of the presence of both cultural and other forms of countertransference and to take appropriate steps to alleviate the situation. These steps include consultation, supervision, and, if the problem is not immediately resolvable and is detrimental to the client, referral to another provider.

Another process issue that may emerge in cross-cultural situations is presented by the children or families who reject their cultural heritage. Some children might want to reject the part of themselves that is culturally different, often because of the negative experiences that they have suffered at the hands of other children and adults. Renouncing personal heritage thus occurs as children's attempts to "fit in" more completely and to avoid future harassment. Such situations present potentially difficult ethical dilemmas to clinicians. On one hand, clients may have set this as a treatment goal, and clinicians have the responsibility at least to consider it as a legitimate goal for treatment. On the other hand, providers might want to focus on helping children incorporate, not reject, all parts of themselves, including those that are a result of the child's ethnic or cultural heritage. There is no easy solution to such a conflict, but it certainly needs to be explored thoroughly with the children, and their parents might need to be consulted on this matter before intervention takes place.

Another situation that may arise for child clinicians is the possibility of child clients having been subjected to discrimination or abuse by peers because of their parents' minority status. For example, children of gays or lesbians may be exposed to verbal and physical insults by other children at school. This can be extremely difficult for those children, as they often experience very mixed emotions about the situation. Such children may incorporate the negative self-perceptions and direct them against themselves or their parents and develop feelings of anger or disgust. They may incorporate a misdirected fear within themselves that they too may be gay or lesbian, and their confusion about the situation may be aggravated by society's general lack of acceptance of gays and lesbians. Thus, general societal prejudice can alienate children from their parents. Similarly, children who have a culturally different stepparent might be subjected to verbal and physical abuse by other children.

Children from biracial parental relationships may present another unique situation for a child clinician. These children are often subjected to verbal abuse from and rejection by children of both parental cultures. As a result, biracial children can become confused about personal cultural identity and begin to feel different and separate from both cultures. To reconcile feelings of confusion, these children might reject one of the two cultures and thus push away part of themselves as well as the parent of that culture. This withdrawal from or rejection of the parent and self may then generalize to a rejection of all members of that culture. Helping such children attain a positive cultural identity can present a considerable challenge to child clinicians.

Even the most culturally sensitive care provider may face instances when cultural differences necessitate referral of a child to a clinician of the child's own cultural background. Although this may occur under numerous circumstances, perhaps the most common situation is one wherein parents or children resist treatment from a provider whose background is different from theirs. The therapist or counselor recognizes that although this may be due to resistance based on other issues, such as the parents' own stage of ethnic identity or the parents' or child's personal biases, the most appropriate solution in this situation might be to refer the child to a different care provider. However, a sensitive therapist or counselor uses discretion in this situation to ensure that the transfer is not done hastily and that it is handled in a therapeutic and educative manner.

Summary and Concluding Thoughts

In the process of becoming child clinicians, trainees have much to learn. They need to learn about children and their development, various aspects of the therapy and counseling process, including assessment and intervention, and application of various treatment techniques. Clinicians go through a process of learning and self-exploration that, it is hoped, leads to becoming a skilled provider of children's mental health care. A crucial part of this learning process is the journey toward cultural sensitivity. Cultural sensitivity is crucial not only for ethical, personal, and humanitarian reasons, but also because of the demographic reality that it is most likely that child clinicians will interact with children from a wide variety of cultural heritages and ethnic groups. Indeed, cross-cultural interactions in the work with children are inevitable, owing to the presence of different cultures and minorities within contemporary society.

Gaining cultural sensitivity is an ongoing process for all child clinicians that begins with self-exploration and awareness and is followed by the acquisition of knowledge and skills. Owing to the presence of an overt and covert racist, sexist, and heterosexist atmosphere in which most people grow up, becoming culturally sensitive can be a very challenging and difficult process. To maintain growth in the area, constant self-monitoring is necessary, and occasional supervision and consultation might need to be sought. However, the benefits provided by the cultural sensitizing process in terms of personal growth for the clinician far outweigh any costs that may be incurred along the way.

Providing treatment to a child who is culturally different from the clinician can be a challenging situation. However, cross-cultural therapy and counseling can be extremely rewarding, resulting in considerable growth for provider and child. Unique situations can arise within the cross-cultural context that present potential obstacles. By striving for cultural sensitivity and through seeking additional learning opportunities, experiences, and supervision, mental health care providers are not only prepared to deal with these situations, but also are more prepared to deal with a culturally diverse society in general. Sensitivity to diversity, especially in the context of working with children, also relates to the ability to adapt to the developmental needs of an individual. Especially in the work with children, clinicians must have some awareness of how interactions and verbalizations have to be adapted to assure that the child's developmental level is commensurate and that messages can be received and understood. The next chapter explores this issue in some detail.

3

A Developmental Context for Child Therapy and Counseling

> *States Parties shall ensure to the maximum extent possible the survival and development of the child.*
>
> —Article 6.2 of the UN Convention on the Rights of the Child

Just as clinicians have to evaluate their overall readiness to work with children and especially children of diverse backgrounds, they must attend to their ability and skills as related to the developmental diversity presented by children. In fact, no discussion of children can be complete without giving significant thought to their developmental levels and needs. Not too many years ago, childhood and development were treated synonymously, with many clinicians disregarding the impact of development on, and its continuation throughout, adult life. Nevertheless, there is general agreement that developmental events are at their peak during childhood and that development progresses more rapidly during this part of life than any other (Kail, 2007; Newman and Newman, 2006).

This rapid development brings with it rapid changes and profoundly influences the lives of children. Any adult who works with children in any capacity must have a genuine appreciation of these changes and of the milestones children must reach in their early years (Schroeder and Gordon, 2002). Only then will adults remember never to treat children like miniature adults, as used to be the case (Russ and Freedheim, 2001), but rather to keep aware and abreast of the special needs and behaviors that development brings for children. Only then will adults remember that children constantly evolve and that the perception of them has to change to follow their development. In other words, the adults in a child's life must have the flexibility to revise their view of and approach to the child with each new developmental task that has been mastered to maintain a realistic and respectful relationship with the child. It is often the very lack of this flexibility on parents' part that brings families to treatment. Many therapists and counselors have encountered parents who were not able to allow an adolescent daughter to separate when she was ready to do so, or parents who did not think their 10-year-old son would understand why they were divorcing because they had lost track of his ever-advancing cognitive complexity. Thus, a thorough appreciation of development is essential for care providers to keep up with their child clients and to set realistic therapeutic goals.

Development: Definition, Influences, and Types

Definition of Development

Although there are several models of development, only one is quite comprehensive in its look at the interaction between the individual and the environment. This dialectic model stresses that development occurs in a context, not only guided by physical or biological factors that occur within the individual, but also affected by psychological, cultural, and external factors (Lerner, Skinner, and Sorrell, 1980). Given this complex interaction, development is viewed as a never-ending process that is shaped by individuals' experiences in their greater context and environment. Development resembles evolution and results not only in the acquisition of behavior but also, and perhaps even more importantly, in "the maintenance and transformation of useful skills and the extinction of formerly adaptive behaviors" (Wimbarti and Self, 1992, p. 37). Thus, the focus of the dialectic model is on change, rather than on a predetermined end state.

The dialectic model of development harmonizes extremely well with the focus of therapeutic work with children. In both developmental psychology and psychotherapy or counseling, children are observed and encouraged to change and grow. In the former, observation and encouragement occur within the normal or healthy context of self-perpetuating evolution of behavior, self, and relationships; in the latter, observation and encouragement occur in the context of helping children to return to their healthy developmental trajectories after they were derailed for one reason or another. However, both watch children grow, and both make an attempt to understand each individual child from her or his unique developmental perspective at any given time in life.

Influences on Development

When attempting to determine a child's developmental maturity and adjustment, the dialectic developmental perspective takes a look not merely at the child's age, but also at the biological, psychological, cultural, and "outerphysical" (Wimbarti and Self, 1992, p. 33) factors that have occurred or are occurring in the child's life. For instance, a dialectic developmentalist would not assume that a child who is referred for aggressive behavior evidences "normal" manifestations of an autonomy struggle just because the child is 3 years old but would also explore whether the child has been subjected to any psychological, biological, cultural, or outerphysical events that may have contributed to this behavior. Perhaps the child is aggressive not because of an age-determined milestone (i.e., Erikson's autonomy versus shame and doubt conflict) but because of the death of a parent (psychological factor), frequent severe headaches (biological factor), or having survived a recent earthquake (outerphysical factor). Considering all of these influences on development, as well as when and how they occur, helps professionals understand children much better and can help place children's actions, needs, and affects in a developmental context that is unique to each one of them.

Biological Factors.   Biological factors that may affect children's development are often easy to spot. Some are related to age-specific bodily changes, such as the onset of puberty. Others are related to larger historical changes, such as malnutrition due to a long-term drought-related food shortage or low socioeconomic status. Who has not seen pictures of African children whose development was delayed because of their starvation diets? Finally, some biological factors occur out of the blue, completely unexpectedly, such as a head injury after a bicycling accident. Such an injury is likely to affect the child's development, especially if it is severe.

Psychological Factors.   Psychological factors, like biological factors, can occur at expected age-related times, can be products of historical occurrences, or can arrive unpredictably. The sudden and unexpected death of a parent can affect a child's development just as profoundly as the historically driven equal rights movement of women. Finally, the age-specific development of peer group relationships can affect the child's maturation and behavioral evolution.

Cultural Factors.   Age-relevant cultural factors impact a child's development. For example, children's lives are greatly altered when they begin school at age 6. Historical cultural events can also affect children's maturation. Early contact with alcoholic beverages in a community that endorses their free and unlimited use may have serious effects on a child's cognitive and behavioral development. Finally, cultural events, such as being born and raised in an inner city, may have significant impact on a child.

Outerphysical Factors.   Outerphysical factors include events such as earthquakes, storms, pollution, and threats of nuclear war over which the individual has virtually no direct control. They can affect development significantly. For instance, lead poisoning can retard cognitive maturation, and living through a tornado may result in phobias about wind.

Types of Development.   The mental health care provider who is sensitive to developmental issues in children and who attempts to see their symptoms within a dialectic developmental framework pays attention to these influencing factors and has an appreciation of age-normed expectations within various realms of development. However, age-normed factors are never used in isolation, but rather are always explored within the framework of the child's whole experience. Thus, although hundreds of books exist that outline tables for normal motor development, emotional development, cognitive development, language development, and so on, none of these guidelines should ever be abused by attempting to determine where a child should be on the developmental continuum merely because of her or his chronological age. To expect a 3-year-old boy to deal with autonomy issues when he has just survived an earthquake is irresponsible. More than likely, this outerphysical event has affected the child to such a degree that he may once again be grappling with simple trust in his world. Helping him deal with the experience of the environmental event is the better course of action. Nevertheless, all child clinicians must have some awareness of the stages of development.

Although discussing them individually would be beyond the scope of this book, there are several arenas of development in which expected (or "normal") behaviors have been plotted against normative age ranges. These have been alluded to above and include motor development (Gallahue and Ozmun, 2005; Haywood and Getchell, 2005), language development (Owens, 2008), cognitive development (Berk, 2006; Piaget, 1967), moral development (Killen and Hart, 2000; Killen and Smetana, 2006), self-development (Stern, 1977, 1985, 1989), emotional development (Kail, 2007; Thomas, 2005), psychosocial development (Erikson, 1950), and psychosexual development (Freud, 1952). A thorough overview of these therapeutically relevant arenas, grouped according to children's expected age ranges, is provided in Tables 3.1 to 3.7 (at the end of this chapter). To be able to appreciate the developmental needs and milestones of the children they treats, responsible mental health care providers for children must have familiarity with all of these developmental models in much more detail than is provided in these tables; the reader is referred to developmental texts for that purpose (Newman and Newman, 2006; Shaffer, 2005; Thomas, 2005).

Development Made Relevant to Child Clinicians

In addition to the use of the dialectic developmental viewpoint to better understand the factors affecting overall level of development, consideration and knowledge of development are also important because of the "overriding importance of interaction among developmental dimensions in determining functioning during any developmental period" (Wimbarti and Self, 1992, p. 48). In other words, the overall developmental level of a child, as assessed dialectically through exploration of psychological, biological, cultural, and outerphysical determinants, does indeed have profound effects on expectations about that child's behavior, cognition, emotion, language, activity level, types of activities, and needs. Further, the distinct subareas of a child's overall development interact to present an even more complex picture that must be appreciated by the child clinician. Achievement or lack of achievement in one developmental arena can strongly affect reaching a milestone in another. For instance, a child cannot be expected to master separation-differentiation from a primary caretaker (psychological arena) if she or he has not yet mastered object constancy (cognitive arena).

Further, knowledge of developmental stages, milestones, and tasks is useful in determining whether therapy or counseling is successful in helping a particular child return to the healthy developmental trajectory that was left behind when the referral was made. Knowing what to expect from children of certain ages or developmental stages helps therapists and counselors evaluate whether the child is back on track, is making satisfactory progress, or needs to continue to stay in treatment (Newman and Newman, 2006).

As development continues across the life span and is clearly influenced by a number of factors, clinicians aware of dialectic approaches to development remember that the environment has not only influenced development up to the time when the child is seen in treatment, but it also continues to affect the child beyond the termination of the treatment. A dialectic approach helps the clinician focus on environmental factors and modifications that can contribute to change in the child. Similarly, the knowledge of developmental milestones sensitizes the counselor to the presence of vulnerabilities in the child (or the adult for that matter), thus recognizing when stressors may have more of an impact and when problems are merely an issue of failed adaptation, as opposed to disease (Sameroff, Lewis, and Miller, 2000).

Not unlike the dialectic approach to a definition of development, recent research on infants has pointed toward the importance of the context and the many contributing and shaping factors that affect children in the interpersonal matrix in which they mature (Brems, 1998a; Chess and Hertzig, 1990; Zeanah, Anders, Seifer, and Stern, 1991). Research is beginning to provide evidence that the infants are indeed very active from the moment of birth, interacting with and affecting their environment and the people within it (Lichtenberg, 1990, 1991). Further, these developments are continuous and present across the life span, indicating that development moves forward regardless of context but may be altered by it significantly. This model suggests that regression or fixation is not the best way of defining psychopathology (Westen et al., 1991) and that clinical issues such as dependence, trust, autonomy, and industry are not tied to a particular period of development, but rather are continuously relevant throughout the life span.

"Shifts in the social 'presence' or 'feel' of the infant . . . [are thus not] attributed to the departure from one specific developmental-task-phase and the entrance into the next" (Stern, 1985, p. 10) but rather to the changes in the infant's self-experience and interaction with important people in her or his environment. Such self-experience and interaction must be understood by the child therapist to appreciate the needs of each individual client and to be capable of developmentally sensitive assessment and treatment planning. In addition to plotting such normal development, the novice child counselor must have familiarity with literature outlining particular problem behaviors or disorders and when in a child's life they are likely to occur in a nonpathological manner (e.g., Wenar and Kerig, 2005). For instance, stubbornness has been attributed to the 1- to 2-year-old child, disobedience to the 2- to 5-year-old child, lying to the 5- to 6-year-old child, and self-consciousness to the adolescent (Berk, 2006; Brooks, 2008; Thomas, 2005). Similarly, disorders such as phobias have been reported more commonly among 2- to 5-year-olds (Kronenberger and Meyer, 2001), whereas eating disorders appear commonly among adolescents (Cooper and Stein, 2006).

Although such facts can be helpful to the child clinician, they are counterproductive if used in isolation or to make diagnostic decisions. Instead, responsible use of this information results in nonpathologizing, developmentally appropriate behaviors or affects and recognition of nondevelopmentally appropriate symptoms. One framework for such assessment was originally provided by Wenar (1982), who suggested that behavior and affects be evaluated as to whether they are developmentally expected, regressed, or fixated. In other words, the child therapist assesses whether a given problem is common among children of the developmental level presented by the current child client (Wenar and Kerig, 2005). If the answer to this question is negative, the counselor follows up by assessing whether the behavior or affect reflects a regression or a fixation. If the behavior began at an expected age, then disappeared developmentally appropriately but recurred, a regression has taken place. However, if the behavior never disappeared once the child progressed developmentally, a fixation has occurred. In either case, intervention is recommended (Wenar and Kerig, 2005). Behaviors and affects are best evaluated according to their severity and effect on day-to-day functioning (Johnson, Rasbury, and Siegel, 1997). Thus, whereas high activity levels are reportedly common and generally not treated among 5-year-old children, this behavior might not be considered normal in a 5-year-old whose general functioning (e.g., concentration and new learning) is interfered with by her or his excessive activity.

Given the critical need of a child clinician to be knowledgeable about expected maturation in the areas of emotional expression, cognition, language, motor activity, psycho-social crises, and self-development, following are descriptions of healthy development among children grouped into three categories: early, middle, and late childhood. This information is also shown in a traditional stage format in Tables 3.1 to 3.7 at the end of this chapter. Common symptoms are included in the descriptions to sensitize the beginning therapist or counselor to the fact that children at different ages may manifest some behaviors or affects that, while considered indicative of psychopathology at some ages, are considered perfectly normal or nonpathological at others. These descriptions are rendered to provide a framework against which to compare children who are referred for treatment. It is important to recognize that not all children, in fact only very few, evidence delays in all arenas of development. Instead, it may be noted that only one or no developmental deficit exists. Any deficits that are noted invariably become part of the treatment plan and are considered when the presenting problem is conceptualized. Obvious deficits in language, motor, and cognitive development are addressed most completely by involving a pediatrician or developmental psychologist to rule out physical or neurological deficits as causative factors. Deficits in psychosocial, emotional, and self-development can generally be addressed by the child therapist or counselor.

Early Childhood

Early childhood for the purposes of this book is defined as the period of life between birth and 5 years of age, that is, the time of life most children spend with their families before they enter the school system. Early childhood is a time of rapid and intriguing change, as it includes infants, toddlers, and preschool children. Infants are never and toddlers are rarely seen in psychotherapy or counseling. Hence, although infants and toddlers are fascinating human beings, here descriptions are provided only of healthy 4- and 5-year olds.

Four- and 5-year-old children are motorically quite sophisticated. They have advanced to an age at which they are quite capable of walking, running, and generally moving very independently of adult help. They have become mobile also through their ability to ride a tricycle or bicycle, to make their way past obstacles, and to climb stairs effectively. Five-year-old children master these tasks more effectively and easily than 4-year-olds, who still fight for balance and full control of their bodies. For instance, although both can run very well, only the 5-year-old has the full ability to change direction while running and to start and stop easily and quickly. Some 4-year-olds, although able to climb to the top of obstacles, may find themselves unable to climb down and need the help of verbal instructions rendered by a nearby adult to master this task. Five-year-olds, on the other hand, generally are able to climb up and down obstacles freely and without help.

Four-year-olds have developed sufficient motor control to dress themselves, working large zippers and snaps easily and independently. They are generally able to brush their own teeth, feed themselves, help themselves to tools and utensils, and help with small chores. Five-year-olds become more sophisticated and are able to tie their own shoes and work buttons easily. Fine motor control continues to improve, readying the child for school. Large motor movements are easily mastered by 5-year-olds, who learn to skate, kick balls, walk on balance beams, and skip with one foot. These children enjoy being creative and love to learn new tasks that challenge their motor development. They enjoy drawing, cutting and pasting, and simple arts and crafts. However, they also continue to be very fond of unstructured activities that stimulate them kinesthetically. They love to play in mud and water, feel gooey materials, and create nondistinct shapes from Play-Doh. These activities are gratifying not because of the creation of products, but rather because of the process and kinesthetic stimulation they provide.

The independence brought on by the young child's motor development is supplemented by her or his sophisticated use of language. By this age, children can communicate extremely well through language while still being very much attuned to nonverbal communication. They still prefer to model after others, rather than following verbal instructions but, if necessary, are able to do the latter if it is kept simple and direct. Much of their play remains symbolic and nonverbal, and some 4-year-olds may be quite sparse in their use of language while playing intently. Nevertheless, language is sophisticated by this age. These children use complex sentences, have an ever-increasing vocabulary, and understand simple instructions. They have become skilled conversationalists who can stick with a topic at hand and can focus in on their communication partner. Many 4-year-olds continue to struggle with the pronunciation of some consonants and various grammatical rules. They are aware of global language rules and apply them indiscriminately, which results in the overgeneralization of rules that leads to common grammatical mistakes, such as "goed" instead of "went" or "do-ed" instead of "did." Such mistakes are best not corrected by adults around the child. Instead, adults are better off striving to model appropriate language by obeying grammatical rules and exceptions in their own speech (Schickedanz, Schickedanz, Forsyth, and Forsyth, 2001). Grammar improves among 5-year-olds, who also are more skilled at engaging their conversation partner. They can begin to take the listener into account and acknowledge her or his communication and response. Children at this age have become excellent listeners who understand language well, even if it is not directed at them. They can follow clear instructions, as long as only one or two steps are involved. They listen to conversations, and much incidental language learning takes place through this activity. However, findings from a longitudinal study tracking children over several decades revealed that only communication that is directed specifically toward the child actually enhances the child's ultimate cognitive performance (Hart and Risley, 1995, 1999).

It is not surprising that as language skills develop, children's cognitive development also grows by leaps and bounds. Although children below the age of 4 were unable to consider others or to understand complex tasks, 4- and 5-year-olds begin to recognize relationships and to consider the perspective of others. Nevertheless, the 4-year-old still might not understand that her or his mother can also be the sister of an aunt. Mother can only be one thing: mother; additional relationships are difficult to fathom given this child's preoperational thought. Children at this age are very inquisitive and curious. They are beginning to understand that there are rules and generalities and are exploring these eagerly. This process is related not only to their increasing cognitive sophistication but also to their need for structure and rules as they learn to differentiate right from wrong. These children desire cognitive stimulation, and they love to listen to stories and leaf through picture books.

Their thinking is becoming decreasingly perception-bound; as their ability for symbolic thought increases, they are more and more capable of symbolic play and make-believe. These children's ability to think can be mistaken as a level of cognitive complexity that allows logic and reasoning. However, this is not so. Children at 4 and 5 years of age cannot yet transfer the knowledge they have accumulated from one situation to another, in other words, they cannot yet generalize and reason logically. Thus, while their cognition has moved beyond being perception-bound in the sense that these children can engage in symbolic thought, in fact, can even engage in simple imagery, their logic remains largely bound to perception, as it does not yet formally contain the crucial elements of thought underlying conservation and perspective, as defined by Piaget (1967).

Conservation refers to the ability to realize that although a quantity of material may appear in different shapes, it ultimately remains the same or, inversely, that although the appearance of a container may be identical, the contents may vary in quantity. For instance, 4- and 5-year-olds are unable to realize that two rows of objects that are laid out so that the rows are of equal lengths may actually contain different numbers of objects because the spacing between objects may be different in each row. Similarly, they cannot yet understand that a cup of water poured from a large round container into a skinny square container is still a cup of water. They claim that there is more water in the second container because the water level reaches higher than it did in the first container. They are unable to compensate (the example of the number of objects in a row), nor can they reverse (the example of the water in two different containers). This inability is related to the same reason that mom can only be a mother, not a sister: These children only focus in on one dimension—the length of a row, the tallness of a container. Conservation requires a person to manipulate a minimum of two dimensions at a time (e.g., the tallness of the container and the circumference of the container), thus remaining theoretically out of the 4- and 5-year-old child's cognitive range. Findings, however, have challenged that 4- and 5-year-olds are unable to conserve, and clever experiments (Bjorklund, 2004) have indicated that if children are challenged with conservation tasks in practical settings, they are more likely to be able to solve them. Hence, although it appears that preschoolers have difficulties with tasks involving more than one dimension, these tasks are not impossible for them. They may merely require more practice, patience, and some guiding help by an adult (Schickedanz, Schickedanz, Forsyth, and Forsyth, 2001).

Similarly, 4- and 5-year-olds were once thought to be exclusively egocentric, that is, capable only of taking their own physical perspective. However, research (e.g., Flavell, Shipstead, and Croft, 1978) has revealed that even preschoolers are able to see the world from another person's perspective if they are encouraged to do so. They merely prefer to view things from their egocentric perspective, perhaps because this

task is less cognitively challenging. The egocentric perspective of the child was originally also explained by the fact that the child can view only one dimension at a time
(as noted above in the discussion of conservation). However, this dimension does not
have to be the child's perspective. It could be the other person's perspective, enabling
the child to view the world from a different focal point than her or his own. This cognitive concept has been supported by research focusing on interpersonal situations,
that is, emotional perspective, which has demonstrated that children are indeed capable of empathic attunement even at this very young age (Stern, 1989).

Four- and 5-year-olds are also becoming aware of and able to differentiate between
reality and appearance. For instance, if they are shown a bogus spider or snake, they
can recognize that it is not real. This ability was not present in the 3-year-old and
hence is tenuous in the 4-year-old child. Because this is a new skill, it can be the source
of great excitement and approach-avoidance for children. They may waver in their
amount of certainty about their estimation of an object or activity as real versus fake,
approaching it with some hesitancy, then delighting in it when they have convinced
themselves that what is presented is really only make-believe. Children use their ability
to pretend in their symbolic play and to gratify needs. They may recognize when they
cannot do something or accomplish a task but can pretend that they have completed it.

Emotionally, children become more sophisticated at this time. They can identify
how they feel and begin to relate specific emotions to specific situations. They are
now able to communicate their feelings to others, providing an excellent example of
the interaction between language and cognition. Specifically, the child would not be
able to understand emotion without her or his increasing cognitive complexity and
would not be able to communicate it verbally without the acquisition of necessary language skills. Nevertheless, 4- and 5-year-old children can express and experience only
one emotion at a time, being incapable of feeling nuances of feelings or mixed emotions. They remain clear-cut in their emotional expression, dealing with one affect at a
time. This singular experience of affect may result in the quick changes in emotion
that can be observed in 4- and 5-year-olds. A young child who might have just been
observed playing contentedly and happily might suddenly break into tears when
another child destroys her or his creation or attempts to take away a toy. Children at
this age do not verbally express emotions easily but talk about their feelings if they are
encouraged to do so. Pressing a 4- or 5-year-old for subtle description and sophisticated explanation, however, is inappropriate and taxes her or his ability. Similarly,
these children cannot yet understand that situations that evoke a strong and specific
type of emotion for them may result in an entirely different feeling for another person.
Hence, pressing a child to take the emotional perspective of another person in a highly
emotionally laden situation is equivalent to requesting the impossible.

Children at this age feel that they are now individuals in their own right. They can
initiate actions, are aware of their past and present, recognize consequences of
actions, and desire to share themselves with others and for others to share themselves
with them. Children become curious about what they can and cannot do and, in their
attempts to find out what kind of people they are, begin to take initiative in their own
lives (Erikson, 1950). They become curious about parents, friends, and environment,
always asking questions, engaging in play, experimenting, and role-playing new situations. If parents act in an understanding manner and guide the child's motives and

behaviors into socially acceptable avenues, there is a sense of purpose that ultimately leads to the child's setting of life goals and identification with parents. If initiative is punished by parents, the child might feel guilty about attempts to find out about self and others and may be stunted in development. Preschoolers are very much concerned with what their family members think of them and have a strong desire to fit in and be appreciated. They model after parents, friends, and preschool teachers, thus becoming socialized to the rules and regulations of their culture and community.

In summary, 4- and 5-year-old children are complex and enjoyable human beings with whom it is easy to interact. Their language skills have grown to an extent that results in easy conversation with adults, even adults who are exceedingly verbally focused. Although preschoolers' cognitive complexity is growing rapidly, their thought remains somewhat illogical, and their increasing facility with language is not to be mistaken for logic and reasoning. The child's emotional expressiveness becomes more sophisticated and is more easily shared with adults, though it still lacks the complexity of mixed emotions and recognition of nuances. Socially, they become curious as they discover their own mission and interests. They like to take charge of their actions but generally evidence very socialized behavior due to their desire to be loved and to fit into their community of family and friends. Nevertheless, 4- and 5-year-olds may show some stubbornness and have occasional temper tantrums. They demand much attention from the adults in their lives and may easily become jealous. Fears are common among 4- and 5-year-olds, but tend to resolve themselves as the child's cognitive skills mature.

Middle Childhood

Middle childhood for the purposes of this book is defined as the period of life between 6 and 10 years of age, that is, a time of life when children adjust to and become comfortable in the school environment and learn to interact with adults and children outside of their families. Middle childhood involves great strides in motor development and skills learning, with particular emphases on cognitive and fine and gross motor skills in the schools.

By 6 years of age, children have achieved excellent balance and coordination. They walk like adults, ride bicycles easily, run faster and with fewer falls, and are working on perfecting fine motor skills. These children love games that challenge their gross motor skills, and it is of no surprise that this is the age when children begin to play team sports. Baseball, soccer, volleyball, and similar physical activities serve to enhance the child's large motor control and overall physical mastery. Fine motor tasks gain in importance and are slowly honed in many academically related activities. It makes developmental sense that children at this age enter school, as their fine motor control is only now sufficiently sophisticated to allow for the practice of neat handwriting, careful drawing, and other fine motor skills, such as sophisticated arts and craft. Younger children would have faced these tasks with too much frustration, and learning may have been hindered by physical or emotional, rather than cognitive, factors and limitations. Special skills often emerge at the age of 7 or 8 when children may begin to play musical instruments or choose a particular sport over others. Tennis, skiing, and similar physical activities can now be attended to with an eye on technique and a goal of improvement. Motor skills clearly continue to develop and a lot of growth takes place between the ages of 6 and 10. But major physical development milestones—namely, balance and coordination—were attained by age 6 and continued development from this age forward reflects refinement of skills, a quantitative rather than qualitative shift.

Language skills continue to be refined at this age. Children become aware of exceptions to grammar rules and are more correct in their use of language. Vocabulary explodes, especially as children add reading to their activities. They continue to be excellent listeners and now are able to track conversations easily. They can follow instructions and can remember several steps at a time that may be involved in following directions. However, young school-age children still have some difficulty with syntax of language as they remain very focused on context. Toddlers spoke only through grammatical morphemes that were understood in the context of their speech. For instance, a toddler's statement "mommy look" could be interpreted in two different ways, depending on context. If the child was playing and attempting to draw the mother's attention to a tower she or he had constructed, the utterance can be understood as a request for mother to take a look. However, if the child entered the room and noticed mother looking out the window, the utterance may be a mere reflection of the mother's current activity. This focus on content remains intact even among children of early school age. Much of their understanding of language still is created on the basis of context. However, it is at school age that reading activity and more complex instructions require that the child begin to analyze language on the basis of syntax, not content. For instance, an early school-age child still may have difficulty recognizing that the sentence "the doll is hard to see" does not indicate that the doll has difficulty seeing, but rather that it is difficult for another person to see the doll. The child's focus on context makes it difficult to focus on syntax, that is, to recognize that a different rule applies to analyzing the phrase "hard to see" than the phrase "can see." Fine syntax-related rules of language begin to develop slowly as the 6-year-old child matures. By age 10, subtle rules are learned and used with ease.

On the way to learning sophisticated language and syntax rules, children discover that language can be used to surprise and play as they hit upon language-based jokes, such as riddles and puns. Third- and fourth-graders love to play word games in which they use unexpected meanings of words (also called lexically based ambiguity), alike pronunciation (also called phonologically based ambiguity), and unexpected interpretations (also called syntactically based ambiguity). The latter is the most difficult type of joke or riddle and generally is not acquired until the child is about 10 years old. Some easy phonologically based jokes, on the other hand, can even be understood by bright 6- and young 7-year-olds. A favorite lexically based joke for school-age children might go like this:

> *Why did the robot eat electric light bulbs at noontime?*
> *I don't know, why?*
> *Because she wanted a light lunch!*

Or like this:

> *You can't park your car here!*
> *Why not??? The sign said: "Fine for Parking!!"*

A phonologically based joke might go like this:

> *I saw the robber running down the road! Did the police catch him?*
>
> *No, he stepped on a scale and got a weigh.*

Additional easy phonologically based jokes that even young school-age children enjoy are the famous knock-knock jokes:

> *Knock, knock*
>
> *Who's there? Boo.*
>
> *Boo who?*
>
> *Oh, don't cry!*
>
> *Knock, knock*
>
> *Who's there?*
>
> *Ida.*
>
> *Ida who?*
>
> *Ida baked a cake if Ida known you were coming!*

A more difficult syntactically based joke for older school-age children goes as follows:

> *Did you hear about the stick-up on the barn?*
>
> *No! What happened?*
>
> *Some kid threw it up there!*

Or like this:

> *The police are looking for a man with one leg named Smith . . .*
>
> *Oh? What's the other leg called??*

School-age children's ability to grasp jokes and riddles also reflects their increased cognitive complexity. Unlike preschoolers, 6- to 10-year-olds develop increasingly sophisticated reasoning skills and logic. They can easily consider more than two dimensions or perspectives at a time, thus mastering tasks involving conservation. They can also explain conservation concepts, being able to point out that quantity did not change because nothing was added or taken away (i.e., identity was preserved), that quantity did not change because while one is taller, the other is fatter (i.e., one dimension was compensated for by another), or that quantity remained the same because the new arrangement could be turned back into the previous one (i.e., reversibility). As was pointed out previously, post-Piagetian research has indicated that even younger children can conserve if they are given time and advice. Hence, the qualitative cognitive change that takes place in the school-age child discussed here is that she or he is not only able to conserve, but can explain why this process works! These reasoning skills, however, are still tied to what the child can see or experience directly and cannot yet be carried out abstractly; that is, the child cannot yet develop new hypotheses or advance her or his own logic. Children's logic remains relatively concrete, and they continue to interpret meanings directly and concretely. For instance, sayings such as "The grass is always greener on the other side of the fence" might prompt this child to look over a fence to observe this phenomenon. Children have not yet learned to abstract that meanings might not be concrete, but rather symbolic. Symbolic thought and abstract interpretation do not emerge until late childhood or even adolescence (around age 12 or 13).

However, by age 8, children are beginning to think more and more logically and become able to analyze thinking itself. They can plan strategy and begin to play games such as chess wherein they have to anticipate moves and think through the consequences of their own actions analytically and indirectly. They become more capable of responding to complex directions or instruction in the absence of a model. Before this age, most instructions either were simple commands or were accompanied by the modeling of a skill if new task learning was involved. By age 8 or 9, children can listen to taped instruction of activities and figure out how to engage in the task by themselves. These children are also able to recognize if instructions are incomplete or do not make sense. If instructions contain unfamiliar words or skip important steps, children are left confused or attempt to make up their own meaning. This can lead to mislearning and misconceptualization of problems and procedures. Clear instructions in children's language hence remain important even at this age.

Children's emotional expressiveness and understanding becomes more complex at this time. Just as they are able to consider two dimensions to explain conservation, so too are they now becoming increasingly aware of two emotions at a time. Mixed emotions were impossible for the 5-year-old, remain difficult for the 6- and 7-year-old, and become increasingly possible for the 8- to 10-year-old. Seven-year-old children can be aware of two emotions at the same time if these do not appear incompatible—that is, two positive emotions such as happiness and excitement, and are directed toward the same situation. Eight-year-olds are aware that two compatible emotions can be felt at the same time and about two different situations. However, not until 10 years of age can children acknowledge two incompatible emotions, such as excitement and fear, and even then only if the two emotions are evoked by two different situations, such as excitement about going to the fair and fear about the train ride to get there.

In addition to recognizing more than one emotion, school-age children also become more aware of nuances in their affects. They can recognize that certain situations may result in more intense emotions than others. Their expression of emotions is becoming more complex and differentiated. They are able to share the nuances with others, in part because they are developing the language skills to communicate fine differentiation. Further, they are able to express emotion in a modulated manner much more so than the preschooler, for whom emotion was still an all-or-none phenomenon. The school-age child, especially with increasing age, can feel very angry but might not express this anger violently. This development is both good and bad, as this is also the age when children may recognize that certain emotions are not well tolerated by their environment and may begin to repress or deny certain affects within themselves.

Social development for these children is highly correlated with the fact that school, teachers, and peers have developed great salience for the child. Teachers become important role models for these children, who work diligently toward becoming competent and industrious individuals. Children learn how to create things and complete tasks and feel satisfaction through their accomplishments. Continuous failure or critical adults may lead the child to feel uncertain and may result in feelings of inferiority. To maintain a positive sense of self and to accept feelings of competence and the associated willingness to attempt new tasks, the child needs responsive and supportive adults in her or his environment. Although for the 6-year-old child, adults have more salience than children, this preference changes quickly, and as the child ages, peers gain in importance until adolescence, when adults are not uncommonly rejected as role models and significant persons.

Popularity becomes important to children at this age, and they strive to meet many peers and attempt to initiate interactions. Almost all 6- to 10-year-olds are outgoing, but only the friendly and positively outgoing children tend to be considered popular by their peers. Aggressively outgoing children tend to be rejected by peer groups. As the school-age child matures, groups become increasingly important. Whereas the 6-year-old might prefer a few special friends, the 10-year-old seeks to belong to a larger group. Children in this age group tend to favor children of their own gender for interactions and play. Further, they model more after adults of their own gender. Given these social interaction patterns, it is not surprising that this is a critical period in children's lives with regard to gender role socialization. Certainly, even younger children (in fact, even infants) experience external gender-bound socialization, but it is at this age that patterns of gender-specific behaviors tend to be established. Finally, children's understanding of right and wrong is internalized by the age of 10, and moral reasoning, not unlike cognitive development, is becoming more complex at this time. Much like gender role socialization, endorsed morality for children of this age tends to reflect the rules and beliefs of her or his family, community, and culture.

In summary, the time period between ages 6 and 10 is one replete with major changes in the child's cognitive and social functioning. Although motor and language development have seen the last of their major qualitative changes at this time in life, cognition and socialization continue to undergo major qualitative shifts as these children enter late childhood. Middle childhood is a time of great sensitivity to environmental factors as social and moral aspects of the self are internalized. Any biases that are expressed and reinforced by the child's environment are likely to be perpetuated from here on out in the child's development. Important patterns of behavior and judgments are set at this time. Common developmentally tied problems encountered among middle childhood children may include arguments, bragging, showing off, and self-consciousness. These issues tend to resolve as the child continues through her or his healthy developmental trajectory.

Late Childhood

For the purposes of this book, late childhood is defined as the period between 11 and 12 years of age, that is, a time of life when children begin to grapple with social interaction issues that will follow them into adolescence, when largely hormonally driven physical changes become of great importance. The differentiation between 12- and 13- to 15-year-olds can be quite arbitrary as many children in Western (industrialized) countries are beginning to enter puberty at earlier and earlier ages (Schickedanz, Schickedanz, Forsyth, and Forsyth, 2001). Nevertheless, the distinction is made here, but with the provision that the child clinician must remember its arbitrariness.

As was mentioned previously, motor and language development do not undergo any further qualitative shifts once a child enters late childhood. However, this is not to imply that development in these arenas is complete. Nothing could be farther from the truth. In fact, late-childhood children increase their vocabulary and improve their grammatical skills by leaps and bounds. Their language skills receive a great boost from the increase in reading and writing required through schoolwork or motivated by individual children's interests and hobbies. Motor skills become increasingly refined and sophisticated as children develop interests in certain sports and practice to improve fine and gross motor skills. However, the crucial aspect of development is refinement and sophistication, not qualitative shifts.

Qualitative shifts, on the other hand, are still necessary to move along the child's cognitive complexity to a level from which continued development would imply mere refinement and increasing sophistication. Specifically, the child has to master the task of moving to formal operations as defined by Piaget (1967). Such thinking involves complex logic and symbolic thought, independent generation of hypotheses and new learning, and abstract reasoning. Although children as young as age 11 may enter the phase in which such qualitative shifts are noted in thought, it is not guaranteed that all children or even adults will ever have equal abilities to think abstractly and symbolically. Nevertheless, most late-childhood children begin to be capable of pure thought that is not tied to current experience or independent action, are able to reason deductively, and form hypotheses about their world. These cognitive skills are supported by school curricula that stress science and mathematics, that is, abstract thought and hypothesis testing and generation.

Closely tied to cognitive sophistication and language skills, emotional shifts take place at this time of life as well. The child is now able to experience and acknowledge two incompatible or competing emotions about a single event. She or he can begin to recognize novel affects never experienced before and begins to make sense of feelings, tying them to specific events. Children are now fully aware of blends and nuances not only in their own affects but also in the feelings of the adults and children around them. Expression of emotion continues to take place in a modulated manner and verbal communication about feelings becomes increasingly sophisticated. Late-childhood children are willing to discuss their feelings and can analyze them carefully. They recognize that the same situation can evoke different feelings at different times and for different people. These children's ability to perceive and accept their own widely varied affects greatly facilitates empathy for and understanding of others' feelings as well.

Socially, no great qualitative shifts are noted between middle and late childhood. The next large social shift does not take place until adolescence, at which time children begin to struggle with future planning, self-identity, budding sexuality, and sexual relationships. Until adolescence, late-childhood children remain concerned about same-gender peer groups, seek popularity, internalize moral standards, and develop interests and gender-specific behaviors.

In summary, the primary marker of late childhood is the continued refinement and increasing sophistication of motor, language, and social skills acquired in middle childhood. Cognitively and emotionally, late-childhood children evidence qualitative shifts that ready them for the greater complexities of adolescent life. Adolescents will continue the pattern of refinement in skills and, while faced with different psychosocial challenges, will continue development not through qualitative but through quantitative changes. It is the lack of qualitative shifts in motor, language, cognitive, and emotional development that may have contributed to the old notion that the developmental phase of life ends at age 18. However, development is clearly not dependent on qualitative shifts alone but also on refinement of "old" skills and talents. Social tasks continue to change throughout the life span, and new challenges face people in different ways at any age. These new tasks challenge people to continue to grow regardless of age and result in lifelong development in psychosocial terms.

Summary and Concluding Thoughts

This chapter presented a developmental framework to emphasize the importance of developmental knowledge when working with children. The dialectic approach to development endorsed in this chapter is considered very useful to the work of the child clinician because of its integrative and thorough nature. It challenges the counselor to recognize that development is not merely the acquisition of new or qualitatively different tasks and behaviors; instead it is an evolution that reflects increasing refinement and sophistication across many arenas of development. Child therapists who have not had a lot of contact with young children, and hence have not observed firsthand the rapid developmental changes (both qualitatively and quantitatively) that occur between birth and adolescence might want to consider seeking out opportunities for additional learning. Such opportunities may include reading some of the many references provided in this chapter; observations in nurseries, preschools, or schools; volunteer work with healthy children; and viewing tapes about childhood and development.

It is essential for a child therapist or counselor to be knowledgeable about developmental milestones and sequences to be able to engage in appropriate diagnosis, case conceptualization, and treatment planning. The child therapist or counselor must also remember that all age norms must be taken with a grain of salt, as they merely represent an average at which to expect certain developments to take place. Individual children, different cultures, and all the factors (e.g., psychological, biological, outerphysical) discussed in the dialectic approach to development remain important variables in determining whether a given child remains on a healthy developmental trajectory. Development has many implications for the environment in which a clinician works with children, as equipment, materials (especially toys), and furnishings have to be appropriate to the developmental levels and needs to the children who are using them.

Table 3.1   A Model of Cognitive Development in Childhood as Developed by Jean Piaget

Type of Thought and Subphases	Characteristics	Age
Sensorimotor	preverbal; growth is estimated via infant's vision, taste, smell, hearing, and tactile perception	Birth to 2 years
Reflex Activity	exercising inherited reflexes tracking objects without reaction to their disappearance imitation of facial expressions	0 to 1 month
Primary Circular Reactions	repetitious act to practice skills staring reaction to disappearing objects repetition of behavior that was responded to	1 to 4 months
Secondary Circular Reactions	repetition of purposeful acts searching reaction to disappearing objects	4 to 8 months
Secondary Schemata	searching for concealed object crude attempts at imitation	8 to 12 months
Tertiary Circular Reactions	experimenting with new situations searching and finding concealed objects sophisticated imitation of action	12 to 18 months
Mental Combinations	symbolic thought; cognitive representations object concept and permanence deferred imitation	18 to 24 months
Preoperational Thought	language development has strong impact on cognitive development progression from perception-bound to symbolic thought	2 to 7 years
Preconceptual Period	inability to consider more than one aspect of a situation egocentric social communication	2 to 4 years
Intuitive Period	increasingly decentrated (more than one aspect) intuitive impressions of social situations (not purely perception-bound)	4 to 7 years
Concrete Operations	increased ability to deal with hypotheticals progression from concrete logic to sophisticated logic and abstraction mastery of conservation and compensation ability to carry out action in thoughts only (internalization) recognizes reversibility and reciprocity	7 to 11 years
Formal Operations	thought no longer bound by time and immediate perception progression from already logical and abstract thought to higher levels of sophistication and flexibility; creativity recognition of transitivity thought completely independent of action hypothetico-deductive reasoning	11 to 15 years

Table 3.2 Emotional Development across the Life Span Adapted from Lane and Schwartz

Period	Experience of Affect	Expression of Affect	Differentiation of Affect
Early Sensorimotor Period	bodily sensation only; no cognitive experience or understanding	inability to express affect either for self or other	undifferentiated arousal
Late Sensorimotor Period	global arousal and tendency to act upon it	specific actions are now associated with specific emotions	global perception specific actions associated with specific emotions recognizable by others
Pre-Operational Thought	limited range of experience only either-or experience (no "mixed" feelings)	stereotypic and unidimensional expression of limited repertoire	can identify only one affect at a time can only tie one affect to one distinct situation
Concrete Operations	awareness of blends of feelings	complex, modulated, and well-differentiated expression	recognition of concurring as well as opposing emotions recognition of subtle change with specific times or situations
Formal Operations	peak differentiation and blending experience of nuances	rich expression of quality and intensity	simultaneous recognition of blends in self and others recognition of novel feelings and patterns

Source: This table was adapted from "Levels of emotional awareness: A cognitive-developmental theory and its applications to psychopathology" by R. D. Lane and G. E. Schwartz, 1987, *American Journal of Psychiatry*, 144, pp. 133–143. Copyright 1987, the American Psychiatric Association. Reprinted by permission.

Table 3.3 Psychosocial Development across the Life Span as Established by Erik Erikson

Age	Conflict	Characteristics of Success	Outcome
Birth to 1 year	Basic Trust vs. Mistrust	learning to trust others and to see them as dependable and trustworthy; becoming trustworthy oneself	Hope
2 to 3 years	Autonomy vs. Shame and Doubt	learning self-assertion and rudimentary independence; taking pride in one's actions and exercising judgment	Will
4 to 5 years	Initiative vs. Guilt	becoming curious and participating purposefully in the environment; exploring and asking questions	Purpose
6 to 12 years	Industry vs. Inferiority	learning how to do and complete tasks; trying out new skills and discovering interests	Competence
13 to 19 years	Identity vs. Role Confusion	sense of independence and personal efficacy; integrating interests and skills into a whole that is identity	Fidelity
20 to 24 years	Intimacy vs. Isolation	entering relationships and learning to compromise and sacrifice; caring for others outside the self	Love
25 to 64 years	Generativity vs. Stagnation	establishing careers and meaningful life; guidance of the next generation; creation of ideas, works, or children	Care
65 years to death	Ego Integrity vs. Despair	reviewing life and feeling satisfied and successful; continuing to contribute to society or family	Wisdom

Table 3.4   Psychosexual Development across the Life Span as Proposed by Sigmund Freud

Age	Stage	Desire	Purpose	Characteristic	Outcome
0 to 1 years	Oral	pleasure from activity of the mouth—sucking	taking in food for physical survival rudimentary ego development	primary narcissism pleasure principle immediate gratification	identification accept other's beliefs object cathexis
1 to 3 years	Anal	pleasure from activity of the anus—defecating	delay gratification develop reality principle ego differentiation	autonomy struggles control issues clash with objects in way of wish fulfillment	enhanced frustration tolerance
3 to 6 years	Phallic	pleasure from the genital area	superego acquisition ego development self-identification	object cathexis focus on sexuality Oedipal/Electra Complex external prohibitions	healthy superego parental cathexis
6 to 13 years	Latency	dormant—focus on peer relationships	skill development discovery of interests	nonsexual play activity	competence in skills academic achievement
13 years →	Genital	gratification in sexual love-making	mature love to satisfy instincts affection	marriage aim-inhibited lust and affection empathy and caring	maturity in self maturity in relationships

Table 3.5   A Model of Self Development as Proposed by Daniel Stern: The Five Senses of Self

Age	Sense of Self	Critical Developments	Critical Contributions from Others
Birth	Sense of Emergent Self	emergence of organization around invariants (e.g., first around physiological regulation)	strong need for an object that helps the child regulate physiological needs and helps meet them appropriately
2 to 7 months	Sense of Core Self	awareness of self-agency, self-coherence, self-history, and self-affectivity self and other are sensed as separate entities	strong need for an object that helps the child self-regulate affects and need states need for another who facilitates repetition which is critical to the child's need to order her or his world
7 to 18 months	Sense of Subjective Self	recognition of shareability of self and affect development of intersubjectivity through shared attention, shared intentions, and shared affective states	critical need for another who is willing to share her or his own affects, intentions, and attention with the infant critical need for another who is capable of affect attunement
15 to 18 months	Sense of Verbal Self	objective (or conceptual) as opposed to experiential self-experience deferred imitation symbolic play language	need for models who can be imitated in play and day-to-day activities need for another who facilitates language development and who listens and shares personal knowledge
3 to 4 years	Sense of Narrative Self	placing of self and others into historical contexts consideration of past and future	need for other who will listen to and show interest in child's life story

Table 3.6 Milestones of Motor Development in Early Childhood

Developmental Period and Approximate Age	Motor Movement Milestones
Infants and Toddlers	
1 to 2 weeks	sucking response; fetal position
1 month	lifts head
2 months	holds head up; lifts chest
3 months	reaches by swiping at objects
4 months	rolls over; sits with support
5 months	reaches and grasps; sits on laps
6 months	sits on high chair
7 months	sits up alone
8 months	stands with help
9 months	stands holding on to furniture; develops pincer grasp
10 months	crawls or creeps on hands and knees
11 months	walks when led
12 months	pulls self up to stand; plays with large objects; gains control of grasping and letting go of objects
13 months	climbs stairs on all fours
14 months	stands alone
15 months	walks alone with a waddle; controlled and intentional placement of objects
18 months	runs alone; steps off low heights
24 months	climbs alone; strings beads on stiff string; puts together simple two- to four-piece puzzles; waves and points; jumps off low heights; walks using arms for balance; throws with awkward, jerky movements
30 months	runs stiffly; walks upstairs; jumps up with both feet; climbs up, but not down; throws ball with rigid arm movement unsupported by other body movement
Preschool Children	
36 to 48 months	rides tricycle; alternates feet while climbing; gallops; hops on one foot for a few steps; walks downstairs two feet on a step; runs smoothly; exerts control over stopping quickly from running; leaps over obstacle with one foot at a time; maintains basic balance; works large zippers and snaps; brushes teeth; dresses self; skips on one foot; cuts and pastes; draws; begins to learn how to throw a ball
48 to 60 months	leaps over obstacle with both feet simultaneously; broad-jumps; hops 8 to 10 steps; catches objects while balancing self effectively by assuming a wide-legged stance; walks and runs a curved line with good control over stopping and starting; changes direction while running; walks stairs with alternating steps; climbs up and down obstacles; balanced jumping up and off; roller skates, ice skates, and kicks balls; throws with overhand motion from the elbow; walks balance beams; skips with one foot

(continued)

Table 3.6 *(continued)*

Developmental Period and Approximate Age	Motor Movement Milestones
60 to 72 months	walks like an adult; bicycles; skips, alternating feet; runs faster and with fewer falls; jumps rope; jumps high and far; perfects the skill of throwing a ball; throws using coordinated whole-body movements
Early School-Age Children	
72 months and older	plays games involving gross motor skills (e.g., baseball, football, soccer, tennis); engages in physical activity that challenges gross-motor coordination (e.g., swimming, gymnastics, skiing); engages in activities that develop fine motor control (e.g., knitting, sewing, arts and crafts); develops special skills (e.g., playing a musical instrument, singing); learns excellent fine motor control to write and draw; achieves excellent balance and coordination

Source: Based on Schickedanz, Schickedanz, Forsyth, and Forsyth, 2001.

Table 3.7   Receptive, Expressive, and Pragmatic Language Development in Childhood

Age	Receptive	Expressive	Pragmatic
Birth to 1 month	differentiates, turns to, and prefers voices	differentiated cries (e.g., pain, hunger)	nonverbal expression of needs
1 month to 4 months	uses eyes to search for speaker	cooing all vowels and some consonants (s, k, g)	nonverbal expression of needs collection of information
4 months to 8 months	responds to own name and familiar tones of voice	babbling four distinct syllables	expression of needs nonverbal requests (e.g., raises arms to be picked up)
9 months to 12 months	listens selectively responds to "no" and verbal requests understands new words	first real words symbolic gestures words with idiosyncratic meaning	expression of needs nonverbal requests protestations
12 months to 18 months	points to named body parts can identify objects understands commands	many single words: average of ten words by 18 months echoes words heard	verbal expression of comments protestations verbal requests
18 months to 24 months	follows series of two to three commands points in response	telegraphic speech (i.e., two-word sentences)	can report to someone else enters into dialogue
36 months and upward	increasing ability to follow commands increasing ability to understand spoken language	some complex sentences grammatical mistakes (e.g., "goed")	skilled conversation maintenance of topic role playing indirect requests
60 months and upward	acknowledges listener takes listener into consideration	better grammar complex syntax increasing vocabulary	good conversational skills (to be refined into adulthood)

Sources: Based on Berk, 2006; Bjorklund, 2004; Thomas, 2005

Environments and Materials for Child Therapy and Counseling

> *The institutions, services and facilities responsible for the care or protection of children shall conform with the standards established by competent authorities, particularly in the areas of safety, health, in the number and suitability of their staff, as well as competent supervision.*
> —Article 3.3 of the U.N. Convention on the Rights of the Child

By now, it is clear that children are a unique group of clients in that clinicians who choose to work with children have to explore a number of background issues that can contribute to the success or failure of their work with children. Clinicians must have assessed their overall interest and aptitude for work with children, explored their ability to work in a culturally sensitive manner with children of diverse backgrounds, and learned about the many implications of developmentally based needs, skills, and abilities. One additional topic that requires forethought and reflection has to do with the physical environment in which the work with children takes place. Although a simple office suffices for most work with adults, children have special needs that are directly related to their uniqueness as less verbal and more exploratory human beings. Hence, it is important to assess whether the available surroundings can be rendered conducive to the therapeutic work with children.

For clients, entering a clinic is much like entering the house of a new friend. Clients look at furnishings, artwork, cleanliness, and layout to glean information about the people working and living in this environment. Judgments may be made on the basis of these first impressions, and it is certainly worthwhile for the enhancement of rapport to keep a mental health clinic as inviting as possible. It is not important that the furnishings and equipment be shiny, brand-new, or even expensive. They merely must be arranged in such a way as to communicate privacy, safety, and caring to the children and their families. The environment is best if it is clean and warm and obviously designed with children in mind. Entering a mental health center that is disheveled, dirty, or dark may communicate a lack of caring and concern that could leave the child frightened and the parent concerned. Of course, excellent work can potentially be done in such an environment, but if disarray and a negative atmosphere can be avoided, it is preferable to do so to set the best stage for beginning the work with children and their families.

There are a number of considerations with regard to clinic design and equipment. None is written in stone, but all are to be carefully weighed before making the decision to begin seeing children. These considerations include the general physical layout and design of the center, the arrangement of the waiting area, decisions about appropriate places and cleanup arrangements for child therapy, and the playroom itself with all its necessary play or activity materials and furnishings. In pondering each of these facets of child counseling or therapy, there are four factors that appear to have been agreed upon (e.g., Coppolillo, 1987: Landreth, 2002a; Simmons, 1987; Spiegel, 1996) as foremost on the clinician's mind: the atmosphere and safety of the setting, the child's and family's privacy, the child's and care provider's comfort, and the convenience of all individuals involved. All four aspects are addressed for each of the considerations that go into successful environmental design. For all of the considerations, optimal design and solutions are discussed. These optimal conditions are not supposed to keep committed clinicians from attempting to make less optimal conditions work. It is surprising how well clinics can function under less than the best conditions. Optimal conditions merely give the care provider something to strive for if the flexibility for change in the physical environment should arise. Less than optimal conditions are also described below to illustrate how with some ingenuity and tenacity, even difficult situations can be mastered. However, as the examples show, there is always the danger that something might go wrong, at the wrong time in treatment when the conditions are not as good as they could be. The discussion that ensues is based on the assumption that the primary means of working with children will be play therapy. Recent research, including a large meta-analysis, clearly demonstrates the effectiveness of play therapy, especially humanistically or child-centered play therapy and makes a compelling argument for the central value of play in the treatment of children with psychological, emotional, or behavioral presenting concerns (Bratton, Ray, and Rhine, 2005; Muro, Ray, and Schottelkorb, 2006).

Physical Layout and Design of the Clinic

The optimal layout of a mental health center addresses foremost safety and privacy, but also comfort and convenience. If sacrifices have to be made, they should be made in descending order, with safety being most and convenience least important. Safety is an extremely important feature in working with children. It has many therapeutic implications and plays strongly into the psychotherapeutic process and counseling relationship. Safety is often something that children who present for treatment do not experience in their everyday lives. Therefore, to provide a corrective experience, safety must be ascertained as completely as possible in the clinical setting. If a child does not feel safe in the treatment room in particular and clinic as a whole, the uninhibited unfolding of the child's necessary growth-oriented work might not occur.

Safety is important inside the therapy room itself, but also with regard to where the room is placed in the larger center. Clinics are often located within office buildings, rather than being a building in and of themselves. This provides an excellent extra safety feature that can be used in choosing which room will serve as the children's therapy room. Specifically, the counseling room proper is safest if it does not have a door that opens to the outside of the mental health center itself. The door best faces into the clinic and even then is best chosen in such a manner as to maximize the distance that must be traveled from the playroom door to the exit door of the agency. On the way to the exit door, the child should have to pass the reception area.

Although play therapy is generally confined to the play therapy room, it does happen that children "escape" because of the overwhelming psychological tasks and emotions that often face them, especially early in the therapeutic work before the relationship with the care provider has solidified and presents safety in and of itself. In such an instance, it is a relief for the clinician to know that the child not only would have to travel quite a distance to get to the exit door but also would have to pass by the reception area and cannot leave the clinic undetected. For instance, one child, who had been brought for treatment on the recommendation of a teacher because of suicidal ideation and severe social withdrawal, managed to escape the therapy room of a clinic that was less than optimally designed. The therapy room was located next to the exit door, which facilitated leaving without being seen by the receptionist, and the exit door faced into a busy street. This child's escape presented a major problem to his safety and certainly was dramatized further by the fact that one of his prior suicide attempts had consisted of running in front of a moving car.

In considering floor plans, placement of the waiting area is addressed as well. In working with children, there is almost always an adult who will be waiting for the duration of the session. Placement of a waiting room next to the counseling room may result in the child's questioning of session privacy, especially if soundproofing is poor. For example, in the therapy of one 12-year-old girl, the poor design of the center resulted in great hesitation on her part to open up to her therapist. Several sessions were spent dealing with issues of privacy and confidentiality. It was very difficult for the therapist to deal with the child on these issues, as she herself had doubts about the appropriateness of the center's design.

Of course, there are always exceptions to rules. For instance, one 3-year-old child, who was referred because of severe abandonment fears secondary to her custody and visitation arrangements, had such a hard time separating from her parents during the first few sessions that she had to peek out of the therapy room door when particularly difficult themes emerged in her play. For her, the faulty design of the clinic, where the waiting area was placed immediately adjacent to the therapy room, presented a saving grace that ultimately resulted in this child's ability to tolerate being apart from her parents, as she knew that they were always just outside the door.

Another consideration is to locate the therapy room where the noise that is unavoidable in the work with children is least intrusive or disruptive for others. In one university clinic, the play therapy room shared a wall with a classroom that was not actually part of the center. This therapy room was used for a children's therapeutic play group every Monday afternoon. As the children began to feel safe and comfortable in the counseling environment, noise levels often escalated, especially around ending time. Students in the adjacent classroom quickly began being complaining to the clinic supervisor. Finally, during one particularly noisy group session, the instructor of the class that was held at the same time as the group opened the therapy room door and intruded into the safety of the therapy process. She had waited as long as she could and had reached her own limit of what she could tolerate for her students. Needless to say, her decision to intrude had repercussions for the therapy of these children.

The previous example also points toward a broader issue of privacy. Often, clinics are located in larger office buildings, university buildings, or other larger structures. Although this arrangement increases safety, it may compromise privacy and confidentiality. Certainly, no mental health center wants to operate in such a manner that a complete stranger can proceed through an entire clinic and into a treatment room without being stopped. But on a lesser scale, clinic designers must also be aware that glass doors into a clinic that allow an easy look into the waiting room are a violation of privacy for the individuals who a waiting for their session. The absence of bathrooms or water fountains inside the mental health center present equal challenges to privacy, as clients should be able to access such facilities without having to leave the center itself. It is not uncommon for people to cry during treatment and to search for a bathroom where they may put themselves together again physically before they reenter the outside world. The repercussions of the absence of a bathroom inside the clinic are obvious.

Further, although children seldom have to use the bathroom during their session (especially if they are reminded to go beforehand), occasionally this cannot be avoided. Therefore, a bathroom best does not require crossing of a waiting area, is easily accessible, and is designed with children in mind. In all of these design features, the first one is the most important. As was mentioned earlier, usually a parent is waiting for the child in the waiting area. Having to cross the waiting areas for a trip to the bathroom can result in contact with the parent in the middle of a session and may interfere with the therapeutic process. Similarly, although there is little need for a child to ever leave the therapy room for a drink of water, preferably there would be more than one water fountain so that one can used by people in the waiting room and a different one by those in the counseling rooms. If there is only one water fountain, it is best most easily accessible from the waiting area.

The size of the treatment room needs to be considered as well. It appears that a 120- to 150-square-foot area works very well for most individual work with children. A room that is also used for group work with children might need to be slightly larger, perhaps up to 250 or 300 square feet, without being so large that individual treatment is hampered. A room that is too big can be just as difficult to manage one that is too small. Although children, especially in groups, might need personal space to diffuse emotions, there must not be so much space that the child has to be chased around during treatment. If the choice is between a room that is slightly too large and one that is slightly too small, it may be preferable to use the smaller room. It is easier to contain a child in a smaller room; the atmosphere is generally warmer and more conducive to self-disclosure. However, children need space to be active, so a room that is too confining or claustrophobic may inhibit the child.

Some thought needs to be given to windows. Windows can help to make a very small room appear larger, yet they may present a source of distraction. A room without windows minimizes distractions from the external environment but may appear closed-in and threatening. A good compromise appears to be to have a few windows equipped with blinds that can be drawn if necessary. Blinds are important not only to screen out distractions but also to maintain privacy and confidentiality, especially if the clinic is on a first floor or if children are being seen when it is dark outside. Activities in a lighted room are easily visible when it is dark outside. Windows in a playroom must either not open at all or open only so far that no child can fall out.

Beyond the general layout of the mental health center and its rooms, design and furnishings are an important consideration as they greatly influence the atmosphere of the center. A clinic where children are seen must be furnished and designed in such a way that children feel safe and welcome. Breakable knickknacks, inaccessible bookshelves, and lack of children's reading or activity materials in the waiting area all communicate that the clinic is not truly responsive to the special desires of children. Furniture must be sturdy enough to survive being climbed on, water fountains low enough to be reached even by the occasional 3-year-old, and carpets sufficiently water resistant and stainproof to endure spills and dirty shoes without problems. Artwork must be tasteful and versatile enough for a clientele of a large age range. A separate children's area can solve problems of appropriate artwork selection and entertainment.

The Waiting Area

Design and furnishing are most obvious in the waiting area, and it is here that the tone of welcome for children is set. Child-size furniture, children's activity materials, and children's books and magazines communicate caring and respect for children. In choosing children's books, care providers may include some of the many existing picture books that have specific therapeutic value (e.g., Aboff, 2003; Bakur Weiner and Neimark, 1995; Blomquist and Blomquist, 1990; Cain, 2000; Clarke, 2006; Crary, Katayama, and Steelsmith, 1996; Koplow, 1991; Marcus and Marcus, 1990; Nemiroff and Annunziata, 1990; Rashkin, 2005; Zeckhausen, 2007). The area has to be safe and sturdy, as well as relatively soundproof so that waiting children do not disrupt work that is ongoing in adjacent rooms. There is some controversy about what materials should be available in a waiting area for children. Some therapists endorse televisions or radios because the noise generated from these devices can mask sounds emanating from therapy rooms. Others, this author included, believe that televisions are strictly off limits and that radios should be limited to neutral or soothing music. This has to be an individual decision of each clinic's staff. Any clinic rules are best posted in the waiting room, clearly visible to all individuals using it. The only such rule that appears quite universally enforced in an environment serving children is that of no smoking.

In addition to designing the waiting area with children in mind, clinic personnel also must remember that the waiting area will be used by parents waiting for their children. Privacy must be guaranteed for the waiting parent, as well as for the working child. A waiting area that is too close to the therapy room may interfere with the child's therapy or may result in a very concerned parent. For instance, the 3-year-old child with abandonment fears mentioned above became very spontaneous and uninhibited in her doll play during one session. She pretended to cry and be sad in her play, doing an excellent job of mimicking these feelings. In fact, she did such an excellent job, that her mother, who was waiting in the adjacent, too closely located waiting room, became very concerned and knocked on the door to ascertain that her child was fine.

Appropriate Places and Clean-Up Arrangements

Before moving on to a discussion of the playroom itself, it is necessary to detour to some related topics, namely, the decisions about where treatment with children is conducted and who cleans up once a session is completed. The most common approach to the former, is to restrict the therapeutic work to the therapy or counseling room. However, there are clinicians who have presented arguments for the opposite (see Landreth, 2002a; Santostefano, 2004). They believe that there may be occasions when work with children can be better conducted in cafeterias, basements, attics, or even outside (Landreth, 2002a). Such decisions may be driven by therapeutic goals, such as generalization of treatment progress, or by limitations of the clinic, which might not be equipped with a playroom per se. Low-income clinics are likely to have to strike compromises that result in the use of creative and unconventional therapy spaces. Good work can still be done in less than optimal spaces. However, in using such spaces, the mental health staff has to pay attention to the safety and privacy issues discussed previously. The decision to move therapeutic work out of the counseling room has to be one that is made only after careful consideration of the potential advantages and disadvantages. It is important to discuss liability issues with parents and insurance carriers before moving therapy out of a safely confined and defined space.

Beyond privacy and safety issues, there are also treatment issues to be pondered. Specifically, it is questionable whether a public place, such as a playground, allows for the development of a relationship wherein the child can be fully uninhibited and spontaneously self-disclosing. The relationship is seen as central to therapeutic progress from the perspective of children who have participated in play therapy (Carroll, 2002), and thus its development needs to be protected. The possibilities of escaping the relationship with the clinician or evading difficult emotions and topics in public places or wide-open spaces are almost endless, allowing for the possibility of a dilution of treatment that may present too large a trade-off for the advantages inherent in the choice of such alternative settings. Finally, the use of a well-defined and circumscribed space can allow for the development of a special feeling or atmosphere that may never be created if the setting varies and has undefined and unclear boundaries. One rule of thumb may be to avoid the use of alternative spaces except if there is an overriding therapeutic need for a child to develop gross motor skills, if generalization of treatment progress calls for it, or if a child tends to be so highly agitated around the ending of a session that she or he needs to run or act out physically in some way other than what can be managed safely in the playroom to calm herself or himself before being able to return to the parent in the waiting room. However, even then, it is prudent to stay within parameters the clinician can manage comfortably and safely and in which limit-setting is possible (Landreth, 2002b). In fact, even counselors who do use settings other than the therapy room can be firm about setting physical boundaries and limits in these alternative environments.

Sometimes the decision is not one of using the playroom or an alternative larger environment but is instead one of using a general counseling office because of lack of a designated playroom. The absence of space reserved for children's work does not have to be entirely prohibitive of doing play therapy with children. Although it may be challenging to approximate the atmosphere of a playroom in a regular office or alternative space, this can be done. If the use of a regular office is necessary, it is best to designate a particular area in that office as the therapeutic play area and to inform the child of the (somewhat imaginary) boundary that runs through the room. The equipment placed in this section of the room is comparable to the equipment that is stocked in a regular children's counseling room, though there may be somewhat fewer materials and perhaps more limitations in how some materials may be used. For instance, whereas Play-Doh may be used quite freely in a special playroom with plastic tile floors or washable carpet, the same material may be present in the general office, but its use might be restricted to a tabletop.

With regard to design and furnishing, the cautions that were applicable to the waiting area in a children's clinic apply to the therapy office or other alternative space that doubles as a play area. Specifically, breakable objects are best avoided, carpets must be easily cleanable, wallpaper washable, and furniture sturdy. Personal items are generally kept to a minimum to avoid the confounding of transferences that tend to arise in child clients. Photographs of family members and pictures of or by other children should especially be avoided. Artwork in the children's area is best if appropriate to children, and materials need to be easily accessible for them.

Regardless of where the work takes place, a decision must be made about who is responsible for cleaning the playroom or area after its use. There are differing philosophies about this issue. Some care providers believe that a person should be hired specifically for that purpose so that neither the clinician nor the child has to become preoccupied during the session about cleanup. This approach brings to bear at least two obvious problems. First and therapeutically, it might not be realistic to suggest to a child that she or he can create messes or disarray without having to take some responsibility for cleanup. Second and pragmatically, such an approach would suggest either that a cleanup person has to be available immediately after each session with a child or that the room is cleaned only once a day, making it impossible for more than one child to be seen per day.

The second approach asks for the care provider to clean after the child client has left. This practice can present problems in several ways. First, again the child is not asked to take responsibility for actions in the playroom. Second, the clinician might become preoccupied with having to clean messes that are being created, thus possibly inhibiting the spontaneous unfolding of play activity in the child. Third, the counselor might resent having to do this task for the child and might feel rushed if cleaning has to take place in the brief ten minutes between two consecutive sessions.

The third approach is one in which child and clinician cooperate in the cleanup of the room during the last few minutes of each session. This approach is recommended because it represents the highest level of realism in that the child is held responsible for her or his actions by having to help deal with their consequences. Further, it allows for an additional act of cooperation and positive interchange between the child and the counselor as they engage in the activity together. It is often quite a new experience for a child to be helped freely by an adult. Finally, in this approach, the room is in order when a session is over, and the therapist does not have to be concerned about the readiness of the room for the next appointment. If this recommended approach is chosen, it must be introduced to the child during the first session to clearly delineate what is expected of the child and prepare the child for responsible interaction.

Features of the Playroom

Once a care provider has chosen to work therapeutically with children, has determined the best location of a playroom within a clinic, and has decided on a space for the work with children, decisions must be made about furnishings and equipment to be used in this work space. Several straightforward and commonly agreed-upon guidelines exist in both regards.

Furnishings

Preferably, the room contains a child-size table with at least two chairs: one for the child and one for the clinician. If children's groups will be conducted in the room as well, extra chairs need to be available to create space for all group members. Cabinets along the bottom third of the walls of the room are very useful for the storage of toys. Some of these cabinets may be lockable for materials to which the care provider wants to have access if necessary but may want to reserve only for a few children. Some of the cabinets should not have any doors at all, displaying the materials contained within them for easy surveying of the available toys. Such open spaces in a cabinet can also serve as an excellent hiding place for the child who needs to withdraw during the course of a session. If shelves are placed sufficiently low, this can be quite safe. Shelves that are high up, yet accessible to the child, can be dangerous, as a child may decide to climb into them; therefore, such shelving is best avoided. The main characteristic of cabinets and shelves is their accessibility for all ages of children. To give the child a true choice of materials so that this choice may be used for interpretive purposes, the child must have free access to all materials. Such unlimited access also encourages autonomy, creativity, and trust on the child's part.

Floor coverings in playrooms should be safe but easily cleanable. Stain-resistant carpet or soft vinyl tile is best. Hard tile can present problems and tends to give the room a cold atmosphere. Walls should be washable and the color cheerful yet relatively neutral. It is important to remember that it is the child who should set the mood for the session, not the environment. Light paints, such as ivory or peach, are sufficiently bright yet neutral to allow for this. Wallpapers are generally not recommended, for the same reasons that artwork should not be displayed. Both introduce content that is unnecessary and may affect the child's mood externally.

Some playrooms have a sink. If this is so, hot water is best avoided to prevent burns. Clinics without running water in the playroom can easily deal with this problem by having a plastic tub with a secure lid that contains fresh cold water. This arrangement can accommodate children who want to play in the water or who want to be sure to wash their hands or faces in the course of or after a particular play activity. For instance, one young child was very hesitant to use the sandtray for several sessions. She would stick part of her hand or foot into the tray, then withdraw it and inspect it for dirt. She became much more at ease with the use of sand when she was made aware that a tub of water and a towel were available if she needed them. Ultimately, this led to her willingness to use the sand freely and creatively—and, after a while, even without cleaning herself so meticulously after each use. This ability represented significant progress in her treatment as it showed that some of her inhibitions that had been overcome and made her affect more commensurate with her 4 years of age. A water tub in a room without sink need not be large; in fact, it should not be too large so that spills can be managed easily. One size that has been found successful is a tub that is approximately 5 inches deep and 10 inches square.

Sandtrays or sandboxes are another common feature in playrooms. Again, not all clinics come equipped with this, and a very large plastic tub with a tight-fitting lid can easily be substituted. One size that has been found very useful is approximately 7 inches deep, 2 feet wide, and 3 feet long. This tray holds enough sand or rice that it is too heavy for most children to overturn and that spills stay small. If a sandtray or sandbox is available, so should a small broom and dust pan for the child to be able to clean up spills. Further, a water sprayer must be handy to be able to wet sand to avoid dust that can irritate children's eyes or mucous membranes. An assortment of toys should be available for use in the sandtray; this is addressed in detail later. Finally, a free-standing or mounted easel and chalkboard facilitates drawing activities; it should be easily accessible and fully equipped with paints and chalks.

General Guidelines for the Selection of Materials

A foremost consideration in the selection of toys is safety. Often, children come to therapy or counseling from very unsafe and disorderly environments. It is hoped that the treatment can be used at least in part as a corrective experience in which the child can learn that there are safe and organized places that can be used to put a life back in order. Safety and orderliness can be expressed through the equipment of the playroom. Specifically, all materials that are freely accessible need to be safe for children of all ages who might choose to use them. All materials must be as sturdy as possible and in good working order; damaged toys are removed, repaired, or replaced immediately. Toys are such that a child does not have to worry about breaking them through regular use. In other words, very fragile or meticulous toys defeat the purpose of the playroom. There are some materials, such as paper and crayons, that need to be replenished from time to time, and it is best to keep a supply handy so that this can be done immediately when the need arises. Paper can be easily obtained in large rolls from local newspaper companies. They are generally willing to make tax-deductible donations to clinics of unused newsprint that is too short to be of use in the printing of papers. Other materials, such as Play-Doh, clay, and paints can spoil over time and must be replaced. Again a supply is best kept handy.

Toys and materials need to be chosen carefully and with the premise that all of children's play in the work with the clinician is an expression of their self and their experiences in relation to their families and larger contexts (Chazan, 2002; Rubin, 2006), including culture (Gil and Drewes, 2005). Landreth (2002a) makes the point that the materials in a playroom should be a selection not a collection of toys and equipment. In other words, care providers do not accumulate toys randomly, but rather choose toys according to a meaningful, therapeutically relevant rationale. Toys and play are a child's language and primary means of communication (Norton and Norton, 2006). They represent the tools and work of a child and thus are serious business for children. They can be used to facilitate interaction or to encourage solitary play. They can be used to communicate encouragement or inhibition, and they can be presented in a manner that stimulates or squelches creativity. All of these features must be on the clinician's mind while equipping the room.

Although it is still true that there are few *researched* guidelines for the selection of therapy room materials, child clinicians have developed several helpful hints and lists of materials that have proven useful in the selection of toys. First, many decades ago Ginott (1960) presented an approach wherein toys are selected for one of several purposes. Specifically, he suggested that a therapy room have toys that facilitate the therapeutic relationship, toys that allow for catharsis of affects and needs, toys that can enhance the development of insight, and materials that allow for defense, especially sublimation. Landreth (2002a) suggests that toys should be chosen to facilitate emotional and creative expression and play, to stimulate exploration and interest in a child in a nonverbal manner, to support relationship building, to allow for limit-testing, and to develop a sense of self-control. Coppolillo (1987) suggests keeping toys to a minimum to be sure that "toys are [merely] for the purpose of offering vehicles for expression of the child, not dazzling or seducing him [sic]" (p. 25). Thus, the final choices reflect very personal decisions of the mental health worker. But the overriding consensus appears to be that the toys have to facilitate the unfolding of therapeutic process and the development of a special relationship between child and clinician, not the entertainment of the child. The diversity, yet convergence, of opinions about the selection of playroom materials results in several points of consensus that a counselor might want to consider in selecting materials.

Self-Expression.   First, there appears to be a consensus in the literature that toys must facilitate a child's self-expression. This self-expression is to be as unstructured as possible. Not surprisingly, toys that have a prescribed use, such as board games or theme toys (e.g., Star Wars figures or Power Rangers figures) tend to be avoided unless they can be used in creative ways that support self-expression (Bellinson, 2002). Instead, toys that allow for a free flow of self-expression without being limited by prescribed rules are preferred. For instance, Play-Doh can be used for successful self-expression in a nonverbal manner that is very easily understood by the therapist. One 8-year-old boy who had presented to treatment as a very angry and aggressive child quickly chose Play-Doh as his primary mode of self-expression. He used the medium to create exploding volcanoes when he was angry, biting "wiener dogs" when he felt he had to defend himself against external intrusions from his family, or airplanes when he wanted to escape difficult situations. He found a literally unlimited number of uses for Play-Doh and very successfully expressed his needs and affects through this medium.

Self-expression also has to be understood in a context of culture and toys have to be culturally appropriate and varied. All children, regardless of background, need to have access to toys that reflect the objects commonly available and used in their environments. At times, this means getting special toys if clinicians provide care in highly unique ethnic or other contexts. For example, in working with children in rural Alaska, it is very helpful to have doll clothing that includes parkas and fur, specially tailored to the cold climate. It is also useful to have miniatures for the sandtray work that are not often found in the generic playroom, such as sleds and sled dogs, harpoons, seals, polar bears, and even igloos (even those actually are only emergency shelters).

Creativity.   The second consensus that appears to emerge from the literature is that the materials need to stimulate creativity. Self-expression and creativity are difficult to differentiate and often go hand in hand. It is possible for a child to be self-expressive without being creative; however, it does not appear possible for a child to be creative without also being self-expressive. Thus, materials that enhance creativity also work well in the area of self-expression. Further, creativity and the development thereof are likely to affect self-esteem and self-confidence positively and are desirable in that sense as well. Creativity also is related to the symbolic use of toys and hence requires careful evaluation and understanding by the clinician in the interpretation of play (Norton and Norton, 2006). The creative use of several wooden toy trucks that were available in the playroom was demonstrated by one 10-year-old girl. She used them as barricades as well as missiles, showing creativity and functional flexibility in the use of the toy, in addition to expressing symbolically her feelings of having been violated and hurt. Pride in her accomplishments in the use of the toys also appeared to be a strong factor in her repeated choice of these materials.

Societal Consensus.   A third consensus emerges with regard to toys that carry a societal consensus about their appropriate use. Toys in this category are theme toys that are patterned after TV shows or movies, athletic gear such as baseball bats and balls, and board games. Any toy that has a rigidly prescribed use tends not to work very well in the therapy setting, as it provides the child with an opportunity to play without working, that is, without being creative or self-expressive. The presence of a Snoopy doll in one therapy room resulted in the acting out of a Charlie Brown Christmas television special by a child who was very hesitant to use the materials in the room to self-disclose. He quickly found the toys that should not have been in the playroom to begin with and easily used them to hide himself from his counselor. Similarly, the often-used "bobo doll" appears to be of little interpretive value because it is very much equated with a punching bag. Thus, if a child hits a bobo doll, what is really communicated? Probably not much beyond the fact that the child can correctly identify a toy that has a definite and predetermined societal use. Pillows, on the other hand, can serve the same function as the bobo doll without that purpose being immediately obvious to the child (though it appears to become more and more obvious to some adult clients!).

Variety of Uses.   A fourth consensus deals with the variety of uses presented by a particular toy. Paper, glue, and crayons can be used for a multitude of activities by the creative and self-expressive child. They can be used to draw, fold, construct, build, tear, shred, throw, cover, mend, or repair. Further, within each of these uses, many sub-themes can emerge that are directly related to what the child is attempting to communicate. This can help the clinician understand the child better and ultimately facilitates the child's self-understanding. For instance, one 5-year-old child used the pencil and paper for drawing only. He repeated the same drawing over and over. This drawing depicted a poisonous mushroom that was large enough to serve as the house for a large family, yet with doors that were out of proportion to other features of the drawing. This child expressed several things through his rigid use of pencil and paper. First, he exhibited functional fixedness in that he could not think of alternative uses for paper and pencil. Second, he was very constricted in his affect and need expression, as evidenced by the monotony of the drawings and the repetitiveness of the task. Third, he demonstrated where his problem originated: in a poisoned environment in his own home!

The same materials were used by another child, a 5-year-old girl, in a much different way. She used the paper to build airplanes and to tear into little pieces, depending on affects she needed to express. She was much less inhibited in her emotional expression and had freer access to her needs than the little boy who had chosen the same materials. These examples demonstrate that materials with multiple uses can add several interpretive dimensions to their specifically chosen use by a particular child client.

Safety.   A fifth consensus relates to the safety of the items that are available in the playroom to children of various ages. It is important to differentiate safety from appropriateness. Although optimally, all items would be equally appropriate for all ages, this is not practically feasible. A baby doll and baby bottle are often found in playrooms but are not often used by 11- or 12-year-old children. However, their presence is appropriate in the room, as they are clearly not unsafe for any of the children. However, a pair of regular scissors, while perhaps appropriate for an 11-or 12-year-old child, is clearly inappropriate for the 3-year-old who does not know how to use them and is also unsafe and should therefore be avoided. Safe toys are those that are soft, do not break, and have no sharp edges. Sand and water are generally considered safe, though their use can be rendered unsafe if not monitored closely by the care provider. Their potential for unsafe use is greatly outweighed by their therapeutic potential and excellent potential for creativity and self-expression.

Therapeutic Value.   The requirement for therapeutic value is the sixth area of consensus about therapy materials. This requirement clearly is more subjectively evaluated by each individual counselor and may even differ from child to child. Thus, occasionally a therapist may introduce and have available a particular toy for one child only. This happens rarely but is possible and should be kept in mind. Therapeutic value refers to the potential of the toy to be used by the child in a meaningful way that enhances her or his working through problems and expression of needs and affects. Dolls and dollhouses have great therapeutic value because of what children can project on them. They tend to result in more meaningful verbal expressions and self-talk than toys such as puzzles or books (Lodhi and Greer, 1989), thus being much more facilitative of actual therapeutic work and exchanges.

The therapeutic value of dolls and a dollhouse was demonstrated by one 6-year-old child who used these materials to reflect upon her parents' divorce situation. She chose the dollhouse and then indicated that she also had to build a second house with the available blocks, as she needed two houses. She proceeded to place the mother doll in the dollhouse and the father doll in the newly created house. Three children were placed in the mother's house first, then in the father's house, and ultimately between the two houses. This child clearly expressed her ambivalence about living with her mother, who had failed to meet all of her affective needs. However, she also did not feel entirely comfortable with her father, who only since the divorce had begun to show significant interest in his children.

Symbolic Value.   The seventh consensus regarding toys and materials has to do with their symbolic value. Almost any toy that is not clearly defined as a theme toy (e.g., a movie or TV character) can have symbolic value. Symbolism is an excellent and safe medium for children to share their life story without having to do so through words. The symbolic value of a toy is determined by the child and is generally guided by the child's real-life experiences. The same toy can have completely different meanings for two different children—or for the therapist, for that matter. Thus, to be able to understand the symbolism of a toy or an activity, the counselor must thoroughly understand the child and her or his situation. It might require several uses of a toy by one child before the clinician can be sure to have correctly understood the meaning or symbolism expressed by a child. The more nondescript and ill-defined an object is, the more symbolic value can be endowed upon it by a child. In fact, in many cases, but especially with abused children, less obvious toys might be more appropriate in helping them to reenact trauma or to express emotions than more explicit toys. For instance, in one study, abused children tended to prefer larger, softer dolls and teddy bears to the standard human-shaped family figurines that come with dollhouses (Sinason, 1988). Although the larger teddy bears were less humanlike, they were also less threatening to the children and more easily endowed with the symbolism or projections children had to express to reenact their trauma and the associated feelings.

Therapist Needs.   The final consensus refers to whether toys are chosen for the clinician's or the client's benefit. Toys should not be bought because the therapist always wanted one like it when she or he was a child, just as parents need to avoid this pitfall in selecting gifts for their children. Toys that have symbolic or therapeutic value for the counselor may not at all speak to the child or facilitate a projection or self-expression. Thus, a toy that is laden with emotion for the care provider is best avoided in equipping a room.

Addressing these points of consensus about child therapy room equipment (summarized as questions in below) proves to be very helpful when materials are being selected. If all questions in can be answered affirmatively, the toys or materials are probably appropriate for use.

1. Does this toy promote a wide range of unstructured self-expression of feelings and needs?

2. Does this toy encourage meaningful creativity that enhances the child's self-esteem and self-confidence?

3. Is this toy free of societal connotations for its use?

4. Does this toy have multiple uses to encourage self-exploration and enhance self-understanding?

5. Is this toy safe for use by children of all ages?

6. Does this toy have potential therapeutic value to allow working through problems and the development of self-esteem and skills?

7. Does this toy have potential symbolic value to allow for expression of the child's real-life experiences?

8. Is this toy free of the therapist's own unfulfilled desires?

Certainly, not all materials will be equally appropriate for all children who will pass through a playroom. However, children like to make their own selections and are generally very capable of recognizing materials that can be useful to them in their growth work. They become more creative and self-expressive as they become more familiar with the therapist and the counseling process and once they have figured out the uniqueness of the clinical environment. If a child does not immediately make use of a wide variety of toys, this does not mean that the counselor has to buy more materials. It may merely indicate that the child needs some time to get accustomed to the new environment and nothing but patience must be added to the equipment list. Again, the room merely sets the stage for successful therapeutic work, and the materials within it are merely props that can be used in a variety of ways. It is the child who determines how the stage and props are used, what type of play is performed, and what purpose is expressed (Schaefer and Kaduson, 2006).

Toys and Materials to Support the Work

There are a number of toys that meet most, if not all of the requirements expressed by child clinicians as outlined above and the use of which is documented consistently throughout the child therapy literature (see Coppolillo, 1987; Dodds, 1985; Landreth, 2002a). Empirical investigation has confirmed the usefulness of these toys and has provided a ranked listing of materials (Lebo, 1998). These toys represent the basics or essentials of a well-equipped playroom and are discussed here briefly with regard to their therapeutic usefulness and an example of their use is provided. An overview of the essential toys and materials is provided in the list below. A few extras are also discussed, pointing out potential benefits and pitfalls. Many of these materials are readily available online in great variety and at reasonable cost (e.g., http://www.selfhelpwarehouse.com/play-therapy.html or http://www.childtherapytoys.com/store/index.html).

Checklist of Essential Therapy Room Toys and Materials
_____ Puppets (predator, prey, humanlike, nondescript)
_____ Large dolls of ethnic variety
_____ Family of anatomically correct dolls
_____ Doll families of ethnic variety sized for a dollhouse
_____ Two dollhouses
_____ Nondescript, humanlike figures or dolls
_____ Schoolhouse (e.g., Fisher-Price) and school bus
_____ School figures
_____ Baby bottle
_____ Pretend food
_____ Cookware, dishes, and silverware
_____ Construction and drawing paper (large newsprint rolls)
_____ Easel and/or chalkboard
_____ Paints, finger paints, pencils, markers, and glitter glue
_____ Glue and children's scissors
_____ Clay and/or Play-Doh
_____ Blocks and/or Tinker Toys

_____ Two sandboxes or sandtrays (one with sand, one with rice)
_____ Sandbox figurines (humans, animals, houses, vehicles)
_____ Plastic animals (farm, zoo, prehistoric)
_____ Dress-up clothes, shoes, and accessories
_____ Telephones
_____ Cash register with play money
_____ Soft pillows and a blanket
_____ Stuffed animals

Puppets

Puppets are perhaps the single most important piece of playroom equipment. They provide excellent means for the child to act out fantasy material and to express needs and feelings in indirect, nonthreatening ways. They come in a variety of shapes and symbolic values and should be selected carefully. As a rule of thumb, four to five puppets are enough. However, if a children's group is conducted in the room, there should be enough puppets for each child to have access to at least one. Of the available puppets, there should be at least one animal of prey and one predator. In the former category, sheep, lambs, and rabbits are popular. In the latter category, lions, tigers, and bulls work well. One additional neutral animal is also generally helpful to allow for completely symbolism-free projection on the child's part. Pigs, dogs (especially puppies), and bears (despite being predators, bears appear to have neutral value to children because of their use as teddy bears) fall into this category. A couple of fairly nondescript humanlike puppets are also useful. These may come in the form of a fairy-tale character or an anthropomorphic animal. Puppets that are based on television or movie characters are best avoided for all or the reasons discussed above.

Puppets are very useful because they allow for direct expression of feelings and needs, as well as for opportunities for problem solving and skill development, without the child having to own directly any of the material that is being expressed. Thus, they can be used for very direct diagnostic and intervention work without the child or clinician ever having to acknowledge or openly interpret this directness. For example, one 11-year-old boy who had a chronic sense of failure and overall lack of self-esteem had clearly begun to favor one of the humanlike puppets that was available in the playroom. Whenever he chose to play with this puppet, he also chose a second puppet for the clinician to handle. Early in the treatment, the two puppets would have long conversations about safe topics that were basically designed to get to know one another. As counseling progressed, so did the depth of the topics for the puppet play. Often, the boy's puppet would ask for advice from the therapist's puppet, and slowly, the boy's puppet was encouraged to find its own solutions. In a much later session, after a several-week hiatus in the use of puppet play, the boy was observed during a particularly anxiety-provoking activity in the session to pick up his favorite puppet and a second puppet. Here is the conversation they had, both parts being played by the boy, some time after the boy had drawn a picture of his science project that he had worked on with his dad (a very judgmental man with high expectations for his three sons):

SECOND PUPPET: You are so stupid! Why did you do that?

FAVORITE PUPPET: I am not . . . (*meekly*)

SECOND PUPPET: Yes you are. You always do it that way even though you know it's wrong, Stupid!

FAVORITE PUPPET: Do not! (*quite forcefully*)

SECOND PUPPET: Stupid!

FAVORITE PUPPET: Stop it. Don't call me stupid. I am sick of it. I did what you told me to do. Leave me alone!

The child then returned to another activity in the playroom and within three minutes returned to the incomplete drawing of his science project, indicating that even though he had not gotten it to work yet, he would finish it today because he thought he had finally figured out what had gone wrong! Although this is not the most profound example of puppet play, it illustrates very well how a child can use puppets without being directly aware of what she or he is working on. Further, it demonstrates that puppet play is quite conducive to letting the child do the questioning and the answering both, without the counselor getting trapped into giving advice. Finally, the sense of accomplishment felt by the child can be real, despite the imaginary scenario of play.

Dolls and Doll Families of Ethnic Variety

Four types of dolls should be available in a therapy room: anatomically correct dolls, ethnically varied large dolls, ethnically varied dollhouse-size dolls, and human-like figures. Dolls, much like puppets, present an excellent medium for realistic self-expression of needs, affects, and desires. They allow children to project as much of their own conscious and unconscious material as they can tolerate and yet keep them often safely unaware of their own metacommunication. Obviously, the added use of a dollhouse that is scaled to the dolls is highly recommended. However, children are often quite ingenious in their ability to make do with available materials, so the absence of a dollhouse might not necessarily be seriously detrimental to the work that can be done. If possible, two dollhouses are optimal, given the reality that many child clients spend their lives in split homes and more than one household.

One of the most important considerations in purchasing dolls for a therapy room is that of ethnic and gender stereotyping perpetuated by doll manufacturers. Many dolls—family dolls and professional dolls alike—are still stereotypic in how they are depicted. They tend to be White, and males are depicted in professions of high responsibility, such as physician, engineer, police officer, or fire fighter, whereas females are depicted in stereotypic low-power positions, such as nurse, secretary, or homemaker. However, many alternatives are now available that are gender and ethnically sensitive. Buying dolls that fail to consider gender and ethnicity issues is irresponsible and delivers a sad message to the non-White or female child. Similarly, this may put unnecessary strain on the male child, who receives a clear message of a strong need on his part to become a high achiever. Lack of availability of ethnically varied dolls is a disservice to ethnic children, who then have to use one additional level of abstraction in their use of dolls, as identification with White dolls may be much more difficult for them. Further, it is a disservice to all children, ethnic minority or White, not to have ethnically correct dolls because children need to have role models from their own ethnic group available for use and need to learn that their ethnic identity is an important and proud aspect of their self-identity. These days there are many sources for ethnically varied dollhouse-size dolls and large dolls, and there is no excuse for not having them available. It is best to have a set of White dolls, African American dolls, Hispanic dolls, Native American dolls, and Asian American dolls (the latter can double very well as Alaska Native dolls, which are hard to find, by simply changing their dress). These dolls can be purchased in all shapes and sizes, even in wheelchairs and with special needs (cf., http://www.sew-dolling.com/dollys_friends.htm). Fortunately, many distributors of play therapy materials are now also selling professional dolls of all genders and ethnicities as well as grandparents and babies to complement the nuclear family dollhouse doll set. These additional dolls add reality to the doll assortment and can serve to expand the repertoire of the child's play.

Anatomically correct dolls do not have to be specifically identified as such and can actually often serve the dual purpose of being used as the large human dolls. When dressed, there is really no difference. The anatomically-correct doll set or large human doll set should include an adult male and adult female doll, a child male and female doll, as well as a baby doll. Extra clothing for all dolls stimulates exploration of the dolls and is more likely to result in the discovery of the anatomical doll's "private parts." Although some clinicians believe that sexually correct dolls may be frightening to some small children (e.g., Spiegel, 1996), this is generally not the case if the dolls are tastefully designed. Further, the presence of anatomically correct dolls is becoming more and more important as the reported incidence of child sexual abuse continues to escalate. Children should, of course, never be forced to use any particular toy, including the anatomical doll. Although such prescribed play may have its place in an assessment of a child, it is inappropriate in the context of therapeutic play work.

For some children, the use of human dolls is too threatening, as it is too directly or obviously related to their actual trauma or problem. They may prefer humanlike dolls, such as anthropomorphic animals, fairy-tale figures, or Gumby dolls. Even then, attention must be paid to gender and race stereotyping, and a good variety of dolls should be available. Sometimes children use dolls of a different ethnic group to gain additional distance from their real-life experience. In this instance, the use of the ethnically different dolls should be interpreted not as a rejection of the child's own ethnic background, but rather as the child's need to distance from reality, much in the same way that use of humanlike figures would imply. For instance, one 10-year-old African American boy refused to use the Black family that was available for the dollhouse for several weeks early in his therapy. Instead, he chose the White family and played with it extensively and aggressively, killing various family members and burying them in the sandbox. As his anger began to be worked through, he slowly and one by one began introducing African American dolls into his play activity. Ultimately, he shifted completely to the use of Black dolls. This shift did not represent acceptance of ethnic identification, but rather a working through of familial conflict.

School Figures

A useful set of toys includes a schoolhouse, school bus, schoolchildren, teachers, and playground equipment scaled to match the dollhouse and its families. Again, preferably, human figures should be available in both genders and from a variety of ethnic backgrounds. School figures are important especially if a referral was initiated by a teacher or if the social/interpersonal adjustment of the child is in question. School is a large part of a child's life and therefore is likely to be the setting of conflicts and problems. The school bus can often double as a regular bus, thus adding more variety to the repertoire of available toys.

Nurturance Toys and Materials

Nurturance materials include baby bottles, pretend food, and kitchen equipment. All of these materials share their ability to evoke themes of nurturance, as well as the expression of emotional neediness or dependence. They are extremely useful in assessing and working through problems related to being overwhelmed by a parent who is not sufficiently nurturing, can be used in the context of working through abandonment fears, and can be used by children to calm or soothe themselves when faced with difficult therapeutic or real-life situations. For example, one very young boy who was seen in treatment because of his biological mother's concerns over the joint custody situation with the biological father made extremely good use of food and cooking materials. This child would spend one week with his father, then three weeks with his mother. After each week with his father, he returned quite emotionally depleted and overwhelmed. During his play session, these feelings and needs were expressed through increased use of pretend food. Although he always used food and cooking activities in his sessions, upon the return from his father, he would often sneak food and would refuse to share it with the counselor. He would ask the counselor to prepare the food for him and serve him. This behavior was very unlike the behavior that he displayed once he had been with his mother for a week. Then, he would freely share food with the counselor and "cook" for himself and her.

Some clinicians endorse the use of actual foods (e.g., Haworth and Keller, 2002; Straus, 1999). This practice should be well thought through before engaging in it. Therapy is not a real-life situation, and the actual nurturance is quite a different way of approaching therapy from the symbolic psychological nurturance or the understanding of the need for nurturance. The decision to use real food versus pretend food is thus driven largely by the counselor's theoretical orientation. A clinician who does not know which way to decide is best advised to use pretend food. The use of real food can result in very strong emotions on the child's part and is often driven by countertransference reactions on the therapist's part. Too often, food is provided by the counselor who would like to give the child something or who desires to take care of the child. However, the temporary provision of food to children does not help them learn how to nurture themselves psychologically.

Creativity Materials

Creativity materials include anything from paper products to paints and crayons to glue and paper clips, as well as clay and Play-Doh. Cultural issues are important to consider even in this context in terms of color choices that are available to children in the playroom. For example, crayons are now available in many skin colors and the well-stocked playroom provides a variety (Chang, Ritter, and Hays, 2005). In terms of paper, an excellent possibility is rolls of leftover newsprint, which can generally be obtained at no cost from the local newspaper. Creativity materials are some of the least structured toys that leave the most up to the child's imagination and creativity. They are excellent and varied tools of self-expression that are often very appealing to older children, who might find the rest of the playroom materials too immature or demeaning. In fact, clay and drawing materials are often very useful in the treatment even of adolescents. The definite advantage of these types of materials is that there is not only a process of creation and expression that is to be observed but also a final product that can be explored for its symbolic value. How a drawing is created can tell an important story; the end product adds yet another essential component.

For example, in a group therapy session, the children decided to make a group drawing. The group drawing ended up being much of an individual activity for each child and then became a group process once again when each child spoke about her or his drawing. In the course of this process, a 7-year-old girl who had recently been faced with a painful parental divorce drew a colorful rainbow, clouds, sunshine, and two houses. The process of her drawing was interesting to watch, as she had begun the drawing with the rainbow. As she added the houses and then the unique features of each house, she also added the clouds. This process helped the therapist to understand that although this girl wanted her life to be happy and full of rainbows, there were some intrusions (the separation of the parents as symbolized by the separate houses) that literally clouded her life. As the girl explained her drawing to the other children in the group, she took a black marker and slowly marked across her drawing until the entire rainbow had been covered in black. The end product of her drawing left no doubt that she felt strongly affected by her parents' divorce and that she was still struggling to come to terms with the brighter side of this process.

The use of three-dimensional materials such as clay can be equally telling. One 14-year-old adolescent who had been extremely reluctant to open himself up to treatment was finally able to commit himself to the process when he discovered the availability of clay in the therapy room (this was a regular office, not a playroom; the latter would be quite inappropriate for a child of this age). He began by merely using the clay for the sensory experience, molding it into nonspecific shapes of various sizes. Slowly, he began using the clay to underscore the stories he told the therapist, giving significant clues as to which parts of his tales were most important to him. Thus, once while telling of how he had wrecked his brother's car, he shaped a human figure. Although his verbal account of the incident stressed the car (he described it in great detail), his clay figure gave away the true concern, namely, the strain that had been placed by the incident on the relationship with his brother.

Construction Materials

Construction materials simply consist of blocks of various sizes and shapes or Tinker Toys. Although more complex and expensive building sets exist, for instance, Lego's Technic Series, these are rarely necessary. Children often use building blocks to represent their daily life experience of having to create things, accomplish things, and master tasks. The construction of a tower can tell a lot about a child's ability to delay gratification, to deal with frustration, to persevere under difficult circumstances, and to work independently and consistently. The construction of sophisticated buildings or even creatures can give hints as to the things that are important to a child's life, as well as being proof of the child's creativity and level of determination. Constructing with building blocks can give a child a new sense of mastery and accomplishment that can greatly enhance self-esteem. For example, a 5-year-old boy whose father had died from a drug overdose came to therapy because he appeared quite depressed and withdrawn. He was a very quiet child who was afraid of new activities and environments and who had difficulty separating from his mother for his sessions. When he discovered a wooden block set in the therapist's office, he became animated for the first time. He asked for much help building his first tower but, across several sessions, developed and honed his skills to the degree of being able to build a tower reaching all the way to his elbow by himself. Upon this accomplishment, he felt and expressed pride for the first time in his sessions. His activities in the therapy room became much more spontaneous after this experience and he appeared more self-assured.

Sandtray Materials

Two sandtrays or sandboxes are great assets to a playroom, as they provide the opportunity for a completely unstructured activity that most children have not been allowed to encounter indoors or around an adult. Two trays are best so that one may be filled with sand and one with rice. This not only provides two different media, but also accommodates children who cannot use sand because of allergies. They generally present a very new experience for the child and one that allows for the free flow of affective expression and catharsis. Children of all ages enjoy sand activities, once they have overcome their initial shyness about making a mess or doing something that often results in reprimand from an adult. Sand is a wonderful medium for constricted children who have not been allowed to get dirty physically or psychologically, that is, who are not allowed the free expression of affects in their home. Sand activity is productive in and of itself but can be greatly enhanced by the presence of figurines that can be used in the sand. These figurines can simply be in the form of inexpensive plastic zoo, farm, and prehistoric animals; tiny plastic humans; tiny plastic houses and cars; and many other humanlike figures. In selecting these miniatures for the sandbox, it is becoming easy to reflect the ethnic diversity of children seen in play therapy as many ethnically diverse figurines are now available and used by conscientious clinicians (Chang, Ritter, and Hays, 2005). The possibilities of what can be used in a sandbox are endless. The figures for the sandbox are easily stored in a plastic fishing gear chest with drawers and small compartments. This renders them easily accessible and makes cleanup easy.

Children use the sandtray both to manipulate the sand or rice itself, for the tactile stimulation this provides, and for the playing out of familiar scenes using the figurines (Homeyer and Sweeney, 2005). An example of a therapeutic use of the sandtray with figurines is that of an 11-year-old boy who had been severely physically abused by his father, felt very insecure, and had a poor self-image. He created an entire city in the sandtray with homes, trees, people, and animals. In the midst of this scene, he buried a treasure, not allowing the therapist to see the exact placement of the treasure. In his play with the sand and the figures, he actively involved the therapist, whose task it was to find and exhume the treasure. This activity was repeated several times upon the request of this child. Each time the therapist found the treasure, this usually somber and serious child was delighted. It quickly became evident to the therapist that the hidden treasure was representative of the child's own strength and positiveness that he was about to discover in his therapy. The fact that the therapist could find it for him delighted and strengthened him. The success of this therapeutic activity, however, became most obvious when the child asked the therapist to bury the treasure so that he could find it himself. When he did so, he was truly excited and also very relieved. He left this session with a newly discovered sense of security and self-confidence.

An example of a child who used the sand without figurines for the tactile experience of it is that of a 9-year-old parentified child who had been the caretaker of her 4-year-old sister ever since the latter's birth. She was very afraid of getting herself dirty during her counseling sessions and avoided the sand, as well as the water activities that were available. She often referred to the fact that sand was dirty and should not be played with in the house. However, it was also noted that she appeared quite torn about her own statement, apparently very much wanting to feel and use the sand. After many sessions of being encouraged by her counselor to use the sandtray, she finally did. Once she began, she was quickly taken in by the experience, to the degree of asking to take off her shoes and socks to step in the sand. Once she began to use the sand in this manner, she opened herself to new challenges and more childlike behaviors in many ways. She had finally found within herself permission to be a child.

Pretend Play Materials

Materials in the pretend category include dress-up clothes, shoes, and accessories, as well as telephones and play money. These items allow the child to try on various roles and to act out fantasies or real-life scenarios (Spero, 2002). Pretend clothing with accessories allows the child to become an adult who is capable of dealing with a difficult situation or a baby who needs to be taken care of and nurtured, merely by choosing what to wear. Thus, both ends of the spectrum of adaptation can be enacted: the healthy end of self-care and self-soothing as well as the less developmentally advanced end of physical and psychological dependence. One young child often chose red dress-up shoes in the therapy room when she was faced with a situation that caused her insurmountable anxiety and then referred to herself as Dorothy. In her pretend world, she had found a way to escape difficult situations.

Play money can be useful for a child who does not know how nurturance and control are given and accepted. This child can experiment by either controlling the money or letting the counselor control it. In one example, a 6-year-old boy was quite thrilled upon the discovery of a cash register and play money in the playroom. He immediately fetched the pretend food and set up a store, then asked the counselor to come shopping at his store. However, although the counselor was supposed to do the shopping, the child controlled the money and gave the clinician only as much money as he found fit. His delight over being in control of the dispensing of food was great and was understood in the context of his family, in which he generally had little control over his own life, being almost ruled by a very controlling father who did not allow him to make his own decisions. The fact that the male counselor allowed the child to have control over psychological nurturance represented an important corrective experience for this boy.

Pretend telephones are yet another means for a child to communicate with the therapist without having to do so directly. Children often surprise therapists with what they are willing to disclose over the toy telephone that they would not otherwise be able to say. One 5-year-old boy managed to disclose physical abuse by his biological mother using the telephone, whereas he had repeatedly refused to talk about his visits with his mother in direct face-to-face contact with his therapist.

Soothing Materials

Although they are not truly therapeutic materials, pillows and one or two stuffed animals do have their place in a playroom. Children do occasionally overwhelm themselves with their own self-disclosures, whether these be direct or through meta-communications. At these times, they may seek nurturance and soothing from an external object that reminds them of a safe place. Such a transitional object is best represented by a large huggable stuffed animal, a pillow, or a soft blanket. One 4-year-old girl, after having worked very hard in her session, indicated that now she needed a nap. She grabbed a blanket and teddy bear and lay down to rest, asking the clinician to tuck her in. After no more than 45 to 50 seconds of thus soothing herself, she was ready to continue her session.

Extras

Extras are toys or materials that might not be routinely available in a well-equipped playroom but that might occasionally have their place in a particular child's therapy. Often their use is more serendipitous than properly planned. For instance, one 8-year-old boy had evidenced significant difficulty in accepting his therapist as trustworthy and sufficiently strong for his needs. During one session, a checkers game, not usually available in the playroom, had been left behind by another care provider. The child, much to his therapist's chagrin, immediately spotted the game and asked to play. The therapist, somewhat unprepared for the request, agreed. He was not sure of his role in the game and decided to let the child win. The child became increasingly agitated as the therapist's mistakes became obvious and ultimately made several moves for the therapist to ascertain that the therapist would not lose the game. Finally, the therapist realized that this was his chance to demonstrate to the child that he would indeed be able to be strong and capable for the child, thus becoming more trustworthy in the child's mind. He realized that he had to win the game. Once he had noticed the child's need for his strength, he was able to use the checkers game for a definite therapeutic advantage that had many positive future implications for the child–therapist relationship. This example demonstrates the serendipitous therapeutic use of a structured board game along with the falseness of adult assumptions that children always want to win a game lest their self-esteem be destroyed. Clearly, this child needed a strong therapist, and a strong therapist cannot lose a simple game of checkers to a child.

Other extras may consist of materials that are more useful for assessment than for treatment. For instance, large floor puzzles can be an excellent means of assessing a young child's independent problem-solving ability. However, their use in counseling is questionable. The Talking, Feeling, Doing Game (Gardner, 1973) can be very useful in assessment, as well as in the early phases of treatment. Various sizes and shapes of toy cars can be useful for some children, as they may be used to present the child and her or his family. Balls or other athletic equipment may be used to assess a child's physical prowess or to help a child develop a sense of physical self-confidence in the therapy.

The use of tape recorders has also been documented as a valuable way of helping children express themselves therapeutically (Durfee, 1998). For instance, one severely psychotic 3-year-old boy had been seen in daily psychotherapy at an inpatient facility for over a month with little change and little attachment to the therapist. One day, he discovered the therapist's tape recorder on the windowsill. He was very curious about this machine, as he had never encountered anything like it in his home. The therapist decided to show him the recorder, as the child had never displayed this amount of interest or affect in a session before. She played back the last few minutes of the session, and the child became elated when he recognized his own voice. For the remainder of the session, he recorded his voice, then listened to it, over and over again. He had for the first time recognized his continued existence across time, and this presented a major breakthrough in his treatment. It should be evident by now that most extras are to be used with specific children for a specific purpose. They should not be routinely kept in the playroom, or at least not out in the open, as they may be too structured or too specific for most child clients.

A word must also be said about the use of games in the work with children. There is some controversy about the use of games. Some therapists argue that games are too structured and specific to be considered useful therapeutic tools (Ginott, 1999). Proponents of the use of games, on the other hand, point toward their usefulness in addressing specific topics or making assessment decisions about a child who is being seen for an intake or early in treatment (Schaefer and Reid, 2000). These therapists argue that games are an important day-to-day activity in the latency period of childhood (ages 6 to 12) and thus can play an important role in the treatment. They tend to group games into three categories: games of chance, games of strategy, and games of skill. Schaefer and Reid (2000) have discussed games in these three categories and have placed them in the context of therapeutic usefulness. As such, they demonstrate how games can be used to enhance the relationship between child and counselor, to facilitate self-expression, socialization, communication, and ego enhancement, and can be introduced merely to add a component of pleasure or enjoyment to the early stages of treatment. They discuss a number of games, and it is notable that many of these are chosen for their lack of competitiveness and freedom from structure. Thus, some excellent games that are compatible with the rules outlined in the list of questions provided previously do exist and can be considered even by care providers who believe in little structure or direction in their interaction with children. These include, but are not necessarily limited to, the Imagine! game (Burks, 1978), the Talking, Feeling, Doing Game (Gardner, 1973), the Ungame (Zakich, 1975), the Reunion game (Zakich and Monroe, 1979), and the Talking/Listening Game (Shadle and Graham, 1981).

Summary and Concluding Thoughts

In summary, the furnishings, design, and equipment of a mental health center that serves children must be carefully planned and implemented. Children as clients have diverse needs that must be acknowledged and addressed through the general layout of the center, as well as through the materials that are available for the child's and care provider's use. The more thought that can be put into the design of a clinic before children are first seen, the more likely it is that the work with them becomes successful. Just as novice child clinicians have to take inventory of themselves, so do they have to take inventory of the clinical environment to assess its potential for successful work with children. Just as therapists must prepare mentally and dress appropriately for the down-to-earth activity with children, the environment must be designed in an indestructible and pragmatic manner. Once the counselor and the setting have been prepared for the child, the clinician is ready to consider the final background topic, the ethics and legal matters involved in the work with children.

5

Legal and Ethical Issues in Child Therapy and Counseling

> *The child, by reason of his (or her) physical and mental immaturity, needs special safeguards and care, including appropriate legal protection, before as well as after birth . . .*
>
> —Excerpt from the Preamble to the
> UN Convention on the Rights of the Child
> (parenthetical material added by this author)

The years 1989 and 1990 marked a significant worldwide advance in children's rights that have affected children's mental health laws and public policy. In 1989, the 159-member states of the United Nations adopted the UN Convention on the Rights of the Child (known as the CRC), a treaty that went into effect after being ratified by twenty UN members less than one year later, in September 1990 (United Nations General Assembly, 1989). Since then, all but two UN member-nations have ratified the convention, the two exceptions being Somalia and the United States. In the United States, Madeline Albright, then U.S. Ambassador to the United Nations, signed the UN Convention on February 16, 1995, for President Clinton; however, ratification was never completed through a vote in the U.S. Congress. Currently, the official position of the U.S. expresses concern about the erosion of parental rights through the CRC and is summarized by George W. Bush who stated that "the Convention on the Rights of the Child may be a positive tool for promoting child welfare for those countries that have adopted it. But we believe the text goes too far when it asserts entitlements based on economic, social and cultural rights. . . . The human rights-based approach . . . poses significant problems as used in this text" (Anderson, 2001).

In the eighteenth century children in the United States began to be treated as valuable property. The nineteenth century saw a primarily societal attitudinal shift in that children were now considered pure and malleable, therefore worthy of protection by the state and church. At this time, child labor laws were enacted, and school attendance became compulsory. However, it was not until the twentieth century that children were regarded as persons, and not until the middle of that century did the courts recognize children as persons under the law. In this context, nurturance and protection rights were emphasized. The UN Convention is significant in that it endorses four core principles previously not bestowed on children, namely, nondiscrimination; actions in the best interest of the child; respect for the views of the child; and the basic right to survival, healthy development, and life. The CRC balances basic human rights for children with basic protections and self-determination and autonomy rights that were previously not viewed as in the purview of children at all. The UN Convention granted these rights to the children as individuals, not as family members. Thus, the rights of the child were placed ahead of the rights of the family (Cohen and Naimark, 1991; Walker, Brooks, and Wrightsman, 1999).

Several of the rights of children spelled out in the UN Convention can have a potentially strong impact on mental health practitioners' attitudes and behaviors toward children. One of the most applicable articles is the granting of the right to privacy to children. Further, children are granted the right to live with their parents, to express an opinion, to be protected from any form of abuse or neglect, to receive protection if no adequate family environment is available, to receive special help and training to aid in the achievement of self-reliance and an active life, to receive a high standard of health care, to be educated in and enjoy their own culture, to be protected from economic exploitation or hardship, and to receive all necessary physical and psychological help to recover from victimization of any kind (full text is available at http://untreaty.un.org/English/TreatyEvent2001/pdf/03e.pdf).

Thus, the UN Convention recognizes the dignity of the child, the child's right to protection and treatment, and the child's right to self-determination. It also places the child in a developmental context, advocating treatment of the child that is developmentally relevant and appropriate. These privileges and rights clearly have implications for the mental health practitioner. Melton (1991) has summarized the major implications in six principles, which he suggests as relevant to future public policy regarding children's mental health.

In his first principle, Melton (1991) suggests that "the provision of high-quality services for children should be a matter of the highest priority for public mental health authorities" (p. 68). This implies that children should have free access to medical and mental health care—that is, that many more resources need to be allocated for such social services in the future. Second, "children should be viewed as active partners in child mental health services with heavy weight placed on protection of their liberty and privacy" (p. 69). This implies not only that the child should be free to express opinions but also that the child should be involved in treatment planning and should not be subjected to treatments that she or he could now or later perceive as demeaning or belittling. Third, "mental health services for children should be respectful of parents and supportive of family integrity" (p. 69). This principle implies shared decision making and respect, not blame, for all parties involved. It is clearly aimed at ascertaining that the family be made the best place to foster the child's continued health and growth. Fourth,

> states should apply a strong presumption against residential placement of children for the purpose of treatment, with due procedural care in decision making about treatment and with provision of community-based alternatives. When out-of-home

> placement is necessary for the protection of the child, it should be in the most fam-
> ily-like setting consistent with those objectives. (p. 69)

This principle has already gained widespread acceptance among mental health practitioners who have for years attempted to provide least restrictive environments. It protects the integrity of the child's family, as well as the child's dignity. Fifth, "when the
state does undertake the care and custody of emotionally disturbed children, it also
assumes an especially weighty obligation to protect them from harm" (p. 69). In other
words, it is not enough to place a child; the placement must provide care and safety.
Finally, "prevention should be the cornerstone of child mental health policy" (p. 69).
Although this is yet again a principle that has been widely promoted (though not necessarily always practiced) among mental health practitioners, it has found little financial support among social policy makers. The UN convention would suggest that such
social policy is not only prudent, but it is also required of any state that wishes to
respect and honor its children.

These six principles, as well as the entire UN Convention, need to be kept in mind
as current mental health laws and ethics are reviewed. It is quite likely that the reality
of the current mental health law will remain in conflict with some of the UN Convention articles or with Melton's (1991) principles for some time, especially since the
United States remains one of only two nations not to have ratified the convention.
However, it is unlikely that conflicts between the convention and current law are great
or that they affect a clinician's work profoundly. It may be necessary for individual clinicians to find their own viable and morally acceptable compromises. Most important, children's rights to protection and nurturance need to continue to be weighed
against their rights to self-determination and autonomy. There are not always easy
answers to ethical questions that surround work with children, but keeping the child's
best interest at heart helps give the clinician the guidance to make the best choice possible in each individual case.

Laws and Ethics Codes

In the current court system of the United States, individual actions of all citizens
can be prosecuted under criminal or civil law. Criminal law covers crimes such as
assault, murder, and robbery and is always prosecuted by the government. Even the
aiding and abetting of such crimes can result in a criminal trial. Civil law, on the other
hand, is reserved for noncriminal offenses and is generally prosecuted by individuals.
Most mental health laws or statutes that govern the behaviors and actions of mental
health service providers fall into this category.

Further, professional affiliations' ethical guidelines or principles, such as the
American Psychological Association Ethical Principles for Psychologists (American
Psychological Association, 2002), the American Counseling Association (2005) Ethical Standards, the Ethical Standards of the American School Counselors Association
(2004), the National Association of Social Workers (2000) Code of Ethics, the Principles for Professional Practice of the National Association of School Psychologists
(2000), and the International Union of Psychological Science (2005) Universal Declaration of Ethical Principles for Psychologists provide necessary guidance for the men-

tal health practitioner. Although these ethical guidelines are not laws or legally binding, they are generally enforced by the professional organizations that developed them. Thus, breaches of ethics by a psychologist may be reported to the American Psychological Association (APA), which may choose to expel the psychologist from the organization if the behavior was indeed found to conflict with APA principles. Further, and perhaps more important, "Courts may also look to the self-imposed standards of the profession to determine liability" of a practitioner if there is no applicable law or precedent to guide the court in its decision-making process (Anderson, 1996, p. 9). Familiarity with the professional ethical standards is paramount to the successful work of any clinician. The provider's primary professional affiliation determines which code of ethics to follow. All codes of ethics that are relevant to mental health service provision share certain commonalities: All guarantee confidentiality, subscribe to appropriate mental health laws such as the duty to warn and the duty to protect, and have behavior codes for therapists regulating the nature of the therapist–client relationship. In the work with children, four topics emerge that are of particular relevance: informed consent, confidentiality, duty to warn and to protect, and duty to report. Each issue is dealt with in detail, first from a perspective of legal and ethical technicalities, then from a perspective of practical implications for actions by the therapist or counselor.

Informed Consent

Legal and Ethical Aspects of Informed Consent

The doctrine of informed consent requires that all patients genuinely understand and freely make choices within the context of a professional relationship characterized by trust and integrity. Informed consent is predicated on three principles: voluntariness, information, and decisional competence (Roberts and Dyer, 2004). Voluntariness refers to the fact that no one can force an individual to be in therapy against her or his will or without a signed informed consent. The decision to participate in counseling and to sign an informed consent has to be the client's and has to be made freely and authentically, never under duress. Voluntariness can only be genuine if the individual consenting voluntarily has done so based on accurate and complete information regarding the reason for and nature of the proposed intervention, risks, benefits, and alternatives, including no intervention, and other ramifications (e.g., economic or social consequences of the decision). Thus, information about taping, observation, risks and benefits of treatment, and confidentiality and its limits must be provided to the client and must be understood. The understanding of this material refers directly to the final aspect of informed consent, namely the competence or capacity to make clinical care decision and to express preferences (including the ability to communicate, take in new information, understand and apply it, and make sense of its meaning and repercussions). Competence is defined in the United States arbitrarily via the age of the client, and the age that determines competence can vary from state to state. Given the focus of this book on children up to age 11 or 12, it can be safely assumed that these children do not qualify in any state to be *legally* competent to render informed consent.

When informed consent cannot be obtained from a client because of legal incompetence, as defined by age or disability, the parents, legal guardians, or any agent in loco parentis is required to provide the informed consent in lieu of the client (Prout and Prout, 2007). Because states differ somewhat in their definitions of competence, it behooves each practitioner to investigate her or his state laws and statutes so as to avoid breaking them. Ethical principles generally agree with the legal definitions of competence and imply that minors cannot give voluntary and competent informed consent. They urge clinicians to use their judgment of what is in the best interest of the child when tricky issues arise and to consider developmental, not just legal, information and guidelines when making decisions about informed consent issues, especially with children from educationally deprived background or highly dysfunctional families (Foreman, 1999; Tan and Fegert, 2004). Generally, care providers agree that it is worthwhile to attempt to obtain consent from children who are cognitively capable of understanding the request for such consent (Paul, Foreman, and Kent, 2000). Children from approximately age 14 on should be cognitively capable of and be involved in making informed consent decisions at a level comparable to adults, whereas children under the age of 9 generally are not considered to have sufficient cognitive complexity to do so (Billick et al., 1998, 2001). Regardless of these opinions, all states do require parental consent for treatment of minors with only few exceptions that are relevant to adolescents only, such as birth control counseling and services, abortions, substance abuse treatment, and crisis or emergency intervention (Corey, Corey, and Callanan, 2007). Parental consent always has to be provided by the parent or guardian who is identified as the *legal* custodian of the child in the cases of divorce, separation, or restriction of parental rights.

Practical Considerations Related to Informed Consent

Most prudently, a signature on the written informed consent form is collected from a family before the intake interview begins. This informed consent is a critical piece of paperwork that must include information about confidentiality, limits of confidentiality, duty to warn, duty to protect, duty to report, clinic procedures, observation and recording policies, and possibly even fee schedules. Any tape-recording practices and observation provisions must be shared with the family. If the therapist has a supervisor, the family must be told, preferably with a disclosure of the supervisor's name. The informed consent is a written document, and care must be taken to ascertain that there is one literate, legally competent (i.e., above the state's legal age of competence and capable of sufficient cognitive complexity) member in the family group, who not only is an identified legal guardian or can respond in loco parentis but also can comprehend and respond to the document. If no one in the family can read it, a clinic staff member must be available to read and explain the form to the family and to collect signatures from the appropriate guardian as defined above. If the identified child client is above age nine years and the clinician so chooses, the child's signature may be collected as well, since it has been suggested that involving children in treatment without assuring that they understand what is happening is coercive and unethical, even if it is legal (Paul, Foreman, and Kent, 2000). A suggested format of a generic informed consent is provided in Figure 5.1; an informed consent that could be read by the child is presented in Figure 5.2, both shown at the end of this chapter.

Despite having obtained written informed consent, it behooves the clinician to cover the informed consent information again verbally at the beginning of the initial session. This coverage should be such that it is comprehensible even to the youngest child in the group (unless that child is below approximately 3 to 4 years of age). In this discussion, the clinician should reiterate all of the issues covered in the informed consent form and should take care to define them well and in a therapeutic context. Thus, confidentiality may be introduced as a privacy issue, the duty to warn or protect as a safety issue, and the duty to report as a protection issue.

Confidentiality

Legal and Ethical Aspects

Confidentiality is defined as a care provider's ethical duty not to disclose information obtained or discovered in the course of caring for a client without permission (Roberts and Dyer, 2004). It is generally believed among therapists and counselors that confidentiality not only protects the interests of clients, but it also facilitates the development of trust and rapport. Without confidentiality, clients are thought to be more hesitant to initiate treatment, more likely to end treatment prematurely, and less likely to disclose all therapeutically relevant and necessary information (Pope and Vasquez, 2007; Reamer, 2005). Although children hardly ever initiate treatment on their own, which means their decision to *begin* treatment might not be affected by confidentiality rules, the other two advantages presented by maintaining confidentiality are still applicable.

Confidentiality in general is a common cause for lawsuits and a particularly touchy topic for work with children (Bersoff, 2003). Although all clinicians certainly agree that there is to be strict confidentiality as far as other agencies and nonparental figures are concerned, the approach to the disclosure to children's parents varies greatly, from complete disclosure to none. Generally, confidentiality decisions and release of information to parents are based on the clinician's judgment about what is in the best interest of the child and legally defensible according to procedural standards of care (Reamer, 2003, 2005). Legally, however, parents who provide consent are to be granted access to records and information upon their request (Prout and Prout, 2007), as parental rights to information have to be honored. However, most clinicians attempt to reach a compromise by getting the child's informed assent before making disclosures, by inviting the child to participate in feedback sessions with parents, and by providing access only if it is in the best interest of the child. Refusal by the child, however, would not be sufficient to deny a parent access to records if she or he insisted upon it.

Although parents have the right to access information about their child's treatment, they do not necessarily have the right to release such information (Melton, Ehrenreich, and Lyons, 2001). It does not appear to be usual clinical practice to receive permission of the child to release records. However, legally speaking, additional consent by the child may actually need to be obtained to be able to release information to other agencies and individuals, especially if the child has sufficient cognitive complexity to give such consent (Melton, Ehrenreich, and Lyons, 2001). Local state laws may need to be investigated by the individual practitioner on this topic if a conflict between the child's and parents' wishes should arise. Finally, although parents have the legal right to access their child's records, children do not have this right in all but three states (Melton, Ehrenreich, and Lyons, 2001). This differential treatment of child and parents certainly should be discussed with the child before treatment begins.

Practical Considerations

During the first in-person contact with a family, the care provider must take time to define confidentiality and must explain what confidentiality means in practical terms for both the child and the parents. Parents and children should be informed about counselors' rules regarding disclosure to the parents of information provided by the child and vice versa. Although, as was noted above, legal guidelines are not clear on this issue, and individual practices vary widely, each therapist can adopt a uniform stance that is carried out with all clients consistently to avoid misunderstandings and the lack of open and clear communication about the issue of privacy. Using one approach with one client and another with a different client is bound to cause confusion and mistakes. If a care provider has decided to disclose all information to everybody, regardless of when and how it was obtained, the family must be informed of this procedure. However, if the therapist has a policy of sharing only progress reports without specific details, then this approach must be explained and justified. Explanations and procedures may need to be repeated with the child or children individually, in addition to having been covered at the beginning of the intake session, to make them more understandable at the appropriate developmental level.

It is often crucial to inform children, especially older children, of disclosure policies vis-à-vis parents. Many children feel much more at ease with a progress report policy than a detail-by-detail disclosure policy. It is possible to negotiate with the child what information can and cannot be shared with the parents within the appropriate confines of legal requirements. Regardless of how disclosure about treatment progress and process is made to parents, ethical guidelines for clinicians do require that parents be informed of progress; in fact, they have the right to be informed objectively and caringly (Brems, 1996; Pope and Vasquez, 2007). Just as confidentiality in the work with adults facilitates the adult's decision to seek therapy, a well-established parental disclosure policy for children facilitates the establishment of therapeutic rapport and trust. Further, children need to be informed that they themselves do not have to share information about their sessions with their parents. Sometimes, parents pry and ask many questions of their children. It is acceptable for the clinician to inform parents that this is inappropriate and that it is the child's choice when and what to disclose about an individual session (Brems, 1996; Dishion and Stormshak, 2007).

A therapist also needs to decide how to handle information obtained between sessions. It does occur that parents or child protection workers may contact the clinician between a child's sessions with important new information. One way of handling such data gathering is to let the child know at the beginning of the next session what new information was obtained and how. This sharing of information and information sources can avoid suspicion and lack of trust on the child's part and discourages parents from calling the clinician without a very serious reason. Taking phone calls from parents between sessions about minor issues may lead the child to feel that the clinician cannot be trusted and is in cahoots with the parents.

Also related to confidentiality are release-of-information procedures involving other agencies and schools. Given the legal guidelines, clinicians are required to collect signatures from the legal guardian or parent if communication with schools or other agencies is necessary. Only if a child is considered legally "competent" would her or his permission also need to be secured. Competent children, and obviously most adolescents, should be involved in this decision-making process, not merely because of legal requirements, but also for therapeutic reasons. The more children are involved in their own treatment decisions, the more likely they will feel that this treatment is helpful and growth-promoting. This approach is also in line with recommendations put forth by the UN Convention that stress privacy rights of children and children's involvement in treatment planning.

When releases of information have been obtained, it is important to outline for the family and child the exact nature of the information that can be communicated among various agencies and individuals. This issue holds particular importance in interactions with schools, in which the flow of information must be carefully controlled so as not to result in stigmatization or prejudice. If teachers need to be involved in treatment implementation, such as developing a behavior modification program in the classroom, the parents and child may need to be involved in the meeting between clinician and teacher to ensure that everyone knows how much information is exchanged. Even when teachers are asked to implement treatment plans in the classroom, they generally do not need to find out everything the counselor knows about the child client. Thus, a verbal information exchange is often more appropriate than a release of clinical paperwork, such as intake reports or treatment plans, to the school. If paperwork is released from a clinic, it is best to clearly mark "Not for Re-Release" to prevent a report reaching undesired targets.

Limits to Confidentiality: Duties to Warn, Protect, and Report

Hardly any rights are absolute, and this is true for the right to confidentiality. There are circumstances in which the right to confidentiality has to be forfeited for the sake of securing the safety of a client or others. The Model Act for State Licensure of Psychologists (American Psychological Association, 1987b; currently under revision), which serves as a model for most state licensing agencies and laws, outlines eight reasons why confidentiality may be breached in an individual case:

1. Where abuse or harmful neglect of children, the elderly, or disabled or incompetent individuals is known or reasonably suspected;
2. Where the validity of a will of a former patient or client is contested;
3. Where such information is necessary for the psychologist to defend a malpractice action brought by the client;
4. Where an immediate threat of physical violence against a readily identifiable victim is disclosed to the psychologist;

5. In the context of civil commitment proceedings, where an immediate threat of self-inflicted damage is disclosed to the psychologist;

6. Where the patient or client, by alleging mental or emotional damages in litigation, puts his or her mental state at issue;

7. Where the patient or client is examined pursuant to court order or,

8. In the context of investigations and hearings brought by the patient or client and conducted by the board, where violations of this act are at issue (p. 703).

Despite this widely accepted standard, states vary a great deal in how they have integrated these reasons into their own laws and statutes. Although it is best for care providers to familiarize themselves in detail with the laws and statutes of their state of residency and licensure, the only unequivocal common reason agreed upon by all states for sharing information with other agencies or individuals is that of having obtained a written release of information by the client or, in the case of a child, the client and the parent or legal guardian who signed the informed consent for treatment. Other reasons have various precedents in U.S. courts, though specifics may vary slightly from state to state. Most importantly and universally, the duties to warn, protect, and report have been well-established reasons for releasing privileged communication without the client's (and/or parents') consent.

Legal and Ethical Aspects

The duty to warn as covered in the Model Act (American Psychological Association, 1987b; item 4) dates back to the *Tarasoff* v. *Regents of the University of California* case in 1976. In this case, the California Supreme Court set a precedent for holding liable any mental health practitioner who fails to warn a victim who is identified as such, even potentially, in privileged communication by a client. In other words, if a client discloses the desire to hurt or kill an identifiable victim and the clinician deems the threat to be serious and likely to be carried out, she or he has the responsibility to warn the victim directly about the client's intent. In the *Tarasoff* case, the court implied that the confidentiality of the communication remains such, as long as the threat is vague and not directed against one identifiable person.

Since 1976, the duty to warn has been expanded by various court decisions (Swenson, 1997). For instance, in 1985, the duty to warn was extended to being applicable to identifiable groups, not just individuals, by the Vermont Supreme Court in *Peck* v. *Counseling Services of Addison County, Inc.* In 1989, the Arizona Supreme Court further extended the duty to include any general threat to a general group of people in *Hamman* v. *County of Maricopa*, as did the Colorado Supreme Court in *Perreira v. Colorado* (VandeCreek and Knapp, 2001).

The expanded version of the *Tarasoff* decision, now called the unidentifiable but foreseeable standard, thus refers to a generic risk for others posed by a client and indicates that if the client refuses hospitalization or confinement, and if commitment is not deemed appropriate, the clinician has the duty to warn family members of the client, the police, and any other likely person the client may contact (Pope and Vasquez, 2007). This is a vague standard and leaves much room for error. However, the clinician is released from the duty to warn once she or he has warned all relevant individuals and/or has been successful in arranging hospitalization for the client (Bersoff,

2003). The duty to warn is likely to be applied by the courts in future cases to clients who have HIV/AIDS and are threatening to spread the infection (Chenneville, 2000; Stevenson and Kitchener, 2001).

The duty to warn might not need to be invoked often by child clinicians; however, even children occasionally express the desire to hurt or kill someone else or themselves. If this desire is expressed in a therapy session, the clinician must be prepared to invoke the duty to warn. The warning is made to the potential victim, if there is a clearly identifiable one; if a vague victim or group of victims is specified, the police may need to be notified (Bersoff, 2003). The duty to warn in the case of child clients also includes the need to let the child's parents know of the threat and of the warning that has been issued either to the victim or to the authorities.

The duty to warn is also applied if the threat is against the self; that is, if suicide is the violence planned by the client and has come to be called the duty to protect (Corey, Corey, and Callanan, 2007). In this case, parents or police must be warned of the client's threat, or the client must be hospitalized, perhaps even committed involuntarily or by a parent. This ethical and legal issue has caused much controversy, since some clinicians, as well as a good number of clients, believe that suicide is a personal right (Firestone, 2006). However, the legal responsibility is clear, and the failure by a therapist to report suicidal ideation and planning is currently the number-one reason for lawsuits against mental health practitioners (Corey, Corey, and Callanan, 2007). Interestingly, at least one preliminary study suggests that care providers who believe in a client's right to commit suicide are less effective in terms of intervening successfully when a suicide threat is made by a client (Neimeyer, Fortner, and Melby, 2001). The issue of protecting a client from self-harm can be complicated with adults (Brems, 2000) but is relatively straightforward with children, in that a threat of self-harm or suicide is immediately relayed to the parent or legal guardian who signed the informed consent to treatment.

The duty to report refers to the mandated report of child abuse and neglect. Most U.S. states have specific statutes requiring mental health professionals to report in good faith any suspicion of abuse or neglect (Barnett, Miller-Perrin, and Perrin, 2004; Miller-Perrin and Perrin, 2007). In fact, by 1967, all states had some type of relevant law in this regard (Zellman, 1990) and the U.S. federal government and all the states now have active child abuse reporting hotlines that can be easily identified online (e.g., http://www.loveourchildrenusa.org/reportingchildabuse.php). The states with reporting statutes usually include a provision that gives the mental health care provider immunity from liability for such reports; that is, despite the breach of confidentiality, the clinician cannot be prosecuted for her or his disclosure of privileged communication (Corey, Corey, and Callanan, 2007; Pope and Vasquez, 2007).

Different states define abuse and neglect in slightly different terms, as do different researchers (Wise, 2006). Physical abuse has been defined as "as inflicting injury such as bruises, burns, head injuries, fractures, internal injuries, lacerations, or any other form of physical harm lasting at least 48 hours. . . . [This] may also include excessive corporal punishment and close confinement" (Walker, Bonner, and Kaufman, 1988, p. 8); and "when a child younger than 18 years of age has experienced an injury (harm standard) or risk of an injury (endangerment standard) as a result of having been hit with a hand or other object or having been kicked, shaken, thrown, burned, stabbed, or choked by a parent or parent-surrogate" (Sedlak and Broadhurst, 1996, as quoted in

Myers et al., 2002). Emotional abuse is defined as "the use of excessive verbal threats, ridicule, personally demeaning comments, derogatory statements, and threats to the extent that the child's emotional and mental well-being is jeopardized" (Walker, Bonner, and Kaufman, 1988, p. 8) and "if one instance is highly likely to produce or has produced mental or developmental harm . . . or if a continual pattern is likely to produce or has produced mental or developmental harm" (Myers et al., 2002, pp. 94–95). Sexual abuse has been defined as "any childhood sexual experience that interferes with or has the potential for interfering with a child's health development" (National Center on Child Abuse and Neglect, 1985); "the use of a child for the sexual gratification of an adult" (Crosson-Tower, 2008, p. 123); and "the involvement of dependent, developmentally immature children and adolescents in sexual activities they do not fully comprehend, are unable to give informed consent to and that violate the social taboos of family roles" (Helfer and Kempe as quoted in Walker, Bonner, and Kaufman, 1988, p. 8). Finally, neglect is defined as "acts of omission in which the child is not properly cared for physically (nutrition, safety, education, medical care, etc.) or emotionally (failure to bond, lack of affection, love, support, nurturing, or concern)" (Walker, Bonner, and Kaufman, 1988, p. 8); and "the persistent failure to meet a child's basic physical and/or psychological needs, likely to result in the serious impairment of the child's health or development" (Browne, Hanks, Stratton, and Hamilton, 2002, p. 7).

Regardless of whether an act of commission (abuse) or omission (neglect), definitions of child abuse and neglect (especially the latter) have evolved over time and are viewed also within the greater context of the child (Myers et al., 2002; Miller-Perrin and Perrin, 2007). It is important for the child therapist to recognize that almost all state statutes written to protect children from abuse or neglect require the mental health provider to report not only actual proven incidents of abuse and neglect but also the mere suspicion thereof (Myers, 2005). Thus, even indirect evidence that emerges in the treatment with a particular child needs to be reported. Most states have provisions for criminal prosecution of care providers who fail to make a good-faith report. As is the case with the duties to warn and protect, the duty to report supersedes confidentiality laws and holds the therapist or counselor harmless. Although practical suggestions about how to best make reports are covered later, it should be pointed out here that if providers believe that the reporting of abuse to the appropriate state agency would result in the family's fleeing or other behavior to avoid prosecution, they are obligated to keep the child on the premises of the clinic while the report is being made—in fact, until a child protection worker arrives (Swenson, 1997).

The consequences of a report of child abuse can vary widely. If the reported offense is the first reported perpetration and is relatively minor, often nothing happens to the family. Investigations tend to result only after more than one report about the same offender or if the child's life appears to be endangered. At the other extreme, if the reported offense represents a repeated incident or if it is considered severe, the child may be removed from the home and placed in foster care immediately. Often, treatment rather than prosecution is ordered after few or mild offenses. Child abuse can be prosecuted in court as a criminal offense if the perpetrator is not a family member or as a civil action if the offender is a family member. Child sexual abuse may be tried twice—once in civil court if perpetrated by a family member, and again in criminal court (Swenson, 1997).

Practical Considerations

In the context of discussing informed consents and, more specifically, the limits of confidentiality, clients must be informed by clinicians of their duties to warn, protect, and report. The related facts are generally shared in a matter-of-fact manner and not discussed in detail unless a duty has to be invoked owing to a concrete threat or action by the child or the parent. If a parent threatens to harm the child, the clinician is legally responsible to inform the police. However, in this case, it is best also to involve the appropriate child protection agency to ascertain that alternative care can be arranged for the child. If the parent is considered a significant danger, commitment procedures might need to be initiated. This generally involves contacting a local psychiatric institution and getting help from a physician and the court system, because few states allow psychologists to make involuntary commitments.

If a child threatens to harm a parent or sibling, it may be sufficient to notify the parents of the intent if the clinician is confident that the parent is able to protect herself or himself or the sibling sufficiently. If there is doubt about the parent's ability to protect, the police must be involved. Threats of suicide from children must be shared with their parents, who also need to be involved if the clinician believes that hospitalization is necessary. Each therapist, when she or he begins to work with children, needs to identify a hospital to which children can be referred if they are considered a threat to themselves or others. It is important for the counselor to be familiar with that clinic's intake and emergency procedures so that when a referral has to be made, she or he knows what to do and can help the parents deal with the stresses of that situation. Helping parents while at the same time trying to find out procedures does not instill much confidence in the parents and leaves them feeling unsure and vulnerable.

Although care providers must keep progress notes and records of all interactions with clients at any time, particular care should be taken to document any situation that may involve the limits of confidentiality (Brems, 2000; Pope and Vasquez, 2007). Good record keeping is crucial to the documentation of situations that involve the possibility for a duty to warn or protect or a duty to report, to safeguard the clinician from legal liability. This liability may involve the disclosure of privileged information, if the mental health care provider does not document that the duty to warn or protect was invoked, or may involve the failure to report. Whenever a child or parents makes a threat, the exact nature of the action must be recorded along with the procedure that was followed by the counselor either to rule out the threat or action and maintain confidentiality or to validate it.

When a therapist has suspicion or evidence of child abuse or neglect, a report must be made to the local child protection agency. Obviously, to be able to conform to this law, a counselor must be prepared to identify children who have been abused or neglected. Although there are no foolproof ways of so doing, there are some guidelines on which care providers may rely. Physical neglect is relatively easy to identify by inspecting the child's relative height and weight, her or his grooming and hygiene, and the cleanliness of clothing. There may also be a decrease in intellectual functioning, as well as overall developmental delays. Common symptoms include repression of feelings, violence, and inability to empathize (Crosson-Tower, 2008; Myers et al., 2002). Emotional neglect is not only difficult to identify with tangible signs, but it is also difficult to prove to a child protection worker. Nevertheless, emotional neglect is extremely harmful and must be reported. An emotionally neglected child may be identified by signs of insecurity, overly anxious relating, inability to trust, caretaking behavior toward younger siblings, or denial of obvious family problems. Common symptoms include behavior problems, low self-esteem, parentified role in the family, and attachment problems (Crosson-Tower, 2008; Fong, 2003). Although all of these signs and symptoms can have other reasons, they warrant further investigation of the child–parent relationship to assess whether the child receives the emotional support and nurturance necessary to facilitate her or his growth and maturation.

Physical abuse, if it is ongoing, is obviously easier to identify than sexual abuse, which rarely leaves physically visible marks. The clinician must be aware of bruises, cuts, and other unusual marks or evidence of physical trauma on the child's body. Reports of frequent accidents, unusual injuries, and frequent trips to the emergency room for serious injuries should alert the clinician to the possibility of physical abuse. Common presenting problems include oppositionality or withdrawal, hypervigilance, pseudomaturity, elimination disorders, behavior problems, and low self-esteem (Barnett, Miller-Perrin, and Perrin, 2004; Myers et al., 2002). Obviously, none of these factors in isolation can be considered evidence of abuse. However, frequent occurrence or joint occurrence implies that the therapist must question of the child and the family regarding abuse. If inquiries lead to further suspicions in the clinician, as opposed to alleviating her or his concerns, a report is warranted.

Sexual abuse victims are difficult to spot. However, reported sudden changes in the child's academic performance or daily routines, such as appetite, sleeping, or behavior, may hint at added stress in a child's life (Barnett, Miller-Perrin, and Perrin, 2004). If these signals are accompanied by increased aggressiveness or fearfulness, sexual preoccupations, above-normal levels of sexual play and sexual exploration, above-expected level of sexual knowledge or interest, or overly sexualized behavior in the company of adults, the clinician must investigate further. Common presenting symptoms include, but are not limited to, depression, fears, anger, school problems, and runaway behavior (Crosson-Tower, 2008; Mannarino and Cohen, 2006). Again, as with physical abuse, none of these indicators in and of itself is sufficient. However, it must be stressed that in most states, a suspicion suffices for a report to be made.

Once a child has been assessed and the clinician believes that the child has been victimized in some form, a report must be made. The best preparation for having to make such a report is to have investigated the procedures beforehand. Just as was discussed in relation to the duty to protect, the clinician needs to be familiar with local agencies and procedures of reporting abuse and neglect. It is good practice to phone local agencies and make an appointment to discuss procedures to glean a sense of how families are treated once a report has been made. This helps the parents anticipate more exactly what will happen and leaves them feeling more trusting of the counselor. Although the question about whether reporting laws interfere with therapeutic rapport with parents is an important one, it remains somewhat academic. That is, the laws are completely clear: There is no leeway. If there is a suspicion or evidence of neglect or abuse, a report must be made. Once the report has been made, the therapeutic relationship can once again be addressed.

It does appear that there is some consensus in the clinical literature that getting the abusing parent to make the report herself or himself in the clinician's presence is preferable to the therapist making the report (Brems, 2000). These clinicians indicate that when a suspicion or evidence has been discovered, the abusing parent is reminded of the provider's duty to report. The parent is then asked to make the report from the counselor's office in the counselor's presence. Then the counselor follows up with a personal phone call. Generally, the parent can be reassured that this procedure will result in more leniency from the child protection agency toward the perpetrator. Further, it places responsibility for the behavior squarely in the perpetrator's lap and often serves to preserve a relationship between the therapist and abusing parent. If the abusing parent refuses to make the call, the therapist best makes the call in the abusing parent's presence. Once the agency has been informed, the therapist asks about the agency's immediate plan so that this information can be discussed with the family before leaving the office.

If a report is to be made, there are certain pieces of information that the child protection worker is likely to request. It is best to be prepared by having the child's chart available during the conversation and to have ascertained that it contains sufficient detail that very specific questions can be answered. The counselor must be prepared to identify the child, the perpetrator, the child's family, potential witnesses, as well as the exact circumstances of instances of abuse and neglect and the child's current state of health and safety. Crucial information to have one's fingertips is summarized below:

Information Needed for the Duty to Report

- biographical data of the victim
- location of the victim
- current location and addresses of the family of the victim
- current location and addresses of the perpetrator
- current location and address of the reporter
- nature, severity, and chronicity of the situation
- current status of the victim (e.g., extent and description of bruises or injuries)
- dates of recent incidents
- names of witnesses
- immediate safety issues concerning the victim

Once a report has been made, it is advisable to schedule a quick follow-up appointment with the family to enhance the chances of retaining them in treatment. At the follow-up appointment the clinician can help the family deal with the investigation by the child protection agency. More importantly, the family and care provider can build trust and rapport during a follow-up appointment. The therapist must be very sensitive to hurt feelings and feelings of rejection and betrayal by the family and each individual member. The individual child, on the basis of whose disclosure the report was made, must also be seen individually to explore issues of trust, rejection, and guilt. Dealing with a family in the wake of a report of abuse or neglect is not easy. However, not dealing with them is even more detrimental to everyone involved.

Miscellaneous Other Legal and Ethical Issues

There are many other legal issues a counselor may encounter, though perhaps none as disheartening as the necessity to report abuse of a child. Search and seizure is a problem that can have a profound impact on client–therapist relationships even if the warrant was not for the particular child (Bersoff, 2003). In search and seizure cases, law enforcement officers may go through all of a therapist's client files, thus breaching confidentiality for the clinician's entire caseload. When such a court order was obtained for an Anchorage, Alaska, school counselor because of a case of suspected sexual abuse of a student by a teacher, police ransacked all of the counselor's confidential files in the attempt to gather evidence about the case in question. When the information about police officers reading confidential files became known among students, they felt extremely violated, and trust became a difficult issue in student–counselor and student–teacher relationships.

Dual relationships, an extraordinarily important issue in the practice with adults, may also become of issue in the work with children. Dual relationships are defined as relationships wherein the clinician and the client have a relationship other than that contained within the treatment room. Such other relationships may include, but are not limited to, sexual relationships, friendships, instructor–student relationships, and employer–employee relationships (Brems, 2000, 2001). They are not only ethical transgressions, but also inhibit the development of a healthy, therapeutically valuable relationship. Dual relationships are less likely to occur between a clinician and a child client than between a clinician and an adult. However, some dual relationships with children may not involve the child directly. For instance, a counselor's friendship or familial relationship with a child's parent may preclude this child from seeking counseling from that particular clinician. If the therapist is the parent of the potential child client's friend, the child should be referred to another provider. If the clinician already sees another member of the child's nuclear family, the child is best not taken on as a client. Thus, although dual relationships with children may not be as straightforward as those with adults, they do exist, are unethical, and must be avoided. All ethical codes of the helping professions that include child therapists, counselors, or other types of care providers contain strong guidelines against dual relationships with clients, and violations may result in a report to local licensing boards or professional ethics committee.

Another ethical issue is that of adequate training of new (Corey, Corey, and Callanan, 2007) and ongoing continuing education of already seasoned child clinicians. It is important for therapists or counselors to treat only those client groups whom they are qualified to treat. Professional organizations, including the American Psychological Association and the American Counseling Association, have specified this requirement clearly, and, as is the case with other ethical violations, noncompliance may result in a report to a local licensing board or a professional ethics committee.

Despite the coverage of this legal and ethical information, questions probably remain. Exact legal language may vary slightly from state to state as laws differ and as procedures vary from agency to agency. For instance, in some states, the office to be notified in the case of suspected abuse is housed in the Department of Health and

Human Services (e.g., Oklahoma), in others the Office of Children's Services (e.g., Alaska). All clinicians need to take the responsibility to review local laws and statutes and to familiarize themselves with relevant mental health laws, professional ethical codes, and specific reporting procedures for the state in which they practices.

Summary and Concluding Thoughts

A number of ethical and legal issues emerge in the work with children. However, none is insurmountable and, in most cases, the duties to warn, protect, or report never have to be invoked. Being prepared for having to move beyond any of the limits to confidentiality protects clinicians from legal liability and makes it more likely that treatment success can be achieved. Familiarity with the UN Convention on children's rights gives clinicians an appreciation of the special issues involved in the treatment of children and places this work in the proper context of balancing children's rights to self-determination and independence with needs for protection and nurturance.

Having now considered all the preliminary aspect of therapy or counseling with children, clinicians are ready for actual contact with children and their families. The first contact is usually focused on assessment and treatment planning and requires careful evaluation and deliberation. Clinicians must resist the temptation to rush directly into treatment and must take the time to assess what is happening with a child and in a family and how presenting problems have come about. Only after therapists or counselors have a clear understanding of all issues from a broad systemic perspective, can therapy or counseling begin.

(Clinic Name)   Date:

(Clinic Address)   Name:

Welcome to the *[Clinic Name]*. This document contains important information about our center's professional services and business policies. Please read it carefully and note any questions you might have so you can discuss them with the clinician conducting your screening appointment. Once you sign this consent form, it constitutes an agreement between you, you on behalf of your minor child (if applicable), your therapist(s), and the *[Clinic Name]*. In this document, the term "client" is used for the individual or individuals seeking services. Thus, "client" may refer to an individual adult client, a family, or a part of a family (e.g., a child, or a parent).

Nature of Psychological Services

Psychotherapy is not easily described because it varies greatly depending on the therapist, the client (whether an individual, a family, or a part of a family), and the particular problems a client presents. There are often a variety of approaches that can be utilized to deal with the problem(s) that brought a client to therapy. These services are generally unlike any services you may receive from a physician in that they require your active participation and cooperation.

Psychotherapy has both benefits and risks. Possible risks may include the experience of uncomfortable feelings (such as sadness, guilt, anxiety, anger, frustration, loneliness, or helplessness) or the recall of unpleasant events in your life. Potential benefits include significant reduction in feelings of distress, better relationships, better problem-solving and coping skills, and resolutions of specific problems. Given the nature of psychotherapy, it is difficult to predict what exactly will happen, but your therapist will do her or his best to make sure that you will be able to handle the risks and experience at least some of the benefits. However, psychotherapy remains an inexact science and no guarantees can be made regarding outcomes.

Procedures

Therapy usually starts with an evaluation. It is our practice at the *[Clinic Name]* to conduct an evaluation that lasts from 2 to 4 sessions. This evaluation begins with a screening appointment and is followed up with an intake interview (that may last 1 to 3 sessions). During the evaluation, several decisions have to be made: the therapist has to decide if the *[Clinic Name]* has the services needed to treat your presenting problem(s), you as the client (whether an individual, a family, or a part of a family) have to decide if you are comfortable with the therapist(s) that has(ve) been assigned to you, and you and your assigned therapist(s) have to decide on your goals for therapy and how best to achieve them.

In other words, by the end of the evaluation, your therapist will offer you initial impressions of what therapy will involve, if you (as an individual, a family, or a part of a family) decide to continue. Therapy generally involves a significant commitment of time, money, and energy, so it is your right to be careful about the therapist you select. If you have questions about any of the *[Clinic Name]* procedures or the therapist(s) who was (were) assigned to you, feel free to discuss these openly with the therapist. If you have doubts about the *[Clinic Name]* or your assigned therapist(s), we will be happy to help you to make an appointment with another mental health professional.

Figure 5.1   Informed Consent Form—Adult

If you decide to seek services at the *[Clinic Name]*, your therapist(s) will usually schedule one fifty-minute session per week at a mutually agreed-upon time (under some special circumstances sessions may be longer or more frequent). This appointment will be reserved for you on a regular basis and is considered a standing appointment (i.e., if you miss one week, you will still have the same appointment time next week). The overall length of psychotherapy (in weeks or months) is generally difficult to predict but is something your therapist(s) will discuss with you as the initial treatment plan is shared with you after completion of the evaluation.

Fee-Related Issues

The [*Clinic Name*] works on a sliding fee schedule that will be discussed with you during your initial appointment. Screening appointments always cost [*insert clinic fee*]. Fees for therapy range from $ [*insert range of fees*], depending on income and therapist. In addition to charging for weekly appointments, the *[Clinic Name]* also charges special fees for other professional services you may require (such as telephone conversations that last longer than 10 minutes, meetings or consultations with other professionals that you have requested, etc.). In unusual circumstances, you may become involved in litigation wherein you request or require your therapist's (and her or his supervisor's, if applicable) participation. You will be expected to pay for such professional time required even if your therapist is compelled to testify by another party.

You will be expected to pay for each session at the time it is held, unless you and your therapist agreed otherwise. Payment schedules for other professional services will be agreed to at the time that these services are requested. In circumstances of unusual financial hardship, you may negotiate a fee adjustment or installment payment plan with your assigned therapist(s). Once your standing appointment hour is scheduled, you will be expected to pay for it (even if you missed it) unless you provide 24 hours' advance notice of cancellation.

To enable you and your therapist(s) to set realistic treatment goals and priorities, it is important to evaluate what resources are available to pay for your treatment. If you have a health benefits policy, it will usually provide some coverage for mental health treatment if such treatment is provided by a licensed professional. Your therapist will provide you with whatever assistance possible to facilitate your receipt of the benefits to which you are entitled, including completing insurance forms as appropriate. However, you *(not* your insurance company) are responsible for full payment of the fee. If your therapist is a trainee, you will not be able to use your insurance benefits.

Carefully read the section in your insurance coverage booklet that describes mental health services and call your insurer if you have any questions. Your therapist will provide you with whatever information she or he has based on her or his experience and will be happy to try to help you understand the information you receive from your carrier. The escalation of the cost of health care has resulted in an increasing level of complexity about insurance benefits that often makes it difficult to determine exactly how much mental heath coverage is available. "Managed Health Care Plans" such as HMOs and PPOs often require advance authorization before they will provide reimbursement for mental health services. These plans are often oriented toward a short-term treatment approach designed to resolve specific problems that are interfering with level of functioning. It may be necessary to seek additional approval after a certain number of sessions. Although a lot can be accomplished in short-term therapy, many clients feel that more services are necessary after the insurance benefits expire. Some managed care plans will not allow your therapist to provide reimbursed services to you once your benefits are no longer available. If this is the case, *[Clinic Name]* staff will do their best to find another provider who will help you continue your psychotherapy.

Please be aware that most insurance agreements require you to authorize your therapist to provide the insurance company with your clinical diagnosis and sometimes additional clinical information, such as treatment plans or summaries, or in rare cases, a copy of the entire record. This information will become part of the insurance company's files, and, in all likelihood, some of it will be computerized. All insurance companies claim to keep such information confidential, but once it is in their hands, your therapist has no control over what your insurer will do with the information. In some cases, the insurer may share the information with a national medical information data bank.

It is best to discuss all the information about your insurance coverage with your therapist, so you can decide what can be accomplished within the parameters of the benefits available to you and what will happen if the insurance benefits run out before you are ready to end treatment. It is important to remember that you always have the right to pay for psychological services yourself if you prefer to avoid involving your insurer.

Contact Hours

The *[Clinic Name]* is open from 9 AM to 5 PM daily but some evening and weekend appointments may be available. Your therapist is generally not available for telephone services but you can cancel and reschedule sessions with the assistance of the receptionist or through leaving messages on the confidential answering machine. If you need to reschedule an appointment, your therapist will make every effort to return your call on the same day, with the exception of calls made after hours or on weekends and holidays. If you are difficult to reach, please leave some times when you will be available. If you have an emergency but are unable to reach your therapist, call your family physician, emergency services at *[insert name of local crisis line],* or the emergency room at *[insert name of local hospitals].* Please note that the *[Clinic Name]* itself does not have emergency services or facilities.

Videotaping and Record-Keeping Procedures

All client sessions are videotaped. These tapes are made for supervision or consultation purposes only and are kept in a confidential locked placed until the therapist has reviewed them with a supervisor or consultant as needed. Once tapes have been reviewed, they are erased. Most tapes are erased within less than one week; no tapes are kept for more than two weeks. In addition to videotapes, therapists also keep case notes. These notes are also kept under lock and key and are strictly confidential. The case notes are reviewed by the therapist, by his or her supervisor or consultant (if applicable), and then are filed permanently in a client's record. All records are locked and kept confidential. Information in the client records may be used for evaluation, research, and service planning purposes. Such use is entirely anonymous, and no individual client data will ever be used. No client names are ever associated with data extracted from records for research or evaluation purposes, and all data will merely be presented in group data format, a format that preserves anonymity and never reveals individual client data.

Both law and the standards of the profession of psychology require that therapists keep treatment records. You are entitled to receive a copy of these records, unless your therapist believes that seeing them would be emotionally damaging to you. If this is the case, your therapist will be happy to provide your records to an appropriate mental health professional of your choice. Although you are entitled to receive a copy of your records if you wish to see them, your therapist may prefer to prepare an appropriate summary instead. Because client records are professional documents, they can be misinterpreted and can be upsetting. If you insist on seeing your records, it is best to review them with your therapist so that the two of you can discuss what they contain. Clients will be charged an appropriate fee for any preparation time that is required to comply with an informal request for record review.

If a client is under eighteen years of age, the law may provide parents with the right to examine the minor child's treatment records. It is *[Clinic Name]* policy to request an agreement from parents that they consent to give up access to the child's records. If they agree, the therapist will provide the parents only with general information on how the child's treatment is proceeding unless there is a high risk that the minor client will seriously harm herself or himself or another person. In such instances, the therapist may be required by law to notify the parents of her or his concern. Parents of minors also can request to be provided with a summary of their child's treatment when it is complete. Before giving parents any information, the therapist will discuss this matter with the minor client and will do the best she or he can to resolve any objections the child client may have about what will be discussed. Please note that the *[Clinic Name]* does not provide treatment to minors without their parents' consent.

Confidentiality

In general, the confidentiality of all communications between a client and a psychologist is protected by law, and your therapist can release information to others about your therapy only with your written permission. However, there are a number of exceptions:

- In most judicial proceedings, you have the right to prevent your therapist from providing any information about your treatment. However, in some circumstances (such as child custody proceedings and proceedings in which your emotional condition is an important element), a judge may require your therapist's testimony if the judge determines that resolution of the issues before her or him demands it.

- There are times when it may be helpful for other professionals to gain access to all or parts of your treatment records. Under such circumstances, data can be released from your *[Clinic Name]* record if you give your therapist written permission (in the form of a Release of Information) to do so. Such release cannot take place unless you consent in writing.

- There are some situations in which your therapist is legally required to take action to protect others from harm, even if such action requires revealing some information about your treatment:

  - If your therapist believes that a child, an elderly person, or a disabled person is being abused, she or he is required by law to file a report with the appropriate state agency (in Alaska this is the Department of Family and Youth Services).

  - If your therapist believes that you are threatening serious bodily harm to another person, she or he is required by law to take protective actions, which may include notifying the potential victim, notifying the police, or seeking appropriate hospitalization.

  - If you threaten to harm yourself (e.g., suicide), your therapist is required to make all necessary arrangements to protect your safety, a process that may include seeking hospitalization for you or contacting family members or others who can help provide protection.

- At the *[Clinic Name]*, some therapists are working under the supervision of licensed psychologists who meet with the therapists on a weekly basis in a one-on-one meeting to review client cases. If your assigned therapist is one of these, you will be told so. Your case will be then discussed during the weekly meetings between your therapist and her or his supervisor. The supervisor is a part of the [Clinic Name] staff and is bound by the same confidentiality laws as your therapist. The supervisor and therapist will also review therapy tapes as necessary to the therapist's education.

- At the *[Clinic Name]*, some therapists occasionally seek consultation to assist with treatment decisions. Such consultation occurs only as needed and is done in such a manner as not to identify the client in any way. Additionally, consultants are bound by the same confidentiality laws as therapists and hence are prohibited by law to disclose any of the information they receive from the therapist about clients.

- At the *[Clinic Name]*, all therapists participate in weekly staff meetings. These meetings are used as opportunities for consultation, and each week a client case is presented. Your case may be one of the cases that will be presented during these meetings. The meetings are confidential and only *[Clinic Name]* staff participate. Only first names of clients are used and all members of the *[Clinic Name]* staff are bound by the same confidentiality laws as your therapist.

Signatures Verifying Agreement

Your signature below indicates that you have read the information in this document, that you have understood it, and that you agree to abide by its terms as long as you are a *[Clinic Name]* client.

_____   _____
Client/Parent/Guardian Signature and Date   Witness Signature and Date

Special Note: This informed consent was developed on the basis of a sample provided by Drs. Bruce Bennett and Eric Harris of the American Psychological Association during a workshop on Risk Management in Psychology in Anchorage, Alaska, in November 1995. The original sample (called an Outpatient Service Contract) can be requested from the APA Insurance Trust at 750 First Street NE, Suite 605, Washington, DC 20002-4242.

Informed Consent

I understand that I am about to start therapy at this clinic. That means that I will sit down with a therapist and talk about myself and about my family and any problems or fights we might be having. I know that my therapist has a video camera and uses it to record us when we talk or play. I also know that these tapes are secret and are erased every week.

I know that I don't have to talk about anything I don't want to talk about. My therapist can't make me do anything I don't want to do. I also know that I have the right to say that I don't want to come back.

I understand that what I tell my therapist is between me and the therapist, and my therapist only tells my parents if I am feeling better or worse. My therapist does not tell my parents what I say about them or my family.

The only time my therapist has to talk to other people about what I told is if I tell the therapist that somebody is hurting me badly in some way. For instance, if somebody beats me so hard that I have bruises, my therapist would have to tell. If I told my therapist that I wanted to hurt myself, then my therapist would have to tell.

If my therapist wants to talk to anybody else besides my parents about me, my parents and I first have to say in writing that this is okay to do.

I agree to talk to my therapist now that I know all these things about therapy. I have put my name on this paper to show that I agree to start therapy.

_____
Child's Name (written by the child)

_____   _____
Child's Name (written by the therapist)   Date

Figure 5.2   Informed Consent Form—Child

PART II

Assessment

Chapter

6

The Intake Interview

> States Parties shall assure to the child who is capable of forming his or
> her own views the right to express those views freely in all matters
> affecting the child, the views of the child being given due weight in
> accordance with the age and maturity of the child.
> —Article 12 of the U.N. Convention on the Rights of the Child

The intake interview is probably the single most important assessment tool available to clinicians who work with children and their families. In fact, this process is so important that entire books have been dedicated to only this purpose (Bourg et al., 1999; Greenspan and Greenspan, 2003; McConaughy, 2005; Zwiers and Morrissette, 1999). It is during the intake interview that clinicians become familiar with the child and the family in which the child resides. It is during the intake interview that clinicians interact with all or most of the important figures in a child's life. It is largely on the basis of the information derived during the intake interview that clinicians negotiate treatment plans and treatment recommendations with the family. The intake interview represents the unique opportunity to view and assess children within the dynamics of their current interpersonal environment, and hence, much thought needs to be given to this interview. Clinicians need to be clear about what type of information to collect, how to structure the interview, and what their goals are *before* sitting down with a family.

The intake interview is lengthy and might appear overwhelming to a new care provider. However, given the ample time clinicians can take to collect the necessary information, they can rest assured that this task is indeed possible. Further, although this chapter suggests one 4-hour session with the family, it is certainly possible to break up this session into various parts that are conducted on separate days. Such a structure perhaps provides beginners with some necessary breaks to collect their thoughts, plan additional questions, and consult with a supervisor. The intIake interview, regardless of how many sessions therapists decide to commit to it, always includes several components: sessions with the entire family to assess family dynamics, individual sessions with the children and the adults in the family, and a feedback session to share findings. Preliminary information can be collected through a thorough intake form that may guide clinicians' work throughout the intake interview.

Preliminary Data Collection

To be optimally prepared for each specific family, clinicians can send child intake forms to the parents before the intake interview is scheduled. Enough of these forms are mailed that a family may complete one form for each child, so that prior to work with the presenting child, specific information can be gathered about all the children in the family, not just the identified client. The intake forms need to give the clinician a thorough history of each child's life within the current, and any previous, family. As such, it inquires about a number of details with regard to the child's life that are summarized below:

Intake Form Topics

- preferred name or nickname
- age and date of birth
- mother's pregnancy and delivery
- current family
- other families (adoptive and foster families)
- medical history and developmental milestones
- legal involvements
- living arrangements
- previous treatment

The use of a formal intake form for gathering this information is recommended because much of it may be forgotten during the interview when other present-time features of the child and family are being observed. Sample forms are provided in various books (e.g., Hecker and Sori, 2007; Wiger, 2005; Zuckerman, 2003) and can be found online through any Web search engine. The intake forms are mailed to and received by the family before their appointment for the actual intake interview to assure that they have ample to time to complete the form and to bring it with them for their intake appointment. Intake forms are never used as substitutes for an actual interview, nor do they give clinicians permission to take shortcuts during the interview. They are simply helpful supplements to a thorough in-person assessment for the type of information that may be a bit more difficult for families to remember and for clinicians to note (e.g., specific dates of accidents or hospitalizations; birth weights and heights). Intake forms are best not completed during the interview, neither by the family nor by the therapist. If a family does not have any members who are literate or sufficiently fluent in English, the therapist or family might attempt to find an individual, perhaps a staff person in the clinic, who can sit down with the family before the appointment to complete the form. This needs to be done in a very courteous manner to avoid offending the family.

Necessary Information to Be Derived from the Intake Interview

Before beginning an intake interview, clinicians need to know what information to gather, so as not to be caught off guard or lack thoroughness. It is often too difficult to try to reconvene families after an initial intake interview has taken place to gather missing information. Thus, the better prepared the counselor is for the interview, the less difficult any follow-up work will be later. There are a number of questions about several topic areas that the therapist wants to be able to answer after the intake interview has been completed. These topic areas are summarized below. Once the care provider knows *what* information needs to be collected, the structure of *how* to collect this information can be addressed.

Interview Topics

- presenting problem
- family relationships
- school or preschool issues
- social and peer relationships
- sociocultural factors
- recreation, interests, and hobbies
- developmental and health issues
- plans for future, fantasies, and daydreams
- behavioral observations

What to Ask about the Presenting Problem

Usually a lot more than a single or simple presenting problem needs to be explored as most families present not with one, but rather with a list of problems. Therefore, the first important step is to find out about *all* presenting problems in the family, not just with regard to the identified child client, but also with regard to other family members. For each presenting problem, a number of issues are clarified.

First, each problem itself needs to be defined in detail. Clinicians need to know *when* the problem occurs: Are there certain situations that are more likely to result in the problem behavior? Are there certain people who are usually present when the child presents with a specific symptom? Clinicians need to know *where* the presenting problem occurs: Are there certain places that are more likely to elicit the problem than others? Is the problem confined to one specific locality? If so, what are the features of that locality? Clinicians need to know *how* the presenting problem occurs: Is there a certain way in which the problem develops? Does the problem behavior start in a certain manner and then escalate to other symptoms? Clinicians need to know *with whom* the presenting problem occurs: Is the symptom more likely in the company of certain individuals? Is the symptom's occurrence restricted to the company of adults or children? Clinicians need to know *how long* the presenting problem occurs: Is this problem consistently present, or does it occur briefly? Does the problem repeat itself in exactly the same sequence each time, or does it vary slightly? The better the definition of the problem, the easier it is for care providers to decide whether a problem is a valid concern, a developmental issue, or a normal presentation.

Second, a history of each presenting problem provides important information. It is useful to know when the problem was first noted and who identified it as a problem. It is necessary to find out whether the problem has changed over time and whether it tends to go away for time periods, only to recur later. If the family can pinpoint the exact time of onset, it is important to explore what changes might have been occurring in the child's life at that time. This information helps the therapist to put the problem in perspective and often gives useful information for a conceptualization that explains the presence of the symptoms. This type of information is likely to affect treatment recommendations. For instance, the treatment of depression may vary for two children, despite similarity in actual symptoms, based on historical information. If one child's depression had a clear onset after the death of the child's father who was a primary caretaker and is present at all times, whereas another child's depression began on the first day of classes and is present only during school hours but never at home, then these two children will receive very different treatments.

Finally, the impact of each presenting problem on the child and the family is worthy of exploration. Certain problems may affect only the individual child; others affect the family as a system or individual family members. Each presenting problem may also affect the identified client differently in different environments. It may restrict the behavior of the child or the entire family, thus creating additional problems with which the child and the family have to cope. For instance, children who are enuretic or encopretic often are severely affected by the disorder as far as their social lives are concerned. They frequently are less likely than other children to spend the night with friends and to belong to clubs that have overnight outings, such as scouts. Thus, the presenting problem has a variety of impacts on the child's life that can hinder psychological growth in other arenas of development.

What to Ask about Family Relationships

Several aspects of family relationships are important to inquire about in detail. These include discipline strategies, parental family histories, spousal relationship, sibling relationships, and extended family issues. Thorough data collection about parenting or discipline strategies reveals the approaches parents take toward their children and, if there is more than one parent, whether they agree on how to discipline and raise children. Specific preferred strategies need to be investigated, as does the degree of consistency with which they are applied. This assessment needs to consider implicit and explicit family rules, as well as consequences for members who break the rules. Consistency is investigated not only with regard to consistency in the use of particular strategies and the application of rules, but also with regard to consistency across children and situations. For example, it is important to note whether parents use different disciplinary strategies with one of their children (unless there is an age-appropriateness reason) or whether they use different strategies for the same misbehavior depending on whether the family is at home or in public. The family's actual behavior during the interview provides important clues about parenting and disciplinary styles.

Parental histories are taken with regard to all parents' unique backgrounds. Issues to be explored include how the parents themselves were parented when they were children; relationships of the parents with their own parents; parental social, academic, and professional backgrounds; and medical as well as mental health histories for their extended and nuclear families. The more background information can be gleaned from and about each individual parent, the better. Such information lends an enormous amount of understanding to the family's presenting problem if the counselor understands the parents' histories. For instance, the presence of child abuse in a family that is being assessed can be better understood if it is revealed that one or more parents were the victims of abuse during their own childhood, as these behaviors tend to be passed along from generation to generation.

If there is more than one parent in the home and these two individuals are in an exclusive sexual (whether heterosexual or homosexual) relationship, this relationship becomes a crucial component of the family assessment. A thorough dating history is often important, as is assessment of conflicts, shared and disagreed-upon values, attitudes, common interests, and shared activities. It is not uncommon for tension in the parental dyad to lead to symptoms in the children. If only one parent is currently living in the home, the relationship of that parent to the other biological parent of the child or children in the home becomes a focus of assessment. Two people need not live together to have an impact on their children. If two biological parents fight frequently, even if they do not share the same residence, their behavior affects their children. Further, the possibility exists that children become the bearer of messages between the parents, thus being pulled into the middle of arguments and conflicts.

Attention needs also to be paid to the relationships among the siblings who live in the same household. This is true whether the siblings are full, half, adoptive, or foster siblings. It is important to find out how well the various children in the same household get along and how they interact with one another. Further, siblings who do not share the same residence also need to be inquired about, especially if they come for visits on any regular basis. Sibling relationships help clinicians gain insight into why one child may present with more symptoms than another.

One suggested format for collecting family data is the construction of a genogram. In a genogram, the counselor and clients plot out the family history by creating a family tree showing all family members on the maternal and paternal (biological and/or adopted and/or step) side of the child who is presented as the problem person. The tracing goes backward to grandparents, great-grandparents, and aunts and uncles, as well as forward to siblings, and nieces and nephews if applicable. For all mentioned family members, salient information is noted. An example of a genogram for a child who presented to treatment because of depression is provided in Figure 6.1 on the following page. A thorough description of the process of constructing a genogram is presented in McGoldrick and Gerson (1999), as well as in Scarf (1987).

What to Ask about School or Preschool Issues

For each client, the clinician needs to assess school performance and related school behaviors. Specifically, academic capacity and intellectual/cognitive functioning need to be evaluated. This can be done through interview or releases of informa-

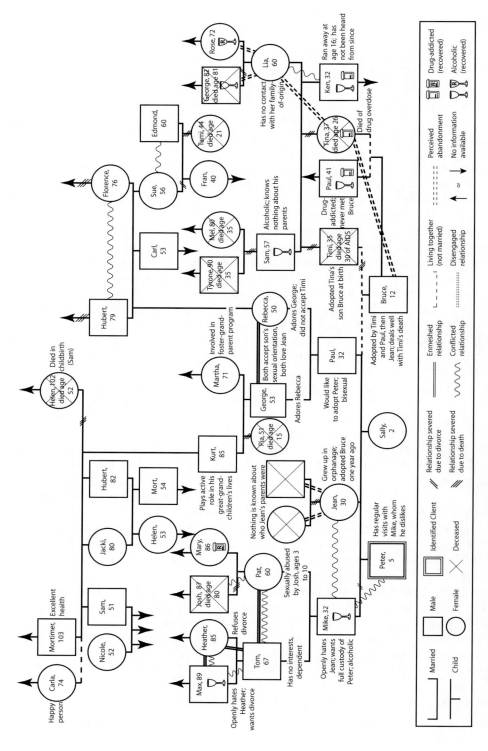

Figure 6.1 Genogram for a Depressed Child

136

tion to obtain school records. Rating forms and behavior rating scales can be very helpful in this process (these assessment tools are discussed in the next chapter). If there is any question about the cognitive functioning of a child, or the possibility of learning disabilities or neuropsychological deficits, evaluation needs to go beyond existing data and interview. Referral to another professional such as a neuropsychologist or educational/school psychologist might be in order (referrals are discussed in the next chapter).

In addition to purely academic performance data, care providers also need to evaluate the child's performance with regard to relationships with fellow students and teachers. A thorough history of any problem needs to be taken. Just as with the presenting problems, time frames and situational components of the behavior, affect, or attitude need to be assessed. Behavior rating scales can add useful information about school behaviors and relationships.

What to Ask about Social and Peer Relationships

Information about a child's peer relationships and social involvement is extremely helpful in assessing the degree of pervasiveness of a presenting problem. Often, children who may experience significant problems in one setting do not have these in another, revealing that the problem may be largely a situational one. With regard to this area of information, the therapist needs to investigate whether the child has or ever has had a best friend. The gender of this friend is important, as well as a description of that friend as provided by the child. Children often choose friends for characteristics in the friend that are either alien to but desired by the child or very similar to those of the child. Therefore, asking children to talk about what they like and dislike about a particular friend may have implications about what they like and dislike about themselves. The absence of a best friend is reason for concern, more so than the absence of a large number of occasional playmates.

In addition to exploring relationships with best friends, it is helpful to ask about playmates and their ages. Preferred games and activities that are engaged in during play are important to inquire about. Care providers should not easily accept children's simple "yes" or "no" about whether they have many playmates but should rather inquire about names, positive traits, common interests, and common shared activities. Only then can the counselor assess whether a child's perception of an adequate social network is realistic. A sociogram collected by the child's teacher can also be useful.

A differentiation may be made about whether children's playmates are encountered primarily during school hours or whether the children actually meet outside of school. Questions about sleepovers and after-school activities are helpful in this context. Finally, it is important to investigate whether there has been a change in playmate relationships and numbers over time. This information is helpful in pointing to the possible onset of the child's (i.e., the family's) presenting problem. It is not uncommon for children's friendship patterns to change after a major move, a divorce, or similar experiences. Of course, a change in and of itself does not indicate that there is a problem; rather, how the change is perceived by the child is of importance and clinical value.

In summary, children's friendship patterns provide helpful hints about their personality traits and problem behaviors in social settings. Therefore, friendship patterns should not be overlooked, nor should they be taken for granted. Parents' perspectives on children's friendship patterns with best friends and playmates are often useful supplements to the information provided by the children themselves.

What to Ask about Sociocultural Factors

Children are influenced not only by the psychological and emotional climate of a family, but also by its socioeconomic and sociocultural background. It is therefore important for therapists to have accurate information about these aspects of children's lives. Specific information needs to be collected about the family's financial status, about the neighborhood in which they currently live and where they have lived previously, about the family's general attitudes about money and possessions, and about the family's self-assessed socioeconomic status. This information is very important for follow-up planning as well as for referral decisions. For instance, a family that is unable to pay is unlikely to follow through when referred to high-cost private practitioners. Ignoring this information not only leads to inappropriate referrals but also may affect treatment recommendations. A family that has a hard time making ends meet financially cannot be expected to adhere to costly treatment recommendations. Similarly, they may be quite unable to come to the clinic if they have no regular means of transportation. Failing to consider true financial needs and limitations may set a family up for failure with regard to their ability to follow through on recommendations if those recommendations are not made in a thoughtful and considerate manner.

Even more important, care providers need to be sensitive to cultural backgrounds and attitudes of children's families. Children are socialized very early in life, thus carrying forth the cultural beliefs, attitudes, and values of their parents. Clinicians must grasp these values and ideals, as they have a profound impact on the harmonious functioning of a family. Specific information needs to be gathered about the ethnic group's attitudes toward mental health, toward normal family functioning with regard to generational attitudes, toward normal affective expression, toward accepted academic functioning, toward self-expression, and many other facets of day to day functioning. All providers need to have cultural sensitivity through education and by reading about the values and ideals of various cultural groups and as they relate to mental health issues. However, it is negligent not to assess the degree to which these cultural beliefs fit for a specific family that is seen in treatment. In other words, clinicians need to be sensitive not only to the ethnic background but also to the degree of acculturation or adherence to the traditional ways of a family's ethnic heritage.

The impact of culture or ethnicity on a family's life cannot be underestimated and needs to be strongly considered, in both assessment and treatment planning. For instance, a project in the state of Alaska involved the training of assertiveness skills in high schoolers of Alaska Native cultural backgrounds (Gasta, 1976). This was considered a very worthwhile effort, as teachers had noted that Native high schoolers were less assertive than their White counterparts and therefore often appeared less academically skilled because of less involvement in the classroom. The training program was indeed effective in training students to become more assertive but was found to have profound side effects in these students' home lives. Specifically, given their Alaska Native heritage, assertive skills toward parents did not fit the cultural norm and resulted in increased conflicts between parents and children. This is an excellent example of good intentions about the improvement of children's mental health that failed to consider the children's ethnic backgrounds and values. Imposing White, or majority, values and beliefs on clients of other ethnic backgrounds, and hence values and needs, is not only insensitive but also possibly iatrogenic.

Within this category of sensitivity to personal or familial belief and value systems, it is important to explore religious affiliation and involvement. Religiosity or spirituality are components of family life that can have potentially profound influences on how likely a family is to become involved in the treatment process and can have implications for treatment planning. Family lore, family secrets, familial ways of doing things, and similar aspects of a family's functioning are all important aspects of a thorough assessment that respects the family for who they are and what they have created for themselves over generations.

What to Ask about Recreation, Interests, and Hobbies

Interests, hobbies and recreational activities are an important aspect of family and personal functioning. They should be assessed for each family member, as well as for the family as a whole. Absence of these is as important as finding out specific preferences. Treatment interventions may be structured to make use of existing interests and shared hobbies.

Related to this issue is the family's social involvement. Are there other people in this family's life who can offer a potential social support network? If there are no such external resources, counselors need to assess the reasons for their absence. Again, it is important to investigate whether the children in this family have friends and acquaintances and how often they interact with them. The existence of friendships needs to be explored with some detail to assess how important and enduring they have been. Sensitivity to the number of family moves, as well as to changes in family structure (e.g., due to divorce or foster-parenting) is valuable in this regard.

What to Ask about Developmental and Health Issues

Although developmental and health information is most important about the identified client, other family members may need to be assessed in this regard if it appears to be of importance to the family's level of functioning or to the identified client's adjustment. For instance, if there is a sibling with a chronic illness or a parent with a terminal illness, these issues need to be discussed with regard to their relevance to the family and the children within it. Specific developmental and health-related information includes, but is not limited to, information about the pregnancy with the identified client, birth/delivery information, postnatal physical state (e.g., APGAR scores), developmental milestones of the identified client, childhood illnesses, accidents, hospitalizations, frequency and circumstances of mild illnesses (e.g., stomachaches, headaches), and frequency and circumstances of minor injuries (e.g., bruises, scratches).

Particular attention is paid to the potential contribution of abuse or neglect to the state of the child's health and development. For instance, frequent minor injuries or a series of bone fractures need to lead to questions related to the potential for physical abuse. Medical problems involving vaginal infections, bladder infections, or similar symptoms need to lead to questions regarding sexual abuse. Similarly, a child who failed to reach developmental milestones within age-appropriate limits needs to be assessed with the potential for neglect in mind. Previous reports to federal or state agencies need to be inquired about.

What to Ask about Plans for the Future, Fantasies, and Daydreams

On a more positive note, and for prognostic purposes, the clinician also needs to find out information about a family's aspirations, as well as each individual member's daydreams and hopes for the future. Planning and goal setting are important components of a well-functioning family.

What to Observe While Asking Questions

Behavioral observations are collected throughout the intake process. They include observations of individuals, as well as of the family system as a whole. Things to look for in all members of the family include cleanliness and appropriateness of dress and appearance, physical characteristics and mannerisms, adjustment to the intake process and the meeting with a stranger (the counselor), affect and mood, communication and general interaction styles, capacity for cooperation and negotiation, willingness to listen and compromise, changes in mood and behavior as the intake session progresses, psychological mindedness and attitudes toward treatment, level of interest and curiosity, and estimates of cognitive ability and verbal skills. Sometimes, behavioral observations can be augmented through the use of mental status examinations (to be discussed in the next chapter). However, most commonly, all necessary information about overall physical and psychological functioning of all family members can be gleaned from good behavioral observations throughout the various sections of the intake.

Once the therapist is cognizant of the type of information that needs to be collected, the purpose of the intake interview becomes much clearer. The interview is then much easier to conduct, as a clear plan has come into focus. However, the actual structure of how to see a family is another important consideration that is worthwhile thinking about *before* beginning the intake process.

Structure of the Intake Interview

As the actual intake process is discussed, reference is made repeatedly to parents, mothers, fathers, spouses, and partners. This is done merely to facilitate writing and reading and has no implications for the actual gender, marital status, or sexual orientation of the adults within the family system. In fact, most of what is said applies directly to blended families, foster families, adoptive families, and even single-parent families. Thus, as readers peruse the material, they should not assume that what is discussed is applicable only to the "American dream" family. Quite to the contrary, most family interviews do not occur with intact biological nuclear families but rather with blended, single-parent, or other types of families. Nevertheless, the intake process as described below still applies.

Preparing for the Interview

Information about the topic areas outlined in the previous section is gathered through various processes implemented during the intake interview. By the sheer amount of necessary information, it becomes evident that a child therapy intake interview is generally quite lengthy. Each individual therapist needs to decide how long an intake ought to take to ascertain sufficient time to collect the necessary data. As previously mentioned, a recommended time frame is four hours. Given this lengthy process, families need to be warned about the length of the appointment at the time of scheduling so that they can arrange to take time off work and to take the children out of school. Clinicians who are willing can accommodate families by scheduling afternoon or Saturday appointments. Stressing to the family that only the initial appointment requires this much time enhances their cooperation and willingness to commit to the assessment period. Surprisingly, many families are very uncertain about the therapy or counseling process and need to be educated about parameters that therapists and counselors often take for granted. As such, during their initial phone contact, families need to be told about the expectation that therapy and counseling involve more than one appointment and in fact may mean weekly appointments for several weeks. Families need to learn that sessions last for a certain amount of time (generally either 50 or 90 minutes) and are scheduled on a regular basis. The better informed and prepared the family is *before* committing to the intake, the more likely they are to follow through with their commitment not just to the initial appointment but also to the treatment process as a whole.

The family also needs to be informed of who is to be included in the family interview. Generally, it is preferable to have all persons who reside in the same home as the child come for the session. However, if there are other primary caretakers who do not live in the home, but who are willing to participate, they are excellent resources to include. Further, if the child lives in a blended or single-parent family, some thought needs to be given to inviting all biological parents. This, of course, needs to be discussed with the custodial parent who legally is the only person who can make the initial contact with the clinic. It is often difficult to get the entire family to cooperate and to appear for the initial intake. However, treatment and the family are best served by maximizing the number of family members who can be convinced to come for the first session. Some therapists or counselors refuse to see a family if not all members are present for the first appointment, whereas others hold the philosophy that one should work with whomever can be attracted to join the process. There is no correct approach to this problem, but a clinician is better off being clear about which approach is to be taken. The decision to see only entire families versus subgroupings willing to come is best not made on the day of the appointment, but rather is a decision that clinicians make and inform their clients of beforehand. Thus, a therapist who does not conduct sessions unless all relevant members present must inform the family of this requirement before the family appears for their first appointment. This eliminates confusion on the family's part, as well as arbitrary decision making on the counselor's part when a particular situation arises.

Building rapport with the parents is crucial to the success of children's treatment and begins at first contact (Kottman, 2002). During the first phone conversation with a parent, counselors must be aware that they need to build a relationship with the parent that is supportive, empathic, and respectful so as not to jeopardize a parent's willingness to support a child's therapy. The phone contact can be utilized to ensure that parents know what to expect from therapy and that they are clear that they need to prepare the child for the intake session. Parents can be given support by referring them to existing literature that has been designed to facilitate entry into therapy by children, such as Nemiroff and Annunziata's excellent *Child's First Book about Therapy* (1990).

Table 6.1 provides an overview of the topics that are best covered with parents during the initial phone contact to help them prepare themselves and their child(ren)

Table 6.1   Preparing Parents for the Intake Interview and Subsequent Treatment

Information to Provide	Additional Details
• introduce reason for return phone call	→ provide name, reason for call, other detail as needed
• provide opportunity for a brief discussion of presenting concerns	→ limit this interaction to 2–5 minutes as clinical material should not be discussed in detail on the telephone
• length of the intake session	→ 3–4 hours
• reason for the long intake session	→ to glean a thorough understanding of child and family
• who is best present for the intake session	→ all members of household and/or involved caretakers
• what happens if not all invited show up	→ provide clinician's rules about this (e.g., reschedule session, proceed without all members)
• how to prepare the child for the intake session	→ recommend a book or explain in clinician's own words
• explain the need to prepare the child for the intake session	→ increases cooperation and removes negative expectations
• explain that therapy or counseling involves more than a single session	→ there will be more sessions after the intake; these sessions will be much shorter; their number cannot be predicted at this time
• provide cost information	→ details about fees, charges for additional services, cancellation policy, and so forth
• discuss intake forms that are mailed and must be completed before the intake session	→ helps to orient and prepare family and clinician; saves time during the interview
• if needed, explain legal and ethical issues	→ if parents inquire, cover issues dealing with confidentiality, dual relationships, duty to report, and so forth
• if needed, help parents understand that problems may get worse before getting better	→ prevents later questioning of the clinician's skill and expertise; makes expectations about treatment more realistic
• if needed, discuss insurance issues	→ explain clinic policies and, if possible, insurer requirements
• if possible, schedule the intake session	→ if parents cannot yet commit to a meeting time, schedule a phone time to follow up
• if requested, provide clinician credentials	→ provide information about professional qualifications

for the assessment interview and possibly for any subsequent treatment. Because this initial phone contact can be very important to ultimate cooperation by the family and may elicit clinically relevant information, it is best made by the clinician, not a receptionist or secretary.

Format of the Interview

The actual intake interview can be structured in many different ways. One suggested format is to see the entire family together, then to split the family into various subgroups or holons. The term *holon* is preferred to the term subgroup because of its special connotation. Specifically, holons denote subgroupings of a family that are both part of a greater whole, and thus incomplete, and autonomous and self-preserving wholes in and of themselves (Minuchin, Lee, and Simon, 2006; Nichols and Schwartz, 2006). Each holon carries its own unique information, process, and communication, as well as containing the whole family's program or integrative energy. From this definition, it becomes clear why it might be important to meet with separate holons individually, as they can all provide a sense of the overall family structure, but additionally, they can give information about the impact of the whole on its parts and of the parts on the whole. This interdependence is crucial not only to the overall functioning of the family, but also to the clinician's understanding of the family and each member.

In splitting up the family into appropriate holons, clinicians need to decide which are the important subgroupings. There is much uniformity in this regard and a general approach might be as follows. After the family has been seen together, parents are identified and seen as one holon, siblings as another, and identified client as a third; each holon requires interviews of varying lengths. Finally, the whole family is reconvened for feedback and recommendations. However, there are other potential options for the intake interview, such as to see the family as a whole only, to see only the child and not insist on the presence of other family members, to see only the parental holon to assess their relationship, or to see individual holons without seeing the family as a whole unit. Although there are no hard empirical data that point toward the superiority of one particular structure for the assessment interview, each of these options has clinical advantages and disadvantages that have to be weighed by the clinician. In deciding on how to proceed, each clinician needs to develop a unique and workable personal style.

The format suggested here has the advantage of providing maximal access to all family members, both as a system and as individuals. Thus, clinicians are exposed to a large number of dynamics that involve intrapsychic as well as interpersonal processes. Observation of the entire system, as well as its subsystems or holons, becomes possible. Further, this approach may reduce resistance, as family members start out in a conjoint meeting; thus, there is less concern about blame being placed, scapegoating being fostered, or secrecy being encouraged. Having the whole family present for the initial section of the intake may well result in greater trust in the process of treatment, therefore being a great way of addressing one of the most common resistances to treatment (Becvar and Becvar, 2005; Gunn, Haley, and Lyness, 2007). However, there are disadvantages. Specifically, some children may be very concerned about confidentiality, not trusting that providers indeed do not discuss the topics that arose between them and the child or between them and the parents. Similarly, parents sometimes attempt to abuse the structure to keep a hidden agenda that they refuse to discuss with the family as a whole, thus perpetuating dysfunctional communication patterns within the family. Each provider has to consider the risk factors inherent in all the different approaches and then needs to decide which approach has the least disadvantages and the most advantages from the individual clinician's perspective.

The Interviewers

Next, it is necessary to decide whether a therapist wants to work alone or with a cotherapist. In the structure discussed above, if two clinicians are working together, both are present during the initial interview with the entire family, then one sees the parents and the other sees the children. After all holons are assessed by the clinicians, they take some time together to evaluate and process the data they have gathered so far. A clinician working alone needs to go through this process without the valuable input from a second care provider. A preliminary conceptualization is developed at this time, a treatment plan is made, and then the family is reconvened for a feedback session. The treatment decisions are discussed with the family in the form of presenting them with and negotiating treatment choices. It is up to the family to decide which treatment suggestions to take.

The whole intake process from the initial family session to the feedback session, if conducted according to the model provided above, takes approximately four hours. Related to the feedback process are decisions about who follows through with the various treatment options that are presented to the family. If two clinicians are collaborating, they decide before they meet the family who works with the parents (both during the intake and during treatment if that should be one of the recommendations), and who works with the identified child client. If only one therapist is involved, that individual needs to decide whether it is wise to see various holons of the family for treatment (it is necessary to do so during the intake). This decision is important because conflicts can easily arise for the counselor who sees parents in couple's counseling while seeing their child for individual work. Parallel therapies such as this often present threats to confidentiality, as it is easy to forget which piece of information about the family was derived from which member. However, parallel treatment may create the advantage of the counselor being aware of everybody's perception of family dynamics and struggles. Again, each clinician needs to decide which process is most efficient and workable within the theoretical perspectives and practical limitations of the treatment that is being conducted.

Final Thoughts about the Interview

The format of the interview with the identified client and with the siblings is determined largely by their ages and personality styles. It is more focused on free play without questioning for younger children, whereas more structure is possible, but not always necessary, with older children. The use of the playroom needs to be considered for its appropriateness. A general guideline is to use the playroom and play as a technique for children under age 10; for children 10 and over, play and conversation may be mixed as determined by the child's spontaneous choices; with adolescents, talking probably proves most productive and appropriate.

Decisions about confidentiality among family members need to be made before the session starts and need to be shared with the family. Legal and ethical guidelines were discussed in a prior chapter. Families, including young children, have the right to be informed of these legal and ethical issues at the time of the intake interview. As was mentioned before, this takes place during the first section of the intake interview when all family members are present. Once the therapist(s) or counselor(s) have decided the structure of the intake interview, they are ready to begin the intake session. For each subsection, certain goals and purposes with regard to data collection emerge. These are discussed below and summarized in Table 6.2.

Table 6.2   Outline, Order, and Goals of the Sections of the Initial Interview

Section	Holon Members	Goals
Family Interview	all members of the household who are willing to come	1. gather information about the presenting problem 2. overcome family resistance 3. build rapport with all family members 4. assess family structure 5. assess family competence 6. assess family process 7. assess family relating
Parent Interview	all adults who function in a parental role	1. collect specifics about the presenting problem 2. gather background information about the identified child 3. assess parenting styles and discipline strategies 4. gather parents' family of origin information 5. gather information about the spousal relationship
Sibling Interview	all siblings who are present for intake	1. get a fresh perspective on the presenting problem 2. assess siblings' roles within the family
Client Interview	identified child	1. establish rapport 2. gather information 3. set the stage for the intervention
Feedback Session	all members of the household	1. provide feedback 2. make specific treatment recommendations 3. set treatment goals 4. prepare the family for treatment

Intake Interview with the Family

In addition to obtaining information about the presenting problem and its history, a major goal of this initial joint interview with the entire family is to interest the family in therapy or counseling and to get away from the concept of there being one identified client. Instead, clinicians attempt to get the family to collaborate in a joint effort to help the child who was identified as having the problem in the family within the context of the entire system. The joint family interview is best used not for the collection of very specific data but rather for a general assessment of the presenting problem and the overall character and functioning of the family. Thus, observations of family interactions are more important than asking specific questions to solicit detailed information; the latter can be accomplished in the individual interviews that follow.

While using the session to observe the family, counselors also focus on joining the family system and building a relationship with all family members. Such rapport building can be accomplished through a myriad of strategies. Perhaps the easiest and most commonly used strategy that is often not even recognized as joining behavior is that of nonverbal communication (Brems, 1999). A friendly tone of voice that reflects warmth, acceptance, and respect, as well as a smiling face, may go a long way to help a family feel welcome and comfortable in this new situation. Greeting all of them through shaking hands acknowledges every individual as important, and can put people at ease.

Verbal communication is equally important and has many aspects. First, verbal communication in a family session is adapted so that it is appropriate for the adults as well as the children in the family. This may mean communicating the same message in two different ways. Clinicians need to avoid talking above children's heads; if it does happen, they later turn back to help the children understand what was communicated. Second, therapists make every attempt to match a family's vocabulary. With a very sophisticated, psychologically minded family, some jargon may be appropriate, whereas with a less-interested or less well-informed family, the use of jargon only serves to alienate and distance. As a rule of thumb, jargon is best avoided, especially for the children's sake.

Third, a time-honored verbal means of building rapport or joining family members is through matching predicates that reveal a preferred sensory modality (Grinder and Bandler, 1975). Different people have different sensory modalities (seeing, sensing, hearing, feeling) that are primary and most commonly relied upon. Information conveyed through the use of predicates of that modality is more salient to that person and more likely to be picked up on. For instance, using an "I see" with a visual person may be perceived as much more understanding than an "I hear." On the other hand, "I hear what you are saying" with an auditory individual may communicate powerfully that understanding has occurred. Kinesthetic people focus on feeling statements and perceive statements that are prefaced with phrases such as "I can sense that . . ." or "it feels to me as though. . . ." as most understanding. A person's sensory preference is easily recognized by listening to choice of language. Matching can then take place individually with each family member.

Fourth, attunement and cross-modal attunement have gained significant importance in the developmental literature (Stern, 1985) and are excellent rapport-building strategies. Attunement involves the verbal and nonverbal reflection that the clinician has understood what a person is expressing on a content and process level. A typical example of attunement may be a statement such as, "I am hearing you say that you are very unhappy in this situation and that you feel like no one understands quite what you are going through." This statement reflects the person's affect without parroting what she or he said directly. Cross-modal attunement accomplishes the same thing, except that rather than choosing the same medium of communication, the therapist switches to an alternative one. For example, a client who may be rapidly tapping a foot might be responded to verbally with a statement such as "You are feeling quite anxious right now." Similarly, a child who has just started crying, thus revealing sadness, may be responded to with a calming, low voice that matches the affect that is being expressed (as opposed to responding with a cheerful, everything-will-soon-be-better voice). Such attunement is extremely successful in communicating a thorough understanding of affective states and leads to greater levels of trust and self-disclosure.

Finally, there are several joining strategies borrowed from family therapists. Specifically, several behaviors, grouped under the label *confirmation* (Minuchin, Lee, and Simon, 2006; Nichols and Schwartz, 2006), may be used to help family members feel understood and cared for. For instance, recognizing holons or individuals and rewarding them; responding with sensitivity to what is being said or done; sympathetic responding with statements such as "I understand"; and describing transactions as they occur and are observed by the clinician. Strategies labeled *tracking* (Minuchin, Lee, and Simon, 2006; Nichols and Schwartz, 2006) ask clarifying questions that help the family gain understanding and insight and help them feel understood and accepted more deeply.

In addition to rapport building, or perhaps as part of it, the family interview focuses on overcoming any possible resistance brought to the room by one or more family members. This is the first time the clinician meets with this family and the stage for a positive and collaborative working relationship is to be set. Issues of distrust, resistance, and perceived differences tend to become more evident during this portion of the interview than at any other time during the intake contact. It is very important to pay attention to the family's hesitations about treatment and to their resistance about seeing the presenting problem from a family perspective, as well as an individual perspective. Such resistances are always present; it is only a matter of degree as to whether they actually interfere with therapy or counseling or whether they can be worked with successfully. It is never worth ignoring resistances in hopes that they simply disappear if not attended to; resistances are best dealt with openly and addressed directly with the parents, though not in necessarily the presence of the child(ren) (Greenspan and Greenspan, 2003). Resistance is not labeled as such; rather it is addressed from a perspective of the parent(s) trying to protect the child and the family. Most resistances have purposes, at least historically they were adaptive or functional, and cannot be overcome by challenging them outright (Brems, 1999; Kohut, 1984). Instead, it is best to join with the parents, explore their concerns and fears, and then attempt to help them feel understood and respected enough that they are willing at least to give work with the child or family a try. The family interview also helps clinicians become aware of potential pragmatic barriers to treatment that are part of a family (e.g., financial or time constraints) and provides an opportunity to educate the family about therapy or counseling and the assessment process.

While rapport is being established and resistance and barriers are being explored and dealt with, the interview begins with introductory statements about what the family can expect of their time with the care providers. Confidentiality and ethical issues (as discussed in a prior chapter) are presented to the family in a manner that is sensitive to every member's cognitive capacity. The same concepts may need to be explained in various ways: once for the cognitive level of the parents and once for the cognitive capacities of each child. Although this approach is more cumbersome than speaking to only one holon of the family, it also models for the family appropriate behavior in groups that include adults and children. It reaffirms that for the clinician, the inclusion of the adults *and* children in the process is equally important.

Once the stage has been set, it is time to elicit information about the reasons for the family's decision to seek treatment. It is recommended that every family member is permitted, and in fact encouraged, to offer her or his unique perspective on the presenting concerns. Ensuring that family member is heard and respected lays important groundwork for the work that might follow. It is during the exploration of the different perspectives on the presenting problem that the counselor has the best opportunity to observe family interaction. In this regard, four major components of family functioning are assessed: family structure, competence, process, and relating.

Family Structure

Family structure deals with family functioning as far as boundaries and alliances are concerned. It addresses family stability, cohesiveness, divisiveness, closeness, and distance. All families have to have several sets of boundaries that are acknowledged and respected by all family members. Not always are these boundaries considered healthy or productive from a family therapist's point of view, but they always exist. Healthy boundaries delineate the holons of a family. For instance, children are not part of the spousal holon; there should be a clear dividing line that the children in the family are not allowed to traverse. For example, if there is conflict in the spousal holon, the boundary is such that the children are not drawn into this conflict. As becomes evident, in problem families, this healthy boundary often does not exist. Frequently, it is replaced by an unhealthy boundary. One of the spouses might engage in an alliance with a child against the other spouse, thus rearranging the boundaries within the family. Obviously, boundaries and alliances often go hand in hand in families and can be used to estimate the level of psychological health of the system (Minuchin, Lee, and Simon, 2006; Nichols and Schwartz, 2006). Boundaries have a direct impact on who is close to whom and on how family members interact. Alliances function in much the same manner.

Family structure and boundary issues also deal with how engaged various members of the family are with others. In some systems there may be overengagement, or enmeshment, between two members, whereas another member may be disengaged from the family. An often cited example of the disengaged member is the parent who has withdrawn from the family and has redirected personal energies to work instead. An example of an enmeshed parent is one who has trouble letting go of a child even once that child is an adult and is attempting to leave home. Family structure also has to do with a family's affective status. The character or emotional state within a family system is often quite obvious. Like individuals, families can be angry, anxious, depressed, reluctant, and so forth. It is interesting to note what a family's overall affective state is and then to compare that affect to the affect of the separate holons, particularly to identified child client. Certainly, much more can be said about family structures and their effects on the mental health of the children in that family (and of the adults, for that matter). The interested reader is referred to the vast family therapy literature for a more in-depth discussion of this topic.

A simple, and by no means conclusive, way of assessing family boundaries and alliances is to pay attention to who is seated where. Do the parents sit together? Is there a child who squeezes between the parents even after they have chosen adjacent chairs? Is a child crawling onto a parent's lap? Are there family members who are turning their backs to the rest of the family? Another simple clue is to pay attention to who speaks and when. Do certain family members speak more than others? Are some family members always interrupted? Is there one spokesperson for the family? All of these patterns are interesting to note and can help form hypotheses about this aspect of family functioning.

Family Competence

Family competence refers to the capacity of a family to carry out the tasks assigned to families. A well-functioning family's primary task is that of raising children and providing an environment that fosters growth and mental health for all members. The specific duties or tasks involved in this mission of the family depend on the developmental stage of the family. As family therapists point out, a family begins through the establishment of a spousal holon that decides to have children. When the first child is born, the spousal holon has to reorganize around the new tasks involved in the role of being parents. Parenting patterns are set and the spouses need to rearrange their relationship to include the child or children, without jeopardizing their couple relationship. As children begin school, the family is once again faced with a new developmental task. Children come into contact with the outside world more frequently, which leads to a reorganization of control and power within the family. Issues of autonomy and self-sufficiency become important as the child or children near adolescence. Finally, as children leave the parental home, whole new ways of relating have to be worked out (Minuchin, Lee, and Simon, 2006; Nichols and Schwartz, 2006).

Family competence has to do with how effectively a family adapts to the new demands of passing to a new developmental stage and the task of providing a mentally healthy environment for children. It also has to do with smaller issues, such as the family's ability to problem solve together, to work out compromises, and to weather crises. Their capacity for cooperation is crucial to their everyday functioning and has implications for therapeutic work. The more cooperative and competent a family is, the more likely they are to be supportive of a child's treatment. Further, their psychological mindedness and degree of psychological health strongly affects prognosis for each individual member, the system, and most of all, the identified client.

Family Process

Family process refers to characteristic sequences of interaction among members and between the family and its environment. It has to do with a family's capacity for communication and the potential role the presenting problem plays in the family system. For instance, a family process issue that may affect the presenting problem is that of triangulation. In triangulated families, conflicts between spouses may be diverted through the problem behavior of a child. Thus, it may be noticed that as a mother and a father begin to fight more intensely, a child may suddenly begin to act out or complain of various physical symptoms. This family has learned to avoid facing conflict between the parents by redirecting all attention to a child's symptoms.

Communication patterns are particularly important to observe. Who speaks to whom, who speaks first when the family is asked questions, who interrupts whom, and who listens are all important features of family interaction of which the clinician needs to become aware. These dynamics identify dominant versus submissive individuals in the family and provide insights into who is in charge of this family. Identification of family patterns or characteristic sequences of interchanges also gives clinicians a better understanding of how conflict and crises develop in a family and how this might affect the functioning of the identified client.

Family Relating

Family relating, the final aspect of family functioning, reaches outside the family system and therefore depends more on verbal interchange than on mere observation of the system in action in the treatment room. Family interaction has to do with how the family relates to the outside world. The clinician assesses whether a family is isolated, distant, or involved with their environment. An isolated family is likely to spend all their free time only with immediate family members or each alone individually, and interaction with, as well as observation of, the community is nonexistent. A distant family behaves very similarly in that there is minimal interaction with the outside world, but here members actively observe what happens in their community and stay abreast of environmental developments. An involved family seeks out interaction with their community, is involved in social activities, and is most likely to have a good support network that can be used therapeutically or for support during crises.

Family relating is often directly tied to family values, which are often strongly influenced by the cultural or social network with which a family identifies. For instance, families who are very involved in a particular religious group are likely to carry that religion's values into their everyday family life. Active membership in an ethnic group results in an acceptance of that group's values and traditions. Awareness of these factors assists counselors in several ways. First, it provides additional insight into a family's functioning and hence the presenting problem. Second, it has implications for the compatibility between family and therapist. A clinician must never pretend to understand a family's social, cultural, or religious beliefs. If therapists are not familiar with a family's choice of values and beliefs, they need to ask the family to explain. Although this may seem awkward, it is actually a wonderful joining strategy if done respectfully and with genuine interest.

In conclusion, the family interview provides a wealth of information that enhances the counselor's understanding of the identified client, the family, and the role of the presenting problem within the family system. The interview provides therapists with hypotheses about contributing, precipitating, and reinforcing factors within a family system that affect the behavior of the identified child. The importance and implications of contributing, precipitating, and reinforcing factors is addressed in depth when conceptualization and treatment planning are discussed in a later chapter.

Intake Interview with the Parents

The major goals of this session are fourfold. First, the parental interview serves to gather background information about the identified client and the family. Second, it is used to gain a thorough understanding of parenting styles and discipline strategies. Third, it serves to obtain a thorough history of the parents' own families of origin. Fourth, it gleans a thorough understanding of the parents' spousal relationship. The fourth purpose is relevant primarily in families in which there are indeed two parents (who of course by no means have to be married, heterosexual, or living together for this interview to be useful!). In single-parent households, this information is still gathered, but the purpose of exploring the spousal relationship is primarily to be one of looking at this aspect of the family from a historical perspective. The four purposes are introduced to the parents at the beginning of the interview by providing them with an overview of the topic areas to be covered. Then these areas are addressed separately. Generally, it is easiest for parents to begin talking about the child and then their parenting styles, as this material is the least personal and least intrusive of the four. The parenting discussion is followed logically by an exploration of parents' backgrounds, as this is where parents have learned most of the parenting strategies they employ. Finally, it is hoped that the clinician and parents hopefully have developed a sufficiently trusting relationship for the parents to feel comfortable discussing their spousal relationship.

Throughout this interview, counselors continue to think about rapport building and joining. It is not helpful to this interview for therapists to be blaming; the parents need to be understood from their own unique perspectives. They are not cold people who consciously want to hurt their child. Instead, they are often people who are in pain and suffer with and for their child. After all, they no doubt see themselves in their child and see their child as an extension of themselves that validates their capability as parents. It can be a significant narcissistic injury to parents to see their child embroiled in emotional or psychological difficulties (Greenspan and Greenspan, 2003). Additionally, many parents have read articles in magazines that have placed the burden of responsibility for children's problems entirely on the shoulders of the parents. Even mental health professionals have played a role in adding much guilt to the pain that is often already experienced by parents through coining phrases such as schizophrenogenic mothers, disengaged fathers, cold or absent parents, and many more. The more the clinician can be attuned to the pain, guilt, and needs of the parents, the better understood they feel, and the more they cooperate with the counselor and their child's therapeutic work.

Background Information about the Identified Client

The need for this information has been explained above. Some of this information is gleaned from the intake form, and it might be useful for the clinician to refer to this form during the session to complete any gaps that remain. This interview section is focused primarily on the identified child and developmental milestones, developmental task resolution, relationships with peers, medical history, accidents, and similar issues. It is an information-gathering section and, as such, is largely directed by the clinician. It is best to warn parents that this section of the interview is structured, as there is a certain amount and type of information that needs to be explored. During this interview, the clinician can also collect any additional family information that did not emerge during the family interview.

Parenting Styles and Discipline Strategies

Discipline strategies are the next important topic, as most parents have never taken classes in this area and often operate on belief systems that stem from their own childhoods. It is helpful to explore types of strategies the parents use, how consistently they are applied, who enforces or implements them, and whether parents agree about the appropriateness of certain strategies. Disagreements between parents about what constitutes adequate disciplinary strategies are not uncommon, and it is helpful to identify them. When disagreements arise, it is likely that the child is aware of the conflict and uses it to her or his advantage (though neither consciously nor maliciously so). Often, it is necessary to ask very specific questions to gain an understanding of how the parents discipline their children. It is generally worthwhile to investigate whether the same strategies are employed with all children, by both parents, in all situations, and at all times. Specific questions include, but certainly are not limited to, the ones provided below:

Questions about Parental Discipline Strategies

- How do you reward good behaviors of your children?
- How do you discuss disagreements about rules with your coparent?
- Do you think that all strategies work equally well with all of your children regardless of their ages? Explain.
- Can you explain what active listening is and how you use it?
- When do you use active listening with your children?
- How do you encourage your child to solve her or his own problems?
- Would you explain what time-out is and when best to use it?
- When and where do you use time-out with your children?
- Would you explain what extinction is and how you use it?
- When and where do you use extinction with your children?
- What are logical and natural consequences?
- How and when do you use logical and natural consequences?
- Do you take into consideration what motivated a child's behavior?
- Do you ever spank your child?
- Where on the child's body do you hit?
- How often do you hit your child?
- Do you ignore or shame your child to punish her or him?
- Do you want your child to feel guilty after a misbehavior?
- Do you react to your child without asking reasons for behavior?

- Do you tell your child you do not love her or him when she or he misbehaves?
- Do you threaten your child? How?
- Do you ground your child for misbehavior?
- Do you think that all strategies work equally well in all situations? Explain.

These questions demonstrate how specific clinicians need to be to do an adequate assessment of parents' disciplinary strategies. Whenever clinicians ask about whether parents know of a certain strategy, they also ascertain that parents know the correct definition and application of that technique if they answer affirmatively. Knowing about a strategy and using it correctly are often two completely different things. If parents are unfamiliar with a strategy, the counselor can define it briefly—parents may be using it without being aware of its label. Throughout this line of questioning, therapists need to be sure to check with all parents. Thus, information about how consistent parents are with each other is gained automatically. It is often very illuminating to ask parents about their favorite and best parenting strategy, as well as about what they perceive to have been their worst intervention as a parent. Also, a question about what strategies seem to work and not work with the children in this household can be helpful.

Finally, it is important to talk with parents about their philosophy of parenting (Brooks, 2008), again exploring the issue for all parents. Parenting styles long ago were defined as taking one of three forms: authoritarian, permissive, and authoritative (Baumrind, 1973). Authoritarian parents tend to be restrictive, expecting their children to follow rules without questioning. They are strict disciplinarians who have little tolerance for negotiating compromise or for letting children work toward their own solutions to problems. These parents have strict rules and expect the child to abide by them. Violation is punished, usually without asking about purpose or reason for the transgression.

Permissive parents have very loose rules, and children are often not clear about what is expected. Rules that do exist are often not consistently enforced and limits are notoriously unclear. This lack of structure often has the child guessing about appropriateness of behavior and acceptability of affect. As children are not born with an innate sense of rules, this permissive style can be unsettling and anxiety provoking for them. Permissive parents are often found not in a parental but rather in a peer relationship with their children. Thus, as children need adults in their environment to figure out what is right and wrong in their society and neighborhood, they are often left guessing and unsure of themselves.

Authoritative parents have developed a compromise between having no rules, like permissive parents, and having too many rigid rules, like authoritarian parents. They generally have several sensible rules that are explained to the child and are often agreed upon and renegotiated as the child develops and matures. Although these parents are in charge of the family, they are tolerant of input from their children and are more likely to run a democratic household in which every member is perceived as having input about what is and is not appropriate and acceptable. Authoritative parents are not personally threatened by a child's misbehavior or stubbornness, but see it in perspective and can deal with it constructively. Of the three parenting styles, the authoritative style is the most psychologically sound approach to parenting. Clinicians need to assess which style is favored by the parents and whether both parents have the same style. Disagreements in styles are a major problem that often results in conflict and arguments for parents.

One additional aspect of parenting is the setting and clarification of rules in a household. As mentioned above, a well-functioning family has to have rules that are explicitly stated and that have certain predictable consequences associated with their violation. These explicit rules, as well as the consequences of violation or transgression, need to be investigated. Further, most families also have several implicit rules. Although these are more difficult to assess directly, they are still worth pursuing. The origin of all rules needs to be explored, as well as parents' willingness to renegotiate them according to the developmental needs of their children. For instance, rules about bedtime are very appropriate and common in most families. However, they need to be renegotiated as children grow and need to differ for different children in the same family depending on ages. It is not uncommon for a family to have instituted a 9 PM bedtime only to continue to enforce it for all children, despite the fact that the eldest child has reached adolescence.

Finally, if the child spends considerable time with other adults who have parental or disciplinary roles vis-à-vis the child, the clinician needs to inquire about these individuals' parenting or discipline strategies and styles as well. Just as conflict between two parents affects the child, so does conflict between parents and other adult caretakers who are important in the child's life.

Family of Origin Information

A very convenient way to lead into gathering family history is by exploring the parenting that the parents received as children within their own families of origin. Specific questions as outlined in the previous section can be asked, now not in terms of the parents endorsing and using these strategies and philosophies, but in terms of having been the recipients thereof. Most parents have some awareness that their own parenting has been affected by the parenting they received from their own parents. Many are quick to point out that they are doing certain things to be different from their parents, whereas they do others because they are modeling their parents' behavior. Nevertheless, much of their interaction with their children remains automatic and unexplored. Careful questioning can help parents recognize that much of what they do is a direct reaction to what they experienced as children. This recognition often leads to the desire to learn more and to change. Thus, this aspect of the interview is not only relevant for assessment purposes but often provides the basis for therapeutic intervention.

The specifics about and importance of other pieces of information about family history have been described previously. The mechanics are such that it is best to include both parents and gather parallel information from both partners at the same time. There are several advantages to this approach. First, by using this approach the clinician does not inquire about a certain set of circumstances regarding one parent and then forgets to explore the same issue with the other parent. Second, the clinician needs to introduce a specific topic only once; thus, time is saved. Third, and most important, through this procedure, the parents gain a new awareness of the similarities and differences in their own family histories and backgrounds. It is not uncommon for parents to have significant valuable insights about their bases for conflict and approaches to their children during this interview. They often recognize for the first time how their own background has shaped their behavior and how the partner has a similar experience of being steered by her or his experiences within the family of origin. The construction of a genogram may facilitate the process of collecting family histories.

Of particular importance during this aspect of the parental interview is the assessment of abuse histories in both parents' family backgrounds. Specific questions about sexual, physical, and emotional abuse are asked. Neglect, physical and emotional, needs to be ruled out or ascertained. Similarly, substance abuse histories, as well as current substance use (or abuse) patterns, are important to assess. These topics are often very sensitive, especially as both parents or partners are present. However, their open exploration conveys the message to both parents that this type of information needs to be discussed openly and honestly and is not kept secret. It is hoped that modeling this communication style can generalize to the extent that both parents feel more comfortable investigating the topic of abuse with their children.

Finally, this section of the interview provides a unique opportunity for counselors to assess how empathically attuned the two parenting partners are to one another, how respectful they are of one another, and how much they have communicated with each other about themselves. The setting allows the therapist to evaluate the potential of open communication between the two parents and the potential for negotiation of compromise. It also leads to a natural transition to talking about the spousal relationship.

Spousal Relationship

Once the parents' family backgrounds have been explored, it is necessary to investigate their intimate relationship. This can be accomplished in the most nonthreatening way by beginning this section of the interview with an investigation of how the couple met, what they liked about one another, and how long they dated before getting married or living together. Exploring the relationship in a time sequence keeps the discussion focused and less intrusive. Parents feel less need to defend themselves and their relationship if the initial focus is not on what is wrong between them but rather on what is positive and healthy. If only one parent is in the family at this time, this information is gathered from a historical perspective. Then the therapist needs to investigate whether there is any contact between the two partners, for instance around visitations of children. The nature of these contacts is explored to assess its impact upon the child. Additionally, the presence of new significant others in the respective parents' lives needs to be inquired, and the prominence of that person's presence in the child's life is estimated.

This approach allows clinicians to explore changes in the intimate relationship as a function of the birth of the children that make up this family. Thus, it provides important information about the emotional climate in which the identified client grew up. Once all of this information has been collected, clinicians have a wealth of data that can facilitate understanding the child. For instance, strict parental discipline may contribute to a child's stubbornness; a parental history of physical abuse may put harsh punishment of the child in a historical context; frequent fights between parents may make somatic concerns without physical basis more understandable in the child.

A final and secondary purpose of the parental interview is to assess how likely the parents are to support the therapy or counseling of their child. There are several parental traits that have been identified as corollary to the facilitation of a child's treatment. These include, but are not limited to, parents' willingness to supply information, to report on the child's behavior between sessions, to encourage the child to trust the care provider, to recognize their role in the child's problem, to trust the therapeutic or counseling process even though there is no advice for them, to tolerate confidentiality between child and clinician, and to bring their child to treatment on a regular basis (Adams, 1982). The more these factors can be answered positively for the identified client's parents, the more likely the therapy of the child actually becomes reality. Parents who have ambivalence about these issues may end up undermining the child's work by missing sessions, coming late, and dropping out prematurely.

Intake Interview with the Siblings

The major goal of the sibling interview is to get a fresh perspective on the presenting problem from individuals who may be less directly involved or less emotionally invested. Siblings can be interviewed as a group or individually, depending on the clinician's preference and the children's ages. For instance, if there are very young and older children, it might be more productive to see these two sets of children separately. Occasionally, the counselor might choose to begin the interview with all children present and then move to separate interviews with various subgroupings of children.

Siblings are an important holon to consider during the assessment phase, as they represent the identified client's first peer group. If all siblings are seen together, patterns of negotiation, communication, cooperation, and competition among the siblings can be observed directly. If siblings are seen separately, this information can only be inferred. Roles of various siblings may emerge during this interaction. For instance, it may be observed that an older child has assumed a parental role with the younger children in the family; one child may have assumed the role of clown who distracts when problems emerge; another child may be in charge of decision making. These roles, and their relationship to the presenting problem, can provide important information about the dynamics of the identified child's difficulties.

The sibling interview is also helpful in assessing why a specific child member of this family was presented as the identified client. The clinician now has the opportunity to observe all the children in the family without the perhaps limiting presence of the parents. Watching the dynamics that unfold helps the counselor understand whether other children in the family evidence emotional or behavioral difficulties, whether one child is being scapegoated, and whether the children who were not identified as having problems indeed function appropriately. Further, the siblings are able to offer additional information about the family's concerns by giving their opinions about causes and implication of the identified client's behavior or about the effect on the family as a whole.

Strategies that are used in this interview to solicit information are very similar to those used with the identified client. They are selected on the basis of clinician preferences and clients' ages. Strategies include, but are not limited to, free play, open-ended questions, projective questions, drawings, and storytelling. All of these strategies are discussed in detail below. If they are used in the sibling interview, all children who are present need to be given the opportunity to answer or engage in each activity.

Intake Interview with the Identified Child

The major goals of the interview with the identified child are the establishment of a meaningful relationship and the gathering of information. For these purposes to be fulfilled, the child must feel trusting, supported, and free to feel emotions while working with the provider. The importance of the establishment of therapeutic rapport cannot be overemphasized, as it is during this interview that the stage is set for the therapeutic relationship between the child and therapist or counselor if a recommendation for individual treatment of the child is made (Lovinger, 1998). Many ingredients are necessary for a therapeutic interaction, and it is impossible to give a firm recipe that works with all children—selecting the right approach with a child is a bit like trial-and-error learning. The counselor needs to meet the child with a number of available strategies already in mind, but how and when to use them is determined through the process that unfolds. Some of the basic ingredients are discussed here. Some are clinician characteristics; others are strategies that can be used by the provider. All can be acquired by a committed therapist or counselor, though some may be more natural than others.

Characteristics and Strategies to Build Rapport and Gather Information

One of the most important characteristics of the clinician that is often instrumental in creating an atmosphere conducive to rapport building and information gathering with a child is that of flexibility. It is best not to follow a fixed or rigid interview schedule (Brems, 1999) but rather to rely on creativity and spontaneity to guide the interview or interaction with the child. It is important to be nondirective, to follow the child's lead, all along thinking about the symbolism and dynamic implications of the child's choices (verbalization of these issues, however, is reserved for later stages of treatment). Nevertheless, nondirectiveness is not equal to passivity. The clinician might well choose to comment, reflect, and mirror a child's feelings. Further, the expression of emotionality when reflecting and mirroring for the child can be quite appropriate.

Another important trait is that of permissiveness, which is not to be misunderstood as the absence of rules and structure, but rather has to do with creating an atmosphere in which the child is encouraged to express all feelings openly, even negative ones, and in which the child can do whatever she or he chooses to do (within limits of safety). It implies that the clinician does not try to hurry things along, but rather allows the process to unfold at the child's speed and ability. Being accepting is another important ingredient for rapport building. It implies that the counselor pays attention to a child's feelings, is empathic, mirrors needs and feelings, and fosters understanding and trust. All of this requires that the clinician be nonjudgmental about the child's feelings, needs, and self-expressions. The counselor needs to be capable of reflecting feelings, as appropriate, through verbal or nonverbal modes of communication.

Further, the use of simple language is crucial to communicating with children. In fact, therapists have to learn to adapt their language. Being highly educated individuals, clinicians generally are used to speaking on a sophisticated level when communicating verbally. Some relearning is in order when the client is a child. Additionally, counselors need to be capable of understanding metaphors and idioms. Much communication with children takes place through the use of symbolism. In using this mode of communication, it is preferable to use the child's metaphors and idioms (see chapter 1).

Another important component of the clinician–child relationship is respectfulness of the child and the child's choices. This implies that the counselor must at times be satisfied to follow the child's lead when it comes to choosing activities, follows the child's exploration of topics, follows the child's approach to self-expression, and understands the importance and impact of various topics from the child's perspective. Respectfulness also implies not belittling the child's feelings and not undoing a child's work.

Another good practice is the avoidance of questions that begin with "why." All too commonly, "why" questions indicate to children that they did something wrong or that their choices are being challenged. Simple rephrasing lowers a child's resistance and makes a meaningful response more likely. For instance, rather than asking a child who is using Play-Doh to build a volcano that then erupts with a sudden burst of energy, "Why did the volcano erupt so suddenly?" the clinician might ask, "What happened when that volcano erupted?" Open-ended questions are preferable to questions that allow for a simple "yes" or "no" in response.

The counselor can also use various projective strategies to elicit additional material from the child. For instance, the use of projective questions often produces helpful unconscious material that corroborates or refutes hypotheses that are forming in the counselor's mind. Common projective questions include the three wishes, people to take to a desert island, the animal the child would choose to be, the age the child would choose to be, and naming of a favorite color or number. In the three wishes, therapists ask children what they would wish for if they had three chances to wish for whatever they want. Children's answers are often quite revealing. For instance, the following response was given by a 7-year-old girl who was brought for an intake because of severe sexual abuse by her father during visitations with him in prison: "I wish that my daddy would have a smaller lap." When the girl was asked further questions about this wish, she indicated that if he had a smaller lap, as she had wished for, she could not sit in it during visitations. As it was revealed that her father had been forcing intercourse on this little girl during these visits, her wish was very revealing indeed.

The desert island question asks children to indicate whom they would want to have with them should they become stranded on a desert island. Once children have invited one person, clinicians may give two more choices. Again, responses often reveal important family dynamics. For instance, it is interesting to note whether children choose a parent, a sibling, or another family member or whether all the choices directly exclude any family members.

Asking children what animal they would like to be can provide useful information. For instance, the children in a family of five (three children, two adults) made the following choices, revealing several of their family dynamics and their impact on the children. The youngest child, the only girl, wished to be a bear because bears were soft and cuddly and always had enough food to eat. Her older brother, the middle child, wished to be a horse because horses were able to run fast and could get away from dangerous situations. The oldest child in the family wished to be a turtle because turtles had a shell that could protect them from harm. These children were being raised in a family with chronic marital strife between the two biological parents. The amount of nurturance was minimal ("not enough food"), and physical abuse of the oldest child was not uncommon ("shell that protects from harm"). The middle child had found that he could have many of his needs met by leaving the family and searching for important adults among his teachers ("run fast and get away").

The question about what age children would be if they had the choice can be similarly revealing. For instance, one 8-year-old boy indicated that he would like to be 80 years old and, when asked further, revealed that this age was appealing to him because then his life would be behind him, rather than ahead of him. This desire was understandable in the context of his family, in which constant arguing and conflict contributed to his significant level of depression and occasional suicidal ideation. Similarly, favorite numbers and colors can provide information about mood and the number or nature of important individuals in a child's life. Favorite jokes, daydreams, fantasies, dreams, and similar material may also be solicited to gain more information about the child.

Although the purely diagnostic use of projective drawings must be reserved for the appropriately trained and educated psychologist or art therapist, any clinician can use drawings to corroborate hypotheses. Useful drawings are those of the child's family and those of a person. Both the execution of the task and the finished product can provide the provider with useful information. Interpretation of drawings, however, is complex and must be done carefully. Excellent resources are available on this subject (e.g., Goodenough, 1926; Knoff, 2003; Malchiodi, 1998).

Another useful tool to extract more information from the interview without direct questioning is the *Talking, Feeling, Doing Game*, distributed by Creative Therapeutics (Gardner, 1973). This game involves the child in answering questions that either address the cognitive, affective, or behavioral realm. Many of the questions are similar to projective questions and challenge children to develop their own solutions and responses to difficult situations. Questions range from difficult to relatively nonthreatening, and the counselor can choose stack the deck before engaging children in this task. For instance, children may be asked to respond to questions ranging from asking about secret wishes about their mother to asking to hop around the room on one foot.

Storytelling is another way of getting children to share information without direct inquiry. The formal technique as developed by Gardner (1993a, 2002) is described in detail later; simple modifications of the strategy can be used even during the intake session. Specifically, the clinician can encourage the child who is unable to play or talk freely to make up a story. These stories can be very meaningful to the assessment process. For instance, a 7-year-old girl told the story of a treasure that was well hidden beneath the sand in her backyard. Only one person knew where the treasure was, and she refused to dig it up to buy food for the starving children in the city. This child had been placed in a foster home after her parents were charged with severe physical neglect of their five malnourished children.

Finally, and perhaps most important, a child's free play is used to gain an understanding of the presenting problem. The interpretive use of play is discussed in detail in the chapter about play therapy. Suffice it to say here that the child's play behavior is viewed symbolically and metaphorically and generally has representative value that gives the counselor new insights into the child's life (Gitlin-Weiner, Sandgrund, and

Schaefer, 2000; Schaefer and Kaduson, 2006). For instance, an 8-year-old boy very much enjoyed playing hide-and-go-seek with the therapist. He delighted in being found but was threatened when the therapist was hidden too well for the child to find her. It appeared that this child, who had been abandoned by his biological mother and was severely abused by his biological father and stepmother, was working on his abandonment fears through this advanced form of peek-a-boo that infants so delight in as they gain object constancy. Play can be viewed as an outline of a child's problem, much like the free association of an adult client.

Limit Setting

Despite the fact that good child clinicians are permissive and nondirective as defined above, they also need to set limits in the intake session and the therapy. There are three important reasons for setting limits. First, clinicians are responsible for children's safety, as well as their own, in the playroom. Therefore, there are certain actions that are not permitted because of their threats to physical safety. Further, limits anchor therapy to real life, in which the child is also unable to engage in certain behaviors because of their impact on others. Finally, limits serve to make children aware of their responsibility within the therapeutic relationship. Children are not born with an innate sense of right or wrong, but rather need to learn rules from the adults in their environment. The creation of an environment in which there are neither rules nor limits is artificial and not conducive to the generalization of change. This is not to imply that the intake interview is restricted by rigid rules and regulations. Quite to the contrary, only those rules are set that are directly necessary for the assurance of the physical safety and integrity of client, counselor, and room. Each therapist needs to decide what rules to have and enforce. A few universal rules include no physical aggression (hitting, kicking, etc.) toward self or clinician, no willful destruction of playroom equipment, no removal or taking home of playroom equipment, and no leaving the therapy room.

Setting the stage for limit setting involves providing the child with the information about the existence of the limit. Thus, clinicians might choose to accompany their introductory statement about the playroom with a simple and matter-of-fact statement of rules, such as "This is the playroom. In here you can do whatever you choose as long as what you do does not hurt you or me. You can play with anything in this room, and everything stays here when you leave, so it will be here when you come back." Thus phrased, the statement of the limits can be done in a very positive, rather than restrictive, manner.

If children attempt to violate limits that have been set, therapists need to address this violation consistently and immediately. However, the first step in this process generally involves a mere comment on the possible meaning of the behavior rather than restricting the behavior, with the expectation that the comment gratifies the child's underlying need and terminates the inappropriate behavior. If the child does not respond to the comment about the behavior, the clinician needs to move to the next step. This involves a statement about the therapist's own feeling or thought in response to the child's violation of the rule. It is only if the child again fails to respond to the clinician's intervention that the counselor verbalizes (i.e., reminds the child of) the limit. If the child continues the behavior, a consequence for the behavior is verbalized. If this does not serve to change the child's actions, the consequence is enforced as it was stated. Thus, therapists must never state consequences they are not willing to enforce and justify in their own mind. An example of an instance follows that demonstrates how a therapist had to move through all stages of limit setting.

> A 9-year-old boy, who had arrived for his session very anxious and upset after having been teased in school about several bruises on his forehead, became very angry during his therapy session. As was his tendency, he expressed this anger outwardly by attempting to attack the therapist by kicking and hitting in the direction from where she was watching. The therapist remained calm and did not speak until the boy began to hit her directly, at which time she said, "You want to fight with me."

Note that according to the first step in the limit-setting procedure, the therapist merely commented on what she perceived as the meaning of the behavior. Also note that she avoided the labeling of the underlying affect, which was anger that covered abandonment fears. She avoided the labeling of the affect "anger," as she had experienced previously that the child was unable to tolerate the verbal expression of negative affects and that his behavior tended to escalate whenever this occurred.

> Since the child continued to hit, the therapist immediately stated, "It makes me uncomfortable and it is not safe when you hit."

Note that the therapist did not wait long before moving to the next step in the limit-setting procedure. It was unnecessary for her to endure the hitting any longer than a few seconds. However, also note that she did not skip any stages in the limit-setting procedures, giving the child a fair chance to stop his behavior before she intervened behaviorally.

> The child hesitated momentarily, then continued to hit and kick, so the therapist said, "You may want to yell at me to let me know that you want to fight with me, but you may not hit or kick me."

The therapist at this point restated the limit of the restriction of physical acting out in the playroom. However, even while doing this, she allowed the child his affect and his desire to fight with her; in fact, she provided him with an alternative means of self-expression.

> Because there was no change in the child's behavior, the therapist followed up her previous statement with an immediate outlining of consequences: "If you continue to hit and kick me, we need to end our session for today because, remember, I have to make sure that we are safe as long as we are in this room."

Although this consequence appears quite severe, and perhaps rejecting, this child had a history of physical violence outside of the therapy room that led to the gratification of his needs by motivating his parents to pay attention to him by physically holding him down. Therefore, to avoid repeating a pattern of reinforcing physical acting out through making physical contact with this child, the therapist chose the termination of the session as the consequence for the child's behavior. This should not be misunderstood as a common strategy or solution for dangerous behavior—every strategy is carefully adapted to the circumstances of each specific child.

> The child hesitated, but this was the first time that the therapist and child had been faced with this type of situation, and he was not sure whether she would enforce the limit. When he continued to hit (he did stop kicking), she turned and opened the door of the room. When he refused to leave, she took his shoulders and guided him out of the room to the waiting room, where his mother received him.

Fortunately, it is quite rare that a therapist has to go to this length to convince a child client that limits in the therapy room are firm and that behavior does have limits and consequences. More often than not, children obey the limit once the consequence has been spelled out verbally. Not all consequences have to be as severe as the one in the example. However, they must be of sufficient strength that the gratification derived from the acting-out behavior is counterbalanced by the noxiousness of the consequence once it is imposed.

Outline of the Interview

Equipped with useful strategies, helpful personal characteristics, and the ability to set limits, clinicians are ready to begin the interview with the identified client. The first task of the interview is to observe how children separate from their parents. Given that the child interview follows a lengthy interaction between the family and the clinician, most children separate easily from their parents to follow the counselor. It is notable if the child clings or cries upon the request to leave the parents. It is important to note whether the child clings to both parents, to the mother, or to the father. Further, it may be interesting to observe the parents' reactions as the children leave. Some parents may show no concern; others may feel the need to warn children to behave, to do what they are told, and so on.

Once the provider and child have entered the playroom, the work begins. As was mentioned previously, there is no firm approach to this interview, unlike the interview with the parents. Instead, it is up to the counselor to allow the process to unfold. The child is briefly introduced to the room and the limits, but no other structure needs to exist. Therefore, it is of the utmost importance to observe how children adjust to the situation and what they choose to do. The succession of different play activities, attention span, and interests are important components to note. If children evidence difficulty with this unstructured situation, counselors may choose to introduce some structure through questioning or through some of the strategies outlined above. It is important to remember the primary purposes of this interview: information gathering and rapport building in preparation for individual therapy work with the child.

The session is also to define therapy or counseling, preferably through play activity that is shared with the child. For instance, therapists can set the stage by communicating that this is the child's time to choose what to do, to assure the child that the clinician is there for her or him, to allow the child to lead while the therapist follows. More about the intake process may be explained verbally if a child asks, with the counselor always attempting to address anxieties that might underlie the questions.

Some clinicians prefer to conduct a semi-structured interview, exploring presenting problems, family dynamics, friendship patterns, and hobbies or interests; this choice is driven somewhat by the age of the child. However, much of this material can be gathered more spontaneously and less intrusively through interaction with the child through play activity. Generally, children have some awareness of the reasons for the interview and spontaneously volunteer information. This is a sign for the therapist that additional questioning is appropriate and tolerable for the child. However, if a child signals discomfort with direct questioning (e.g., by withdrawing, turning away, occupying herself or himself with various other activities, ignoring the therapist, or refusing to answer questions), that line of approach is perhaps best abandoned. This can be done easily if the counselor can remind herself or himself that much of the specific information about behaviors and family dynamics can be gleaned more easily through the intake interview with the parents.

Once enough corroborating information has been gathered and children appear to feel comfortable in the playroom and with the relationship that was established, the interview can be closed. A fair warning about ending this aspect of the intake is given, so that the child can complete tasks or finish explorations that remain incomplete. It is important to note how the child anticipates the return and how the child actually does return to the parents. It is not uncommon for children to attempt to stretch out the interview as long as possible. Very few children have ever had the experience of having an adult pay attention to and respect their behavior for an extended period of time. Thus, they often do not want to conclude this gratifying and unexpected experience. Other children become notably anxious about the return to their parents. Perhaps they have paint on their hands or clay on their clothing and they are worried about their parents' response to their perceived messiness. Perhaps they have recognized that they do not feel as comfortable in the adult company of their parents, as in the adult company of the clinician. Some children, on the other hand, are quite eager to meet their parents to tell them about their experiences in the playroom. Others may welcome the end of the session as the prolonged contact with s stranger proved very anxiety provoking to them. These patterns provide the clinician with additional material that can be used diagnostically and conceptually.

The identified client interview is often the lengthiest of the interviews and the most important with regard to establishing rapport and setting the stage for individual work with a child (Greenspan and Greenspan, 2003). This outline of the session, as well as the discussion of strategies, characteristics, and limits cannot guarantee successful completion of the interview, but it can enhance the clinician's chances of having a positive first contact with an identified child. The session with the identified client concludes the interview section of the intake contact with the family. Now that all interviews have been completed, the clinicians need to take time to review all materials, develop a preliminary conceptualization that is sufficient to develop recommendations, and set preliminary goals that can be discussed and negotiated with the family. This information is shared with the family during the feedback and recommendation section.

Feedback and Recommendations
Section of the Intake Interview

Once an intake interview is complete, the therapist or counselor must take time to provide thorough and understandable feedback to family. Although such feedback includes providing assessment and treatment information, feedback is free of jargon and labels and is delivered respectfully and without condescension. It is presented as a means of enhancing the family's understanding of the situation that brought them to treatment. As such, it is best to talk about observations and summaries of situations, not conclusions and problems; to start with descriptions of behavior, not labels or diagnostic codes; and to point out patterns within a developmental and systems context, not to wax philosophical about abstract concepts such as interpretations about underlying dynamics.

In giving feedback, it is a primary goal to come to an agreement with the family, especially the parents, about what is going on with the child and the family and about what needs to be done to improve the situation or presenting concern (Brems, 1996). Failure to communicate feedback in such a manner may be the reason why 50 percent of parents fail to follow through with recommendations made by child clinicians (Greenspan and Greenspan, 2003). Agreement is reached most easily if clinicians have taken into consideration parents' expressed resistance, the family's unique histories and needs, and everyone's emotional and social circumstances. On the basis of such information, therapists are able to join with the family, helping them see that treatment of the child is a joint venture of the whole system to promote the child's psychological health, emotional growth, and developmental adjustment, not a threat to the parents or the family.

Before discussing specifics about the feedback session, an important clarification must be made. Although it is important to structure an assessment period, and although this assessment period remains separate from the actual therapy or counseling, this distinction is somewhat arbitrary. Many interactions and events happen during the intake interviews that have a profound *therapeutic* effect for the family and its members. Similarly, even once counseling has begun, clinicians continue to *assess* and gather new data with each contact. The arbitrary distinction between assessment and counseling becomes most noticeable to clinicians during the feedback session with the family. Technically, this section of the interview is still part of the assessment. However, it may also be viewed as the beginning of therapy or counseling.

The prior establishment of positive rapport with all family members, particularly the parents, is crucial to the success of the feedback session. The feedback session includes all family members and clinicians who have been involved with the intake sessions and contains four distinct phases. First, clinicians share with the family what they have learned about them from the various interviews that have taken place, and what conclusions were drawn. Second, treatment recommendations follow and are a direct outgrowth of what has been shared about the understanding of the family system and the presenting problem. This is an important and sensitive task, as it often shatters illusions and dreams that parents and children have built up about their families (Ellis and Bernard, 2006; Schaefer and Kaduson, 2006). It may represent the shattering of explanations parents and children have produced to explain their interactions and behaviors. Thus, some families may react with guilt, anger, shame, or disappointment. Others, however, react with relief upon hearing that their problem is not unsolvable and that, through hard work, they can help themselves change. When this happens, clinicians can feel comfortable in making positive prognostic predictions. Third, once the family has accepted a set of recommendations, they need to be involved in setting treatment goals. Fourth, the family receives preparation for therapy or counseling if they have agreed to return for treatment. If the family refuses all recommendations, obviously phases three and four become obsolete. The family is then encouraged to reconsider, and their file is closed. How therapists prepare for recommendations and goal setting is discussed in the next chapter. Mechanics of the feedback session are briefly discussed below.

Sharing the Conceptualization

The purpose of the feedback section of the intake interview is to share the understanding the clinician has derived from the interview with the family. Many of the same rules that were discussed relative to the family interview apply with regard to language, to whom to speak, and so forth. However, all of these issues are slightly more complicated now that the therapist faces the task of putting in laypersons' terms complex psychological dynamics of individuals and families. Preparation for a brief statement before the counselor enters this final meeting with the family is of utmost importance so that the therapist does not appear scattered or arbitrary in the feedback. A sample of a simple feedback statement developed for the benefit of the adults and the children in the family follows. It is presented by one clinician, even though two clinicians were involved in the assessment.

> We have spent the last three and a half hours getting to know one another, and you have given us a lot of information about each of you individually and about your family as a whole. Thanks to all of your help, we feel that we now have a pretty good understanding of what is going on with your family and each one of you and would like to share our understanding with you to see if it rings true for you. Please stop us any time you have any questions or comments.

This introduction helps everybody to capture the purpose of this section of the interview. It is a standard introduction; that is, it is the same for all families and can be used for a variety of circumstances.

> You came here today because Nancy has been having a lot of stomach problems in the last 9 weeks and was diagnosed last month by Dr. Chad to have a pre-ulcer condition.

It is recommended that before delving into an explanation, clinicians repeat the original presenting problem. The amount of elaboration with which this is done is up to the clinician and depends on the complexity of the problem. In this example, the presenting problem was straightforward, and not much time needed to be spent on its summary.

> We think Nancy's stomachaches have something to do with how the whole family works together. You told us that mom and dad are fighting a lot, dad is really

working too hard, and mom is upset because she has to do most of the work that has to do with chores around the house and with Nancy and Tom. That has made everyone in the family pretty nervous, and you told us that sometimes it's like walking on eggshells. Well, often when these kinds of things are going on in a family, one of the kids gets stomachaches or headaches because they are reacting to the stress in the family around them.

In this example, a simple systemic explanation was offered as to why the identified client is evidencing certain symptoms. The conceptualization is offered in simple terms so that even the children can understand what is being said, and it is phrased so that no one member in the family is blamed. The explanation is neither detailed nor sophisticated but reflects the essence of the conceptualization derived for this case by the two clinicians.

If a family cannot relate to or agree with the conceptualization at all, the therapist tries to explain it in more detail or to investigate why the family is resisting. The counselor needs to ask the family whether they have an alternative explanation for their problems and then searches for common threads between the counselor's and family's explanations. It is never worthwhile to force the family to accept a clinician's explanation. Instead, it is hoped that the clinician and family can arrive at an understanding that is mutually acceptable. It might not be as thorough as the initial conceptualization offered by the therapist, but the family has more ownership of it, and therefore it is more meaningful to them.

Sharing the Recommendations

Once the feedback has been received—that is, heard, understood, and more or less accepted—by the family, the next task becomes the outlining of treatment recommendations. These recommendations are based on the assessment or conceptualization of the presenting problem, the goals set for treatment, and an assessment of the family's level of cooperation. How to arrive at conceptualizations and treatment goals is discussed in detail in chapter 8. Reading that chapter is crucial to being able to do a skillful feedback session with a family. Generally, clinicians come to certain conclusions about what is best for an identified client with regard to future treatment contacts. This understanding is then conveyed to the family in very simple and practical terms. The context for the recommendations has been set through the feedback about how to understand the family and its presenting problem.

Outlining a menu of treatment options for a family is preferable to providing only one solution, especially if some resistance to the recommendations is expected. Thus, if it is the therapist's opinion that the underlying dynamic of the presenting problem in actuality is one of marital conflict between the parents, the treatment of choice that is offered first to this family is marital therapy for the parents. However, if the parents refuse, possibly because they are not yet capable of openly admitting to their conflicts with one another, a second option of family therapy can be offered. This approach is still an appropriate treatment of choice as the children in this family obviously have become entangled in the parental conflict, but the focus is less directly on the parents, thus perhaps making them more willing to comply with treatment. If the family refuses again, a third alternative of parenting education may be offered. This is a viable alternative, as the conflict between the parents in the spousal relationship doubtlessly interferes with their parental relationship and results in unfortunate parenting choices. Finally, if this treatment modality is also refused, some individual intervention might be appropriate with the children in this family. This intervention then focuses primarily on helping the children adjust to and deal with the conflict evidenced in the spousal relationship of their parents.

It becomes obvious from this example that clinicians need to have some flexibility yet remain within appropriate boundaries with regard to the treatment strategies that are offered. Before clinicians agree to move to less preferred treatment strategies, it behooves them to explore the family's resistance and to attempt to overcome it. It is in this role that the feedback and recommendation session clearly leaves the boundaries of assessment and enters the boundaries of therapy or counseling.

Setting Goals

In the work with any client, three sets of goals emerge: goals that the clinician and client agree upon, goals the client has that are of lesser importance to the clinician, and goals that are important to the clinician but of lesser importance to the client. It is the purpose of this aspect of the feedback and recommendation session to define all goals, focusing primarily on the shared goals. Once everyone has articulated goals, it is crucial that the family or individuals to be seen in treatment agree on goals that become the direct and overt focus of treatment. Parents' agreement is very important in this regard, as they are more likely to follow through with treatment if they agree with the hoped-for outcome. Specifics about goal setting and prioritization are discussed in another chapter.

Preparation for Treatment

If the family agrees to return for therapy or counseling, they need to be prepared for the parameters of treatment. Although issues of confidentiality were already discussed when the parents rendered informed consent, it is good practice to reiterate the limits of confidentiality at this time. Care is taken to inform parents about reporting laws, the duty to warn, the duty to protect, and the duty to report (Brems, 1996). The boundaries of treatment are explained thoroughly, as much of the success of the child's work hinges on the parents' cooperation. As such, clinicians review their rules about cancellations (e.g., no more than three in a given period of time), no-shows (e.g., no more than two), being on time, payment (i.e., how much, when it is expected), and commitment to treatment in general (i.e., not undermining the work of the clinician). The frequency and length of future sessions is decided, as well as an estimated overall length of treatment. It is helpful to settle on a certain number of sessions after which time the family meets again as a whole to renegotiate and evaluate treatment and progress so far. The importance of consistency and timeliness in coming to scheduled appointments is stressed and explained. Policies about fees, payment schedules, cancellations, and no-shows are reemphasized. Finally, it is important is to acknowledge that although the parents have the legal right to the child's records and to be updated on treatment progress, the clinician generally does not disclose specific contents of what the child talks about or does while in the playroom. Therapists may also need to reiterate that they cannot serve as parents' therapists but are available to parents in other capacities (Kottman, 2002). To maximize the likelihood of consistent and conscientious follow-through, clinicians may highlight the potential effects on the child in case parents choose to undermine treatment. By the time the family leaves, they should have no unanswered questions about procedures, policies, ethics, and legal issues related to the treatment plan or treatment process.

Summary and Concluding Thoughts

The intake interview is a lengthy process that serves several purposes. First, it is used to glean as much information about the identified client and family as possible. Second, it serves to build rapport and to interest the family in treatment. Third, it sets the stage for therapy or counseling by informing and educating the family about their presenting concern from a professional perspective, providing the family with a thorough set of recommendations for treatment procedures and goals, and thoroughly preparing the family for the therapeutic process that is yet to come. A well-executed and prepared intake interview provides the family with a feeling of trust and safety that makes them more likely to return. It answers their questions and alleviates their anxieties about the counseling process.

Once treatment has begun, it is important to keep in close touch with the parents to keep them interested and involved. This is best accomplished through regular session updates with the parents. The frequency of updates varies depending on the type of case. More complex cases might require that updates occur every two weeks; for many cases, monthly updates suffice. Session updates have a twofold focus. First, they serve as a means for the clinician to assess whether the child is making changes at home and at school by soliciting this information from the parents. Second, session updates serve as a means for the clinician to keep the parents interested in the child's treatment by filling them in on noted progress and explaining the therapeutic process that is taking place. What is not done is discussion of specific content or play activity. For some parents, session updates do not suffice. They may be quite emotionally needy themselves, or they may be faced with social circumstances that are overwhelming. With these parents, the clinician takes on the additional and perhaps more active roles, such as providing emotional and logistical support.

"Given the importance of parents in the lives of children, it seems vital that any kind of professional intervention in relation to the child should be concerned with supporting and strengthening the parents" (Fine and Gardner, 1991, p. 33). By listening to parents' needs (Chethik, 2003) and reflecting their feelings (Kottman, 2002), the child's clinician can become such an important emotional support. This is true especially for parents for whom session updates do not suffice to maintain enough motivation to keep bringing a child to counseling. Although a child clinician cannot become the parent's therapist as well, she or he can nevertheless help parents through making appropriate therapy or counseling referrals, hooking them up with social support networks, assessing them for eligibility for social services (e.g., financial support, respite care for children) and helping them to apply for these, and being generally supportive and understanding. Often, just being willing to listen to parents' concerns is sufficient to help them feel supported and understood.

The approach the clinician takes with parents in such supportive work does not come from a deficit perspective, even if the family is in crisis. Instead, it focuses on empowering parents—on helping them recognize that they can bring about change and can influence their own and their children's fate and adjustment to difficult circumstances. It is best in such work to recognize the interconnectedness of family roles, functions, relationships, and behavioral patterns and to be sensitive to each family's unique needs and requirements. Families are not a group of independent individuals; rather, they are a system and have to be dealt with from that perspective (Becvar and Becvar, 2005; Gunn, Haley, and Lyness, 2007). Further, families are not an independent unit; rather they are thoroughly tied into a culture and environment that again represents an interdependent context that must be considered for the family and parents to feel understood, represented, and supported.

7

Supplementary Assessment Strategies

with Mark E. Johnson

> *States Parties shall take all appropriate measures to ensure that the child is protected against all forms of discrimination or punishment on the basis of the status, activities, expressed opinions, or beliefs of the child's parents, legal guardians, or family members.*
>
> —Article 2.2 of the UN Convention on the Rights of the Child

Once the intake interview has been completed, the care provider is left with a wealth of information that needs to be organized, understood, and utilized to develop the best possible treatment plan for the child. However, although many questions were answered during this interview, it is not uncommon that some remain unanswered. These are often best addressed through supplementary assessments, such as obtaining school records and previous treatment records, consulting with other professionals, and conducting psychological evaluations. Clinicians should not hesitate to receive permission from the child's legal guardians for these types of assessments, as they can fill in information gaps that might prove crucial to successful treatment. A summary of relevant sources of additional information is shown in Table 7.1. It is evident from inspection of this table that there are two modes of additional data collection. First, the counselor can gain access to records that already exist, either from the child's school(s) or from the child's previous service provider(s). Second, the therapist can gain additional information by asking for further evaluation, either in the form of consultation with and treatment by other professionals or through additional psychological assessment.

School Records

School records are the most accessible records and are often of great value in that they may validate or clarify information gathered during the interview. School records

170

Table 7.1   Sources of Additional Information

Type of Record or Service	Type of Professional or Test
Obtaining Existing Information	
School Records	• educational/academic tests • psychological evaluations • teachers' observations • teachers' ratings • sociograms
Previous Treatment Records	• therapy/counseling • hospitalization • medicine • hearing • speech
Creating Additional Information	
Referral Sources/Consultations	• medicine • pediatrics • neurology • speech • audiology • developmental psychology • classroom observation
Psychological Assessment	• mental status examination • behavior rating forms • personality assessment • projective testing • achievement testing • intelligence testing • neuropsychological testing

can only be obtained if appropriate releases were obtained from the child's legal guardians, which can also be used to communicate with the child's teacher(s). School records are particularly helpful when presenting problems include issues of attention or concentration, peer relationships, learning difficulties, developmental concerns, separation anxiety, deterioration of grades, frequent parental meetings with teachers or principals, behavior problems at school, or referral of the child by school personnel. However, as children spend a large part of their lives within the school setting, obtaining records from the educational environment—be that preschool, Head Start, kindergarten, or grade school—may be necessary for all children.

The most obvious components of school records are the child's grades and test scores on standardized educational or academic achievement tests. This information provides data about the child's intellectual potential and correlated achievement. However, these scores can also be used to investigate whether there was a significant change in a child's performance, when this change occurred, and external factors to which it might be tied. For instance, a sudden drop in grades after a change to a new school or teacher might reveal that a child is having difficulties adjusting to a new environment. A drop in performance after a hospitalization that resulted from a severe head injury during an episode of physical abuse toward the child may indicate either that the child missed much material while hospitalized or that the child's neurological system was compromised. Vast differences in academic achievement versus actual cognitive capacity can give clues about the child's emotional state or the possibility of specific developmental disability. Although many of these hypotheses need to be investigated further through additional testing or consultation, school records may be the crucial documents that point the way for the clinician to consider these factors. In addition to academic testing and grades, school records also contain psychological evaluations. Access to these assessments can save the counselor from repeating them unnecessarily and may provide new insights and information that did not emerge during the intake interview. Further, the very existence of such evaluations in a school records indicates that there have been concerns about this child in the school setting.

Communication with the child's teachers often provides much insight. Teachers, especially in the lower grades, tend to know their students very well, have an appreciation of changes in their pupils, and can compare the child to peers in the same classroom. They are generally very willing to share their observations and tend to be able to verify or dispute information obtained from parents. Although not entirely objective, teachers are less subjective than parents in their evaluation and tend to have a standard against which to compare a child. It is also possible to ask teachers to evaluate the child formally through the use of behavior rating scales and checklists (more detail below). Further, teachers sometimes are able to provide sociograms of the child's classroom. It is important to remember not only to talk to current teachers, but also to interview previous teachers. This is especially helpful when the behavior of a child appears to have changed or a current teacher is the person raising complaints.

Teachers are best involved when the presenting problem is relevant to the child's school performance, such as in cases of attention deficit hyperactivity disorder, learning disability, or developmental disability. In these situations, a phone interview with a teacher can be an unobtrusive yet valuable source of information that neither stigmatizes the child nor takes much time. Getting information from more than one teacher provides additional corroboration or validation of information collected from all individuals. One final reason to contact schools and teachers has to do with treatment implementation. Teachers tend to be more cooperative with treatment recommendations that involve them or their classroom if they were part of the assessment period and feel that they had some input.

Despite the advantages of obtaining school records, this discussion would not be complete without also mentioning disadvantages of involving schools and teachers. Contacting schools for records, and especially communicating directly with teachers, makes them aware that a child has been identified as having "a problem." The risk thus becomes one of creating a self-fulfilling prophecy, especially if the teacher never perceived the child as problematic to begin with. In instances in which the presenting problem of the child appears clearly contained outside of the classroom, a release of school records should be weighed carefully against the potential risk of marking the child. If there appears to be some question about the child's academic performance but no concern about peer relationships and classroom behavior, the least intrusive approach might be simply to obtain a release of records, without communicating with teachers.

Previous Treatment Records

Although it appears obvious that a clinician would obtain previous treatment records for a child, this is probably one of the most neglected sources of information available. The reticence to obtain previous treatment records is partly due to long waiting periods, as many agencies take a long time to respond to requests for information. In fact, it is not unusual to have to follow up written requests with a telephone call to receive any records at all. Nevertheless, these data are very important, and utilizing them can save much time and expense for the child, family, and service provider. It is not sufficient to obtain releases merely if the child previously has had mental health services. It is very common for parents to take children who evidence some problematic behavior or affect to physicians or pediatricians. Therefore, the investigation of medical records can often be quite illuminating. Further, speech problems or hearing deficits can contribute to problems or behavior that appears psychological or emotional in nature. For instance, it is not uncommon for very young children who present with slight developmental delays to have ear infections that have prevented them from hearing well enough. Because of this hearing deficit, these children develop more slowly, not because of an emotional problem, but rather because of a physiological problem. Obtaining records from physicians can clarify these types of etiologies.

Obtaining records from hospitals where the child may have been hospitalized is also important. Not only is it possible that the emotional trauma of being separated from parents has contributed to a child's difficulties, but it is also possible that hospital personnel have noted behaviors that are still present or exacerbated. The trauma of hospitalization at a young age should not be underestimated, and hospital records may help the counselor assess how traumatic the experience was for the child. For instance, one child who presented for treatment had a prolonged hospital stay at age 5. He was an inpatient for 6 weeks and, during that time, had no contact whatsoever with his family. Upon his return to the family, extended family members frequently commented on the personality change he had undergone. Whereas before, he was fun-loving and outgoing, he now was shy, reserved, and afraid to seek out others for simple interactions. He tended to play by himself and was most comfortable alone or around adults. Clearly, the experience of being hospitalized had a great effect on this child's psychological adjustment and must be considered in understanding the etiology of his current presenting problem and in treatment planning.

Referral Sources and Consultation

Just as it is important to realize that past treatment records—medical, psychological, academic, or otherwise—provide a wealth of information that might otherwise be missed, it is crucial to recognize when a presenting problem might be beyond a therapist's expertise and requires a referral to another professional. There are many common childhood problems a mental health professional should not encounter without making a medical contact. This contact may simply consist of a release of information if the family had previously sought medical consultation for the same problem; it may involve a consultation with a medical professional; or it may necessitate a referral to and subsequent collaboration with a physician, pediatrician, psychiatrist, or neurologist. Examples of disorders requiring such action include, but are not necessarily limited to, enuresis, encopresis, tic disorders, attention deficit hyperactivity disorder, eating disorders, severe depression, and psychosis. The rationales for involving a medical practitioner are slightly different from disorder to disorder. For instance, with regard to enuresis and encopresis, a referral to a physician is important to rule out a physiological reason, as opposed to a psychological one, for the child's inability to exercise control over bladder or sphincter. Children with symptoms of anorexia, bulimia, overeating, or rumination often need to be evaluated for weight issues and nutritional deficits; blood tests can ascertain that they have no severe vitamin or mineral deficiencies and that their electrolytes are properly balanced. Thus, while the referral for elimination disorders happens to rule out a functional or physiological cause, the referral for eating disorders occurs to rule out negative consequences of the disorder as far as physical well-being is concerned. For disorders of attention or psychoses, the primary reason for referral has to do with assessing the need for medication to relieve the negative side effects of the severe symptomatology that is often involved. Tic disorders may have neurological bases and therefore should never be treated without a thorough examination by a neurologist.

It behooves the mental health practitioner to identify a few physicians in the community to whom referrals can be made. A positive working relationship between the counselor and medical professional can facilitate the referral, is easier for the child and family, and results in cooperation. These types of professional relationships can often be started successfully by asking other mental health care providers for references to physicians who appear most capable of forming such a liaison. Then a letter, followed by a phone contact, can pave the way for a good working relationship. It is best also to have such a relationship with a child psychiatrist. Pediatricians and family practitioners are next in order of preference, with general practitioners after that. Once a relationship has been forged with one of these types of physicians, they can assist with making more specialized referral recommendations, such as for neurology or surgery.

Medical referrals are not the only sources of consultation in the work with children. Speech and hearing deficits can significantly affect children's psychological well-being; therefore, a referral is crucial for any concern about a child's speech or hearing. Many child guidance centers across the country provide these services, as do many schools. Thus, these referrals can often be made at low cost to the family. The relative payoff if an actual speech or hearing problem is detected is worthwhile indeed. If developmental delays appear to be present but speech and hearing evaluations are negative, it is a good idea to involve a developmental psychologist. Although mental health service providers have some understanding of human, and especially child, development, it is not their area of expertise. Developmental psychologists are specifically trained to assess a child's developmental appropriateness, assessing children's developmental levels across many domains, including language, social adjustment, fine and gross motor movement, cognition, emotional expression, and others.

Finally, one easy consultation that is often neglected is direct observation of the child in the classroom. This observation involves a conference with the teacher as well and can generally be conducted by the counselor herself or himself. This is not a referral in the usual sense, but it does move the assessment of the child beyond the therapy room. In conducting observations in the classroom, the therapist receives firsthand information about the child's peer relationships, involvement in the classroom, learning capacity, interactions with teachers, and general behaviors in a structured and challenging setting. Further, it can corroborate information obtained from the child or family. This process is similar to obtaining releases of information for school records or conversations with teachers but is preferable, as the information is obtained firsthand and independent of another individual's assessment or interpretation. Details about how to do classroom observations are beyond the scope of this book; however, many sources of information are available (e.g., Shapiro and Clemens, 2005; Shapiro and Kratochwill, 2000).

Psychological Assessment

A final excellent source of creating additional knowledge about a child for etiological understanding and treatment planning is that of psychological assessment. Literally hundreds of tools have been developed to help clinicians learn more about children and their families in an objective manner (Sattler, 2005). These tests can be grouped into several large categories:

- mental status examination
- behavior rating forms
- achievement testing
- intelligence testing
- objective personality testing
- projective personality testing
- neuropsychological testing

These categories are ordered according to the amount of specialized training necessary to utilize the tests contained within each. In other words, the farther down on the list the strategy is that is desired for further assessment, the more crucial it is to identify a professional who is appropriately qualified through specialized intensive training to render the service. Specifically, mental status exams and behavior rating scales can be administered by any conscientious counselor or therapist who has thorough familiarity with the procedure and interpretation of data derived from it. On the other hand, the use of projective tools is restricted to professionals who have taken several courses covering tests. Finally, neuropsychological testing can be conducted only by neuropsychologists whose entire graduate (or postdoctoral) training was devoted to the study of neuropsychology. Table 7.2 provides an overview of minimum qualifications necessary for the various categories of psychological testing. The approach taken in Table 7.2 may be perceived as very conservative. However, in considering that important treatment decisions can be based on the findings derived from such instruments, it become clear that such conservatism is more than justified.

Inspection of Table 7.2 reveals that the only mental health professionals who are qualified to administer psychological testing beyond the level of mental status exams

Table 7.2   Minimum Qualifications Required for Various Types of Psychological Assessment

Category of Testing	Minimum Qualification
Mental Status Examination	Master's degree in a mental health service profession and thorough familiarity with mental status procedures
Behavior Rating Forms	Master's degree in a mental health service profession and thorough familiarity with the chosen instruments
Achievement Testing	Master's degree in a mental health service profession and formal training in the use of the chosen test
Intelligence Testing	Doctoral degree in an applied mental health service profession (i.e., clinical, counseling, or school) and formal training in the use of the chosen test
Objective Personality Assessment	Doctoral degree in an applied mental health service profession (i.e., clinical, counseling, or school) and formal training in the use of the chosen test
Projective Personality Testing	Doctoral degree in clinical or counseling psychology and formal training in the use of the chosen test
Neuropsychological Testing	Doctoral degree in neuropsychology or doctoral degree in clinical or counseling psychology with postdoctoral training in neuropsychology

or behavior rating forms are those trained within the field of psychology. Although counselors, clinical social workers, or psychiatrists are capable of providing excellent therapeutic services for children, they were not trained to conduct psychological testing. Much specialized and formal classroom instruction is necessary for this purpose, and neither social work nor psychiatry provides such training. Nevertheless, a broad understanding of the categories of psychological assessment tools is important for any mental health professional, if only because it is helpful when it comes to making a referral or reading an assessment report. What follows is a brief discussion of some of the major instruments by category to provide a broad understanding of commonly used assessment tools for children. In this discussion, more emphasis is placed on the categories of tests called "Mental Status Examination" and "Behavior Rating Scales," as these two categories are amenable for use by most mental health professionals who are willing to read more about these procedures.

Mental Status Examination

A mental status examination is not a psychological assessment tool in the true sense. It actually tends to fall more in the realm of assessment tools utilized by physicians or psychiatrists. Nevertheless, conducting a mental status examination with children is a skill every mental health care provider who works with children needs to have. The mental status exam provides a context in which to gather certain types of information. It structures what type of behavior, affect, cognition, and so forth, to look for when working with a child. Because there are several well-accepted components of a mental status exam, its conduct also facilitates communication among professionals, as it provides a focus for questioning and a structure for reporting (Morrison and Anders, 1999).

Although the mental status exam has distinct categories of information, it is an interview that can be conducted in a very structured or a very informal manner, depending largely on the style of the individual clinician and the needs and age of the child that is being assessed (Casat and Pearson, 2001). Entire books have been written on the subject and should be referred to for specific details if the clinician plans to use this strategy (Goodman, 1994). In fact, formal checklists exist that can be used for the purposes of conducting and recording this type of interview (Dougherty and Schinka, 1989). A brief outline of the crucial components of mental status interviews is provided here. The primary categories of a children's mental status exam always include, not necessarily in this order, appearance and level of physical activity, mood and affect, sensorium and perception, cognitive functioning, health and development, behavior, interpersonal relations, self-concept, and coping strategies and psychological defenses. For each of these broad categories several subsections of exploration and assessment exist. A sampling of these is outlined in Table 7.3.

Appearance and Level of Physical Activity.   This category involves information that need not be inquired about but rather is gleaned from behavioral observations. It directs the counselor's attention to factors such as a child's height and weight, grooming and hygiene, manner and style of dress, eye and hair color, posture, gait, psychomotor movement, and physical characteristics such as scars, bruises, physical handicaps, and prosthetic devices. Several of these characteristics are simply descriptive, whereas others can be evaluated with regard to appropriateness or can be rated and further defined. Specifically, traits such as eye and hair color are simply described. Hygiene and grooming can be rated as to whether they are appropriate given societal health standards and grooming habits. Size, weight, and height can be judged according to their developmental and health appropriateness. Motor movement must be further defined as agitated, fidgety, unusual, normal, or as including tics, tremors, or motor abnormalities.

Overall, the assessment of appearance and physical activity of children can give many clues about them. For instance, physical characteristics such as dirty clothing, unkempt appearance, or emaciation can be overt signs of parental neglect. Unusual scars, large numbers of bruises, and seductive or cowering body postures can be the first evidence of abuse. Particularly small size, abnormal height and weight can point toward health problems or developmental problems that can affect the child's psychological adjustment.

Mood and Affect.   This information can often be solicited through observation as well as some cautious questioning of the child. It assesses a child's primary emotions, paying attention to clinical signs of depression, anxiety, fears, and phobias, but also simply assessing how cheerful, optimistic, angry, irritable, hostile, friendly, or antagonistic a child is during the interaction with the clinician. The stability of these moods needs to be described, especially if the clinician notes that moods appear to fluctuate widely and change quickly. Affect needs to be rated with regard to its range and its appropriateness to the topic of conversation or the theme of play activity and should be described with regard to its most outstanding features. As such, judgments need to

Table 7.3 Components of Mental Status Examinations for Children

Main Components of Exam	Subcomponents
Appearance and Physical Activity	• size, height, and weight • mannerisms and habits • type and cleanliness of dress • body, hair style, and hygiene • notable physical characteristics • psychomotor movement
Mood and Affect	• predominant emotion • range and appropriateness of affect • variation in mood or affect • fluctuation of moods
Sensorium and Perception	• orientation (time, place, person) • reality appraisal • functioning of senses • hallucinations
Cognitive Functioning	• intelligence • complexity and type of thought • academic performance • speech and verbalization • reality of thought and delusions
Health and Development	• physical well-being • medical history • developmental appropriateness
Behavior	• general patterns of conduct • self-destructive behavior • hobbies and interests
Interpersonal Relations	• family relationships • peer relationships • adult relationships
Self-Concept	• esteem and confidence • self-identity and appraisal • values, ideals, and goals
Coping Strategies and Psychological Defenses	• capacity for coping • types of strategies • behavioral manifestations of coping and defense

be made about whether affect is blunted or restricted, labile or rigid, dramatized or constricted. It is also important to note whether the child is comfortable in the expression of affect. It is not uncommon for some families to have unwritten rules about the appropriateness of some affects over others. Thus, a child may be quite at ease with affects that are positive and may show appropriate expression in that realm. However, as the same child encounters negative affects, expression may be inhibited and clearly uncomfortable for the child.

Sensorium and Perception.   This realm of functioning has to do with a child's contact with reality and orientation to surroundings and can be observed or directly questioned. With regard to orientation and awareness, even very young children need to have awareness of where they are in time and space, as well as of who they are. They should be able to provide their name and age, tell the counselor where they are or where their family lives, and say during what part of the day (morning, afternoon, evening) the interview is taking place. Older children are much more sophisticated about this information and should be able to name the current date and approximate time (within about 30 minutes to one hour), know the name of the clinic where the interview takes place, state their full address, identify by name their primary caretakers and teachers, and share information about themselves that goes beyond name and age.

With regard to reality contact, the functioning of the child's senses must be assessed. This is important in that malfunctioning of certain senses can result in severe developmental delays that, in turn, may affect psychological adjustment. Thus, the child's ability to hear, see, feel, speak, and taste can be inquired about. It is also interesting to note any obvious preferences of certain senses. Some preferences are developmentally driven. Infants, for instance, prefer to utilize their sense of taste in the exploration of new surroundings. Clearly, such a preference in a 4-year-old would be somewhat disturbing. Similarly, whereas the sense of touch is an important one for the 8-year-old who explores the new therapy environment, an adolescent is more likely to explore simply through the use of the sense of vision.

Further, and perhaps more important, the therapist ascertains if the child can differentiate fantasy from reality and that there is no hallucinatory process in any of the realms of sensing. Fantasy can be differentiated from reality to some degree already by age 3; however, full separation may occur as late as age 8. Hallucinations are important to rule out through direct questioning if the presenting problems include related concerns by parents and teachers, such as excessive fantasy life, distractedness that appears and disappears suddenly, nightmares or night terrors, and physical concerns or strange physical sensations. Finally, the child's level of consciousness must be assessed through questions about loss of consciousness, such as fainting or blacking out. The intrusiveness of certain environmental stimuli into the child's consciousness must be assessed and gives clues about the child's level of distractibility and ability to pay attention. Dissociations or similar lapses in consciousness need to be recorded, and the presence of seizure disorders must be inquired about.

Cognitive Functioning.   The first category of information within the realm of cognitive functioning concerns itself with intelligence, cognitive complexity, and memory. The amount of formality that is used to make these assessments can range from using formal intelligence testing to making judgments based on the child's verbalizations, grammatical correctness, and logic of thought. The clinician can ask the child to perform simple tasks such as counting backwards from 10 to 0 (or from 100 to 0 by intervals of three, depending on the child's age), can ask the child to interpret simple proverbs such as those included in the Wechsler Intelligence Scale for Children (see below), and can assess memory by asking for recall of birthdays, breakfast food on the day of the interview, and similar questions. Much information can be assessed through simple conversation that challenges the child to converse in different topic areas. Abstracting ability can generally best be evaluated by observing the child's problem-solving skills and problem awareness.

The exploration of speech and verbalizations also falls into this category. The counselor can pay attention to the spontaneity of the child's speech, the adequacy of word choice and word finding, and the age appropriateness of the child's language. Academic performance is an important topic to inquire about and must be seen in relation to the child's estimated (or formally assessed) level of intelligence. Academic performance can simply be inquired about with the child or parents or can be formally reviewed through school records.

Once the normal cognitive processes of the child have been assessed, it is necessary to evaluate the presence of cognitive features that may be pathological in nature, such as delusions, preoccupations, and obsessions. These thought contents need to be specified with regard to the topic that is prevalent. Common themes that emerge in children include guilt, violence, religion, spirits (demons, ghosts, devils), worthlessness, persecution by peers, and physical complaints. Additionally, the child's thought processes must be evaluated in terms of coherence, circumstantiality, tangentiality, neologisms, unusual associations, and blocking or evasiveness; distortions such as overgeneralization, catastrophizing, black-white thinking, perfectionism, and mind reading should be noted. Finally, the effects of the child's cognitive processes on judgment and level of insight must be estimated.

Health and Development.   This category of information relies on observation, releases of information to receive medical records and conversation with the child or parents. The child's current and past level of health must be assessed through inquiry about past illnesses, accidents, and hospitalizations. The child must be observed to make judgments about developmental appropriateness in the areas of cognition, emotional differentiation and expression, interpersonal relationships, self-development, language, fine and gross motor movement, and morality. Health and development in combination may be used to obtain important information about the possibility of fetal alcohol spectrum disorder (FASD). Suspicions about FASD based on the child's health, appearance, and developmental delays should be corroborated through an interview with the child's (preferably biological) parents. General health and developmental information were discussed in detail in chapter 3 and are not repeated here.

Behavior.   Information about a child's behavior can best be gathered through careful observation and talking to parents and teachers, with general patterns of conduct as the primary focus. The therapist notes information about how a child reacts during activities, how well a child can manipulate toys and execute tasks, how a child responds to frustration, how well a child delays gratification, whether a child withdraws or seeks to be the center of attention, and whether a child behaves aggressively or meekly. Behavioral tones can include apathy, distractibility, unresponsiveness, demandingness, withdrawal, histrionics, manipulation, and so on. Also in the realm of behavior are patterns such as overeating, bingeing and purging, refusing food, and other self-destructive acts. Acting out behaviors and involvement with legal authorities are behavioral issues, as are school truancy and suspension. If these are of concern, their exact nature and the setting in which they occur must be noted. Their history needs to be inquired about, and the nature of the actions should be described in detail (e.g., aggressiveness toward peers, fire setting, lying, stealing, cruelty to animals). Leadership ability versus follower characteristics is included as well, and hobbies and interests should be noted in detail.

Interpersonal Relations.   This category includes a thorough assessment of peer, adult, and family relationships. As this aspect of the mental status exam is redundant with the type of information that should already have been collected during the intake interview, it is not discussed in further detail at this time.

Self-Concept.   Information in this category often becomes obvious simply through carefully observing the child with this aspect of personality adjustment in mind. Two important components of self-concept—self-esteem and self-confidence—are often clearly expressed in play and in the interaction with the counselor. A self-confident child explores the playroom and makes spontaneous verbalizations directed toward the therapist, whereas a child with little confidence may remain reticent, withdrawn, and unable to exhibit spontaneous behavior or speech. Sometimes children with low levels of confidence overcompensate by being destructively exploratory or overly garrulous without maintaining safe boundaries and limits. Similarly, self-esteem helps the child regulate actions in the playroom and toward the counselor. It emerges in the child's play, especially when play becomes self-revealing. A child with healthy self-esteem is be much more willing to try a new task or play with an unfamiliar toy than a child with little self-esteem, who might be afraid of handling materials incorrectly.

Self-identity, also an important aspect of self-concept, is often directly expressed through play and conversation. A child who has established some preferences and who has a sense of identity is assertive in choice of materials and conversation topics. The child who lacks identity has no preferences and takes cues from the environment to determine behavior and selection of toys or activities. This latter child tries to please the adult by performing in line with what she or he perceives the counselor to desire. Realistic self-appraisal is an important characteristic that children must develop early in life. It is demonstrated by the realistic choice of materials that reflect that the child has knowledge of what she or he can and cannot do, without shying away unnecessarily from new situations. Thus, a 4-year-old who has developed appropriate self-appraisal within her or his developmental capacity will not choose to play with a 1,000-piece puzzle or a game that necessitates reading skills. A 4-year-old who has not developed realistic self-appraisal and has negative self-esteem will not even explore the puzzle or the game and might shy away even from small blocks that require manual dexterity. She or he will be unwilling to try new things for fear of failure. On the other hand, another 4-year-old who has not developed a realistic sense of self-appraisal might be unaware of the inappropriateness of certain toys and will attempt to use them over and over, will fail, and then will feel devastated.

Finally, self-concept also includes the establishment of values, goals, and ideals. Absence of any of these features points toward lack of self-identity that would be appropriate to the child's developmental level and may indicate that the child has not experienced an environment that has helped her or him learn about consistency, boundaries, and limits. Care must, of course, be taken to assess these aspects of self in a developmental context. Thus, a 3-year-old may have the goal of establishing some autonomy in the choice of play materials while interacting with the counselor by refusing what is offered. A 10-year-old, on the other hand, may be more interested in using toys that can be manipulated to simulate interaction among peers, such as puppets or dolls in schoolhouses. An adolescent chooses activities and materials that help to establish direction and sophisticated skill building, such as the use of clay or paints.

Coping Strategies and Psychological Defenses.   The information in this category refers to the child's capacity and means to deal with a number of circumstances that might evoke anxiety or feelings of threat or danger. Such circumstances may involve placing the child in a new, uncommon situation; asking the child to meet a stranger; taking the child out of a familiar environment; or placing the child in situations that facilitate or evoke needs or desires that the child may consider inappropriate or impossible to have met. A final coping situation is that which stimulates or encourages strong affect. The mental status situation may fit any of these descriptions, as it involves a new situation, a stranger, a conversation, questioning that may stimulate material that is difficult or painful for the child, and interactions that may evoke strong affects. Observation of the child in any of these circumstances can give the therapist clues not only to whether a child is capable of coping but also to preferred strategies. Capacity for coping is evidenced by a child's ability to tolerate and adapt to new situations and strangers, to express difficult needs and desires and accept them as important, and to express even strong or difficult affects as they emerge and to deal with them (e.g., diffuse them) successfully. Examples of positive coping within each of these circumstances are provided below.

> A 7-year-old boy was asked to go with the examiner to the play therapy room for a mental status exam. He was hesitant to go with the stranger and asked his mother whether it was okay to go. When she indicated that she knew the person and that she was safe to go with, he accompanied the examiner to the room. Once in the room, he was quiet and withdrawn for a few moments. When he was encouraged to explore the room, he cautiously picked up toys, looked at materials, and put his hands in some of the puppets. He occasionally glanced at the examiner to ascertain that his behavior was acceptable, and as he realized that it was, he became more active and engaged in some puppet play and conversation. Finally, he was able to engage the examiner in his play and was open to being questioned.

This is an example of a child who evidenced good coping skills in a new situation. He first ascertained that the situation was safe by checking with his mother. He then separated from the familiar adult and entered the new setting. Once he had established that the stranger was safe and that the environment was stimulating, he relaxed and opened up.

> A 6-year-old girl who had been seen in therapy for some time often felt very needy and emotionally depleted. During one particular session, immediately after her father had been suddenly and dishonorably discharged from the military, she was overwhelmed by her fear of abandonment and her need for nurturance. She spontaneously began telling a story of a mouse who woke up one morning and was all alone. The mouse was very frightened because it was breakfast time and she was hungry, but no one was around to make her breakfast. After some

affective discharge of fear and need, the girl finally indicated that the mouse must now be strong and find her own food. She related that the little animal got out of bed and went to a neighbor's house to tell them that she was home alone and hungry. The neighbor invited her in for breakfast, and the little mouse felt better.

This is an example of a child coping effectively with the emergence of strong needs (need for nurturance and being taken care of). Although the resolution is not one of complete autonomy (the mouse did not find her own food, after all, but rather received it from a helper), it nevertheless indicated that the child had accepted the necessity for the need (the mouse had to find the food because it could not survive without it) and was aware of the need for her to take some part in ascertaining that the need would be met (the mouse got out of bed and went to a neighbor's house).

A 12-year-old boy was seen for an initial interview and had engaged in exploration for some time. He was now attempting unsuccessfully to work a crane set in the playroom. It was obvious that he was becoming very frustrated because he could not figure out how to work the crane. As his frustration mounted, he appeared tempted to smash the crane. He then talked loudly to himself, saying, "Okay, maybe this thing is broken. Why do they have broken toys in here? It's not nice to make kids play with broken stuff. Maybe it's not broken; maybe there is a trick to how it works." At that point, he turned to the examiner and asked whether there was a trick and whether he could get some help.

This is an example of a child who is coping successfully with a strong affect that was about to get out of control. As he was about to break the crane set in anger, he calmed himself by using a strong voice and self-talk to vent his frustration. As soon as he began to talk, he visibly relaxed. He talked himself through the height of his affect and then was able to ask for help.

Children do not always cope this successfully, and sometimes, rather than coping, they use defenses to deal with difficult situations. Kohut (1984) reconceptualized defenses as protective mechanisms that are used by people to protect vulnerabilities within themselves. In the work with children, this conceptualization of the defensive process appears extremely appropriate. Children are very vulnerable in the sense that they still depend on adults in their environment to help them care for their physical and psychological needs. If the availability of adults for such purposes is sparse, children have to learn to protect themselves through various mechanisms. These self-protective mechanisms are commonly called defenses. A large number of defenses have been identified in the work with both adults and children, and it is impossible to define and mention all of them here. The reader is referred to works by Anna Freud (1946) and Henry Laughlin (1983) for details. However, a few defensive strategies are common enough to warrant some discussion and examples, as the mental status examiner must note not only whether a child has the capacity to cope but also the types of self-protective, or defensive, strategies a child employs in coping situations.

Many children try to use avoidance, evasion, or diversion when difficult coping situations arise. For instance, a 9-year-old girl was playing interactively with the examiner with the dollhouse family. She placed the mother and father figures in their large bed and removed their clothing. When the examiner asked what the adults were doing, the girl began to cough and said that her throat was hurting. She asked for a glass of water and moved away from the dollhouse. This child's behavior in response to the (somewhat unfortunate) question of the examiner was one of diversion ("my throat hurts") and avoidance (moving away from the dollhouse). Similar maneuvers may include the child's failure to respond to a question, the sudden changing of topics, or the attempt to direct the interaction or questioning to avoid certain subject matter. Somatization was also involved in this example of diversion, in that the chosen diversion was one of physical complaining. This is not uncommonly noted in family interviews, when children suddenly develop stomachaches or headaches as their parents or siblings begin to discuss sensitive information or are fighting loudly.

Withdrawal is a common defense in children and may range from quite severe manifestations to lesser forms of contact shunning. For instance, a child might hide in a closet when a difficult affect emerges. Often, children engage in a defense called undoing. In the following instance, the child had allowed a piece of information to emerge that she or he would then like to make go away. An 11-year-old girl was painting at the easel, indicating that she was drawing her family. She proceeded to draw her father and her brother. Her father had no hands and was placed in the bottom left corner of the page. Her brother was prominently placed in the middle of the page with big muscles and a smirk on his face. She drew her mother and herself only as an afterthought. She then stated that her brother always got all the attention in the family and that he was big and fat. Suddenly, she blushed and stopped talking. She turned away from the examiner, back to her painting, and covered the entire page in black paint. This child had revealed some information that was too difficult for her to deal with at this time. She undid her action by literally covering it up.

Acting out is another common defense among children. If the boy in the crane example had not been able to calm himself through self-talk and asking for help, but had actually kicked the crane, he would have evidenced acting out. However, acting out does not always occur in the context of angry affect, but might also be used to relieve anxiety or fear. For instance, one 6-year-old girl who suffered from severe abandonment anxiety frequently kicked toys and furniture in the playroom when this fear emerged through play activity. Other defenses that are frequently used by children but are not elaborated on here include denial, rationalization, internalization, projection, and projective identification.

This discussion of the mental status exam reveals that there is some degree of overlap between a mental status exam and an initial interview in terms of the information included. The mental status exam, however, is more evaluative in the sense of making actual judgments about appropriateness of cognition, perception, behavior, and so forth, whereas the initial interview simply collects information. There is also some overlap between the mental status exam and a good conceptualization. However, the mental status exam merely lists the findings and judgments from each area, whereas the conceptualization goes beyond the mere listing of data by making sense of how the data fit together to *explain* the presenting problem of the child and to determine a useful treatment plan. This difference is crucial and must be understood. A mental status exam is a tool for obtaining and organizing information. A conceptualization, on the other hand (as discussed in chapter 8), is a tool to integrate information and understand a child and family system.

Behavior Rating Forms

First in the category of assessment instruments (as summarized in Figure 7.1), behavior rating scales, forms, and checklists provide an easy means of obtaining more objective data about a child's behavior than interviews and observations. They are focused on expanding the pool of information about behavior in various types of settings from the perspective of the adults in the child's life. They do not provide information about personality, intelligence, or ability but are strictly focused on overt behavior. A variety of such scales exists, and most were developed in such a manner that they are best cross-validated by administering them to all primary caregivers, including parents, baby-sitters, and teachers. A brief overview of the most commonly used behavior rating scales are provided here, with a discussion of each instrument's purpose, psychometric properties, special features, and information about purchasing sources.

Achenbach System of Empirically Based Assessment.   This assessment (ASEBA; Achenbach and McConaughy, 1996) comprises a set of integrated scales that assess children's behavioral problems and social competencies by having behaviors and actions rated by a variety of informants. Separate forms are available for parents or guardians (Child Behavior Checklist), teachers (Teacher's Report Form, Caregiver-Teacher Report Form), and clinicians (Direct Observation Form, Semistructured Clinical Interview for Children and Adolescents, Test Observation Form). A Youth Self-Report (YSR; Achenbach and Rescorla, 2001) is available for older children ages 11 to 18 years.

Depending on age of the child, either the Child Behavior Checklist for Ages 1½ to 5 with Language Development Survey (CBCL/1½–5/LDS; Achenbach and Rescorla, 2000) or the Child Behavior Checklist for Ages 6 to 18 (CBCL/6–18; Achenbach and Rescorla, 2001) is to be completed by adults who know the child well. The CBCL/1½–5/LDS consists of 99 problems, descriptions of problems, disabilities, concerns, and best things about the child. Item ratings are summed to yield scores representing seven syndromes: Emotionally Reactive, Anxious/Depressed, Somatic Complaints, Withdrawn, Attention Problems, Aggressive Behavior, and Sleep Problems. Further, two second-order scales, Internalizing and Externalizing, and a global scale, Total Problems, are calculated. This form also yields five scales that are related to the DSM-IV-TR diagnostic categories of Affective Problems, Anxiety Problems, Pervasive Developmental Problems, Attention Deficit/Hyperactivity Problems, and Oppositional Defiant Problems. Finally, the CBCL/1½–5/LDS incorporates items to help identify possible language delays.

The CBCL/6–18 consists of 20 competence items within the realms of activities, social relations, and school performance; 118 specific behavioral and emotional problems; and two open-ended questions for reporting additional problems. The competence areas are based on the competence demonstrated as compared to other children in activities in which the child participates. The problem areas are rated on a three-point scale ranging from 0 (not true) to 2 (very true or often true), based on their presence. Eight areas of problem behaviors and three areas of social competence are derived from the responses. The problem behavior areas are descriptively labeled Aggressive Behavior, Anxious/Depressed, Attention Problems, Rule-Breaking Behavior, Social Problems, Somatic Complaints, Thought Problems, and Withdrawn/Depressed. Some of these problem areas are combined into two second-order sub-

Category and Instruments

Behavior Rating Forms

Achenbach System of Empirically Based Assessment (ASEBA)

Child Behavior Checklist for Ages 1½ to 5 with Language Development Survey (CBCL; Achenbach and Rescorla, 2000)

Child Behavior Checklist for Ages 6 to 18 (CBCL; Achenbach and Rescorla, 2001).

Teacher's Report Form (TRF; Achenbach and Rescorla, 2001)

Youth Self-Report (Achenbach and Rescorla, 2001)

Caregiver-Teacher Report Form for Ages 1½ to 5 (C-TRF; Achenbach and Rescorla, 2000).

Direct Observation Form for Ages 5 to 14 (DOF; Achenbach and Rescorla, 2001)

Semistructured Clinical Interview for Children and Adolescents Ages 6–18 (SCICA; McConaughy and Achenbach, 2001)

Test Observation Form (TOF; McConaughy and Achenbach, 2004)

Behavior Assessment System for Children-2 (Reynolds and Kamphaus, 2002, 2004)

Parent Rating Scales (BASC-2 PRS)

Teacher Rating Scales (BASC-2 TRS)

Self-Report of Personality (BASC-2 SRP)

Structured Developmental History (BASC-2 SDH)

Student Observation System (BASC-2 SOS)

Parent Relationship Questionnaire (PRQ)

Conners Third Edition (Conners, 2008)

Parent Rating Scale

Teacher Rating Scale

Self-Report Rating Scale

Vineland Adaptive Behavior Scales (VABS-II; Sparrow, Cicchetti, and Balla, 2005

Achievement Testing

Kaufman Test of Educational Achievement (KTEA-II; Kaufman and Kaufman, 2004a)

Peabody Individual Achievement Test-Revised/Normative Update (PIAT-R/NU; Markwardt, 1997)

Wechsler Individual Achievement Test, Second Edition (WIAT-II; Wechsler, 2001)

Wide Range Achievement Test, Fourth Edition (WRAT4; Wilkinson and Robertson, 2006)

Woodcock-Johnson III Normative Update Complete (W-J III; Woodcock, McGrew, and Mather, 2007).

Intelligence Testing

Kaufman Assessment Battery for Children, Second Edition (KABC-II; Kaufman and Kaufman, 2004b)

Kaufman Brief Intelligence Test, Second Edition (KBIT-2; Kaufman and Kaufman, 2004c)

Peabody Picture Vocabulary Test, Fourth Edition (PPVT-III; Dunn and Dunn, 2006)

Stanford Binet Intelligence Scale, Fifth Edition (SB5; Roid, 2003a, 2003b)

Wechsler Abbreviated Scale of Intelligence (WASI; Wechsler, 1999)

Wechsler Intelligence Scale for Children, Fourth Edition (WISC-IV; Wechsler, 2003)

Wechsler Preschool and Primary Scale of Intelligence, Third Edition (WPPSI-III; Wechsler, 2002)

Objective Personality Assessment

Beck Youth Inventories, Second Edition (BYI-II; Beck, Beck, and Jolly, 2005)

Children's Depression Inventory (CDI; Kovacs, 1992)

Multidimensional Anxiety Scale for Children (MASC; Marsh, 1997)

Personality Inventory for Children Family of Tests

Personality Inventory for Children-2 (PIC-2; Lachar and Gruber, 2001)

Personality Inventory for Youth (PIY; Lachar and Gruber, 1995)

Student Behavior Survey (SBS; Lachar, Wingenfeld, Kline, and Gruber, 2000)

Piers-Harris Children's Self-Concept Scale, Second Edition (Pier-Harris 2; Piers, Harris, and Herzberg, 2002)

Projective Personality Assessment

Children's Apperception Test-Animal (CAT-A; Bellak and Bellak, 1949)

Children's Apperception Test-Human (CAT-H; Bellak and Bellak, 1965)

Draw-A-Person (DAP; Goodenough, 1926)

Kinetic House-Tree-Person Drawing Test (K-HTP; Burns, 1987)

Rorschach Inkblot Test (Rorschach, 1942)

Thematic Apperception Test (TAT; Bellak, 1943)

Tell-Me-A-Story (TEMAS; Constantino, Malgady, and Rogler, 1988)

Figure 7.1   Assessment Instruments

scales: Internalizing and Externalizing. A Total Problems score is obtained by summing most of the problem behaviors. The three competence areas are Activities, Social, and School, and a global scale, Total Competence, can be calculated. This form also yields six scales that are related to the DSM-IV-TR diagnostic categories of Affective Problems, Anxiety Problems, Somatic Problems, Attention Deficit/Hyperactivity Problems, Oppositional Defiant Problems, and Conduct Problems. For both CBCL versions, a profile is plotted that provides percentile ranks and T-scores for the child's performance in each area. Thus, a comparison of relative problem areas is easily accomplished by analyzing the profile obtained.

Additional forms can be used to supplement the data obtained through the CBCL. The Teacher's Report Form (TRF; Achenbach and Rescorla, 2001) is appropriate for use with children ages 6 to 18. It consists of 118 items, 93 of which correspond with items on the CBCL/6–18 and 25 of which are related specifically to school behaviors. Using the same rating scale as on the CBCL, teachers rate the child for presence of a behavior within the last two months. The TRF yields scores for the same eight syndromes, six DSM-IV-TR-related scales, and Internalizing, Externalizing, and Total Problems scales obtained from the CBCL. Additionally, the TRF yields scores for Academic Performance, Total Adaptive Functioning, Inattention, and Hyperactivity-Impulsivity. As with the CBCL, raw scores, percentiles, and T-scores are plotted on a profile for easy comparison of problem areas within the child and between the child and the normative sample. Similarly, a Caregiver-Teacher Report Form (Achenbach and Rescorla, 2000) can be used with children ages 1 1/2 to 5 years that parallels the CBCL/1 1/2–5/LDS.

To gain further information, the Direct Observation Form (DOF; Achenbach and Rescorla, 2001) can be used for children ages 5 to 14 years. The DOF consists of 96 problem items scored on a four-item scale and allows for an objective observer to observe the child in a natural setting. The DOF yields scores for On-task, Internalizing, Externalizing, and Total Problems. Additionally, six syndromes scales (Withdrawn-Inattentive, Nervous-Obsessive, Depressed, Hyperactive, Attention-Demanding, and Aggressive) can be calculated. The Semistructured Clinical Interview for Children and Adolescents Ages 6–18 (SCICA; McConaughy and Achenbach, 2001) provides questions and probes that guide the interviewer to rate the child on eight syndrome scales (Aggressive/Rule-Breaking Behavior, Anxious, Anxious/Depressed, Attention Problems, Language/Motor Problems, Self-Control Problems, Somatic Complaints, and Withdrawn/Depressed) as well as on the Internalizing, Externalizing, and Total Problems scales. Finally, the Test Observation Form (TOF; McConaughy and Achenbach, 2004) provides 125 items to which the counselor rates the child or adolescent on a 4-point scale ranging from 0 (no occurrence) to 3 (definite occurrence). The TOF yields scores on Withdrawn/Depressed, Language/Thought Problems, Anxious, Oppositional, and Attention Problems; Internalizing, Externalizing, and Total Problems; and DSM-IV-TR-related scale of Attention Deficit/Hyperactivity Problems. These additional forms can greatly enhance the confidence a therapist may have in the results. They can be invaluable in evaluating a child's behavior across several settings, information that may prove useful in determining a treatment plan. The ASEBA forms can be obtained through the University of Vermont, Research Center for Children, Youth, & Families, Burlington, VT 05401-3456; http://www.aseba.org.

Behavior Assessment System for Children-2. This instrument (BASC-2; Reynolds and Kamphaus, 2002, 2004) consists of a set of rating scales and self-report forms that were developed to assess the behaviors and emotions of children and adolescents: Parent Rating Scales (BASC-2 PRS), Teacher Rating Scales (BASC-2 TRS), Self-Report of Personality (BASC-2 SRP), Structured Developmental History (BASC-2 SDH), and Student Observation System (BASC-2 SOS). Three versions of the Parent and Teacher Rating Scales are available depending on a child's age (2 to 5, 6 to 11, and 12 to 21); they comprise 100 to 160 items and take 10 to 20 minutes to complete. Each item is a brief description of behavior, rated on a four-point scale from "never" to "almost always." Depending on the form used, the PRS provides scores on five adaptive scales (Activities of Daily Living, Adaptability, Functional Communication, Leadership, Social Skills) and nine clinical scales (Aggression, Anxiety, Attention Problems, Atypicality, Conduct Problems, Depression, Hyperactivity, Somatization, and Withdrawal). The TRS forms yield scores on these same scales (except Activities of Daily Living), as well as information about Learning Problems and Study Skills. For both versions, second-order scales can be calculated, including Externalizing Problems, Internalizing Problems, Adaptive Skills, and Behavior Symptoms Index; a School Problems factor can be calculated on the basis of TRS responses. Additionally, with the use of the test publisher's software program, the following content scales are available: Anger Control, Bullying, Developmental Social Disorders, Emotional Self-Control, Executive Functioning, Negative Emotionality, and Resiliency.

The BASC-2 Self-Report of Personality has four versions, one for young children (ages, 6 to 7), one for children (ages 8 to 11), one for adolescents (ages 12 to 21), and one for college-aged adults (ages 18 to 25). The young children's version involves asking questions to which the children responds with a yes or no. The other versions rely on the child or adolescent completing the questionnaire. Depending on the form used, the BASC-2 SRP yields 18 primary scales (Alcohol Abuse, Anxiety, Attention Problems, Attitude to School, Attitude to Teachers, Atypicality, Depression, Hyperactivity, Interpersonal Relationship, Locus of Control, Relations with Parents, School Adjustment, Self-Esteem, Self-Reliance, Sensation Seeking, Sense of Inadequacy, Social Stress, and Somatization); four content scales (Anger Control, Ego Strength, Mania, and Test Anxiety); and five composite scales (Emotional Symptoms Index, Inattention/Hyperactivity, Internalizing Problems, Personal Adjustment, and School Problems) All forms include validity scales that help examiners evaluate the quality of the responses.

To supplement these forms, the Student Observation System (SOS) provides a system for recording observations of a child's behavior in both timed and untimed situations. The SOS assesses both adaptive and maladaptive behaviors and can be used by a variety of trained individuals. Information gathered from this form can help to fine-tune the assessment process by helping identify behaviors in different settings. The Structured Developmental History (SDH) provides the equivalent of a thorough intake form, asking detailed questions about various areas in the child's life, including social, psychological, educational, and medical history. It can be completed in a structured interview with the parent or caregiver or can be sent home with the adult to be completed and returned at the next session. Finally, the Parent Relationship Questionnaire (PRQ) provides an avenue to quantify a parent's perspective on the parent-child relationship. The PRQ has two forms, one for preschool children (ages 2 to 5) and one for children and adolescents (ages 6 to 18). Taking 10-15 minutes to complete, it yields scores on the following scales: Attachment, Communication, Discipline Practices, Involvement, Parenting Confidence, Satisfaction with School, and Relational Frustration The BASC-2 is available from Pearson Assessments; http://ags.pearsonassessments.com.

Conners Third Edition.   These ratings scales (Conners, 2008) have seen their greatest use in evaluating and screening children for disruptive behaviors and in tracking these children's progress in treatment. For use with children and adolescents ages 6 to 18, three different forms are available for gaining and comparing data from multiple informants, namely, parents, teachers, and self. Long and short versions exist for parents (the long version with 110 items and the short with 43), teachers (the long version with 115 items and the short with 39) and self (the long version with 99 items and the short with 39). Each of the items represents a problem behavior that is rated on a 0 to 3 scale on the basis of degree to which the child has demonstrated it within the last month. Depending on which form and the length of form chosen, the Conners third edition yields scores on the empirical scales of Hyperactivity/Impulsivity, Executive Functioning, Learning Problems, Aggression, Peer Relations, Family Relations, and Inattention; DSM-IV-TR associated scales of ADHD Hyperactivity/Impulsivity, ADHD Inattentive, ADHD Combined, Oppositional Defiant Disorder, and Conduct Disorder; validity scales of Positive Impression, Negative Impression, and Inconsistency Index; two global indices of Conners third edition ADHD Index and Conners 3 Global Index; two screening items for Anxiety and Depression; impairment scales in the domains of Schoolwork/Grades, Friendships/Relationships, and Home Life; and critical items for Severe Conduct. Additionally, the two indexes, ADHD Index and Global Index, can each be used independent of all other items to provide quick measures of ADHD and general psychopathology, respectively. *T*-scores are calculated for all subscales, scores of 61 to 65 being regarded as mildly atypical, 66 to 70 as moderately atypical, and 70 or greater as markedly atypical. The Conners 3 is available from Multi-Health Systems; http://www.mhs.com.

Vineland Adaptive Behavior Scales-II.   These scales (VABS-II; Sparrow, Cicchetti, and Balla, 2005) represent a second revision and reorganization of the Vineland Social Maturity Scale (Doll, 1953). It is a measure of adaptive behavior administered to an adult who is very familiar with the child's behavior in various settings. Adaptive behavior for the purposes of this instrument is defined as the child's assessed ability to perform the types of daily activities that would make her or him self-sufficient with regard to social interaction and personal care. Three versions are administered to a parent or caregiver. The first version (Survey Interview Form) is administered as a semi-structured interview in which open-ended questions elicit in-depth information that is rated. The second version (Expanded Interview Form) provides additional questions to be administered during a survey to gain more in-depth information on the child. The third version (Parent/Caregiver Rating Form) covers the same content as the Survey Interview Form, but does so using rating scales. Additionally, there is a version (Teacher Rating Form) that is completed by a teacher or day care provider.

Within this context, the VABS-II assesses the child's behavior in five domains: Communication, Daily Living Skills, Socialization, Motor Skills, and Maladaptive Behavior. The Communication Domain includes the three domains of child's Receptive, Expressive, and Written; Daily Living includes the three domains of Personal, Domestic, and Community; Socialization includes the three domains of Interpersonal Relationships, Play and Leisure Time, and Coping Skills; Motor Skills includes the two domains of Fine and Gross; and the Maladaptive Behavior Index rates three domains of Internalizing, Externalizing, and Other. The VABS-II may be obtained from Pearson Assessments; http://www.ags.pearsonassessments.com.

Achievement Testing

Achievement tests are standardized and well-normed tests that are administered in a highly structured and well-prescribed manner. Their purpose is the assessment of a child's achievements in various academic or vocational skills that are a result of instruction or training. Most commonly, skills such as reading, comprehension, spelling, and mathematics are evaluated; however, literally hundreds of other specialized achievement tests exist to measure a child's accomplishment in a particular area of instruction (e.g., foreign language, science, logical thinking, geography, problem solving). Achievement test administration must be conducted by a well-trained examiner, as it has to be exactly identical from child to child. Only under such highly standardized, structured conditions can information be obtained in such a manner that a child's scores can be confidently compared to those of other children of the same age to make judgments about delayed or accelerated performance. Achievement tests are often administered when there are questions about the possibility of specific developmental disabilities, such as dyslexia. Further, their administration is warranted if a child has to participate in remedial instruction (Anastasi, 1997). Achievement tests cannot provide information about personality or behavior, nor should they be misunderstood as evaluating a child's *aptitude*, such as intellectual functioning. Much controversy exists about the cultural fairness of these tests, and this must be considered for children of ethnic backgrounds other than White American. Achievement tests are structured in such a way that they tap information and achievement that are most relevant in the dominant White culture, neglecting important aspects of minority cultures (Sattler, 2001). A brief overview of some of the most commonly used achievement tests is provided here, with discussions of their purpose, psychometric properties, and special features and information about purchasing sources and restrictions.

Kaufman Test of Educational Achievement-II.   This achievement test (KTEA-II; Kaufman and Kaufman, 2004a) is for children ages 4 1/2 years through 25 years, is individually administered, and takes approximately 15 to 80 minutes, depending on the version. Two versions of the KTEA-II are available: a Comprehensive Form and a Brief Form. The Comprehensive Form yields norm-referenced scores on six composite scores, namely, Reading (comprised of Letter & Word Recognition, and Reading Comprehension), Reading-Related (Phonological Awareness, Nonsense Word Decoding, Word Recognition Fluency, Decoding Fluency, Associational Fluency, and Naming Facility), Math (Math Concepts & Applications, and Math Computation), Written Language (Written Expression and Spelling), Oral Language (Listening Comprehension and Oral Expression), and Comprehensive Achievement. The subtests have excellent scoring criteria. For instance, spelling is not merely scored as correct or incorrect, as for instance on the WRAT-3, but rather it is evaluated with regard to phonemic, morphemic, and syllabic components of each word. Thus, scoring takes into consideration not only error or actual performance but also the process through which the child arrived at a given response (Kaufman and Kaufman, 2004a). The Brief Form is used for quick screening and yields norm-referenced standard scores on Reading, Written Expression, and Mathematics. It does not provide the in-depth analysis that is available through the use of the comprehensive version.

Scoring results in standard scores for each subscale, as well as a composite score, all of which have a mean of 100 and a standard deviation of 15. Raw scores can also be converted into age and grade equivalents to investigate the child's relative grade placement or age performance. KTEA-II Manual and Kit are available to appropriately credentialed professionals from Pearson Assessments; http://www.ags.pearsonassessments.com.

Peabody Individual Achievement Test-Revised/Normative Update.   This is an individually administered scale (PIAT-R/NU; Markwardt, 1997) for children enrolled in kindergarten to high school that requires approximately 60 minutes. It consists of six subscales that assess Reading Recognition, Reading Comprehension, Spelling, Mathematics, General Information, and Written Expression. Administration is facilitated by the use of an easel format and by the fact that three of the six subtests are arranged in multiple-choice format. Only the Reading Recognition task requires the child to read out loud, and the General Information task requires the child to give spoken answers, as opposed to pointing. Reading Recognition assesses the child's ability to use letters and read aloud; Reading Comprehension assesses the ability to make sense of what is read by the child; Spelling assesses the ability to identify letters of the alphabet and spell words; Mathematics assesses the ability to do simple computation, recognize numbers, and use simple geometry and trigonometry principles; General Information assesses the general fund of knowledge acquired by the child in areas such as arts, sports, science, and social studies; and Written Expression assesses written language skills for two levels: prewriting skills (grades K to 1) and ability to write a story (grades 2 to 12) (Markwardt, 1997). The PIAT-R/NU also provides a Written Language Composite (combining Spelling and Written Expression subtests) and a Total Reading score (Reading Recognition and Reading Comprehension subtests).

Administration of the PIAT renders grade equivalents, age equivalents, standard scores with a mean of 100 and a standard deviation of 15, and percentile ranks. Scores can be calculated for each of the five subtests, as well as for overall achievement performance. The PIAT-R/NU Manual and Kit are available to appropriately credentialed professionals from Pearson Assessments; http://www.ags.pearsonassessments.com.

Wechsler Individual Achievement Test, Second Edition.   An individually administered test (WIAT-II; Wechsler, 2001), it assesses achievement of individuals aged 4 to 89 in nine areas: Word Reading, Pseudoword Decoding, Mathematics Reasoning, Spelling, Reading Comprehension, Numerical Operation, Listening Comprehension, Oral Language, and Written Expression. Word Reading assesses sight-reading ability; Pseudoword Decoding involves ability to decode words; Mathematics Reasoning evaluates problem-solving strategies and skills and includes items from geometry, measurement, and statistics; Spelling assesses encoding and spelling ability; Reading Comprehension measures skills that include comprehension of detail, sequence, cause-and-effect relationships, and inference; Numerical Operations assesses ability to write dictated numerals and solve basic addition, subtraction, multiplication, and division problems and problems with whole numbers, fractions, decimals, and algebraic equations; Listening Comprehension incorporates reception of sounds and words, as well as comprehension as demonstrated by understanding details to draw inferential conclusions; Oral Language gauges the ability to name targeted words, describe scenes, give directions, and explain steps in a sequential task; and Written Expression addresses idea development and organization, as well as writing mechanics. The scales also provide four composite scores for Mathematics, Reading, Language, and Writing. These scales meet the regulatory requirements of the Individuals with Disabilities Education Act (IDEA) and can be useful for learning disabilities screening, special education placement, and curriculum planning. The items are structured in such a way that they provide information about not only test takers' achievement but also their problem-solving strategies. The WIAT-II is directly linked to the WISC-IV and WPSSI-III, allowing for more precise comparisons between achievement and ability scores when both instruments are administered. Such comparisons provide more in-depth analysis of the tested child, leading to more individualized treatment plans. Administration time is 30 to 60 minutes, depending on the age and abilities of the child. Standard scores are derived (mean = 100, standard deviation = 15), and normative data are provided for fall, winter, and spring grades for more precise comparisons.

An abbreviated version of the WIAT-II is available that includes three subtests from the complete instrument. These three subtests (Spelling, Word Reading, and Numerical Operations) can be administered in 10 to 20 minutes. The WIAT-II and the WIAT-II-A are available from the Psychological Corporation; http://www.psychcorp.com.

Wide Range Achievement Test, Fourth Edition.   This test (WRAT4; Wilkinson and Robertson, 2006) is a very popular achievement test because its administration time is brief and the procedure is relatively easy, especially considering that it is an individually administered instrument. Overall administration time is approximately 15 to 30 minutes. The test is considered most useful for quick screenings, as it renders only four subtest scores: Word Reading, Sentence Comprehension, Spelling, and Math Computation. The Word Reading subtest assesses ability to pronounce or recognize words and letters; the Sentence Comprehension subtest measures ability to understand information included in sentences; Spelling subtest focuses on ability to write from dictation; and Math Computation subtest evaluates knowledge of simple counting and computation. None of the subtests provides detailed or sophisticated information about the examinee, and the use of the test appears inappropriate for clinical assessment beyond screening.

Items on the WRAT4 are arranged in ascending order of difficulty. Scores obtained for each subscale can be expressed as stanines, normal curve equivalents, scaled scores, age equivalents, grade equivalents, percentiles, and standard scores. The latter four types of scores are most commonly used and interpreted. Age and grade equivalents indicate what chronological age or grade the examinee would be expected to be, based on the score that was obtained on a given subtest. Standard scores compare the child's performance to that of other children the same age and have a mean of 100 and a standard deviation of 15. Percentiles indicate what percentage of all children in that age range perform worse than the examinee.

Unlike the previous version of the WRAT, in which the test had two separate levels, one for younger children and one for older individuals, the current version consists of only one form that can be used with individuals ages 5 to 75. Two alternative forms of the WRAT4 are available for instances in which multiple testing is needed. Results from these two forms can be combined to provide more detailed information about an individual's performance. The WRAT4 Manual and Kit are available from Psychological Assessment Resources; http://wwwparinc.com.

Woodcock-Johnson III Normative Update Complete.   This test (WJ-III; Woodcock, McGrew, and Mather, 2007) represents a revision of the commonly used Woodcock-Johnson Psycho-Educational Battery (Woodcock and Johnson, 1989) and consists of two co-normed but distinct tests: the WJ-III Tests of Achievement and the WJ-III Tests of Cognitive Abilities. These tests are designed to evaluate an individual's general intellectual ability, specific cognitive abilities, scholastic aptitude, oral language, and academic, achievement. The Complete Battery can be used with individuals ages 2 to 90, with administration time varying depending on the form used and the age of the individual. The Tests of Cognitive Abilities consist of twenty-one subtests that assess the following eight cognitive abilities: Long-Term Retrieval, Short-Term Memory, Auditory Processing, Visual Processing, Comprehension-Knowledge, Fluid Reasoning, and Quantitative Ability. The Tests of Achievement consist of fourteen subtests that assess achievement within the four domains of Reading, Mathematics, Written Language, and Knowledge. The battery can be completed in two forms: standard or comprehensive. The standard form includes seven cognitive tests and eleven achievement tests; the comprehensive form includes administration of all subtests and yields more detailed information about strengths and weaknesses of the examinee. The Tests of Achievement have two alternative forms, allowing for repeated testing of the individual.

Cluster scores can be calculated on the basis of combinations of different subtests. For each cluster, standard scores with a mean of 100 and a standard deviation of 15 can be obtained and converted into percentile ranks. Grade-level scores are provided for the clusters, as well as for the individual subtest scores. In addition to inter-individual comparisons, intra-individual comparisons are available. For example, within the individual's achievement scores, comparisons are made to identify relative strengths and weaknesses. Further, the achievement subtests can be used in connection with the cognitive ability subtests to construct an ability-achievement profile that compares relative ability with actual achievement. The WJ-III is available from Riverside Publishing; http://www.riverpub.com.

Intelligence Testing

Intelligence tests are literally used for the purpose their name suggests: the evaluation of a child's intellectual performance. Originally, intelligence tests provided a global score of intelligence that did not assess or emphasize differential skills in various subcategories of intellectual functioning. In more recent decades, however, a more commonly accepted approach has been to differentiate at least verbal versus performance functioning. Intelligence as tested by these tools is supposedly an aptitude, not an achievement, and hence independent of instruction or training. Intelligence can theoretically be measured before any instruction has taken place in a child's life (of course, there are some obvious practical limitations to this theoretical idea). They are often used as screening instruments before other aptitude or achievement tests are administered. They are also used to identify or classify mental retardation. Intelligence tests share many features of achievement tests. For instance, their administration is equally rigidly standardized and to be followed exactly, they are lengthy, there is a question about their culture fairness, and they are used in the assessment of learning disabilities. One of the most recent uses of intelligence tests is in the area of neuropsychological assessment (along with a number of other tests). Like achievement tests, IQ tests cannot be used to assess personality or behavior. There are only a few intelligence tests, and the most common ones are outlined briefly, with a discussion of their psychometric properties and special features and information about purchasing sources. It is important to note that the intelligence tests that are described here are those used with populations of children that have no physical or sensory handicaps. Nevertheless, a number of intelligence tests have been developed over the years for use with children who have physical disabilities; who are blind, mute, or similarly specially abled; and who have special needs or concerns (Sattler, 2001, 2005).

Kaufman Assessment Battery for Children, Second Edition.   This test (KABC-II; Kaufman and Kaufman, 2004b) represents a significant revision from the earlier version. The most significant change is the incorporation of two theoretical models and the allowance for examiners to select the model most appropriate for their examinee. The first model is based on Luria's (Luria, 1973, 1976) neuropsychological model that excludes measures of acquired knowledge and yields a global score referred to as the Mental Processing Index (MPI). The second model is based on the Cattell-Horn-Carroll (CHC) approach to categorizing specific cognitive abilities (Carroll, 2005; McGrew, 2005). This model includes measures of acquired knowledge and yields a global score of Fluid-Crystallized Index (FCI). The CHC model is preferred for most children; however, the Luria approach is recommended for children from bilingual or other backgrounds that may have influenced knowledge acquisition and verbal development. Prior to administration, the examiner must select which model to follow, as this dictates which subtests are administered.

The KABC-II is intended for children ages 3 to 18. In addition to the global scales described above and an additional global index (Nonverbal Intelligence), the KABC-II yields from one to five scales, depending on the age level of the child and the model chosen by the examiner. For children age three, only global scales are provided; for children ages 4 to 6, scale scores for Learning, Sequential, Simultaneous, and Knowledge are obtained; and for children aged 7 to 18, an additional scale of Planning is obtained. To obtain these scales, up to seventeen subtests are administered. All KABC-II subscales have a mean of 10 and standard deviation of 3. The global scales have means of 100 and standard deviations of 15.

Administration is highly standardized but facilitated through a convenient easel format. Nevertheless, it requires thorough training and practice on the examiner's part. The KABC-II Manual and Kit are sold to appropriately credentialed professionals by Pearson Assessments; http://www.ags.pearsonassessments.com.

Kaufman Brief Intelligence Test, Second Edition.   This test (KBIT-2; Kaufman and Kaufman, 2004c) serves as a brief screening instrument to obtain quick information about a child's intelligence and can be used with individuals ages 4 to 90. It takes approximately 20 minutes to administer and provides measures of verbal (crystallized) and nonverbal (fluid) intelligence. Verbal intelligence is measured through the Crystallized scale that contains both Verbal Knowledge and Riddles subtests; nonverbal intelligence is measured through the Fluid scale that includes a Matrices subtest, which consists of pictures and abstract designs. Similar to other recent intelligence tests, all items are contained on an easel. Results are provided in the familiar format of a mean of 100 and standard deviation of 15; percentile ranks are provided as well. Comparisons between verbal and nonverbal scores can provide the basis for further assessment for learning disabilities. As with other quick screening tools, this instrument can provide the basis for further assessment, can answer secondary questions, and can be used to verify previous test results. The KBIT-2 can be obtained from Pearson Assessments; http://www.ags.pearsonassessments.com.

Peabody Picture Vocabulary Test, Fourth Edition.   This test (PPVT-IV; Dunn and Dunn, 2006) is a quick way to measure an individual's receptive vocabulary and to screen for verbal ability. It is normed for ages 21 to 90, consists of 228 sets of four pictures, and takes approximately 10 to 15 minutes to administer. In administering the test, the child is shown four pictures while the tester says a single word; the child then indicates which picture best represents the word stated by the tester. Arranged on an easel, test administration is straightforward and easy. Two alternative forms are available for situations in which retesting is needed to assess changes or in which the child has previously taken the test. Standard scores (mean = 100; standard deviation = 15), NCEs, stanines, and age and grade equivalents are available. The PPVT-IV can be obtained from Pearson Assessments; http://www.ags.pearsonassessments.com.

Stanford Binet Intelligence Scale, Fifth Edition.   This version (SB5; Roid, 2003a, 2003b) represents the fifth edition of the original Binet Intelligence Scale, which was the first test of this nature to be developed and used in the history of intellectual assessment. The SB5 is appropriate for use with individuals ages 2 to adult. Conceptually, the SB5 is based on a three-level hierarchical model of intelligence. In this model, an overall Intelligence Quotient is obtained at the first level. This score supposedly measures g, or general ability, which comprises an individual's general cognitive makeup and cognitive complexity involved in problem solving. On the second level, the overall Intelligence Quotient is divided into verbal and nonverbal intelligence. The final level are the five cognitive factors of Fluid Reasoning, Knowledge, Quantitative Reasoning, Visual-Spatial Processing, and Working Memory, each of which are assessed through nonverbal and verbal means. These scores are obtained by administering a series of nonverbal and verbal subtests. However, in administering the SB5, examiners start with two subtests, namely, Object Series/Matrices and Vocabulary. The child's performance on these tests allows the examiner to individualize the test administration to maximize information gained while minimizing time. Then, administration of subtests proceeds by establishing ceiling performance (i.e., determining a point within each test beyond which the subject can no longer correctly respond to subtest items) and moving to the next subtest. This procedure of testing prevents frustration as it does not require children to move through all items of each subtest. Total testing time is approximately 60 to 90 minutes depending on speed of work and cognitive performance.

Parallel to the three-level hierarchical model, three levels of scores can be obtained from the SB5. For each subtest, a subtest score is derived with a mean of 10 and a standard deviation of 3. Scores can be combined according to second-level membership as outlined above to make up Verbal and Nonverbal IQ scores, which have means of 100 and standard deviations of 15. Combined, they result in the Full Scale IQ, also with a mean of 100 and a standard deviation of 15. Given these three levels of scores, there are three levels of interpretation. At the third level, the child's strengths and weaknesses can be assessed based on differential subscale performance. Second, analyzing the second-level scores, the child's relative strengths in larger subareas of cognitive functioning can be assessed. At the highest level, an appreciation of the child's overall cognitive functioning is gleaned. Testing with the SB5 is highly standardized and requires thorough training of the examiner. It follows a multistage testing model, in which performance on one of the subtests (namely, Vocabulary) is used to determine at which level to enter subsequent tests. The SB5 is available from Riverside Publishing; http://www.riverpub.com.

Wechsler Abbreviated Scale of Intelligence.   This scale (WASI; Wechsler, 1999) provides a quick screening tool for estimating an individual's verbal and nonverbal intelligence and can be used with individuals ages 6 to 89. The WASI can be administered with either four subtests (Vocabulary, Similarities, Block Design, and Matrix Reasoning) or two subtests (Vocabulary and Matrix Reasoning). Taking approximately 30 minutes to administer, the four-subtest form yields Verbal, Performance, and Full Scale IQ scores in the same manner as the WISC-IV and WPPSI-III. The two-subtest form takes about 15 minutes and yields only a Full Scale IQ score. Although the content is different, the format of these subtests is the same as their counterparts in the other Wechsler scales. Indeed, the WASI can be used to estimate Full Scale IQ scores on the more comprehensive Wechsler Scales. Results are provided in standard score format analogous to other Wechsler scales (mean = 100, standard deviation = 15). The WASI can be obtained from Harcourt Assessment; http://www.harcourtassessment.com.

Wechsler Intelligence Scale for Children, Fourth Edition.   This scale (WISC-IV; Wechsler, 2003) represents the third revision (first revised in 1974 and again in 1991) of the WISC, which was developed in 1949 as a downward extension for children ages 6 to 16 of the original Wechsler-Bellevue Intelligence Scale. The WISC-IV is based on the concept of global intelligence defined by Wechsler as the overall capacity to cope with and understand the world. As such, the concept of intelligence assessed through the use of the WISC-IV is one of a multifaceted, multidetermined global entity, as opposed to one well-defined and unique trait. The WISC-IV yields four composite scores, namely, Verbal Comprehension (including subtests of Similarities, Vocabulary, Comprehension, Information, and Word Reasoning), Perceptual Reasoning (subtests of Block Design, Picture Concepts, Matrix Reasoning, and Picture Completion), Working Memory (Digit Span, Letter-Number Sequencing, Arithmetic), and Processing Speed (Coding, Symbol Search, and Cancellation), as well as a Full Scale IQ score. The WISC-IV is appropriate for children ages 6 to 16 years.

The information derived from the Wechsler scale is multifold. Most obvious is the overall interpretation of the child's Full Scale IQ that provides an estimate of intellectual functioning. Next, performance on the four composite scores can be examined with information being derived not only about skills in each area but also about any discrepancies between the two subareas of intellectual functioning. Finally, inspection of subtest scores results in a profile of strengths and weaknesses. This profile analysis can be particularly helpful in assessing where a child evidences signs of problems in an academic or learning setting, versus where a child may be capable of adequate performance (Sattler, 2004).

The WISC-IV is administered according to a strictly standardized procedure. Entry level for each subtest is determined by a child's age. Ending of each subtest is determined by a cut-off criterion of a certain number of consecutively failed items. As in the SB5, testing procedures are such that administration of items clearly beyond the cognitive capacity of the child is avoided, thus minimizing examinee stress levels. Total testing time is approximately 60 to 90 minutes and can vary widely depending on number of items administered and on the speed of the work. Administration of the Wechsler scale results in scaled scores for each subtest, each of which has a mean of 10 and a standard deviation of 3. They are combined to result in four index IQ scores and one Full Scale IQ score. These IQs have a mean of 100 and a standard deviation of 15. The WISC-IV Manual and Test Kit are available from Harcourt Assessment; http://www.harcourtassessment.com.

Wechsler Preschool and Primary Scale of Intelligence, Third Edition.   This version (WPPSI-III; Wechsler, 2002) is the second revision (first revised in 1989) of the original scale developed by Wechsler in 1967 as a downward extension of the 1949 Wechsler Intelligence Scale for Children. The WPPSI-III was developed in such a way as to minimize gender, ethnic, and socioeconomic biases present in earlier versions. Further, it was revised to be easier to use and more aesthetically appealing to young children. It can be used with children ages 2 1/2 to 7 years. Its format is similar to the WISC-IV. As earlier versions, the WPPSI-III provides three types of IQ scores (Full Scale, Verbal, Performance). However, the current version also adds a General Language Composite (GLC) and, for older children, a Processing Speed Quotient (PSQ). The WPPSI-III includes fourteen subscales, several of which are optional and administered depending on examinee age. Verbal IQ includes the subscales of Comprehension, Vocabulary, Receptive Vocabulary, Similarities, Word Reasoning, and Information; Performance IQ includes Picture Completion, Coding, Matrix Reasoning, Picture Concepts, Block Design and Object Assembly; Processing Speed Quotient includes Coding and Symbol Search; and General Language Composite includes Picture Naming and Receptive Vocabulary. Subscale means are 10 with standard deviations of 3, and IQ, GLC, and PSQ means are 100 with standard deviations of 15. Testing procedure is standardized, requires thorough training on the examiner's part, and is highly similar to that of the WISC-IV (Sattler, 2004). Total testing time is approximately 90 minutes. The WPPSI-III Manual and Test Kit are available from Harcourt Assessment; http://www.harcourtassessment.com.

Objective Personality Assessment

Objective personality assessment tools are standardized tests that provide the counselor with information about a child's general level of functioning or about a specific subset of personality, such as mood, motivation, attitudes, self-concept, and so forth. Although items may be focused on some facets of a child's overt behavior, the instruments typically are not used to assess *behavior* per se, nor are they helpful in assessing ability or intelligence. Their primary purpose is to help the therapist understand the personality makeup of a child with regard to emotional, motivational, attitudinal, and interpersonal styles and functioning. These tools are usually normed and provide a means of comparing scores to population scores to allow for a judgment about a child's personality traits as compared to other children of the same age. The administration of these tests varies, some relying on parental reports and others relying on children's self-report. A brief overview of some commonly used personality measures for children follows, with a discussion of each instrument's purpose, psychometric properties, special features, and information about purchasing sources.

Beck Youth Inventories, Second Edition.   This instrument (BYI-II; Beck, Beck, and Jolly, 2005) consists of five separate self-report inventories for use with children ages 7 to 18. The five measures are the Beck Depression Inventory for Youth, Beck Disruptive Behavior Inventory for Youth, Beck Anxiety Inventory for Youth, Beck Anger Inventory for Youth, and Beck Self-Concept Inventory for Youth. Each of the BYI-II inventories consists of twenty statements about the respondent's thoughts, feelings, and behaviors and takes about 5 to 10 minutes to complete. The child taking the inventory answers how true each statement has been for her or him in the past two weeks. These scales are intended for screening children for emotional and social difficulties and can be used for monitoring treatment outcome. For each of the five inventories, norms allow for comparisons with similarly aged children, and profiles can be developed to compare the child across all five affective domains to determine particular problem areas. The Beck Youth Inventories are available from Harcourt Assessment; http://www.harcourtassessment.com.

Children's Depression Inventory.   This instrument (CDI; Kovacs, 1992) was developed to assess depressive symptoms among children ages 7 to 17. The CDI consists of twenty-seven items, each of which includes three sentences from which the child chooses the one that best describes her or him during the past two weeks. The CDI yields scores on five factors, namely, Negative Mood, Ineffectiveness, Negative Self-Esteem, Interpersonal Problems, and Anhedonia. Separate norms are provided for girls and boys, and for children ages 7 to 12 and ages 13 to 17. A short version of the CDI, consisting of ten items, provides a quick screening measure. The CDI is available from Multi-Health Systems; http://www.mhs.com.

Multidimensional Anxiety Scale for Children.   This tool (MASC; Marsh, 1997) was developed to provide comprehensive screening and assessment of anxiety symptoms in children and adolescents. Children respond to the 39 items in the MASC on a four-point scale that ranges from 0 (never true for me) to 3 (often true for me). The MASC is useful for children ages 8 to 19 years and takes approximately 15 minutes to complete. The MASC yields scores on four scales: Physical Symptoms (which include subscales of Somatic Symptoms and Tense Symptoms; Social Anxiety Scale (subscales of Humiliation Fears and Performance Fears); Harm Avoidance Scale (subscales of Perfectionism and Anxious Coping); and Separation/Panic. It also includes two global indexes, namely, Anxiety Disorders and Total Anxiety, as well as a validity index, Inconsistency, to identify random or careless responding. Standard t-scores are derived to allow comparisons with age-appropriate normative samples. A ten-item version of the MASC (MASC-10) is available and takes approximately five minutes to complete. The MASC-10 can be used in group settings for quick screening and can be used for repeat testing to evaluate treatment progress. The MASC and MASC-10 are available from Multi-Health Systems; http://www.mhs.com.

Personality Inventory for Children Family of Tests. This set of scales includes the namesake instrument, Personality Inventory for Children-2 (PIC-2; Lachar and Gruber, 2001); Personality Inventory for Youth (PIY; Lachar and Gruber, 1995); and Student Behavior Survey (SBS; Lachar, Wingenfeld, Kline, and Gruber, 2000). Each of the three instruments is an independently designed and validated instrument that can be used separately or combined to provide a multisource assessment of a child. Specifically, a parent or other adult completes the PIC-2; the child completes the PIY; and a teacher or other adult completes the SBS on the basis of the child's school behavior.

The Personality Inventory for Children (PIC-2; Lachar & Gruber, 2001) is the first complete revision of the PIC, an instrument with a research history that stretches back more than 40 years and through two previous forms of the test (Wirt, Lachar, Klinedinst, and Seat, 1977; Lachar, 1982). It is completed by a parent or other adult who is thoroughly familiar with a child ages 5 to 18 years (or older if they are still secondary school students living at home). The PIC-2 provides a thorough assessment of a child's behavior, affect, and cognitive status, as well as family climate. Two formats exist, Standard Format or Behavioral Summary. The Standard Format is completed in about 40 minutes, includes 275 test items, and is scored for nine adjustment scales: Cognitive Impairment, Impulsivity and Distractibility, Delinquency, Family Dysfunction, Reality Distortion, Somatic Concern, Psychological Discomfort, Social Withdrawal, and Social Skill Deficits. Each adjustment scale consists of two to four nonoverlapping subscales that can be scored for more content specificity. This format also includes three response validity scales: Inconsistency, Dissimulation, and Defensiveness. The PIC-2 Behavioral Summary is completed in about 15 minutes and includes the first 96 items of the longer format. The Behavioral Summary short adjustment scales correspond to eight of the nine adjustment scales from the Standard Format (all except Cognitive Impairment). In addition, three longer composite scales are derived for more sensitive measurement of change, namely, Externalizing, Internalizing, and Social Adjustment, and there is a Total Score.

The Personality Inventory for Youth (PIY; Lachar and Gruber, 1995) was designed to assess the emotional and behavioral adjustment of children and adolescents ages 9 to 19. Whereas the PIC is completed by an adult, the PIY is designed to be completed by the child. It consists of 270 items written approximately at a third-grade reading level to which responding children answer either true or false; it takes approximately 45 minutes to complete. The PIY provides scores on four validity scales and nine clinical scales. The validity scales measure inconsistent or random responding, faking bad, and defensiveness. The clinical scales correspond to those measured by the PIC-2, namely, Cognitive Impairment, Impulsivity and Distractibility, Delinquency, Family Dysfunction, Reality Distortion, Somatic Concern, Psychological Discomfort, Social Withdrawal, and Social Skill Deficits. Each clinical scale has two or three non-overlapping subscales, for a total of twenty-four subscales. Each subscale measures a more narrowly defined content dimension associated with the overall scale and thus provides more detailed information about the respondent. A screening short form is incorporated within the first eighty items. *T*-scores are calculated for each scale and subscale on the basis of gender norms but not age norms. For the clinical scales, *T*-scores of 60 and higher are interpreted, while more varied interpretation limits are provided for the subscale s and scales of response validity.

The Student Behavior Survey (SBS; Lachar, Wingenfeld, Kline, and Gruber, 2000) is a brief, multidimensional assessment of student adjustment for use in the evaluation of children and adolescents from grades K through 12 (five through 18 years of age). It consists of 102 statements rated on a 1 (never) to 4 scale (usually), and takes approximately 15 minutes to complete. The SBS provides fourteen scales: four scores assess a student's Academic Resources (Academic Performance, Academic Habits, Social Skills, and Parental Participation); seven others address Adjustment Problems (Health Concerns, Emotional Distress, Unusual Behavior, Social Problems, Verbal Aggression, Physical Aggression, and Behavior Problems); and the final three address Disruptive Behavior of clinical concern (Attention Deficit Hyperactivity, Oppositional Defiant, and Conduct Problems). Conventional, age- and gender-based *t*-scores are calculated, with *t*-scores of 60 and higher being interpreted and explicit interpretive language provided for the clinically significant *t*-score ranges on all scales. The PIC-2, PIY, and SBS can be obtained from Western Psychological Services; http://www.wpspublish.com.

Piers-Harris Children's Self-Concept Scale, Second Edition. This instrument (Piers-Harris 2; Piers, Harris, and Herzberg, 2002) was developed as a measure of children's psychological health. It consists of 60 items written at a second-grade reading level. The Piers-Harris 2 yields scores on six subtests, namely, Physical Appearance and Attributes, Freedom from Anxiety, Intellectual and School Status, Behavioral Adjustment, Happiness and Satisfaction, and Popularity. The questionnaire is completed by the child herself or himself and is appropriate for children ages 7 to 18 years. The instrument can be administered to individuals or groups and is an excellent screening tool that can be used with an entire classroom. The PHCSCS Manual and Kit can be obtained from Western Psychological Services; http://www.wpspublish.com.

Projective Testing

Projective testing provides a global approach to the assessment of personality that emphasizes a composite picture of a child's personality, as opposed to being trait-focused as are objective personality assessment techniques (Smith and Handler, 2007). Projective testing situations are highly unstructured because of the hypothesis that the lack of structure provides the child with the opportunity to project personal needs, affects, thought processes, conflicts, and characteristics onto the test situation. These features of a child's global personality are reflected in test performance so that the projective test is basically viewed as a screen onto which the child projects salient personality characteristics. Projective tests require a highly trained examiner who is familiar with personality theory as well as with detailed scoring procedures and theories of interpretation. Test administration always has to involve the child and is quite lengthy. Projective instruments have wide clinical utility despite the fact that reliability and validity data are often very dissatisfying or discrepant, depending on the source. Projectives are extremely useful testing tools; however, they are also the most commonly abused psychological instruments. This is so because they appear easy to use to the layperson but actually involve a high level of experience and sophistication in scoring and interpretation. The sole use of projective tools is rarely warranted. Rather, projectives are best used in conjunction with other personality assessment procedures, behavior rating scales, and personal interviews. Although some clinicians hire psychological technicians to administer the test, this is not recommended, owing to the wealth of information obtained through the actual testing interaction with the child. Many excellent books have been written about various projective assessment tools. A brief overview of some of the major projective tests is provided here, with a discussion of their purposes, special features, and information about purchasing sources.

Draw-A-Person Test.   Although originally developed as a quick screening measure of intelligence that did not require verbal interaction (DAP; Goodenough, 1926), upon repeated use, Goodenough noted that the picture drawn by the child often reflected important aspects of the child's personality style and functioning. Today, the DAP is used almost exclusively in the latter context and, in fact, is used very widely, being considered one of the top five projective instruments in use (Hammer, 1997; Handler, 1996). As the title implies, the DAP involves asking the child to draw a person. No more guidance beyond this instruction is provided, to make certain that the drawing situation remains ambiguous and unstructured so that the child can embellish it according to personal interpretations, needs, and desires. It is believed that the artwork created through this process reflects not only the child's overt approach and style but also unconscious material such as intrapsychic conflict, psychological defense, interpersonal adjustment, and similar personality features.

These characteristics are assessed through exploration and interpretation of various components of the child's completed drawing. Specifically, the placement of the drawing on the page, its orthographic features (e.g., pencil pressure, shading), its elaborateness, and its completeness are analyzed and used for interpretation. Much research has been done in all four of these areas and has resulted in many commonly accepted hypotheses about the meaning of various features expressed in a drawing. This body of literature provides an important backdrop for interpretation and must be updated constantly as new findings and understandings emerge. Further, the validity of these general symbolisms and meanings still has to be corroborated for each individual child through other tests and information obtained about and from the individual. Several well-accepted features that can be confidently assessed through the use of the DAP are self-concept, self-identity, coping styles, affect, and presence of psychopathology (Rabin, 1974). The test is an excellent tool for reticent or shy children who cannot be easily approached verbally. It is often used as a starting point for discussions of conflicts and has utility in tracking treatment progress and outcome. Again, as with other projectives, care has to be taken to refer to a properly credentialed, trained, and experienced examiner. This warning is even more appropriate about the DAP, as this is the single most commonly abused tool in terms of being used by individuals without adequate training. No ordered materials are necessary for the administration of the DAP, as all that is required is a clean white sheet of 8½ by 11-inch paper.

Kinetic House-Tree-Person Drawing Test.   This tool (K-HTP; Burns, 1987) was developed to expand on the DAP as used by clinicians today. Specifically, Burns developed this instrument to make the drawing technique that had found wide acceptance among mental health professionals through the DAP more amenable to additional interpretations that had to do with the child's or examinee's interactions with the environment, with other people, and with his or her own image. Thus, while the DAP is focused primarily on intrapsychic dimensions of personality, as discussed above, the K-HTP is more concerned about interpersonal dimensions (while also lending itself extremely well to intrapsychic interpretations). In being administered the KHTP, a child is asked to draw a house, tree, and person in the same picture while introducing some activity or action into the drawing. Burns suggests that the artwork derived from these instructions lends itself not only to all interpretations that have been discussed here with regard to the DAP but also to interpretations that have to do with the story line depicted in the picture, the type of action that is suggested, the placement of all objects on the page, and the relative distances of the objects from one another. Also, spontaneously introduced objects (e.g., a sun or clouds that are added to the picture though the instructions did not mention them) can be of symbolic and interactive value. The K-HTP represents a more dynamic assessment of the child's personality and considers more dimensions. However, it is a relatively new technique and therefore does not enjoy the research base that has been generated for other drawing techniques. Until more research is available on the topic, interpretation rendered from the K-HTP must be viewed with caution and within a wider context of information. Nevertheless, its conceptualization promises that this will become a major assessment tool for children.

An additional note is warranted about the fact that the K-HTP represents the merging of two other techniques that have found wide acceptance among clinicians, the House-Tree-Person Drawing Test (Buck and Hammer, 1969) and the Kinetic Family Drawing Test (Burns, 1982; Burns and Kaufman, 1970, 1972). The K-HTP combines these two established techniques in that it borrows the objects (house, tree, person) from one and the concept of introducing kinesthesis from the other. The merging of the two techniques allows the K-HTP to rely somewhat on the research that has been accumulated for these assessment procedures to date, providing additional support for its use. No ordered materials are necessary for the administration of the K-HTP, as all that is required is a clean white sheet of 8½ by 11 inch paper.

Rorschach Inkblot Test.   This personality assessment technique consists of ten inkblots, each printed on one cardboard card (Rorschach, 1942). The test can be administered to children as young as age 5, as well as to adults of any age. The inkblots that are still being utilized today were developed by Hermann Rorschach in 1921, and originally were conceived of as a measure of perception or imagination. However, Rorschach quickly recognized that his examinees varied greatly in their approach to the task of describing what they saw in the inkblots and began to explore the instrument as a psychological assessment tool of personality functioning. As such, the Rorschach is said to have utility in personality description, identification of type and severity of pathology, evaluation of coping ability, and general interpersonal and intrapsychic style.

In completing the Rorschach task, children are first asked to describe what they see in each card without any prompting. Once they have described their percepts for each inkblot, they are asked to elaborate on their original response, providing information about why they chose a particular percept and defining its location and boundaries. Some clinicians, in an attempt for additional data collection, then ask the child to choose a favorite and a worst card. The information gleaned from this administration process is complex and very difficult to interpret. It cannot be understood by the layperson but rather relies on a well-trained and experienced examiner. There are several ways of approaching the information, and four types of analyses are always included. These are called structural analyses, location analyses, content analyses, and sequence analyses. Norms have been developed for the first two approaches by various researchers and clinicians, including Rapaport, Klopfer, Beck, and Exner. Of these, Exner (1994, 2002; Exner and Erdberg, 2005) has been particularly successful in developing norms and standards for comparison across ages, genders, and diagnostic groupings that are now widely accepted and used by clinicians.

In a sequence analysis the examiner explores the child's responses in terms of when they occurred and how one percept may have affected another. Thus, if a child had a very disturbing association to one area of a particular inkblot, the clinician may evaluate the next response with regard to how the child dealt with that disturbance—specifically whether the child is withdrawing, becoming aggressive, getting depressed, and so forth. Content analysis refers to the symbolism or latent meaning of the percepts, especially in the context of the specific inkblot for which it was rendered. Examiners' overgeneralizations and abuses abound in the area of content analysis (i.e., it must be done cautiously and with care not to let the clinician's own associations intrude).

Location analysis refers to where in a blot a child sees something and whether the child has a well-balanced selection of responses that include either whole blots or parts of the blot. Finally, structural analysis of Rorschach responses involves the most complex process of interpretation. It first involves the use of an objective scoring system to which every single response rendered by the child is subjected. As such, each verbalization is scored with regard to certain characteristics that are projected onto the card by the child (e.g., use of color, movement, texture). Not only can the particular scores be interpreted, but they can also be combined to provide ratio scores that have been associated with various personality traits. For instance, a depression index has been developed that can be scored for each child and can then be compared to other children's norms to indicate level of depression for this examinee.

Clearly, the analysis and interpretation of a Rorschach protocol are very complex and easily abused. No mental health professionals should attempt to make interpretations without training, nor should they neglect their responsibility in making appropriate referrals. In other words, before referring a child for projective testing with the Rorschach, the clinician should investigate the credentials and training background of the referral source (Brems, 2000). After all, it is the clinician who utilizes the report rendered by that examiner and therefore must be able to have confidence in the examiner's performance. The Rorschach Inkblot Test is available from Psychological Assessment Resources (http://www.parinc.com), one of the U.S. distributors of the cards that are manufactured in Switzerland. Sale is restricted to properly credentialed professionals.

Thematic Apperception Test, Children's Apperception Test-Animal, and Children's Apperception Test-Human.   The Thematic Apperception Test (TAT; Bellak, 1943) and its successors (CAT-A; Bellak and Bellak, 1949; CAT-H; Bellak and Bellak, 1965), which were developed specifically with children in mind, was developed to assess personality style and to help with differential diagnosis. The TAT consists of 31 cards depicting a variety of scenes that are thought to have differing stimulus values. Generally, clinicians choose a subset of ten cards, the stimulus values of which appear particularly relevant to the history and/or identified pathology of the examinee. The CAT-H and CAT-A consist of 10 cards each, which depict various family or interpersonal scenes that are considered relevant to children. They are identical in terms of picture and stimulus value, but the actual characters depicted in the drawings are humans in the CAT-H and animals in the CAT-A. The rationale behind this difference is that younger children are more likely to be able to respond to the animal cards, whereas older children relate better to human content. However, not all clinicians use either of the CAT versions with children, as subsets of the TAT are quite useful with young examinees. While the stimuli (i.e., the pictures on the cards) are very different across the TAT and the CAT versions, the basic administration and interpretation processes are identical, making a joint discussion of the three tests possible.

Administration of an apperception test requires the child to tell a story about each picture. This story is supposed to include current happenings, antecedents, consequences, and thoughts and feelings of the story's characters. As with all projectives, the apperception test user assumes that the child projects unconscious material onto the card and that responses provide insight into personality functioning and style. Whereas the Rorschach, for instance, has formal scoring criteria and systems that have found wide acceptance and use, the apperception tests do not. Although attempts have been made at such systems (Bellak, 1997), they have not been widely adopted by clinicians. Instead, most clinicians use their own informal system to evaluate the stories that are provided by the children about the pictures (Dana, 1996). Interpretation generally focuses on manifest content, types of characters, thoughts and feelings that are expressed, conflict resolution and coping patterns, latent contents and symbolisms, interpersonal styles, intrapsychic conflicts, and similar issues. Themes, styles, and patterns that emerge across several stories are explored and given more credence than those that occur only once in an entire protocol. Because of the lack of accepted scoring criteria, the potential for abuse of the apperception tests is great. However, a very vast literature exists about these instruments that suggests their clinical utility, and they are generally identified as frequently used by clinicians (Dana, 1996). This reality makes careful consideration of the clinician to whom one refers children very important. As with referrals for Rorschach testing, care needs to be taken to ascertain that the examiner has training and experience in using the tool. Only then can faith be placed in the report that is subsequently issued about a child's performance. The TAT and CAT cards are available from a number of test publishers, including Harcourt Assessment; http://www.harcourtassessment.com.

Tell-Me-A-Story (TEMAS). This projective test (TEMAS; Constantino, Malgady, and Rogler, 1988) was designed for use with culturally and linguistically diverse children and adolescents. The technique is similar to the CAT and TAT in that stimulus cards are used to evoke stories that are then evaluated. However, it differs in that the TEMAS has a focus on interpersonal dynamics, whereas the CAT and TAT focus on intrapsychic dynamics. Further, the stimulus cards in the TEMAS are more culturally relevant, gender balanced, and less ambiguous (Constantino, Dana, and Malgady, 2007).

The TEMAS consists of 23 chromatic stimulus cards, most of which depict individuals in urban settings. To assess a range of responses, the cards depict positive and negative emotions and interactions. Two sets of parallel cards exist with one set depicting primarily Latino and African Americans and the other set depicting primarily Whites. Designed for children ages 5 to 18, the TEMAS takes up to two hours to complete. The children's stories are recorded in a booklet and scored using an objective system, resulting in scores for 10 Personality Functions, 18 Cognitive Functions, and 7 Affective Functions. A shorter administration of only nine cards allows for a testing time of less than an hour. The same scoring system and scores are obtained using the shorter form; however, less information and fewer details are gained. The TEMAS can be obtained from Western Psychological Services; http://www.wpspublish.com.

Neuropsychological Testing

Neuropsychological assessment is the newest testing discipline in psychology. Its characteristic feature is the establishment of a relationship between brain functioning and behavior. Although Freud himself was extremely interested in this connection, it had received very little attention and study in the field of psychology until the last four decades. Only then did the discipline catch up with tendencies in the neurosciences and medicine, and now neuropsychology represents the primary link between these disciplines and psychology. Neuropsychological testing is perhaps the most sophisticated and well-standardized type of assessment in psychology today. It was well founded in research from its inception and continues to generate hard data. Neuropsychological testing is concerned primarily with assessment of pathological, neurological, and brain processes and their effects on behavior and personality. It is not just a diagnostic discipline; it is also a necessity to treatment planning and intervention. It assesses the cognitive, psychological, and behavioral strengths and deficits and relates them to brain functioning. Thus, this assessment requires great amounts of training not only in traditional clinical or counseling psychology but also in areas of neuroanatomy, neurochemistry, and neurophysiology. It requires the examiner to be extremely familiar with the standardized testing procedures of the various instruments and with the need to adapt testing procedures appropriately to individual clients. Neuropsychology was developed originally with and for adult clients. However, child versions of most of the major instruments have now been developed. Further, neuropsychological testing always includes an intelligence scale (of which there are many specifically designed for children), and the use of the Bender Gestalt Visual Motor Test, a tool that was originally developed for children.

The most commonly used neuropsychological test instruments for children include the Halstead-Reitan Neuropsychological Test Battery for Children (age 9 to

14) and the Reitan-Indiana Neuropsychological Test Battery for Children (age 5 to 8). Both are modifications of the adult version of the battery and include child versions of the Category Test, the Tactile Performance Test, and the age-appropriate Wechsler Scale. In addition, the Halstead-Reitan includes the Trail-Making Test and the Speech Sounds Perception Test, whereas the Reitan-Indiana includes the Aphasia Screening Test and the Sensory Perceptual Exam (all in age-appropriate modified versions). All testing materials can be obtained from Reitan Neuropsychology Laboratory; http://www.reitanlabs.com.

Neuropsychological testing is used to assess a child's level and pattern of performance, left-right differences, and pathognomic (signs of a disease process) neurological indicators. This information is used to answer specific questions regarding severity and type of dysfunction (lesion, tumor, trauma, etc.), type of pathological process (e.g., progressive), cognitive and behavioral strengths and deficits, day-to-day functioning, and implications for treatment and prognosis (Stein, Barrueco, and Halperin, 2004). Given the extreme need for specialization of training, no specific neuropsychological tests are discussed here. The reader is referred to primary references such as Lezak, Howieson, Loring, and Hannay (2004).

Summary and Concluding Thoughts

This chapter has provided an overview of various procedures a mental health professional can utilize to expand on information gathered about a child in the intake interview. Primary sources of previously gathered data include school records and teachers, as well as medical and other treatment records and corresponding professionals. Primary sources for creating new information entail referrals to other professionals for consultation and specialized data gathering, including psychological testing. With regard to psychological testing, a wealth of data can be obtained from a variety of sources in a variety of contexts, ranging from mental status to behavior to personality, both general and specific, to achievement and intelligence, as well as neuropsychological processes.

8

Conceptualization and Treatment Planning

with Mark E. Johnson

> *Protective measures should, as appropriate, include effective procedures for the establishment of social programmes to provide necessary support for the child and for those who have the care of the child, as well as for other forms of prevention and for identification, reporting, referral, investigation, treatment and follow-up of instances of child maltreatment described heretofore, and, as appropriate, for judicial involvement.*
> —Article 19.2 of the U.N. Convention on the Rights of the Child

Once the care provider arrives at the point at which a conceptualization and treatment plan must be formulated, much information has been gathered from the child and her or his family, environment, teachers, and other sources. This information must now be combined in such a way as to make sense of the symptoms or concerns with which the child and family are presenting. It is crucial to formulate a conceptualization and related treatment plan before proceeding with treatment. All the work with the child and the family up to this time has been considered assessment, though some therapeutic work may have been initiated on the sidelines of the interaction with the clients. All too often, clinicians proceed from the assessment phase to the therapy or counseling phase before clarifying in their mind a thorough conceptualization and a treatment plan that is determined by this understanding of the client. The failure to conceptualize and put on paper a treatment strategy results in treatment without direction, based strictly on trial and error, and may perpetuate the problems in the child's life, in which the lack of direction or organization is often an integral part of the presenting problem. A thorough understanding of what is involved in conceptualization and treatment planning is crucial to the success of the treatment. Only then can counselors effectively use their tools without wasting their potential.

Preparing for Conceptualization: Diagnosis

A conceptualization is the means of pulling together all information gathered about the child to make sense of what is happening to the client and the family. It involves reiteration of the problems that have been identified through the assessment phase, formulation of these problems into a diagnosis, and understanding the dynamics that contribute to the development and maintenance of the concern. The first step is the careful collation of data to arrive at a diagnosis that can be shared with other health-care providers and insurance companies. Diagnoses in and of themselves have limited utility for preparing the clinician for making a treatment plan; a full conceptualization is much more helpful for that. However, a diagnosis is nevertheless the first step in organizing the information about a child client in preparation for making a treatment plan. The process begins with the problem list.

Problem List

Although creating a problem list might appear unnecessary and redundant with the assessment of the presenting concerns, this is not so. Often, as assessment progresses, therapists make note of a number of problems not mentioned by the family as part of the reason for their presentation. The problem list focuses the counselor's attention on all potential areas of impact in the child's life, rather than restricting the view merely to the psychological. As such, there are several problem areas that need to be addressed: psychological, medical/physiological, academic, social/cultural, familial, and other problems. Although not all problems or issues are obviously related to the presenting problem, all are listed.

Psychological Problems.   Psychological problems are those that involve the child's emotional, psychological, intrapsychic, and interpersonal adjustment. Emotional adjustment involves affect and mood, including fears, moodiness, depression, and variability in affect. Psychological adjustment refers to perception, cognition, awareness, or development, including hallucinations, delusions, lapses in consciousness, delays in development, functional elimination difficulties, and so on. Intrapsychic adjustment refers to issues of self-perception, self-understanding, conflict with self, and life direction, including low self-esteem, lack of interests or hobbies, nightmares, obsessive hand-washing, conflicted expression of affect, indecisiveness, and similar problems. Interpersonal adjustment refers to problems that manifest in the context of relating to others, such as family and friends, including difficulties in peer relationships, fighting with parents, ambivalence about attachment and trust, or school anxiety.

Social and Cultural Problems.   Social and cultural problems are those that refer to the social situation, hence are focused on environmental, socioeconomic, religious, and similar issues. Environmental problems may include issues such as inappropriate shelter or nourishment, whereas living in a deprived neighborhood represents an example of a socioeconomic issue. Clearly, the two are often directly and inextricably related. However, sometimes environmental problems may not be as obvious. For instance, exposure to lead-based paint is an environmental issue that can have psychological implications but is not tied to socioeconomic status. Religious problems may involve concerns such as school prayer, ostracizing because of religious affiliation, and forced church attendance by the family. Other social problems may include concerns over school curricula by parents. Cultural issues may include lack of appropriate role models of the child's culture in the mass media or living environment or unfamiliarity with the cultural context in which the child is educated or cared for, such as might be true for immigrant children.

Academic Problems.   Academic problems refer to issues that emerge in the school setting but focus primarily on actual academic performance, such as grades, changes in functioning, exceptional performance, learning disabilities, and so on. There may be some overlap with psychological problems in that there may be some interpersonal problems, such as peer or teacher relationships that are confined to the academic setting. It is an arbitrary decision as to where to list these types of problems, as long as they are included somewhere.

Medical/Physiological Problems.   Medical or physiological problems obviously refer to the child's general level of health and accident proneness. Medical problems can vary from severe (e.g., frequent hospitalizations for a chronic illness) to mild (e.g., allergies). Regardless of severity, they should be listed. Developmental deficits and delays (although occasionally not physical or physiological in nature) are placed in this category, as are family history of mental or other illness. It is wise to note obvious medical problems of other family members because of their potential impact on the child. Neurological and neuropsychological problems are listed if they were formally assessed.

Familial Problems.   Familial problems refer to conflicts that arise in the family setting. As with academic problems, there is overlap with psychological problems. Focus is on a detailed description of family problems, not merely a statement of conflict among family members. For instance, triangulation, crossing of generational boundaries, frequent fighting in the marital dyad, lack of trust, history of divorce, and similar issues are appropriate matters to note.

Other Problems.   Other problems simply refer to any other concerns the counselor has that do not appear to fit any other category or are not clearly defined. This category may include speculations about problems that are suspected, but have not been substantiated. An example of such a problem may be the suspicion of child abuse in a case in which members of the family are denying the allegation. If a listed problem is a hypothesis, it must be identified as such.

   In writing down these concerns and issues, it is best literally to make a list of problems within each of the areas, rather than trying to write a narrative. To help put identified problems into a context of time and a time-referenced relationship to one another, it helps to note onset or nature in terms of chronicity or acuteness. Timing issues are clarified by identifying the number of weeks since a problem or behavior has been noted, defining a problem or behavior as chronic if it has a long history and is still occurring, and noting an issue as acute if the onset is recent and of particular importance or salience in the present. Problems that wax and wane are noted as such, as are problems that occurred recently but have been resolved. An example of a problem list contained in the conceptualization for a child who came to counseling after the divorce of her parents is presented in Table 8.1.

Table 8.1   Problem List for a Child Presenting after Parental Divorce

Problem Area	Onset	Specific Problem
Psychological	20 wks	pervasive sadness and mood swings
	12 wks	weight loss and refusal to eat
	12 wks	frequent crying and complaining
	10 wks	decreased interest in play and hobby
	20 wks	decreased self-esteem
	10 wks	nightmares and initial insomnia
	1 year	refusal to sleep at friends' homes
	1 year	isolation from play with peers
Social/Cultural	12 wks	decreased income in the primary home
	12 wks	move to new inner-city neighborhood
	8 yrs	conflicting religious values in father's (Asian American) and mother's (white) home
	12 wks	lack of Asian cultural role models
Academic	20 wks	deterioration of grades (As to Cs)
	10 wks	difficulty concentrating
	1 year	withdrawal from schoolmates
	12 wks	pending school-initiated assessment of developmental reading disorder
Medical/Physical	10 wks	frequent stomachaches (2x daily)
	Chronic	maternal history of alcoholism
	10 wks	many recent accidents (burned hand, fell off bike, ran into a wall)
	20 wks	occasional nighttime bed-wetting
	1 year	delay in emotional development
Familial	12 wks	parental divorce
	Acute	continued custody battle
	Chronic	different values in parental homes
	Chronic	attempted triangulation
	Chronic	overinvolved maternal grandmother
	10 wks	significant decrease in paternal contacts
Other	12 wks	suspected neglect in maternal home
	4 wks	recent death of only younger sister (severe abuse as possible cause)
	Chronic	suspected substance abuse by mother
	10 wks	possible suicidal ideation (e.g., accident proneness)

DSM-IV-TR Diagnosis

Diagnosis is the second aspect of a thorough, all-inclusive conceptualization. Diagnosis is generally made based on the nosology provided by the Diagnostic and Statistical Manual of Mental Disorders (Fourth Edition—Text Revision; DSM-IV-TR; American Psychiatric Association; 1994, 2000). This manual provides a symptomatology-based, checklist-type nosology that is used to classify problems in a manner that is as standardized, research-based, and objective as possible. Even though concern has been expressed that the DSM fails to consider the larger circumstances of an individual, especially a child (Jensen, Knapp, and Mrazek, 2006), it nevertheless is the most commonly accepted diagnostic system among mental health professionals, thus facilitating communication and identification. Further, DSM-IV-TR coding is accepted by insurance companies and Medicaid for third-party reimbursement purposes. A brief discussion of the DSM-IV-TR multiaxial system is presented here, followed by some of the most commonly used Axis I and Axis II diagnoses available for children.

Multiaxial System. The DSM-IV-TR uses a multiaxial system of diagnosis that classifies problems along five dimensions, or axes, for purposes of ensuring that counselors make the broadest assessment possible of each client. The five dimensions represent evaluations along the lines of clinical syndromes (Axis I), personality disorders and mental retardation (Axis II), physical disorders (Axis III), psychosocial stressors (Axis IV), and overall level of functioning (Axis V). Once a problem list has been prepared, diagnosis of the child and family using the DSM-IV-TR axis system is relatively easy, as diagnosis with the DSM-IV-TR is symptom driven and structured somewhat like a checklist; the problem list provides the information necessary to make diagnostic decisions. Nevertheless, very thorough familiarity with the manual (American Psychiatric Association, 2000) and related resources (Frances and Ross, 2001; Spitzer, Gibbon, Skodol, Williams, and First, 2002, 2006; also see Meyer and Weaver, 2007) is required for its successful and responsible use. In fact, formal classroom training in its use is preferable to mere studying of the manual and related books.

Axis I—Clinical Syndromes. Axis I of the DSM-IV-TR is focused on the identification of major mental disorders such as depression, anxiety, and schizophrenia that generally have periods of florid symptomatology and do not necessarily begin in childhood or necessarily continue in stable form across the life span. More likely, these disorders have later onsets and fluctuations in the severity of their symptoms across time. This fluctuation is not to be mistaken as the absence of chronicity. It merely indicates that although the disorder itself may be chronic, its actual manifestation through obvious symptoms may wax and wane. Despite this definition of Axis I disorders, there is one category of mental illnesses, Disorders Usually First Evident in Infancy, Childhood, or Adolescence, coded on this axis with onset during the developmental period of life. Further, disorders in the other categories may also begin early in life. It is possible for a child to warrant more than one diagnosis on Axis I. For instance, it is common to have a pairing of Adjustment Disorder with Mixed Mood and Enuresis. Sometimes a child may meet most of the criteria necessary for a given diagnosis but does not fulfill all. It is then possible to note this diagnosis as a "Rule Out" category, implying that this diagnosis is a possibility but that more information must be gathered before it can be established for certain.

Axis II—Personality Disorder and Mental Retardation. In contrast to Axis I disorders, Axis II disorders always have to have their onset during the developmental period of life (birth to age 18). They are always called either Personality Disorders or Mental Retardation, considered chronic, and have stable symptoms. Fluctuations in symptomatology that are characteristic of Axis I disorders are not present in Axis II disorders. Axis I versus Axis II differentiation was made by the DSM-IV authors to assure that therapists are satisfied look not only at the most florid, or obvious, symptomatology but also at less obvious but more stable and chronic symptomatology of long-term disorders that have their onset in childhood. It is not uncommon to have diagnoses on Axis I and Axis II for the same individual. If this is the case, the counselor is urged to make a judgment about which diagnosis is primary or seen as chiefly responsible for the current referral of the child. This diagnosis is labeled clearly as Principal Diagnosis. As is true for Axis I, a "Rule Out" category can be provided.

Axis III—Physical Disorders. Axis III allows for the formal coding of any physical condition or disorder that is seen as relevant to the diagnoses on Axis I or II. The physical condition is relevant either etiologically or in terms of its impact on the person's mental health. Sometimes the condition is a result of the mental disorder; sometimes it is only loosely or potentially associated. Technically, Axis III diagnosis is only in the purview of physicians; however, all clinicians have the responsibility to note already diagnosed disorders or symptoms. Obviously, whenever there is a notation on Axis III, there must have been some involvement of a physician (through study of previous treatment records, referral, or collaboration).

Axis IV—Psychosocial and Environmental Problems. Axis IV requires notation regarding the presence of psychosocial or environmental problems in a child's life that may affect the etiology, diagnosis, prognosis, or treatment of disorders noted on Axes I or II. The manual provides a listing of psychosocial problem categories that warrant attention: problems with a primary support group (e.g., death of a parent, parental divorce), problems related to the social environment (e.g., stigmatization of a child because of cultural differences, social isolation), educational problems (e.g., academic performance difficulties, problems with a teacher), occupational problems (e.g., unemployment of a parent), housing problems (e.g., a child living in a shelter, homelessness), economic problems (e.g., poverty), problems with access to health care services (e.g., lack of health insurance, lack of transportation), and problems related to interaction with the legal system/crime (e.g., victim of a crime, incarcerated parent). Each category is assessed for absence or presence; multiple problems are usually present and all are listed. Problems noted on Axis IV are often contributory to the development, maintenance, or recurrence of a disorder. Occasionally, they may be the consequence of a disorder; for instance, enuresis may lead to a disturbance of peer relationships, resulting in social isolation.

Axis V—Global Assessment of Functioning. Ratings on this axis are accomplished via the Global Assessment of Functioning Scale (GAF), which ranges from 0 to 100 and indicates a child's overall level of functioning, considering social, academic, and psychological aspects of the client's life. A rating of zero is used only for inadequate information (equivalent to absence of a functionality rating). The better a child's functioning, the higher the GAF. For example, a rating of 90 indicates minimal symptoms of a disorder and good functioning in all three areas mentioned above; a rating of 100 refers to exceptional functioning. A rating of 1, on the other hand, indicates extremely severe pathology with persistent danger of suicide, severe disruption in communication, or gross inability to care for oneself. Examples of ratings are provided in the manual (American Psychiatric Association, 1994, 2000). Ratings are made via a four-step process that leads the counselor to the most objective evaluation possible. Step 1 involves reviewing all ranges of functioning from the top down; Step 2 directs the therapist to identify the range of functioning most indicative of the child's symptoms or level of functioning, whichever is worse; Step 3 involves a process of double-checking the correctness of the chosen range; Step 4 helps the counselor choose a specific index in the chosen range of functioning.

An example of a DSM-IV-TR diagnosis is provided in Table 8.2, for the same child whose problem list was presented in Table 8.1. This example shows the useful-

Table 8.2   DSM-IV-TR Diagnosis for a Child Presenting after Parental Divorce

Diagnosis	Symptoms Present
Axis I:	
296.22 Major Depression, Single Episode, Moderate	• depressed mood for more than 1 week • decreased interest in activities • weight loss • (failure to make expected weight gains) • loss of energy • insomnia • difficulty concentrating
307.60 Enuresis, nocturnal only	• nighttime bed-wetting frequency of twice per week
309.0 Rule Out Adjustment Disorder with Depressed Mood	• stressor within 3 months (divorce) • impairment in academic functioning • R/O: above and beyond what would be expected for the circumstances
Axis II:	
315.0 Rule Out Reading Disorder	• reading level is markedly below expected level (standardized test is pending) • academic achievement is affected
Axis III:	
No formal diagnosis	• physical was completed and ruled out physical causes for bed-wetting and headaches
Axis IV:	
Problems with Primary Support Group Problems Related to the Social Environment Educational Problems Occupational Problems Housing problems Economic Problems Problems with Access to Health Care Problems Related to Interaction with Legal System Other	• Chronic parental arguments • Recent parental divorce • Sister's death
Axis V:	
Current Functioning—45	• moderate impairment in school and social functioning • severe impairment in psychological functioning
Highest Level of Functioning in Past Year—80	• only slight impairment in all areas

ness of the careful preparation of the problem list in making a DSM-IV-TR diagnosis. The example in Table 8.2 goes somewhat beyond the information that would be included in a child's actual conceptualization, in that for purposes of demonstration, the actual symptoms that matched the DSM-IV-TR checklist used for diagnosis are provided ("Symptoms Present"). This reiteration of symptoms would not be necessary in the actual case because of its redundancy with the problem list.

Once the care provider is familiar with the DSM-IV-TR diagnostic system, the actual differential diagnosis must be made. This process can be aided by the use of decision trees provided in the DSM-IV-TR manual (American Psychiatric Association, 1994, 2000). However, thorough familiarity with the individual disorders is crucial. The most common disorders that are relevant to the work with children are presented briefly. The first nine broad categories—Mental Retardation, Attention-Deficit and Disruptive Behavior Disorders, Learning Disorders, Motor Skills Disorders, Communication Disorders, Pervasive Developmental Disorders, Feeding and Eating Disorders of Infancy or Childhood, Tic Disorders, Elimination Disorders, and Other Disorders of Infancy, Childhood, or Adolescence—are all Disorders Usually First Diagnosed in Infancy, Childhood, or Adolescence. The last few—Schizophrenia and other Psychotic Disorders, Mood Disorders, Anxiety Disorders, Sexual and Gender Identity Disorders, Sleep Disorders, Adjustment Disorders, and Other Conditions That May Be a Focus of Clinical Attention—can have their onset at any time during a person's life.

This presentation can in no way substitute for the use of the actual manual. It focuses merely on listing symptoms within each category, making no attempt to provide etiological or prevalence data. The reader is referred to child psychopathology books such as Achenbach and Rescorla (2007), Mash and Barkley (2002, 2006), Wicks-Nelson and Israel (2006), and Wilmshurst (2005) for this type of information.

Mental Retardation.   Mental Retardation is characterized by significantly subaverage levels of intellectual functioning, significant deficits in adaptive behavior skills, and onset of symptoms before age 18 (Beirne-Smith, Patton, and Kim, 2005). There are several levels of severity, which are determined by the level of impairment in cognitive functioning as determined by the intelligence quotient (IQ) obtained on a standardized intelligence test (Handen and Gilchrist, 2006). Levels range from mild (IQ of 50–55 to 70) to moderate (35–40 to 50–55) to severe (20–25 to 35–40) to profound (below 20–25). Unlike all of the other diagnoses noted in this chapter, the diagnosis of Mental Retardation is coded on Axis II.

Attention-Deficit and Disruptive Behavior Disorders.   This class of disorders is well described by Barkley (2000, 2005) and consists of three major diagnostic categories: namely Attention-Deficit Hyperactivity Disorder, Oppositional Defiant Disorder, and Conduct Disorders. These diagnoses "comprise a spectrum of disruptive behaviors that exist along the dual continua of age and severity" (Morrison and Anders, 1999, p. 214). Attention-Deficit /Hyperactivity Disorder is diagnosed when for at least six months, a child evidences either six distinct symptoms of inattention (e.g., is easily distracted, does not follow through on instructions, has difficulty sustaining attention, is forgetful, has difficulty organizing activities) or at least six symptoms of hyperactivity-impulsivity (e.g., fidgets with hands or feet, talks excessively, acts as if "driven by a motor," blurts out answers, interrupts others). Three types of this disorder are differentiated: If only the inattention symptoms are present, Predominately Inattentive Type; if only the hyperactive-impulsive symptoms are present, Predominately Hyperactive-Impulsive Type; if both sets of symptoms are present, Combined Type. Oppositional Defiant Disorder is characterized by at least four distinct symptoms of negativity, hostility, and defiance that are above and beyond what might be expected given a child's age, such as argumentativeness, externalization of blame, loss of temper, vindictiveness, annoying or bratty behavior, and so on. Finally, Conduct Disorders are characterized by at least three distinct symptoms that indicate lack of respect for others' rights and for social norms or rules in a number of settings. Such symptoms include stealing, fire setting, lying, truancy, cruelty to animals or people, physical fighting with or without weapons, destruction of property, and other even more severe behaviors. Conduct Disorders can be differentiated according to whether the behavior first occurs before (Childhood-Onset Type) or after (Adolescent-Onset Type) age 10.

Learning Disorders. Learning Disorders are characterized by a child's performance on a standardized achievement test that is substantially below what would be expected given her or his age, education, and intellectual level (Wodrich and Schmitt, 2006). The primary subcategories of Learning Disorders are Reading Disorder, Mathematics Disorder, and Disorder of Written Expression, and each requires specific diagnosis and management (Whitmore, Willems, and Hart, 2000).

Motor Skills Disorders. The only diagnosis in this category is Developmental Coordination Disorder (Dewey and Tupper, 2004). This diagnosis is given when a child evidences marked impairment in the development of motor coordination, such as dropping things, delays in achieving motor milestones (such as walking, crawling, sitting), and clumsiness. To diagnose this disorder, impairment must interfere with daily life and not be due to a physiological disorder.

Communication Disorders. This class of disorders consists of four major diagnostic categories: Expressive Language Disorder, Mixed Receptive-Expressive Language Disorder, Phonological Disorder, and Stuttering. All of the disorders interfere with the child's ability to communicate with others (Gulley, 2005). Expressive Language Disorder is indicated when scores on standardized tests of expressive language are considerably lower than both nonverbal intellectual capacity and receptive language. The disorder can manifest as limited vocabulary, errors in tense, or difficulty in producing sentences with developmentally appropriate complexity; these problems must interfere with the child's academic or social life. In Mixed Receptive-Expressive Language Disorder, the child must have lower test scores on both receptive and expressive language as compared to nonverbal intellectual ability. In addition to symptoms of Expressive Language Disorder, the child has difficulties understanding words. Phonological Disorder involves difficulties using developmentally appropriate speech sounds. In Stuttering, fluency of speech is affected, with elongation or repetition of sounds or syllables.

Pervasive Developmental Disorders. The primary diagnoses within this category are Autistic Disorder, Rett's Disorder, Childhood Disintegrative Disorder, and

Asperger's Disorder. All are marked by "severe and pervasive impairment in several areas of development: reciprocal social interaction skills, communication skills, or the presence of stereotyped behaviors, interests, and activities" (American Psychiatric Association, 2000, p. 69). Autistic Disorder is characterized by impairment in social interaction, verbal and nonverbal communication, and repetitive and stereotyped patterns of behavior and activities. Impairment of social interactions may manifest as lack of empathy for or awareness of others' feelings, inability to form relationships with other children or adult caretakers, absence of comfort-seeking behavior even in situations of clear distress, absence or impairment of nonverbal cues used in social interactions, lack of social play, or lack of spontaneous seeking out of others. Communication impairment may manifest as delay or lack of spoken language, inability to sustain conversation, lack of imaginative play activity, unusual speech (e.g., echolalia), and similar disturbances. Finally, restriction of behavioral repertoire may manifest as stereotypy, distress over minor environmental changes, insistence on precise routines, and preoccupation with parts of objects. Autistic Disorder is very poorly understood and perhaps the most profound of the developmental disorders (Volkmar, Paul, Klin, and Cohen, 2005a, 2005b). In Rett's Disorder, following an apparently normal first five months of development, a marked change in physical and behavioral development begins to manifest. This change includes a deceleration of head growth, loss of hand skills previously demonstrated, loss of social interests, loss of coordination, and severely impaired expressive and receptive language development. Onset of this disorder occurs prior to 4 years of age and usually in the first or second year of life. Childhood Disintegrative Disorder is marked by substantial regression in several areas of functioning after a period of at least two years of normal development. Such regression must occur in at least two areas of language, social skills, bowel or bladder control, play, or motor skills, resulting in significant impairments in at least two areas of social interaction, communication, and repetitive or stereotyped patterns of behaviors and activities. Finally, Asperger's Disorder is characterized by significantly impaired social interaction and some demonstration of repetitive and stereotyped behaviors (Attwood, 2006). In contrast to Autistic Disorder, these problems manifest in the absence of significantly delayed cognitive and language development. Further, in Autistic Disorder, the repetitive and stereotyped behavior and activities are varied and usually involve motor mannerisms; in Asperger's Disorder, repetitive and stereotyped behavior usually centers on a "topic to which the individual devotes inordinate amounts of time amassing information and facts" (American Psychiatric Association, 2000, p. 82).

Feeding and Eating Disorders of Infancy or Early Childhood.   This class of disorders consists of three major diagnostic categories: Pica, Rumination Disorder, and Feeding Disorder of Infancy or Early Childhood (Cooper and Stein, 2006). All three are marked by "persistent feeding and eating disturbances in eating behavior" (American Psychiatric Association, 2000, p. 103). Pica is marked by the eating of substances that are not considered food, such as soil, paint, and cigarette butts. Pica is not uncommonly associated with Mental Retardation. In Rumination Disorder, the child regurgitates and rechews food without associated nausea or stomach upset, a process that can result in weight loss or failure to gain weight. Feeding Disorder of Infancy or Early

Childhood is characterized by a persistent failure to eat adequately, resulting in either weight loss or the failure to gain developmentally appropriate weight. This disorder is diagnosed when such problems exist in the absence of a physiological reason.

In the DSM-III-R (American Psychiatric Association, 1987), Anorexia Nervosa and Bulimia Nervosa were categorized as disorders usually first diagnosed in infancy, childhood, or adolescence and included with the previously noted feeding and eating disorders. In the DSM-IV-TR (American Psychiatric Association, 1994, 2000), these two eating disorders form a category of their own and are no longer listed as disorders first diagnosed in childhood. Anorexia Nervosa is defined as weight loss or failure to gain weight that results in at least 15 percent underweight, along with a refusal to eat for fear of being fat. It is generally accompanied by a distorted body image and, in adolescent (or adult) females, by the absence of at least three menstrual cycles. Bulimia Nervosa is a similarly self-destructive disorder that manifests as episodes of binge-eating, during which the person feels an utter loss of control over her or his eating behavior. Bingeing is followed by behaviors designed to prevent weight gain, such as purging, using laxatives, vigorous exercising, or fasting. As in Anorexia Nervosa, there is great concern over body shape and weight. Both diagnoses are unlikely to occur in children, instead usually first manifesting in adolescence; however, child clinicians need to be aware of them nevertheless as they can be present among children as well.

Tic Disorders.   This class of disorders consists of three major diagnostic categories: Tourette's Disorder, Chronic Motor or Vocal Tic Disorder, and Transient Tic Disorder. All three are marked by rapid, stereotyped, and recurrent motor movements or vocalizations that are not under the child's voluntary control (Kurlan, 2004). In Tourette's Disorder, these tics involve multiple motor and one or more vocal movements that occur several times per day. Symptoms are identical in Chronic Motor or Vocal Tic Disorder, except that there is either a motor or a vocal tic (never both). In a Transient Tic Disorder, multiple motor and/or vocal tics occur nearly every day; however, the disorder is time-limited to 12 months, at which time it either becomes a Tourette's Disorder or disappears.

Elimination Disorders.   This class of disorders consists of two major diagnostic categories, namely, Enuresis and Encopresis (also well described by Christophersen and Friman, 2004; Von Gontard, 2006). Both are marked by the child accidentally or purposefully not maintaining control over either bladder or sphincter. Two types of these disorders have been described: Primary, in which the child has never established continence, and Secondary, in which the disorder manifests after a period of continence. In Enuresis, urine is voided in an inappropriate place at least twice per week after age 5. In assigning this diagnosis, Enuresis is further coded as Nocturnal Only, Diurnal Only, or Nocturnal and Diurnal. In Encopresis, feces are passed at inappropriate places at least once a month for at least three months after age 4. Functionality always has to be ascertained by a physician and should never be assumed even if the child at one time had complete bladder or bowel control.

Other Disorders of Infancy, Childhood, or Adolescence.   Four other disorders that usually first manifest in Childhood or Adolescence are Separation Anxiety Disorder, Selective Mutism, Reactive Attachment Disorder of Infancy or Early Childhood, and Stereotypic Movement Disorder. These disorders do not share any specific traits or symptoms other than their childhood onset. Separation Anxiety is characterized by at least three distinct symptoms of anxiety about being separated from a major attachment figure, such as refusal to go to school, distress upon separation, refusal to go to sleep alone, worries about harm befalling the attachment figure, or fear of being kidnapped or otherwise separated from the person (Bowlby, 1999). For this diagnosis to be made, the duration of the disturbance must be at least four weeks and must cause significant impairment in the child's life. Selective Mutism manifests as a child's refusal to talk in some or all social situations despite the ability to use and comprehend language (Kehle, Bray, and Theodore, 2006). Reactive Attachment Disorder is primarily characterized by disturbances in a child's social relationships that manifest either as failure to initiate social interaction or as inappropriate sociability, in the absence of other severe disorders that might explain this behavior (e.g., mental retardation). It is accompanied by pathogenic care, which may be evidenced as a complete disregard for the child's basic emotional or physical needs by the caretaker or as repeated changes in caretakers that serve to hinder stable attachment (Stafford and Zeanah, 2006). Finally, Stereotypic Movement Disorder is diagnosed in the presence of intentional, repetitive, and nonfunctional behavior that interferes with normal activities or results in injury to the child. Such behaviors include body rocking, head banging, self-biting, hand waving, and so forth, and are not accounted for by other diagnoses (such as Obsessive-Compulsive Disorder or a Tic Disorder).

In addition to the previous 10 categories of disorders that are usually first evidenced in childhood, other diagnostic categories of which a child clinician must be aware include Schizophrenia and other Psychotic Disorders, Mood Disorders, Anxiety Disorders, Sexual and Gender Identity Disorders, Sleep Disorders, Adjustment Disorders, and Other Conditions That May Be a Focus of Clinical Attention. These categories include disorders that can have their onset at any time during a person's life, making it possible for a child clinician to encounter them in the practice with children.

Schizophrenia and Other Psychotic Disorders.   Although disorders in this category are most likely to manifest for first time in early adulthood, some occasionally begin during adolescence or (even more rarely) during childhood. The disorders in this category that are most likely to be evidenced in childhood are Schizophrenia, Schizophreniform Disorder, Schizoaffective Disorder, and Shared Psychotic Disorder. Additional disorders in this category that manifest almost exclusively in adulthood, and thus are not reviewed here, are Delusional Disorder and Brief Psychotic Disorder (Tsai and Champine, 2006). Schizophrenia is characterized by a marked decrease in functioning over a minimum period of six months, along with psychotic symptoms such as delusions or hallucinations, incoherence or loose association, catatonia, or inappropriate affect. Schizophrenia is subdivided into more specific manifestations based on specific symptoms evidenced by the individual (e.g., Paranoid Type, Disorganized Type, Catatonic Type, Undifferentiated Type, Residual Type). In Schizophreniform Disorder, the child meets the criteria for Schizophrenia, but the disorder has not necessarily resulted in severe impairment in life functioning and has occurred for less than six months. Schizoaffective Disorder is marked by the presence of a mood disorder (i.e., Major Depressive Episode, Manic Episode, or Mixed Episode) in conjunction with psychotic symptoms, such as delusions or hallucinations, incoherence or loose association, catatonia, or inappropriate affect, as well as the presence of delusions or hallucinations in the absence of the mood symptoms. Shared Psychotic Disorder is characterized by development of a delusion similar in content to the delusion held by someone to whom the child is close. Diagnosis of childhood psychosis must be made cautiously because of the stigma and negative connotations attached to the label. Nevertheless, they exist and must be identified as such when they are present to ascertain correct treatment.

Mood Disorders.   The primary disorders in this category are organized into Depressive Disorders (Major Depressive Disorder and Dysthymic Disorder) and Bipolar Disorders (Bipolar I Disorder, Bipolar II Disorder, and Cyclothymic Disorder). All are marked by a disturbance in the child's mood, such as either depression, irritability, or elation (Stark et al., 2006). Major Depressive Disorder involves a constellation of symptoms that are commonly associated with depression, including depressed mood, irritability, diminished interest in previously rewarding activities, insomnia or hypersomnia, fatigue, lack of concentration, significant weight loss or gain, suicidal ideation, and so on. These symptoms represent a change in level of functioning for the child and are present for at least two weeks. Dysthymic Disorder can be considered a milder version of Major Depressive Disorder in that the child manifests depressed mood or irritability with symptoms of poor appetite or overeating, insomnia or hypersomnia, fatigue, poor concentration, and feelings of hopelessness. The difference is that with Major Depressive Disorder, there are discrete episodes of severe depression that represent a change from previous functioning, whereas with Dysthymic Disorder, there is an ongoing presence of less severe symptomatology with few, if any, breaks from the depressed symptoms.

Bipolar disorders, marked by mood swings cycling from depression to elation (or mania), primarily manifest for the first time in late adolescence and early adulthood (Youngstrom, Findling, and Feeny, 2004). The exception to this general rule of age of onset is Cyclothymic Disorder, which may occur among children. Cyclothymic Disorder is characterized by mild depression or irritability that takes turns with mildly elevated mood for at least one year (two years for adults) without major interruptions. That is, the child's mood is rarely at a normal level, but rather cycles through symptoms of mild depression versus mild elation (hypomania). Full manic episodes, required for the diagnosis of Bipolar Disorder I, are rare among children.

Anxiety Disorders.   Included in this diagnostic category are Specific Phobia, Social Phobia, Obsessive-Compulsive Disorder, Posttraumatic Stress Disorder, Acute Stress Disorder, and Generalized Anxiety Disorder. Other diagnoses in this category, generally only applicable to adolescents and adults and not discussed here, include Panic Attack, Agoraphobia, and Substance-Induced Anxiety Disorder. Specific Phobia (formerly called simple phobia) is characterized by persistent fear of an identifiable object or situation and manifestation of anxiety in its presence (Chorpita and Southam-Gerow, 2006). Subtypes of this diagnosis are Animal Type, Natural Environment Type, Blood-Injection-Injury Type, Situational Type, and Other Type. In diagnosing specific phobias in children, care must be taken not to confuse a diagnosable phobia with a normal age-appropriate and transient phobia. In Social Phobia, the child experiences a persistent fear of a social or performance situation in which the child fears that she or he might act in an embarrassing manner. This fear leads to an avoidance of the situation and results in significant interference with the child's life. If the fears include most social situations, the disorder is further specified as Generalized. Obsessive-Compulsive Disorder is diagnosed in the presence of obsessions or compulsions that interfere with the child's life (Franklin, March, and Garcia, 2007). Obsessions are recurrent and persistent thoughts, impulses, or images that cause anxiety and are not simple worries about real problems and which the child recognizes are within her or his own mind and attempts to ignore or suppress. Compulsions are repetitive behaviors that the child feels driven to perform and that are intended to prevent or reduce distress or prevent a negative event to occur. Posttraumatic Stress Disorder and Acute Stress Disorder are both reactions to traumatic events, in which the person was confronted with actual or threatened death or serious injury and to which the person responded with intense fear, helplessness, or horror. Both disorders involve the re-experience of the traumatic event through dreams, recollections, flashbacks, or similar occurrences; persistent avoidance of stimuli associated with the event; and anxiety symptoms, such as poor concentration, irritability, hypervigilance, and motor restlessness. Acute Stress Disorder is diagnosed when the symptoms occur within one month of the traumatic event, whereas Posttraumatic Stress Syndrome is diagnosed when symptoms persist for more than one month. Finally, Generalized Anxiety Disorder (which incorporates what was previously referred to as Overanxious Disorder) is characterized by at least three distinct symptoms of excessive and unrealistic worrying, such as irritability, muscle tension, sleep disturbance, difficulty concentrating, easy fatigue, and restlessness (Morris and March, 2004). Such anxiety must have occurred for at least six months, caused significant interference in the child's life, and is not confined to features of another disorder.

Sexual and Gender Identity Disorders.   Most of the diagnoses in this category are only applicable to adolescents or adults; the exception is Gender Identity Disorder in Children (Zucker, 2006). To be diagnosed with this disorder, children must demonstrate a strong cross-gender identification *and* discomfort over their assigned sex. Cross-gender identification is marked by the desire to be, or insistence that she or he is, the other sex, preference for wearing stereotypical clothing of the other sex, preference for taking the role of the other sex in make-believe play, desire to participate in stereotypical activities of the other sex, and preference for playmates of the other sex. Discomfort over assigned sex is demonstrated in a boy through expressed disgust toward his genitalia, rejection of stereotypical male activities, and aversion to rough-and-tumble play; in a girl, it is demonstrated through the assertion that she may grow a penis, rejection of urinating in a sitting position, stating that she does not want to grow breasts or to menstruate, and aversion to stereotypical feminine clothing.

Sleep Disorders.   Sleep disorders are organized into the four categories of Primary Sleep Disorder, Sleep Disorder Related to Another Mental Disorder, Sleep Disorder Due to a General Medical Disorder, and Substance-Induced Sleep Disorder (Stores, 2006). The category that is most applicable for children and therefore is reviewed in this chapter is that of Primary Sleep Disorders. Primary Sleep Disorders are broken down into Dyssomnias (marked by disturbances in quality, quantity, or timing of sleep) and Parasomnias (marked by abnormal events occurring in association with sleep). Dyssomnias can manifest as Primary Insomnia, Primary Hypersomnia, Narcolepsy, Breathing-Related Sleep Disorder, and Circadian Rhythm Sleep Disorder. Primary Insomnia is characterized by difficulty initiating or maintaining sleep, which in turn causes difficulties in life functioning, lasts for at least one month, and is not related to another mental or physical disorder. In Primary Hypersomnia, the child exhibits excessive sleepiness for at least one month, experiences impairment in life functioning due to this sleepiness, and has no other mental or physical disorder that explains the disorder. Narcolepsy involves attacks of sleep that refresh the child but are invariably followed by renewed sleepiness after a brief period of time. Additionally, the child evidences either cataplexy (brief loss of muscle tone, often in association with intense emotion) or recurrent rapid-eye-movement sleep during the transition between sleep and wakefulness, which can result in hypnagogic hallucinations or sleep paralysis. Breathing-Related Sleep Disorder refers to sleep disruptions caused by difficulties or abnormalities in breathing, resulting in excessive sleepiness during the day or insomnia during the night. Circadian Rhythm Sleep Disorder manifests as excessive sleeping and insomnia that results from a repeated disruption in sleep patterns due to a mismatch in the child's sleeping schedule and her or his circadian sleep pattern. Four types of this disorder are coded: Delayed Sleep Phase Type, Jet Lag Type, Shift Work Type, and Unspecified Type.

The category of Parasomnias includes Nightmare Disorder, Sleep Terror Disorder, and Sleepwalking Disorder. In Nightmare Disorder, the child experiences repeated awakenings with detailed memory of very frightening dreams. Upon awakening, the child becomes rapidly alert. The dreams cause significant impairment in the child's life functioning and are not associated with another mental or physiological disorder. Similarly, Sleep Terror Disorder involves recurrent awakenings from sleep. However, in this disorder, the child awakens with intense fear and arousal, has difficulty getting oriented, and cannot recall the dream. Finally, Sleepwalking Disorder involves the child getting up while asleep and walking about. During the sleepwalking episode, the child has a blank and staring face, is difficult to awaken, and is unresponsive to others; upon awakening, the child has no recollection of the event.

Adjustment Disorders.   This class of disorders consists of numerous diagnostic manifestations of the same disorder that are not unique to children: Adjustment Disorders with various emotional and/or behavioral features (Hill, 2006). Adjustment Disorders always involve a major known stressor that has occurred in the child's life within the past three months and must be noted on Axis IV (e.g., a parental divorce). The child evidences a maladaptive pattern of affect or behavior in response to this stressor that goes above and beyond any reaction that would normally be expected. Although this maladaptive reaction involves more than one overreaction, it never lasts longer than six months beyond the moment when the stressor ends. If the stressor has been eliminated but symptoms persist after six months, another diagnosis must be given; on the other hand, if the stressor persists, symptoms may persist, and the diagnosis of adjustment disorder remains appropriate. Type of impairment that characterizes the maladaptive response defines type of Adjustment Disorder. Notably, there are Adjustment Disorders With Depressed Mood, With Anxiety, With Mixed Anxiety and Depressed Mood, With Disturbance of Conduct, With Mixed Disturbance of Emotions and Conduct.

Other Conditions That May Be a Focus of Clinical Attention.   The DSM-IV-TR includes a number of other disorders that may be relevant to the child clinician. These diagnoses are problems, not mental disorders, though they may coexist with a diagnosable mental disorder; however, the problems are sufficiently severe in and of themselves to require intervention. Many of these are called V codes because the diagnostic number starts with a V. Parenthetically, this is important to note because insurance companies often do not reimburse for V-code diagnoses. Briefly, some of the diagnoses within this broad category are as follows: Relational Problems (including Parent–Child Relational Problem and Sibling Relational Problem); Problems Related to Abuse or Neglect (including Physical Abuse of a Child, Sexual Abuse of a Child, and Neglect of a Child); and Additional Conditions That May Be a Focus of Clinical Attention (including Child or Adolescent Antisocial Behavior, Borderline Intellectual Functioning, Bereavement, Academic Problem, Identity Problem, and Acculturation Problem).

Although only DSM-IV-TR categories of disorders that appear most relevant to the work with children are covered here, others exist and can manifest in children. They are discussed in detail elsewhere (e.g., Achenbach and Rescorla, 2007; Mash and Barkley, 2002, 2006), and the reader is referred to these references for more information. Before diagnosing a child, mental health professionals must familiarize themselves more thoroughly with the DSM-IV-TR.

Conceptualization: Understanding Case Dynamics

Once the problem list is prepared and used to aid the diagnostic process, the clinician attempts to understand *why* the problems or symptoms exist. This attempt at understanding the etiology of the child's disorder is crucial to treatment planning and involves taking a look at several factors surrounding the child and her or his family. The counselor needs to explore the three Ps of a case conceptualization: predisposing, precipitating, and perpetuating factors. As such a clinician looks at factors in the environment that may have predisposed the child for the development of symptoms, factors that may have precipitated current symptoms as well as the timing of presentation to the clinic, and factors that serve to perpetuate or reinforce the symptoms and dynamics evidenced by the child and family. The three Ps, in combination with observed dynamics within the child and the family, give the clinician a sense of direction for the child's treatment, as well as a sense of understanding and empathy for the development of the disorder (Brems, 1999).

Predisposing Factors

A variety of factors predisposing children to mental illness or emotional conflicts have been identified over the years. They have been explored in general, as well as related to particular disorders. Although some generalizations can be made (for instance, the genetic predisposition for mental retardation), it is important to assess particular predisposing factors that appear to function in the life of a child who is presenting for treatment. Predisposing factors can be societal, environmental, social, familial, personal, biological, and genetic. For each area, the clinician looks at the possibility of influences on the child's mental health and current presenting problems. Often such factors are quite obvious, but rarely can all be assessed accurately. A comprehensive listing of all possibilities assures that no possible component that has contributed to the child's psychological development and adjustment is missed. Rarely does one of these factors alone account for the symptoms that are presented at intake.

Societal Factors.   Societal factors can include issues such as Zeitgeist and moral attitudes, prejudice, ostracism of certain groups of people, or media-induced societal values. Eating disorders can be said to have a strong societal predisposing component because of the strong focus on certain acceptable body types. Even children as young as 10 or 11 years of age are aware of the strong societal preference for slim, muscular bodies. In an attempt to conform to such body typing, children may fall into unhealthy eating habits or patterns (Gordon, 2000). Adolescent suicide behavior among Native children may have a strong societal predisposing factor, as the Native culture currently is nearly devoid of heroes or role models. This absence of positive role models or ideals leaves children wanting self-esteem and a sense of life direction, resulting in depression and hopelessness that may culminate in suicide (Alcantara and Gone, 2007; Sullivan and Brems, 1997).

Environmental Factors.   Environmental factors can range from issues such as moving to a new neighborhood or a new school to surviving a traumatic environmental event such as an earthquake or a tornado. Absence of stimulation, such as might occur in an institutional setting, can be a grave environmental factor that may predispose children for numerous concerns, including depression, selective mutism, or pervasive developmental disorders (American Psychiatric Association, 1994, 2000). Separation anxiety is thought to have an environmental predisposing component, as affected children often have a history of loss, such as death of a friend, moving to a new neighborhood, or similar experiences (Bowlby, 1999). Adjustment disorders by definition have a strong environmental predisposing component, in which the child is responding very strongly to an environmental stressor. Finally, environmental factors are crucial to the development of posttraumatic stress disorder, in which a major environmental stressor is a required part of the diagnostic picture of the disorder (Putnam, 1996; Silva, 2004).

Social Factors.   Social factors are often closely related to environmental issues. They include malnutrition, neglect, living situation (e.g., growing up in a rural or inner-urban area), socioeconomic status, acculturation problems, stress levels, and similar influences. Social concerns are important predisposing factors in the development of disorders such as drug or substance abuse (Reinherz, Giaconia, Paradis, Wasserman, and Hauf, 2000), even in children. Aggressive behavior disorders and juvenile delinquency are correlated with socioeconomic status, suggesting a potential predisposing link between this social factor and subsequent pathology (Brems, 1995, 2000). Malnutrition may be involved in pica behaviors, as well as being related to developmental disorders. The possibility of these factors as important influences on a child's behavior or affects must not be underestimated.

Familial Factors.   Familial factors include issues such as parental divorce or discord, parental inconsistency in parenting, birth order of siblings, intergenerational conflicts, emotional absence of one parent, abuse of the child by a family member, mental illness of a parent, and other family processes. Obviously, these factors can have a variety of effects on a child, ranging from phobic reactions to depression, to conduct disorders, to reactive attachment disorders (Abela and Hankin, 2007; American Psychiatric Association, 1994, 2000; Beidel and Turner, 2007; Stafford and Zeanah, 2006).

Personal Factors.   Personal factors may be difficult to differentiate from familial patterns but include such unique factors as temperament (Seifer, 2000). They may account for the particular style a child evidences in adapting to situations or stressors and may be involved in the development of adjustment disorders. They may consist of relatively stable personality patterns that are potentially related to the development of personality disorders (Brems, 1999).

Biological Factors.   Biological factors include a variety of possibilities, such as neurological deficits, biochemical disturbances, various disabilities (e.g., physical, sensory), a range of severe or chronic illnesses (e.g., temporal lobe epilepsy, encephalitis), psychoactive substance use or abuse by the mother during pregnancy (e.g., alcohol, caffeine, sleeping pills), and allergies. Fetal alcohol spectrum disorders are considered a primary predisposing factor for a number of behavioral disorders in children, including but not limited to mental retardation, attention-deficit hyperactivity disorder, and learning disabilities (Autti-Raemoe, 2000; Sokol, Delaney-Black, and Nordstrom, 2003). A large number of childhood disorders may have other biological predisposing components, including stereotypic movement disorder (American Psychiatric Association, 1994, 2000), autism (Volkmar, Paul, Klin, and Cohen, 2005a), attention-deficit hyperactivity disorder (Bradley and Golden, 2001), mental retardation (Beirne-Smith, Patton, and Kim, 2005), and depression (Birmaher et al., 1996). Genetic factors have been found similarly important and may play a role in schizophrenia (Robertson, Hori, and Powell, 2006) and mood disorders (Zalsman et al., 2006). They are best traced through family histories of mental illness.

Predisposing factors are not noted to determine a definite cause of the child's problems but rather to obtain a better overview of all possible life components that may have contributed to the development of current symptoms. It is not possible to trace definite causes for specific disorders, only high correlations are known. Nevertheless, the possibility of predisposing factors must be considered and noted for each child who presents for treatment.

Precipitating Factors

Precipitating factors are the triggers either for the child's symptoms or the presentation of the family to treatment. Sometimes precipitants may be as simple as a big family fight that made everyone aware that the family needs to seek help. Sometimes, the precipitant is the complaint of a teacher about a child's behavior. Perhaps the parents had not even noted the child's particular behavior until it was pointed out as problematic by another adult. Precipitants are often most helpful in understanding why a family presents for treatment when they do, especially when it appears that a problem has existed for quite some time. However, sometimes the precipitant is responsible not only for triggering the referral but also for the manifestation of a particular concern. Thus, certain factors may be precipitants as well as predisposers. For instance, sudden divorce may result in extreme withdrawal behavior in a child. It is likely that although the divorce precipitated the child's symptoms, chronic parental conflict may have predisposed her or him for the development of such symptoms.

Perpetuating Factors

Just as mental health professionals consider what might have predisposed a child for a concern and what may have precipitated a symptom, so do they need to look at why the symptom is maintained. Not uncommonly, symptoms serve a purpose that perpetuates or reinforces their display. For instance, if somatic concerns such as frequent headaches in a child distract from parental fighting, the symptom may be maintained because it is less painful for the child than its alternative. Similarly, although enuresis may keep the child from being able to participate in sleepovers, this may be a small price to pay for the reward, which might be nightly attention that helps the child deal with separation anxiety. Perhaps the development of night terrors has convinced a single parent to allow the child to share the same bed. Many more examples are possible. Thus, a symptom, although being reported as uncomfortable or even painful, may have a larger purpose that can be described as secondary gain derived from the disorder. Clinicians need to assess what potential rewards may be inherent in a symptom to evaluate the possible reinforcing factors that maintain it. This provides information with regard to understanding the problem and has implications for treatment planning.

The exploration of reinforcing factors must not be mistaken by the client as an attempt to blame the child for the symptoms or as the belief that the child is aware of the reinforcing patterns. Secondary gain is an unconscious process, and there is hardly ever purposeful (or conscious) production of symptoms on a child's part. Further, not all reinforcing, or maintaining, factors are of a secondary gain nature. Sometimes, the failure of a parent to recognize the impact of her or his own behavior on the child may maintain a problem that would not be as severe if the parent were to change that behavior. For instance, use of inappropriate parenting strategies may result in the escalation of a child's acting out or may result in the inadvertent rewarding of misbehavior. An excellent example is that of a father who chooses to buy a tantruming child a treat at the grocery store to get the child to stop screaming. His inappropriate choice or timing of intervention has reinforced the child's misbehavior and has made it more likely to recur in the future.

Examples of predisposing, precipitating, and reinforcing factors are presented in Table 8.3, using the same child presented in Tables 8.1 and 8.2. Once the various factors that may have contributed to the development and maintenance of a presenting problem have been explored, this information is combined with all other aspects of this case to arrive at a thorough understanding of the child with regard to intrapsychic, family, and interpersonal dynamics. Defenses that are used must be reiterated and understood in the context of the child's intrapsychic adjustment, familial context, and interpersonal matrix. This integration of materials represents the heart of the case conceptualization and is done thoroughly and with care. It is this section of the conceptualization (and the diagnosis) that is included in a child's intake report.

Table 8.3   The Three Ps in the Case of a Child Presenting after Parental Divorce

Factor Type	Specific Example
Predisposing Factors	• chronic parental fighting that often involved the children • history of substance abuse by mother and suspected current abuse • cultural differences in parental and extended family backgrounds • conflicts around religious practices between parents • intrusive maternal grandmother (fails to respect child's privacy) • possible abuse (physical and emotional) • physical and psychological neglect • inconsistent discipline and unpredictability of consequences of behavior • psychologically unavailable mother who is incapable of adequate mirroring • psychological strain on child who had to take a parental role with the younger sister • absence of cultural belongingness because of maternal refusal to allow child to participate in father's religious rituals and cultural beliefs
Precipitating Factors	• sister's death • parental divorce • decrease in frequency of contact with father • move to new neighborhood • custody battle
Perpetuating Factors	• maternal attention for stomachaches and nightmares • paternal attention for accidents (he has medical benefits, thus is called when child needs medical attention) • avoidance of visits to maternal grandparents' home due to enuresis • attention and intervention at school for deteriorating performance • temporary "cease-fire" between parents after accidents and other symptoms • maternal discipline that tends to reward acting out behavior

Intrapsychic Dynamics

Not all clinicians emphasize the same contents, or even this entire aspect of a conceptualization, in the same manner. Of all parts of a conceptualization, it is perhaps this one that most strongly reflects counselors' primary theoretical approach to the work with children and therefore may vary greatly depending on the use of psychoanalytic, psychodynamic, person centered, cognitive-behavioral, or other systems of psychotherapy. However, all therapists take a look at the individual child and her or his personal adjustment (though behaviorally oriented therapists may take offense to the label "intrapsychic"), making this an integral part of the case formulation. Whether conceptual work focuses on interpreting belief systems, values, interests, behavioral patterns, development, reinforcement histories, or other facets of a child's psychological being is determined by the theoretical approach of the counselor. The common themes, however, always center on the attempt to gain an understanding of the child from her or his unique personal perspective and an appreciation for how the child has dealt with and adjusted to her or his living situation. For example, behaviorists look at the child's reinforcement or learning history, assessing how the child has learned various behaviors or symptoms and how well the child is coping. Cognitive-behaviorists emphasize aspects such as distorted thought patterns, irrational beliefs, and automatic thoughts that affect the child. Developmental theorists assess the developmental phase of the child, and developmental tasks and challenges faced by the child. Psychodynamic theorists assess the child's ego strength, developmental stage, conflicts, defenses, self-development, and similar intrinsic forces.

It is neither possible nor prudent to dictate a particular approach for this aspect of the conceptualization. Research has indicated that there is no one theoretical approach that is clearly superior to any other in terms of conceptualization and treatment (though a specific problem may indeed warrant a specific approach; Mash and Barkley, 2006). However, it has been established that *having* a firm theoretical background of any type *is* crucial to the success of treatment. Thus, therapists about to embark on clinical work with a child need to take a look at their beliefs about human behavior and life and best try to approach each case from a consistent theoretical point of view. Knowledge of various systems of psychotherapy is helpful in making a choice about to which theoretical system to employ (Todd and Bohart, 2006). Changing conceptual understanding, and thus the practical approach to treatment, of a child's case midstream is likely to be confusing not only for the counselor and supervisor, but primarily for the child and the family. It tends to indicate that the counselor is floundering and treatment does not have a sense of direction. Lack of consistency and direction are clearly counterproductive. Careful formulation of a child's intrapsychic processes is thus considered a necessary prerequisite to successful treatment. Using a self-psychological perspective for understanding human behavior, the intrapsychic dynamics of the child presented in the examples in this chapter so far can be summarized as follows:

> This 9-year-old girl appears to have been on her way to stable adjustment and self-development when a sudden parental divorce and other changes in her environment occurred. Although she shows slips in her capacity to appraise her own abilities and to maintain her sense of self-esteem in the absence of nurturing others in her environment, she was, until recently, capable of taking care of her own needs, in fact, using these skills to parent her younger sister. She now feels less able to comfort herself, and her moods have become sufficiently severe to feel out of control and overwhelming to her. Because she is overwhelmed by the severity of her moods, she is no longer able to regain a sense of stability and equanimity on her own. Several aspects of her developing self, for instance, her internalized sense of strength, are becoming vulnerable and less resilient than they used to be. In an unconscious attempt to help herself regain a sense of safety, she has withdrawn from others and has begun evidencing symptoms (stomachaches and accidents) that may activate potential helpers in her environment at least temporarily. Her stressful situation has also contributed to her decreased ability to attend and concentrate, with a subsequent deterioration in academic performance. Lack of adequate nurturance and positive feedback from others in her environment have resulted in decreased coping energy and a sense of helplessness and hopelessness that has culminated in her wish to die or hurt.

Situational stressors are now extremely difficult for her to face, as her internal resources to help herself have been taxed to the limit and currently are not working for her. Stress now manifests through somatic and physical channels, as evidenced by her stomachaches and enuresis.

Family Dynamics

As was true for the formulation of intrapsychic processes, all clinicians must and do integrate the family context to arrive at yet another component of the case conceptualization. Children are firmly embedded in an interpersonal matrix of adults and caretakers whose roles must be neither ignored nor underestimated. Thus, their impact on the child's life, their interactions with the child, their effect on the child's behavior, and their own psychological makeup are crucial to understand and place in the context of the child's symptomatic presentation. Family processes can be phrased in terms of a number of theoretical approaches, and again, no one superior approach has emerged in the literature. However, there appears to be much less divergence across clinicians from various systems of psychotherapy when it comes to understanding family systems. Generally, the focus is on understanding how behaviors, attitudes, mental health, and interactions of the child's primary caretakers affect the child's current and past psychological adjustment and behavior. Extended family influences are also considered, especially if there is frequent interaction and visitation. The family dynamics, consistent with a self-psychological perspective, surrounding the child presented in the examples in this chapter so far can be summarized as follows:

> It appears that the child's mother has been unable to nurture and enjoy this child from the moment of her birth given her own needs and psychological pain. She has relied on her daughter for her own nurturing and strength, thus often overburdening the child and failing to nurture her daughter's psychological growth and self-development. The mother does not have a healthy, integrated self and is in great need of others to help her maintain her sense of balance, esteem, and purpose (e.g., alcohol, this child, her own mother). The mother's own vulnerability has resulted not only in the use of the child as a helper but also in the inconsistency of her own ability to lend support to her child.

> The child's father has been emotionally distant and unavailable. However, he is a highly successful surgeon who has received much acclaim in the medical community. As a result, apparently the child's father has had some positive influence on her and has been a figure in her life from whom she could glean strength even when he was physically absent. His strength supported her development of the capacity for self-regulation as she followed his role modeling for healthy coping and willful living. His lack of warmth, however, left her yearning for an emotional connection that would have supported her needs for nurturance and caring support.

> The child's sister was an important person in her life in the sense that caring for her gave her a purpose (though it was also a source of distress and feelings of being overburdened). When her sister died, the child lost her sense of purpose and may even have experienced feelings of guilt and self-blame that have under-

mined her self-esteem. When her father left the family, she lost her role model for strength and with him her budding ability to care for herself and to regulate her own affects. The absence of his sense of strength and coping has contributed to a deepening of her depression and sense of hopelessness. Her decreased contact with her father and his extended family have left her feeling more vulnerable and distanced from her most important coping resource. As she had not completely internalized a permanent sense of strength and self-confidence, the removal from her father may prove detrimental to her continued self-development, especially since her mother is not emotionally available to provide supportive nurturance and guidance.

The child's intrusive grandmother frequently interferes with this child's attempts at nurturing and strengthening herself, for example, by reading her diary and making fun of her entries, by admonishing her for not taking better care of her mother, by scolding her for trying to be like her father, and by constantly comparing her negatively with her cousins. The grandmother's negativity fails to support the child's healthy attempts at coping and self-nurturing.

Interpersonal Matrix Dynamics

Family dynamics, as outlined above, are only one aspect of a child's interpersonal matrix. Children interact with other children, babysitters, day care personnel, teachers, and many other individuals every day. All of these people represent potential sources of conflict or support and are considered part of the child's overall life. Exploration of the interpersonal matrix is driven by the therapist's theoretical framework and may be considered more important by some than by others. However, most mental health professionals agree that interpersonal relationships are an important aspect of a child's mental health and day-to-day functioning. After all, ultimately, any gains that are made in therapy are hoped to generalize to the child's interpersonal matrix. This is the final aspect of the case conceptualization, and it leads to a summarizing statement about the child's overall adjustment and driving forces. The dynamics of the interpersonal matrix and the summary of the case of the child presented in the examples in this chapter so far are as follows, again taking a self-psychological perspective:

The move to an unfamiliar neighborhood and the removal from cultural values and religious beliefs that she had just started to accept as her own took away opportunities from being with others, leaving her feeling alienated and different from other children. Subsequent withdrawal from her peers has initiated a vicious cycle of isolation and self-protection. She is now so unsure of herself and unable to take care of her own needs that she maintains an interpersonal distance as a final effort to maintain some sense of self-protection and safety. She avoids interpersonal contacts for fear of being hurt or used and is withdrawing from others completely. Yet at the same time, she is starved for emotional nurturance and a source of strength and attempts to meet some of these needs by mobilizing resources in her academic environment.

In summary, this child grew up in an environment in which her nurturance needs were not met given her mother's own psychological needs and her father's emotional distance. Although she received some adequate opportunities for learning strength, coping, and values from her father, she was generally overburdened and undernurtured. A chronic sense of not being adequately cared for and nurtured has impaired her developmental ability to grow into a capable individual with internalized strength and self-esteem. Her lack of perceived coping ability and self-efficacy has left her prone to falling apart when she is under stress and has contributed to the current symptomatic picture.

Once the case conceptualization has been prepared, clear avenues for intervention should have occurred to the counselor. The conceptualization is a direct precursor to treatment planning. However, even once a treatment plan has been written, it is never written in stone. Throughout the work with the child, the counselor learns new information, gains new insights, and is encouraged to modify the conceptualization and the treatment plan as appropriate to these new understandings. However, any reconceptualization best remains consistent with the original theoretical approach, and updating treatment plans does not imply changing direction. Only rarely is an initial conceptualization so off the mark that a major therapeutic shift is necessary.

Treatment Planning

The process of treatment planning occurs upon completion of the thorough assessment phase that has been outlined to this point. It represents the transition between assessment and treatment. Treatment does not begin before a treatment plan has been formulated, even if the child and family have been seen repeatedly. Any session before the formulation of a treatment plan is considered assessment and has as its purpose the better understanding of the client in the hope of arriving at the best possible treatment plan. Once the treatment plan has been developed, treatment begins, and the focus of the interaction becomes change and growth. Desired counseling or therapy outcomes must be mutually agreed upon by the care provider and the client(s); that is, treatment goals are discussed with the child and family. It is neither uncommon nor problematic for the clinician and the family to have slightly different perspectives on the goals for treatment. Parents may simply be interested in the removal of symptoms, whereas the counselor may also be interested in enhancing a child's self-esteem. Such differences are discussed and explained in the context of the presenting symptom to help parents understand that symptom removal alone is often not enough in the long run. It is unwise to argue with parents or children about treatment goals even if they differ. Rather, respect and, as appropriate, education are indicated. The family is sided within their stated goals, tying these goals in with the larger context the clinician would like to address. Treatment is more successful if all parties involved agree on what is being worked on.

Treatment Goals

There are often three sets of treatment goals that can be identified: the care provider's, the child's, and the parents'. There is significant overlap among these three, but all are noted and identified in terms of who views a particular goal as most important. Treatment strategies are developed in such a manner as to maximize the number of goals that can be accommodated. They are clear and quantifiable or measurable; they are directly related to the presenting problems and the underlying dynamics noted in the conceptualization. For example, if a primary presenting problem of depression was revealed, a related treatment goal is a measurable decrease in severity of depressive symptoms. Goals can be arranged hierarchically so that larger goals can be broken into component parts that may make treatment progress more obvious and likely. For example, in decreasing the severity of depression, it is best to have smaller goals that relate to specific symptoms, such as better sleep, increased self-esteem, weight gain, enhanced interpersonal involvement, and renewed interests.

Treatment goals can be divided into two major categories: resolution of the presenting problems and rehabilitation of the underlying case dynamics. Thus, there are various ways in which treatment goals can be dealt with. The most thorough approach integrates them all and is demonstrated here. In this approach, treatment goals are grouped according to the two broad categories of resolution of presenting problems versus rehabilitation of the underlying case dynamics. Within each category, goals are arranged according to whether they are global goals or subgoals of an overall symptom. Further, they are identified with regard to who is most concerned about the particular goals. This process results in a hierarchy of goals, an applied example of which is provided in Table 8.4 (on the following page) for the child discussed above. The format of the table can be used as it is in a child's treatment plan, but is generally not included in the intake report.

Treatment Strategies

Once goals have been identified, strategies have to be chosen with which to address them. This process can be quite detailed, as very detailed descriptions can be provided about how the clinician plans to approach each particular problem (see Table 8.5 on p. 233). However, more often, the strategy choices are global, as it is often difficult to anticipate how a particular problem (and hence its associated) goal might manifest in treatment (e.g., Table 8.5; the specific techniques within each global strategy have been deleted). Flexibility in terms of actual in-session interaction with the child is maintained to enable the counselor to respond according to her or his best judgment. It is likely that each therapist has a repertoire of skills she or he prefers in varying situations. Again, the actual strategies used by mental health professionals vary according to their theoretical orientation.

Although consistency in overall approach and in conceptualization is crucial, flexibility in the use of strategies is paramount. Thus, a psychodynamically oriented therapist may have a rehabilitation goal of helping the child to internalize an idealized pole of the self. This aspect of self has to do with self-regulation and requires the knowledge of limits, boundaries, rules, and values. In the process of pursuing this psychodynamically oriented treatment goal, the therapist might utilize behavioral principles that reinforce for the child the necessity and adequacy of certain behaviors, depending on the setting in which they are displayed. In other words, although a theoretical orientation must be firm with regard to conceptualizing a case, the use of strategies must be adaptable, creative, and flexible. Fortunately, many techniques are

Table 8.4   Hierarchy of Treatment Goals for a Child Presenting after Parental Divorce

Goal Category Global Goal	Subgoals	Individuals Concerned about This Goal
Resolution of Presenting Problem		
Resolve Depression (Goal 1)	(1a) increase activity level	clinician, child, parents
	(1b) decrease social isolation	child, clinician
	(1c) weight gain	parents, clinician
	(1d) increase mood	parents, clinician
	(1e) increase self-esteem	child, parents, clinician
	(1f) enhance concentration	parents, clinician
	(1g) decrease crying spells	parents, clinician, child
	(1h) grieve sister's death	parents, clinician
Resolve Academic Problems (Goal 2)	(2a) improve grades	child, parents
	(2b) enhance concentration	parents, clinician
	(2c) increase attention span	clinician, parents
	(2d) test for learning disability	clinician, parents
	(2e) enhance achievement	parents, child
Resolve Physical Problems (Goal 3)	(3a) decrease stomachaches	clinician, child, parents
	(3b) decrease nightmares	clinician, child, parents
	(3c) decrease enuresis	clinician, child, parents
	(3d) increase to age appropriate weight	clinician, parents
Rehabilitation of Underlying Dynamics		
Enhance the Psychological Environment (Goal 4)	(4a) decrease mother's drinking	clinician
	(4b) decrease mother's neglect	clinician, father
	(4c) monitor abuse, report as needed	clinician, child, father
	(4d) monitor neglect, report as needed	clinician, father
	(4e) increase visitation with father	clinician, father, child
	(4f) exposure to Asian culture, religion	clinician, father
	(4g) increase parenting knowledge	clinician, child, father
	(4h) open communication between parents	clinician, child
	(4i) decrease contact with grandmother	clinician, child
	(4j) increase contact with other adults	clinician, child
Promote Healthy Self-Development (Goal 5)	(5a) develop capacity to self-nurture	clinician
	(5b) develop inner strength	clinician
	(5c) increase coping ability	clinician, parents
	(5d) support desire to be with others	clinician, parents, child
	(5e) facilitate skill development	clinician, parents, child

available to the counselor. The remainder of this book is dedicated to the thorough discussion of many of these techniques (e.g., play therapy, art therapy, storytelling, behavior modification) and specific strategies and approaches within them. Strategy choices are noted (though often in abbreviated form) in the child's intake report in the form of recommendations, and are presented in detail in the treatment plan. Table 8.5 exhibits strategy choices as noted in a treatment plan. The list below shows the corresponding recommendations that would be noted in the intake report.

Table 8.5   Treatment Strategies for the Therapy of a Child Presenting after Parental Divorce

Global Strategies Specific Techniques	Treatment Goals Addressed (by numbers)
Play Therapy for Child	1, 1a–h, 2, 2a–2c, 2e, 3, 3a–3d, 5, 5a–5e
• activity therapy	1a, 1d, 1f, 2a, 2b, 2c, 2e, 5a–5e
• storytelling	1c, 1d, 1e, 1h, 2e, 3b, 3d, 5a–5e
• art therapy	1d, 1e, 1f, 1h, 2a, 2b, 2c, 2e, 5a
• mirroring transference	1d, 1e, 1g, 1h, 3a, 3b, 3c, 5a
• idealizing transference	1d, 1f, 1g, 2a, 2b, 2c, 2e, 5b, 5e
Group Therapy for Child	1, 1a–g, 4, 4f, 5, 5a–5e
• twinship experience	1b, 4f, 5c, 5d, 5e
• activity therapy	1a, 1b, 1d, 1f, 5a, 5c, 5d, 5e
• art therapy	1d, 1e, 1f, 1h, 5a, 5d
School Consultation	2, 2a-2e, 3a, 4, 5, 5c–5e
• communicate with teacher	2b, 2c, 3a, 4f, 4j, 5c, 5e
• academic testing	2d, 2e, 5d
Parent Education and Consultation	4, 4a–4g, 5, 5a–5c (indirectly: 1–3)
Relationship Therapy for Parents	4, 4h–4j, 5, 5a–5c (indirectly: 1–3)
Individual Therapy for Mother	4, 4a–4d, 4i–4j, 5, 5a–5c

Treatment Recommendations for a Child Presenting after Parental Divorce

1. Offer once-weekly 50-minute play therapy sessions for the child.
   (Therapist: Dr. X)

2. Offer attendance of once-weekly 75-minute group therapy sessions for the child.
   (Therapist: Dr. A)

3. Consult with school, especially teacher, to open communication and initiate academic assessment; consider intervention in the classroom with teacher.
   (Therapist: Dr. X)

4. Enroll parents in clinic's Parent Education Workshop as space becomes available.
   (Workshop Leaders: Drs. A and F)

5. Offer regular meetings between parents and child's individual therapist to keep parents apprised of child's progress in therapy and to keep communication open.

6. Offer relationship therapy to parents to attempt to resolve their fighting to provide a healthier interpersonal matrix for the child.
   (Therapist: TBA)

7. Offer individual therapy for the mother to help her integrate herself to make her better capable of serving as a healthy parent for the child.
   (Therapist: TBA)

8. Once-monthly consultation of all therapists involved in this case to coordinate treatment.

Expected Treatment Resistances/Hindrances

Another integral part of the treatment plan is the counselor's assessment of possible resistances that may be encountered. The treatment of children includes a number of people and hence is much more prone to being boycotted or sabotaged in one way or another than work with adults. It can be quite frustrating to recognize that even though the child and counselor are quite committed to the child's counseling, the parents are unwilling to bring the child consistently or on time. Thus, the child's treatment is impeded by a third force over which neither child nor the clinician has much, if any, control. However, parental resistance is not the only potential problem. Several sources of hindrances exist.

A child client might resist treatment because of fear of not being loyal to a parent, fear of the interpersonal setting, inability to trust, and a number of other reasons that are as unique as the specific presentation for treatment. The child's family might resist because they are threatened by the intervention of another adult or for fear of being reported for child abuse or neglect. Often, parents resist not because of malicious intent, but because of their own psychological problems or emotional needs. Thus, they may fail to recognize the severity of their child's symptoms, may downplay their own role in their child's adjustment, or may be offended by a school-initiated referral. As most parents are not entirely certain of their ability to parent "correctly," the challenge of facing a professional might be too great for them to have the strength to deal with this situation effectively and nondefensively.

Resistances do not always come from the child or the family. Sometimes, the environment in which the family lives is not conducive to compliance. Perhaps the extended family questions the action by the family who sought the intake consultation, a challenge that can result in the family's failure to follow through with treatment recommendations. Perhaps the particular cultural group to which the child belongs is not convinced of the value of therapy or even attaches stigma to a person's need for counseling. Sometimes, socioeconomic factors get in the way, in that families are unwilling to disclose their inability to pay. Occasionally, families make the best attempt at coming for treatment together, but realistic work schedule limitations get in the way. Not often, but yet sometimes, a child's school may negatively influence a family's ability or willingness to follow through with treatment, either by scapegoating the child, not allowing the child to leave school early on a regular basis, making negative comments about the child's progress, or similar interactions.

Finally, there are resistances or hindrances that arise from the therapist or the mental health agency itself. Agencies without sliding fee schedules and with rigid business hours tend not to be conducive to the treatment of children. It is very difficult for families or children to come to treatment between 8 AM and 5 PM, yet many agencies expect parents to do so. Failure to provide flexible fee schedules might set families up for failure. Often families who have been identified for referral by an outside agency are not able to cover the cost of treatment. Resistances that arise from the clinician can be multifold and were addressed in detail in chapter 1. They may involve prejudices, stereotypes, expectations, or personality characteristics. It is also possible that a particular case results in a very specific countertransference. Resistances due to the therapist are often difficult to note, and are best dealt with through consultation.

Some signs of provider-induced problems in the counseling process include, but are not limited to, failure to make progress even though the child and family have complied with treatment, failure to collect outstanding bills from a family whose fee was set according to ability to pay, dreading the session with the child, avoiding the child's parents, unwillingness to discuss the child's case at staffings, resistance to letting go of the child, or difficulty terminating a case. Anticipating resistances, whether from the clients, the environment, or from the therapist, is the best protection against letting them undermine a child's therapy.

Strengths

In making a treatment plan, the clinician focuses on the problems the family brought to the intake interview(s). However, it is important to remember in this process that families and children also bring strengths that facilitate treatment. Noting these strengths and using them in the treatment planning process can significantly improve and speed up interventions. Just as resistances were noted in the child, the family, the environment, the agency, and the therapist, so too are strengths. Thus, a child who is bright and has a good social support network brings two definite strengths to treatment. Parents who are cooperative and concerned can be a great asset to the work with a child. A school setting that is supportive of the family's decision to seek services can make a big difference. For instance, one little boy who was referred for treatment had very poor parents who were unable to provide transportation between the agency and his school. As he had been referred by the school because of abuse and neglect in his home, his school made a commitment to transport him to his sessions. He made tremendous strides in treatment, something that would not have been possible without the help of his school. Similarly, teachers who are open to incorporating various strategies used with the child in the classroom often greatly facilitate generalization of progress. Finally, geographic, schedule, and cost compatibility between family and agency is a great asset.

Summary and Concluding Thoughts

This chapter has outlined a careful, step-by-step process for conceptualizing a child's situation and for making a treatment plan. Emphasis was placed on comprehensiveness, which plays a crucial role in treatment implementation. Ignoring any facet of a child's life and adjustment can result in treatment errors with grave consequences. Following the guidelines presented in this chapter helps the clinician, child, and family get well on their way to a successful counseling or therapy experience for everyone involved.

PART III

Treatment

A Framework for
Child Therapy and Counseling

> States Parties shall take all appropriate measures to promote physical and psychological recovery and social reintegration of a child victim of: any form of neglect, exploitation, or abuse; torture or any other form of cruel, inhuman or degrading treatment or punishment; or armed conflicts. Such recovery and reintegration shall take place in an environment which fosters the health, self-respect and dignity of the child.
>
> —Article 39 of the U.N. Convention on the Rights of the Child

It is difficult to decide on a logical progression for a chapter on therapy or counseling process, as it superimposes a structure or order that does not exist in exactly the same manner in the room. Treatment in reality is the occurrence of many simultaneous events, and the ordered discussion of these events often gives the false impression that they occur in a predictable manner and sequence in the real-life situation. The reader must understand that this is not so. Instead, therapy and counseling processes, tools or catalysts, and challenges, all of which are described and discussed here, are intermingled, facilitate one another, and coexist. In fact, they depend on one another for their existence. There can be no therapeutic goal without a process leading to it; there is no process without the necessary tools; there is no change without catalysts. Despite the coexistence of these events, they are addressed individually here to provide the reader with a sufficiently thorough, yet coherent, overview of what happens between a child and clinician when treatment progresses well. The arbitrariness of the orderly approach chosen for this chapter, however, must be borne in mind throughout.

Goals for the Therapy and Counseling Process

The discussion of the therapy or counseling process is best begun with a brief overview of goal setting, despite the fact that this is largely within the realm of assessment and intake. Goals for each child are generally straightforward and well planned out by the time actual treatment begins. They are listed in detail in the child's treatment plan and are used to monitor progress, as well as to determine when treatment is complete. Goals are very specifically tailored to problems that emerge during the intake interview and through any additional assessment. Despite their specificity, goals can be grouped into three categories in a manner appropriate for all child clients. First, there is the category of goals that has to do with resolving the child's presenting problems. Second, there is the category of goals that deals with strengthening the child's psychological and emotional adjustment overall. And third, there is the category of goals that relates to helping a child reenter a healthy point on the developmental trajectory with regard to all developmental functions (e.g., self-development, language development, motor development, psychosocial development; Russ and Freedheim, 2001). All three sets of goals deserve equal attention and are important in the work with children. However, the latter two are often overlooked even by the most experienced clinicians.

The goals pertaining to the resolution of presenting problems are the most measurable and observable goals in a child's treatment and are more commonly used to monitor progress and determine the timing of termination than the other two categories of goals (Brems, 1999). They are couched in terms of behavior that is observable, as well as measurable, as opposed to terms that are global and vague. For instance, two goals that commonly fall into this category of goal setting for children who are depressed are increasing the child's daily intake of food and increasing the child's weight. Both goals can be easily monitored by parents who may track caloric intake and chart weight and height. Even increases in self-esteem fall into this category, as long as they are observed and measured. Thus, if a child were administered a self-esteem inventory and given the same test at regular intervals throughout treatment, scores could be used to track changes in self-reported well-being.

Goals pertaining to the strengthening of the child's overall psychological adjustment are often more difficult, though not impossible, to measure. These goals are important as they keep the therapist from focusing on details or separate aspects of the child at the expense of monitoring overall improvement and change. Not uncommonly significant gains have been made in a child's overall psychological health before specific behavior changes are noted. On the other hand, it is possible for children to have made progress with regard to several very specific aspects of functioning without having improved their overall well-being. Goals that fall into this category reflect the theoretical beliefs of the counselor about the important aspects of a child's individual adjustment, a child's family, environment, reinforcement histories, and so forth, and about where changes need to be facilitated. Specific goals within this category vary greatly depending on the theoretical approach of each care provider. This is unlike the goals in the first category, which are strictly problem-, not theory-, driven.

For instance, for a cognitive-behaviorist, an overall goal may be the general improvement of a child's ability to use self-talk in a number of situations to avoid depressive or anxiety-provoking thoughts. For a family therapist, an overriding goal may be changing the family structure. A humanistic therapist may use this category of goals to ascertain that a child has developed a way of being that feels genuine or coherent and is free of a false sense of self. A psychodynamic therapist of the Kohutian school may focus on helping the child gain a strong sense of self-confidence, a clear sense of direction, and a set of skills that can support and guide both of these aspects of the child's self. In other words, this set of goals is less directly measurable, but nevertheless equally important as the first set of goals.

The third set of goals, dealing with the developmental trajectory of the child, refers to the fact that treatment must help children master developmental milestones and achieve a certain level of maturity. This maturity is not to be understood in the adult sense of behaving rationally and appropriately but rather in the sense of "maturity that is relatively appropriate" to the child's age (Spiegel, 1989, p. 24) and developmental level. This set of goals is often left implicit by therapists and is rarely included in the written treatment plan. Developmental goals can take many different forms. For one child, it might be an appropriate goal to help her or him reach a sense of core self or self-regulation (Stern, 1985). For another child, the focus may be on helping her or him achieve a sense of initiative (Erikson, 1950), while for a third child the most important developmental trajectory may be that of developing appropriate language skills. An overall developmental goal is always the bringing all aspects of development in line with one another. In other words, it is desirable to ascertain that a child's psychosocial development is consistent with cognitive development, that moral development is at the same level of sophistication, that self-development is equally advanced, and so on. Inconsistencies in developmental levels produce problems in and of themselves and always deserve to be included as treatment goals.

Once clear goals have been identified and providers have made some preparations for measurement of these goals, treatment is ready to commence. It remains important throughout the treatment process that therapists remain aware of all treatment goals and monitor them carefully. This is generally best done by eliciting help from parents and teachers who have daily contact with the child. These individuals can provide the counselor with valuable information about improvements and changes that are too intrusive for clinicians to monitor. For instance, weighing the child during each session would be quite disruptive. Receiving monthly feedback from parents about this issue, on the other hand, can be very helpful.

Phases of Child Therapy and Counseling

Once the therapeutic work with a child has begun, there are several processes or stages the clinician needs to keep in mind. Superimposed on the stages of change that the child is likely to go through in the adjustment to the therapy or counseling process is a progression of process behaviors that repeats over and over in the course of treatment. This progression is likely to begin once the child has moved beyond the anxious, exploratory stage and has moved into a stage in which affect is being expressed freely and the relationship with the therapist has become important. This progression of behaviors moves from *recollection* of events to their *reconstruction* and *reexperience* in play and finally to their *resolution* (Brems, 1999). Although this sequence is likely to occur in this order for any one problem or event, the child may be at different phases of this progression for different problems. In other words, while recollecting one event, the child may already be at the stage of resolving another. Thus, while this progression is easily discussed in an orderly manner, it is less likely to be quite as clear-cut in the actual therapy or counseling sessions. It must also be noted that sometimes entire phases are skipped, with a child moving directly into a reconstruction or resolving a problem without reexperiencing it. Often, reexperience and resolution are closely tied together for minor problems, and the child may progress through these phases in such quick succession that they are no longer distinct. Finally, the four phases, which are discussed below in some detail, are facilitated by the clinician through the use of various therapeutic tools or counseling strategies. For ease of presentation, the phases are discussed first and displayed in Table 9.1; specific facilitating tools are addressed later.

Table 9.1   The Phases of the Therapy or Counseling Process

Phase	Content	Level of Understanding	Strategies
Recollection	sharing of memories provision of information	no tie to presenting problem or etiology	listening questioning probing
Reconstruction	affective involvement in play and memory	still no direct tie to etiology, though affect is recognized as out of proportion	clarifying statements communication of understanding
Reexperience	affective expression in here-and-now with recollection of past event	beginning recognition of a tie between current issues and past events	use of transference explaining strategies projective identification
Resolution	strength confidence coping	tie between presenting problem and other issues is formed	internalization insight

Recollection

In the recollection phase, the child begins to share recollections or memories of issues that are related to the major area of concern. Children typically exhibit recollection by presenting their conflict or problem in play activity and, less often, by sharing it verbally. In this phase of the process, recollection is often vague, not consciously related to the presenting concern by the child, and rarely endowed with much affect or strong need states. It is a relatively matter-of-fact restating or replaying of events that is generally more meaningful to the clinician than to the child. This phase of a child's treatment is much like the early stage of an adult's treatment, wherein clients give much information about their life without making connections between the information that is given and its relevance to the presenting problems. Not uncommonly, adults in this phase of treatment talk about past events, especially from childhood, without being very certain about why these memories are emerging. The connection between the memory and the presenting problem does not occur until a later phase in the process of treatment. Given the fact that no connection has been made by the child or the adult client, interpretation at this time is premature. The clinician best serves the process of treatment by facilitating recollection through listening, probing, and asking questions to gain a better understanding of each event's relevance.

An example of a child in this phase of treatment is the interaction with an 8-year-old boy in his third session. He had been referred for aggressive acting out with peers and engaged in a very interesting play activity without much awareness of its revealing and applicable nature.

> Eight-year-old Jason chose to play (for the first time) with the dollhouse and doll family. He picked up the male adult doll and called him Frank (the child had a live-in grandfather named Francis), the female adult doll and called her Linda (his mother's name was Lisa), and a female child doll named Susan. The three-some ate dinner together, and much focus was placed on Linda serving food to Frank, on Susan having to eat everything on her plate, and then on Linda cleaning up after the meal while Frank smoked a cigarette and had a beer. After cleanup, Susan was put to bed by Linda, who read her a bedtime story and kissed her goodnight. After Susan fell asleep, Linda went to bed and locked her door. Frank tried to get into her room, banged on her door, and finally climbed through her window. He made a lot of noise, and Susan awoke.

The boy went through this scene quickly and with little affect. After the female child had awakened, he turned to another activity and refused to play with the dollhouse again during this session. However, he did return in his next session and enacted a very similar scene. This scene was understood by the therapist as indicating that the child indeed was witness to abuse of his mother by the grandfather. (This was later confirmed in a session with the mother, who soon thereafter began treatment of her own.) Further, the scene confirmed in conjunction with previously obtained information that the boy felt helpless and unable to protect his mother, yet would have liked to do so. He developed very angry feelings against his grandfather, which found an outlet in his aggressive behaviors against peers who were not as powerful as his grandfather. This is an example of a recollection, as the child showed no significant affects in the reenactment of the scene. Further, he had distanced himself from the imparted information by making the child in his play a girl, indicating that although he was ready to share information, he was neither ready to deal with it directly and openly nor able to make a connection between the memory and the presenting concerns of aggressive behavior.

Reconstruction

In the second phase of therapy or counseling process, the child reconstructs personal emotional or psychological states as related to recollections and memories that emerged in phase one. This shift in the process involves the child's affective involvement in play activity and reenactments. It is paralleled in adult treatment by a client who becomes tearful while discussing a painful childhood event without fully recognizing its relevance to the current problem. The experience is moved beyond mere recollection in that the client recognizes that the experience evokes affects or need states that are as powerful as they are somehow meaningful. Children often reconstruct entire relevant scenarios in their play with full expression of affect yet little awareness as to the direct relevance to current problems. The differentiation between a recollection and reconstruction is important, as the clinician's response varies depending on how the event is understood. As was mentioned earlier, in response to a recollection, the clinician merely gathers more information. However, in response to a reconstruction, the counselor can make a clarifying statement that communicates to the child that the expressed affect or need has been understood. No attempt is made to give an interpretation or to tie the event directly to the current presenting problem.

For instance, reconstruction was at the heart of an event in the work with a 3-year-old girl who had been referred because of recent severe night terrors and nightmares that had begun to interfere with her sleep.

> Three-year-old Sally liked to retreat to the floor cushions when painful affects emerged that related to memories or current events. In one session, she pretended that the cushions were her bed and asked the counselor to go through her bedtime rituals with her. She directed the counselor in what to do, telling her how to tuck her in, how to read a bedtime story, and how to kiss her goodnight. She then would close her eyes and pretend to have gone to sleep. When she "awakened," it was morning and the breakfast routine began. This scene was played out several times, and during the third time, the child began calling the counselor "mommy" and told her not to leave the side of bed while she slept. She became very agitated at this time and indicated that her stepmother and biological father, whom she had to visit every other weekend, refused to tuck her in and read her a story.

This event in this girl's work was a reconstruction of both positive and negative bedtime experiences that represented one aspect in the etiology of her nightmares and night terror disorder. It is an example of a reconstruction, as opposed to recollection, as the child became visibly agitated in the absence of the ritual and was visibly soothed and comforted by the presence of the ritual. Her expressed need to have her "mommy" by her side when she went to sleep was reflected by the counselor who responded to the child's calling her "mommy" by saying, "You really want your mommy when you go to sleep." The relief on her face validated that the counselor had understood her correctly and had correctly identified the event as a reconstruction and the need of the child as one for a nurturing and reliable figure in the child's life.

Reexperience

In the third phase of treatment, the child begins to relate present psychological or emotional states to past ones that may have contributed to the current issue or presenting problem, at least affectively. This type of reexperience is evident in children when they express an affect or need in the present and then spontaneously reenact scenarios from the past that resemble the current situation, or if they respond to a current situation with unwarranted vehemence. Whereas reexperience with adults generally involves making a verbal connection between the relationship of a past event, a particular style of thinking, or a particular way of looking at oneself to the presenting concern, the child does not have to do so verbally. Reexperience in child treatment can occur without conscious or verbal expression of the relationship, as long as nonverbal communication clearly ties present and past, or current problems with a particular style of thinking, and so on.

It is in this phase of treatment that the relationship between the child and the provider takes on special significance; this is when rapport is crucial, or, in psychodynamic terms, when transferences occur. For instance, in this phase of treatment, children may respond to actions by the clinician as they would to similar actions by parents or other significant individuals in their life. It is in this phase that children endow the relationship with the clinician with a special significance that stems from what they have learned and experienced over the years. This phase of treatment with adults often involves some irrational behavior on the client's part, some unorthodox interpretations of therapist behavior or verbalization by the client, and other more traditional transference reactions. It involves the expression of ingrained patterns that have developed over the course of a client's life (regardless of age) without regard to their appropriateness in the current context. Thus, a child may express an exceedingly strong affect in response to a here-and-now occurrence that can be explained only by the activation of a related earlier event or the stimulation of a related affect that is not truly relevant in its full force in the current situation.

Reexperience is a powerful occurrence for client and counselor and is easily differentiated from recollection and reconstruction. Most important, recollection and reconstruction are not tied to current happenings in the playroom or in the therapeutic relationship. They are relatively (though obviously not completely) independent of what occurs in the here-and-now. Reexperience, however, by definition always involves a here-and-now component and, because of this, generally results in more potent affective expression and impact. It is during this phase of treatment that interpretation can be appropriate, though certainly not required. An example of how reexperience may manifest in the work with a child is the case of a 5-year-old boy who was referred because of fearfulness and inability to make friends.

Five-year-old Mike had become very comfortable in the playroom and had begun to trust the clinician as evidenced by much spontaneous play and sharing. In one session, he became severely agitated and frightened by the sight of a small moth on the outside of the therapy room window. The following verbal, though metaphorical, exchange took place:

> MIKE (*panic-stricken, with a high pitched voice*): It's going to get me! It will come and get me.
>
> THERAPIST: You are afraid the moth will get you.
>
> MIKE: It will come after me. (*panicked and almost crying*) Make it go away.
>
> THERAPIST: You want me to help you be safe.
>
> MIKE (*crying*): Yes! Kill it . . . (*screaming*) kill it!
>
> THERAPIST: We can walk up to it and look at it and be safe because it can't come in. We are safe.
>
> MIKE (*sobbing less severely*): Go up to it . . . ?
>
> THERAPIST: Will you come with me and take a closer look at it?
>
> MIKE (*no longer crying*): Will you carry me?

THERAPIST: I will hold your hand and we will be safe.

(*They walk up to the moth, and the therapist explains about the moth, shows him its wings, and explains that it cannot come through the glass. This moth flies up, and Mike flinches, then relaxes, though grabbing on the therapist's hand a little harder.*)

MIKE (*forcefully*): Steve can't get me now!!

THERAPIST (*equally forcefully*): You feel safe!!

This reexperience process was a powerful moment in this child's therapy. The response of the boy to seeing the moth was an exaggerated response, yet one that was understandable once its symbolic meaning was understood by the therapist and linked to the child's past experiences. She focused on his need for safety because this had been a recurrent theme in his treatment. Mike had been severely sexually abused by his stepfather, Steve, who was now incarcerated. Nevertheless, Mike continued to have frequent nightmares, was very frightened of men, and generally refused to be with other children. The verbal intervention offered by the therapist was an interpretation despite the fact that it stayed within the child's metaphor, that is, it focused on the behavior of the moth, exemplifying that interpretations can be metaphorical rather than direct in the work with children. The mere fact that the child stopped crying could have been used as evidence that he felt understood and at some level not only had heard but also had accepted the intervention of the therapist. However, he spontaneously made the connection between the current event and his ultimate fear by indicating that he felt safe because he knew his stepfather could not reach him anymore. It must be pointed out that such verbalization of the connection between the here-and-now, the historical development of the problem, and the presenting problem is rare among children. Mike was a very bright and verbal child who had spent several months in treatment by the time this event occurred.

Resolution

Once a child has progressed through the phase of reexperience, resolution is often imminent. In this phase of treatment, the child resolves the presenting problem, often either through gaining understanding of why the problem occurred or through the process of internalization. Internalization means that the child has gained sufficient strength, understanding, and self-confidence that she or he can either cope with the presenting problem or let go of it. With children, this work can be done completely nonverbally and symbolically; insight does not need to be verbalized, as it is not the primary medium of change. Resolution is often much less emotionally powerful than reexperience, as it merely represents the logical conclusion of this earlier phase of treatment. It is often almost an afterthought and not uncommonly occurs immediately after a reexperience. The mark of a child having gained resolution is her or his ability to do the work formerly done by the clinician. In other words, during this phase of treatment, children can provide their own explanations of presenting problems or their own strategies for coping. An example, using the case of a 7-year-old girl who was referred because of severe separation anxiety, clarifies how this phase of treatment may manifest in the treatment of children.

Seven-year-old Janine was seen for her sixteenth session. Despite still engaging in some exploratory behavior, she appeared to become more spontaneous in her affective expression and had begun to trust the counselor. She was moving around the playroom, which had a large column in one corner that was a remnant of an earlier use for the room. The column was placed such that a child could hide behind it and lose sight of the counselor. Janine moved behind the column and hid for a very brief moment and then screamed for the counselor to come and help her. The counselor approached far enough for Janine to see her and said, "You are afraid of what might happen when you can't see me." The child nodded, calmed significantly, and no longer insisted on help. She repeated this behavior several times during the session, each time expressing strong affects. Finally, while approaching the column and the child's field of vision, the counselor said, "I know you are there even when I can't see you. And you know that I am here even when you can't see me." The child came out from behind the column with a big smile and said, "I know."

This interaction exemplifies a resolution immediately following a reexperience. Janine overreacted to the visual separation from the counselor, yet this response was understandable in light of her presenting problem and historical information that had been obtained during the intake. The repeated reexperience, along with the counselor's expression of understanding and then suggestion of reality, led very naturally to the resolution of this particular problem in the therapy. Resolution of the larger problem of separation anxiety had not yet obtained completely, but this small progress had paved the way.

Catalysts for Change

To facilitate the progression through the four phases of the therapy or counseling process, the clinician relies on a number of tools, or catalysts, for change. These tools are independent of a specific theoretical framework (e.g., behavioral, humanistic, psychodynamic) or preferred technique (e.g., group therapy, art therapy, storytelling). They transcend theories and are generally agreed upon as important facilitators of change. Each clinician needs to develop a personal repertoire of tools, and their variety and style of use will differ widely. However, several catalysts for change are sufficiently universal and important to warrant discussion. Nevertheless, it must be remembered that they represent merely a sampling of all the means that are available to help children change and work in treatment. Often, it is only the care provider's own level of creativity and willingness to take risks that limits the choices of interventions that are being made. The tools presented here are summarized in Table 9.2.

Creation of a Therapeutic Environment

In the early stage of treatment, the clinician must create an environment that communicates to the child that therapy or counseling represents a safe setting wherein free emotional expression is valued and never punished and where trust and confidentiality are fostered. The creation of the therapeutic environment, of course, begins

Table 9.2   Catalysts for Change

Catalyst Category	Specific Tool
Creation of a Therapeutic Environment	
Physical Safety	• no physical aggression • cleanup rules
Psychological Safety	• length of session • interval of sessions • structure of session • sameness of setting • continuity of therapist presence
Creation of a Therapeutic Relationship	• exclusive focus on child • reassurance and comfort • respect • physical touch • tolerance of nonverbal communication • transference awareness • countertransference awareness
Empathy and Understanding	• vicarious introspection • communication of understanding • cross-modal attunement
Methods and Levels of Explaining	• running commentary • reflection • pointing out patterns • asking clarifying questions • identification of feelings • identification of sources of feelings • catharsis • as-if explanation • interpretation
Internalization	• self-assurance and realistic self-appraisal • relevant rules or regulations and life-direction
Projective Identification	• projection of affect onto the therapist • acceptance of the affect by the therapist • metabolization of the affect • reintrojection of the affect by the child • projective counteridentification
Use of Defense, Symptoms, and Resistance	• definition as self-protective device • teaching coping skills • environmental modification • teaching parenting skills • effecting familial change

long before the actual treatment with any child commences. Specifically, therapeutic environments are equipped for the safety of the child and the clinician and the conduciveness of self-disclosure and affective expression, as outlined in the chapter concerning the physical environment. However, beyond the actual physical surroundings, a psychological environment or atmosphere must be created for each client. This environment involves several components. Most important, it involves physical and psychological safety (Landreth, 2002b; O'Conner, 2000). Second, it involves the facilitation of physical and psychological self-expression (Axline, 1947; Chethik, 2003; Schaefer and Kaduson, 2006). (See also chapter 4.)

Physical and psychological safety are best ascertained through the creation of some psychological structure. This structure refers to the setting of limits and the delineation of therapy or counseling rules that protect the child and clinician and that are clearly stated and presented to the child once treatment begins (Landreth, 2002a, 2002b). Leaving the child guessing about rules, limits, and parameters of the session invites unnecessary limit-testing on the child's part and anxiety about expectations, and it hinders the free flow of creativity and play that is so essential to the work with children. Thus, structuring the environment might appear rigid or inhibiting upon first reading, yet this must not be so. Rigidity and inhibition emerge only if rules and regulations are unreasonable and go above and beyond their purpose of ensuring safety. Rules that are clearly set only for the purposes of safety do not intrude or hinder. There are only a few general rules. Individual clinicians may need to add a few of their own, depending upon their unique environments and clinical settings.

Most commonly, rules that ascertain physical safety are clearly presented to the child in those terms. Specifically, a child client has to be informed that physical aggression in the room is fine as long as it does not result in physical injury of the child or the clinician and as long as no toys or furniture are broken willfully. Hitting the care provider is not allowed. Although the rules are introduced gently as is appropriate to the content and context of the first one or two sessions, contingencies or enforcement rules are introduced only when a rule is broken by the child. Limit-setting, as was outlined in a previous chapter, should then be used to deal with the individual situation.

Rules for psychological safety are often more difficult to explain to a child than to an adult but are equally important. These rules have to do with informing the child about length of sessions; the general structure of sessions, with a beginning, a middle, and an end; and the intervals between sessions. Further, it may be stressed that the toys in the room are always available from session to session for the child's use and that they always remain in the room. Some discussion of whether toys may be taken home may follow at this time. These rules have generally already been discussed in the feedback session of the intake interview but are best repeated in the first treatment session. Providing structure as far as length and process of sessions is concerned is quite important, as it lets the child know that there are limits to how much work has to be done in any one session, and it confirms for the child that there is regularity to the work that can be counted on. Providing information about the consistency of the room's equipment and the clinician's presence in each session helps some children transition more easily from one session to the next. Reassurance about the counselor's predictability, consistency, presence, and stability are particularly important in this context. Reiterating psychological safety rules can be as easy as reflected in the following dialogue between a therapist and a 6-year-old boy who had just begun his first session and had been seen for an extensive intake interview two weeks prior by the same therapist:

> CLINICIAN: Do you remember this room?
>
> TIM (*nods shyly*)

This is a good introduction for a child who has been in the playroom before. Most children have been through an intake in the same clinic and have had some experience with the room in that context. Reminding them of this initial contact subtly points out for the child that the room and toys are stable and consistent across sessions.

> CLINICIAN: Remember, you may use any of the toys that you want, just like last time you were here.

This reminder is necessary only with timid children, such as Tim in this example. More outgoing or active children not only remember the freedom of the room, but also quickly make use of it upon their return.

> TIM: I liked the dollhouse . . .
>
> CLINICIAN: Yes, you did. You very much liked the dollhouse last time you were here!

The therapist's response here communicates to the child that she remembers him and that she noticed his preferences. Although this might not fall into the category of establishing a therapeutic environment as defined above, it certainly falls into the next category of catalysts: the therapeutic relationship.

> TIM (*walks to the dollhouse*): It's still right here!

This comment reaffirms for the therapist that this child has concerns about being left or abandoned and signals for her that a reiteration of the constancy of the therapy environment is important.

> CLINICIAN: Yes, all the toys stay in this room, and they will always be here for you when you come each week.
>
> TIM: The paints too?
>
> CLINICIAN: Yes, everything stays, including me. I will be here every week for you; always at the same time, always for 50 minutes.

The therapist chooses to stress not only the constancy of the room, but also the constancy of her presence and availability. Stressing this environmental factor is particularly important for children who have had little stability of relationships in their own home, have experienced abusive parents, or have parents who abuse substances. The latter is the case for this child.

> TIM (*continues to explore the room, a bit more vigorously now*): I get to come back every week?!

The new vigor in the boy's behavior at this time confirms for the therapist that he picked up on stressing the continuity, and it relieved some of his fears. His last statement was hesitant but was followed by a firm nod of the head. The therapist decided to respond to the hesitation by restating the permanency of her presence.

CLINICIAN: Yes, every Tuesday at four o'clock I will be here for you.

The therapist chooses in her restatement to focus on her presence, rather than on the child's, as she has no control over his presence, only hers. For his presence, she depends on his parents who have to bring him, but she wants the child to know that she is there for him no matter what. At this time, the child turns and begins to play with the dollhouse, indicating that for now he feels safe in this new environment. No physical safety rules are approached at this time, as this child is very subdued and the mention of anger and physical aggression is more likely to intimidate than relieve him. A more obviously angry child may therefore receive a differently focused introduction.

Creation of a Therapeutic Relationship

The above example already points toward another important set of catalysts for change, namely, the establishment of a therapeutic relationship. The therapeutic relationship is a crucial aspect in the treatment of any client and care must be taken early in the work to facilitate its development and throughout the work to maintain it. There are many traits in a counselor that enhance rapport with children, and some of the main ingredients that make the development and maintenance of a positive relationship possible are quickly listed here.

Child Focus.   Perhaps the most unique aspect of interaction between a child and a care provider from the child's perspective is the exclusive focus on the child and the child's wishes. There is no self-disclosure on the therapist's part, no imposition of unnecessary rules that serve merely to enhance the adult's life, a complete acceptance of the child and her or his behavior (within the framework provided above), and a willingness to let the child lead and choose activities.

Reassurance and Comfort.   In addition to the acceptance that is expressed verbally and nonverbally, the counselor is reassuring and comforting. Especially early in treatment, while the child is still struggling with the concept of treatment and with trust issues, the counselor does not allow anxiety levels to rise out of control and is caring and nurturing. The therapist reassures the child in her or his exploration of the room, choices of self-disclosure, and tenuous affective self-expression. Clinicians comfort the child when psychological pain mounts but also when physical pain is present. They do not ignore pains the child brings to the room, such as cuts and bruises or stomachaches, and take even minor complaints seriously. Accidents in the playroom do occur and require caring and comforting. This stance toward the child is often unique in the child's experience and helps her or him learn to trust the counselor quickly and easily.

The therapist's comforting and reassurance are certainly not done to allow the child to shed all responsibility for proper behavior. Quite to the contrary, counseling introduces responsibility for behavior to children. Cleanup is generally required, and acting out behaviors, while accepted, are discussed with regard to their consequences. However, even in stressing the responsibility, the clinician remains warm and accepting of the child. Above all, the child's needs and desires are respected and responded to with flexibility.

Respect.   Respect for the child can be communicated through silence (Schaefer and Kaduson, 2006). Often, adults interrupt children's stories or play behavior. Clinicians rarely do so. They observe the child in silence and allow the child to complete thoughts and activities before intervening or commenting. Despite, or perhaps because of, this silence, clinicians must remain obviously available for communication and the exchange of information. This may include the tolerance of silence during play, as well as the encouragement of dialogue in the absence of any obvious nonverbal communication. Counselors' availability for communication is best expressed through simple questions or reflections about the child's activity. For instance, a child who is engrossed in dollhouse play may well be communicating with the therapist on a nonverbal level. However, without a response from the therapist, the child cannot be certain whether the clinician is receiving the communication initiated by the child. Thus, rather than sitting passively, the therapist may choose to accompany the child's behavior with some running commentary that is merely reflective of, and does not intrude into, the child's action. Similarly, simple reflection of the child's overt behaviors and affects are adequate strategies to inform the child that the counselor is paying attention and available for communication.

Physical Touch.   Despite some cautions against this, physical contact can be an important component of establishing rapport. Children like to express affection through physical contact and may feel quite alienated, if not rejected, by refusal of the clinician to reciprocate. Obviously, care has to be taken that physical contact is never sexualized, but the fear of this possibility should not interfere with the occasional hug, tap on the arm, or pat on the back. On the other hand, physical contact must not be overused. Like all strategies used in treatment, it must be well-timed and must have a purpose. It is never a good idea to have a routine of physical contact that is practiced with all children. For one thing, not all children like to be touched. For another, children recognize the difference between a routine touch and a genuine expression. A good rule of thumb is to wait for the child to initiate physical contacts beyond pats on the back. It is not unlikely that children change their attitude toward physical touch in the course of treatment, moving from shrinking from physical contact to its spontaneous initiation or moving from attempted aggressive contact to caring contact.

One 9-year-old boy, who was being seen because of significant physical aggression, never initiated physical contact with his counselor unless attempting to hit him. Therefore, the counselor was very respectful of the child's boundaries and never touched him. However, in one session, the child's behavior escalated, and the counselor had to restrain him for approximately 10 minutes. After the session, the counselor was quite distraught, as now the only physical contact that had been established by him toward his client was negative. He decided that despite the fact that the child had shrunk from physical touch, he would use some pats on the back and taps on the arm of this boy to begin to introduce positive physical touch. The child responded beautifully. He enjoyed the positive expression of feeling between the counselor and him and reduced the amount of attempted aggressive touching. He soon began to initiate hugs at the beginning of the session and developed warmth in the relationship with the counselor that was very healing for him.

When physical touch is used with children, their parents should be informed that this is done so that the parents do not misunderstand or misinterpret the actions. In this day and age of sexual and physical abuse, clinicians must protect themselves from false accusations. Further, they may also model for nontouching parents that the physical expression of caring is appropriate. It is quite sad to see parents, especially fathers, who have stopped touching their children for fear of being falsely accused of inappropriateness with them.

Transference.   Related to the establishment of a therapeutic relationship is the concept of transference. Transference has many different definitions, ranging from traditional psychoanalytic concepts to very broad interpretations. In the psychoanalytic tradition, transference referred to those needs, feelings, and desires that found expression in the therapy relationship without a here-and-now reason, instead stemming completely from earlier life experiences. These types of transferences were always viewed as inappropriate to the relationship at hand and interpreted in the context of previous, usually parental, relationships. Later and less traditional definitions include all needs and feelings brought to the work by either the child or the clinician, regardless of how relevant they are to the here-and-now relationship between the two (O'Conner, 2000). It is argued that everyone is affected by all past life experiences, and therefore, all interactions with significant people in one's life are somehow a function of earlier relationships and hence never pure. In this approach, the importance is placed on helping the child become aware of how the past has influenced or patterned the present.

Transference in the context of this book is viewed from a perspective somewhere between these two extremes. It is suggested that transference is never as pure as we suggested traditionally and that there is always a component of the here-and-now relationship that triggers old feelings and needs that are also related to past relationships. Thus, transference is not seen quite as completely independent of what the counselor brings to treatment as in the traditional approaches. It appears much more likely that the personality of the clinician and therapeutic style influences which feelings and needs emerge at any given time in the treatment process. However, in the approach taken here, transference is not seen quite as broadly as suggested by O'Conner (2000), wherein every single component of the child–therapist interaction is viewed as transferential. Instead, the definition of transference as proposed in this book is as follows:

> Transference refers to the fact that there are aspects of the child–clinician relationship that are catalyzed more so by clinicians' overt and intentional behavior and less so by their covert or unintentional personality style and that reflect or express a child's unique feelings, needs, and desires, as they were formed through the child's interpersonal environment up to this time in her or his life.

This definition deserves some detailed exploration. It suggests first of all that both child and clinician contribute to the transference. The therapist or counselor contributes in two ways. First, she or he contributes through overt and intentional behaviors, behaviors that are designed to facilitate and stimulate certain affects and need states in the child. This is the true definition of a catalyst. The clinician does not *create* feelings or need states in the child but merely provides a relationship and environment in which previously existing affects and needs can emerge, be freely expressed, and then understood. Second, the counselor inadvertently contributes characteristics that may further stimulate or hinder the expression of these affects and needs. The inadvertent contribution is generally secondary to personality style, personal feelings, beliefs, and affects and is truly in the spirit of what is generally labeled countertransference. The child contributes in the most important way to the transference relationship with the clinician. Children are not blank slates—not even very young children. They have grown up in unique environments with very individualized interpersonal relationships. These factors, environment and relationships, have impacted the child to such a degree as to strongly influence what the child's needs and affects are, particularly in intense interpersonal contexts, such as that presented by play therapy. The child responds to the treatment environment from that unique historical perspective. The therapist's behavior merely facilitates the expression; it does not alter it in the sense of producing needs or affects that would not otherwise be there. Thus, self-disclosures and affective expressions by the child in counseling can be confidently understood as arising from the child's unique history and family environment. It is this aspect of the child–clinician relationship that represents the transference between them and can be used to gain further insight into the child's development, environment, needs, and directions for change.

Transference thus defined is used to understand the child and to determine where deficits or problems have arisen and how to go about effecting change. This understanding of transference can accommodate various theoretical frameworks as well, as it implies neither the content of the expressed affects and needs of the child, nor specific interpersonal development. Thus, a cognitive behaviorist may argue that the transference is due to cognitions learned in the home and that certain cognitive patterns, which are reinforced by the family, have led to current feelings and behaviors. A humanist might argue that the needs and feelings are secondary to the lack of genuineness in a child's family that has resulted in the development of a false or incongruous self with which the child is struggling. A family systems theorist might indicate that the feelings and needs are due to family patterns that have resulted in a certain role that is played by the child within the family system. A self-psychologist might conclude that the child feels a certain way and expresses specific needs because the needs were not adequately provided for by caretakers in the child's earlier life. No matter how the transference feelings and behaviors are explained, the fact remains that they are present in the child–clinician relationship and that they present the counselor with the unique opportunity to work on these feeling and need states in the playroom, despite the fact that they originated in a different setting. The following example uses a self-psychological conceptual perspective and demonstrates how transference can be used as a catalyst for change.

> Angie, a 7-year-old girl who was referred because of several phobias, developed a very powerful relationship with her male therapist. She expected him to hold her and cuddle her when she felt frightened and overall wanted him to protect her, even from events and interactions outside of the playroom. She often asked that he tell her mother not to ask her to do certain things and occasionally became upset when he did not comply with her demands. The transference in this case was the child's view of the therapist as all-powerful and her demand that he protect and help her in all possible life circumstances. These demands and perceptions are viewed as transferential because they are not entirely realis-

tic within the therapy relationship, yet their development was certainly facilitated by the warm, nurturing attitude of the therapist, which had stimulated the expression of these needs in the child. She had lost her father 4 years earlier to a drunk-driving accident after one of his bingeing weekends. Since then, she had been placed in foster care off and on when her mother, who was diagnosed with schizophrenia, had to be hospitalized. Angie had no stability in her life and often felt unprotected, owing to the absence of a father and the inability of her mother to be counted on consistently. Her needs for protection had been rechanneled into various phobias and now found expression in the transference relationship with the therapist. Therapy focused on helping her to recognize her need for protection, on helping her to mobilize her own resources to protect herself, and on building realistic means of protection into her day-to-day life. It had been the powerful transference that revealed the depth of the child's needs and fears and paved the way for change.

Empathy and Understanding

Going hand in hand with the establishment of a therapeutic relationship and rapport is the expression of empathy and understanding in the work with children. Empathy is defined here as understanding the child from her or his unique perspective and history, just as the transference is expressed as a result of a child's unique background (Kohut, 1982). This definition requires an experience-near approach, which means understanding the child, as well as the presenting symptoms in the here and now and in the context of a specific situation as a reflection of how and where the child developed and grew up. Thus, empathy is not merely a warm, fuzzy feeling of caring; rather it is an important tool that facilitates insight. This type of empathy has also been referred to as vicarious introspection (Kohut and Wolf, 1978) to indicate that it goes beyond a recognition of how the clinician or other children would feel in a similar situation; that is, it is an understanding of how a particular child feels, given the unique experiences in that child's life. This type of empathy requires an in-depth understanding of the child, the child's history, and the child's interpersonal environment.

Furthermore, merely having empathic understanding is not enough; it must be communicated to the child, confirming that empathy is indeed an interpersonal, not a one-sided, process. The cycle of empathy always begins with the self-expression of the child. This self-expression is received by the clinician, who attempts to put the self-expression into the framework of the child's entire life. That is, the clinician attempts to understand the meaning of the self-expression based on the knowledge of the child's background. Once the clinician is relatively certain to have understood the child correctly, the understanding is communicated back to the child. The communication of understanding can take place either verbally or nonverbally, directly or symbolically. It is never to be confused with an interpretation. In other words, the communication of understanding is an expression of empathy but not a method of explaining. It is designed merely to tell the child that the clinician understood what the child expressed. Thus, it may consist of the mere labeling of an affect, or it may consist of a behavior on the part of the therapist, such as joining the child's play. This interpersonal cycle of empathy has been described in the social psychology research literature for many years (Barrett-Lennard, 1981; Brems, 1989a) and certainly appears to apply to the therapy context as well, as demonstrated by the following example:

> Eight-year-old Alex was using clay in her sixth session with her counselor. She created two dogs—one small, the other rather large. The small dog was doing its homework, which was reportedly very difficult and important. It could not finish the task and began calling for help, only to be ignored by the large dog, which was portrayed as watching TV. The small dog became more and more rambunctious and finally tipped over the TV. At this point, the large dog made snoring noises, a way of indicating that it was still not paying attention to the small dog. The small dog then got out of control, as Alex pretended that the dog was tipping over the furniture in the dollhouse. At this point, to avoid further escalation, the counselor decided to communicate that she had understood the child's communication. To do so, she picked up the large dog and, pretending that it was waking up slowly and beginning to watch the small dog, said, "Oh, you are so upset. I think you need my help to calm down."

This is an example of a symbolic communication of understanding, as the counselor remains within the chosen metaphor. It demonstrates that the reflection of understanding is merely that; in other words, no attempt is made to interpret the behavior or activity for the child. In this example, the child is communicating that she does not yet possess internalized controls over her behavior and needs external limits to be prevented from acting out aggressively when faced with frustration. This is the understanding that the counselor reflects back to her. It is not interpreted for her that the absence of internal controls is directly related to the absence of external controls in her life, as her caretakers are overly permissive and do not care in the least about what the girl does.

The ability to empathize and communicate understanding is quite dependent upon or analogous to the process of attunement as described originally by Stern (1985). Attunement requires the clinician to listen carefully, to make inferences about the meaning of a child's behaviors and verbalizations, and to reflect these back to the child in a meaningful, nonredundant manner. Like attunement, empathy helps the child develop self-understanding, self-respect, and self-confidence.

Once therapists have understood a child and have reflected the understanding either verbally or nonverbally, they begin to help the child develop empathy with herself or himself. Children need to learn to understand their own feelings and self-expressed needs and affects, and they need to learn to place labels on them. This process of gaining better self-understanding is an important first step in therapeutic change. Just as empathy by the counselor serves to help children feel better by virtue of letting them know that the feelings are real, understandable, and accepted, so does children's own empathy with themselves serve to build up and enhance their self-esteem and self-confidence.

Methods and Levels of Explaining

Care was taken in the discussion of the interpersonal cycle of empathy to differentiate the communication of understanding from the process of making interpretations or giving explanations. Explaining the relationship among behavior, affects, thoughts, interpersonal relationships, and environment is an important component of treatment (Russ and Freedheim, 2001). However, it is generally confined to the later phases of therapy or counseling, as it does not occur during the recollection and reconstruction phases, which are limited to information gathering and empathic understanding. Explaining can be done in numerous ways, ranging from the simple pointing out of patterns to very direct intervention in the form of straightforward verbal interpretation. Like the communication of empathic understanding, running commentary and reflection, two commonly used interventions mentioned in the context of establishing a therapeutic relationship (e.g., Landreth, 2000), are not true forms of explaining, as they merely communicate that the counselor is listening or paying attention. This does not reduce their value as interventions but merely places them in a different category from true explaining strategies.

True explaining strategies have as their purpose much more than the communication of attention and understanding. At their heart is the communication of understanding affects, needs, and behaviors in the here and now together with their relationship to the child's life as a whole. Explaining strategies are used to communicate conceptual understanding, as opposed to empathic understanding. They not only reflect what the counselor observes in the child, but they also explain it on the basis of the knowledge the clinician has of the child's background and history. Sometimes explaining strategies are aimed simply at imparting information. For instance, a child who is awaiting the birth of a sibling but whose parents are unsure, unable, or unwilling to help the child understand the biological processes of conception and birth may benefit greatly from learning how babies are conceived and born. Most commonly, however, explaining strategies are less educational and more process-oriented.

Pointing Out Patterns.   The most basic form of explaining is that of pointing out patterns. It requires the clinician to recognize that certain behaviors, needs, affects, and desires are repeated by the child, either in the playroom or in other settings. The presence of these patterns is then shared with the child, as in the following example:

> Six-year-old Tanya spent several sessions preparing and shopping for food using the anatomical doll family whom she had given names. A pervasive theme in her play was the lack of sufficient food to feed everybody and the running out of money before the shopping trip was completed. When this pattern was once again played out in a session, the counselor decided to make this comment: "Lucy [name of the female child doll] is trying and trying, but it seems like there is never enough food around to fill her up. She keeps asking her mommy and daddy for more, but there is just not enough to go around."

Asking Clarifying Questions.   Sometimes it is necessary to help a child gain better self-understanding by asking questions to clarify thoughts and perceptions for the child (O'Conner, 2000). This is a method of explaining that is slightly more advanced than pointing out patterns, as it is designed to develop cognitive insights. This type of questioning must be differentiated from information-gathering questions. In information gathering, clinicians asks questions for their own benefit of clarification. In explaining questioning, the questions are designed to lead the child to an insight that the clinician already has. The following example should clarify the difference:

Twelve-year-old Terrence had been seen for ten sessions when he used two puppets to express himself. He played out a scenario wherein one puppet, a rabbit, was picking on another one, a lion, until the lion kicked the rabbit. The rabbit was terribly hurt by the lion and retreated, crying and whining. The therapist knew that Terrence chronically got into fights with older boys at school, fights that he often provoked by name-calling. As the puppet play was a perfect reenactment of this process that Terrence had denied up to this point, she decided to ask some clarifying questions to help him recognize the contributions he made to the fights. She chose a third puppet, a bear, through which to ask her questions.

BEAR (*touching the rabbit carefully*): You are hurt. What happened?

RABBIT: That stupid lion hit me!

BEAR (*turning to lion*): Is it true that you hit the rabbit?

LION: I sure did. I hate him—he is so stupid, so I hit him!

BEAR: How come you hate him?

LION: I don't know . . .

BEAR (*to rabbit*): Why do you think he hates you?

RABBIT: Beats me. I didn't do anything!

BEAR: You didn't pick on the lion or anything?

RABBIT: Hell no—he's too big and strong.

BEAR (*to lion*): I saw what happened, and I thought the rabbit picked on you. Didn't he pull your hair and call you a nerd?

LION: Yes, I guess he did.

BEAR: How do you feel when someone calls you a nerd and pulls your hair?

LION: I don't like it!

BEAR: Do you sometimes pick on the person back?

LION: Oh yeah—gotta show 'em who's the boss!

BEAR (*to rabbit*): Do you remember picking on the lion?

RABBIT: Yeah . . . I guess I did.

BEAR: Do you think the lion was just defending himself when he hit you?

RABBIT: Yeah, I suppose. I guess I kind of started it.

The child was quite able to play both parts, the rabbit and the lion, throughout this exchange. Through the use of the puppets, he was able to distance enough from the real-life situation to take an objective look at the events and to realize that behaviors have causes and consequences.

Identification of Sources of Feelings. Although labeling and identification of feelings often fall into the realm of communicating empathic understanding, it can also be an explaining strategy, if it incorporates the identification of the source of the feelings. In this process, therapists not only are empathically attuned to feelings expressed by a child, but they also make a connection between the feeling and its origin. The child, on the other hand, does not appear to have made this connection, and needs some help in so doing. Helping children recognize the sources of their feelings imparts a sense of control over their affects they did not previously have (Russ and Freedheim, 2001). It also helps them become more altruistic, as they can then recognize that there are sources for other people's feelings and that these need to be respected.

Following is an example of an interaction oriented toward helping a 5-year-old girl recognize why she was mildly school-phobic (well, kindergarten-phobic). This child's mother was severely asthmatic and had almost died on two occasions. One time, she was saved by the girl's brother, who ran to a neighbor, who then alerted emergency medical personnel. The other time, the girl was home alone with the mother and was unable to help her. The mother fortunately recovered on her own.

> Michelle was telling a story in which a little bear cub was afraid to leave the den when summer came. She wanted to stay in the den with her mother and brother and just spend the summer there instead of learning how to fish for salmon and graze in the meadows. The therapist told a story back, designed to label, identify, and explain the little bear's feelings. This was her story: "The little bear cub does not want to leave the den because she would rather stay in for the summer than to learn how to fish and graze. She is afraid of what might happen when she leaves the den because when her little brother left the den the week before, he got hurt by a big grizzly cub that was born last year. The little cub doesn't want to leave because she is afraid she might get hurt too, because her mother is very weak and can't protect her because she is sick. The little cub would rather stay with her mom and take care of her to make sure that she doesn't die. Soon the little cub will learn that she can leave the den and learn how to fish and graze from other mommy bears, and then she can get strong and can eat a lot and feed herself really well. Maybe she can even come back and bring her mom a fish she caught."

The therapist's story identified and labeled the feeling as one of being vulnerable to and unprotected from the world. She proceeded to explain the feeling as the child's fear for her mother's life, and hence her own abandonment. She also identified the child's helplessness and decided to make a suggestion aimed at addressing this feeling therapeutically by explaining that the girl might have to seek alternative sources of support to overcome her vulnerability.

Catharsis.   It should be noted in this context that mere catharsis, that is, release of emotion and expression of feeling, is very therapeutic for children (Russ and Freedheim, 2001). Therapists have the responsibility to provide an environment in which even the expression of negative affects feels safe to the child.

As-If Explanations.   Sometimes feelings cannot be labeled directly because they might be too threatening for the child to own them. The clinician then best makes these statements using an as-if scenario (O'Conner, 2000). In the as-if situation, an interpretation is stated in general terms to make it more acceptable to the child. Rather than requiring the child to own a feeling or need that was expressed in play or symbolically, the therapist may choose to draw the conclusion for children in general. Thus, the counselor might say something like "Some girls/boys might feel depressed/angry/anxious if this were to happen to them."

More direct explanations of obvious feelings or their dynamic sources can be used with children if a process becomes clear within a child's play, indicating that the child has already gained a certain level of awareness of the situational dynamics (O'Conner, 2000). Thus, the child who pretends that a girl doll is very angry because a brother doll got to go to camp might be responded to with a statement such as, "This doll says she is very angry at her brother because he got to go to camp. I wonder if she is really angry at her parents because they let him go but told her she was too young."

Interpretation.   Similar to the explaining of sources for feelings is the connection of past experiences and present behaviors or of thoughts and subsequent feelings and actions. This type of explaining is sophisticated and requires significant cognitive capability on the child's part. It requires a level of abstraction and insight that is not necessarily present in all child clients. Thus, it is a strategy that is less often utilized with children than used with adults. Nevertheless, an occasion may arise when explaining is appropriate. For instance, one 12-year-old girl who had severe nightmares benefited from learning about the connection between her nightmares and her history of being sexually abused by her father at age 4. Her father used to come to her room late at night after she had gone to sleep and have intercourse with her. She often pretended to sleep through the entire process and then spent the night trying to stay awake for fear of his return.

This type of explaining is traditionally called an interpretation and, as such, is reserved for the reexperience and resolution phases of treatment. Interpretations can be tailored to children's needs and cognitive development if they can be rendered symbolically or nonverbally. These alterations of the traditional interpretation make it amenable to the work with children. However, it is important to remember that interpretations are most generally oriented toward helping a client achieve some level of insight, which might not always be a necessary outcome in the work with children. Children are often very well-served through the internalization of strength, direction, and self-esteem—processes that do not require sophisticated insight (Kohut, 1984).

Internalization

Internalization is an important catalyst or medium for change in the work with children; in fact, this is perhaps the most important one of all. Internalization is a process as much as a catalyst and thus is not as concrete a strategy as the other catalysts discussed thus far. It permeates all therapeutic work and often is involved when other catalysts are used as the more overt or noticeable strategies. Yet despite, or maybe because of, its covert nature, internalization represents an extremely important aspect of child therapy or counseling. Internalization is the process of helping children make certain processes, beliefs, feelings, needs, behaviors, and values their own through the use of imitation, modeling, and similar normal developmental occurrences. Children observe their environment very curiously and intently from very early on in life. Much of what they learn, they learn through imitation and modeling. In fact, some clinicians claim that as much as 80 percent of what human beings know and believe is acquired through modeling. Children pay particular attention to models who are important to them in some way or another. Children's earliest models are no doubt their primary caretakers during infancy, toddlerhood, and childhood—often their biological, adoptive, step-, or foster parents. From these models, children learn many concrete skills. However, these persons or models also serve more subtle purposes related to the child's general self-development. Specifically, there are two major components of a child's self, one having to do with self-esteem and realistic self-appraisal and the other dealing with life direction, values, and self-perceived strength and ability to cope, that are developed through the process of internalization. (The interested reader is referred to Kohut [1984] for more information.)

If children do not internalize certain capabilities or aspects of the self in their relationship with prominent figures in their lives, they are able to use the therapeutic or counseling relationship to do so. Thus, interactions with the clinician serve to strengthen the child's internalized self-representations and serve to strengthen the child in many ways without the need for insight or explaining. The child can glean strength from the clinician through the mere interaction, in much the same way as an infant in a healthy interpersonal environment learns to do by modeling after, imitating, and internalizing parents' responses, values, and so forth. This process of internalization is crucial to the work with children, as it takes place nonverbally and preverbally, does not rely on cognitive insights, and builds the basis for a strong, goal-directed and self-confident self.

To be able to serve as such a model, the clinician has to recognize where the primary needs of the child lie. Thus, for some children, internalization of self-esteem and realistic self-appraisal may be more important, whereas for others, the internalization of rules and regulations may be paramount. Empathic attunement with the child and communication of empathic understanding greatly enhance the process of internalization.

An often used example of internalization of rules and regulations is the child who is observed in front of a cookie jar in the absence of a regulating parent. The child approaches the jar and is ambivalent about whether to take a cookie. This child is often observed to mimic a parent's voice to talk herself or himself out of taking a cookie. An example of a therapeutic internalization is presented here by describing an interaction between a female counselor and a 9-year-old girl:

> Sally had been referred by her teacher because of severe constriction of affect and inability to play and let herself get dirty. She was always very intent on following rules and could not relax. Sally had been seen for several sessions, during which she had learned some relaxation techniques and had begun to trust the counselor. However, she was still very controlled in her play and had difficulty letting go of her severe approach to life. The counselor had been intent on helping her realize that rules are fine but are there to keep you safe and not to keep you from being playful and explorative. She had modeled on various occasions that getting dirty was okay and safe. For instance, in Sally's play with clay the counselor had purposefully gotten clay in her own hair and on her clothes and reacted with complete unconcern. Often, Sally would get angry or worried about what might happen. She was clearly worried that if she let go just a little bit she would be completely out of control. Thus, she stopped herself from even approaching the limits of a rule for fear of the consequences. Her severe constriction was thus understood as resulting from severe externally imposed rules, as opposed to resulting from a healthily internalized sense of right or wrong.

After many sessions, she finally began to relax and explored the room more freely. In one session, she took the clay and smeared it into her hair, clearly imitating the counselor's earlier actions. Several sessions later, she chose the clay again and this time played without concern. When she got it on her dress, she turned to the counselor and said assertively, "I don't want it in my hair, but it's okay on the dress." The counselor interpreted this behavior as a sign of a beginning internalization of rules. The child could now choose for herself what was appropriate and acceptable for her. She neither followed the strict external rules modeled in her daily interpersonal environment nor completely followed the example of the counselor. Instead, she had internalized her own individualized sense of right and wrong without the need for this ever having been verbalized or discussed directly.

Projective Identification

Internalization was discussed as a catalyst that is of importance because of its nonverbal quality that can be used to influence behavior, attitude, value, or emotional changes. The direct or verbal expression of affect is perhaps the most difficult form of self-expression for many children. Thus, it is useful for clinicians to be aware of a way of understanding and influencing a child's affects without the need for a verbal exchange. Projective identification is such a nonverbal method. Projective identification was first described by Melanie Klein as a defense mechanism (1955). She described it as a process wherein an individual splits off negative aspects of the self and projects them onto another person in an attempt to control this person and get her or him to act in accordance with the projector's own needs. Bion (1959) viewed projective identification as a normal developmental process that young children use to explore strong affects while these emotions are safely contained within another person. This process involves projection and reintrojection of strong affects in such a way that there is no threat to the developing self. This definition of projective identification implies that it is an interpersonal process, or a mode of interaction, that is relevant in everyone's development, as well as in the developmental setting of psychotherapies, individual or otherwise (Grotstein, 2000).

Bion's conceptualization of the interpersonal nature of the projective identification process is most closely related to the view of a contemporary writer, Ogden (1993, 2004), who views projective identification as serving four functions: defense mechanism, mode of communication, means of object relatedness, and pathway to psychological change. He indicates that as a defense mechanism, projective identification helps the individual to rid herself or himself of undesirable or frightening affects (Klein's definition); as a mode of communication, it helps the individual to feel understood by others by imbuing them with her or his own feelings; as a way of relating to others, it constitutes a relatively safe way of being with others; and finally, as a pathway of psychological change, it makes difficult feelings, that had been projected, available to the individual in altered (i.e., less threatening or frightening) form for reintrojection. It is this latter view of projective identification that makes the concept most relevant in the context of therapeutic catalysts in the work with children (Brems, 1989b; Tansey and Burke, 1995).

As a therapeutic catalyst or technique, projective identification consists of three stages. First, the child projects an unacceptable or frightening affect or self-aspect onto the therapist to calm and soothe herself and himself and keep hidden from the developing self-disturbing aspects thereof. Second, the projection of the child is met by the clinician with acceptance and recognition or understanding, to then be metabolized, that is, altered in some fashion that makes the affect acceptable to the child. Acceptance is communicated nonverbally; recognition of the particular type of feeling is facilitated by the clinician's empathic understanding of the client and by the clinician's exploration of her or his own feelings in the work with the child. Metabolization of the affect refers to the counselor's recognition that the affect she or he is experiencing with the child originated from the child, is overwhelming to the child, and must be made less frightening and more acceptable before the child can identify with and own the affect again. Third, once thus altered or metabolized, the affect is identified by the child as her or his own and is reintegrated into her or his developing self-image or self-definition. This process of reintrojection is critical to the therapeutic impact of projective identification, as without the introjection, no change in the child has occurred.

Without reintrojection, the projective identification would merely have served as a defense against the affect that was successfully concealed from the developing self of the child by projecting it. Without the metabolization of the projected affect by the clinician, reintrojection is impossible in a therapeutic way, as the unaltered affect remains unacceptable or overwhelming to the child, cannot be reintegrated into the child's conscious concept of self, and continues to be rejected by the child. However, if the clinician is successful and accepting, recognizing and altering the affect, it will be acceptable to the child and can be incorporated successfully. Although this process sounds technical and abstract, it is actually very experience-near. It always contains some affective involvement on the care provider's part. It is this affective involvement that occasionally causes the cycle to derail and to end unsuccessfully. In other words, if the clinician receives the affect but does not recognize it as the child's, instead perceiving it as her or his own, a projective counteridentification is set in motion. In this scenario, the therapist feels equally overwhelmed or disturbed by the affect and cannot contain or alter it, and the therapeutic cycle cannot be closed.

For instance, if a client is utterly confused about life and the direction she or he wants to choose for life, it can occur that the counselor takes on some of the client's projected confusion, only to begin to feel disoriented and ambivalent about the client's treatment. One supervisee was observed to begin to avoid talking about a particular client's case. When this avoidance was addressed, she confessed that she felt very confused and unclear about her treatment goals with this individual. Her therapy had been unfocused, and no themes had begun to emerge across sessions. Upon some exploration with the supervisor, this therapist came to realize that much of her confusion had originated from her client, who was utterly unable to give any focus to his life. When she recognized that the confusion she experienced was not entirely her own, she was able to formulate some treatment goals and was able to begin to direct the sessions.

Projective counteridentification, as described in the following example, is most likely to occur around affects that clinicians have not completely mastered themselves. Thus, novice counselors who have not worked with very many children and feel somewhat anxious in sessions with child clients are particularly vulnerable to projections of anxiety. This occurred in the treatment of one particularly anxious child. This child had experienced life in a household that had little structure or direction, few rules, and little caring. His feelings were similarly unfocused and not governed by the normal rules and moral developmental regulations that are normally expected of a 10-year-old. Consequently, his behavior was often out of control, destructive toward others, as well as suicidal. Early in his treatment, which occurred early in the counselor's career, he was extremely out of control in the treatment room, often threatening to and actually throwing furniture or climbing on shelves and threatening to jump and hurt himself. The counselor began to dread her sessions with this child and often felt very upset and anxious for half a day before his scheduled appointment. She felt as though she had lost control over the sessions, which indeed she had. In exasperation, she consulted with a supervisor, who recognized the projection of affect and helped the counselor differentiate between her own level of anxiety and the child's exaggerated projected anxiety, orient her treatment through the setting of definite and revised treatment goals, introduce structure into the play environment, and set limits assertively and consistently.

Successful use of projective identification resulted from the above examples of the almost derailed processes. Once the clinicians in the examples recognized the origin of the strong affects, they were able to accept the affects and to tolerate them in milder forms. They were able to make environmental and attitudinal changes that rendered the affects manageable and tolerable. Once the affects were thus metabolized, the clients could recognize them in their milder forms as acceptable and tolerable, identified with them, and reintrojected them into their own repertoire of feelings in the milder, more tolerable form. This change in affect was achieved entirely through nonverbal interpersonal processes that never had to be discussed or interpreted. A detailed example of the therapeutic use of projective identification with children is presented in Brems (1989b).

Use of Defenses, Symptoms, and Resistance

One final common catalyst for change is the skilled therapeutic use of a child's defenses, symptoms, and resistance that are evidenced in the therapy room. Defense and resistance are always part of treatment and, despite having been dealt with mainly as processes that disturb the therapy, can actually be used as therapeutic aids. To understand defense and resistance as therapy catalysts, they must be redefined, and, some therapists recommend, even relabeled (e.g., Brems, 1999, 2000; Kohut, 1984). The new recommended label for defense or defensive symptom is protective mechanism, a label that suggests the new definition. Defenses are developed by children early on in their lives and generally serve a self-protective purpose. They develop when threats arise either from within or without and represent the child's attempt to deal or cope with this threat as positively and effectively as possible. Thus, all defensive maneuvers ultimately share one trait: they are designed to protect and keep harm away from the developing self. It is irrelevant whether this protection is from intrapsychic processes, as defined by psychodynamic or psychoanalytic theorists; from negative cognitions, as defined by cognitive behaviorists; from family dynamics, as defined by family systems theorists; or even from reinforcement contingencies, as defined by behaviorists. Regardless of how a defense works and why it is developed, it always serves to protect or to help the child cope as best as possible.

The child clinician must recognize the need for the defenses or symptoms that developed as means of self-protection. The particular context in which the defense and the symptoms developed must be known for the care provider to understand from what the child is seeking protection. For instance, a young boy who has developed stomachaches as a defense against seeing his parents fight should not be confronted about the defensive nature of his physical complaints; rather he needs to be understood within his dysfunctional family system. His stomachaches are the one thing he can use (not consciously, of course) to control an aversive and difficult situation. In other words, clinicians need to develop *understanding* for defenses or symptoms, *not confront* them with reality testing. To go back to the boy in the example, the therapist does not challenge the reality of the stomachache, arguing that there is no physical cause, but rather helps the child understand that the stomachache is his way of coping. In this approach, the defensive symptom is not attacked and stripped away. Rather, it is understood and empathically placed into the context wherein it developed.

Stripping away the defense leaves children vulnerable and without coping strategies. Clinicians need to learn to understand children's defensive affects and symptoms before unmasking and challenging them; understanding rules and explaining take the backseat. Once children have grown stronger through treatment, familial changes, or environmental modifications, and they have learned other coping skills, symptoms or defenses can be challenged. Learning alternative problem-solving and coping strategies is a crucial aspect of intervention. It can be facilitated through direct problem solving in the session or via modeling and redirection (Russ and Freedheim, 2001). Stripping away symptoms before other forms of coping or strength have been imparted or developed is dangerous and not helpful to the child's continued growth.

This interpretation of defenses and symptoms is very similar to the concept of "going with the resistance." Rather than challenging a child's resistance to treatment, the clinician explores why the resistance has developed to begin with. Most often, the resistance serves the same self-protective purpose as a defense or symptom. Coming for treatment is frightening, and resisting the process appears to be the only way in which children can protect themselves from further intrusions or pain. Children who come to treatment are there because they have been hurt in more or less direct physical or psychological ways. They have often learned not to trust adults and to protect themselves through withdrawal, acting out, or other behavioral or emotional patterns. To expect them to shed these defenses quickly and easily is unrealistic. Allowing the children to bring these patterns into the playroom and to manifest them there, observing them, and attempting to understand them, on the other hand, communicates respect and is more likely to result in sufficient trust to help children give them up. Challenging resistance only results in more resistance. Treatment resistances present unique challenges to treatment. They are addressed further below.

Although a number of strategies, or treatment catalysts, have been discussed, many more exist. It is likely that each clinician develops preferred means of intervening. However, the strategies presented here are likely to remain in the repertoire of all child clinicians, as they are relatively theory-free. Catalysts ultimately allow clinicians to help children address the established treatment goals. Additionally, clinicians often observe changes in children that were not predicted, and new behaviors emerge that were not necessarily targeted directly by the treatment goals. These outcomes are typically positive and useful for the child and fall into the category of therapeutic by-products. These by-products tend to involve the resolution of problems that were related to the presenting problem without being obvious or overt. For instance, as a fearful child improves, she or he may also feel an increase in self-esteem and a decrease in loneliness. Seeing children improve over the course of treatment is a gratifying process. It is the recognition of change and improvement that reinforces clinicians and maintains their zeal and enthusiasm for their chosen career. However, the process of change is not always an easy one. There are a few common challenges presented specifically by child clients. These problems and their potential solutions are discussed in the final section of this chapter.

Challenges to the Therapy or Counseling Process

The challenges of child therapy are many (Chethik, 2003; Landreth, 2002b), and the better prepared clinicians are to face them, the more likely that they do not interfere with treatment, but perhaps even enhance it. Often, challenges presented by children are resistances or defensive maneuvers. Thus, they are understood as self-protective—understood, used therapeutically, and slowly replaced by more appropriate behaviors. They are not challenged, criticized, or confronted. The creativity and sensitivity of the counselor are often the best tools for handling the challenges presented by an individual child. A few suggestions are provided here. They are by no means exhaustive but are included merely to get clinicians prepared to think on their feet.

"NOOOOO—I Don't Want to Go in There!!"

For the child with separation anxiety, the first trip to the playroom can be fraught with fear and dread. This child may be full of negative feelings about the interaction with the therapist, as it requires the child to leave the caretaker. Mild forms of refusal are best dealt with by reassuring the child that the clinician understands that the child is frightened but that the playroom is a safe place, and the parent remains in the waiting room where the child is greeted after a specified time period. Sometimes it is necessary to allow the child to leave the door to the room open to maintain some visual contact with the person in the waiting room. For extremely anxious children, however, it may be necessary to invite the parent into the playroom with the child to break the ice and let the child do initial exploration in the parent's presence. If this is the case, the child is slowly weaned by asking if the child is ready to let the parent go.

Once a child has been weaned or has been to the playroom once, there is usually no problem in future sessions of getting the child to agree to come to the room. However, the child might have other difficulties reaching the room. For instance, impulsive children may not be able to move along hallways quietly and without disrupting other work in rooms along the way. Some children may have some remaining apprehension about going to the playroom and may attempt to prolong the journey as much as possible. Other may use the trip to the room to act out and test limits. One 11-year-old child who was seen in a room on a second floor consistently refused the stairs and insisted on riding the elevator. Once in the elevator, he predictably attempted to push the emergency button.

For children with these types of problems, it is best to develop a ritual or firm procedure to help them travel to the playroom. The situation with the 11-year-old child in the above example was solved with the following procedure. He was informed that if he were able to ride the elevator quietly and without pushing the emergency button on the way to the session, he could ride it to the very top of the building before going down to the floor on which the waiting room was located. If he forgot to be quiet on the way to the session, the stairs had to be taken on the way to the waiting room after the session. In this example, the therapist chose to reinforce an incompatible behavior (riding the elevator quietly) to eliminate the problem behavior on the way to the session (pressing the emergency button). Her reinforcer was the extra-long elevator ride after the session, as she knew this to be an exciting experience for the child.

For an anxious child, a parent might need to be involved in the transition ritual from the waiting room to the playroom. One 4-year-old girl was allowed to show her mother the way to the room as a means to reduce her anxiety of the trip. Again, the actual procedure chosen by the clinician has to be uniquely adapted to each individual child. The most important thing is not to panic when a child refuses or acts out on the way to the therapy room. There is always a creative solution (O'Conner, 2000).

"Just One More Time!?"

Often children enjoy their sessions and have difficulty ending them. Sometimes, their refusal to end is a means of testing limits or manipulating the clinician. Occasionally, a child would rather stay because of the real-life situation she or he faces after leaving the safety of the session. No matter what the reason, children generally have excellent excuses why the clinician should allow them to stay just a little bit longer. They may express the need to complete a drawing, the desire to finish a game, or share the sudden memory of some important information. Regardless of what the excuse, the session must end on time. Landreth (2000, 2002a) points out that one aspect of treatment is always to help children internalize control and responsible behavior. Ending sessions on time requires them to exercise this self-control and also provides for the consistency and stability of rules that makes therapy and counseling so safely predictable. Bending the rules for a child makes the clinician unpredictable and manipulable. It can create problems of respect in the child–clinician relationship.

The key to ending sessions on time is to warn children and to develop ending rituals. A common procedure is to warn the child that only seven to ten minutes remain of the session and that cleanup needs to begin soon. This reminder gives the child a chance to finish ongoing business. It also prepares the child for the cleanup time, which represents an excellent ending ritual in and of itself. For some children, a concrete reminder might be necessary, such as an egg timer that is turned 5 minutes before the session's end. For most children, the verbal reminder suffices. Once cleanup begins, the child has a chance to wind down from the session's work and to ready herself or himself to face the world. If cleanup is not enough to prepare the child, an additional ritual might be added. For one child, a trainee had devised a method of taking off and putting on shoes. For this child–clinician dyad, the beginning of a session was signaled by both of them removing their shoes. The ending was ushered in by both of them putting on their shoes. Even then, the child occasionally had difficulty transitioning out of the room. She played helpless, asking the therapist to help her with her shoes. The clinician responded by putting on her own shoes and emphasizing that she knew the child could handle putting on her own shoes. This was an important message, as it told the child several things. First, she could not manipulate the clinician; second, she was reminded that she was capable of putting on her shoes; and third, she was symbolically assured that she could handle the life once she left the session.

In the absence of an established ritual, a child who refuses to leave the room only on occasion might merely need to be reminded that the session must end regardless of the child's wishes. The child should be reassured that she or he will return during the following week and that everything will stay the same. If an issue has remained unresolved, that is, a play activity remained incomplete, the clinician can reassure the child that the activity can be completed during the following week. The counselor may also acknowledge understanding that it is difficult for the child to end the session.

"I Want to Go Home . . . "

Quite to the contrary of the child who refuses to end is the child who wants to leave early. Therapists appear somewhat split in their opinions about how to handle this issue. For instance, Gardner (1994) believes that it is the child's right to determine when she or he has had enough and therefore advocates allowing an early ending. Ginott (cited in Spiegel, 1996), on the other hand, advocates a rigid refusal to the extent of actually blocking the door if this becomes necessary. A more balanced approach is advocated by Spiegel (1996), who suggests that the clinician attempt to find out why the child wishes to leave and then decide whether the request should be met or refused. It appears that if a therapist is firm about ending on time, this stance is maintained, whether the limit is tested by the child to extend or shorten the interaction. As such, it appears most sensible to explore why the child wants to leave early but not allow the departure.

Often, children who ask to leave have reached a point in their session that is anxiety provoking for them. They wish to avoid this anxiety by removing themselves from the stimulus. This is an unrealistic approach to life, in which no one can always escape difficult situations. Counseling can model appropriate ways of handling such difficult situations by helping children verbalize their feelings and dealing with them constructively rather than through avoidance. If children are extremely anxious and not able to connect with the reasons for their anxiety, it may be permissible to let the child visit the parent in the waiting room to refuel and regain some security. However, such visits should be well structured, short, and infrequent.

One 6-year-old boy who had severe abandonment fears was helped to remain in his sessions by being allowed to visit his parents for brief 30-second visits when his anxiety threatened to overwhelm him. This practice was allowed for approximately five weeks; then he was allowed to visit them only once during the session, while being allowed to look out the door and make visual contact during other times. The next step in the desensitization process was that no more visits were allowed, only visual contact by opening the door and looking out. The next stage involved allowing him to open the door only once and asking him to imagine his parents sitting on the couch in the waiting room during the other times. Finally, only visualizations were allowed. This desensitization and visualization process helped the child to settle into the work and proved a useful strategy for other concerns with which he had presented for treatment.

"Do You Have Kids?"

Questions regarding personal information about the clinician should never lead to an autobiography. Instead, the clinician must explore the fantasy underlying the question before responding to it. More often than not, the question has a dynamic, or transferential, meaning that must be understood. These types of questions tend to occur early in the treatment and often deal with underlying issues of trust and rapport building. For instance, children commonly ask if clinicians have children of their own. This question can have a number of underlying meanings, depending on the specific context of a child's situation. For instance, it might in reality be a question about whether a therapist can love the child as she or he loves her or his own children; it might be a matter of sibling rivalry; it might be related to a child's concern whether the counselor has enough concern and caring to go around for everyone and for this child in particular. Sometimes, children ask the clinicians if they love their spouses (parents, children, etc.). This question often really inquires whether the therapist loves the child. Often, children ask about other children the counselor sees in counseling. This is a particularly common question if the child has observed the counselor leave the playroom with another child. The concern typically is again one of whether the counselor can care for everyone and may imply jealousy or competition.

No matter what the content of the personal question is, the clinician considers its hidden meaning before answering it. If a therapist ever decides to answer a personal question, this response should be brief and directed not only toward the surface issue but also toward the deeper meaning. Thus, in response to questions about whether the therapist has children, a self-disclosing yet process-oriented response might be, "Yes, and I have enough love and caring for them and all the children I work with." Such a self-disclosure, however, must be made for a good reason, not because it is the easiest way to respond. In other words, the counselor must have reason to believe that the surface content must be answered before moving to the process issue. This might be true in this example if the therapist is aware that the child lives in the same neighborhood and is likely to see the therapist with her or his family outside of the playroom. When in doubt, however, the clinician best refrains from self-disclosure.

"I Have to Go to the Bathroom!"

Questions that have to do with more general process issues tend to occur later in treatment than personal questions about the clinician. They are more commonly oriented toward resistance and defense than trust and rapport. For instance, children sometimes express the urge to go to the bathroom. Although this request might be genuine, more often than not it reflects the child's attempt to leave the playroom at a moment when difficult affects are expressed or when overwhelming needs are mobilized. The first time the request is made, the therapist generally grants it, as there is no certainty that it is not genuine. For the following sessions, however, the therapist remembers to ask the child to use the bathroom before entering the playroom. Thus, bathroom requests can then be explored with the child in the context of the process that is occurring. For instance, one 10-year-old boy had been asked, after the first such occurrence, to use the toilet before entering the next session and nevertheless asked to go to the bathroom during this session as well. The counselor had noticed that the context of the request was very similar to that of the previous session. Specifically, in both sessions, the child had made a self-disclosure about having witnessed abusive behavior on the part of his father in the family home. (Appropriate reports had been made by the counselor about this family.) The child had been struggling for several months with his ability to trust the counselor enough to deal with these issues, and it was very clear that this disclosure, made in the context of dollhouse play, was extremely anxiety provoking for the boy. In response to his request, the counselor chose not to address his request at all, but rather responded to what she perceived to be the process issue. Picking up a boy doll in the dollhouse, she said, "I am very scared about talking about what has been happening in my house. But I should remember that my counselor can keep a secret and that she can protect me." The boy did not repeat his request to go to the bathroom. However, he still chose to turn to less frightening play activities, rechanneling his anxieties within the playroom.

"I Am Going to Tear This Place Up!"

Although threats of physical aggression and the actual aggressive acting out of children are one of the most frightening prospects for child clinicians, this need not be so. Aggression can be contained through various processes. Basic limit-setting skills are crucial to the management of aggression and knowledge of safe physical restraining techniques are definitely recommended. When aggression is threatened or just beginning, the child needs to be reminded of the physical safety rules that were previously introduced. Often, the reminder suffices to end the acting out. If the behavior continues, a contingency is set up. The child is informed of what will occur if she or he chooses to continue to escalate the behavior. It is important to remember to set contingencies that are in the clinician's power to enforce and that have therapeutic value. Thus, a contingency of "You won't get dessert tonight" is clearly inappropriate, as it is neither under the clinician's control nor related to the behavior. Contingencies are best chosen according to logical consequences (Dreikurs and Grey, 1990). If the child does not interrupt the aggression upon hearing the contingency, the counselor must be prepared to enforce it. A last-resort contingency can always be the early termination of a session.

If a child escalates despite limit setting and enforcement of contingencies, physical restraint may be necessary. In fact, physical restraint procedures occasionally are also used to keep a child safe from injury. In one group for middle-childhood children facing parental divorce, physical restraint was used with two sisters who were becoming extremely aggressive with one another. The constraint served to contain their aggression, as well as to communicate support and guidance to them. The two children were held one each by the two cotherapists after verbal interventions had failed to keep the sisters from hitting one another. They were taken in a loose arm hold with the therapists kneeling and the two girls sitting. As soon as the restraints had been initiated, the girls stopped kicking and hitting, but any loosening of the grips on their arms resulted in escalated behavior. It was interesting to note that the hold that had been placed on both girls did not interfere with kicking, but neither continued to kick as long as they were held. As they were restrained, they began talking to one another, a process that had been extremely difficult for them. They discussed their feelings of jealousy and rivalry. They felt secure in the hold and remained calm and capable of communicating as long as they were held. Slowly, the holds were loosened, but body contact remained necessary for approximately 10 minutes.

This example demonstrates that even if aggression escalates to the point at which it necessitates physical restraint, the actual use of holding does not need to be aversive or countertherapeutic. In fact, it can signal concern and caring and can be a concrete means of helping the child to contain affect.

"Can I Bring My Ice Cream Cone?"

Almost any child at some point arrives for a session with food. Different opinions exist about whether food is appropriate in sessions, with some clinicians arguing that it interferes and others claiming that it can be used therapeutically. Thus, the important issue is to decide beforehand whether food is tolerated in session. If a clinician decides against food, this limit must be enforced within realistic and therapeutic boundaries. Children who arrive for an after-school session with a half-eaten sandwich might need to be allowed to finish the food in the waiting room to ascertain that they are not too hungry to concentrate on their session. However, routine arrival with food might need to be addressed if it appears to have become a means of avoiding the session. Nonnutritious foods can generally wait to be eaten until after the session. However, occasionally, the impact on rapport of forbidding the child to finish an almost-gone candy bar might need to be weighed against the benefits of allowing the child to finish the candy. If therapists choose not to allow children to finish their food or drink before going to the playroom, they should take care to remember to leave the food in a safe place outside the playroom where the child can predictably retrieve it after the session.

"Can I Take This Home?"

Invariably, children ask to take home with them an item that they found in the playroom. This request is best explored for its therapeutic meaning as it may represent a longing to extend the session, reflect an attachment to something the child made in the playroom, be a way of testing limits that were set previously, or be a request for a gift. Depending on how the request is interpreted, the counselor may respond in different ways. If the request is meant to prolong the session, a mere reiteration of the rules might be sufficient to end the child's behavior. If it is a request for a transitional object, a different path may be chosen. If the desired object was a project created by the child, such as a painting or small clay figure, the request is granted. If the object is large and essential to treatment, the request cannot be granted but needs to be discussed with the child. In this instance, children might be encouraged to create a small object that they can take home instead that may serve the same purpose. One thing that works quite well is to make a drawing of the actual desired object. Occasionally, a clinician might choose to allow the child to take home an item as a transitional object if there is a good reason. For instance, one boy who had been seen in therapy for several weeks and who had large difficulties learning to trust and to make use of the therapy process became particularly attached to a humanlike puppet. During a session that immediately preceded a two-week break in treatment due to his family's vacation, he requested to take the puppet with him. He was allowed to do so, with the provision that he return it during the next meeting (which he did).

"It's My Birthday! Do You Have a Present for Me?"

The request for gifts is quite another matter. Often, children's direct requests for a gift have a hidden meaning, such as a request for affection. Opinions vary widely about whether clinicians should or should not give and receive gifts. Some theoreticians claim that the giving of gifts is natural and should be a normal part of treatment. Others believe that no gifts should ever be given. A middle-of-the-road position is presented by Dodds (1985), who advocates that small gifts or edible gifts are fine, especially if they can be justified therapeutically or perhaps are used to communicate special caring to a child who might not otherwise understand this message. As in most cases, it is probably best for counselors to ask themselves why they would like to present the child with a gift. If the reason is therapeutic and not countertransferential, the gift may be given. If there is doubt, the clinician should refrain from the temptation of giving until having consulted with a colleague to make sure that there are no hidden countertransference issues and to collect a second opinion about the appropriateness of the action.

The receiving of gifts is equally debatable, but perhaps less so than with adult clients. Children are not likely to bring expensive gifts, nor would they understand why therapists cannot accept gifts. Thus, the acceptance of modest gifts may be warranted. In fact, rejection of such spontaneous gifts may be more countertherapeutic than beneficial, as long as the gift truly came from the child and not the parent. Food is a common gift presented by children and, if brought for the counselor, is best shared with the child in the session. One young girl was delighted to bring cookies for her counselor late in the treatment. For her, the process of sharing cookies symbolized her ability to nurture herself and others and her growing emotional independence. Rejection of her gift would have communicated that the counselor did not agree with her assessment of her own capabilities and would have been countertherapeutic. It is perhaps possible to conclude that almost anything can be done in the treatment with children, as long as the clinician has thought about the action, has determined it to be therapeutic, and is certain that it did not develop from a personal countertransferential need.

"Guess What This Is?"

The most important thing to recognize about this commonly asked question is that it almost never is intended as it is stated (Landreth, 2000, 2002a). The child usually already has something in mind when asking the therapist about the nature of a drawing or clay model. If the counselor were to answer in this instance and be wrong, the child would be likely to be disappointed, if not disillusioned. It is best for the clinician to lay the responsibility on the child by saying that the child must have something in mind and asking the child what the drawing, the model, and so on, represents to her or him.

Often, children also ask clinicians what they think about a certain project, behavior, action, or affect. Again, responsibility is given back to the child by asking the same question of her or him. Not uncommonly, these questions are not questions to be taken literally but are to be understood as requests for permission by children to share their own thoughts and fantasies. Thus, an answer by the therapist would short-circuit a potential self-disclosure or self-exploration by the child.

Sometimes, these types of questions are also attempts by children to shirk responsibility and to shift it to the counselor. In these instances, it is best to acknowledge that the child would like to have an answer from the therapist but that the child needs to figure out the answer. The following interaction resulted between a therapist and a 6-year-old girl and demonstrates how to use a child's invitation into a guessing game to help the child self-disclose or grow, without ever answering the original question:

> SARA (*trying to complete a drawing she had begun earlier in the session*): What color should this be?
>
> THERAPIST: What color would you like it to be?
>
> SARA: It's a big house. It should be white. Do you think I should color it? Or should I leave it white?
>
> THERAPIST: What would you rather do?
>
> SARA: I don't know . . . It should be white, shouldn't it?
>
> THERAPIST: You are worried to give it the wrong color, and you want me to tell you what to do.
>
> SARA: It has to be just right . . .
>
> THERAPIST: You are afraid to do the wrong thing. But remember, everything is okay in here. It's all up to you.
>
> SARA: I think I'll make it all black (*proceeds to color; as she progresses she continues to talk, more to herself than the clinician*) . . . it's a very sad house. It has to be all black because black is sad . . .

This example demonstrates that questions and requests are often loaded with unmentioned values, affects, and needs. Direct responses keep the child from uncovering these needs and affects and are generally not in the best interest of advancing treatment.

"I Didn't Take It . . ."

Fortunately, it does not occur often that a child engages in theft. However, it is an incident that is likely to baffle the new clinician and needs to be addressed. Occasionally, children, knowing that all playroom toys must remain in the room upon ending the session, attempt to steal a small toy from the room. They might put it in a pocket and "forget" to remove it before leaving the room. If this happens, direct, though gentle, confrontation is necessary. It is not recommended to pretend that the clinician is not aware of the child's action. Rather, a direct approach is preferred (Landreth, 2000, 2002a).

Similarly, if children succeeded in taking an item from the playroom, they need to be asked about their behavior during the next session and need to be asked to return the item (Spiegel, 1996). No moralizing is necessary. Children tend to feel guilty anyhow, and extended scrutiny, moralizing, or perseverating about the incident is counterproductive. One 10-year-old boy was observed by a person in the waiting room to go into another clinician's office while waiting for his father to pick him up. The waiting room person alerted the clinician after the child had already left the center that he had carried a stopwatch when his father arrived. Sure enough, a stopwatch was reported missing from the other clinician's office. When the child returned the following week, the following conversation took place:

CLINICIAN: After you left last week, I noticed that you took a stopwatch that belongs to someone who works here. Please bring it back next week.

TIM: What are you talking about? I didn't take no stopwatch!

CLINICIAN: Someone saw you take it, and you need to return it.

TIM: Who saw what?

CLINICIAN: I know that you have the stopwatch, and you need to give it back. It is not yours to keep.

TIM: So I took it. Big deal. Why don't you just get a new one?

CLINICIAN: I know you don't want to give it back, but it does not belong to you.

TIM: I'd like to keep it.

CLINICIAN: You really like the stopwatch.

TIM: Yeah, it's neat. I took it to show-and-tell, and everyone liked it.

CLINICIAN: The other kids really admired the watch.

TIM: Yeah, Bill even wanted to borrow it, but I didn't let him.

CLINICIAN: You didn't even let anyone borrow it!

TIM: No, they might steal it!

CLINICIAN: . . . Hmm

TIM: I guess I have to give it back.

CLINICIAN: Yes, please bring it with you next week.

TIM (*retrieves the watch from his pocket*): Here it is.

The example is not complete without mentioning that the conversation then continued on to explore why Tim liked the watch. It became clear that he often was unable to bring items to show-and-tell and felt embarrassed. The watch had served as his way of ascertaining some attention and recognition from his peers. It is best always to explore why a child took an item as often an important meaning is attached to the theft. Again, this exploration is not focused on a moralizing investigation of the theft but on the emotional significance of the event. It is done directly, not condescendingly.

It must be reemphasized that the examples here are not exhaustive of all the special circumstances that may arise in the work with children. In fact, entire volumes have been written just on this topic (e.g., Gabel, Oster, and Pfeffer, 1993). The above scenarios were included merely to sensitize new clinicians to the types of difficulties that are encountered with some predictability to ready them to deal with these common challenges in a therapeutic and meaningful manner. It is good to establish some preformed rules to deal with challenging situations to prevent being taken by surprise, though at times a sudden gesture (such as sharing food) can actually serve a positive therapeutic purpose (Terr, 2006).

Summary and Concluding Thoughts

In this chapter, the reader was introduced to a general framework of working with children, which can be used with diverse theoretical approaches as well as with the wide range of specific techniques. The remainder of the book is devoted to introducing clinicians to a diversity of techniques. They are dealt with individually, but can be and most often are used concurrently. Obviously, not all available techniques can be covered in one volume; only a few of the major techniques are covered. It is hoped that the interested reader seeks additional guidance from books dedicated to each one of the specific techniques that exist.

The techniques covered in this volume include play therapy, storytelling, behavioral strategies, art therapy, and parent consultation. Other techniques include, but are not limited to, bibliotherapy (Doll and Doll, [1997]; Thompson and Rudolph [2007] present an excellent annotated bibliography of therapeutic children's books), cognitive-behavior therapy (Kendall, 2005; and Kratochwill and Morris, 1998), rational-emotive therapy for children (Ellis and Bernard, 2006), family therapy (Kaslow, Kaslow, Celano, and Farber, 2001; Minuchin, Lee, and Simon, 2006; Satir, 1967), relaxation training (Koeppen, 2002; Pearson, 1998), modeling and social skills therapies (Dowrick, 1986), biofeedback (Schwartz and Andrasik, 2003), hypnotherapy (Olness and Kohen, 1996; Wester and Sugarman, 2007), use of metaphor (Mills and Crowley, 2001; Stine, 2005), pharmacotherapy (Green, 2006), sandtray therapy (Boik and Goodwin, 2000); therapeutic games (Cheung, 2006a); and many others (for useful summaries of techniques, see Kendall [2005] or Mash and Barkley [2005]). Collections of case examples have been compiled by Roberts and Walker (1997) and Landreth, Sweeney, Ray, Homeyer, and Glover (2005).

10

Using Play in Child Therapy and Counseling

> *States Parties recognize the right of the child to rest and leisure, to engage in play and recreational activities appropriate to the age of the child and to participate freely in cultural life and the arts.*
>
> —Article 31.1 of the U.N. Convention on the Rights of the Child

Play is perhaps one of the most common techniques utilized by child therapists. Its use for that purpose has been widely documented, described, and supported (O'Conner, 2000; Landreth, 2002a; Landreth, et al., 2005; Schaefer, 2000; Schaefer and Kaduson, 2006). To understand the importance and relevance of play in the therapeutic work with children, it is first necessary to take a look at the normal, everyday impact that play may have on a child's life and development.

Conceptual Background

The fact that play is guaranteed by the United Nations as an inalienable right of childhood for children all over the world reveals the great importance placed upon play as an important task that facilitates a child's growth and maturation. Play was once described as a child's occupation (Erikson, 1950), and the toys used as the child's tools (Woltman, 1964). However, this definition has been questioned as merely being a way of legitimizing play in adults' eyes (Landreth, 2002a), since play is important in and of itself, even if not viewed as a child's work. It is the most "natural medium for self-expression" (Axline, 1947, p. 16), and an excellent means of communication among children, as well as between children and adults. Child's play communicates without words. It is person dominated, and toys or simple objects are used for the purpose of enhancing the child's growth or helping the child to enact an important life situation (O'Conner, 2000). Play is noninstrumental; in other words, it is the process that is important, not the product or a defined end goal (Cheung, 2006a). In fact, there rarely is an end goal in the free play of a child, even when such a goal appears to have been defined by the child. Often an activity is started that appears to lead to a certain outcome, only to be altered in its overt purpose before the child is done. However, despite being thus noninstrumental, play is nevertheless unconsciously purposeful (Landreth, 2002a; Landreth, et al., 2005). Although there might not be an overt goal or end state of play, it nevertheless serves a purpose for the child, even if this purpose is not always readily observable or understandable (Homeyer and DeFrance, 2005).

The unconscious purposefulness of play is at the crux of play's symbolism. Play is not always only what is seen on the surface. Play has an indirect meaning through which the child may work through everyday problems or may find solutions to problems. The unique meaning of each play activity, both its content and its style, can be understood only over time and through intensive exploration of content, form, associations, accompanying feelings, and fantasies expressed by the child in the activity. Play, understood in this context, serves as an effort at mastery of the environment and often the self, a mastery that is obtained through the planning and experiment (Chazan, 2002) that are inherent in all children's play. This mastery function of play was already recognized by Sigmund Freud, who wrote that "every child at play . . . creates a world of his [sic] own or, more truly, he [sic] arranges the things in his [sic] world and orders it in a new way that pleases him [sic] better" (1952, p. 174). This definition clearly implies the purposefulness of play. What specifically are the purposes of play? They are multifold, though they may be grouped into three larger categories; namely self-development (or intrapsychic) purposes, maturation (or growth) purposes, and relationship (or interpersonal) purposes. These three functions and their subgoals are summarized in Table 10.1.

The Self-Development Function of Play

Intrapsychic purposes are those that help the child in the task of defining and developing a sense of self. This is a large task of early childhood, and therefore, it is of no surprise that this is also a major task of play activity. Through play, the child can begin a rudimentary definition of self. Play helps children express themselves freely and without having to fear negative consequences. Such self-expression always includes a component of self-exploration. Many activities are engaged in—some are experienced as more pleasurable than others and therefore are repeated and result in an observable pattern of preferences and interests, which the child may later use to define likes and dislikes.

Expression through play is not merely expression of interests, but also expression of affect. Children express and work out feelings through play. Feelings that might not be allowed expression in a child's family are often tolerated when disguised in play activity. For instance, although children might not be allowed to shout at their mother when angry, they are rarely punished or even chastised if they allow two dolls to shout at each other. Even if one doll is clearly a child doll and the other an adult doll, parents usually grant children the freedom to engage in doll play freely. This expression of feelings is a very important aspect of play, as it not only allows for catharsis but also teaches the child that affect can be expressed freely, can be controlled through expression, and

Table 10.1   Purposes of Play in a Child's Everyday Life

Overall Function	Specific Purpose
Self-Development Function	• to engage in self-expression • to define the self • to express and explore feelings • to discover likes and dislikes • to gain a sense of control • to cope with difficult situations • to express complexities beyond verbal capacity • to meet the need to be engaged in an activity • to feel stimulated
Maturation Function	• to explore the environment • to explore relationships among objects • to gain a sense of mastery • to practice language skills • to practice motor skills • to practice cognitive skills • to learn moral judgment • to learn problem-solving skills • to organize experiences in meaningful ways
Relationship Function	• to communicate with others • to learn about roles • to learn about culture and environment • to learn social skills • to explore relationships among people • to work through conflict in relationships • to feel connected to others • to use others as models

can be rendered manageable when expressed. Children become aware of nuances of affect through their play, recognizing that there are different levels of the same emotion that may require different levels of expression. Play is important in this regard also, because even if children wished to express some of these affects and needs verbally, their cognitive or language skills (or limitations) might have prevented them from doing so. The nonverbal nature of play allows for the expression of complexities that children might not be able to master through any other medium or means of communication.

Through the free expression of affect and through the exploration of interests and other aspects of self, children also gain a sense of control over themselves. Rather than being driven by emotions or needs, children drive, express, and solve them. The subsequent feeling of control serves to enhance children's self-confidence and sense of mastery. It ultimately helps them feel competent to cope with life's difficulties.

Finally, as all living organisms have a need to be stimulated and to feel somehow purposefully engaged in activity, play can serve this function as well. Through play, children remain stimulated, keep boredom from taking over, and experience a sense of meaning in their existence. The importance of this function of play is best demonstrated by observing children who cannot find a play activity or who are unable to self-initiate a game. These children grow bored, then experience self-doubts, which may ultimately be rechanneled either into internalized feelings, such as anxiety or depression, or externalized feelings, such as anger or hostility.

The Maturation Function of Play

In addition to enhancing self or intrapsychic development, play promotes children's general growth. Play leads to maturation in a number of developmental arenas, including language skills, motor skills, cognitive skills, problem-solving skills, and moral judgments. Through play, children not only learn new skills in all of these areas but are also given the opportunity to practice skills in a meaningful and nonthreatening manner. Play can serve as an arena to act out skills modeled after parents or friends. This opportunity helps children gain a sense of mastery as well as enhances their ability to problem solve in general and to cope with new situations. In fact, even modeling in play activity is never done in a truly replicating manner. Instead, children modify what they have seen to make it fit their own unique perspectives, needs, and capabilities. In addition to skills learning and practice, maturation is facilitated through play's 0exploratory function. Play leads children to explore the environment, relationships between objects, cause-and-effect relationships, and connections between events. This facilitates the meaningful organization of experiences.

The Relationship Function of Play

Closely related to the self-development and maturation functions of play is the relationship function. Through this aspect of play, children apply what they have learned about themselves and what they have mastered and learned through practice to relationships with other people. As children learn new problem-solving skills in general, they can now learn to apply these skills in interpersonal situations. This may initially be done in solitary play that involves puppets, dolls, or other objects that may represent important figures in a child's life. Later, this is accomplished through actual interactive play with playmates in which compromises have to be worked out and conflicts solved.

Play helps children communicate with others, regardless of whether this is an intended component of a given activity. Thus, communication can take place in solitary play in which an observer becomes the incidental recipient of information or through interactive play in which the playmate is the intended target of communication. The nonverbal nature of play removes the need for language between sender and recipient, making communication independent of shared language. Communicating with others through play helps children feel interpersonally connected and enhances their feelings of belonging.

Through play with others, children also learn about roles in relationships and roles that are connected to family rules or cultural and environmental attitudes. Play can be used to practice roles in children's family and friendships and within their larger communities and cultures. Learning about roles is related to learning social skills, as both involve interaction with others that is acceptable and appropriate to the context in which the interaction takes place. In the play with other children, all players have to learn to negotiate and to assert themselves. This has to be done in a manner that is acceptable and well received by the targets, or it may result in ostracism of the child.

However, even as children create conflict in their play, learning takes place. Conflicts have to be resolved, and there is no better activity to learn conflict resolution than through interactive play. The advantage of interactive over solitary play in the relationship function also stems from the fact that interactive play necessitates the presence of others, who may serve as models. Children not only learn from watching adults, but learn perhaps even more from watching and playing with their peers and friends.

By now, the developmental advantages of play are quite self-evident. Further, these advantages and functions of play are readily apparent as the reasons why play is an important technique in the work with children. Many of the normal, everyday functions of play are relevant in the therapy or counseling context.

Application to Child Therapy and Counseling

As one aspect of the normal function of play is the establishment of relationships, it is easy to see that play can be used to facilitate the relationship between a child and a clinician. Through play, interaction can be initiated, can be made to feel familiar to the child, and can introduce a feeling of safety. A second aspect of play's usefulness in therapy and counseling is its use for self-disclosure by the child, whether consciously or unconsciously. Specifically, through play, a counselor can learn about the child without having to ask intrusive questions and instead by observing and becoming a careful recipient of the nonverbal communication sent by the child. Using the symbolism of play, a therapist may receive information that would be too difficult or painful for the child to put into words. Finally, play can be used to help the child resolve problems and legitimizes nonverbal strategies as a proper or appropriate means of facilitating and understanding the therapy or counseling process. These three aspects of play can be labeled the relationship, disclosure, and healing functions of play, in much the same way as everyday play entails the self-development, maturation, and relationship functions. These functions of play in treatment and their subpurposes are summarized in Table 10.2.

The Relationship Function of Play in Treatment

The most obvious function of play in the work with children is that of facilitating the development of a trusting and special relationship between child and clinician. There are not very many places where adults watch children play or engage in play initiated and completely controlled by the child. There is no doubt that this interactive or observing style of play is conducive to the building of trust on the part of the child in the adult. Further, the relationship is, by definition, special because of its difference in terms of the play activity from other relationships with adults experienced by the child.

The Disclosure Function of Play in Therapy

In addition to facilitating the rapport building between child and clinician, play also aids the clinician in understanding and learning about the child. As mentioned above, in play, emotions, conflicts, problems, and relationship difficulties are reenacted directly or symbolically. This process of communication and interaction helps

Table 10.2   Purposes of Play in Child Therapy or Counseling

Overall Function	Specific Purpose
Relationship Function	• to establish a trusting relationship • to establish a special relationship
Disclosure Function	• to facilitate diagnosis • to facilitate assessment • to allow expression of feelings • to act out unconscious material • to act out fears • to allow the expression of forbidden affects • to allow the expression of forbidden needs • to allow the expression of conflicts • to reconstruct conflict • to reconstruct experiences
Healing Function	• to provide an arena for intervention • to provide a sense of direction • to deal with defenses • to resolve resistances • to relieve tension • to facilitate catharsis • to provide corrective emotional experiences • to teach coping skills • to experiment with new behaviors

the clinician put together the pieces of the puzzle that is the child's life and presenting problem. It provides information that may be too threatening or frightening for the child to share through any other medium. Obtaining information through play not only helps the care provider better understand the child but also facilitates the process of diagnosis, conceptualization, and treatment planning.

The disclosure that takes place in play is healthy for the child in addition to being useful for the clinician. Often, merely having the opportunity to express feelings and conflicts freely is therapeutic for the child. Thus, the disclosure (or cathartic) function of play is closely, almost inseparably, linked to its healing function.

The Healing Function of Play in Therapy

In its simplest form, play provides an opportunity for healing merely through the facilitation of catharsis and free self-expression. The child is given complete freedom of self- and emotional expression, and the simple opportunity to vent is often quite relieving. Having an adult witness the self-expression and respond empathically and understandingly further sets the stage for corrective emotional experiences that can help children change their attitude toward a problem or conflict and greatly relieves tension.

More important, however, play becomes a technique through which the clinician and child cooperate toward the solution of the presenting, and related, problems. It provides an arena for intervention and direction and sets the stage for many opportunities for internalization. With the help of the counselor, children learn to recognize their defenses and symptoms as self-protective and may choose to substitute new behaviors and more adaptive coping skills. In play, a counselor can model and help children develop new problem-solving strategies that prepare them to cope better with life's problems. The play activities that occur allow children to experiment with new behaviors in a safe setting where failures do not have to hurt or worsen a situation. Play makes it possible for all of these processes to occur nonverbally or symbolically, thus making therapy possible even for very young or low-verbal children (James, 1997).

Finally, one goal of therapy is always generalization of the changes to relevant external settings. Once therapeutic goals have been obtained in the playroom, children are encouraged to transfer these gains to other environmental settings and future experiences. Play facilitates this process, as it occurs naturally not only in the playroom but also in all types of settings outside of the treatment context. Thus, it is likely that skills gained through play are more likely to generalize than skills gained through talking because the former are part of the child's natural, rather than learned, repertoire of behaviors.

Variations on the Technique

Although the functions of play in the work with children have been discussed somewhat generically so far, theoreticians from different schools of thought have attributed different specific therapeutic roles to the play technique in their style of treatment. Clinicians who utilize play as an important means of facilitating therapeutic change are oriented to at least one of the four largest schools of thought: psychoanalytic/psychodynamic, relationship-centered or humanistic, behaviorists, and release. All take a slightly different conceptual approach to understanding pathology, and all consequently attribute a slightly different role to the counselor and the use of play. Because all of these approaches are important, they are briefly reviewed here.

Psychoanalytic/Psychodynamic Theories

Psychoanalytic and psychodynamic child therapists are often labeled directive, because in this school of thought clinicians "assume responsibility for guidance or interpretation" (Axline, 1947, p. 9), as opposed to merely following a child's lead and focusing on empathic relating. Two of the most important figures in the psychoanalytic tradition of working with children were Melanie Klein (e.g., Klein, 1975) and Anna Freud (e.g., Freud, 1928). Both adhered to a conflict model of psychopathology. Simply put, in the conflict model, a clinician assumes that there is a conflicting relationship between one or more aspects of the child's personality. Traditionally, this conflict is seen as arising from the differences between wishes and desires emanating from the person's id versus the needs and direction stemming from the superego. The id is seen as pleasure-seeking and purely hedonistic, whereas the superego is the moralistic aspect of the person's self that keeps behavior and desires under control and within acceptable limits. When conflict between these two aspects of the client's psyche can no longer be mediated by the ego, the reality-oriented aspect of the person's self, it begins to create problems for the person. These problems are avoided through the use of defense mechanisms and through the development of symptoms.

For instance, in the conflict model, a boy with a simple phobia of snakes may be viewed as having developed this phobia to avoid awareness of an inner conflict between id wishes and superego guidance. The phobia perhaps served to keep him from situations wherein this conflict might find expression. Thus, if the assumed conflict involves the id wish of sleeping with his little sister, a wish strongly opposed by the incest taboo protected by his superego, his snake phobia may be viewed as having developed to keep him from participating in family camping trips where he might have to sleep in the same tent as his little sister. Similarly, a girl who believes that the world is a hostile place and is unable to trust anyone might simply harbor strong feelings of anger against her father. As anger toward a parent is not an acceptable affect as far as her superego is concerned, direct expression of this emotion is not allowed. Thus, the girl might use a defense of projection, wherein her own anger is projected on her environment. Perceiving the environment as an angry place certainly explains why she might perceive it as hostile and untrustworthy.

In the psychoanalytic, or conflict, model of psychopathology, play is used therapeutically in a symbolic fashion and equivalent to free association in the treatment of adults. It is perceived as offering an avenue into the child's psyche, providing a clear look at the conflicts that are hidden or defended against. Play is not to be taken literally, but to be interpreted with its relevance to the conflict of the child. For instance, if the play of the little boy with the snake phobia included play with dolls who are engaging in sexual play, this would be interpreted as a manifestation of his incestuous wishes toward his sister. In addition to being used symbolically, play is also used to establish a therapeutic relationship between the child and the clinician and sets the stage for interpretation. Only through the play activity of the child does the therapist find the opportunity to interpret the child's conflict, with the assumption that the interpretation serves to resolve the child's conflict, reducing the symptom and making the defense unnecessary.

Thus defined, the therapist in the psychoanalytic model is the interpreter—the person solving the riddle behind the symptom and the person who explains the riddle to the child, which in turn relieves conflicts. The goal is insight, and the curative factors are the interpretations made by the clinician and the transference relationship between the clinician and the child. The relationship between child and therapist is perceived as purely transferential, so that whatever feelings emerge in treatment are viewed as by-products of the child's history and personality conflict. The relationship, much as the child's play, is used to corroborate the counselor's theories about the child's inner conflict and is interpreted in the same way as the child's play. Thus, should the boy in the example express love for the clinician, this love would be interpreted as transferential, transferred from the sister onto the provider. A real (nontransferential) relationship between clinician and child is not acknowledged.

Relationship Theories

Quite opposed to the psychoanalytic therapist, the relationship therapist is nondirective. All direction and responsibility for the therapy session and therapy contacts are left to the child (Landreth, 2000; Landreth, et al., 2005). The counselor follows the child's lead, reflects the child's feelings, and focuses on the establishment of a warm and empathic relationship with the child. The model of pathology—or, rather, the model of recovery from pathology—is a growth model. In this model, the clinician believes that children have innate strivings for mental health and maturation and, if placed in the correct atmosphere, rekindle this growth through their own resources. Pathology is viewed as developing in an environment in which natural expression of growth and maturation is somehow stunted, usually owing to the absence of genuine or empathic caretakers who help children discover their ideal future self. Consequently, treatment is focused on helping the child to regain this capability.

Play is viewed as the tool through which children can reacquaint themselves with their true life direction and desires. Play is viewed as the way through which children communicate with the clinician, and it ascertains growth and maturation in the same way that talking is supposed to help adult clients to solve their problems. Thus, play facilitates the relationship between the client and the care provider. It is a therapist's role to listen empathically and extract from the child's play true feelings and desires. This understanding is reflected back to the child in an accepting and understanding manner. The acceptance and understanding confirm for the child that feelings are valid, important, and a vital part of the self. The permissiveness and respectfulness communicates to the child that the child has the answers to problems and has control over her or his life to such an extent as to be able to change it. In other words, the counselor gives the child the responsibility to direct treatment and to rediscover a healthful growth trajectory.

The goal of this approach to child treatment is not insight, as in the psychoanalytic model, but rather self-actualization and self-acceptance. Children learn to be who they want to be and feel accepted for this choice. The curative factor in this type of treatment is the empathic, warm, and secure relationship between the child and clinician. The relationship is important as it unfolds in the here and now and is not merely interpreted transferentially, as in the psychoanalytic model. The structured atmosphere or environment in which the relationship develops includes supportive limits that are set by the clinician to facilitate safety and feelings of security of the child and to inject the treatment with a dose of realism (Landreth, et al., 2005). However, the prime focus is on the relationship and the empathic, warm, and respectful relating between the two people.

In this model, the boy with the snake phobia would be viewed as being frightened of allowing himself to become who he wants to be. He is viewed as having developed this symptom in response to an environment that has not supported him appropriately for authentic self development. Perhaps, upon his first sight of a snake, he was frightened and this fear was responded to nonempathically. Perhaps his first camping trip was traumatic, yet his fear was ridiculed and not accepted. In this treatment approach, the child would be allowed to explore his feelings and to express them in an environment where they would be empathically reflected and accepted as important and valid.

Behavioral Theories

The behavioral therapist has an altogether different treatment approach with children. The relationship between the child and the clinician is of little importance, other than to convince the child and parents to comply with prescribed treatment. Behaviorists may follow a strict conditioning or a social learning model (Bandura, 1999; Patterson, 1977; Skinner, 1976). The boy's snake phobia in this model is explained as having developed because of the reinforcement or learning history he encountered. For instance, perhaps the first time he saw a snake, he was with his father, who was also frightened of snakes. His father responded with fear and ran from the snake, sweeping up his son in his arms, telling him not to be afraid. Despite the verbal message, the boy recognized the father's fear and learned that snakes are dangerous. His fear might have been further reinforced by a friend who also responded with fear to snakes when the class was on a field trip. By now, the child's fear has become strengthened to a point of complete avoidance of snakes. His fear has nothing to do with internal personality conflicts, as in the psychoanalytic model, nor is it secondary to not having been empathically responded to as in the relationship model. It is plainly understood as a learned response, in fact a socially learned response wherein the child simply models his father's affects.

In the attempt to treat a child, behaviorists view play as a mere by-product, not a focus, of treatment. Play provides a means of establishing rapport and a stage on which reinforcement contingencies or modeling can be implemented that will change the child's behavior. It becomes a therapist's role to dispense reinforcers or to punish, to serve as a model, and to implement relaxation or desensitization programs. The clinician does not need to explain these issues to the child, as insight is not important; nor does the counselor have to treat the child with empathy, warmth, and respect, as this is not crucial to change. (This is not to say that behaviorists do not do these things; they are merely not viewed as essential therapeutic ingredients to effect change.) The goal of treatment is neither to interpret and understand conflicts nor to help children feel accepted and self-actualized; rather it is to define what maintains, shapes, eliminates, or alters their behavior and to gain control over it. The curative factors in the behavioral treatment process are the reinforcers and punishers that are found to be effective in producing behavior change.

For the boy in the example, this might mean that a counselor develops a desensitization program for the child. In this process, the child may be taught how to relax. Then, while relaxed, the child is slowly and incrementally exposed to the feared stimulus, namely, snakes or snake-related items. The child is reinforced for remaining calm in the presence of such fear-producing stimuli until, in the end, the child can tolerate the presence of a snake and remain calm. Obviously, much of this work can, and often does, take place outside the playroom. Relaxation programs, reinforcement schedules, and so forth can easily be implemented in a child's classroom or home, making behavioral treatment methods very helpful for generalizability of progress.

Release and Structure Theories

In release and structure therapies, as originally developed by David Levy (1939, 1998) and Gove Hambridge (1955, 2002), the cathartic or abreactive effect of treatment is stressed. These clinicians subscribe to a catharsis model. In this model, the expression of affect in a lifelike situation is viewed as essential to growth and healing. Play is used to introduce or re-create anxiety-provoking situations that are thought to have precipitated the child's problems. It is the therapist's larger theoretical model that determines what is believed to be the problem's precipitant. Thus, going back to the boy in the example, one release therapist might expose the child to a structured play situation wherein two children engage in incest. Another therapist might create a play scene wherein the child is attacked by a snake. The critical piece that ties these theorists together is the structured play activity that is designed by the clinician to evoke a strong, cathartic affect in the child.

Some free play is allowed by these clinicians, primarily for exploration of the problem and for building a relationship. Sometimes, free play is permitted to help children recover from the intervention of the structured play activity. The role of the counselor is one of introducing the anxiety-provoking play scenes and to set the stage for the child's emotional expression and acting out behavior. There is little, if any, focus on a therapeutic relationship beyond the establishment of sufficient rapport to gain the child's and family's cooperation for treatment. No interpretations are made; no reinforcement contingencies are planned. The goal of treatment is simply abreaction and catharsis. The curative factors are the structured play scenes introduced by the clinician and the child's emotional responses to them.

This brief overview, summarized in Table 10.3, of these four approaches to the use of play activity with children was provided not to train the reader in these particular theories. Much more time would have to be spent discussing them if that were the purpose. They were presented merely to point out that play can be and has been used in a number of different ways and contexts and can be equally effective in all. The presentation of these models demonstrates that no one of these approaches sufficiently prepares a child clinician to work with the wide range of problems that children present to treatment. Specifically, it is unlikely that very many modern clinicians would treat a child's snake phobia from a traditionally psychoanalytic paradigm. It appears similarly unlikely that a behaviorist would not explore family circumstances in which the child's phobia developed, to intervene not only through reinforcement plans but also through the involvement of other family members in the treatment process. Finally, few contemporary clinicians disregard the here-and-now relationship that develops between a child and a clinician in the course of play therapy. Consequently, a mixture of the above approaches appears to provide the most solid conceptual base from which a play therapist might choose to intervene (James, 1997; Webb, 2007).

This eclectic or integrative approach is promoted by many play therapists today (Landreth, et al., 2005; O'Conner, 2000; Schaefer and Kaduson, 2006), despite not always being labeled as such, as clinicians prefer to identify themselves with a specific conceptual model. However, if actual treatment dialogues and transcripts are reviewed, significant overlap can be found among the interventions and responses from clinicians of various schools of thoughts. It is the eclectic integration of a number of approaches to play therapy that is presented in the following pages as the practical implementation of the play technique is discussed. For conceptually pure discussions of play therapy, the reader is referred to the primary references provided above.

Table 10.3   Four Conceptual Approaches to Play in Therapy and Counseling

Approach	Model	Role of Play	Role of Therapist	Goal	Curative Factor
Psychoanalytic	Conflict	establish relationship symbolism— like free associations stage for interpretation	interpreter who creates insight transference object	insight	interpretation transference relationship
Relationship	Growth	establish relationship self-exploration means to achieve maturation communication	create a warm, caring environment reflect and accept feelings	self-actualization self-acceptance	here-and-now, warm relationship accepting environment
Behavioral	Conditioning; Social Learning	establish rapport stage to implement treatment	developer of reinforcement, relaxation, and desensitization programs	learn child's reinforcement contingencies	reinforcers punishers relaxation training desensitization
Release/ Structure	Catharsis	establish relationship means to act out structure medium for abreaction	prepares and directs structured play scenes sets stage for emotional catharsis	catharsis or abreaction	structured play scenes emotional release

Practical Implementation

In the eclectic integrative model of play therapy, the counselors enter the assessment phase of intervention with conceptually open minds. They explore a number of aspects of the child's life and current presentation and use all of these factors to develop a conceptualization and treatment plan. Although the case conceptualization is likely to reflect a clinician's preferred theoretical framework, the implementation of strategies to achieve treatment goals is flexible and wide-ranging across all four models of play therapy. Thus, an integrative play therapist does not necessarily adhere to one single strategic approach to the child in treatment but rather uses the technique that appears most relevant to a specific problem that occurs in the here and now in the playroom. For instance, although a relationship-centered or psychodynamically oriented play therapist may not hand out tangible reinforcers for a positive action by the child, social reinforcers nevertheless are used constantly. Counselors smile at children after they have accomplished a difficult task, they express pride in a child who has mastered a new skill, and they ignore behaviors that they deem inappropriate. They may even set up specific contingencies in the process of enforcing and implementing safety limits. Both social and coping skills are often and inadvertently modeled and reinforced by the clinician.

Not uncommonly, the eclectic integrative play therapist uses here-and-now opportunities to help the child develop relaxation techniques, such as breathing exercises, muscle tension–relaxation exercises, visualization, and even some calming self-talk (Kaduson and Schaefer, 1997, 2001, 2006). For instance, one 5-year-old girl was helped to visualize her parents sitting on the couch in the waiting room to help her tolerate separation from her parents. In this process, she was first asked to draw a picture of her parents, then the picture was left in the room for the child to look at whenever she needed the reassurance of her parents' presence. Slowly, the picture was moved to less and less obtrusive places in the playroom, until the child was able to merely look in the direction of the picture (at this time kept in a closet, completely out of sight!) to reassure herself. This internalization of a vivid picture of her parents also generalized out of the playroom to help this girl cope better with visitations with her biological father and stepmother every month.

Similarly, the behavioral use of the therapy stage is generally complemented by a solid appreciation of the interpersonal relationship that is developing between the child and the clinician, along with overt to covert interpretations of this relationship as relevant to the child's history and present living situation, even by strictly behavioral therapists. The eclectic integrative clinician is sensitive to how children feel in the presence of the therapist and strives to construct an atmosphere of warmth and caring wherein children feel safe and sufficiently trusting to engage in self-disclosing play activity. Counselors engage in play with the child when invited to do so, not remaining passively and aloofly uninvolved.

For instance, one 9-year-old girl, who had been referred by her teacher because of her phobic fear to speak out in class, was evaluated for treatment and referred for a desensitization program to deal with this social phobia. In the course of assessment, the clinician was stunned by the amount of trauma that had occurred in this child's life. She had been a victim of repeated sexual abuse by her stepfather after her biological mother had died of a drug overdose. Her biological father had been sentenced to a life term in prison after a drug-related murder shortly after her birth, and she had neither met him nor had any recollection of him or stories about him. She was placed in a number of foster homes after being taken from her stepfather's home and was desperately wishing to be adopted. With this knowledge, the therapist decided that merely implementing a desensitization program to help this girl deal with her fears was not sufficient. He also provided a nurturing and supportive environment that conveyed stability and guidance. As such, while in every session the two worked on her fears, they also engaged in interactive and gentle play. When the girl encountered difficulties in moving from one step in her program to the next, it was not uncommon for her to sit cuddled up to the clinician for support and the warmth of knowing that he cared for her and was prepared to face the difficult task with her.

In addition to using the relationship with a child to provide support and nurturance, it can also be used to explore anger, sadness, isolation, or other interpersonal affects, needs, and desires expressed by a child. The integrative play therapist is open to making interpretations about the current relationship in the context of the child's history. Often, this historic explanation can also be accomplished symbolically through the child's play activity. This symbolic explanation requires that the counselor be not merely a spectator but also an active participant in the child's play.

For instance, the girl described in the previous paragraph often chose to play with the anatomical dolls, without yet having discovered their genitalia. One day, the therapist prepared for the session by laying out a change of clothes for the dolls to encourage exploration by the child (i.e., he used a technique that is certainly related to structured play). The child indeed recognized the invitation and began to undress the girl doll. She evidenced fear and shock upon discovery of the doll's vagina, threw the doll down, and turned to an alternative activity in the room. The therapist, trusting that their relationship was secure enough to endure a challenge, interpreted her behavior for her by indicating that it appeared that the girl was very frightened by the sight of the naked doll. He encouraged her to look closely and to pick up the doll, indicating that he would help her and keep her safe. Together, they picked the doll back up and began to explore. This interaction was very important based on the trusting relationship that had already developed in the girl's treatment. It led to an opportunity for the child to speak through the use of the dolls about her experience of being raped by her stepfather. The opportunity for her to tell of her victimization was cathartic, and it also helped her process feelings of shame and guilt that had remained with her for several years. These feelings had found their expression in her interpersonal reticence and fearfulness, particularly in the classroom around other children.

In summary, although eclectic integrative play therapists may well prefer one particular play therapy model for case conceptualization, they remain flexible with regard to the implementation of techniques that can facilitate change in the child. Integrative play therapists adapt strategies of intervention to the specific needs of each individual child, rather than imposing a particular approach on every child. The flexibility and willingness to try different techniques that maximize a child's sense of safety and being care for so they can work on growth and maturation are crucial to successful play therapy.

Case Example

The unfolding of play therapy is best experienced by each clinician personally. Recognizing the usefulness of play to help a child enter into a relationship, self-disclose, trust, and ultimately change is an extremely satisfying process. As clinicians new to the work with children are not likely to have had this experience, a sample case is presented here to help them gain an appreciation for this development. However, as readers review this case example, they must understand the purpose for which it was chosen. It was chosen because of its quick success and its model case quality. Not all cases unfold this quickly and easily, but it is hoped that all play therapists have at least one case in their careers that is similar to the one presented here. This case occurred early during the therapist's training, an opportunity that is rare indeed. Perhaps this example can best serve to encourage new clinicians without suggesting that, if their first few (or even first one hundred cases) are not similarly successful, they are not good play therapists.

The example is based upon the 14-week treatment of a 7-year-old girl who was referred by her foster mother after being placed in her current home following the sudden death of her father and mother in a car accident. The girl had lived with her foster family for 10 weeks by the time she was seen for an intake. The therapist was a psychology trainee doing a one-semester practicum. She anticipated being able to see a child for approximately 15 weeks, the length of the semester. This case was referred to her after the intake interview, as it appeared to be of relatively short-term nature that would allow for a natural termination rather than a transfer.

The intake, which included the foster mother, foster father, and Tracy, the 7-year-old girl, revealed the following information. Tracy was born healthy and developed normally. She was very attached to her biological father and his wife, Tracy's stepmother. Her biological mother had left her husband 15 months after Tracy's birth and had not been heard from since. Tracy's father always claimed he did not know why his wife had left him and her daughter and knew nothing of her whereabouts. Tracy's biological mother had no family; she had claimed to have been orphaned at an early age, thus remaining a mystery. Tracy's father met his second wife when Tracy was almost 2 years old and married her after a six-month courtship. This woman was very loving toward Tracy, and Tracy called her "mommy," though she knew the true relationship. Tracy had seen pictures of her biological mother but never had asked many questions about her, being quite happy and content in her nuclear family (father and stepmother). Tracy's father's parents had died before Tracy's birth. They had been in their forties when Tracy's father was conceived, and he himself was 43 when Tracy was born. There was an aunt, who lived in Chicago, and an uncle in Los Angeles, neither of whom felt capable of or was willing to take Tracy in after the accident. Her current foster family was a family with whom she had been familiar, because they attended the same church as Tracy's family. They had decided to take her in when they heard of the tragedy and at the time of the intake were thinking of adopting her. They had no children of their own for unknown reasons.

Tracy's school performance had always been quite good, with special abilities in math. She had several friends, both in her school and in her original neighborhood where she had lived since birth. She had never presented any problems to the knowledge of her foster parents and her teachers. Immediately after the accident, Tracy moved into her current home. Although there were no problems for the first two weeks in her new home, Tracy then developed severe nightmares, as well as night terrors and wet the bed on three occasions. Her teachers reported that her performance was deteriorating, that she failed to concentrate and attend, and that she had withdrawn from her friends. Everyone in her environment appeared concerned about her yet also indicated that they believed that her behavior would change spontaneously once she adjusted to the death of her parents and new surroundings. When her behavior continued to worsen after 8 weeks in her new home, her foster family called to make an appointment.

The intake clinicians, after having met with the family and all family holons, diagnosed Tracy as suffering from an adjustment disorder with mixed emotions and academic problems. No diagnosis was made on either Axis II or III. Her stressors were identified as acute, naming the death of her parents as well as the move to a new neighborhood. Her current GAF level was judged to be 63, compared to a past year level of 95. Treatment goals revolved around helping her deal with her parents' death and new living situation, with expected resolution of the current presenting problems if these issues could be resolved. In other words, the clinicians judged that her nightmares, bed-wetting, academic performance, and friendship difficulties were secondary to her life changes and needed no specific treatment at this time. The recommendation was for individual play therapy for Tracy, as no family problems were noted. Tracy was assigned to the trainee therapist, who had also conducted the individual intake interview with the child and thus had already begun to establish a relationship with her.

In her first session, Tracy was shy and refused to do much exploration in the playroom. This continued the pattern that had been set in the intake. She was very hesitant to involve herself in conversation with the therapist and did not wish to speak or play. The therapist, believing that the child had been sufficiently challenged by her previous traumata, accepted this stance and chose not to challenge or prod Tracy. For quite a while, the two sat together in silence, with the therapist letting Tracy know that she was there for her and it was up to Tracy to determine how her time would be used. She chose simply to follow Tracy's lead by using the same material used by the child and modeling after her behavior. For instance, Tracy had picked up some clay and was molding various shapes, always destroying one before advancing to the next. The therapist tentatively followed Tracy's lead by also making shapes with the clay. However, in a slight variation on Tracy's theme, the therapist, Ruth, did not destroy her previous shapes when making new ones. Ruth had decided that Tracy's destruction of the shapes might symbolize her parents' death or the ephemeral nature of relationships in general and did not want to reflect to the child that she held the same belief. Instead, her message was that new shapes (i.e., relationships) can be formed without destroying old ones.

Later in the session, Tracy became more interactive, asking Ruth for permission to use the various toys. She also checked with Ruth on several occasions about the appropriateness of her actions. Ruth interpreted Tracy's inquiries as a means of establishing a relationship with the therapist (not wanting to offend or anger Ruth), but also a reflection of the child's insecurity (not trusting her own judgments and desires). She responded to the child's inquiries with reassurance to communicate that she also wanted to build a relationship with Tracy and with encouragement to communicate that Ruth was certain that Tracy could make good decisions herself. One such interaction was as follows:

TRACY: Is it okay to take my shoes off and walk in the sandbox?

RUTH: In this room we can take our shoes off and feel comfortable because we don't have to worry about getting hurt. Also, in here you can decide for yourself what you would like to do. It's really all up to you because I know that you can decide for yourself.

Although this is a quite lengthy response to a simple question, the therapist justified her response by the importance of the message. It might have been preferable to give the message in chunks, that is, choose the most relevant issue in this case, and wait for a second opportunity to deliver the second message. Children hear messages much more clearly if they are delivered one at a time.

However, Tracy not only appeared to have heard both messages, but also was able to trust their genuineness. When she returned for her second session, she immediately took off her shoes and appeared much more comfortable in the room. She asked whether she could play with the dollhouse and proceeded to do so without waiting for a response. Using the dolls, Tracy began to tell her story. Here is a description of the play and conversation that followed:

TRACY: This doll should not be in this room, she does not belong there!

RUTH: She should be somewhere else.

TRACY: She left a long time ago. Maybe she died because she sure hasn't been around (*throws the doll forcefully over the house, where it landed out of sight*).

RUTH (*forcefully*): Now she's gone.

TRACY: . . . gone . . . (*grabs two other dolls and puts them in the kitchen*).

LARGE FEMALE DOLL: Hello sweetie, good morning, did you sleep well? Did you have any dreams?

SMALL FEMALE DOLL: Oh yes, I dreamed that a little bear came up to our house and chewed up the apple tree. And then dad came and chased it away so we could eat the apples ourselves.

LARGE FEMALE DOLL: Let's eat breakfast. I am very hungry.

SMALL FEMALE DOLL: Me too!!!

(*The dolls eat cereal, then clean the dishes and go into the bathroom; the large doll gives the small doll a bath and helps her get dressed; the large male doll comes in.*)

LARGE MALE DOLL: Ohhhh! I am still so sleepy. Could you take Teetee to school today?

LARGE FEMALE DOLL: Sure and then we can pick her up together in the afternoon.

(*Tracy throws the dolls away and turns to another activity. The therapist does not understand what just happened.*)

RUTH: You are done playing with the dollhouse.

TRACY: Yes, it's just fake anyway.

RUTH: What you played wasn't real?

TRACY: No!!! No!!! No!!!

(*Ruth backs off, sensing that Tracy is protecting herself.*)

Session 2 ended with Tracy painting a picture of Ruth. She wanted to take it home with her. Because the paint was still wet, Ruth promised to keep the picture until the next session and to allow Tracy to take it home after that session. Tracy agreed. Tracy immediately asked for the picture at the beginning of her next session. Ruth retrieved it and Tracy put it back on the easel, adding a few brush strokes in various places. She then turned to the dollhouse. The following dialogue took place:

TRACY (*sadly*): My mommy can't take me to school anymore.

RUTH (*tenderly*): You are very sad that your mommy can't take you to school.

TRACY: I liked it when she took me to school. Dad took me more than mommy did, but I liked mommy doing it because she always walked to my room with me and looked at my pictures.

RUTH: It was very special when mommy took you because she came in with you.

TRACY: She liked my pictures!

RUTH (*realizing that it was not the coming in per se, as much as the looking at her pictures that was important to Tracy*): You sure liked showing her your pictures. She thought they were pretty.

TRACY: She even took some home and hanged them up! She had a bunch in the car . . .

RUTH (*very tenderly, fearing the obvious*): She had pictures in the car with her when she came to pick you up with daddy the day they had the accident. (*Ruth now also connects the behavior from session 2 and reaches out to Tracy to touch her.*)

TRACY (*weeping quietly*): She wanted to hang them in her room!

RUTH: She really liked your pictures and kept them for a long time.

TRACY: Forever!

RUTH: She never got rid of them.

TRACY: Do you want to see my pictures?

RUTH: Yes! I would very much like to see your pictures.

Ruth had stumbled upon a means to connect with Tracy in a meaningful way by having kept Tracy's picture for her from one session to the next. This action revived sad memories in Tracy, who was surprisingly able to deal with the day of her parents' death. Ruth attempted to give support to Tracy by lowering her voice and using some cautious physical touch. Tracy had begun to trust Ruth and was establishing a transference relationship with her, having invited Ruth to care for her pictures much as her stepmother used to do. Tracy failed to take Ruth's picture home with her, and Ruth wondered whether this was a test of their relationship.

In session 4, Ruth put Tracy's picture of Ruth on the easel to communicate her understanding of the importance of pictures in Tracy's life. Tracy saw the picture immediately upon entering the room, ran up to it, and kissed it on Ruth's cheek. She turned to Ruth and then began playing with the dollhouse, going back to the scene of session 2. She replayed the scene almost identically, but this time was able to go further. Here is what happened:

SMALL FEMALE DOLL: I can take the bus. Don't pick me up!

RUTH: She doesn't want her mommy and dad picking her up.

TRACY: No, she wants to ride the bus.

RUTH: Why does she want to ride the bus?

TRACY: All her friends ride the bus, and she is old enough to do it too.

RUTH: She is old enough to get home on her own.

TRACY: But she is such a scaredy-cat. She never wants to ride the bus, always cries and whines! So mommy or dad pick her up every day.

RUTH: Her friends take the bus, but she is too scared, so mommy or dad picks her up.

TRACY (*to small female doll*): Stupid crybaby! Can't you ride the bus? You stupid crybaby.

RUTH: You don't like her much right now . . .

TRACY: She is such a crybaby!

(*Tracy turns away from the dollhouse and begins to paint again.*)

Ruth had learned important information today. She now knew that the guilt and shame she had suspected in the little girl had a very deep root and would not be easy to break. She clearly had blamed herself for her parents' death and probably was quickly losing the self-confidence and self-esteem that her parents had helped to build so beautifully.

Session 5 began with Tracy asking to play in the sandbox, an activity in which she had not engaged since her first session. She took off her shoes and stepped into the box. She brought several of the dollhouse figures with her, including also several children. She enacted playground play in which several children were happily engaged in interactive play. One doll remained outside the circle. Ruth, being aware of the child's current problems in friendship, chose to comment on the lonely doll.

RUTH: This little girl isn't playing?

TRACY: She is too sad to play . . .

RUTH: What's making her so sad?

TRACY: She has no one to play with.

RUTH: She feels like she has no one to play with even though there are lots of children in the playground.

TRACY: But these kids don't like to play with her because she is bad.

RUTH (*not yet sure where this will lead, chooses merely to reflect*): She thinks she is a bad girl, and the other kids don't want to play with her.

TRACY: She is bad!

RUTH: What makes her bad?

TRACY: She whines and complains a lot. She is a crybaby. Even her dad tells her that she cries too much and acts like a baby sometimes.

RUTH (*aware that they have returned to a theme from session 4*): She feels she is a crybaby, and because of that people don't like her—sometimes even her dad gets mad at her!

TRACY: He used to want her to ride the bus, but she wouldn't.

RUTH (*feeling it is time to be direct, a questionable decision as the metaphor was working*): Your dad used to think you were a crybaby because you wanted mommy to pick you up from school.

Tracy got out of the sandbox and started to paint, ignoring Ruth. Ruth realized her mistake (interpretation instead of understanding) and attempted to reconnect with Tracy by once again following her lead rather than imposing her own need for clarification and directness. Session 5 ended with Ruth and Tracy reconnecting around Ruth's willingness to keep Tracy's paintings for her.

In session 6, Tracy painted for a long time. Ruth allowed her to do so without challenge, still aware of the breach in their relationship. Toward the end of the session, Tracy turned to Ruth, and the following conversation took place:

TRACY: You think I'm a crybaby too!

RUTH: I hurt your feelings, and now you think I don't like the way you act.

TRACY: You think I whine too much.

RUTH: You are worried that I think you whine too much, just like your dad sometimes said you whine too much.

TRACY: He didn't like it that mommy picked me up from school all the time. He told her she spoils me.

RUTH: You liked it that she picked you up from school. That was special.

TRACY: The other kids were mad 'cause they had to ride the bus and I had my mommy pick me up.

RUTH: You were special!

TRACY: Do you think I am a crybaby?

RUTH: I don't think you are a crybaby at all. Sometimes you like for someone to take care of you. You liked your mommy to take care of you, and now you wonder if that was bad.

TRACY: Will you keep my drawings for me?

RUTH: Yes. I will keep them safely in this room till you come back next week.

In session 7, Tracy returned to the dollhouse and finally finished the scene. She reenacted the accident her parents had on the way to work in the morning after they had dropped her off at school. She played out her guilt and her belief that if it were not for her whining, they might still be alive. Ruth attempted to help her understand that nothing she did or could have done would have changed anything and that the event was not her fault. Tracy was hesitant to hear the message. However, at the end of the session she drew a picture. This drawing was of her mommy and daddy in heaven, looking down at Tracy. Tracy was lying in bed having bad dreams. Her parents watched and looked very sad. The following dialogue ensued:

RUTH: They are very sad about your bad dreams every night.

TRACY: Mommy always liked to listen to my dreams. We told our dreams every day! (*This explained the story in session 2.*)

RUTH: You really miss your mommy in many, many ways.

TRACY: My dad too . . .

RUTH: You love them and they love you, and you wish you could keep telling them about your dreams and show them your drawings and ride home from school with them.

TRACY: I have bad dreams a lot.

RUTH: I would like to hear about your bad dreams, just like your mommy used to listen to your dreams. How about next time you tell me about your dreams?

It is very difficult to end a session when a child has made an important and painful disclosure, but for the sake of continuity and consistency, the boundaries of treatment must be observed. Ruth chose to help Tracy bridge the gap by tying in the events of this session with events that would occur in the next session.

Tracy came to session 8 prepared to tell Ruth her dreams. She had dreamed of a wild bear that was eating up all the berries in an old woman's garden. The old woman could not walk very well, so she was afraid she might have to starve because the bear ate all her berries and she could not walk to the store. Ruth noted several important themes in this dream. First, the bear, which had also inhabited Tracy's first dream in session 2, was again included in this dream but in a more threatening form. Second, food was once again a theme in her dream. However, whereas the dream related in session 2 had a positive ending with her dad protecting the family and ascertaining that they would have enough food, this dream ended on the frightening note of potential starvation. Ruth chose to empathize with the old woman in the dream and told Tracy that she was sure that someone would come to save the old woman and would bring her many berries so she could survive the winter. Tracy at this time turned to the dollhouse and began to set up the kitchen.

TRACY: It's dinner time, and they are all going to eat together.

RUTH: They are hungry, and they are looking forward to eating dinner together.

TRACY: They always eat dinner together. Eating alone makes the food go bad.

RUTH: They don't like to eat alone.

TRACY: My mommy says the food spoils—you have to eat as a family. Dixie [her foster mother] never eats with Pete [her foster father] and with me because she works late.

RUTH: You are worried about the food with Dixie not eating with you and Pete!

TRACY: Do you think I will die because I eat bad food?

RUTH: The food you eat with Pete is good food, and there is lots of it, so everyone can get enough even though you can't always eat together. (*Ruth tried to avoid saying that Tracy's mommy was wrong in saying what she said because she did not want to tarnish Tracy's memory of her mother, nor did she want to engage Tracy in a struggle wherein Tracy would have to convince Ruth that her mommy was right.*)

TRACY (*picking up the small female and large male doll*): Dinner time. Let's save some food so Dixie can eat when she comes home.

Ruth realized that the food arrangement in the new home was also symbolic of a more basic concern of Tracy's, namely, a fear about whether her foster parents would be able to protect her and nurture her in the same way her parents used to. Ruth's response was designed to address this issue indirectly.

In session 9, Tracy drew another picture, this time of her mommy and dad watching her eating with Pete. She then turned to the dollhouse and enacted bedtime and breakfast themes. These scenes appeared to show that as she was dealing with her parents' death, she was able to begin to draw closer to her foster parents. For instance, in the breakfast scene, it was Dixie who asked her about her dreams, and for the first time, the small female doll had a happy dream to report. Checking with the foster parents, Ruth also uncovered that the number of nightmares had decreased and that there were no more night terrors or bed-wetting. Tracy was still very shy in school, but her academic performance was slowly improving again.

With the security of building a relationship with her foster parents, Tracy was able to return to her feelings of guilt and shame surrounding the accident of her parents. In session 10, the accident was reenacted, and Tracy verbalized that if she only were less of a crybaby, her parents would be alive. Ruth helped her work through her painful affects and allowed Tracy to cry freely. Ruth helped the child to allow herself to feel safe in her pain and to feel supported and loved despite her perceived guilt. Later in the session, Tracy returned to the sandbox.

Tracy took several houses and cars and built a complicated road system. She placed several dolls in front of several houses, then took a car that went from house to house picking up dolls. She narrated that this was a mommy picking up children to go to school because the school bus was late and the children needed to get to school on time. For the first time, Tracy revealed she had some recollection of the fact that there had been a reason other than her whining why her parents had taken her to school the day of the accident. There had been an announcement on the radio that the bus was going to be 30 minutes late in their small rural town. Because Tracy's parents had a long commute to a nearby city, they could not wait for her and decided to take her to school themselves. Just before they left, another mother had called to ask them whether they had heard about the announcement and whether they wanted to drop Tracy off at her house so that she would not need to wait alone. The parents had turned down the invitation, indicating they would just drop Tracy at school. Despite the fact that Tracy did not tell this story directly (Ruth had known about it from her foster parents), Ruth was now confident that Tracy recognized that she was not the cause of the accident.

In session 11, Tracy returned to the dollhouse and enacted more breakfast and bedtime scenes. She revealed through her play with the small female and the large male doll that Pete was responsible for taking her to bed, as Dixie worked late. She appeared to enjoy their bedtime ritual, during which Pete read her a story, then tucked her in with a stuffed animal and plugged in her night light. Tracy revealed some ambivalence about enjoying the ritual, as evidenced by this play activity:

> TRACY: She likes the storytelling, but maybe she should just go to sleep.
>
> RUTH: She wonders if she shouldn't like the story because it keeps him so busy and he can't do what she thinks he needs to do.
>
> TRACY: Oh, he is so busy. He is a writer, and he works very hard. When he tells her a story, he can't work.

RUTH (*knowing that her dad was a writer, whereas Pete is an engineer*): Some dads don't have time to read bedtime stories, but other dads do.

TRACY: She knows that, but she worries what he thinks.

RUTH (*a bit lost, as she did not yet understand the child's message*): She worries what he thinks of her?

TRACY: She likes his story, but he might not like it.

RUTH (*still wondering*): He doesn't like the story, but she does?

TRACY: She likes for him to read to her, but she worries that when he watches he doesn't like him.

RUTH (*acting on a hunch*): Her dad watches them telling stories, and she is afraid he might be jealous because he couldn't read her stories, but her new dad can and she likes it!

TRACY: Yeah! Maybe he wants to read to her too.

RUTH: I bet he is happy to see her happy because he always wanted to tell her stories but didn't have time. Now she gets her bedtime story, and everyone is happy.

TRACY (*confidently, almost assertively*): She sure likes it!

It was not surprising for Tracy to feel conflicted over liking her new family. Often, this is perceived as disloyalty to the biological parents and restimulates old guilt feelings about having felt angry at parents, perhaps even having wished them dead. Ruth was very direct in her instruction that Tracy's dad would be happy for her, and Tracy accepted the message easily.

In session 12, Tracy related that she and Dixie and Pete were going on summer vacation together. She appeared excited and happy. Ruth decided that this was a good time to discuss termination, as reports from school and home revealed that Tracy was beginning to adjust. They discussed ending their special time together and that they would both remember one another even after they no longer met every week. Tracy handled the introduction of the topic very well. She demonstrated her general life gains in her play activity during this session. She had returned to the sandbox to build a replica of Dixie's and Pete's house. She related that she had her own room and that Dixie told her they would redecorate it according to Tracy's wishes. Pete had already begun painting the walls and allowed Tracy to help. Tracy then moved to the easel to draw a picture for Ruth of her new room. She asked Ruth to keep the picture at the end of the session, but then changed her mind and asked whether she could take it home to give to Dixie. Ruth, delighted at the shift of the relationship, allowed her to do so.

Session 13 began with Tracy's return to the dollhouse. She reenacted the original breakfast scene and the continuation of the scene according to the real-life occurrence, including the radio announcement, the phone call from her friend's mother, and the actual accident. She was very sad but able to tolerate this affect. She demonstrated her attachment to Dixie and Pete by staging a funeral during which the three dolls stood so closely that they quite literally supported one another physically. Tracy was able to say goodbye to her parents and to welcome her foster parents. At the end of session 13, Dixie took the therapist aside to inform her that she and Pete had received permission to adopt Tracy. They were planning to tell Tracy that evening and to have a celebration. Dixie wanted to know whether Ruth felt that Tracy was ready for this development. Ruth agreed that it would probably serve to strengthen the family ties, as Tracy had revealed in this session that she had resolved her ambivalence about shifting her attachments.

Session 14 focused on the termination of treatment. Tracy was able to share with Ruth the ways in which she felt better, and Ruth shared with Tracy that she was special and that Ruth would not forget her. The session ended positively.

Summary and Concluding Thoughts

The example was presented to clarify for the beginning clinician that treatment with children not only incorporates a number of techniques, but also requires flexibility and the ability to follow a child's play symbolically. This latter ability improves over the course of a child's treatment as the clinician gets to know the child better and begins to understand the child's unique and individualized symbolism. Responding within this symbolism or within a particular metaphor is generally very useful, as it allows the child to deal with difficult matter in an indirect and hence more tolerable manner. Leaving the metaphor or symbolism represents a big step and is done only if the clinician sees a distinct advantage to dealing with the contents directly. Often, the child leads the way in leaving the metaphor on her or his own, as was evidenced in Tracy's case. When the therapist left the metaphor prematurely in an early session, the child closed up and withdrew. However, until the very end of her treatment, she returned to the metaphor each time she introduced a new feeling or conflict. In later sessions, Tracy abandoned the metaphor and spoke directly and openly about her experiences, which generally symbolized her resolution of the conflict.

11

Storytelling in Child Therapy and Counseling

> States Parties shall:
> (a) Encourage the mass media to disseminate information and material of social and cultural benefit to the child ...;
> (b) Encourage international co-operation in the production, exchange and dissemination of such information and material from a diversity of cultural, national and international sources;
> (c) Encourage the production and dissemination of children's books;
>
> —From Article 17 of the U.N. Convention on the Rights of the Child

Storytelling as a formal therapeutic technique with children was first described by Richard Gardner in 1971. However, even this author conceded that it was unlikely that he was the first therapist working with children to use stories in the work. Storytelling appears to be an almost natural means of connecting and communicating with children, whether for therapeutic or other purposes. Children invent stories as part of their development in an attempt to deal with their environment more effectively. To introduce storytelling as a therapeutic technique, first its history, cultural relevance, and developmental importance are traced. Then its application to and implementation in child therapy and counseling is outlined.

Conceptual Background

Storytelling has been an important means of making sense of the environment and of transmitting information, knowledge, and wisdom from generation to generation among many ethnic groups across the world, including the North American continent. Fables, myths, fairy tales, and legends have been developed for the purposes of transmitting values and knowledge (Pellowski, 1990; Pomerantz, 2007; Renner,

2006). Storytelling has also served as a means for families to transmit family lore and values from parents or grandparents to children and to help children mature, make sense of their world, and learn about their ancestry; storytelling also facilitates parent–child relationships (Pratt and Fiese, 2004; Walkup, 2006). Children, in turn, use storytelling to reveal information about themselves to family members, friends, teachers, and other significant individuals in their lives; to express affects and needs indirectly; to engage in problem solving; and to learn to differentiate reality from fantasy (Engel, 2005). All three of these uses of storytelling are relevant to storytelling in therapy and counseling, which combines the purposes of all, namely, the transmission of information and wisdom, the teaching of values and facilitation of relationships, uninhibited self-disclosure, and catharsis that results in psychological growth.

Transmission of Cultural Beliefs, Values, and Knowledge

A number of purposes have been cited for the use of myths, fables, and stories among and within cultures and other groups. Traditional use of stories appears to have been motivated by its facilitation of understanding or making sense of a people's environment (Pellowski, 1990; Walkup, 2006). Storytelling became a coping mechanism that aided people's sense of control over their lives and environments. Relatedly, stories were used to express spiritual or religious beliefs, as well as moral values of a given culture (Renner, 2006). Thus, stories were used by elders to guide the actions of younger members of a cultural group and to help them adapt their behaviors according to the codes and values of the group. Through storytelling, human beings expressed and communicated their experiences to others around them, helping them feel integrated into a group of others who understood them. The self-disclosing and sharing purpose of storytelling may well have been essential to the maintenance of mental health even among early peoples and cultures. Traditional stories reflect or illustrate typical situations a person in a given group might face, thus preparing her or him for its occurrence and for adjusting to and coping with it. In summary, stories traditionally have "provide[d] recurring themes which reflect a people's perception of their world, hopes, dreams, values, beliefs, customs, frustrations, humor, and problems as well as solving them" (Greenbaum and Holmes, 1983, p. 415).

By depicting typical situations and problems, listeners can gain an in-depth understanding of problems with which a culture or group of individuals is faced (Walkup, 2006) and can identify with the individual characters in a story. Individual identification can enhance the listener's sense of belonging to a group and can provide direction and guidance for decision making. Further, stories can be developed to provide storytellers with the opportunity to express their own or the group's psychological and emotional needs, attitudes, and beliefs (Dundes, 1980). This provides great insight into the emotional and psychological atmosphere of a people or an individual and can give the listener a true appreciation of the culture's needs and requirements (DasGupta et al., 2006). Finally, an additional original and continued purpose of storytelling is that of entertainment. Storytelling allowed early cultures, and continues to allow all who engage in it, to enjoy the beauty of creation and the aesthetics of expressive language (Goldberg, 2003; Pellowski, 1990). Entertainment is likely to draw people together as they recognize their common heritage and their shared psychological and interpersonal climate and can aid in problem solving and growth.

Understanding stories from this perspective renders them extremely useful, as they become reflections of the culture in which they arose (DasGupta et al., 2006; Miller and Moore, 1989) and define the meaning of behavior in relation to the culture in which it is expressed. Stories, myths, legends, and other tales provide readers or listeners with invaluable information about and understanding of a people's lives, customs, beliefs, and even their sense of humor and psychological preoccupations, facilitating insights into cultural differences and similarities. Similar to the transmission of cultural or group information, stories that are passed on from generation to generation within a family can serve a parallel purpose of educating younger members and providing ready insights about a family and its values and traditions.

Transmission of Family Lore, Values, and Wisdom

Cultural storytelling is focused on the sharing of myths, legends, and fairy tales that were developed by the members of a given group; family storytelling involves the sharing of family tales developed and transmitted by parents, grandparents, great-grandparents, and other extended family members. Family narratives are collections of stories made up by family members that are based on real occurrences, embellished events, or fantasy material. Family storytelling has been shown to have numerous advantages; specifically, family narratives help children develop values through communicating limits, boundaries, and family-endorsed morality (Pratt and Fiese, 2004). In addition to providing children with a clear sense of right and wrong as perceived by a given family, family stories are also used to pass along parental insights and knowledge. This process of transmitting knowledge may be important to positive parent–child relationships, as the absence of family stories has been shown to be related to difficulties among parents to establish a caring or meaningful relationship with their children (Sherman, 1990). Similarly, the process of parental storytelling has been related to enhanced parent–child relationships (Godbole, 1982). Family storytelling is a powerful model for individual storytelling, which serves many purposes that are compatible with the larger purposes of cultural myths, legends, and fables or family narratives.

Communication about the Self

Whereas listening to stories told by parents or to myths and legends developed in one's cultural group is a powerful means to gain new information, glean wisdom, and develop problem-solving skills, personal storytelling provides an excellent medium for children to "[work] through some of the problems of growing up" (Schwartz, 1964, p. 384). Children tell stories to communicate with parents, friends, and teachers and to express meaningful material indirectly when the direct approach appears too frightening or threatening. Stories allow free expression of feelings, needs, problems, conflicts, and beliefs and, through this self-disclosure, provide opportunities for mastery and maturation. Through stories, children can symbolically deal with problems, test various solutions, and arrive at acceptable alternatives. Stories help children to confront challenges more openly and confidently, facilitate competent problem solving, and result in enhanced self-esteem (Cattanach, 2006; Freeman, Epston, and Lobovits, 1997; Pomerantz, 2007). Specific situations that have been hypothesized to be amenable to successful working through with the use of stories are those that involve goal setting, grieving, dealing with loss, establishing new and close relationships, and becoming a caring individual (Cattanach, 2006). In summary, personal storytelling is a powerful aid to the socialization process of children (Änggård, 2005; Engel, 1999; Robertson and Barford, 1998). Consequently, storytelling, like play, is an important childhood activity that is encouraged and fostered and lends itself well to therapeutic work with children.

Application to Child Therapy and Counseling

Stories and storytelling in child therapy and counseling serve purposes similar to those of stories in a cultural or developmental context (summarized in Table 11.1). Just as stories told by elders of a Native people give listeners insights into the functioning of

Table 11.1   Cultural, Familial, and Personal Purposes of Storytelling

Setting	Type of Story	Purpose
Culture	myths legends fairy tales fables	• understanding of the environment • control over the environment • coping with the environment • expression and transmission of spiritual and religious beliefs • transmission of moral values to guide actions • self-expression to facilitate identification • cultural identification and belongingness • preparation for problem situations • preparation for and facilitation of coping • representation of the psychological and emotional atmosphere of the group • entertainment
Family	fantasy narratives true event narratives embellished true events	• communication of limits, values, and morals • fostering of value development • teaching of rules and regulations • imparting of knowledge and information • transmission of wisdom • enhancement of parent–child relationships • prevention of problems or conflict between parent and child • transmission of coping skills
Child	fantasy stories make-believe stories	• communication • expression of feelings, needs, conflicts • mastery of feelings, needs, conflicts • alternative problem solving • meaningful, anxiety-free self-disclosure • symbolic working through of conflicts • symbolic confrontation of challenges • enhancement of self-esteem • enhancement of the socialization process

a people and its approach to life and the environment, so does a story told by a child teach clinicians about the child's functioning, approach to life, and beliefs about the family environment. Just as parents can use stories to inform the child about family values and to enhance rapport with the child and development of values, so can providers use stories to facilitate a therapeutic relationship and the internalization of limits and guidelines. Finally, just as children can use stories to communicate and express themselves to family, self, or friends, so can children in treatment use the stories to reveal themselves to their care providers. Clinicians can respond to children on the basis of the story, and a dialogue can be established that is based on the story's language.

The transmission of values, knowledge, and wisdom that has originally been an important aspect of storytelling in different cultures and families is maintained in the treatment setting. The process is altered somewhat, however. Children relate a story, thus transmitting their knowledge and beliefs. Therapists do not merely receive this information, as do listeners in the traditional use of the story, but also respond and provide information, thus becoming storytellers themselves. Thus, in the storytelling technique as applied to treatment, child and counselor switch roles being senders and receivers of information when telling stories. In the traditional use of stories, senders do not become receivers in the same interaction, nor do receivers become senders (though they might take on these other roles in a later interaction or in an interaction with another individual).

The Usefulness of Storytelling

There are two primary purposes that make the storytelling technique useful in child therapy, namely, the giving and receiving of information. Both clinician and child give and receive information through the storytelling process. Most commonly, children give information first and then receive it (that is, the child tells the first story). Therapists receive information first and then give it (that is, therapists tell their story after having listened to the child's story and in direct response to the child's story). This process facilitates not only assessment but also rapport building and understanding of the child. It provides an environment in which a therapeutic intervention can be implemented in a nonthreatening and culturally sensitive manner (Greenbaum and Holmes, 1983).

As pointed out above, children give information by using stories to express and master feelings, communicate about themselves and their families, and share themselves in other ways. Through children's stories, counselors learn about children's problems and frustrations and gain insight into children's defenses, conflicts, and family dynamics (Gardner, 1993b, 2002). Stories are an excellent supplement to other assessment procedures, and can be used to validate hypotheses about children and their family (Brandell, 2000; Mueller and Tingley, 1990; Sherman, 1990). Stories can thus be used to gain a fuller understanding of children given their surroundings, both cultural and familial. The advantage of the story used for this purpose is its nonintrusive and nonobvious nature. Most children are not aware of the vast self-disclosure they engage in while telling a story. In many ways, stories are projective techniques, much like free associations or dreams. They reveal information about the child innocuously, as the child does not need to provide explanations or commentary, does not have to defend or protect self or family, and can share information without needing to feel accountable for it (Close, 1998).

The counselor simply has to listen carefully and has to be able to listen to the underlying message. (This is addressed fully in the Practical Implementation section of this chapter.) There is no need to make the child's metacommunication overt or conscious (Cattanach, 2006). Instead, the therapist can understand the child on the basis of the metaphor that was used and can respond using the same metaphor to communicate directly with the child without bringing the problem up in direct or confrontational language. In Gardner's words, the counselor communicates directly with the child's unconscious and need not worry about making the unconscious conscious for the child (Gardner, 1993b, 2002). In this way, clinicians can give something to the child without an overt process of giving or advising. In fact, through the process of responding in children's metaphors by telling stories back using the same characters and setting, yet a slightly different outcome, counselors can provide a corrective experience, can suggest solutions and coping strategies, can reinterpret (or reframe) events, and can give advice, without ever doing so overtly (Cattanach, 2006; Pearce, 1995; Stiles and Kottman, 1990). This technique of using metacommunication as a therapeutic intervention is very much related, if not equivalent, to the use of metaphor endorsed by Milton Erikson and modified for use with children (Kottman and Ashby, 2002).

Nature and Themes of Therapy Stories

Above and beyond the general purpose and usefulness of stories in giving and receiving information, there are also certain themes that tend to emerge depending on the stage of therapy or counseling that has been reached with a given child. Thus, the nature of the stories of any individual child is expected to change over the course of treatment and can help the clinician track progress and possibly determine when ending the work is indicated. Gardner (1971) highlighted the nature and expectations for five types of stories (summarized in Table 11.2): first stories, early-phase stories, middle-phase stories, late-phase stories, and termination stories.

First Stories and Early-Phase Stories.   The first story children are ever asked to tell in treatment tends to express their attitudes toward treatment and, like the early-phase story, represents an excellent projection of processes that they may not yet be able to share willingly or with full awareness (Gardner, 1993b, 2002). The first and early-phase stories provide an uninhibited, uncensored look at children's problem in their language and from their perspective. Further, they provide the clinician with metaphors that can be used to help children adapt to the treatment process and build trust and rapport. The first and early-phase stories of inhibited children, according to Gardner (2002), can be part of the assessment phase. They can be used for diagnostic and conceptual purposes, hence clinicians can ask children to tell them during the intake process if so desired. An example and discussion of an early-phase story follows:

> Once there was a little horse, and he liked to run on the pasture and chew grass. Sometimes there wasn't a lot of grass. One day a littler horse came along and said, "Go away—it's my pasture and you can't eat my grass." The little horse couldn't eat any more grass, and he got starved. He got very thin. Soon he

Table 11.2   The Nature and Meaning of Stories

Type of Story	Nature	Meaning or Usefulness
First Story	• relatively short • cautiously provided • usually totally uncensored	• expectations about therapy • revelation of the problem from the child's perspective • aid to assessment • provision of a metaphor that can be used therapeutically
Early-Phase Story	• still short • provided more freely • less inhibited or cautious • still uncensored	• provision of insight into the child's and family's dynamics • aid to continued assessment • adjustment to therapy • information about relationship building with therapist • expression of affect
Middle-Phase Story	• longer • themes emerge • story characters may reemerge • more spontaneous	• facilitation of internalization through repetition of themes • desensitization to fears and anxieties connected with the therapy process and therapist • internalization of new solutions and alternative responses • expression of therapy progress • beginning mastery of affect
Late-Phase Story	• changes in story • changes in the moral/lesson • incorporation of alternatives • more flexibility in story line • longer, healthier	• expression of self-growth • expression of improved coping • facilitation of exploration of alternatives and options • mastery of affect • expression of needs in relationships • expression of caring in the therapy relationship
Termination Story	• long, healthy • flexible • many changes • include outside world more	• mastery of affects and needs • reflection upon therapy process and relationship • efficient problem solving • dealing with saying goodbye

thought he was gonna die because he couldn't eat. Then came the big horse and said, "Go ahead and eat, but just a little bit." The little horse ate and ate, but then the big horse yelled, "No more!" Then came another horse and said, "You poor horse. I think you need some more food." And then everything was fine. And the moral of the story is "Don't eat too much or the big horse gets mad."

This story is a typical early story, reflecting strong nurturing needs and hope for the treatment process. It was told by a 9-year-old boy who had numerous learning disabilities and health problems. He had been a difficult infant, had spent much time in hospitals, and was placed in a special classroom. His attachment to his mother was questionable, yet he was fond of his father. His father, however, was somewhat unpredictable in his willingness to interact with his son, sometimes initiating or proposing an activity, only to rescind his offer later. The child's parents had decided not to have another child, yet the mother became pregnant again when this child was 7. The brother was a healthy infant who was admired by and received much attention from parents and maternal grandparents. The elder child felt left out and deprived of the kind of caring his brother received.

The child's story very accurately reflected his home situation. His story indicated that he did receive some nurturance before his brother arrived. Yet after the birth of the second child, the boy felt unwelcome and unnurtured (whether this was so is irrelevant; the child's feeling is what counts). Even when his father offered to give him nurturance, the offer lasted only a limited time and was withdrawn quickly. The moral of the story revealed that the child had learned to ask for little and not to expect consistent nurturance. However, the story did show hope that the treatment process might be helpful. Although this hope was perhaps unrealistically high at this time, it was nevertheless evaluated as positive by the clinician, as it indicated that the child had not given up hope completely.

The Middle-Phase Story.   Middle-phase stories facilitate the therapeutic process of the child beginning to respond to and internalize the changes or alternative solutions suggested in the counselor's stories. Some children maintain some consistency in story character, whereas other children invent new characters almost every time they tell a story. However, all children tend to develop themes that reemerge in most of their stories and are easily recognized by the therapist as relevant to the most pressing or relevant problem or conflict in the child's life. This repetition facilitates the internalization of the clinician's message as many opportunities are provided to reiterate messages in different terms and within different story lines. Themes also serve to decrease children's fears and to help them become desensitized to and deal with anxieties arising in the child-provider relationship. As the comfort level with the counselor increases, children become more spontaneous and more self-revealing, as well as more open to hearing alternative endings to their stories. Stories can be expected to begin to change slightly in the middle phase, as children begin to incorporate new learning and their counseling experience into new story lines. However, large changes in the story do not occur until the internalization of change is more firmly embedded and accepted by the child. This occurs in the late phase of treatment as defined by Gardner (1971, 2002). An example and discussion of a middle-phase story follows:

> I'm going to tell another story with the rabbit that couldn't run. The rabbit that couldn't run decided that taking lessons was a good idea after all. So she went to the head rabbit and she said, "Can you give me lessons in how to run?" and the head rabbit said "Sure." They started to have lessons, and the rabbit could run. But the next day, the rabbit was at a hill, and she couldn't run up the hill. She cried because she couldn't go up the hill. Then she remembered the head rabbit. She went to the head rabbit and said, "Can you teach me to go uphill?" and the head rabbit said "Sure." So the rabbit learned to run uphill. And the lesson is that if you can't do something, go to the head rabbit to learn it.

The 7-year-old girl who told this story in her tenth session had been referred for treatment because of depression and low self-confidence and self-efficacy. She lived with her biological mother and her mother's boyfriend. The mother was severely depressed; the boyfriend was an alcoholic. There were no other children or adults living in the home, and this girl was extremely shy and withdrawn. Her need for help was identified by her first-grade teacher, who had become a major support for this child.

The girl's story is an example of a typical middle-phase story. The girl not only repeated a theme that had emerged in other stories that revealed her feelings of incompetence and insecurity, but also reused one of her favorite story characters. Like most middle-phase stories, her story reflected the incorporation of positive movement and internalization of hope in that the rabbit was able to overcome its problems of not being able to run and to move uphill. This is a significant change from earlier themes in the child's story that were permeated by helplessness and hopelessness about change and the ability to perform or achieve. However, the story is not a late-phase story because the girl had not yet become self-reliant in her attempts to solve her problems. Instead, she relied heavily upon others to give her advice and suggest solutions.

The Late-Phase Story.   Late-phase stories can be recognized by the changes that are beginning to occur in themes and characters. Children begin to incorporate messages heard from the clinician and are beginning to tell stories that suggest solutions, alternatives, and options. Stories at this time become even more spontaneous, longer, and healthier. Child–counselor relationship anxieties tend not to emerge in this stage, as this aspect of therapeutic interaction has been resolved successfully. Instead, stories include more unrelated characters, as the child's world and coping skills expand. Late-phase stories that are elaborate, healthy, and filled with options suggest that termination may approach and may need to be explored. If other events in treatment and in children's lives point toward the same conclusion, the topic is then broached with the parents and finally with each child herself or himself. (See chapter 15 for specifics about termination decisions and procedures.) Once this has occurred, it is likely that the child's stories change once again. An example and discussion of a late-phase story follow:

> This is a story about an alien who fell in a hole on earth after his spaceship crashed. When he first fell down, he was very, very scared. He didn't know nobody, and when people came up to his hole, they scared him because they looked different, and they always screamed so loud, and he thought they didn't like him. Then he figured out that the reason they screamed so loud was that they were scared too. Then he figured out that they were scared of him because he looked different. So the next time the people came to where he was, he said, "Don't scream so loud because I am scared too," and they said, "But how can you be scared? You are so green, and green things shouldn't be scared." The alien said that even green things get scared and that they should help him out of his hole so they could find out he wasn't as mean as they thought. Then the people said, "But how can you be scared? You are so big, and big things shouldn't be scared." The alien said that even big things get scared and that they should help him out of his deep hole. The people talked with each other for a while, and then they came down and got him. When they were in the hole, one man said, "You are smaller than I thought you are." One other man said, "You are less green than I thought you are," and one other man said "You are scareder than I thought you are." The alien said, "You are nicer than I thought you are, so let's

all be glad and let's have a celebration together." The people were happy and carried the alien up out of his hole and invited him for supper. They celebrated and laughed a lot and told stories. And the moral of the story is that when you're scared of something, check it out first because it might be okay, and when you're scared of someone, talk to them because they might be scared too.

This story was told by a 10-year-old boy who was initially referred because of aggressive behavior in the classroom and during break times. Intake revealed severe physical abuse by his mother, a single parent of five boys. The abuse was stopped after involvement of child protection workers and therapy for the mother. The child, in addition to exhibiting aggressive behavior at school, also revealed many fears and anxiety that manifested in frequent nightmares and occasional night terrors. His aggressive behavior quickly diminished once he started counseling and felt protected from his mother's abuse.

His story was an excellent example of a late-phase story. It combined recognition of his previous problems, namely, being afraid of people and making people afraid of him so that they avoid and withdraw from him; internalization of new and adaptive coping skills, namely, being willing to approach people and to explore possible ways of relating positively with people; and hopeful resolution of interpersonal problems despite differences, namely, the ability to celebrate together despite being different. It reflected his increased level of socialization as the story demonstrated that he was now able to use verbal skills, as opposed to bullying and nightmares, to express his fears. It expressed recognition of the superior quality of verbal skills over impulsive behavior in the moral of the story, which emphasized talking as opposed to quick judgment or giving up of hope. Finally, the alien had appeared in several stories before and was clearly a symbol of himself. Over the course of several stories the alien had made great progress in his self-image and level of self-confidence, revealing the same progress in this child.

The Termination Story.   Termination stories are generally healthy stories, much like late-phase stories. However, they also include themes of separation and grieving over the loss of the therapeutic relationship. Termination stories are often used by both child and counselor to test internalizations and coping skills, and they reflect the various emotions that children deal with in separating from their clinician (e.g., denial, anger, depression). However, in addition to these slightly negative emotional themes, there typically are also indications of joy over accomplishment and confidence about future problem-solving ability. Occasionally, a very sophisticated termination story may also recapitulate the treatment process as perceived by the child. An example and discussion of a termination story follow:

Here is the story of the girl who wanted to be an astronaut. She wanted to be an astronaut for a long time. But she never thought she could be an astronaut because her daddy told her she was dumb. Her mommy told her she was dumb too and that she should be a housecleaner, not an astronaut. Then the girl came to school, and her teacher asked what she wanted to be when she grew up and the girl said, "I want to be a housecleaner," and the teacher said, "I think you are too smart to be a housecleaner." And the girl said, "Well, I really want to be an astronaut." So the teacher said, "You'll have to practice real hard, but I think you can be an astronaut if you really, really try." Well, the girl really wanted to be an astronaut, so she tried really hard. She did a lot of math, and she did a lot of drawing, and she did all her homework. But sometimes she still didn't know if she could be an astronaut. She checked with her mommy, and her mommy said, "Well, maybe." So the girl tried some more. Then one day she did really well in her drawing, and then she knew she could be an astronaut because her teacher would show her how. But then the teacher had to go, and then the girl was alone again. But this time she just told her mommy she would be an astronaut, and finally her mommy said, "Yes." Now the girl is an astronaut. And the moral is that, even if your mommy says you can't be an astronaut, maybe you can do it anyway if you try hard and show her how good you can work.

This 11-year-old girl was referred by her maternal grandmother who was concerned that her granddaughter had withdrawn after her biological father remarried and her biological mother moved to a different town. The girl was found to be quite depressed and fearful. She had no goals and felt extremely inadequate. Over the course of counseling, she began to develop several goals and to work toward these with confidence and direction. She needed much guidance, indicating that she was in dire need of an adult whom she could idealize in her life. She responded very well to guidance, ultimately internalizing some structure and direction for herself. Her story was a good example of a termination story because it summarized her treatment process (the teacher represented the therapist), indicated that she had internalized the strength she needs to continue to work toward her goals even if her environment was not always in agreement with these goals, and suggested that she is able to implement her goals even in the absence of the therapist.

In summary, the storytelling technique can be used to receive and give information, explore behavior and affect patterns in the child, assess treatment progress, and explore readiness for termination. However, it must be pointed out that storytelling is never the only technique that is used with a child. Storytelling is best embedded in a larger conceptual and therapeutic context that includes clear goals and other interventions. Storytelling is easily incorporated with play techniques, art, and even behavioral strategies. It does not provide a comprehensive framework for treatment and is simply a strategy that increases a clinician's repertoire of skills available to help a child make the best possible use of therapy or counseling. Obviously, storytelling is also a highly verbal activity and therefore limited in its usefulness with very young children (below the age of 5) or with children who are not easily verbal.

Variations on the Technique

There are no formalized alternative approaches in the literature to the actual procedure of the storytelling technique as outlined originally by Gardner (1993b, 2002). However, clinical use of the procedure suggests and has demonstrated that some variation in implementation is indeed possible depending on the needs of individual children. For instance, Miller and Boe (1990) have used storytelling in conjunction with sand play to assist children in telling their stories and to teach staff to respond to children through the metaphor. Kottman and Stiles (1990) have applied the technique to Adlerian therapy, outlining stories specific to therapeutic foci inherent in this approach to human behavior. Gabel (1984) has adapted the technique by asking the child to draw, not merely tell, the story in order to solicit assessment information from reticent or oppositional children. Cain (2004) has demonstrated that asking children who are less verbal or from a deprived background to draw the story as they tell it provides a richer and more meaningful narrative.

Although Gardner (1993b, 2002) suggests that storytelling always involves the telling of a story by the child, and a subsequent retelling of a similar story by the clinician, this procedure can be modified successfully. For instance, for some children, telling a story for the first time can be almost impossible for numerous reasons. Modeling of the storytelling procedure by the therapist in such instances can break the ice and can prepare children to invent a story of their own. Some children prefer to be involved in the retelling of their story, as opposed to allowing the counselor to do the retelling independently. This tends to be the case in the middle and later phases of treatment, when children begin to do their own problem solving in collaboration with the care provider. In fact, it can be extremely therapeutic to involve a child in the healthier retelling of the story.

For instance, one 7-year-old girl, who was referred for treatment because of adjustment problems to her parents' marital difficulties and possible impending divorce, told the following story:

> A little bear was lost in the woods without her mommy and her daddy. She looked and looked, but they were nowhere to be found. The little bear was very hungry and scared. There was nothing to eat. She kept looking for her mommy and couldn't find her. The little bear starved to death because there was nothing to eat.

In retelling her story, the therapist had to consider that the child's parents indeed had been extremely neglectful of all three of their children, having been reported for physical neglect by the children's school on numerous occasions. Therefore, a retelling of the story could not falsely encourage the child to rely on her parents' help for nurturance and sustenance but instead needed to help her learn skills to nurture herself. The therapist decided to retell the story of the bear, beginning as follows:

> A little bear was lost in the woods without her mommy and her daddy. She looked and looked, but they were nowhere to be found. The little bear was very hungry and scared. There was nothing to eat. She kept looking for her mommy and couldn't find her. Then she saw some fresh green grass, and she remembered that her big brother used to eat fresh green grass all the time and that it had helped him grow big and strong. So the little bear ate all the grass she could find and felt much better. The next day, all the grass was gone, and she was hungry again. She looked and looked, but her parents were nowhere to be found. The little bear again was very hungry and scared. There was nothing to eat. She kept looking for her mommy and couldn't find her. Then she saw some ripe blueberries on a bush, and she remembered that one of her teachers told her that

bears can eat berries when they were ripe. So she ate all the berries she could find, and she felt much better.

At this point in the story, the girl interrupted to inform the therapist that the bear can feed herself with raspberries and strawberries as well. The therapist agreed and decided to continue the story in collaboration with the child. Whenever the bear in the story was hungry again, the girl was asked to invent new food sources for the bear. The child became very excited and indicated several times that she had never realized that there were so many ways to find food and get filled up. She then decided to draw each item of food, using paint and the easel. She drew salmon, trout, trees, clams, and small bushes. She became very excited in the process, and it was clear that she had heard the message. Her parents were no longer considered the only source of nurturance, and she realized that there were things she could do to feed herself. At the end of this session, the child asked to keep her food drawing to remind her of the little bear and her ability to fend for herself. The therapist consented gladly.

A counselor may also choose to prepare a story beforehand to tell the child if the child cannot think of a story. This use of stories is in the spirit of the use of a metaphor. However, unlike the use of a metaphor, the story contains characters chosen by the child previously. Sometimes, if the child has never told a story, the counselor can use other characters the child has created in play or art to create a story. One of the best ways to construct a story is for the clinician to use the child's answers to the projective questions (e.g., favorite animal and color, desired age, desert island) posed during the intake interview. For instance, one boy who had wished himself to be a turtle and who decided that he would not take anyone to the deserted island with him was subsequently told a story of a turtle who was stranded on an island all by itself. Other variations on the technique are no doubt possible, and clinicians are encouraged to follow the child's lead. Flexible use of storytelling can lead to ingenious ways of communicating with children through their own metaphors and symbolisms.

Practical Implementation

The verbatim transcripts of the mechanics of the mutual storytelling technique as originated by Gardner are presented in his books (e.g., 1993b), and clinicians who are planning to use this strategy for the first time are encouraged to read them in the original reference. A thorough summary is presented here according to this author's adaptation and interpretation of the original technique. The guidelines provided here and summarized in Table 11.3 (on p. 316) are presented with the assumption that a child is asked to engage in the process of mutual storytelling for the first time. Obviously, upon reuse of the technique with the same child, the first step in the procedure (i.e., the instructions) is skipped. To implement and capture the stories that are told by both child and counselor, Gardner recommends the use of a tape recorder. However, clinicians can just as effectively use a video camera or another method to provide a framework for the technique (such as a puppet theater or even a mock recording device). A recording device works well; however, it is not essential. Using a tape recorder allows the child and counselor to relisten to the story exactly as it was told the first time. Typically, however, this is really not that important—no more so than it is important for a child to have a visual record of sand play or puppet play. The process of storytelling is therapeutic in and of itself and the message is clear even if there is no permanent record of the product.

Instructions

The instructions inform the child that the story must be original, in other words, not a summary of a TV show, book, or comic book that the child may have read or seen in the past. The child is asked to give the story a beginning, middle, and end, as well as a moral, or lesson, to top off the story. Children are informed that after they have told a story, the clinician will do the same. After all instructions are given, Gardner recommends introducing the child to an imaginary audience. A mock audience is perceived by Gardner as helping the child overcome anxiety or embarrassment associated with the procedure. The child's introduction to a mock audience can be brief or lengthy, depending on the therapist's judgment of how much time the child needs to adjust and prepare. It can consist of asking children simple questions about themselves, such as their age, hobbies, and friends. Once introduced to the mock audience, they are asked to proceed with their story. Although part of the original concept of mutual storytelling as devised by Gardner, the imaginary audience does not appear to be an essential aspect of storytelling; most children are quite content telling their story just to the clinician. What is most important in introducing the storytelling technique to the child is the emphasis on constructing a cohesive story line that leads to a lesson or moral of the story. Other aspects of the process can be adapted as needed based on the child's reactions and desires.

If children have difficulty getting started with a story, the counselor can provide help. Therapists tell the beginning of the story (but also more if necessary) together with the child. In so doing, counselors make every attempt to keep their part of the story neutral, allowing the child to fill in the important blanks. For instance, a clinician might start off with the traditional fairy tale beginning, "Once upon a time, there was a . . ." then turning the story over to the child, asking her or him to fill in the object or person. This procedure can be continued until the child spontaneously takes over the story line. If children's first stories do not have all the components that were mentioned in the instructions (beginning, middle, end, and moral), they may be prompted. The most important prompt is for the moral, or lesson, of the story. Prompting is carefully weighed against rapport—if a child is clearly done with a story and not interested in telling more, the counselor lets the story stand as is even if it is incomplete.

The Child's Story

While the child is telling the story, Gardner recommends that clinicians may want to jot down some notes as they need to tell a second story that will closely resemble the child's story. Depending on how a counselor works, it may be preferable, however, not to take notes but rather to concentrate on the child and the story and to make a point of remembering all the information necessary to retell a new story using the same characters. Taking notes can actually be distracting for the clinician and may feel distancing or anxiety provoking to the child.

The important issue for the therapist is that the main characters and their names need to be remembered as well as the main themes and events. Names of places and order of events are also important to note (whether on paper or mentally). In taking mental or actual notes, the counselor can begin to formulate questions for the child that serve to clarify content, process, and meanings of the story. Many children, especially younger children, need prompts to clarify certain aspects of their story and its characters. Children are not always clear in their differentiation of characters, often referring to them generically. To clarify which character is saying or doing what, the counselor might need to suggest that the child give labels or names. For instance, if the child introduced two girls in a story and frequently refers to one girl or the other, the clinician might suggest that the child either give names or label them Girl One and Girl Two so that the therapist can follow the imaginary dialogue between the two.

If the child alludes to unusual, dangerous, or vague occurrences that give rise to questions in the counselor about such issues as possible delusions or hallucinations and abuse or neglect, these thoughts are clarified. The clinician might follow up by asking children whether they have had similar experiences. Questioning is done cautiously, not in a challenging manner, to neither offend nor create the impression that the child must defend the story. Finally, questions can also serve to clarify the meaning of the story and its characters, which the therapist attempts to determine while the child tells the story. If a clinician cannot create a story to retell as quickly as the child ends hers or his, the therapist can create a delay before telling the second story. Gardner recommends a "commercial break" for this purpose but other delay strategies exist that are equally effective.

Delays between Stories

The commercial break was Gardner's idea for creating a break between stories. Other options exist for delays that help clinicians gather their thoughts. One particularly helpful strategy is creating a picture of the main characters in the child's story (not the story itself; just the characters). This strategy works well in that it also creates visual cues that can be used by both child and counselor to remember names and characters, especially in the absence of a recording device or written notes. Another strategy may be to re-create the story characters and places in the sandtray with small figurines. Asking additional questions to flesh out the characters in the child's story is another means of delaying. Only the therapist's own creativity limits the choices of delay tactics that can be used to allow for a moment between stories.

The time created by a delay between the child's story and the clinician's story is used to collect the clinician's thoughts and to formulate an alternative story. New clinicians or clinicians working with a child for the first time are more likely than skilled clinicians or clinicians who have worked with the same child repeatedly to need a delay between stories. Delays are also more likely helpful early in a child's treatment, when the therapist is still assessing the child's needs, patterns, and themes. Later in treatment, story themes repeat themselves and are typically easily interpretable and usable. Similarly, the counselor formulates alternative approaches tailored to the needs of a given child more and more easily as treatment progresses.

Some helpful guidelines for developing the clinician story process exist and can be used during a delay or simultaneously with the child's telling of a story. First, clinicians need to determine which story figure represents the child and which of that figure's characteristics are most central and important to the child's self-definition and presenting problem. Second, other story figures must be evaluated for their representational value. In other words, they may represent family members, friends, feared persons, loved individuals, and so on. Therapists explore both living creatures and objects in the story according to their symbolic and representational value. It is important to recognize that sometimes several aspects of a single person may be represented by different figures or characters in the story (much as in a dream).

In addition to determining which person in the child's life is represented by which character in the story, it is also necessary to explore the nature and strength of feelings and needs that are being expressed, their origins and targets, and the ease of their expression. Similarly, defenses against the experience or expression of needs and feelings is assessed, as well as coping strategies employed to help the child deal with difficult content in the story. Once a child's feelings and needs have been explored, the same process is repeated for the feelings and needs of other story characters and the real-life people they represent. Once the significance of each figure has been evaluated, the overall atmosphere of the story is attended to. This overall ambiance is very likely to tell the counselor much about a child's emotional state and the emotional ambiance of the child's home. For example, cold weather in a story might be reflective of an emotionally cold atmosphere in the home. Lack of liveliness in a child's tale might be a representation of a lack of joy or interaction in a family. Hostile content might reflect the same sentiment in the child and her or his known world.

Finally, counselors can attempt a dynamic interpretation of the story, in much the same way as an adult client's dream is interpreted. The moral of the story is generally particularly useful in this context, as it tends to synthesize a child's concerns and their origins and meanings. For instance, the moral in the early-phase story above, "Don't eat too much or the big horse gets mad," helps therapists recognize the withholding nature of a child's father, represented by the big horse. Similarly, the fact that the little horse in the story was significantly affected by another small horse suggests a theme of sibling rivalry with the infant in the family. Once clinicians believe that they understand the meaning of a child's story, they construct an alternative story that addresses the needs, feelings, and defenses expressed in the original tale and bring them to an alternative, healthier resolution.

The Clinician's Story

The most important aspect of the clinician's story is the healthy resolution of the conflict or feeling expressed in the child's story. The clinician uses the same characters as the child, places the story in the same frame of reference, but slightly alters the outcome to include a healthier resolution to the child's expressed problem or conflict. This approach serves largely to increase the child's perceived options and alternatives and suggest alternate coping skills or ways to solve problems. It is important that solutions and coping mechanisms offered to a child are acceptable within the child's family environment. To suggest subtly to a child that a parent should be told about angry feelings when the therapist is not certain that the parent can handle the free expression of negative affects is not only inappropriate but is also dangerous. Solutions and alternatives need to be carefully tailored to the child's needs and emotions and to the needs and emotions of the important adults in the child's life. Clinician stories also serve to challenge children to move on to the next level of improvement. Even once a story already incorporates positive rethinking on the child's part, the counselor suggests moving on to the next step. For instance, the following story was told in response to the middle-phase story provided above:

> This is another story about the rabbit that couldn't run. The rabbit that couldn't run decided to follow a friend's advice that taking running lessons might help her improve her running skills. She went to the head rabbit and asked her if she would be willing to teach the rabbit how to run so that the rabbit could feel better and do all the things she would like to do. The head rabbit was happy to do so, and they started the lessons right away. Before long, the rabbit could run. But on the next day, the rabbit came to a hill. She had never seen a hill, so she was not sure what to do. She was sure she couldn't run uphill. She almost started to cry because she had just learned how to run and now she was faced with yet

Table 11.3   Mechanics of the Mutual Storytelling Technique

Step	Purpose	Procedures
Instructions	• acquaint the child with the procedure • relieve any fears or anxieties in the child about the procedure	• introduce parts of the story: beginning, middle, end, moral • help child overcome anxiety about the procedure • help child get started • consider using recording device
Child's Story	• allow children to express themselves symbolically • learn more about the child and family • allow children to explore options and apply new learning	• listen carefully • ask clarifying questions • make mental or actual notes about the story line and all characters • begin to interpret the characters and events • listen for themes, patterns, conflicts, and affects • praise the child's effort
Delays between Stories	• interpret the child's story • prepare a healthy story in response	• explore who is represented by the different characters • explore feelings and needs • explore ambiance • assess dynamic meaning
Clinician's Story	• communicate with the child in the child's metaphor • facilitate internalization of change • communicate respect and caring • communicate alternatives, coping strategies, and options	• recreate the story with identical characters in a similar setting and story line • incorporate new choices, options, and alternatives • revise the moral to underscore alternatives • make resolution healthier • respond to children's expressions respectfully and therapeutically

another problem. But—then she remembered what the head rabbit had told her: "Whenever you come to a new place, just keep using the same basic steps. Put one foot in front of the other and keep moving forward." So the rabbit decided to try it, and lo and behold, it worked. Soon she was at the top of the hill. And the moral of the story is, when faced with a new problem, just remember what you have already learned, and you can find your own solution.

This story demonstrates the essence of the alternative offered by the clinician. The child was reassured that she can find her own solutions and that she need not depend on others to achieve progress in her life. It was suggested that she begin to rely on her own resources instead of passively depending on or waiting for others.

Case Example

The example that follows was chosen because of the excellent verbal skills demonstrated by this 9-year-old girl. Although the focus of the example is on a few select stories—namely, one story in each category—readers must keep in mind that other stories were told as well, and many other interventions were applied. Play therapy and drawing were two additional integral techniques; the child's parents were referred for marital therapy, as well as being seen in parent education classes. The parents had refused family therapy, indicating that they thought that it was unnecessary to involve the older child in the treatment process. Although only samples derived through the traditional use of mutual storytelling are included here, often stories in this girl's treatment also were told or shared not following the traditional techniques. In fact, the first story in therapy was told by the therapist. Only after having the process modeled for her was the child able to use this technique herself.

The girl in this example was referred by her parents because she often vomited, yet no physical illness was diagnosable; she frequently could not sleep at night, again with no physical cause; and she often developed a cough at night that kept other family members awake. The intake session revealed an anxious mother who was concerned about her daughter, mainly because of others' comments about her. The child's father was uninvolved with the family and frequently gone because of his business. He appeared slightly depressed and malcontent with his life. The child's older brother appeared well adjusted, was a high achiever in school, and had many friends. The family had lived with the maternal grandmother until the second child was born. Both parents worked until that time, and the male child in the family had been largely raised by his maternal grandmother until the family moved to their own apartment upon the birth of the second child. At this time, the mother took charge of the primary care of both children. The daughter's presenting problems were described as chronic, and no one in the family could remember a time when they had not been present. Here is the child's first story:

> Once upon a time, there was a rabbit. This rabbit lived in a mushroom. It was a big mushroom that had many rooms. It was a toadstool mushroom. The rooms had very small windows, and the door was in the back of the mushroom. The little rabbit was very small and couldn't reach the handle of the door, so he had to

be in the toadstool a lot. The little rabbit lived in the mushroom with his mommy and daddy and his brother. His brother was very big, and he could use the back door all by himself. Everyone liked his big brother. The little rabbit tried to be just like his brother, but he was too little. His big brother went to have a great adventure, and he saw many things. He was gone for many weeks, and the little rabbit was home all alone with his mommy. His mommy was very sad because the big brother was not home. So the little rabbit asked his mommy to play to make her happy. They played for the whole day, and they had a lot of fun. And the moral of the story is that if someone is unhappy, all you have to do is cheer them up and everything is better.

This first story was somewhat unusual in that it did not appear to incorporate the child's feelings about therapy and the therapist, and it was quite lengthy. There was not a lot of action in this story, and this was interpreted as reflective of the girl's life in general, which did not appear to lead her outside of the family very often. The small rabbit was seen as symbolic of the child, despite being male in the child's story. The toadstool house was interpreted to represent the somewhat poisoned home atmosphere in which the child lived. She did not feel loved and sensed a definite preference by her parents for her older brother. Indeed, her parents had been very disappointed when this child was born, as they had hoped for another son. The child's mother was resentful upon the birth of this child, as her own mother refused to take care of a second child, which necessitated that the mother quit her job and take care of her children from now on. As the older child was already in kindergarten by this time, the mother shared her days primarily with her younger child. They rarely left the home and appeared to have only few interactions.

The child's story was an excellent metaphor of her home environment, her relationship with her mother, and her jealousy of her older brother. Further, it pointed toward a major theme that emerged again and again in future stories, namely, her great need to please her mother at all cost. The following story was told by the therapist in response:

Once upon a time, there was a rabbit. This rabbit lived in a mushroom. It was a big mushroom that had many rooms. It was a toadstool mushroom. The rooms had very small windows, and the door was in the back of the mushroom. The little rabbit was very small and couldn't reach the handle of the door, so he had to be in the toadstool a lot. Now as we know, toadstools are very poisonous. So the little rabbit got very sick from living in the house. The rest of the family didn't get sick because they were big enough to come and go as they pleased and never spent much time in the house. But the little rabbit had to stay there all the time, so he got very sick. Everybody became very worried about the little rabbit because he was so sick. They took him to many doctors, but no one could figure out what was wrong with the rabbit. Finally, they came to a doctor who said, "Oh, well, you live in a toadstool house, and you don't let the little rabbit out very often. No wonder he is sick. Don't you know that toadstool houses are poisonous?" So the family realized that the house had been making the little rabbit sick, and they all learned that they had to make some changes to help the little rabbit get better. The brother was asked to take the little rabbit out to play; the mommy was asked to take the little rabbit out for walks and for good food; and the daddy was told to take the little rabbit out on special adventures. And the little rabbit was taught how to open the back door so that he could let himself out whenever he needed to. So then he made new friends, and he started feeling better. And the moral of the story is, if a little rabbit is sick, you better check that he gets everything he needs to be healthy before blaming him.

In her story, the therapist decided to present her view of the child's presenting problem as a systemic family problem. She also suggested that the child was not to blame for her difficulties and that every family member has some responsibility in the child's recovery. However, realizing that family change might not occur quickly, she also suggested a strategy for the child to find nurturance elsewhere. From this point, therapy progressed slowly, with the child and therapist working on developing a therapeutic relationship. The girl had difficulty establishing trust and often withdrew from the therapy process. However, she discovered several media through which she could uninhibitedly communicate with the therapist. The most important one of these remained storytelling; however, another one was the use of drawing and creating clay models. When the child finally had established a trusting relationship with the therapist, she began to incorporate some of the changes suggested in the therapist's stories. Here is an example of a middle-phase story, approximately 10 weeks into treatment.

Once upon a time, there was a big old camcorder. And this camcorder always took pictures and always worried that every picture had to be just perfect. So one day, she came to a big old house, and it was falling apart, and she was crying and sad because the balcony was falling off and the windows were broken. [The therapist interrupted to ask: "Who was crying?" The child responded: "The house was crying!" The therapist then indicated to the child to go on.] So the camcorder said, "Shape up, I want to take your picture and you are too ugly right now." So the house did everything it could—it polished the windows, it cleaned the floor, it even gave itself new paint and put a new chimney on top. It worked real hard, day and night. Then it called the camcorder and said, "I worked all night and all day and now you can take my picture because I'm really pretty now." The camcorder walked around the house and said, "No, no, no, this is no good. There is still a broken window here and still a little bit of dirt there. I can't take your picture like that! Didn't I tell you to clean up and get pretty? Oh, no, no, no, I just can't take your picture this way," and she left. The house was very disappointed and almost let everything fall apart again. But then she thought, "Well, maybe I'll keep clean and maybe I'll keep fixing me up because who knows, some day another camcorder might come and take my picture for real." And the moral of the story is, even if one camcorder doesn't like you, keep up the good work, because another one might come and take your picture anyway.

This story was clearly a middle-phase story. It was long and elaborate and had moved on to more meaningful interpersonal issues in the child's life. It reflected some internalization of change, but not an entirely healthy resolution. In this case, the child was represented by the house, not by the first character introduced in the story. The switch to a feminine pronoun for the house as the story progressed confirmed this interpretation. The camcorder was interpreted as a symbol for the girl's mother, who was exceedingly critical and never quite satisfied with the girl. She often scrutinized the child's appearance and performance. She appeared to measure her own value as a mother according to how well her children performed, placing a heavy burden on this child to do everything she could to please her mother and earn her praise. The healthier aspect of this story is reflected in the fact that the house decides to maintain her own idea of a pretty appearance even after the mother disapproved and in the fact that the house showed hope for someone else to come along and appreciate her (i.e., take her picture). A healthier approach to this latter issue is for the house to recognize that it only needed to please itself, no one else. Here is the story the therapist told in response:

> Once upon a time, there was a big old camcorder. This camcorder always liked to take pictures of pretty things. One day it saw a house, and it thought it was pretty, but not quite good enough. So it told the house, "Why don't you shape up and change so I can take your picture?" The house looked at the camcorder and said, "I am an old house and this is how I look. If you like it, you can take my picture. If you don't, that's too bad because I won't change for you. I like myself the way I am and that's that!" The camcorder thought and thought, and finally decided to take the picture. She was never completely satisfied with it, but she still liked it very much. And the moral of the story is, if you like who you are, don't change yourself for anyone else.

The therapist decided to address the mother's narcissistic need for the child's perfection and to suggest to the child that she would never be able to meet this need for her mother. Instead, the child was asked to focus on her own needs and to learn to like herself as she was and to present that real self to the world. Although this involves some risk, as the world may respond rejectingly, the likelihood is portrayed as greater that ultimately the world deals with reality. The child's self-acceptance and self-esteem remained important elements throughout her treatment. Her narcissistic mother and uninvolved father were unable to provide help, and much reliance on the child's own resources had to be stressed. Ultimately, the child was able to develop healthy self-esteem and strength and to maintain it through the help of others in her life, as well as her own internalized self-acceptance. Here is an example of a late-phase story that demonstrates this process. This story used a similar theme and the same characters developed for the first story. It was told after one year in treatment and suggested not only that great improvements had taken place in the child but also that the family as a whole unfortunately had not done so.

> Here is our beloved rabbit from the toadstool house again. He was very happy today because he made a new friend. This friend showed her how to plant corn and potatoes and how to water the garden so that lots of fresh vegetables could grow that could help the rabbit grow healthy and strong. The little rabbit ran home very happy and told her mommy and daddy about what she had learned. Her daddy said, "That's nice," and her mommy said, "Oh, but you get so dirty when you work in a garden." The little rabbit was very sad that they did not like her garden. So she decided she would visit her friend and tell her that her

mommy and daddy didn't like her garden. Her friend explained that not everyone can have a good garden because it takes a lot of patience and a lot of work, but that the little rabbit could have a good garden even if she had to take care of it without her mommy and daddy. So the little rabbit kept up her garden, and when the carrots came she ate them all up and was proud. And the moral of the story is, even if you live in a toadstool, you can have a garden.

This story revealed that, most important, this child had developed self-esteem and self-confidence that she had not possessed formerly. She referred to the rabbit as "beloved" and was willing to allow the rabbit to act against her parents' wishes or preferences. She was able to set her own goals, to use outside resources to work toward these goals, and finally to implement them and use the fruits of her labor to gratify her own needs for nurturance. Most interestingly, the gender attached to the rabbit had changed early in this story. This was the first time that the child had referred to the rabbit as female, indicating that her level of self-acceptance as a female child had increased along with her self-esteem and strength. The story was interpreted as an excellent indicator of improvement in the child. Unfortunately, the same did not yet appear to hold true for the family, at least from this girl's perspective. The therapist's story follows:

Here is our beloved rabbit again. She is very happy because she has a new friend and she has learned how to have a garden. She loves to garden because it gives her a chance to be outdoors and to make sure that she has as much food as she needs and wants. She loves her garden very much and plants corn, and potatoes and carrots, and even some flowers. She eats the vegetables, and she uses the flowers to make things around her pretty and enjoyable. She wants very much to share her happiness with her mommy and daddy, and so she tells them all about her garden. But, as it turns out, her mommy and daddy don't like gardening. They prefer to eat other foods and to use other things to make everything look pretty. The little rabbit is a little disappointed, but then she decides that she can like her garden and use it to feed herself, even if her mommy and daddy don't want to do the same. So she keeps gardening and is very happy. And the moral of the story is, other people don't have to like what you do and it can still make you happy.

The therapist decided to inject the reality that this girl's parents may never be able to enjoy her and her activities in the way she would like them to but that this parental attitude need not interfere with her enjoyment of life. She also suggested that there is more to life than being fed and nurtured and that other activities can create pleasures for this girl. This decision was based on the fact that the girl had become an outstanding student who excelled in many subjects. The therapist communicated to the child that she can pursue her interests regardless of external criticisms.

Given the improvements in the child, the therapist decided on the basis of the story that she needed to attempt one more time to involve the family in family therapy. The child's parents had participated in marital treatment with surprising commitment and were reported to have made good strides in their relationship. However, either their improvements had not translated into the family system or the girl was unable to recognize the changes in her family. For either instance, family therapy appeared to be the most appropriate route to create change. As the child's parents finally agreed to give family therapy a try, it was decided to terminate the child's individual therapy in one month, at which time the case would be transferred to a family therapist. Hence, the termination process was initiated with the child. The following story was told by the child in her next to last session:

> There was once a poor woman. She thought that she would never have anything in the world, and she was sick to her stomach about it. She worried so much she couldn't sleep. Sometimes she worried so much she cried very loud, and everyone around her noticed how sad she was. She tried and tried to make things better for herself. But no matter what she did, she failed! Then one day along came a rich woman. The rich woman looked at the poor woman and said, "Oh you poor woman, your life is not treating you right. Let me help you." And the rich woman took the poor woman to her house. She taught her how to plant a garden, how to grow her own food, and how to feed herself. Then she taught her how to sew clothes and how to dress herself. Then she showed her how to talk to other people and how to not be all lonely anymore. Then the rich woman said, "I have to go now, but you just keep doing what you're doing without me." And the poor woman thought, "Oh no, I can't do all this alone!" But then she tried anyway. And guess what happened? She learned that she could feed herself, and that she liked herself, and that she even enjoyed playing with other girls besides the rich woman. So she made lots of friends and lived happily ever after. And the moral of the story is, if you believe in yourself, you will be okay even when times are rough or when you're alone.

This story spoke and still speaks for itself. It was a perfect recapitulation of the child's presenting problem and therapeutic journey. It had a sad tone because of the termination but also expressed great hope for the future. The child had learned her lessons, and the therapist saw no need to add a new one. Here is how she responded:

> Once there was a poor woman who was very sad and ill. She had gone from doctor to doctor, but no one could help her, not even her mommy and daddy. Finally she ran into a rich woman who could help. Together they figured out how to keep the poor woman fed and how to keep the poor woman happy. When it came time for the two women to say goodbye, both were sad that they had to say good-bye, but both realized that they each were richer now than they had been before they did all their work together. They will always remember each other!

Summary and Concluding Thoughts

This chapter summarized the procedures for the mutual storytelling technique as developed by Gardner (1971, 2002) and as adapted slightly. It demonstrated storytelling as an excellent means for metacommunication with children. The procedure makes use of the metaphors and symbolisms that are natural for young children and can easily be fitted into any child's counseling or therapy, regardless of the clinician's theoretical background. There is no technique in adult treatment that can quite compare to storytelling. Dream analysis can uncover an adult's unconscious, but the counselor cannot respond on the same subtle level. Instead, insight has to be created. Metaphors can rely on other, less obvious, processes to affect change in an adult but often rely on symbolism created by the therapist, not the client. Thus, storytelling is uniquely applied to child clients and serves an excellent purpose in that realm. It is one of the richest techniques conducive to the internalization of change without requiring the child to verbalize insights or understanding of how changes occurred. This makes the technique utterly appropriate and immensely helpful for the use in child counseling and therapy.

12

Graphic and Sculpting Art in Child Therapy and Counseling

> *The child shall have the right to freedom of expression; this right shall include freedom to seek, receive and impart information and ideas of all kinds, regardless of frontiers, either orally, in writing or in print, in the form of art, or through any other media of the child's choice.*
> —Article 13.2 of the U.N. Convention on the Rights of the Child

Philosophers and psychologists have long believed that human beings have a very basic need and ability to create, to give form to the unformed, to make shapes from the shapeless (Kohut, 1966; Lasch, 1979; Masterson, 1985). The need to create has received various labels, the most concise perhaps being Buber's "originator instinct" (Buber, 1965, p. 85). The need to create arises from the human desire to see oneself reflected in one's surroundings and to imbue one's surroundings with meaning that is relevant to the self. Art, as the term is used in its widest sense, provides a medium for creation and self-expression that may meet this basic human need. Although art is comprised of many disciplines, such as writing, poetry, music, dance, painting, drawing, sculpting, the focus in this chapter is on self-expression through graphic and sculpting art only. This choice in no way implies that other forms of art, such as music or dance, might not provide appropriate therapeutic techniques; however, to date their use with children is less frequently documented than use of graphic and sculpting art.

The term *art* is used loosely in this chapter. It includes not only the final true art product, or formed expression, that is a symbolic means of self-expression and communication but also the precursors to this final product. Four precursors to the production of art have been identified: namely, precursory activities, chaotic discharge, stereotype activity, and pictographs (Kramer, 1998). Precursory activities are uses of art media such as paints or clay for the purpose of scribbling, smearing, and other exploration of the medium itself. Chaotic discharge refers to the pounding, splashing, or spilling of art materials that may signal discharge of various affects within the child. Stereotype activity, also referred to as art in the service of defense, includes activities such as copying, tracing, and stereotypic repetition of patterns or themes and is clearly not conducive to the free, disclosing self-expression of the child, but rather it keeps conflicts and affects covered up and unexplored because of the noncreative use of art media. Finally, pictographs represent the use of pictures or models to replace words. Although this is true for expressive art as well, pictographs are highly idiosyncratic to specific communication between two people that could not be understood by outsiders (e.g., between the client and therapist). Pictographs frequently emerge in a therapy relationship and can be quite meaningful to client and therapist. The final form of art, and often the only one that is considered a true form (Kramer, 1998), is expressive art, which serves not only self-expression but also communication. All five processes or products are of interest to the therapy or counseling process, as they can serve various functions that aid development, growth, and maturation among children. In fact, some theorists suggest that the *process* through which art is created is more important than the product itself (Creadick, 1985; Rubin, 2005). Hence, all four processes and the product are implied, as art is discussed with regard to its general conceptual meaning, application to therapy and counseling, and actual use in the work with children.

Conceptual Background

Art, like play, is viewed as a typical developmental activity among children. However, art, being somewhat more goal-directed than play, makes more stringent demands on the child's self, is more lasting, is designed to be understood by others, and can greatly affect life decisions (Kramer, 1998). In contrasting play and art, some theoreticians claim that play's function is to maintain equilibrium or to depict an ideal or fantasized self and outcome. Art, on the other hand, is viewed as bringing out problems and hence as depicting the real self or the realistic outcome of a situation. Art, not play, according to this understanding, makes the human being face reality and seek solutions. Additionally, art gives the growing child an opportunity to relive experiences in an active role, whereas the original role may have been passive, overwhelming, or out of the realm of control for the child. Art creates a completely new and creative process or product out of an old situation, thus ushering in mastery and resolution (Kramer, 1998). Art, in other words, has clear developmental purposes and is encouraged as an important activity for children.

Purposes of Art

The purposes of art are multifold. Art has been referred to as "the purposeful making of symbols" (Kramer, 1998, p. 63), "a child's spontaneous means of [self] expression" (Rambert, 1964, p. 340), the purposeful redirection of unacceptable impulses into acceptable behavior through sublimation (Rubin, 1998), and "a way of bringing order out of chaos" (Ulman, 1971, p. 20 as quoted in Rubin, 1978, p. 254). In a strict developmental or utilitarian sense, art serves a number of additional purposes. It can be used by the child symbolically to gratify wishes, control impulses, express affects and needs, and re-create interpersonal processes and relationships without any fear of consequences or retaliation from the environment (Rubin, 2001). In addition to this function, which appears related to normal mirroring or nurturance needs of children (Kohut, 1984), art also serves idealizing or guidance needs. As such, children can use art to learn control of their environment as they learn to control and use certain art media and their related tools. Additionally, organization can be practiced and self-imposed, as evidenced by a child's developmental movement from free-form scribbles or sculptures to drawings or models that are clearly contained by outline boundaries that set self-imposed limits on the child's activity. Skill development needs are addressed through art by providing a medium for learning and practicing new skills, modeled by others or spontaneously through the child's own desire to create. Such new skills can facilitate the development of new coping behaviors and problem-solving strategies, further aiding the child in self-control and meaningful self-expression. In summary, art is a flexible, typical developmental medium that helps children meet the crucial developmental needs for self-exploration, structure, and skill development as they have been outlined by many developmental theorists. Given the developmental role of art, the healthy succession of different developmental levels in the production of art needs to be investigated.

Developmental Framework for the Creation of Art

To understand art and the process of its creation, a clinician has to have an understanding of art's developmental phases to be able to differentiate normal or healthy expression from regression (Rubin, 2001). Rubin (2001) has outlined nine distinct phases through which a child must pass in learning a new art form or medium. These are outlined in Table 12.1 and briefly discussed here. The first phase is a prephase, referred to as *manipulating*. It is highly sensory and kinesthetic, serving primarily exploratory purposes. In the next phase, *forming*, the child begins to gain control over art materials and consciously manipulates the materials to produce different results. This phase may be marked by scribbling, smearing, rolling, or flattening. In phase three, *naming*, the child's creations begin to stand for something, and with the encouragement of adults in the environment, the child begins to name the creations. Although the child names the creations, their actual shape might not be at all related to the product or relationship that it is identified to represent. Not until the fourth phase, *representing*, do creations begin to take on certain features. Actual shapes or representations are still difficult to identify for many adults but do have some shape. These objects or drawings represent and emphasize what the child knows about or focuses in on the object (e.g., the encephalopod [a head with arms and legs without torso] drawn by the child that clearly represents a human being despite the omission of critical aspects of the symbolized object).

The fifth phase, *containing*, reveals a definite shift in the child's approach. Art and its products are no longer a mere mass but become systematic, such as the filling in of an outline. At this point, children learn to stay within boundaries (not just artistically, but also symbolically), demonstrating their ability to control impulses and the self. In phase six, *experimenting*, the child begins to explore ways through which to express and symbolize the same things in different ways or through various media. The child becomes truly creative, and work becomes more detailed as fine motor control improves, more interesting to the viewer, and more elaborate. In the seventh phase, *consolidating*, the child begins to express preferences for and within certain art media and creations begin to look very realistic and less egocentric. Drawings are still two-dimensional but include other people and a wider variety of objects, such as trees and houses. Phase eight, *naturalizing*, evidences the child's increasing elaboration and sophistication. The child in this phase may become frustrated attempting to master proportions, shading, and dimensionality. It is this stage that can lead the child to a self-critical attitude or even to giving up. This frustration stems from the need to move on to new learning and to give up previous, more comfortable schemata that the child had worked with up to this point. Many children, and hence adults, do not move beyond this stage of artistic development.

The final phase, *personalizing*, involves the definition of a personal style for artistic self-expression. The child's or adult's art in this phase becomes a reflection of values and ideas. Any conflicts in the individual find their more obvious expression now

Table 12.1   Normal Developmental Levels of the Artistic Process and Product

Level	Characteristic Process	Characteristic Product
Manipulating	exploratory behavior for sensory or kinesthetic stimulation	splashed or smeared paint or splashed, smeared, or crumpled clay or paper
Forming	conscious manipulation of materials as the child gains control over the medium	scribbles, rolled or flattened clay or Play-Doh
Naming	creations begin to stand for something and can be named by the child with encouragement of adults in the environment	child-identified scribbles or molded clay or Play-Doh, products that represent something
Representing	creations take on features, but are still difficult to identify; there are some shape and definite representative value	objects or drawings that have representative value, though it may be difficult to identify (e.g., encephalopod)
Containing	systematic filling in of outlines; staying within boundaries, literally and symbolically	pictures with definite outlines for objects; clay models with definite boundaries that are representative of reality
Experimenting	exploration between and within media; unfolding of creativity; increase in attention to detail	interesting and elaborate pictures or models that capture viewer's attention
Consolidating	preferences for and within media; realistic, though two-dimensional representations; less egocentrism through inclusion of people and objects	picture of others that are elaborate in their inclusion of objects; realistic sculptures
Naturalizing	elaboration and sophistication; attempts at mastery of proportions, shading, and dimensions	three-dimensional and proportioned pictures and sculptures
Personalizing	self-expression and search for personal style; reflection of values, ideas; conflicts are more obvious now	three-dimensional, elaborate, idiosyncratic paintings or sculptures imbued with meaning

(though this makes their expression no more meaningful as far as the art's usefulness to the therapeutic process is concerned). Understanding the developmental phase reached by children in their artistic development not only provides an understanding of their overall developmental level but is also relevant to the application of art to child therapy and counseling, as it influences clinicians' choices of art media and interpretations of process and product.

Application to Child Therapy and Counseling

Art techniques have been successfully applied in numerous settings and for numerous presenting problems, including coping with illness (e.g., Brown, 2001), nightmares (e.g., Hickey, 2001), sexual abuse (Murphy, 2001), exposure to violence (Malchiodi, 1997), and dealing with death and dying (Goodman, 2005). The use of art techniques in generic child treatment is different from pure art therapy (Rubin, 2005), which is not only therapeutic in the traditional therapy or counseling sense but also focuses on artistic eloquence (Kramer, 1998) and gives advice and help with the artistic process and product. If art is used as a technique in generic child therapy or counseling, however, the clinician uses it somewhat differently. The focus in using art techniques in this setting is on the process of creating art and the symbolism of the end product. The correctness or eloquence of the techniques used is neither attended to nor evaluated therapeutically. Hence, art as a technique applied to the work with children does not require artistic capability on the part of the child but merely a willingness to employ art materials for various therapeutic or counseling purposes (Malchiodi, 2003, 2005a, 2005b).

Purpose of the Process and Product of Art in Child Therapy

The purposes of art techniques can be grouped into three major categories: assessment, catharsis, and growth. All three permeate treatment from beginning to end and are discussed here.

Assessment. One use of art for assessment reasons is focused on soliciting diagnostic and dynamic information that aids the therapist in the conceptualization and problem definition of the child's case. As such, art can be used to facilitate the recognition of conflicts, needs, and affects, through both the process of creation and the resulting product. Another assessment-related use of art is focused on determining treatment progress and readiness for termination. In this process, the counselor assesses changes in the artistic process and product to evaluate growth and maturity in the child. Disappearance of certain themes that formerly were interpreted to express conflict or mood disturbances, changes in the process that suggest more patience, increased self-confidence, or greater goal-directness are only a few examples of how art can reflect treatment progress. The primary use of art by the child for assessment purposes thus is one of communication and self-disclosure. The primary use of art by a clinician for assessment purposes is one of listening to the child's communication and self-disclosure to glean new information.

Numerous formal procedures have been developed to aid therapists with the diagnostic, or initial, component of assessment of using children's art. These include, but are not limited to, the Draw-A-Person Test (Machover, 1952), the House-Tree-Person Drawing (Buck, 1948), the Kinetic House-Tree-Person Drawing (Burns, 1987), and the Kinetic Family Drawing (Burns and Kaufman, 1970). All of these techniques differ significantly in the directions that are provided to the child and the content that is elicited, but their joint purpose is to derive additional information from a child during the assessment phase of treatment. However, the existence of these formal procedures should not imply that unstructured, or free, drawing or scribbling cannot be equally useful in meeting the assessment purpose of art (Kramer, 1998; Malchiodi, 2003, 2005b; Rubin, 2005). This is particularly true, as interpretation (discussed in detail below) proceeds along the same lines regardless of how an art product came about.

Catharsis.   If art is used for purposes of catharsis, expression and mastery of feelings are emphasized. In the cathartic experience, the child is allowed to process past occurrences, through either the process or product of artistic self-expression. For example, a child might pound clay vigorously in recalling an anger-provoking event or may sculpt an erupting volcano. The expression of current events and their associated affects is also in the spirit of allowing catharsis or a free expression of feelings and needs. The primary use of art by the child for the purpose of catharsis thus is self-expression to release and master affect and conflict. The primary use of art by the clinician for purpose of catharsis is the encouragement and facilitation of the child's uninhibited experience of affects and needs and their expression.

Growth.   Finally, art as a growth-promoting medium may be used to facilitate establishment of rapport or therapeutic relationships. It is designed to help children learn alternative means of problem solving and to foster creativity in this regard. Exploration of alternatives and creative multifold use of various media are particularly helpful in this regard. Various solutions can be attempted and can stress for the child that flexibility and alternative approaches are crucial to the growth process. Use of art materials enhances skill learning and encourages talent development. This, in turn, serves to increase self-confidence, as does product completion in and of itself. In fact, the unfolding of the creative process in art therapy has been compared to the unfolding, or development, of a cohesive and vigorous self in clients, especially children (Sanville, 1987). Finally, through enhancing self-esteem, encouraging problem solving, and searching for alternatives, art promotes the working through of conflicts. The child is free to express conflicts through the process and product of creative activity and becomes increasingly likely to experience resolution and mastery. The most important use of art for both child and therapist for the purpose of growth is the interpretation of art's meaning and subsequent resolution of expressed issues or concerns. Art in this context is a true catalyst for change.

For the therapist to help the therapeutic purposes of art (summarized in Table 12.2) emerge in the child–therapist interaction, he or she must have an understanding of the meaning of the creative process and artistic product. In other words, the ability to interpret what the child's behaviors and creations reveal is essential to the useful application and implementation of art as a therapy or counseling technique. Clinicians must spend some time familiarizing themselves with the symbolism of art products, the meaning of the process through which a product is created, and the form of

Table 12.2   The Therapeutic Purposes of Art

Overall Purpose	Specific Sub-Purposes
Assessment	• diagnostic information that aids conceptualization • diagnostic information that aids treatment planning • dynamic and interpersonal information • recognition of conflicts and problems • recognition of affects and needs • determination of change that implies progress • determination of readiness for termination
Catharsis	• free expression of affects and needs • uninhibited processing of past occurrences • expression and re-creation of current events • expression and re-creation of anticipated events • release and mastery of affects and conflicts
Growth	• establishment of therapeutic rapport • exploration of alternative problem solving • fostering of creative problem solving • fostering of creativity in approach and solutions to problem situations • skill learning and talent development • increased self-esteem and self-confidence • increased goal-directedness

the end result. However, it must be noted that, as is true for play and metaphors, identical process, form, or product can have different meanings for different children and in different situations. Therefore, although a few general guidelines for interpretation are provided here, it is most appropriate to approach a child's artistic process with an open mind to fully recognize its meaning and importance on an individual and idiosyncratic basis. Further, although it is important for a clinician to understand a child's drawing to be able to interpret it, this same rule does not hold for the child. In other words, the child may benefit from the process of creating art without any insight or verbalizations whatsoever, merely through internalization of what was spontaneously expressed and felt, as well as symbolically mastered (Oster and Crone, 2004).

Interpretation of the Process and Product of Art in Child Therapy and Counseling

The interpretation of the artistic process and product was long ago described as a process of listening with one's eyes (Landgarten, 1987). This is a particularly apt definition of the essence of using art as a therapeutic strategy for two reasons. First, the use of art can help children recognize feelings or needs they did not formerly acknowledge or have awareness of. As such, the creation becomes a visual reminder of problems, feelings, needs, and, most important, solutions and alternatives. This visual reminder often does not need to be interpreted out loud by the counselor to have a profound impact on a child's therapeutic growth. Second, the use of art can focus a clinician's attention on issues children have not verbalized for one reason or another. Thus, art may literally open the therapist's eyes to new information or processes within children and their families or environments. These insights and new understandings can help care providers revise treatment plans and plan interventions that lead to resolution of such unspoken issues. To facilitate the process of "listening with one's eyes," therapists must be familiar with the three dimensions through which art can be interpreted: process, form, and content (also presented in Table 12.3). In all three areas, interpretations are viewed merely as hypotheses to be corroborated by other materials and data. It is a mistake to believe that art processes and products are definitive in their meaning. Hence, the following discussion of interpretation is best understood in the context of hypothesizing to avoid arbitrary inferences and illusory correlations between a child's art production and reality.

Table 12.3   Approaches to the Interpretation of the Artistic Process and Product

Type	Definition	Behaviors/Products Observed	Example
Process	exploration of the child's approach to the creative process and art media	• response to presentation of media • selection of specific media • handling and use of media • attitude toward the media	Refusal to use clay as the artistic medium because of fear of getting dirty may imply obsessive or compulsive traits.
Form	meaning extracted from the overall shape and impression of the creation	• degree of organization such as in placement, completeness, and symmetry • clarity, movement, color • size and relative size	A family drawing in which the child is significantly smaller than all others may reveal a child's perceived importance.
Manifest Content	evaluation of the actual content	• actual objects • actual figures • actual portrayed relationships	A drawing of a happy scene may reflect happy feelings.
Associative Content	evaluation of titles, stories, etc., as related to the artistic product	• spontaneous verbalizations about the creation • response to questions about the creation • spontaneous/ requested titles	A sculpture that represents a first school day titled, "My worst day," hints at school problems.
Latent Content	analysis of the symbolism of the artistic product	• all objects (e.g., kites, keys) • all human and human-like figures • all other items (e.g., a sun, rain, wind)	Inclusion of knives or other aggressive objects may indicate hostility, aggression, or history of abuse.

Process Interpretation.   Process interpretation refers to clinicians' explorations of children's approaches to the use of art materials. Counselors observe how children respond to the presentation of materials, which materials are selected, how they are handled, and how they are put together. Further, children's attitude toward the creative process is observed carefully to note hesitation, enjoyment, spontaneity, inhibition, and similar reactions. This aspect of interpretation is particularly useful in forming hypotheses about preferred defenses or coping mechanisms. For instance, a child who frequently uses a defense of undoing might create several figures or objects from clay or Play-Doh, only to hide or destroy them immediately after they are completed. Similarly, in using drawing or painting, a child might paint a dark color over the picture to hide it after it has been created. Restrictive defenses, such as isolation or restriction of affect, intellectualization, or constriction, can result in a controlled approach in which a child shows little or no spontaneity or creativity. Such children may adhere to rigid outlines or fail to use color in preparing drawings or paintings. Relatedly, such children might refuse clay altogether because of fear of soiling their hands. Process interpretations have to be made in a developmental context. Certain behaviors are appropriate at some ages or developmental levels, but not at others. Thus, a 10-year-old who merely uses art media to smear or pound might evidence regression; however, a 3-year-old engaging in the same behavior most likely demonstrates age-appropriate use.

Observation of the process can provide hypotheses about contents of conflicts or situations that present problems. For this purpose, therapists watch where and when children appear anxious, disorganized, fearful, saddened, or otherwise emotionally affected. For instance, a child who is drawing a family picture might suddenly become very angry. Upon closer inspection, it might be noted that this anger emerges consistently in the context of drawing a particular sibling. Significant problems in the relationship with this brother or sister can be inferred and subsequently investigated. Similarly, a child who is constructing a pleasant scene with clay figurines, yet suddenly becomes disorganized and begins to destroy figures, may be communicating that the scene that was produced is anxiety producing and overwhelming for the child.

All interpretations are made against a backdrop of carefully completed assessment that helps the clinician gain confidence in interpretations. In other words, interpretations cannot be taken at face value, but must be confirmed by additional observations and data collection. Nevertheless, some commonalities (however tentative) in the meaning of behaviors have been documented. For instance, excessive concern about staying within outlines appears to signal concern with impulse control, whereas excessive erasing appears to be related to anxiety or uncertainty or may reflect a timid request for help (Ogden, 2001). Process information is extremely valuable but can still be enhanced by supplementing the information gleaned from it with hypotheses based on the form and content of the art activity and product (Malchiodi, 2003).

Form Interpretation.   Form interpretation refers to the meaning extracted from the overall shape and impression of a creation. The degree of organization, as expressed in a picture's or sculpture's placement, completeness, and symmetry is one important form component. Additionally, clarity, movement, and color need to be assessed and evaluated (Ogden, 2001). Sizes of objects and their relative sizes as compared to one another add additional important dimensions to be interpreted. For instance, placement of a drawing on the right side of a page tends to be related to intellectualization, introversion, and an orientation toward the future, whereas placement low on a page may signal insecurity and depression (Ogden, 2001). Edge placement may imply insecurity, as well as searching for externally imposed boundaries in the absence of internalized structure (Burns, 1982). Excessively light pressure has been associated with timidity, fearfulness, and low energy levels (Ogden, 2001), whereas excessively heavy pressure is sometimes related to aggression or organicity (Burns, 1982). Excessively large figures tend to be created by expansive, grandiose clients (Ogden, 2001); excessively small figures are made by insecure individuals with depression or withdrawal tendencies (Burns, 1982). However, the relative size of objects in the same drawing may also reflect their respective emotional saliency for the child (Burns, 1987). Excessive shading is not uncommonly associated with anxiety and occasionally with agitated depression (Burns, 1987).

Although the above interpretations have been documented in the research literature, they must be neither overutilized nor treated in any other way than as hypotheses. In other words, as was true for process interpretation, specific meanings of a form may emerge highly idiosyncratically for an individual child. As such, clinicians are always encouraged to attempt to ascertain that their hypotheses are not arbitrarily imposed. Instead, hypotheses must be confirmed through other sources of information and data collection. Regardless, the books and manuals that do exist to guide clinicians in assessing the form of children's drawings can be extremely helpful (e.g., Burns, 1982, 1987; Ogden, 2001).

Finally, form interpretations, as is true with process interpretations, have to be placed in the developmental context of the child. A very young child's activity cannot be scrutinized for its absence of boundaries, as this use of art is not expected until school age. Similarly, a child who has just discovered boundaries and outlines should not be viewed as constricted or defensive when using this approach repeatedly. It is more likely that this child is simply experimenting with a new and developmentally fitting use of the art medium. Another very useful aspect of assessing developmental levels in form interpretation is the comparison of a single child's performance across various projects, or even within the same project. For instance, if a child is capable of drawing at an experimenting level of art development, in other words, can draw meaningful and elaborate figures in general, it is expected that all drawings express this level of elaboration and maturation. However, if this same child reverts to creating encephalopods each time she or he draws or sculpts a figure representative of the self, this may be interpreted as a regression and a meaningful statement about self-esteem and self-image.

Content Interpretation.   Content interpretation refers to the use of the picture's or sculpture's actual end product (Levick, 1998). There are three levels of content interpretations that are attended to glean the maximum amount of information from a final product. First, the manifest (or surface) topic or subject matter is explored. This level of analysis is comparable to the interpretation of manifest contents in dream analyses with adult clients and means that the actual content of a picture is evaluated. For instance, one girl chose to draw two houses within close vicinity of one another.

She then connected them with a sky bridge and labeled one house with her own name and the other with her counselor's name. This manifest content alone suggested to the counselor that this girl felt a very strong need to remain connected with her clinician. Because this drawing was prepared in a session before the child was scheduled to go on a four-week vacation, this interpretation guided the counselor's interventions for the remainder of the session, as it was important to reassure her that throughout the separation, a tie (though merely mental; the sky bridge) could be maintained between the two.

Second, the associative content derived from titles to or stories about drawings or clay models is explored to form additional hypotheses, especially if manifest content is not easily understood. The child whose case example was presented in chapter 11 about storytelling drew a picture that preceded and paralleled the early-phase story she had told. Namely, she drew an unelaborated toadstool devoid of other objects. Although the manifest content was already somewhat informative (e.g., little elaboration; questionable home atmosphere as evidenced by the choice of a poisonous mushroom as a house), the child's commentary while she was drawing the picture was even more illuminating. She indicated that the rabbits living in the house could not run very fast and were not allowed to go far from the home. She related that they would like to go far away but were quickly reined in by their mother whenever they attempted to do so. This commentary suggested that in addition to providing a less than healthy environment, the children's mother prevented them from seeking nurturance elsewhere, forbidding them to interact with other adults who might potentially meet the children's needs for nurturance.

Associative content interpretation becomes even more important when a drawing or sculpture has no recognizable content. Many children begin their experience with art media by producing shapes that reflect a low developmental level and hence are not recognizable. Encouraging commentary about such creations provides access to their meaning, which mere inspection of content denied. For instance, one child drew a picture that had two halves that were solidly separated from one another by a heavy black line. On one side, the child used cheerful colors, wavy lines, and free brush strokes. The other side of the painting was dominated by dark colors and rigid contours. Certainly, content was somewhat useful here in helping the therapist recognize the possibility of a splitting defense or black-or-white thinking. However, it was the associative content that provided the meaningful information. When asked for a title for the painting, the boy indicated that it was a self-portrait based on how he thought his father viewed him. Upon a request for elaboration, he revealed that sometimes his father heaped praise upon the child, especially after the boy had mastered a new skill or was honored for some type of achievement by his teachers. However, at other times, the father deprecated the child, destroying his confidence and self-esteem. Clearly, although splitting did occur in this child's life, it was his father who engaged in the defense, not the child.

Finally, the implied (or latent) content of the product is analyzed. This analysis considers the symbolisms of the drawing or model. There are some symbols that are common within given cultures, communities, and even children (Rubin, 2001). The counselor has the responsibility to learn about these symbols and recognize their latent meanings in each individual child's presentations. As is true for process and form, a few common meanings that can be used with caution have been identified by the research literature. For instance, houses are often symbols of mothers or family life in general, whereas the sun is more likely to represent a father figure. Witches can represent hostility or self-deprecation. Cars or other vehicles can symbolize independence and striving for autonomy (Ogden, 2001). Animals in a tree hole often signal dependency needs (a return to the womb perhaps [Burns, 1987]). Knots or other wounds or scars in a tree trunk might symbolize the experience of a trauma (Ogden, 2001), the specific placement of the scar indicating the time period in the child's life when the trauma occurred. For instance, a scar halfway up a tree implies that the timing of the trauma was halfway through the child's life (if the child is 10 years old, the trauma may have occurred at age 5). A kite might signal escapism from a restrictive home environment, whereas a ladder might reflect tension (Burns, 1987). Water is often considered a symbol of the unconscious (Ogden, 2001). Many other symbolisms have been suggested, and the reader is referred to other sources for more information (e.g., Burns, 1982, 1987; Ogden, 2001).

In assessing latent content, it has also been suggested to approach the child's drawings from two perspectives. First, the clinician views the picture's content while ignoring all human figures; then the figures are viewed, ignoring all other content (Burns, 1982). This helps refocus attention on specific details of the picture and may lead to questions that the counselor can ask for the purpose of illuminating additional meanings. For instance, while looking at a drawing, a counselor might recognize, by ignoring all other content, that all the human figures are shown only from the waist up. Other objects were used to block the view of humans from the waist down. Once this fact is noticed, the therapist can explore directly or indirectly why only pieces of the human figures were visible. Similarly, in viewing another drawing, a clinician might ignore all human figures and realize that the picture is devoid of any other objects. The fact that the child left out other objects can be explored to assess why the child does not recognize other things in her or his surroundings.

Finally, in assessing latent content, clinicians take care to note themes that repeat across a number of creations. Such themes might render additional hypotheses that may have remained elusive had the pattern only occurred once or was not recognized as repetitive. For instance, a child who always includes clouds in her or his picture may certainly have a different approach to or experience with life than a child who always includes sunshine. A child who has an even balance of rain and sunshine across numerous drawings, on the other hand, might have the most realistic perception of the world. A child who never sculpts human figures, but instead focuses on mechanical objects, might have a highly disrupted interpersonal environment. Once themes have been identified, the therapist must also note if sudden or gradual changes occur. Thus, if the child who has never sculpted a human figure suddenly places one inside a sculpture she or he creates, this is a noteworthy occasion and may well signal therapeutic progress or growth.

In summary, facilitation and careful observation of the artistic or creative process and the end result provide clinicians with a wealth of information and the child with rich opportunities for self-expression, catharsis, and problem solving (Malchiodi, 2003). Awareness of basic purposes of art, namely, assessment, catharsis, and growth, provides a useful framework for interpretation. The extraction of meaning from a child's behaviors and creations is carefully conducted along at least three dimensions, namely, process, form, and content analysis. Knowledge of and experience with these dimensions of using art techniques in the work with children and being able to place them in a general developmental framework prepare clinicians to implement this strategy with their child clients (Rubin, 2005).

Variations on the Technique

Although the stated purposes and overall procedures for interpretation of the artistic process and product are relatively stable across clinicians and theoretical approaches, there are a number of variations on the actual use of art media. The two largest schools of thought are represented by Naumberg (1966) and Kramer (1998). These two theorists, although both being credited with developing important art therapy techniques and both utilizing its interpretation and expressive force, differ significantly in their emphases. Naumberg (1966), developing art therapy out of a fairly traditional psychoanalytical model, stresses interpretation and the creation of insight in the client. She believes that expressive media are yet another road to the unconscious. Kramer (1998), by contrast, believes that art therapy can be extremely useful even without the use of dynamic or latent content interpretations. She explains that expressive media provide useful therapeutic intervention strategies in and of themselves. Kramer views art as a means to rechannel, or sublimate, unacceptable impulses into acceptable activities, thus helping the child to solve problems and find solutions without conscious awareness or insight. Regardless of which approach a clinician prefers upon reading both descriptions, it is most likely that art techniques are ultimately used in both ways. With some children, the expressive use of art leads to meaningful internalizations and therapeutic changes, without a need for overt interpretation. However, other children prefer to talk about their creations and to assess their meaning in collaboration with the provider. Thus, flexibility and willingness to tailor the approach to individual children's needs and preferences appear most useful.

Kramer and Naumberg agree on the use of art that has been freely created by children and therefore tend not to encourage prescribing specific projects. Instead, they suggest clinicians merely provide a framework for self-expression. Other art therapists, however, use either formal assessment procedures (see the discussion in Oster and Crone [2004]) or specific instructions tailored to lead to very specific goals (Landgarten, 1987). For instance, Landgarten (1987) might ask for specific tasks from different family members in the context of family art therapy. Parents might be asked to draw themselves at their children's current ages to assess the possibility of projections of feelings or roles. To help a child process an anticipated stressful event, such as a hospitalization, Landgarten might ask the child to draw the hospital, then to draw a picture that expresses the child's feelings about the hospital, and finally to create a drawing that shows both the good and bad components of having to go to the hospital. These pictures can subsequently be used to problem solve or process feelings around the anticipated event. Another example presented by Landgarten (1987), using sculpting, is that of a child who suffered from terrible nightmares. She asked the boy to sculpt a monster and then to use it to show her what happened in his dreams. Then she instructed him to sculpt the figure of a sheriff. She used the latter figure to frighten the monster, thus removing the fearful connotation of this sculpture. Ultimately, she encouraged the child to play both roles himself.

This brief presentation of approaches to the use of art demonstrates that there are almost infinite numbers of approaches to working with expressive media with children. Whereas pure art therapists exclusively use art techniques to facilitate assessment, growth, and catharsis, the generalist can choose art techniques in addition to play, stories, behavioral interventions, and so forth. Regardless of whether art is used exclusively or in combination with other strategies, it provides a powerful approach to working with children that tends to decrease resistance and increase cooperation and trust. Implementations of art can vary as widely as variations on the existing techniques. For the remainder of this chapter, focus is on implementing art techniques within a general framework—using art flexibly to incorporate all of the variations discussed so far.

Practical Implementation

The practical implementation of art techniques is quite spontaneous and generally adapted flexibly to a child's needs and preferences. Thus, art techniques may sometimes be used interpretatively, sometimes expressively, and sometimes in both ways. Freestyle may be most appropriate with some children and in some situations, whereas others may call for a prescription of certain drawings or sculptures. This flexible and nonexclusive approach tends to be particularly useful with resistant or involuntary clients, such as children presented by parents, families mandated for treatment by the courts, and referred adolescents (Riley, 1987).

The function of the therapist who chooses to use art as a technique is somewhat different from the function of a pure art therapist. "Art therapists [serve] children in many capacities: as their auxiliary muscles, as sources of factual information, as instructors in artistic technique, as providers of sanctuary for beneficial regression and for experimenting with new attitudes toward the self and the environment, as recipients of confidences and fantasies, and last but not least, as objects of identification" (Kramer, 1998, p. 158). However, a generalist clinician does not generally address the first three functions of the art therapist. Further, according to Rubin (2001), art therapists are artists themselves. This makes them able to focus on both treatment and also on teaching the technique or medium. This is very much unlike the clinician who merely uses art as a technique. A generalist neither needs to be an artist nor has to worry about teaching anything (in fact, best refrains from teaching per se).

Despite these differences between art therapists and general clinicians, they agree that counselors are responsible for creating an environment that provides a frame or a structure within which a child can self-express freely and uninhibitedly through the use of art media. The environment needs to provide enough structure to provide boundaries, limits, and safety rules without being controlling or imposing unnecessary restrictions. A therapist observes the child's artistic process and creation and does not to imply correct versus incorrect use of materials or evaluation of the product.

Counselors encourage spontaneity and fantasy to promote self-disclosure, catharsis, and growth. Crucial to the ability to provide such an environment is the correct choice of art materials available in the room or offered to the child directly.

The selection of materials has to meet several criteria to assure that therapeutic use will result. First, the materials or media have to be age appropriate. Not all materials are equally useful with children of differing ages. Finger paints tend to be excellent for use with very young children, who do not have sufficient motor coordination to work with a paint brush or felt-tip marker. The latter, however, might be a more relevant choice for an older child. Similarly, clay has been identified as an excellent material to be used with developmentally delayed or very young children because the sensory stimulation it provides is ideally suited to help a child develop a sense of boundaries and object relations (Henley, 1991). Enough materials need to be available that the child truly has a choice, but not so many that decisions are too difficult to make. Media should not be anxiety-provoking for the child. Children who are clearly fearful of clay or Play-Doh should not be unduly encouraged to use this medium. Perhaps as these children grow through the use of other techniques, they might change their approach to this medium; however, the choice is left up to the child. The coordination and fine motor control of children must be considered. For instance, a very uncoordinated child might not be able to handle scissors to assemble a collage. This also exemplifies the fact that special needs of children are best considered when presenting materials to them. Finally, another influencing factor may be a child's prior experience with certain art media. Some media might be more comfortable for a child because they have been encountered before. Others might be less comfortable because a prior encounter was negative and unsuccessful. Thus, while the counselor needs to keep a wide range of materials for drawing, painting, modeling, and constructing available, the encouragement of their use is considered carefully and in the context of each child's needs, talents, interests, and other experiences.

Once a medium has been chosen by a child, either alone or in collaboration with the therapist, the clinician begins to observe the creative process to see what emerges. If the child has difficulty getting started but clearly is attracted to an art medium by having expressed a preference for it over free play activity, storytelling, or other strategies, the counselor can use a number of techniques to help the child overcome this initial hesitation. For instance, the child might be instructed to swing her or his arm freely to relax it and then to make a free scribble on the paper. This scribble can subsequently be explored for potential objects or meanings that emerge spontaneously or can be elaborated upon until such an object or meaning emerges (Rubin, 2001). In another approach, a child might be asked to make a few blots or scribbles and then to connect them to see whether an image emerges (Rubin, 2001). In fact, if an extremely reticent child cannot begin with simple blots or squiggles, the therapist can produce these, and the child can connect them. This procedure is similar to the approach in the Draw-a-Story Game (Gabel, 1984), in which a child is encouraged to tell a story about an image that was created on the basis of a simple line or scribble provided by the clinician.

Once a child is immersed in the creative process, the therapist helps it along through cautiously commenting on the child's emerging creation to indicate interest, caring, and understanding. These comments are not evaluative in nature. Some interpreting may be appropriate as specific themes emerge. However, the communication of understanding and empathy is more important than the creation of insight. Failed attempts at creation are responded to empathically, not condescendingly or chastisingly. The child is never forced to finish an incomplete creation. Instead, the counselor asks why the project was abandoned. Examples of good impulse control may be reinforced and the child may be helped to rechannel negative affects or impulses into creative art activity.

Once the process is complete and has resulted in a product, attention is shifted to the outcome. The therapist can encourage the child to talk about what was created (Rubin, 2001). The clinician may ask questions about the drawings to elicit associations and to corroborate hypotheses forged so far. Sometimes, a story to accompany the creation can shed new light on the creation and can provide useful insight. Additional information may be solicited by asking specific questions about different aspects of the product or about its title and accompanying story line.

Occasionally, a clinician might want to assign a particular art project to help a child explore a particular affect or meaning or prepare for an anticipated event (Landgarten, 1987). Once the process is set in motion, the procedure and interpretation that are followed are identical to what has been described already. One event that can be greatly facilitated by a directed, perhaps even a joint, project is termination of treatment. Client and counselor might attempt a project together that symbolizes or represents the process of their work together or of the changes the child has made. This project can result in a tangible product that can be used to review the treatment process together and as a farewell gift for the child. Similar interventions may be used at crucial points in a treatment, such as before a vacation or other breaks in the work. The creation of a joint project that the child can take home can result in excellent transitional objects. Art projects can also be used to underscore other therapeutic activities, such as stories or play. In the chapter dealing with storytelling, such an example was provided. It introduced a girl who chose to paint the food items in the story about a hungry bear. She then asked to take home the drawing as a tangible reminder of what she had learned in her session.

An example of the implementation of art techniques in a general therapy setting is provided below. This particular example was chosen because the child whose case is presented often spontaneously chose to introduce certain art activities as a corollary to play and storytelling. He was a very talented boy who received a lot of satisfaction from the creative process in and of itself. He also began to generalize the use of art to his life outside of treatment, where it became an excellent coping strategy for him.

Case Example

This 7-year-old boy was presented for treatment by his mother and her partner, who had recently moved in with mother and son. The boy's biological parents had divorced when he was 3 years old because of incompatibility. They had remained on friendly terms, and the child's visits with his father had been very regular. He had maintained a caring relationship with both parents and had always appeared to enjoy his visits. However, approximately two years previously, he had begun to refuse visits to see his father, often cried before having to leave, and was sullen when he returned. His mother investigated changes in the father's life, but he denied any. She also explored with her son why he had a change of heart, yet he refused to talk. Although this mother was greatly concerned about her child, she was not directly aware of the possibility of treatment and therefore had never initiated it. It was not until her partner moved into the home and witnessed the child's behavior that she (the partner) recommended therapy for the child to the mother.

The boy was very reticent during the intake interview, and his mother was unable to give much information surrounding the presenting concern. The partner described the child's affect as increasingly depressed. Both women agreed that he had failed to show age-appropriate weight gains, had become shy and withdrawn, had little self-esteem and self-confidence, and did not appear able to get much enjoyment from play. His visits with his father were still a cause of great distress for the child but continued on a regular basis. An additional interview with the father revealed that he also had noted the changes in his child but indicated that he had no idea why they were occurring. The father described the son as withdrawn and shy and tended to blame this affect on the lesbian relationship of the boy's mother. However, the onset of the child's depression clearly had preceded this relationship. Further, the boy and his mother's partner appeared to have a very positive relationship. The boy's father denied any intimate relationships since the time of the divorce.

The clinician suspected a form of abuse, but direct questioning about physical and sexual abuse of all parents led to denials. Questions to the child were met with silence and refusal to speak. His response indicated to the therapist that the possibility of abuse could not be ruled out at this time. On the basis of the intake information, the child received preliminary diagnoses of dysthymia and major depression. A recommendation for individual treatment was made, as no specific family systemic problems emerged during assessment. Further, the therapist believed that crucial information was still missing and was perhaps known only by the child. Therefore, individual time with the child was deemed most appropriate. The goal was to continue assessment while treating his depression through play, storytelling, and art. All parental figures had also agreed to participate in a parent education course. However, this intervention did not appear crucial as all three showed good parenting skills and were on positive terms with one another.

During assessment, the boy was asked for three routine drawings: the Draw-A-Person Test (DAP), Kinetic House-Tree-Person Drawing (K-HTP), and the Kinetic Family Drawing (KFD). All three drawings comprised stick figures only, remained very unelaborated, and evidenced stereotypic activity, revealing the child's high level of defense at intake. Over the course of his first month of treatment, primary focus was placed on building trust and fostering self-disclosure. Play and stories were the most important media. In his fifth session, the boy spontaneously asked to draw. Using colored pencils and crayons, he drew the head of a woman, once in front view, once in side view. Under the drawing (Figure 12.1), he wrote "Wanted: Liza—You can trust her." His therapist's name was Lisa, and his drawing was his first clear indication that he had begun to trust her. He gave the drawing to his therapist, asking her to keep it safe. She posted it on the wall for the remainder of the current session and during subsequent sessions.

Figure 12.1   Ken's First Spontaneous Use of Graphic Art: Mug Shot Drawing of the Therapist

In his next session, he immediately recognized the picture on the wall and proudly pointed out that he had created it. He then asked to draw again. This time, he indicated he would redo one of the drawings the therapist had asked for in his first session. He proceeded to draw a K-HTP. This drawing appeared to confirm the therapist's suspicions of sexual abuse of the child. As can be seen in Figure 12.2, all objects were highly phallic in nature. Given her suspicions, the clinician asked the child to tell a story about his drawing. Despite his prior willingness to tell stories, he refused. However, he did indicate that he would tell her more later. As he spoke, he proceeded toward the sandtray. He staged a furious war between several monsters and small non-traditional male figures. (The room was equipped with two sets of very alternative male and female figurines; the children were shown in very nongender-traditional activities, with girls lifting weights and boys holding dolls; many figures were pudgy, some had special disabilities.) In his war, the monsters subdued and frightened the boy figures over and over. The child built strong forts of sand for the boys, yet nothing kept out the monsters. He built caves to hide them, but they were found. The clinician initiated the following conversation at this time:

LISA: No matter what they do, the monsters keep coming!

KEN: There is no getting away for these kids.

LISA: They are very afraid, but they don't know what to do because everything they try fails.

KEN: And nobody, nobody knows what's happening . . .

LISA: They aren't telling anyone?

KEN: They can't!!!

LISA: They can't tell anyone because the monsters told them not to?!

(*Lisa is trying to confirm her hypothesis of abuse by suggesting a common theme to the child, i.e., the abuser's warning not to tell.*)

KEN (*surprised*): Yeah!! They told them not to or terrible things would happen. He would slash them open and cook them up for dinner.

(*Lisa notes that the monsters had now been identified as one male person by the use of the pronoun "he."*)

LISA: He threatened to hurt them if they told. In fact, he was gonna slash and cook them. So now they are scared to tell, and they can't get help.

KEN: They want to tell. . . . They are really afraid.

Figure 12.2   Ken's Second Attempt at the K-HTP: The Emergence of a Phallic Theme

LISA (*decides to pursue the abuse topic directly*): They have to tell to feel better. If they don't tell, nobody can help, and things won't get better. There are some secrets that cannot be kept. Monsters have a habit of threatening kids, but they can't really hurt the kids if the kids tell!

KEN: The kids don't know what to do!

LISA (*very gently*): They are so afraid! But they have to tell. It really will help!

KEN (*throwing the dolls in the sand and turning away from the sandtray*): Let's play with the blocks!

LISA (*decides not to allow the child to redirect*): You don't want to talk about what is hurting you. But we need to talk about it. It's too big for you to deal with alone. Let me help you!

KEN (*crying*): The monster makes the little boy do things. . . .

Lisa continued to prod Ken along and uncovered his story of sexual abuse by the father. The abuse did not occur during every visit. However, Ken feared it every time he went. His father had asked him to promise not to tell because then Ken would no longer be allowed to come for his visits. As Ken was deeply connected to his father, he did not want to be barred from visitation. The therapist had to prepare Ken for what would happen next, namely, that his father would be reported and that Ken's fear and his father's threat indeed would become reality. Ken's visitation with his father would stop, at least for a while.

The revelation of abuse and the subsequent events were very difficult for Ken, yet they also resulted in an immediate improvement in many of his depressive symptoms. However, he now began the difficult task of working through his feelings of anger and betrayal against his father, whom he truly had trusted and loved. His drawings became more expressive at this time, and he used them to express his feelings vividly. He used many dark colors, such as dark blue, purple, and brown. He often drew furiously, not creating any specific shape but rather throwing paint on the paper in a very cathartic manner. This regression from using representing and forming art to using paint to smear and release revealed his strong feelings very clearly. He also enjoyed using clay to pound and smash. He often created a number of small clay balls, then smashed them with his hand until they were flat. This became a very repetitive activity for him, and he released a lot of emotion. His mother reported that he engaged in the same art activities at home as well. She was extremely concerned about this, as before his drawing had been very contained and he had seldom used Play-Doh because he thought it was too messy. The mother was helped to understand what the child was doing, to ascertain that she would continue to allow him to engage in the activity both at home and in therapy. Slowly, Ken progressed beyond the angry use of art media and started to contain his affect. As he and the clinician dealt with his anger and betrayal (also at the therapist for having made the report), and as these feelings were resolved, his art became more contained.

He once again used clay to create meaningful shapes, but now the content of his shapes reflected his anger and betrayal. He often created biting dogs and spewing volcanoes. However, the specific shapes of the materials revealed that although his anger was still present, it was contained and had become more manageable for the child.

His drawings also began to take shape again, both in therapy and at home. An example of the types of drawings he created at this stage in treatment is reproduced in Figure 12.3. In this drawing, he revealed his great ambivalence toward his father, who appears to be symbolically represented by the sun in the upper right-hand corner of the picture. Although this sun certainly provides light and brightness for the entire scene, it also has big teeth that look

Figure 12.3   A Sample of Ken's Middle-Phase Drawings: Integrating Nurturance and Aggression

quite menacing. The child in the sandbox is thought to be representative of Ken, who had first revealed the abuse by his father while playing in the sand in the therapy room. Also, the use of a sandbox indicates some containment and protection. This impression is further supported by the rainbow, which provides a barrier between the child and the sun. He can enjoy the sunshine without having to fear the teeth (supervised visitations with his father had been implemented by this time).

Art remained an important medium in this child's therapy and work at home. As he was removed from the abusive situation and as his father received treatment, Ken improved and became more involved with his peers at school. Therapy was terminated after 33 sessions, and a cooperative drawing was used to symbolize the ending and to produce a transitional object that Ken could take with him. The drawing was a recapitulation of many drawings and sculptures that had been of importance in his treatment progress. For instance, the therapist began her contribution by drawing the mug shot that Ken had created of her in the first month of treatment. Ken drew the sun with teeth and the child in the sandbox. Other figures and images were included and led to a reprocessing of what had occurred in the 10 months of therapy. Because Ken was allowed to take this picture home, it is not available for reproduction.

Summary and Concluding Thoughts

This chapter introduced the use of graphic and sculpting art as a therapeutic technique. It emphasized the use of these media in a general therapeutic setting, rather than discussing art therapy per se. The practical implementation of art techniques in that context allows for a variety of uses of the medium. It is always marked by sensitivity, flexibility, respect, and an open mind on the clinician's part. It can be uniquely adapted to the individual needs of a child and can be used as a wonderful supplementary strategy to play or storytelling. It can help overcome resistances and can serve to introduce and discuss difficult topics or affects. Art is an excellent intervention with children and fits well with other strategies introduced in this book. The clinician interested in the use of art is encouraged to read as many of the sources cited in this chapter as possible, as the interpretation of art must be conducted skillfully and responsibly. Art therapy is a specialized discipline with its own unique training programs and requirements. It was not the purpose of this chapter to create art therapists but merely to introduce generalists to yet one more technique that is uniquely adaptable to the work with children.

13

Behavioral Techniques in Child Therapy and Counseling

> No child shall be subjected to arbitrary or unlawful interference with his
> or her privacy, family, home or correspondence, nor to unlawful attacks
> on his or her honour and reputation.
>
> —Article 16.1 of the U.N. Convention on the Rights of the Child

Behavioral techniques are widely used and endorsed by child clinicians. Although there are numerous strategies that are included within this category of intervention, all are based on the premise that most behavior and many fears are learned and can be changed through the application of various learning principles. Behavioral techniques have been submitted to intense scrutiny in the research literature and have survived this process with excellence. There is much empirical evidence that points toward the success of behavioral techniques in creating change in children's behavior (Donohue, Romero, and Devore, 2006; Ollendick, King, and Chorpita, 2005; Watson and Gresham, 1998). This change is not ephemeral or situational; rather it has been shown to generalize to alternative situations and settings and to be maintained across the years. To provide clinicians with a thorough introduction to behavioral interventions, the conceptual background of these techniques is explored first. Then the techniques are discussed briefly with regard to their relevance to child treatment and finally are defined in some detail. An implementation example follows. Excellent additional and more detailed information is available in primary sources such as Martin and Pear (2007), Kazdin (2001), and Kendall (2005).

Conceptual Background

Behavioral interventions are based on the conceptual premise that most behavior and some affects or fears are learned. Unconscious motivations, social interest motivations, drives, and other concepts that are deemed important in other approaches to human behavior are considered less essential and uneconomic, though not necessarily nonexistent. The traditional, or radical, behavioral perspective emphasizes the interaction or relationship between behavior and environmental responses or events that elicit, maintain, or extinguish certain behaviors. All human beings are viewed as directly affected by their environment in a manner that shapes and determines their reactions and future behavior. Children are perceived as neutral at birth, as neither endowed with internal drives or needs nor predisposed to certain reactions through temperament or personality. Children learn behaviors strictly through their interaction with the environment and slowly increase the number of skills and behaviors they exhibit as a function of environmental feedback. They are responders not shapers; they are products of conditioning not agents of environmental change. As behaviors are learned, they are stored in memory and then used as needed and appropriate on the basis of environmental cues. Contemporary behaviorists have also begun to concentrate on cognitions. Such cognitive-behavioral perspectives focus not only on interactions between the child and the environment but also on a child's thoughts or cognitions during a given learning process or response. However, even in exploring cognition, these behavior theorists still view behavior as the primary focal point and end result of learning. There are three primary approaches to learning that are considered the basis of the major behavioral therapy interventions in use today. These are respondent conditioning, based on Ivan Pavlov's (1927) and Joseph Wolpe's (1958) work; operant conditioning, based on B. F. Skinner's (e.g., 1971, 1976) investigations; and social learning theory based on Albert Bandura's (1999) achievements. The former two are identified with the more traditional behavioral schools of thought, whereas the latter is identified with the cognitive-behavioral tradition.

Respondent Conditioning Model

In respondent (or classical) conditioning, learning takes place through the inadvertent or planned pairing of two events. One of these events is considered neutral because it does not in and of itself result in an immediate response in the child. The other is considered a stimulus, as it results in a specific behavior or feeling on the child's part. As this reaction of the child is indeed predictable, given the nature of this stimulus and the child's learning history, the event is labeled the unconditioned stimulus. As the other event does not elicit a response, it is labeled a neutral stimulus. The response of the child to the unconditioned stimulus is labeled an unconditioned response, as it occurs naturally or predictably. If the unconditioned stimulus and the neutral stimulus are paired in such a way that the unconditioned response occurs immediately after both events, the child may begin to associate the neutral stimulus with the response that was originally tied only to the unconditioned stimulus. If this learning is sufficiently strong, future occurrence of the neutral stimulus may result in the same response that was before exhibited only after the unconditioned stimulus. While the response is identical in this situation, it is now labeled a conditioned response as it did not naturally or predictably occur after the neutral stimulus.

Respondent conditioning is often implicated in the development of fears in children. Following is an example of how such a fear developed according to this classical conditioning model of learning. Usually, children are not afraid of being outside playing in a sandbox (a neutral stimulus). However, many young children are naturally afraid of loud noises (an unconditioned stimulus). On a pretty spring day, a babysitter decided to allow a 1-year-old boy to go outside to play in the sandbox. She had just taken him outside when a neighbor began drilling in his back yard. The child began to scream and was almost inconsolably distressed. The babysitter quickly picked him up and brought him back inside the house. When the neighbor had finished his task, she decided to take the child back outside. She no sooner had approached the sandbox with the child than he began to cry. It had taken only one pairing of a neutral stimulus (the sandbox) with an unconditioned stimulus (the noise from the drill) for this child to develop a conditioned response (the crying in response to being placed in the sandbox). Whereas formerly only the noise had produced the screaming (then an unconditioned response), it was now also produced by the sandbox (now the conditioned stimulus). This example, depicted in Figure 13.1, demonstrates the powerful impact the pairing of unconditioned and neutral stimuli can have on children's behaviors and emotional responses.

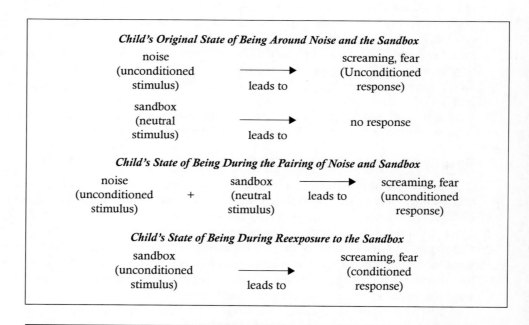

Figure 13.1   Example of Respondent Conditioning

Operant Conditioning Model

In operant (or instrumental) conditioning, learning takes place through the experience of environmental consequences or contingencies that either develop, maintain, eliminate, decrease, or increase a certain behavior. The original behavior that resulted in such an environmental consequence is labeled an operant, as it operates upon the environment to create a particular situation that, in turn, is likely to affect the rate of the original behavior. The environmental consequence is a stimulus that affects whether the child's behavior recurs or disappears. As such, a stimulus-response chain is set in motion, wherein the environmental intervention becomes a stimulus for the child's behavior, the response. Some environmental consequences are perceived by the child as positive and can be used to maintain, increase, or develop behaviors. Others are perceived as aversive or undesirable and thus result in a decrease or the elimination of a given behavior or operant. Positive and negative reinforcement fall within the former category; extinction and punishment reside in the latter.

Positive Reinforcement.   Positive reinforcement is the presentation of a desirable consequence after the demonstration of a behavior to increase its frequency. For instance, a parent might give praise to a child for having cleaned up the play area in the living room without having been asked to do so. This praise is likely to result in repetition of the child's cleaning behavior, as the behavior was followed by a pleasant interaction with the parent. A most critical component of the success of positive reinforcement is the appropriateness of the environmental consequence for the child's behavior. The environmental stimulus in a positive reinforcement situation is called a reinforcer. A reinforcer has to be perceived as such by the child. In other words, a reinforcer does not work unless the child perceives it as a positive or desirable event. For instance, one father decided to use positive reinforcement to increase the number of times his son brushed his teeth. Every time the son brushed his teeth, his father gave him a Matchbox car. The son's tooth-brushing behavior failed to increase; in fact, it decreased. The father could not understand this. He had collected Matchbox cars when he was a child and believed them to be quite reinforcing. When he discussed his distress about the failure of his positive reinforcement plan with his therapist, the clinician was quick to recognize that this father had made a very common mistake. Assuming that an object or event that is reinforcing to him would also be reinforcing to his son, he used it in his program. He never checked with his child whether he liked Matchbox cars as well. When he asked his son whether he liked these toys, he found out that he did not. He then explored what might be reinforcing for his son and realized that his son liked Pokémon cards. When he began to use these stickers as reinforcers, his son's tooth-brushing behavior began to increase in frequency.

In addition to being appropriate to a child's desires, a reinforcer must also be delivered immediately and consistently (with predictable frequency, not necessarily each time). If a reinforcer is not delivered immediately after the desired behavior has occurred, the child might not be able to connect the behavior to the reinforcer. For instance, one mother was attempting to increase her 4-year-old daughter's dressing behavior. She decided to tell the child a bedtime story on each day when she dressed herself alone in the morning. The daughter loved bedtime stories, yet her dressing behavior did not increase. In troubleshooting the mother's approach, it became clear that the two events, the dressing and the delivery of the reinforcer, were spaced too far apart in time for the daughter to be able to make a stable and reinforcing connection between them.

A reinforcer is also only effective if it is not so abundant that the child does not need any more of it and if it is not otherwise easily accessible to the child. Even if a child loves cookies, the use of another cookie to reinforce the child for having played quietly for a while will not be effective if the child feels too full to eat another thing. Similarly, using stickers loses its reinforcing quality if children have accumulated so many stickers that they no longer know what to do with them. This abundance of a reinforcer, referred to as satiation, is a particular problem with young children and in reinforcement programs that rely on food items as reinforcers. Finally, a reinforcer is not a reinforcer if the child can gain easy access to it through other means. For instance, one mother decided to use orange juice as a reinforcer for her son's home-work behavior. Every time he completed his math problems without having to be prompted, he was allowed to have a glass of orange juice. This child loved orange juice, yet he failed to increase how frequently he did his math homework spontane-ously. It was discovered that he was allowed to drink orange juice freely most times of the day. Thus, he failed to see why he should have to work for it through doing his homework if he could have the juice almost any time anyhow.

In determining a reinforcer for a particular child, nontangible rewards must not be forgotten. Although small toys, stickers, foods, and other tangible goods are easily recognized as reinforcers, human interactions and social interactions can also be pow-erful reinforcers. In fact, for many children, time alone with a parent, a hug, public praise, a smile, and so forth may be more powerfully reinforcing and meaningful than yet another sticker or piece of gum. Children generally are very willing to work hard for attention. In fact, it is not unlikely that the source of their misbehavior is their way of searching for attention from a parent who does not otherwise interact freely with the child.

To summarize, positive reinforcement is used primarily to increase existing behaviors. It can also be used to slowly shape new behaviors in children. For the posi-tive reinforcement process to work, the reinforcer must be appropriate, delivered immediately and predictably, not freely available to the child anyhow, and not so abundant as to lose its reinforcing quality. It can be a tangible object or nontangible, such as praise, attention, or time spent together.

Negative Reinforcement.   Negative reinforcement, much like positive reinforce-ment, is used to increase the occurrence of behavior. However, in this instance, the child is not presented with a reinforcer but rather is allowed reprieve from an undesir-able or aversive event that is already present in the environment. For instance, a parent might tell the child that she or he will turn off her or his (the parent's) favorite record, which the child despises, each time the child completes cleaning her or his room. In this case, an aversive event, the record, was removed to increase the child's cleaning behavior. Negative reinforcement is also used by car manufacturers who are attempt-ing to increase the use of seat belts. A buzzer sounds when the ignition is turned on and does not end unless the seat belt buckle is inserted into its slot. As soon as the seat belt is buckled, the aversive event is removed, increasing the likelihood that everyone buckles up. Removal of the stimulus must follow the same guidelines that were pre-sented for the use of reinforcers. In other words, it must be appropriate, not freely pos-sible, not abundantly available, and not too far removed in time.

Punishment.   Punishment is a procedure designed to decrease the occurrence of behavior, that is, to deal with behaviors that the parent wants to eliminate from the child's repertoire. Punishment is achieved through the presentation of an undesirable or aversive consequence when the inappropriate behavior occurs. A common punisher used by parents is spanking. Society uses incarceration as a punisher for people who commit crimes in the attempt to decrease criminal behavior. Obviously, the punisher must be appropriate, presented in a timely and consistent manner, and more undesirable than the behavior itself is reinforcing. For instance, incarceration is not an effective punisher if it is not consistently applied each time a person engages in a criminal act. The problem becomes obvious: If the behavior is not noticed, the punisher cannot be applied effectively. There are several additional problems associated with the use of punishment (Kazdin, 2001). For instance, although it may be effective in the short term, its long-term effectiveness is questionable. Further, the presentation of an aversive or undesirable event may instill conflicts and aversive behaviors or fears in the child. Punishment may actually increase inappropriate behavior by serving as a model for aggressive behavior or as a reinforcer. (For some children, punishing attention may be more desirable than no attention at all.) The use of punishment is therefore not generally endorsed unless other behavioral strategies have failed and the behavior is dangerous to the child. For instance, some punishment procedures may be used with severely developmentally disabled children who engage in self-destructive behaviors such as eye-gouging or head-banging. In these cases, the injuries that result from the behavior are greater than the risks presented by punishment.

Extinction.   Extinction, like punishment, is used to decrease undesirable or inappropriate behaviors. However, unlike punishment, it does not involve the presentation of a noxious stimulus but rather the removal of a positive stimulus present in the environment as the child engages in the undesirable behavior. As such, it is the inverse of punishment, in the same way as negative reinforcement is the inverse of positive reinforcement. For instance, children who like to listen to music might be told that each time they throw a temper tantrum, the music will be turned off. The music (the positive stimulus in the environment), present when the child began throwing a tantrum, is thus removed to decrease the frequency of the behavior. A commonly used strategy is the removal of attention. If children act out in the presence of a parent, clearly to gain additional attention, parents do well to remove themselves from the situation, making it impossible for children to receive further attention unless they stop acting out. Again, as with all stimuli discussed so far, the removed stimulus must be appropriate (i.e., must have had reinforcing quality); must be removed immediately, predictably, and consistently; and must not be freely available or overly abundant (e.g., reattainable without the decrease in the inappropriate behavior).

The four operant strategies, summarized in Table 13.1, can be combined in various ways to develop more sophisticated therapeutic programs for children. This application of operant conditioning is addressed in detail later in this chapter.

Social Learning Theory

In social (or observational) learning theory, learning is hypothesized to take place through observation and subsequent imitation of direct or symbolic models. In other words, a child can learn a new behavior by watching another individual, the model, engage in it. The imitation of the behavior does not have to be immediate, though the

Table 13.1   The Four Strategies of Operant Conditioning

Strategy	Type of Stimulus	Action	Example
Positive Reinforcement	positive stimulus (reinforcer)	presentation	presenting a cookie each time the child does homework alone
Negative Reinforcement	negative stimulus (undesirable event)	removal	turning off a loud noise in the class-room as soon as all children are sitting still
Punishment	negative stimulus (punisher)	presentation	yelling at the child each time she or he forgets to take out the garbage
Extinction	positive stimulus (desirable event)	removal	no longer reading a bedtime story if the child tries to delay bedtime

behavior must have been encoded in the child's memory to be imitated or used at a later time. In place of a live model, a symbolic model may be used, such as a video-tape, movie, or picture. Children learn many new behaviors through modeling, including behaviors needed for adaptive living such as tying shoes, washing hands, and so forth. For the modeling process to be successful, children have to be capable of engaging in four distinct processes, which are displayed and exemplified in Table 13.2. First, they must have a sufficient attention span, as well as attentional ability or motivation, to observe the model's behavior in detail. Second, they must have sufficient memory ability to be able to retain a cognitive representation of the behavior, even in the absence of the model. Third, they must have the motor skills necessary to reproduce the behavior at least somewhat successfully, though correction of the attempted imitation is often not only appropriate but also desirable. Fourth, and finally, they must have sufficient external or internal motivation to engage in the modeled behavior. Although imitation of a model may be immediate, as in the deliberate teaching of

Table 13.2   The Four Processes of Modeling or Observational Learning

Process	Example
Attention	A boy watches very intently as an older boy builds a paper airplane (the older boy is someone this child admires and has often attempted to emulate).
Retention	The boy is too shy to interact with the older boy and has no paper; hence, as he watches carefully, he tries to remember each step of the airplane-folding process the older child models.
Reproduction	After returning home later in the day, the boy asks for a piece of paper and begins to construct an airplane; his mother is watching with interest, wondering where her son had picked up this new skill; she also helps him along with offering several helpful hints when the boy appears uncertain about the next step in the process.
Motivation	The boy is obviously pleased with himself upon completion of the product (internal positive feedback), enjoys flying the airplane around the house (external positive feedback), and receives praise for his accomplishment from his mother (more positive external feedback).

a new skill, it also may be delayed in time, as in the inadvertent imitation of a behavior witnessed previously. In other words, the acquisition and performance of the behavior do not have to be concurrent.

Application to Child Therapy and Counseling

Learning principles serve to explain the acquisition of adaptive behaviors and new skills as well as to explain maladaptive, or problem, behaviors (Martin and Pear, 2007). Hence, behavioral theorists argue that no behavior, regardless of how maladaptive it appears, is abnormal or pathological. Instead, the behavior is viewed with regard to its learning history in the child's life, as well as the reinforcement history that maintains it. Problem behaviors are viewed as no more than bad habits or faulty learning patterns (Kazdin, 2001; Martin and Pear, 2007). This approach to misbehavior or presenting problems of children ascertains that children are not viewed as pathological or abnormal. Regardless of theoretical background, it behooves every clinician to borrow this attitude toward children's behavior from behavioral theorists. Children are shaped by their environment in many ways, regardless of the degree to which a theorist believes in other motivational factors, such as innate personality styles, genetic factors, or biological processes. All behavior is best explored and understood in its context in the child's family and larger cultural and social environment; therefore it is not judged as abnormal or pathological but viewed as a self-protective, even adaptive, learned response.

Some child clinicians may perceive behavioral approaches to explaining human behavior as incompatible with principles of free will, as all children, in fact all people, are viewed merely as responders to their environment. However, it is an indisputable reality that environmental factors do influence behavior in many ways. Behaviorists, particularly Skinner (1971), suggest that becoming aware of how the environment shapes and determines behavior and using that knowledge provides true freedom. Thus, the reader is encouraged not to perceive behavioral interventions as restrictive or authoritarian. Although this point may be disputed, it is important to recognize the usefulness of behavioral principles in many realms of life and learning. Behavioral techniques can be very instrumental in helping a clinician effect change in a child client, without interfering with other beliefs about human behavior. Although behavioral theory might not be accepted by all clinicians as accounting for the entire spectrum of human behavior, affects, motivations, and so forth, its principles can be successfully and respectfully incorporated into interventions with children and their families.

Behavioral techniques used in that manner become strategies that increase a clinician's general repertoire of clinical tools without having to become the theoretical framework used to conceptualize the entire case. Although this approach certainly is prone to some attack by purely behavioral therapists, it is endorsed in this chapter. Behavioral interventions are discussed as extremely useful means of intervening in child treatment without suggesting that they must provide the entire framework for the work with the child. As were play therapy, storytelling, or art therapy techniques, behavioral strategies are viewed as tools taught and used to ascertain that a sufficiently wide spectrum of skills is available to the mental health service provider to maximize likelihood of success in a child's treatment.

Another advantage of the use of behavioral strategies is the fact that it lends itself well to the assessment of change in the child and treatment effectiveness (Kazdin, 2001). To use behavioral principles, therapists do two things: First, they obtain an accurate and extensive history and baseline count of the behavior that is presented as a problem; second, they set clear behavioral goals for the treatment process. This strict focus on observable and quantifiable behavior guides counselors carefully in the treatment process and the measurement of movement toward treatment goals. In other words, behaviorally oriented treatment involves the clear definition, measurement, and quantification of original behavior, as well as behavior throughout treatment until termination. For instance, if a child is presented to treatment because of a tendency to speak out of turn in the classroom, the counselor's first step is to define the behavior and assess the frequency of its occurrence. This may be done through classroom observation or collaboration with the child's teacher. Then the behavioral treatment process is implemented. The child's behavior continues to be observed and counted during predetermined intervals to assess whether an improvement in the number of disruptions in the classroom is occurring. When the frequency of behaviors has dropped to the desired level, treatment focused specifically on this behavior is ended. All therapists can benefit from the incorporation of clearly defined behavioral changes that can be measured and observed. Such measurement can be an objective indication of a child's improvement and can be used to praise the child and motivate the parents to continue treatment or at least view it as a helpful process.

Finally, use of behavioral strategies usually necessitates the involvement of parents or teachers, as well as the cooperation and consultation of the child. Thus, it may enhance the willingness of parents and teachers to cooperate with treatment as they feel more ownership of the therapeutic process. As implementation usually does not occur exclusively in the playroom (in fact, it may never occur in that setting at all), but instead in the environment in which the behavior tends to be problematic, generalization is excellent and virtually built into the treatment program. Behavioral strategies can continue to be used by parents, teachers, and children once treatment has been completed, as they can be diversely adapted to numerous problem behaviors (Barkley, 2000, 2005). Thus, in addition to helping solve a presenting problem, clinicians provide children and their significant others with tools that can be adapted for future use.

Given their diverse applicability, behavioral strategies have a permanent place in child treatment (Mash and Barkley, 2006). Although they may not always be the only strategies utilized with a particular child, some are almost ubiquitously used. Two excellent examples of such ubiquitousness are positive reinforcement and extinction, both of which tend to be utilized by all therapists many times in the course of treatment (whether inadvertently or purposefully). Behavioral strategies consequently can be carefully woven into the network of interventions planned by the counselor regardless of the underlying conceptual framework. They can be taught to parents and teachers for later use with the child, use with other children, and prevention purposes. Clinical application is detailed here; the preventive application is discussed in some detail in the parent education chapter.

Variations on the Technique

Behavioral methods have excellent support in the literature with regard to their usefulness for a great variety of behavior problems among children (for brief reviews of this literature refer to Powers [2001]; Spiegler and Guevremont [2003]; also see journals such as the *Journal of Applied Behavior Analysis, Behavior Therapist, Behavior Therapy, Behavior Research and Therapy*, and *Cognitive and Behavioral Practice*). Although methods of intervention can be as simple as basic reinforcement or extinction, more complex programs have been developed specifically for therapeutic purposes. Sophisticated behavioral programs that have been found highly useful and successful in the treatment of childhood problems can be based on respondent, operant, or social learning theory, and a few examples are discussed in detail.

Strategies Based on Respondent Conditioning

Strategies in this category are based on the pairing of two stimuli that are not naturally paired in the child's environment. (For more information about these strategies also refer to Morris and Kratochwill [1998]). Through the pairing of stimuli, new responses can be produced in the child designed to take the place of the maladaptive behavior. Although only two approaches are covered here, systematic desensitization and aversive conditioning, others exist, such as the bell-and-pad procedure used for functional enuresis (Walker, 2003) and flooding used for phobias (Spiegler and Guevremont, 2003).

Systematic Desensitization.   This procedure is most commonly used with children who have severe anxieties or phobias. It relies not only on respondent conditioning and also on the concept of reciprocal inhibition. Reciprocal inhibition indicates that a person cannot have two conflicting physiological responses at the same time—for example, cannot feel relaxed and fearful simultaneously. In using systematic desensitization, clinicians approach a child's anxiety by pairing relaxation exercises or visual imagery that result in a relaxed response with the feared stimulus until the feared stimulus produces the same relaxed response as the relaxation. In other words, the relaxation training or visualization process is the unconditioned stimulus that results in the unconditioned physiological response of relaxation and peaceful feelings. This unconditioned stimulus is paired with a feared stimulus (the neutral stimulus in the classical conditioning paradigm) until the neutral stimulus becomes a conditioned stimulus that results in the conditioned response of relaxation. Reciprocal inhibition aids this process of conditioning, in that it ascertains that the fearful response to the slow and careful presentation of the feared (neutral) stimulus cannot override the feeling of relaxation and peacefulness produced by the relaxation or imagery.

The first step in a systematic desensitization program always involves teaching children a method of relaxation that results in relaxed and peaceful feelings for them. Two commonly used methods are progressive muscle tension–relaxation procedures and visual imagery. Relaxation programs developed for children are available and highly recommended for use (Cautela and Groden, 1982; Cheung, 2006b; Koeppen, 2002). Once children have mastered a system of relaxation and are able to relax quickly and reliably, they are ready to move on to the next step: the pairing of the unconditioned and neutral stimuli. This pairing is conducted in a carefully paced manner so that children are not exposed to the most feared stimulus immediately. Instead, a hierarchy of feared stimuli is constructed in collaboration with each child to expose the child to anxiety-producing events step by step. The creation of a hierarchy of fearful events is done very carefully. The first item in the hierarchy must not result in a fearful emotional response whatsoever. Each successive item has a slightly larger negative emotional impact on the child than the previous one. The number of items in a hierarchy is dependent on the strength of the child's phobic reaction to the feared stimulus. The more fearful the child, the longer the hierarchy may need to be, as more items may be needed for the child to manage fear successfully. Some hierarchies are developed in such a manner as to make each progressive item merely quantitatively larger than the previous one; others incorporate items that vary qualitatively while all being related to the feared stimulus.

For instance, the hierarchy for a child who fears cats might consist of a first item that requires a 1-second imagined exposure to the animal, slowly increasing the length of the exposure time to several minutes. Another child with the same fear might develop an entirely different hierarchy. In this case, the first item on the hierarchy may be for the child to imagine the house of a friend who owns a cat, without any reference to the animal. Subsequent items might include visualizations of the friend's room with the cat hiding out of sight under the bed. A later item might involve the friend holding the cat, and the final item might require the child to visualize herself or himself holding the cat.

Both quantitative and qualitative hierarchies are likely to work; they merely approach the problem from two slightly different perspectives. In using a qualitative approach, the counselor must take care to order items correctly to prevent premature exposure of the child to an item that might prove overwhelming and break through the relaxed response, resulting in the experience of anxiety. Further, in presenting the progressive items to a child, clinicians need to be very much attuned to the child's emotional response. If the child is perceived to become less relaxed, the clinician backs up, reverting to an earlier item in the hierarchy until the child is once again fully relaxed. At times, if a response appears to approach anxiety, the relaxation procedure might need to be repeated. Systematic desensitization programs can also be carried out in the actual presence of the fear-producing stimulus. This procedure is called in vivo desensitization. It can be used in conjunction with the traditional process, generally being used after several sessions of imagined exposure to the feared stimulus, or may be a corollary to the systematic desensitization process in the playroom. In vivo procedures can be powerful and have to be implemented carefully. They often require the involvement and cooperation of other people in the child's life, such as teachers, trainers, parents, or friends.

For instance, a child with a public speaking phobia that is sufficiently severe to result in attempts to skip school on the day of speech class may be involved in a traditional imagined desensitization program at the same time as participating in an in vivo procedure. The first step in the in vivo procedure might require the child to go to school on the day of speech class. The second step might require the child to remain in speech class for 10 minutes. This time frame could then be expanded until the child can attend speech class without experiencing anxiety. Then the child might be asked to speak publicly for 20 seconds, slowly increasing this time frame to several minutes. All along, the same child may also be working through a similar hierarchy in the playroom with the clinician.

An applied example of systematic desensitization is presented in the case example at the end of this chapter. The hierarchies developed for the systematic and in vivo desensitization programs for this child are presented on pages 369 and 370.

Aversive Conditioning.   Another commonly used respondent conditioning strategy is aversive conditioning. In this procedure, an aversive stimulus is paired with a maladaptive, yet somehow intrinsically rewarding, behavior to decrease the amount of pleasure felt in response to the problem behavior. For instance, a child who frequently doodles during class lectures might be told to snap a rubber band worn on the wrist. In this example, the doodling behavior is the neutral stimulus that is paired with a conditioned stimulus (the snap of the rubber band) that leads to an unpleasant unconditioned response (pain on the wrist). After a sufficiently large number of pairings, the doodling behavior itself results in a conditioned aversive response (anticipation of pain) and therefore decreases in frequency. It must be noted that although this procedure has some merits in reducing undesirable behavior, it is negatively focused. It is best not be used in isolation, but rather is embedded in a larger behavioral (or other therapeutic) program that contains positive interactions with the child.

Strategies Based on Operant Conditioning

Strategies in this category are based on the principle that behaviors are either maintained or reduced on the basis of environmental feedback and stimuli. (For thorough discussions of these strategies, also refer to Kazdin [2001] and Martin and Pear [2007].) Operant conditioning programs are designed to decrease or increase behaviors and teach or eliminate behaviors or emotional responses by manipulating a child's environment in such a way as to reinforce appropriate behaviors while ignoring inappropriate ones (punishment is rarely used). Numerous operant conditioning strategies exist, and new ones can be invented by each clinician or parent. Indeed, the number of applications and variations of operant strategies is limited only by the creativity of the care provider. Presented below are four of the most commonly used operant procedures: shaping, reinforcement of incompatible behaviors, time-out, and token economies.

Shaping.   The shaping process is used to develop new behaviors. Shaping of new behaviors is accomplished by analyzing a behavior according to its component parts and beginning to reinforce the child for the rudiments of the behavior. The child is not expected to be able to engage in the entire or final desired behavior in one large step, but rather is allowed and reinforced for developing the behavior in small steps that increasingly approximate the target behavior. The steps leading toward the desired behavior are called successive approximations, and care has to be taken that a child is appropriately reinforced for each successive approximation. Once a particular step has been mastered, reinforcement for that successive approximation is phased out, and reinforcers are not provided until the next step in the behavior chain is demonstrated. This necessitates watching the child carefully and focusing on positive behavior.

The positive focus of shaping makes the procedure an excellent corollary to more aversive behavioral procedures, such as aversive conditioning. Using the same disruptive child as in the example for aversive conditioning, a shaping program could be added to the rubber band intervention for disruptive behavior, to begin to reinforce the child step by step for more appropriate classroom behavior. A target behavior is defined along with successive approximation toward that target. A reinforcer is delivered by the teacher each time an approximation of the behavior occurs. Immediate and appropriate delivery and careful selection of an effective reinforcer is critical. For example, the target behavior might be defined as active participation in class discussion as evidenced by making at least three relevant comments during each lesson. Successive approximations might involve behaviors such as taking relevant notes that indicate the child is following the lecture, raising a hand to indicate that the child wants to comment, actually making one relevant comment in the course of a lecture, making two relevant comments, and finally making three relevant comments.

Shaping can also be applied to one single behavior that is broken into component parts. For instance, if children need to learn how to make their own bed alone, reinforceable successive approximations may be defined in small steps. The first step might consist of pulling up the covers as they get out of bed. The second step may involve fluffing the pillow in addition to pulling up the covers. The third step might add the requirement of tucking in the sheet. Steps are added in such an additive manner until the target behavior is reached.

Reinforcement of Incompatible Behaviors.   Another procedure that is positively focused and easily added to aversive procedures is positive reinforcement of incompatible behaviors. This procedure, using positive reinforcement, has two emphases: elimination or decrease of an undesired behavior and development or increase of a desired behavior. The desired behavior that is positively reinforced either in its entirety (as in simple positive reinforcement) or in its component steps (as in shaping) is selected on the basis of its incompatibility with the undesirable behavior. In other words, the desired and undesired behaviors cannot humanly be engaged in at the same time. Thus, increasing the desired behavior results in an automatic decrease of the undesirable behavior. The latter is treated with extinction if it does occur.

For example, if a girl presents for treatment because of her chronic tendency to be late for dinner, an incompatible behavior might be to make her responsible for setting the dinner table and sounding the bell to let the rest of the family know that dinner is being served. In this case, the girl is positively reinforced for setting the table and sounding the bell. (Probably a shaping procedure is best utilized, as it is unreasonable for the child to know the entire process of setting a table from the beginning; modeling is useful as well, as may a token economy.) Increasing her table-setting and bell-sounding behavior automatically reduces her lateness to dinner, as she is the person responsible for letting everyone else know when dinner is served. If the child forgets to set the table and sound the bell and is late to dinner, her behavior is ignored (extinction, as no attention is given to the undesired behavior), and she automatically loses out on receiving the reinforcer that she could have earned through having set the table.

Time-Out and Response Cost Procedures.   Time-out and response cost procedures are designed to decrease or eliminate undesirable behaviors by removing reinforcing events from a child's environment. As is true for all negatively focused strategies, alternative positive programs (e.g., reinforcement of incompatible behaviors) are best attempted first. Only if positively focused programs remain unsuccessful are negatively focused programs implemented. Even then, they are best complemented by another behavioral program that uses reinforcers to increase frequency of an existing positive behavior or to develop additional desirable behaviors.

The time-out procedure is essentially a carefully designed extinction procedure that is frequently used by parents and teachers but only occasionally in the playroom. It can be used for an individual behavior or for several behaviors that have the same reinforcement history. The first step in designing a time-out procedure is to investigate which events in a child's environment are maintaining or reinforcing an inappropriate behavior. In implementing the time-out procedure, clinicians, parents, or teachers remove the child from these events for a certain period of time. The time-out area must be designed such that it has no reinforcing qualities in and of itself. For instance, the use of a child's room or a bathroom (both common choices among parents) is inappropriate because of access to many rewarding objects and activities. Relatedly, use of a broom closet or attic (also choices that have been reported by parents) is extremely inappropriate because of the fearful stimuli associated with such settings for many children. Time-out is to be neither reinforcing nor punishing. The best time-out area is one that is specifically designated for that purpose, for instance, a corner in a dining room that is well lighted but unstimulating, where the child has access to neither sounds of radio, television, or family members nor to toys or books. Sitting on a staircase also works if the stairs are inside the home or apartment, not outside or separate from the family's living quarters. In a classroom, a certain corner or table might be specified as the time-out area and all children know not to interact with a child placed in the area. In a playroom, time-out can be implemented by using a corner or chair. Time-out in the playroom is used only in extreme circumstances, since it is easily interpreted as nonacceptance of the child and places the counselor in an adversarial role with the child.

The timing of time-out can be approached in numerous ways. Some clinicians endorse the specification of a certain number of minutes, after which the child is allowed to return from the time-out area. Others suggest that children be given the responsibility to determine when they are ready to return from time-out and behave appropriately. Yet others believe that children should be given permission to return from time-out by the person who implemented it when the child appears ready. Any of these approaches can be either suitable or abused. Leaving a child in time-out for 30 minutes is punitive and not in the spirit of time-out. Leaving children in time-out for 2 minutes and allowing them to return from time-out while they are still having a tantrum defeats the purpose of the procedure. Not letting children know how long they need to be in time-out leaves them wondering and fearful. Allowing children to set their own time-out period is possible only if they are responsible and understand the purpose of the procedure. Therefore, thought has to be given to the determination of the length of the procedure. Perhaps the best guideline is to use time-out with a regulated interval initially, moving to a child-determined interval once the child recognizes the utility of the procedure.

Response cost programs take extinction programs one step further by not only removing the child from reinforcers in the environment but also adding a penalty or fine. For instance, children might lose privileges or tokens earned in a token economy program (see below). Response cost thus can essentially be defined as a punishment procedure yet avoids some of the common disadvantages of punishment proper, such as the modeling or reinforcement of inappropriate behavior and the conditioning of fearful responses or withdrawal in the child.

Token Economies.   Token economies can be as simple as positive reinforcement or as complex as complicated contingency programs that combine a number of operant strategies such as shaping, reinforcement of incompatible behaviors, and response cost (Kazdin, 1977). The underlying similarity of all is the use of tokens as reinforcers. Tokens are items such as stars, points, or chips that are not inherently reinforcing but have gained reinforcing quality by being paired with a powerful reinforcer (i.e., they are essentially conditioned reinforcers, in the same way as neutral stimuli become conditioned stimuli that produce a conditioned response in the classical conditioning model). Using tangible (or unconditioned) reinforcers such as the ones discussed so far is not always practical. Some problems have already been alluded to. Foods and similar small items do not maintain their reinforcing quality for extended periods of time owing to satiation. Social reinforcers, such as praise or attention, might not work right away with all children. Some reinforcers are too expensive to be provided each time an appropriate behavior occurs, and some reinforcers are not possible to administer in all situations. When any of these problems is at issue, tokens can be used as backup reinforcers to be exchanged later for primary reinforcers.

There are literally hundreds of ways in which token economies can be implemented. A few examples are provided here, not to imply that these are the best ways to use tokens, and certainly not the only ways, but rather to stimulate clinicians to look at the process of setting up contingency plans with creativity and an open mind. An example of a simple positive reinforcement token economy is the use of stars to increase a child's hand-washing behavior. Each time a child washes her or his hands before a meal or snack without having to be prompted to do so, she or he receives a star on a chart that is mounted by the sink. When the child has earned five stars, they can be exchanged for a tangible reinforcer from a prespecified shopping list. If a child does not exchange the five stars, but prefers to keep on earning stars, ten stars may be exchanged from another shopping list of even more desirable items or twenty stars from yet another menu.

A token economy that combines positive reinforcement and response cost not only provides children with stars for appropriate behaviors but also has a contingency for what happens if children do not comply. Rather than merely using extinction or reminders, in this case one star might be wiped off the chart each time a child has to be prompted into action. The star chart and reinforcement menus remain the same, but the response cost contingency is added.

A complex token economy may combine positive reinforcement, reinforcement of incompatible behaviors, and response cost. For instance, if parents present a boy for treatment who frequently hits his younger sister, breaks toys, and refuses to play by himself, a token economy can be developed that ties together the behavioral interventions for all of these target problems. The child is allowed to earn one point for each 10-minute interval during which he plays quietly by himself without hitting his sister and without breaking a toy (positive reinforcement of a desirable behavior). He receives an additional point for each toy he played with during a given day that was not broken (positive reinforcement of an incompatible behavior, i.e., of not breaking toys). Bonus points are earned for days when he does not hit his sister at all. Each time he hits his sister, two points are subtracted from his chart (response cost for an inappropriate behavior). The points are backed up by a graded system of tangible reinforcers that allow the boy to self-reinforce in either short (exchange as few as five points for a reinforcer) or long (collect as many as 50 points for a large reinforcer) intervals. This boy's (Billy's) point chart and associated reinforcement menus are presented in Figure 13.2.

To summarize, token economies have numerous advantages over the use of tangible reinforcers. They can be administered immediately and every time the desired behavior occurs. They neither result in satiation nor are impossible to administer in

How to Earn Points
- 10 minutes playing alone and quietly   = 1 point earned
- each toy played with and not broken   = 1 point earned
- not hitting sister all day long   = 3 bonus points earned

How to Lose Points
- hitting sister   = 2 points lost

Monday	Tuesday	Wednesday	Thursday	Friday	Saturday	Sunday
Week One						
Week Two						
Week Three						
Week Four						
Week Five						

(continued)

Figure 13.2   Point Chart for Billy

Billy's Reinforcement Menus

5 points may be exchanged for one of the following:

- 10 minutes of play with mom
- 10 minutes of play with dad
- one short bedtime story
- one board game with mom and/or dad
- one Pokémon card
- one new magic marker
- one sheet of colored cardboard
- one 10-minute phone call to a friend
- one candy bar (may only choose this item once per day)
- one can of soda (may only choose this item once per day)

10 points may be exchanged for one of the following:

- half hour of mom's undivided attention
- half hour of dad's undivided attention
- may stay up half an hour later
- extra half hour of TV watching
- a new book
- one extra trip to the library
- one extra serving of dessert
- two 15-minute phone calls to one or two friends
- may ask mom or dad to take the garbage out for him once
- one long bedtime story

20 points may be exchanged for one of the following:

- a 2-hour trip to the park with mom
- a 2-hour trip to the park with dad
- may stay up till 10 PM on Friday or Saturday
- may watch cartoons on Saturday morning
- may ask mom or dad to make his bed for him one morning
- may ask mom or dad to take the garbage out for him three times
- may make one 15-minute long-distance phone call
- may invite a friend for a sleepover
- may choose a new toy at the store for up to $10
- may choose the destination for a family outing

50 points may be exchanged for one of the following:

- a 1/2-day trip to the park with mom
- a 1/2-day trip to the park with dad
- may choose a new toy at the store for up to $20
- may make one big wish come true

Figure 13.2 *(continued)*

certain situations. The tangible reinforcers that back up the tokens can be individualized for each child, even if used in a group setting such as a classroom. This property of token economies makes them highly applicable in group settings, including classrooms, hospital units, residential settings, or homes that have several children. Again, the actual implementation and combination of strategies is limited only by the creativity of the person developing and implementing the program and can take into consideration changing needs and preferences of each child.

Strategies Based on Social Learning

The strategies in this category are based on observational learning principles that suggest that children learn many behaviors, as well as emotional responses, from watching others in their environment and incorporating the observed actions in a meaningful way into their own behavioral repertoire. The process of observational learning varies primarily according to the type of model used. Caring and powerful models of the same gender tend to be more successfully imitated than other models (Bandura, 1999). Three types of models that may meet these criteria or have been used successfully in the treatment of children are other human beings, videotaped or filmed models, and videotaped or filmed self (Powers, 2001). The use of other human beings is referred to as live modeling, the use of filmed other models as symbolic modeling, and the use of the filmed child as self modeling. A fourth procedure that combines several features of the previous three modeling processes is called participant modeling.

Live Modeling.   In live modeling, the child watches another human being perform a behavior the child is to learn. This may involve a new skill acquisition or the modeling of not fearing a stimulus that is currently feared by a child. A live modeling approach to a snake phobia might be to ask the child to watch another person handle a snake. The child is not expected to touch the snake herself or himself.

A live modeling approach to skills acquisition might be to ask a child to watch a model who engages in the desirable behavior, such as prosocial behavior for a withdrawn child. A live model does not always have to be selected by the therapist. Children can be asked about idealized others in their environments who can serve as models. For instance, a child who has to learn social skills might be asked if there is another child in the same school who possesses the skills the child would like to learn. If there is such a live model, the child can then be asked to observe this child and to identify a number of behaviors in which this other child engages that the client might like to learn and imitate.

Symbolic Modeling.   In symbolic modeling, rather than watching a live model, the child is exposed to a film or video of relevant models. The snake phobic child might watch a video showing several fearless children handling snakes and talking about snakes without anxiety. The withdrawn child might watch a film of children interacting positively or of a social skills training program in progress. An excellent example of symbolic modeling is provided by a film developed by the Department of Pediatrics at the University of Oklahoma Health Sciences Center designed to ready children for a spinal tap procedure. The film depicts a young girl who has been taught numerous relaxation and breathing techniques to cope successfully with this invasive medical procedure. Symbolic modeling can also involve asking the client to visualize engaging in the desired behavior or facing the feared stimulus. However, this procedure has not yet been frequently applied to children.

Self Modeling.   In the self modeling procedure, originally developed by Hosford (1980), successful incidents of the desired behavior engaged in by the child are captured on video and then shown to the child in the attempt to increase their frequency of occurrence. If the behavior is very complex, the child may be taped engaged in behaviors that represent successive approximations for the target behavior. Children, in viewing their own videotape, serve as their own model. This is a powerful application of modeling theory and has been found to be very versatile and successful (Dowrick, 1991; Dowrick, Kim-Rupnow, and Power, 2006).

Participant Modeling.   In participant modeling, children are exposed to a live, symbolic, or self model and asked to imitate the behavior in the presence of the counselor. Feedback is provided about the child's performance as the behavior occurs. If the desired behavior is a very difficult one, the model breaks the process into its component steps and shows the steps one at a time. The child imitates each individual step and practices it to an acceptable criterion level before moving on to the next step. Whereas the counselor provides much feedback and reinforcement early in the process, or early on in the mastery of each step, this external feedback is slowly phased out toward the point of mastery to let the successful completion of the behavior serve as its own reinforcer for the child. Participant modeling has been reported to be one of the most successful and powerful modeling procedures for children (Bellini and Akullian, 2007; Gelfand and Hartmann, 1992).

Practical Implementation

The proper implementation of behavioral strategies requires thorough assessment, goal-setting, treatment planning, and data collection during implementation of interventions. As such, it is a far cry from being the superficial strategy that opponents of behavioral interventions make it out to be. In fact, behavioral assessment is extremely thorough and takes into account numerous and complex familial and environmental factors. The intake information outlined in previous chapters is as crucial for behavioral interventions as any other treatment.

Once assessment of a child has been completed, problem behaviors have to be identified and defined carefully, and their baseline rate has to be established. This procedure requires that therapists, parents, teachers, or other caregivers in the child's life observe the child and record the child's behavior to obtain an exact understanding of when, where, and how often a problem behavior occurs. As such, teachers may be asked to count the number of disruptions during a given lesson and to note the circumstances of the occurrence. Similarly, parents may be instructed to count how often the child acts out aggressively, noting specific behaviors and circumstances. Children may be asked to rate a fear or phobia on a scale from 1 to 10, depending on different settings and occurrences. These measurements then serve as a basis for assessing treatment effectiveness. Only if clinicians know where the child started can they assess whether an intervention has been successful in reducing an undesired behavior or increasing a target behavior (Kazdin, 2001).

Once baseline rates or levels have been established, goal setting becomes more realistic. For instance, a child who is observed to engage in an attention-seeking action at least once in every 30-minute interval cannot be expected to show no attention-seeking behaviors within the first month of treatment. A more appropriate goal for this child might be to reduce attention seeking to no more than five occurrences in one day during the first month of treatment, three occurrences a day during the second month of treatment, and so forth. Similarly, a child whose undesirable behavior occurs only while visiting with a particular friend might not be sufficiently challenged by a treatment goal that does not specify the environment wherein the change is to take place. Goals for behaviors that are to be addressed through the use of behavioral strategies are clearly defined. They specify the exact number of occurrences in specific environments or around certain individuals.

Behavioral goals are rarely set by the provider exclusively. Instead, children, parents, teachers, or any other relevant individuals are consulted about desired treatment outcomes. This involvement of children and others is likely to increase cooperation with and investment in the treatment process by all parties involved. The involvement also continues beyond the goal-setting stage, as many behavioral strategies are not only applied in the playroom but also in other relevant real-life settings. Environments outside the playroom have to be prepared for the implementation of treatment interventions. Parents and teachers have to be taught to implement programs that were selected by the clinician and family. Teachers, parents, and children are essential to the determination of appropriate reinforcers as they have more extended knowledge of the child than a clinician who just made the child's acquaintance. Although the counselor provides the theoretical knowledge and framework for the intervention, family members have to provide the specifics of the child's behavior and reinforcement history to make treatment work. This is particularly true for operant conditioning strategies. Respondent conditioning strategies are more likely to be implemented by the therapist in the playroom.

Although reinforcers are most commonly disbursed by parents or teachers, it is not impossible to make children responsible for their own reinforcer. This is particularly true for token economies, in which children may be asked to record points on the chart or to track the number of tokens earned in other ways. If token economies are used, it is best to have charts and menus highly visible in children's room to provide a good visual reminder of the program. If children are too young to read, contingencies can be displayed not in written but in pictorial form. Magazine pictures of children or photographs of a child herself or himself can be used to display an appropriate behavior and the number of stars earned by this behavior may be pasted next to the picture as a visual reminder for the child that different behaviors may earn different numbers of points. Similarly, pictures of undesirable behaviors may be posted on the board with a heavy red line drawn through them.

Throughout implementation of a behavioral strategy, records are kept of a child's behavior to monitor progress. It is not unusual for baseline behaviors to worsen during the initial stage of treatment, as children are likely to test the limits of the person responsible for the disbursement or withholding of reinforcers. However, after the initial testing of limits, improvements in children's behavior often emerge quickly. As most operant treatment strategies and in vivo desensitization programs are best implemented in the actual environment, generalization of progress is built into treatment.

Behavioral strategies and interventions are best used to supplement other treatment strategies. A counselor can set up token economies in children's homes and classrooms, can conduct relaxation training and desensitization programs in the playroom, and use play therapy, storytelling, art therapy, and other strategies to interact therapeutically with the child. Such a comprehensive approach most likely can reduce undesired and increase desired behaviors, plus it can also address issues that are not purely behavioral in nature, such as the child's awareness and playing out of family roles, affective awareness and expression, recognition of needs, teaching of coping skills, and so forth. The example provided below reflects the case of a child who was treated using such a comprehensive approach.

Case Example

The boy whose case will be presented here was seen once weekly by the therapist for over a year. His parents were seen by the same therapist once weekly for three months and then on an as-needed basis for parent education training, which was to aid them in the implementation of a token economy in the home. One of the child's teachers was involved in the third week of treatment to implement a token economy in the classroom and an in vivo desensitization program in gym class as an extension of the systematic desensitization that was used by the therapist in the individual therapy sessions. The therapist used storytelling to explore family problems and to help the child develop new coping skills. Play was used to facilitate development of a therapeutic relationship, and art therapy helped the child's self-expression, as well as facilitated additional monitoring of treatment progress. As the focus of this chapter is on behavioral intervention, only that aspect of the child's treatment is highlighted here. However, it is exceedingly important to remember that the behavioral intervention was firmly embedded in a larger conceptual context and child–therapist interaction, and is not endorsed in isolation.

This 10-year-old boy was presented for treatment by his parents, who had just been contacted by his teacher and informed that Michael had skipped school twice in one week. When his parents attempted to talk to Michael about the situation, he cried but could not verbalize why he was so distraught. When they further explored the situation with his teachers, they found out that Michael had been very withdrawn and fearful in the past three months. One teacher believed that Michael's mood was particularly depressed on days when the class was scheduled for physical education. Michael routinely attempted to avoid physical education, claiming stomachaches or headaches. Both days of school he had skipped recently were days with physical education class in the morning. During the intake, Michael revealed that he hated gym class because he felt inadequate and was often made fun of by several larger boys. Michael was slight in build and somewhat younger than most of his classmates. He indicated that he hated having to race against other boys because he always lost. Further, he felt very panicky in these situations and one time fell and hurt himself badly.

Michael's father was very upset by his son's failure in gym class. He was a former bodybuilder and still conscious about physical appearance and exercise. He ran several miles daily and often entered races, winning occasionally. Michael's mother was hurt that her son had not confided in her. She revealed that Michael was not very close to her and had withdrawn even more since the birth of his younger sister six months earlier. Also present for the intake was Michael's older brother Steven, a 16-year-old who indicated that he was bored by the intake and wanted to get out of it as soon as possible. Michael adored his older brother, but Steven rarely allowed Michael to play or interact with him. Steven was athletic and had recently received his driver's license, which frequently removed him from the family. He had a 10 PM curfew and rarely arrived home before that time.

Michael was diagnosed with a simple phobia, and the feared stimulus was identified as gym class. He also was assessed for depression and showed several signs, though not enough to diagnose dysthymia. He did appear unusually withdrawn and shy, and his self-esteem appeared compromised. When asked how he rated himself with regard to how positively he felt about himself on a 1 (low) to 10 (high) point scale, he said 3. Michael's teacher volunteered to do some ratings of Michael's withdrawal behavior in the school setting and reported that he refused interactions with children who approached him four out of five times, stayed by himself during breaks the entire time, complained of stomachaches during every gym class, and reported headaches approximately twice per week. On the basis of this information, Michael, his parents, and the therapist set four primary treatment goals. The first goal was to keep Michael from avoiding gym class by reducing the fear and physical pain responses he had developed in connection with this activity. The second goal was to involve Michael more actively with other children by increasing the number of offers to play that he accepted to three out of five offers, by increasing the amount of time spent with children during break to 10 of the 15 minutes, and by increasing his involvement with other children in after-school activities. The third goal was to help Michael increase his self-rated self-esteem to at least a 7 on a 10-point scale. The fourth goal was to continue to work on assessing the family relationships, especially the relationship between father and son and the role change for Michael since the birth of the baby. Parent education was recommended to help the parents implement behavior programs in the home, to prevent future difficulties with the other children, and to explore their own psychological needs. Family therapy was recommended as a follow-up to Michael's individual treatment.

Behavioral interventions were chosen to address the first two treatment goals. Play therapy was chosen to address the third and fourth goals. Only the behavioral strategies are elaborated upon here. To reduce Michael's fear and physical response to gym class, a two-pronged approach was developed. First, a systematic desensitization program was started in the therapy sessions in which a hierarchy was developed. Second, an in vivo program was designed in collaboration with the gym teacher and implemented once Michael had mastered the relaxation techniques. To reduce Michael's withdrawal behavior in school and at home, two token economy programs were implemented, reinforcing him for interacting with other children. A response cost program was part of this token economy.

The therapist and Michael developed a hierarchy of anxiety-producing situations connected to his fear of gym class. Michael was taught progressive muscle tension–relaxation, using Koeppen's (2002) procedure. Once he mastered basic relaxation, the in-session desensitization program began. In the third week of treatment, an in vivo component was added in collaboration with the gym teacher. Michael progressed through the systematic desensitization hierarchy over the course of 18 weeks, indicating just how strong his fear of gym class was. He was able to move to the second item of his in vivo hierarchy in week 6 and required 3 additional weeks before moving to item 3. He progressed to the items graded 22 and higher after an additional 6 weeks and was not able to do the final item until week 24 (his next semester). The hierarchies for the two desensitization programs are presented in Figures 13.3 and 13.4.

In Figure 13.3, the steps are presented and imagined one after the other as they can be tolerated without experiencing a fear or physical response while Michael is fully relaxed. The steps are graduated from zero (no fear or physical response) to 25 (extreme fear and strong physical response) on the basis of how strongly Michael would respond without relaxation.

0	Going to school on a day without gym class
3	Wearing gym clothes at home without any intent to exercise
5	Being in the gym alone without any intent to exercise
6	Going to school on a day with gym class, knowing you won't have to go to gym at all
7	Going to school on a day with gym class, knowing you won't have to participate at all, but you'll have to sit and watch
9	Going to school on a day with gym class, knowing you won't have to participate at all, but you'll have to sit and watch while wearing gym clothes
12	Sitting in gym class in street clothes, just watching the other kids
14	Sitting in gym class in gym clothes, just watching the other kids
16	Going to gym class, but only participating in warm-ups
19	Going to gym class, but only participating in warm-ups and cool-downs
21	Going to gym class, but only participating in warm-ups and cool-downs, and 10 minutes of noncompetitive exercise of your choice
22	Going to gym class, but only participating in warm-ups and cool-downs, and 20 minutes of noncompetitive exercise of your choice
23	Going to gym class, but only participating in warm-ups and cool-downs, 20 minutes of noncompetitive exercise of your choice, and 5 minutes of competitive exercise of your choice
24	Going to gym class, but only participating in warm-ups and cool-downs, all noncompetitive exercise, and 5 minutes of competitive exercise of your choice
24	Going to gym class, but only participating in warm-ups and cool-downs, all noncompetitive exercise, and 10 minutes of competitive exercise of your choice
25	Going to gym class, but only participating in warm-ups and cool-downs, all noncompetitive exercise, and 10 minutes of competitive exercise of your choice, and having to perform a task individually in front of the other kids and doing fine
25	Going to gym class, but only participating in warm-ups and cool-downs, all noncompetitive exercise, and 10 minutes of competitive exercise of your choice, and having to perform a task individually in front of the other kids and messing up
25	Going to gym class, but only participating in warm-ups and cool-downs, all noncompetitive exercise, and 10 minutes of competitive exercise of your choice, and having to perform a task individually in front of the other kids and messing up so badly everyone laughs

Figure 13.3   Michael's Systematic Desensitization Hierarchy

In Figure 13.4, the steps are implemented in real life one after the other as they can be tolerated without experiencing a fear or physical response while Michael is fully relaxed. The steps are graduated from zero (no fear or physical response) to 25 (extreme fear and strong physical response) based on how strongly Michael would respond without relaxation.

5	Going to school on a day with gym class but knowing that he will not have to go to that class
10	Going to gym class but knowing that he will not have to participate in the class; he will sit and watch
15	Going to gym class but knowing that he will only participate in the warm-up exercises, which last 5 minutes and are noncompetitive; then he will only sit and watch
18	Going to gym class but knowing that he will only participate in the warm-up exercises, which last 5 minutes and are noncompetitive; then he will be allowed to sit and watch until closing exercises which are for cool-down purposes and are noncompetitive
20	Going to gym class but knowing that he will participate only in the warm-up exercises, which last 5 minutes and are noncompetitive; then he will be allowed to sit and watch all competitive exercises; he will participate in 10 minutes of noncompetitive exercises of his choice and will join cool-down
22	Going to gym class but knowing that he will participate only in the warm-up exercises, which last 5 minutes and are noncompetitive; then he will be allowed to sit and watch all competitive exercises; he will participate in 20 minutes of noncompetitive exercises of his choice and will join cool-down
23	Going to gym class but knowing that he will participate only in the warm-up exercises, which last 5 minutes and are noncompetitive; then he will be allowed to sit and watch all competitive exercises; he will participate in 20 minutes of noncompetitive exercises of his choice; he will participate in 5 minutes of competitive exercises of his choice and will join cool-down
25	Going to gym class but knowing that he will participate in the entire gym class, including warm-up, noncompetitive exercises, competitive exercises (never more than 10 minutes), and cool-down

Figure 13.4   Michael's In Vivo Desensitization Hierarchy

The therapist, Michael, his brother Steven, and his parents developed a token economy for home and school. Michael's teacher agreed to cooperate with the school component of the program. The program combined positive reinforcement, reinforcement of incompatible behaviors, and response cost for undesirable behavior. Specifically, Michael had a daily reinforcement chart at school and a weekly chart at home. At school, Michael's teacher was responsible for delivery of the tokens, in this case stars, that were placed on the daily chart. Michael received one star for each observed positive interaction with another child during break time (positive reinforcement). He also received a star for each time he was observed to respond positively to being approached by another child (reinforcement of an incompatible behavior). He received two stars for each break time during which he spent less time alone than he spent with other children (reinforcement of an incompatible behavior). At home, he received a star for each time he initiated an interaction with another child, whether in person or over the telephone. He received a star for every 30-minute period during which he interacted with another child. In both settings, Michael lost a star each if he did not interact with any children during all breaks (at school) or free time (at home). Exchange of stars for tangible reinforcers was possible based on a graded menu to allow Michael to determine intervals between receipt of a tangible reinforcer. Simplified copies of Michael's charts and reinforcement menus are displayed in Figures 13.5 and 13.6 on pages 371–373. His original charts and menus were prepared by him and his older brother in a collaborative activity and were quite sophisticated, with pictures of Michael interacting with friends in various settings and activities. The brother had agreed to be involved in this activity after the therapist had met with him and explained his potentially influential role with Michael as a model.

Summary and Concluding Thoughts

This chapter served to familiarize clinicians with behavioral strategies to be used either within a strictly behavioral, or more eclectic, framework. A differentiation was made among respondent (or classical) conditioning, operant (or instrumental) conditioning, and social learning theory. Use of these strategies has a number of advantages, including the thorough assessment of baseline behavior, accurate assessment of treatment progress, involvement of the child and significant others in the goal-setting and treatment implementation processes, excellent generalization, and a nonpathological approach to behavior. In addition to these advantages, it is noted that behavioral therapists do not neglect the child-therapist relationship and understand its importance to the successful outcome of treatment. Thus, rapport building and empathy, though not focused on in this chapter, are not inherently incompatible with a behavioral approach. It is recommended to use behavioral strategies as handy tools, not as the exclusive framework of conceptualization of a child counseling case.

How to Earn Stars
- any positive interaction with another child   = 1 star
- positive response to another child inviting to play   = 1 star
- less time alone during break than with children   = 2 stars

How to Lose Stars
- no interaction with another child during the entire break   = 1 star

---

Stars Earned in School Today

Michael interacted positively with another child and earned _____ stars.

Description of what he did: _____

_____

_____

_____

Michael responded positively to a child who invited him to play or join in an activity and earned _____ stars.

Description of what he did: _____

_____

_____

_____

Michael Spent less time alone that with others and earned _____ stars

How much time did he spend with others during:

Break 1: _____

Break 2: _____

Break 3: _____

Break 4: _____

Michael did not interact with another child during an entire break and lost _____ stars

Breaks without contact:

Break 1 _____

Break 2 _____

Break 3 _____

Break 4 _____

TOTAL STARS EARNED IN SCHOOL TODAY: _____ *STARS*

Figure 13.5   Michael's School Reinforcement Chart

How to Earn Stars

- initiate an interaction with another child   = 1 star
- interaction with another child in a 30-minute period = 1 star

How to Lose Stars

- no interaction with another child all afternoon = lose 1 star
- no interaction all Saturday morning   = lose 1 star

Day and Stars	Initiated Interaction —Describe	Interacted in 30-Minute Period —Describe
Monday		
Tuesday		
Wednesday		
Thursday		
Friday		
Saturday		

TOTAL STARS EARNED THIS WEEK: _____ *STARS*

Figure 13.6   Michael's Home Reinforcement Chart

Reinforcement Menus for Michael

Level One Rewards (worth 10 stars)
- spend half-hour alone indoors any way he wants to
- spend half hour alone outside any way he wants to
- spend 15 minutes daytime with older brother Steven
- two large cookies (may choose no more than one per day)
- a pack of chewing gum
- one can of Dr. Pepper (may choose no more than one per day)
- allowed to read a new comic book
- have a short story read to him by mom or dad
- play a board game with mom or dad
- may listen to a favorite CD on the family stereo system

Level Two Rewards (worth 20 stars)
- spend half a daytime hour with brother Steven
- spend an extra afternoon at the library
- spend an extra Saturday afternoon at the museum
- spend one hour alone indoors
- spend one hour alone outdoors
- have a long bedtime story read to him by mom or dad
- have a short story read to him by mom or dad any time
- have two helpings of dessert, even if he didn't finish dinner
- may buy one new container of Play-Doh
- may buy a new notebook
- allowed to buy a new comic book
- may buy a new T-shirt
- may listen to three favorite CDs on the family stereo system

Level Three Rewards (worth 40 stars)
- spend one daytime hour with brother Steven
- spend one afternoon after school alone indoors
- spend one afternoon after school alone outdoors
- spend one afternoon with dad
- spend one afternoon with mom
- may buy one new set of magic markers
- may buy one new science book
- may buy one new Pokémon figure
- determine the destination of a family outing
- have unlimited access to the family stereo for one afternoon
- have a long bedtime story read by brother Steven

Level Four Rewards (worth 100 stars)
- spend one afternoon with brother Steven
- spend a day at the museum with dad
- spend one Saturday alone indoors and/or outdoors
- buy one new toy for up to $25
- buy new clothes for up to $25
- cash in on one big wish

Figure 13.6   *(continued)*

PART IV

Termination

14

Creating Thoughtful Endings

> *States Parties recognize the right of a child who has been placed by the competent authorities for the purposes of care, protection or treatment of his or her physical or mental health, to a periodic review of the treatment provided to the child and all other circumstances relevant to his or her placement.*
>
> —Article 25 of the U.N. Convention on the Rights of the Child

Termination is the unfortunate word that has been chosen to describe the process of ending treatment and saying good-bye. This choice of terminology appears so unfortunate because of the pictures a mind's eye conjures upon hearing the word *termination*: Some think of death, others think of the cessation of any link between client and clinician, others even link the term with killing. In truth, termination is merely the ending of the relationship between the client and the counselor as it existed to date. However, in reality, the bond between the two people who worked toward the growth of one of them can never be broken completely. Nothing ever undoes the work these people have done together or the special feeling they developed for each other. The memories of their joint efforts and the benefits reaped from their work remains with both individuals for a lifetime.

Ending therapy is a bittersweet event, for both child and clinician. It is bitter because it means severing a relationship that has come to be of great importance to the child, and often also to the counselor. It is sweet because of what it implies: the reduction of symptoms and establishment of emotional stability and health of the client. The ending or termination of treatment is, after all, the universal goal of all therapies, regardless of symptoms and theoretical and practical approach to treatment. Ending is not only inevitable, but desirable. Nevertheless, clinicians and clients alike tend to dread endings and turn terminations into sad occurrences that sometimes overshadow the joyousness of the event. In this chapter, termination is explored from various angles. Some terminations are indeed sad because they were agreed upon neither by the client nor by the clinician but were forced by external factors. Other terminations are indeed happy because they signal arrival and growth. Regardless of how an ending comes about, the clinician is responsible for making it as productive and positive for the child (and family) as possible. Termination need not be unpleasant, but rather can be seen as a cause for celebration, as a reaffirmation of the relationship that is oriented toward growth, and as an integral part of the complete therapy or counseling process (Cangelosi, 1997; O'Conner, 2000). In fact, Sigmund Freud himself is often quoted as seeing therapy from the second session on as a termination process, that is, a process of learning to say good-bye to important people in one's life without feeling overwhelmed, abandoned, alone, or rejected. It is in this more positive light that termination is discussed in this chapter.

Types of Endings

There are numerous ways in which treatment can be ended or interrupted. The most desirable reason for ending is certainly the natural termination that occurs because treatment goals have been reached and both individuals agree that the client is ready to face her or his life on her or his own. Such mutually agreed upon terminations are, if not rare, at least much less frequent than premature terminations. In fact, although exact figures vary quite a bit in the literature, attrition rates due to premature terminations range from approximately 40 to 60 percent (e.g., Nock and Kazdin, 2001). Reasons for premature terminations vary almost as widely as the prevalence figures, but some patterns have emerged. Philips (2007) reported that individuals who have a distancing approach to their presenting concerns (not owning them) are more likely to end treatment prematurely than individuals who are openly approaching their concerns in therapy. Clients who have good agreement with their clinician about the nature of the presenting concerns tend to be more likely to persevere in treatment than clients who have a discrepant view of their problem conceptualization (Corning, Malofeeva, and Bucchianeri, 2007). In working with adolescents, a positive alliance with parents appears to prevent premature terminations (Shelef, 2005). Work specific to children has shown that poorly managed transference and projection can contribute to premature endings (Jany, 2005), as may low expectancies about the helpfulness of treatment (Nock and Kazdin, 2001), lower family income, and certain presenting problems (most commonly run-away behavior and truancy in the part of the child; Christy, 2001). Further, especially with ethnically diverse children, ethnicity match with the clinician, parental education, and parentally perceived barriers to treatment are predictive of whether or not families retain their children intervention treatment (McCabe, 2002).

Reasons for premature terminations can be grouped into three categories: clinician-initiated reasons, client-initiated reasons, and externally initiated reasons. Clinician-initiated reasons include such factors as the ending of a practicum or internship for a trainee, illness or geographic relocation of the therapist, countertransference, or inability to establish a working relationship with a child. Client-initiated reasons for children include not only the child's, but also the parents' or family's actions. Thus, these factors may include a geographic relocation of the family, sudden illness of a child or a parent responsible for the child's transportation to and from the clinic, and a family's or parent's arbitrary reason to quit therapy, perhaps for reasons that are attributable to resistance to treatment. Finally, externally initiated reasons, which, of the three categories, are least likely to occur, may include the closure of a clinic because of lack of funding, incompatible clinic and family schedules, or interference by schools or other agencies in the child's treatment.

Obviously, some of these reasons are quite genuine and are not necessarily under a person's (either clinician, child, or parent) control. For instance, a family move may not be realistically delayed because of a child's therapy needs. However, other reasons are less concrete and justifiable. Parental resistance to a child's therapy is an unfortunately common cause of premature endings for children's treatment. Yet, often these resistances could have been dealt with or avoided. Therapist countertransference could have been addressed through supervision or consultation, in much the same way as a therapist's inability to establish a working relationship. Because of these less concrete and justifiable reasons, many clinicians believe that these types of factors seldom work in isolation (Jany, 2005). For instance, if a family withdraws a child because they believe that no progress has been made and this withdrawal occurs suddenly and without preparation, chances are that the therapist has somehow failed to work sufficiently with the parents to have overcome their resistance or the therapist has indeed mismanaged the case and the child has not improved because of the counselor's failure to seek consultation. Similarly, counselors who fail to establish a relationship with a parent might be victims of their own countertransferences, which might have prevented them from dealing effectively with an abusive parent. Parents, in turn, are more likely to withdraw their children when they themselves feel neglected, uncared for, or attacked by their children's clinicians. Thus, although consultation and supervision certainly are no panacea for premature endings, they may serve to prevent a good number of them. Similarly, although regular meetings with parents for consultation or involvement of parents in their own treatment might be similarly unsuccessful at avoiding all premature endings, they certainly reduce their likelihood of occurrence.

Natural Termination

Premature terminations obviously imply that the child's treatment was not complete when the ending occurred and that further work remains to be done. Sometimes, premature terminations result in transfers; more commonly, they truly are the end of the child's work in counseling. Some children, however, are lucky enough to complete therapy and become part of a natural termination. Such natural terminations can be ushered in through a variety of ways and clinicians have to learn to identify when the ending is near, and it must be approached with the child and family. In other words, there have to be reasons to justify endings, as well as signals from both child and clinician that the timing is right for termination.

Reasons for a Natural Termination

Just as there are many reasons for premature terminations, there are a number of reasons for natural terminations. Different theorists may use slightly different guidelines, but some consensus does emerge. Specifically, there is long-standing agreement that foremost, there must be resolution of the presenting problems and a decrease in or disappearance of symptoms evidenced by the child (Cangelosi, 2002; Horney, 1939; Walsh, 2007). Further, children must have become more developmentally appropriate in a number of realms, including cognition, experience of affect, expression of affect, morality, self development, and interpersonal relating (Ablon, 1988; Kohut, 1984; O'Conner, 2000; Spiegel, 1996). Children must evidence increased problem-solving ability and cognitive flexibility, allowing them to generalize skills and adapt skills to new situations, as well as to recognize options and alternatives (Hutchins and Vaught, 1997; Walsh, 2007). Increased capacity to cope and use adequate defenses should be accompanied by increased spontaneity in behavior, as well as in need and affect expression (Horney, 1939; Joyce, Piper, Ogrodniczuk, and Klein, 2006). Further, the child should feel greater capacity for enjoyment, increased self-confidence and self-value, and an integrated sense of self (Horney, 1939; Kohut, 1984; Landreth, 2000). There should be evidence that the child has become more independent and is now ready to progress and grow on her or his own (Coppolillo, 1987; Norton and Norton, 2006). Finally, the amount of conflict experienced by children, either intrapsychically, interpersonally, familially, or otherwise, should be greatly reduced and manageable, and children should be capable of setting their own limits and boundaries for behavior and affect (Landreth, 2000, 2002a).

Although this might appear to be a rather long list of changes that clinicians must look for to be able to end treatment, it is unlikely that most of them do not automatically develop and become evident in unison, as these improvements are intimately tied to one another. For instance, it is unlikely that the reduction of symptoms would not result in increased spontaneity and self-esteem. Similarly, getting back on track developmentally usually implies that children become more independent and sufficiently cognitively complex to do their own problem solving and limit setting. It is noteworthy in examining this list of changes, however, that nowhere in the literature is there any suggestion that children must be completely free of problems or conflicts to end therapy. The emphasis for all theorists remains on decreasing problems and conflicts and increasing coping ability. Cure, in the traditional sense of removing all symptoms and problems in the present and the future, is not a goal in child treatment. In fact, Freud, speaking about adult treatment, even acknowledged that cure is unrealistic. He believed that "above all, don't try to cure, just learn and earn some money" (Sigmund Freud in a letter to C. G. Jung, as quoted by Ablon, 1988, p. 98). Spiegel echoes this sentiment in the context of work with children, by writing that "the task, at least with children, is to repair, not to remake" (Spiegel, 1996, p. 195). This approach to treatment frees both child and therapist from having to attempt to achieve the unattainable: perpetual happiness and freedom from conflict.

If a counselor believes that there are sufficient reasons (summarized below) for a natural termination to be initiated, there is one final means of double-checking this decision. Teyber (2006) suggests that there be verification of the reasons for termination from three sources: the clinician, the client, and one external source. Obviously, by this time, the first source has been established, that is, the clinician has decided that enough evidence exists to suggest sufficient improvement in the child to warrant ending. Ideally, this evidence is corroborated by the child, who might begin to tell enough stories about change outside the therapy room to imply that progress has been made.

The third source is often a parent or a teacher. In fact, getting corroboration from a third source is much easier in the work with children than in the work with adults. In the latter, this evidence is generally secondhand, delivered by clients as a statement about what other people are beginning to say about them. In child treatment, however, there is always some level of involvement of a parent, caretaker, guardian, or teacher who can be interviewed to assess children's behavioral change outside the playroom. Finally, in addition to corroborating the evidence pointing toward the need for termination through other sources, the clinician can also begin to look for signs and signals above and beyond concrete improvement or symptom resolution.

Reasons for a Natural Termination

- resolution of presenting problems
- reduction or disappearance of symptoms
- developmentally appropriate cognitions
- developmentally appropriate expressions of affect
- developmentally appropriate experiences of affect
- developmentally appropriate morality
- developmentally appropriate self development
- developmentally appropriate interpersonal relationships
- increased problem-solving ability
- increased cognitive flexibility
- ability to generalize and adapt skills to new situations
- ability to see and explore options and alternatives
- better coping ability
- increased spontaneity in behavior
- increased spontaneity in affect expression
- increased spontaneity in need expression
- greater capacity for enjoyment
- increased self-confidence
- increased self-esteem or self-value
- increasingly clear self-definition
- increased independence
- internalized ability to set limits and boundaries
- decreased experience of intrapsychic conflict
- decreased experience of interpersonal conflict
- decreased experience of familial conflict

Signals of an Impending Natural Termination

There are many signals, from both the child and the therapist, that indicate that the end of counseling may be at hand and that the timing is right to terminate treatment. Some of these signs might occur even before the clinician has identified the reasons for termination listed above. In this case, the signals might have to be analyzed to make a decision as to whether the signs are occurring because of resistance or other nontherapeutic reasons, or because the reasons for ending have been reached, but were overlooked by the provider. It is indeed not uncommon for a therapist to rationalize the continuation of therapy even after presenting problems have been resolved, under the guise of working on underlying problems or personality restructuring. Such continued work may indeed be justified in some cases; however, if signals arise from the child that indicate that it is time to end, the therapist may need to explore countertransferences about why continuation is deemed important.

Signs experienced by the counselor that the end may have come are quite varied in nature but are always related to the relationship that has been established with the child. An important signal is given when clinicians begin to note that they are growing increasingly fond of the children they see in treatment and are having fewer and fewer ambiguous feelings about them. At the same time, counselors might consider children increasingly interesting and, while having high hopes for their achievement and health outside of the playroom, feel less responsible for making these things happen. Clinicians feel less burdened by the work with children who are ready to end treatment, less protective, and less in need to provide continuous support. In other words, children are perceived as more capable, stronger, and more of an equal partner in the client–clinician relationship. Thus, when the ending is near, therapists might note that they have to work less hard in sessions and are perhaps are even bored on occasion by the work that is being done. In fact, if counselors find themselves feeling less responsible and justifying lateness or cancellations, it might well be time to reiterate the treatment goals and assess whether the reasons for a natural termination have perhaps been reached.

Similarly, children who are ready for termination begin to spend more and more time talking about issues that concern their future and that are not directly relevant to treatment. They begin to engage in behaviors that are new or unusual—that are "firsts" (Landreth, 2001). For example, a child who has never used the finger paints available in the room might now choose them; a child who was never hostile toward the therapist might now be so; a child who always used to take off her or his shoes after entering the room might now fail to do so; an adolescent who always chose to sit in a particular chair might suddenly switch to a different one. Although children are seldom responsible for their own transportation, thus making coming late for treatment rarely a termination sign (it is for adults!), they might be less interested in getting started right away upon entering the room. Perhaps the child asks to end sessions early or just runs out of things to do or say. Sometimes, a parent begins to cancel sessions for the child, picking up on the child's decreased need for sessions and giving in to requests to let other activities take precedence.

All of these signs can obviously also communicate resistance to treatment. However, their context, timing, and novelty usually help the clinician recognize them for what they are. In other words, if a child has been in treatment for only a brief period of time, has not yet shown a significant attachment to the counselor or the therapy process, and starts running out of things to say, this child's behavior can be interpreted as resistance (or self-protection). However, if the same behavior occurs in a child who has been in treatment for several months, has built a meaningful relationship with the therapist, and has repeatedly evidenced a belief in the importance of therapy, it can be confidently interpreted as a termination signal. None of the signals (displayed below) is foolproof; none can be used in isolation. It is best to view them in their context, to look for additional signs, and to explore whether the reasons for termination are obvious as well. If all of these factors are answered affirmatively, it is time to consider termination.

Therapist Signals for a Natural Termination

- becomes increasingly fond of the child
- finds the child increasingly more interesting
- has high hopes for the child's achievement without feeling responsible for helping the child reach these goals
- feels less protective of the child
- feels less burdened with the responsibility for the child
- feels less need to support the child continuously
- works less hard in session
- may occasionally become bored in session
- may become less responsible about not being late for sessions
- may become less responsible about not canceling sessions

Client Signals for a Natural Termination

- engages in "firsts"
- is less interested in starting sessions on time or right away
- asks to end sessions early
- runs out of things to say or do before session is over
- convinces parent to cancel sessions
- gives other activities precedence
- spends more time talking about things outside the therapy
- spends more time talking about plans for the future

Preparation for Natural Termination

Preparation for termination begins with a clinician who has to come to terms with the fact that the work is coming to an end. Counselors must have correctly evaluated all reasons and correctly read their own as well as the child's signs. Once convinced that the end of treatment has indeed been reached, counselors first explore their own feelings about the impending break with the child. It is unrealistic to expect that no feelings will surface. To have seen a child through to the termination of treatment means having traveled with the child down a road that may have been difficult at times, joyous at times, but most of all, goal directed and intense. It is not always countertransferential to have strong feelings and to be ambivalent about ending. Countertransference becomes an issue only if the counselor has recognized the reasons and signs, yet chooses to continue treatment. Acceptance of feelings is paramount at this stage, as it will be important to model this process for the child once the actual process of ending treatment begins.

Next, the child's parents are consulted. In this meeting, parents need to be questioned about their perceptions of the child's readiness for termination, warned about the impending termination, prepared for behaviors and feelings that may emerge in the child during the process, and consulted about a date for the final session. However, despite the discussion of the topic with parents at this point in time, the child is informed of the ending by the clinician, not by the parents. Thus, the meeting with the parents ideally takes place directly before a session with the child, and the topic of termination is broached with both parties on the same day, requiring no secrecy on the parents' part. However, if such a schedule cannot be arranged, the parents must commit not to disclose the information to the child until it has been shared with the child by the clinician. If therapists are uncertain about parents' willingness or ability to cooperate in this endeavor, they may choose to address the topic with the child first and the parents second.

Addressing the topic of ending with a child client is often easier than anticipated. As has been pointed out, there usually have been signals from both child and therapist about an impending ending. Therefore, an easy way to approach the topic is to begin to interpret the child's hints directly during the session. For instance, one 12-year-old boy who had been seen for 34 sessions began to do many firsts, missed two sessions in one month, and began to talk about his summer vacation plans, despite summer being two months away. The therapist recognized the signals, explored the reasons, and decided that it was time to end. She approached the topic with the boy's parents, who corroborated that he had improved significantly in several realms. They agreed to allow the therapist to introduce the topic to the child and helped her to set a firm ending date, which coincided with the beginning of summer vacation. In the next session, the therapist asked the child what he thought it meant that he was spending less and less time talking about his problems at school and more and more time about his summer vacation. He responded that there were few problems left to work on and that he was ready to start a new phase in his life. The therapist probed the "new phase of life," only to find out that the boy himself had recognized that he no longer felt he needed to see the therapist as often.

In addition to showing how a child's behavior can be used to open the door for termination, this example also introduces the idea that what is a natural break in treatment anyway can be conveniently used as a termination point. In this case, treatment would have been interrupted by the child's visit with his father at the beginning of summer vacation. This natural break was used to specify a logical ending point. Further, the example points toward the importance of setting a firm date for the last session. Although some therapists (e.g., Spiegel, 1996) argue that children might not need this structure as much as adults do, as they often do not yet have a good sense of time, most child clinicians (e.g., Landreth, 2000; O'Conner, 2000) agree that it is good practice to set a date. Not only is setting a date critical, but also weekly reminders should be given to the child about the number of sessions left.

To summarize, the easiest sequence of preparing for termination is for the counselor to recognize the signals and reasons, to process personal feelings about ending, to introduce the idea to the parents, and then to broach the topic with the child in the context of interpreting signals given by the child. However, signals are not always obvious and children are not always sufficiently verbal to hear and process interpretations. In such cases, clinicians, after having met with the parents, might address termination by asking children gently how long they thought treatment might continue on. Often, children at this point express their fantasy, which is that therapy might never end. This fantasy needs to be redirected to a realistic time frame. If the child responds well, a date can then be announced. If the child appears distraught, the topic may be reintroduced again and again over a few sessions before an actual ending date is specified. Most counselors suggest that children be given ample time to process the ending of the therapeutic relationship, suggesting that two to four months be given. During this time, reminders are given, and feelings are discussed. The actual content and process of this last phase of treatment is discussed below. However, first one comment remains to be made about children who have obvious difficulties with the decision to end.

If children have difficulty ending or if parents are concerned about the process, two procedures may be considered to prepare them better. Children and parents may be weaned from treatment, or they may be allowed time to practice termination by using natural breaks to prepare them for saying their final good-bye. In the first procedure, rather than ending treatment from one session to the next, sessions are spaced farther and farther apart to give child, parent, and therapist a chance to evaluate how the child is coping with the decreased contact. This spacing can be very individually tailored to the needs of the child. Often, spacing begins by meeting every other week and then continues to meetings once per month for two to three months. However, there is no rule about how to set the weaning schedule, and this can be negotiated flexibly with the child and parent. Sometimes, if spacing between sessions is too long, the child never returns for a session that was formally defined as the last session. This represents an avoidance of the termination that is best prevented. Thus, if an appointment is missed during the weaning phase, it is crucial for the clinician to call and make an appointment for what is specified as a final session.

In the second procedure, children and parents are helped with termination by introducing vacation breaks that can be used to practice saying good-bye. This procedure obviously carries with it a component of weaning in that it also results in sessions that are spaced farther apart. However, in the weaning procedure, the emphasis is on whether and how the child tolerates the longer breaks between sessions. In the practicing procedure, the emphasis is on saying good-bye and slowly letting go of the clinician. A combination of both procedures is obviously easy to design and often used.

Once children, the families, and therapists have prepared for termination by discussing the ending and setting a date, the actual process of termination has been set in motion. This phase of treatment has some features that are quite distinct from the therapy or counseling process in general and warrants some discussion.

Process of Natural Termination

The process of termination is ushered in and is almost inseparable from the preparation for ending. It is a gradual process that helps children (and clinicians) adapt to the idea that therapeutic relationships do end. If plenty of warning is possible (two to four months), the early stages of the termination process are quite innocuous. During these first few weeks, the clinician might merely remind the child of the termination date and count down the weeks with the child. Up to about the fourth to the last session, not much actual processing of separation might need to be done directly, though it is likely to be expressed in the child's play, stories, art, or behavior.

General Guidelines

When in the last month of treatment, the clinician gently helps the child confront the ending. Not only are the final date and number of sessions remaining mentioned at the beginning of each session, the child is also asked to express feelings about ending. A variety of affects tend to emerge in this phase of termination and these are discussed in detail and context below. In general, regardless of the type of feeling that emerges, children are encouraged to own their feelings and express them. Counselors also own their feelings, in a significant change from how they used to relate to the child. Specifically, although most therapists have chosen not to self-disclose to the child up to this point in treatment, most now disclose their own reactions to ending therapy. They speak to their sadness and disappointment, but also to their excitement about what being ready for ending implies. This self-disclosure paves the way for exploring what termination means and what has been accomplished in treatment. This shifts the focus to a positive one, as the gains tend to outweigh the losses in a natural termination. Thus, child and clinician might discuss the growth they have seen together in the child; they might address the child's increased ability to cope, set limits, and solve problems; they discuss how the child's problems have decreased and how general emotional well-being has improved. In this process, they work toward a true appreciation and enjoyment of the child's improvement, placing termination in a positive and joyous light.

This process of exploring gains is not to imply that there no sadness about ending the special relationship between child and counselor. This sadder aspect of termination is clearly acknowledged. The two individuals might talk about how they will miss one another, what they have enjoyed and endeavored together, and what it will be like not to meet anymore. Also, often some work is left to be done for the child, and this is the time to talk about this work and encourage the child to do it and to feel confident to do it alone, without the clinician. This review of the therapy or counseling process and preparation for the future are done over several sessions and represent an ending ritual in and of themselves (O'Conner, 2000). However, the clinician and child might choose to add an official ending ceremony to their last session. Perhaps they can paint a picture together that the child can keep and that shows the changes in the child; perhaps they share food for the first time; or perhaps they choose a toy from the playroom that the child may keep as a memento of treatment. Most therapists agree that a gift at the end of the last session given to the child may be an appropriate way to provide a transition and to symbolize that children take something away from treatment even if they will never see the clinician again (e.g., Spiegel, 1996).

Some therapists endorse leaving the door open and letting the child know that she or he can return for further sessions if the need arises. For instance, O'Conner (2000) suggests giving children a business card at the end of the last session to signal that they may return and may contact the clinician again. In leaving the door open, it is important to do so in such way as not to suggest that this termination is not really an ending. Termination is final. Termination with the expectation to meet again is never clean and tends to fail. Thus, if the door is left open, it is left open as a generic invitation to seek services again if large problems arise, and it is clear that services can be sought from any, not just this, clinician.

In the process of reviewing treatment progress, anticipating future challenges, and engaging in self-exploration and mutual affective self-disclosure, many feelings and behaviors emerge in the child that are dealt with as they occur. To prevent parental overreaction, parents are warned that some of these feelings or actions may spill over into the child's day-to-day life. Helping parents anticipate a child's potential regression and return to previously conquered symptoms during the termination process makes them accomplices who help facilitate the process as opposed to turning them into critics who begin to doubt the timing of termination or the entire value of treatment. In other words, as therapists and parents are faced with children's termination feelings, they must remain aware of the context and the ephemeral nature of expressed affects.

The types and strength of expressed termination affects are somewhat unpredictable and vary greatly from child to child (Landreth, 2000, 2002a). They can range from easy acceptance to anger, in all kinds of gradations. Common feelings include fear and anger expressed toward the clinician. Sadness may be expressed at the anticipated loss of the relationships, and feelings of "unloveworthiness" (Dodds, 1985, p. 153) might surface. However, the child might also express pride or excitement over the accomplishments of counseling and may be quite delighted to end treatment, viewing it as a milestone of great positive significance. Often, symptoms reappear in children during the last weeks of treatment, and the child may be less able to cope. It is critical to see this regression in the context of termination and not overreact to it. Instead, the behavior is interpreted to the child as an attempt to prevent ending, and the child is reminded that a termination date has been set and will not be altered. Again, keeping parents apprised of this process and involving them in it will greatly support it.

Stages of Termination

The behaviors and affects children tend to show during the termination phase can best be understood if they are placed in a comprehensive framework of how human beings tend to deal with loss. One framework that has been developed in the past for exploring and understanding people's reactions to loss is that of the stages of adaptation to death and dying outlined by Kübler-Ross (1971, 1975). Kübler-Ross observed in her work with terminally ill patients and their families that the patient, as well as the family members, passed through distinct phases of affect in the process of adapting to the thought of death or the loss of a loved one. Specifically, people facing death or the loss of a loved one tended to respond with initial denial, followed by anger, which tended to result in the attempt to bargain with a higher power to prevent the loss, which was followed by depression when bargaining did not result in a change of the situation, and finally by acceptance of the inevitability of the situation. Although the stages tended to occur most commonly in this order, Kübler-Ross conceded that for some individuals, stages overlap, may be skipped, or may occur in a different order.

Although these stages, or reactions, were conceptualized specifically with death and dying in mind, they can be applied to many other situations involving significant losses in people's lives. The loss of a friend can be equally tragic and can result in the same sequence of feelings and behaviors, whether the friend is lost to death, a geographic relocation, or some other ending. Thus, in discussing children's termination behaviors and affects, Kübler-Ross's stage theory is applied as a framework for the conceptual understanding of what is occurring between child and clinician during termination. The stages may occur in any order, though acceptance is always last. Some children may skip a particular stage or go through more than one stage at once. For ease of presentation, however, Kübler-Ross's (1971) original order is maintained in the following discussion and the overview in Table 14.1.

Table 14.1   Stages of a Natural Termination

Stage	Child's Behavior	Clinician's Intervention
Denial	• ignores the clinician • avoids the topic of ending • represses the information • pretends not to have heard the clinician	• works to get the child's attention • brings up the topic repeatedly • discusses the topic until convinced the child heard it
Anger	• behaves aggressively • plays out aggressive, seemingly unrelated scenes • blames the clinician • behaves with anger or hostility toward the clinician	• recognizes child's affect and behavior in the context of ending • interprets child's behavior and affect • helps child express anger, frustration
Bargaining	• reports return of symptoms • reports appearance of new problems • openly tries to negotiate an extension of treatment • finds reasons why not to end treatment	• recognizes old symptoms and new problems in context of ending • interprets child's symptoms, problems • holds firmly to the original ending date
Depression	• expresses sadness over the loss of the relationship • may evidence mild symptoms of depression • fears loss of therapeutic progress without the clinician • grieves the loss of the relationship and the treatment process	• recognizes any symptoms of depression in context of ending • interprets child's symptoms and fears • expresses own feeling of loss and sadness • models grieving process for child • acknowledges/validates feelings
Acceptance	• accepts the inevitability of ending • reviews treatment process • reviews and recognizes own progress • makes plans for future • says farewell to the clinician • has bittersweet feelings	• models acceptance • helps review the therapy process • helps review child's progress • models leave-taking • delights in child's progress • shares own feelings

Denial.   The first introduction of termination with children is not uncommonly met with denial similar to that encountered in family members of a dying patient. In an attempt to deny the inevitability of the ending of the special relationship, the child might ignore the clinician when the subject is broached or might make light of the subject in such a manner as to deny the potential impact of the ending of the relationship. Denial is one of the major reasons why the topic of termination is introduced with sufficient advance warning so that it may be reintroduced repeatedly, each repetition making the child's denial more difficult. Sometimes, denial is so pronounced that special care needs to be taken to ascertain that the client has heard the therapist and has registered the meaning of the message. For instance, one child, upon being asked how long he thought he would keep coming to see the counselor, indicated his belief that counseling would last forever. The counselor proceeded to explain the realistic time limits of treatment and tried to negotiate an ending time with the child. The boy turned away from the counselor and ignored her quite effectively, engaging in a number of activities such as hammering and pounding that made hearing her extraordinarily difficult. The counselor decided to interpret his behavior for him, explaining that she understood his wish to continue forever and that it was difficult and sad for him to imagine not coming back. The child stopped his hammering but never acknowledged the communication of the counselor during this session. His denial made it extremely important for the counselor to continue bringing up the topic in ensuing sessions. The child finally conceded that he understood he needed to end but also explained that it was not time for him to do so because he had started wetting his bed again. This return of symptoms signaled to the counselor that the boy now indeed had received the message of having to terminate. Moving on to a later stage in the process of adjusting to ending, he was now bargaining for at least an extension of the experience.

Sometimes denial is well veiled under a cover of easy acceptance. This form of denial may operate when a child denies the potential impact of ending and responds without affect. For instance, one adult client, when presented with ending the therapy relationship, indicated that she of course had thought of the fact that therapy needed to end and that she was prepared to face this termination when it came. She showed no significant affect or concern, and the therapist proceeded to set a date with the client. Because she accepted the date easily, he assumed that he did not need to remind her carefully and failed to bring up termination during several subsequent sessions. Finally, in the last month of treatment, he reminded her that only four sessions remained for the two of them to say good-bye. The client feigned shock and surprise, indicating that she had no idea that treatment needed to be ended. When the therapist reminded her of their prior conversation, she denied any recollection of it and, even when shown progress notes from that session, insisted that the therapist may have meant to bring the issue up to her but failed to. She then proceeded to get angry, signaling that she had moved onto the next stage of dealing with her impending loss.

Anger.   Denial is most commonly followed by anger, as in the example above. Anger can be expressed by children in a number of ways and needs to be understood in the context of ending, rather than as a reemergence of original anger and hostility. The better prepared clinicians are for children's anger, the easier it is for them to refrain from personalizing the anger and feeling guilty about abandoning the children.

Guilt feelings for the counselor are a possible occurrence at this time because the child's anger often targets the therapist as the reason for the destruction of a beautiful relationship, the source of a felt rejection or abandonment, and the harbinger of unnecessary and unfeeling news. Sometimes, anger is externalized, blame being directed toward parents or school, which serve as reasons the child conjures up to maintain a positive image of the clinician. In either event, the therapy refrains from letting the object of the child's anger become the focus of the interpretation or the anger, keeping firmly in mind that the child is angry at the process of having to end. It is important to realize that the anger might not be expressed immediately after termination is discussed but may become an issue later in the same session or during a subsequent session.

For example, when termination was discussed with a 10-year-old girl, she proceeded to cooperate in setting a date and expressed her agreement with the therapist that she indeed had improved significantly. When the topic felt settled to both child and therapist for the time being, the girl turned to her usual play with puppets. However, her puppet play had an unusual flavor during this session and became increasing aggressive and hostile. Soon two of her favorite puppets (often interpreted by the therapist as a representation of the child and the therapist or the child and her ideal self) engaged in a particularly fierce argument and then began a physical fight. They were quarreling vehemently over preparing a guest list for a birthday party and could not agree upon whom to invite. Rather than settling the problem rationally and calmly, as the child had clearly learned over the course of treatment, the puppets decide to engage in a fist fight and let the winner decide the guest list. The puppet that usually represented the child won the fight and proceeded to tell the other puppet that everyone she knew would be invited except the other puppet (the puppet often representing the therapist). She explained her decision by indicating that the (therapist) puppet had been very mean to her and did not deserve to see her ever again. The therapist easily understood the message delivered by the child so eloquently: She had disappointed the girl by severing the relationship and needed to be punished. The therapist allowed the child her anger and did not attempt to intervene in the puppet play. She decided instead to wait and see whether the girl would be able to resolve her anger on her own, which she was able to do in her next session. Only after having evidence that the child felt less angry and had resolved some of her feelings of rejection and abandonment did the therapist introduce the notion that some of the child's strong feelings might be related to ending treatment. The girl began to cry and revealed that she was very afraid of saying good-bye, fearing that she would once again feel as poorly about herself as she had when treatment began. She had moved to a more advanced stage in the termination process.

Bargaining. Often, facing the inevitability of ending and having expressed anger results in a final attempt on the child's part to change the situation. This attempt, called bargaining, is directed either toward never ending treatment or toward at least extending it for a while. Whereas dying patients are reported to do much of their bargaining with a higher power in the attempt to extend their lives, children bargain with the clinician to stay in therapy or counseling just a little bit longer. Bargaining is not necessarily a conscious endeavor, though it may be. Conscious bargaining may be reflected in children's attempts to negotiate a later ending date or in promises to make certain changes in exchange for additional sessions. However, unconscious bargaining is much more common among children (and adults, for that matter). The return of symptoms or the emergence of new problems represents a child's attempt to bargain for extra time. After all, if one goal was for the child to stop having bad dreams, the return of such dreams may result in renewed efforts on the clinician's part, which may lead to a postponement of the termination date. Or if a child indeed improved in all areas targeted by treatment, perhaps the emergence of a new problem, such as acting out at school, may convince parents and clinicians to continue treatment a while longer.

Return of symptoms and sudden new problems after having negotiated an ending date are understood in the context of bargaining and are not given in to. Instead, the therapist helps the child understand what is occurring. It is typically important not to extend the termination date at this time but rather to stress to bargaining-children that they will indeed be ready to end when the agreed-upon time comes, regardless of the current crisis. Consultation with, and preparation of, parents is crucial during this phase of termination, as they might otherwise become unknowing accomplices of their child. In other words, parents need to be warned about the possible reemergence of problems and need to be helped to understand them in the context of bargaining. This prevents overreaction to the behavior, and thus reinforcement of it, by well-meaning parents.

For instance, in the above example of the boy who once again began bed-wetting, his foster parents had been warned that some return of symptoms could occur during the ending phase of treatment. Therefore, when the bed indeed was wet, in the morning, they responded matter-of-factly, asked him to help remove and launder the sheets, and encouraged him not to worry too much about the problem. Because they had been warned by the counselor, they were able to keep from panicking and reinforcing the child's bargaining position by joining his effort to convince the counselor that treatment must continue. The boy wet his bed twice in one week, then never wet it again as he began to accept termination and began to realize that his treatment gains could be maintained even without weekly sessions.

Depression.   Depression is a common affect expressed by children during the ending phase. It can range from rather severe-appearing dysphoria with decreased psychomotor movement, self-disparaging comments, slight insomnia, or temporary loss of appetite to mild feelings of sadness. Fortunately, the latter is much more common than the former in natural terminations (though not necessarily during forced terminations). The expression of sadness about ending the relationship with the clinician is often a most important component of working through termination. It helps children express their attachment to the clinician and their sadness over the loss. Healthy expression of sadness usually leads to recognition of the positive aspects of the relationship that are not lost even after termination, thus leading to acceptance, and, in fact, to a joyous and proud ending of treatment. Sadness is also often felt by the clinician, and this appears to be accepted as an appropriate time for self-disclosure, even among therapists who do not usually do so. Counselor might share with children that they too feel sad about not seeing the child any longer and model that sadness can be part of saying good-bye without overshadowing the positive implications of ending therapy or counseling.

For instance, in the example of the girl with the puppets, her anger had given way to expressed sadness. This sadness was not just the grieving of the loss of the therapist, but also an expression of her fear that losing the therapist implied a loss of her progress in treatment to date. Addressing the fear of losing ground is an important aspect of working through the depression phase. The therapist helps the child to recognize that progress is independent of continued meetings and can maintain without weekly meetings. Generally, if children are indeed ready for a natural termination, sufficient self-esteem has been internalized by this time in treatment that they are able to hear the clinician's message. The depression stage is therefore helpful in allowing children to recognize the temporary nature of sadness as well as the continuity of change and general strengthening of the self.

Acceptance. Once children have understood the inevitability of ending, expressed anger at it, attempted to bargain an extension, and expressed sadness over their loss, acceptance of the termination typically follows naturally. By progressing through the prior stages, children have explored all possibilities to extend treatment and processed important feelings connected with the loss of the counseling relationship. Child and clinician have come to realize that there is continuity in child's progress, that the child has grown and is capable of saying good-bye in a productive way. Having dealt with these possibilities and affects, child and clinician are ready to explore the positives of their relationship and their work and to move to an acceptance of the termination that is full of joy and pride, despite any sadness over the loss of a relationship. The phase of acceptance, in other words, is the phase during which children and clinicians review treatment progress, explore changes made, acknowledge the special nature of their relationship, and become aware of the positive implications ending treatment. Both recognize the importance of the relationship, and may choose to reveal that they will always keep alive a memory of the other person, even if they should never see one another again. The exchange of a gift or the sharing of a closing ritual can become a symbol of acceptance that the relationship in its present form has come to an end. An example of a last session that was beautifully executed and that reflected acceptance follows:

> Michelle, a 10-year-old girl who had been in treatment with Kate for 24 sessions appeared for her final session with a small book she had prepared for the therapist as a parting gift. The book was her depiction of the treatment process as she understood it. Therapist and child had discussed the child's progress in treatment over the last three to four sessions in preparation of the last session and had agreed in the previous session that their last time together would be spent briefly recapping major milestones in treatment and preparing a picture together that would symbolize their work and relationship. The book Michelle brought had been prepared to help the two individuals look at milestones through the child's eyes and was a beautiful collection of pictures and stories that had been developed in treatment. After having read the book, therapist and child went to work on their picture. Michelle drew a very small heart in blue and black, then a very large heart in shades of orange and red. While preparing her picture, she revealed that when she came for treatment, she felt as though she had a very small heart when she first met the therapist—a heart that had no room for other

people and that she used to protect herself. (Michelle had been passed from foster home to foster home while her parents were abusing drugs; after 5 years they relinquished parental rights, and Michelle was adopted by her mother's brother and his partner; she was referred to treatment at the same time she moved in with this couple.) The large heart represented her at termination, when she felt open to people and felt loved by the world around her. The therapist drew a number of people who all looked quite confused and circled around a little child who sat in the middle crying. She explained that when Michelle first came to therapy, that is how her world looked to the therapist. Then Kate drew a man, a woman, and Michelle in a house with large windows and an open door. Outside were numerous children and adults, whom she identified by names as some of Michelle's friends and herself. She explained that now Michelle's world looked much more orderly and inviting and that Michelle was now able to accept friends into her world without being frightened. The picture was given to Michelle as a parting gift. Both therapist and child reiterated how important their work had become to both of them and that they would never forget each other. The therapist did not deem it important to let Michelle know that she could always return to treatment if the need arose, as Michelle was strong and had supportive parents who had been reminded of this fact earlier. At the end of the session, the following dialogue occurred:

MICHELLE: I know I will miss you, but I have our picture, and if I forget that I am strong now, I can look at it and then I'll remember. But I think I'll still miss you a lot!

KATE: I will miss you too because you are very special. But I can always look at your book, and then you are with me all over again. That way I can be with you without having to see you.

MICHELLE: Just like I can do with the picture . . .

KATE: Yes, and even if you ever lost the picture, you could just close your eyes and remember all the hard work you did, and that will help you make it through tough times!

MICHELLE: Yes, I can just close my eyes and see this room and Trudy (*the name for one of her favorite puppets*).

KATE: Goodbye, Michelle. I'll miss you, and I am a sad, but I'm mainly proud and happy for you. Goodbye (*hugs the child*).

MICHELLE: Bye-bye, Kate. I love you. (*They stop their embrace, and the child goes to meet her adoptive parents in the waiting room; this time the therapist does not accompany her out of the room.*)

Premature Termination

Not all children are lucky enough to experience a natural termination. Many more are forced out of treatment for any number of reasons. However, the process of ending is not neglected, even if it arrives prematurely and quickly. If ending is forced (i.e., therapist-initiated), it tends to be more easily dealt with than if it is unilateral (i.e., client-initiated), because the therapist has taken care to have left a sufficient number of sessions to make the termination process as natural as possible. In this case, the process outlined for a natural termination is almost entirely applicable, only to be modified to include a discussion of work that is left to be done. If the ending is arranged suddenly by client or external factors, the counselor must insist on having as much time as possible to say good-bye to the child (Norton and Norton, 2006; Spiegel, 1996). In these last sessions, the clinician attempts to deal with the child's anger, bargaining, depression, and other feelings to try to facilitate acceptance and readiness to seek services elsewhere. Meetings with parents are crucial and used to review the progress of their child while also pointing out the work left to be done. If the termination results from resistance, this may be difficult to do but is attempted nevertheless. If external factors forced the termination, parents are often grateful for a few final meetings as they want help in setting up continued treatment for their child. The counselor can then help facilitate a transfer.

One feeling that does not generally arise during the natural termination process but is common in premature terminations is a feeling of helplessness. Regardless of how a premature termination takes place, children generally feel as though they had no control over the decision (unless of course it is the child who refuses to return to treatment, in which case the therapist must explore what went wrong in treatment). This sense of helplessness must be dealt with in the same manner as anger and hurt in a natural termination. This may be difficult, especially if the clinician feels helpless as well. For instance, one child was forced to terminate prematurely by external circumstances. Her custodial arrangement between her biological mother and father had suddenly and arbitrarily been changed by a court decision. This change resulted in the child's geographic relocation to a distant city in the same state. The child and her biological father had long opposed and fought this court decision, and both now felt very helpless and frightened. They looked toward the therapist to feel more empowered, but she felt equally helpless and unable to exert control over the situation. Nevertheless, she was very aware that she needed to control her experience of helplessness and must not let it show during sessions to be able to help her clients cope. Therefore, the therapist initiated consultation with a colleague to help her deal with her sense of helplessness and anger at a judicial system that allowed this situation to occur. Consultation made her better able to face the parent and child, yet did not suffice to make termination a positive or happy one.

Fortunately, therapists do not always feel as helpless as children and can usually help the children deal with their sense of helplessness in an efficient and therapeutic manner. For instance, in one case, an 8-year-old boy was quite angry, hurt, and helpless about his mother's decision to leave the state and start a new career. This move was doubly difficult for the boy, as it meant not only leaving treatment prematurely but also leaving friends and, most important, his biological father, whom he visited regularly. The boy felt betrayed by his mother and believed that there was nothing he could do to change his fate. In addressing his sense of helplessness in treatment, it became clear that he had never told his often-absent mother how important his visits with his father were to him. He was encouraged to do so and to explore the possibility of maintaining contact. The child did indeed talk to his mother (as did the clinician) and received permission to initiate a phone call once a week, receive unlimited phone calls, initiate one visit a month, and accept an unlimited number of invitations for visits. The mother agreed to allow the boy to visit his father for three months in the summer and to recontact the therapist during those times. These solutions were very effective in helping the boy overcome his sense of helplessness in this situation and to increase his self-confidence in shaping his own fate.

No doubt, not all cases of helplessness have a solution that is as obvious or easy. However, all generally have some way in which children can be helped to feel more a part of the decision or to be able to at least acknowledge the imposition. Counselors need to help children see opportunities and must not be shy about scheduling meetings with parents to help them gain empathy with their child's plight and right for self-determination.

Special Issues in Premature Termination

There are a at least two noteworthy special issues related to premature terminations, namely, therapy transfers and therapy contracts for therapies that are time-limited from the outset. Therapy transfers are common when premature termination is initiated by clinicians and somewhat likely if client-initiated termination is not due to resistance but other mitigating circumstances. When a therapy transfer is necessary, it is best if the termination process for a natural termination is followed with an eye toward special feelings that tend to emerge in premature termination. However, all along in the process, focus is not on ending a relationship *and* a process, but only on ending the relationship without ending the process of treatment. This procedure is shorter than a strict termination, as the child only needs to say goodbye to the clinician, not the counseling experience. Although this might appear to make the process easier, this is not necessarily the case. Some clinicians have to face their own countertransferences at this time. It is not uncommon to hear therapists discuss with consultants the question of to whom to refer their clients. There is often an underlying fantasy that the client may never be as well served by a new therapist. It is important for clinicians to realize that is not necessarily true so that children are not indirectly set up to reject their new clinician.

Some clinicians recommend that a new therapist be introduced in the last few sessions with the current clinician to let the child and new provider become acquainted in the presence of the trusted clinician. It is possible, however, that such an arrangement may interfere with the process of saying good-bye to the "old" therapist as the child may be encouraged simply to switch attachment to the new person without facing feelings about ending an important relationship. This procedure may also set up the new therapist to be directly compared with the previous therapist, making the new person an easy target of the anger that could not be freely expressed in an individual interaction with the therapist who is leaving the child. Thus, before inviting a second clinician into the session, the clinician should explore whether this procedure indeed serves to enhance the leave-taking or whether it merely serves to make a difficult situation easier by cloaking or avoiding it.

If at all possible, transfers should take place at a natural break in treatment, so that the child has time to process the absence of the previous clinician before entering into a new therapeutic relationship. Some clinicians suggest that the transfer therapist be more experienced than the original therapist, owing to the special needs of a client in beginning work with a new therapist. This may be a justifiable position therapeutically but is often neither possible nor completely free of countertransference issues. In other words, most commonly, transfers occur because a trainee has finished a practical experience in a clinic. Usually, the child is then picked up by the trainee replacing the original counselor. It is rare that the child is transferred to a regular staff clinician. In some circumstances, the child might be transferred to the child's supervisor. This appears to be one of the most successful ways of conducting a transfer, as it provides continuity in the approach to treatment and the theoretical orientation favored by the clinician and meets the criterion of replacing the old with a more experienced therapist.

Some treatments are begun with the knowledge that the relationship between child and clinician will be shorter than the course of therapy will require. This is again most commonly true for cases involving a trainee therapist or counselor. Planning for termination and transfer is important in these cases, as is preparing child and family from the very first session. Children and their families have a right to be informed if clinicians are available for only a certain number of weeks and if this time frame is not long enough to complete treatment. The inevitability of a transfer is introduced from the beginning in the service of ethics and professionalism.

Summary and Concluding Thoughts

Terminations are difficult for clinician and child, yet they are crucial to maintaining the child's treatment progress after having to say good-bye to a clinician. Through a successful termination process, children are able to leave the treatment situation and clinician with minimal difficulty and are able to consolidate and continue the change and growth they attained. A major effect of termination is the practicing of leave-taking from important relationships in a child's life. As such, termination prepares children for the task of separating from parents during adolescence and from taking leave from other important people. Additionally and importantly, children's perceptions of termination may affect their perception of the entire treatment process. With a successful termination, children are more likely to have positive memories of treatment; a negative termination experience may flavor the entire experience in a negative manner. Termination can be difficult for clinicians, especially if they have developed a close relationship with the child. The greatest challenge occurs if clinicians are torn between wanting to continue the relationship and being aware that children must go off on their own to complete their therapeutic growth. Whether symbolically or verbally, all of these issues need to be addressed in the last few sessions, as discussed above. The ending of treatment is indeed as important as its beginning.

Bibliography

Abela, J. R. Z., and Hankin, B. L. (Eds.). (2007). *Handbook of Depression in Children and Adolescents.* New York: Guilford.

Ablon, S. L. (1988). Developmental forces and termination in child analysis. *International Journal of Psychoanalysis, 69,* 97–104.

Aboff, M. (2003). *Uncle Willy's Tickles: A Child's Right to Say No* (2nd ed.). New York: Magination.

Achenbach, T. M., and Rescorla, L. A. (2007). *Multicultural Understanding of Child and Adolescent Psychopathology: Implications for Mental Health Assessment.* New York: Guilford.

Achenbach, T. M., and McConaughy, S. H. (1996). *Empirically Based Assessment of Child & Adolescent Psychopathology: Practical Applications* (2nd ed.). Thousand Oaks, CA: Sage.

Achenbach, T. M., and Rescorla, L. A. (2000). *Manual for ASEBA Preschool Forms & Profiles.* Burlington, VT: University of Vermont, Research Center for Children, Youth, & Families.

Achenbach, T. M., and Rescorla, L. A. (2001). *Manual for ASEBA School-Age Forms & Profiles.* Burlington, VT: University of Vermont, Research Center for Children, Youth, & Families.

Adams, P. L. (1982). *A Primer of Child Psychotherapy* (2nd ed.). Boston: Little, Brown, & Company.

Alcantara, C., and Gone, J. P. (2007). Reviewing suicide in Native American communities: Situating risk and protective factors within a transactional-ecological framework. *Death Studies, 31,* 457–477.

Allen, J. (2007). A multicultural assessment supervision model to guide research and practice. *Professional Psychology: Research and Practice, 38,* 248–258.

Altman, N., Briggs, R., Frankel, J., Gensler, D., and Pantone, P. (2002). *Relational Child Psychotherapy.* New York: The Other Press.

American Counseling Association. (2005). *ACA Code of Ethics.* Alexandria, VA: Author.

American Psychiatric Association. (1987). *Diagnostic and Statistical Manual of Mental Disorders* (3rd ed., Rev.). Washington, DC: Author.

American Psychiatric Association. (1994). *Diagnostic and Statistical Manual of Mental Disorders* (4th ed.). Washington, DC: Author.

American Psychiatric Association. (2000). *Diagnostic and Statistical Manual of Mental Disorders* (4th ed., text rev.). Washington, DC: Author.

American Psychological Association. (1987a). Resolutions approved by the National Conference on Graduate Education in Psychology. *American Psychologist, 42,* 1070–1084.

American Psychological Association. (1987b). Model act for state licensure of psychologists. *American Psychologist, 42,* 696–703.

American Psychological Association. (2002). Ethical principles of psychologists and code of conduct. *American Psychologist, 57,* 1060–1073.

American School Counselor Association. (2004). *Ethical Standards for School Counselors.* Alexandria, VA: Author.

Anastasi, A. (1997). *Psychological Testing* (7th ed.). New York: Prentice-Hall.

Anderson, B. S. (1996). *The Counselor and the Law* (4th ed.). Alexandria, VA: American Counseling Association.

Anderson, M. J. (2001, February 2). Bush team signals new U.N. direction. *WorldNetDaily.com.* Retrieved October 16, 2007, from http://www.wnd.com/news/article.asp?ARTICLE_ID =21590.

Änggård, E. (2005). Barbie princesses and dinosaur dragons: Narration as a way of doing gender. *Gender & Education, 17,* 539–553.

Armour-Thomas, E., and Gopaul-McNicol, S. A. (1998). *Assessing Intelligence: Applying a Bio-cultural Model.* Thousand Oaks, CA: Sage.

Atkinson, D. R., Morten, G., and Sue, D. W. (2003). *Counseling American Minorities: A Cross Cultural Perspective* (6th ed.). Dubuque, IA: William C. Brown.

Attwood, T. (2006). *The Complete Guide to Asperger's Syndrome.* London: Jessica Kingsley.

Autti-Raemoe, I. (2000). Twelve-year follow-up of children exposed to alcohol in utero. *Developmental Medicine & Child Neurology, 42,* 406–411

Axline, V. (1947). *Play Therapy.* New York: Ballantine.

Bakur Weiner, M., and Neimark J. (1995). *I Want Your Moo: A Story for Children about Self-Esteem.* New York: Magination.

Bandura, A. (1999). Social cognitive theory of personality. In L. A. Pervin and O. P. John (Eds.), *Handbook of Personality: Theory and Research* (2nd ed., pp. 154–196). New York: Guilford.

Barker, P. (1990). *Clinical Interviews with Children and Adolescents.* New York: W.W. Norton & Company.

Barkley, R. A. (2000). *Taking Charge of ADHD: The Complete Authoritative Guide for Parents* (revised ed.). New York: Guilford.

Barkley, R. A. (2005). *Attention Deficit Hyperactivity Disorder: A Handbook for Diagnosis and Treatment* (3rd ed.). New York: Guilford.

Barnett, O. W., Miller-Perrin, C. L., and Perrin, R. D. (2004). *Family Violence across the Lifespan: An Introduction* (2nd ed.). Thousand Oaks, CA: Sage.

Barrett-Lennard, G. (1981). The empathy cycle: Refinement of a nuclear concept. *Journal of Counseling Psychology, 28,* 91–100.

Baumrind, D. (1973). The development of instrumental competence through socialization. In A. D. Pick (Ed.), *Minnesota Symposia on Child Psychology* (Vol. 7, pp. 3–46). Minneapolis: University of Minnesota Press.

Beck, J. S., Beck, A. T., and Jolly, J. (2005). *Manual for the Beck Youth Inventories, Second Edition.* San Antonio, TX: Harcourt Assessment.

Becvar, D. S., and Becvar, R. J. (2005). *Family Therapy: A Systemic Integration* (6th ed.). Boston: Allyn & Bacon.

Beidel, D. C., and Turner, S. M. (2007). *Shy Children, Phobic Adults: Nature and Treatment of Social Anxiety Disorders* (2nd ed.). Washington, DC: American Psychological Association.

Beirne-Smith, M., Patton, J. M., and Kim, S. H. (2005). *Mental Retardation: An Introduction to Intellectual Disability* (7th ed.). New York: Prentice-Hall

Bellak, L. (1943). *The Thematic Apperception Test.* Cambridge, MA: Harvard University Press.

Bellak, L. (1997). *The T.A.T., C.A.T., and S.A.T. in Clinical Use* (6th ed.). New York: Grune & Stratton.

Bellak, L., and Bellak, S. S. (1949). *Children's Apperception Test.* Larchmont, NY: CPS.

Bellak, L., and Bellak, S. S. (1965). *Children's Apperception Test-Human Figures.* Larchmont, NY: CPS.

Bellini, S., and Akullian, J. (2007). A meta-analysis of video modeling and self-modeling interventions for children and adolescents with autism spectrum disorders. *Exceptional Children, 73,* 264–287.

Bellinson, J. (2002). *Children's Use of Board Games in Psychotherapy.* Lanham, MD: Jason Aronson.

Berk, L. E. (2006). *Child Development* (7th ed.). Boston: Allyn & Bacon.

Bernstein, I., and Glenn, J. (1988). The child and adolescent analyst's emotional reactions to his patients and their parents. *International Review of Psycho-Analysis, 15,* 225–241.

Bersoff, D. N. (2003) *Ethical Conflicts in Psychology* (3rd ed.). Washington, DC: American Psychological Association.

Billick, S. B., Burgert, W., Friberg, G., Downer, A. V., and Bruni-Solhkhah, S. (2001). A clinical study of competency to consent to treatment in pediatrics. *Journal of the American Academy of Psychiatry and Law, 29,* 298–302.

Billick, S. B., Edwards, J. L., Burgert, W., Serlen, J. R., and Bruni, S. M. (1998) A clinical study of competency in child psychiatric inpatients. *Journal of the American Academy of Psychiatry and Law, 26,* 587–594.

Bion, W. R. (1959). Attacks on linking. *International Journal of Psychoanalysis, 40,* 308–315.

Birmaher, B., Ryan, N. D., Williamson, D. E., Brent, D. A., Kaufman, J., Dahl, R. E., Perel, J., and Nelson, B. (1996). Childhood and adolescent depression: A review of the past 10 years. *Journal of the American Academy of Child & Adolescent Psychiatry, 35,* 1427–1439.

Bjorklund, D. F. (2004). *Children's Thinking: Cognitive Development and Individual Differences* (4th ed.). Belmont, CA: Wadsworth.

Blom, R. (2004). *Handbook of Gestalt Play Therapy: Practical Guidelines for Child Therapists.* London: Jessica Kingsley.

Blomquist, G. M., and Blomquist, P. B. (1990). *Zachary's New Home: A Story for Foster and Adopted Children.* New York: Magination.

Boik, B. L., and Goodwin, E. A. (2000). *Sandplay Therapy: A Step-By-Step Manual for Psychotherapists of Diverse Orientations.* New York: Norton.

Bornstein, B. (1948). Emotional barriers in the understanding and treatment of young children. *American Journal of Orthopsychiatry, 18,* 691–697.

Bourg, W., Broderick, R., Flagor, R., Kelly, D. M., Ervin, D. L., and Butler, J. (1999). A *Child Interviewer's Guidebook.* Thousand Oaks, CA: Sage.

Bowlby, J. (1999). *Separation Anxiety and Anger* (Vol. 2). New York: Basic.

Bradley, J. D. D., and Golden, C. J. (2001). Biological contributions to the presentation and understanding of *attention-deficit/*hyperactivity disorder: A review. *Clinical Psychology Review, 21,* 907–929.

Brandell, J. R. (2000). *Of Mice and Metaphors: Therapeutic Storytelling with Children.* New York: Basic.

Brandell, J. R., and Ringel, S. (2007). *Attachment and Dynamic Practice: An Integrative Guide for Social Workers and other Clinicians.* New York, Columbia University Press.

Bratton, S. C., Ray, D., and Rhine, T. (2005). The efficacy of play therapy with children: A meta-analytic review of treatment outcomes. *Professional Psychology: Research and Practice, 36,* 376–390.

Brave Heart-Yellowhorse, M. (2000). Wakiksuyapi: Carrying the historical trauma of the Lakota. *Tulane Studies in Social Welfare, 21-22,* 245–266

Brave Heart-Yellowhorse, M. (2003). The historical trauma response among Natives and its relationship with substance abuse: A Lakota illustration. *Journal of Psychoactive Drugs, 35,* 7–13.

Brems, C. (1989a). Dimensionality of empathy and its correlates. *Journal of Psychology, 123,* 329–337.

Brems, C. (1989b). Projective identification as a self psychological change agent in the psychotherapy of a child. *American Journal of Psychotherapy, 43,* 598–607.

Brems, C. (1990). *Manual for a Self-Psychologically Oriented Parent Education Program.* Anchorage, AK: University of Alaska Anchorage.

Brems, C. (1995). Women and depression: A comprehensive analysis. In E. E. Beckham and W. Leber (Eds.), *Handbook of Depression* (2nd ed., pp. 539–566). New York: Guilford.

Brems, C. (1996). A model for working with parents in child clinical practice. *Journal of Psychological Practice, 2,* 11–22.

Brems, C. (1998a). Implications of Daniel Stern's model of self development for child psychotherapy. *Journal of Psychological Practice, 3,* 141–159.

Brems, C. (1998b). Cultural issues in psychological assessment: Problems and possible solutions. *Journal of Psychological Practice, 4,* 88–117.

Brems, C. (1999). *Psychotherapy: Processes and Techniques.* Boston: Allyn & Bacon.

Brems, C. (2000). *Dealing with Challenges in Psychotherapy and Counseling.* Belmont, CA: Wadsworth.

Brems, C. (2001). *Basic Skills in Psychotherapy and Counseling.* Belmont, CA: Wadsworth.

Brems, C., and Sohl, M. A. (1995). The role of empathy in parenting strategy choices. *Family Relations, 44,* 189–194.

Brems, C., Baldwin, M., and Baxter, S. (1993). Empirical evaluation of a self-psychologically oriented parent education program. *Family Relations, 42,* 26–30.

Brim, O. G. (1959). *Education for Child-Rearing.* New York: Free Press.

Brislin, R. (1993). *Understanding Culture's Influence on Behavior.* Fort Worth, TX: Harcourt Brace College.

Brooks, J. B. (2008). *The Process of Parenting* (7th ed.). Mountain View, CA: Mayfield.

Brown, C. D. (2001). Therapeutic play and creative arts: Helping children cope with illness, death, and grief. In A. Armstrong-Dailey and S. Zarbock (Eds.), *Hospice Care for Children* (2nd ed., pp. 250–283). New York: Oxford University.

Browne, K. D., Hanks, H., Stratton, P., and Hamilton, C. (2002). *Early Prediction and Prevention of Child Abuse: A Handbook.* Hoboken, NJ: Wiley.

Buber, M. (1965). *Between Man and Man.* New York: Macmillan.

Buck, J. N. (1948). The H-T-P test. *Journal of Clinical Psychology, 4,* 151–159.

Buck, J. W., and Hammer, E. F. (1969). *Advances in House-Tree-Person Techniques: Variations and Applications.* Los Angeles: Western Psychological Services.

Burks, H. F. (1978). *Psychological Meanings of the Imagine Game.* Huntington Beach, CA: Arden.

Burns, R. C. (1982). *Self-Growth in Families: Kinetic-Family-Drawings Research and Applications.* New York: Routledge.

Burns, R. C. (1987). *Kinetic House-Tree-Person Drawings (K-HTP): An Interpretative Manual.* New York: Routledge.

Burns, R. C., and Kaufman, S. H. (1970). *Kinetic Family Drawings (K-F-D): An Introduction to Understanding Children through Kinetic Drawing.* New York: Routledge.

Burns, R. C., and Kaufman, S. H. (1972). *Actions, Styles, and Symbols in Kinetic Family Drawings (KFD): A Manual.* New York: Routledge.

Cain, J. (2000). *The Way I Feel.* Seattle: Parenting Press.

Cain, W. J. (2004). Telling stories: Examining the effects of elaborative style, reporting condition, and social class in preschoolers' narratives. *Merrill-Palmer Quarterly, 50,* 139–158.

Cangelosi, D. M. (1997). *Using Play to Say Goodbye: Planned, Unplanned, and Premature Endings in Child Psychotherapy.* Lanham, MD: Jason Aronson.

Cangelosi, D. M. (2002). Using play and art techniques during the ending phase of treatment. In C. E. Schaefer and D. M. Cangelosi (Eds.), *Play Therapy Techniques* (2nd ed., pp. 27–34). Lanham, MD: Jason Aronson.

Canino, I. A., and Spurlock, J. (2000). *Culturally Diverse Children and Adolescents: Assessment, Diagnosis, and Treatment* (2nd ed.). New York: Guilford.

Carroll, J. (2002). Play therapy: The children's views. *Child & Family Social Work, 7,* 177–187.

Carroll, J. B. (2005). The three-stratum theory of cognitive abilities. In D. Flanagan and P. L. Harrison (Eds.), *Contemporary Intellectual Assessment: Theories, Tests, and Issues* (2nd ed., pp. 69–76), New York: Guilford.

Carter, R. T., and Helms, J. E. (1993). White racial identity attitudes and cultural values. In J. E. Helms (Ed.), *Black and White Racial Identity: Theory, Research, and Practice* (pp. 145–163). New York: Greenwood.

Casat, C. D., and Pearson, D. A. (2001). The mental status exam in child and adolescent evaluation. In V. H. Booney and A. Pumariega (Eds.), *Clinical Assessment of Child and Adolescent Behavior* (pp. 86–97). Hoboken, NJ: Wiley.

Cattanach, A. (2006). Narrative play therapy. In C. E. Schaefer and H. G. Kaduson (Eds.), *Contemporary Play Therapy: Theory, Research, and Practice* (pp. 82–99). New York: Guilford.

Cautela, J., and Groden, J. (1982). *Relaxation: A Comprehensive Manual for Adults, Children, and Children with Special Needs.* Champaign, IL: Research Press.

Chang, C. Y., Ritter, K. B., and Hays, D. G. (2005). Multicultural trends and toys in play therapy. *International Journal of Play Therapy, 14,* 69–85.

Chazan, S. E. (2002). *Profiles of Play: Assessing and Observing Structure and Process in Play Therapy.* London: Jessica Kingsley.

Chenneville, T. (2000). HIV, confidentiality, and duty to protect: A decision-making model. *Professional Psychology: Research and Practice, 31,* 661–670.

Chess, S., and Hertzig, M. E. (1990). *Annual Progress in Child Psychiatry and Child Development.* New York: Routledge.

Chethik, M. (2003). *Techniques of Child Therapy: Psychodynamic Strategies* (2nd ed.). New York: Guilford.

Cheung, M. (2006a). *Therapeutic Games and Guided Imagery.* Chicago: Lyceum.

Cheung, M. (2006b). Muscle-group relaxation. In M. Cheung (Ed.), *Therapeutic Games and Guided Imagery* (pp. 201–203). Chicago: Lyceum.

Chorpita, B. F., and Southam-Gerow, M. A. (2006). Fears and anxiety. In E. J. Mash and R. A. Barkley (Eds.), *Treatment of Childhood Disorders* (3rd ed., pp. 271–335). New York: Guilford.

Christophersen, E. R., and Friman, P. C. (2004). Elimination disorders. In R. T. Brown (Ed.), *Handbook of Pediatric Psychology in School Settings* (3rd ed., pp. 467–487). Mahwah, NJ: Lawrence Erlbaum Associates.

Christy, V. F. (2001). Factors associated with premature termination of psychotherapy in children and adolescents. *Dissertation Abstracts International, 61(12-B),* 6698

Chused, J. F. (2000). Engaging the child in the therapeutic process. In S. T. Levy (Ed.), *The Therapeutic Alliance* (pp. 55–74). Madison, CT: International Universities.

Clarke, L.A. (2006) *Wishing Wellness: A Workbook for Children of Parents with Mental Illness.* New York: Magination.

Close, H. T. (1998). *Metaphor in Psychotherapy: Clinical Applications of Stories and Allegories.* Atascadero, CA: Impact.

Cohen, C. P., and Naimark, H. (1991). United Nations Convention on the Rights of the Child: Individual rights concepts and their significance for social science students. *American Psychologist, 46,* 60–65.

Conners, C. K. (2002). *Manual for the Conners' Rating Scales.* North Tonawanda, NY: Multi-Health Systems.

Conners, C. K. (2008). *Manual for the Conners' Rating Scales* (3rd ed.). North Tonawanda, NY: Multi-Health Systems.

Constantino, G., Dana, R. H., and Malgady, R. G. (2007). *TEMAS (Tell-Me-A-Story) Assessment in Multicultural Societies.* Mahwah, NJ: Lawrence Erlbaum Associates.

Constantino, G., Malgady, R. G., and Rogler, L. (1988). *TEMAS (Tell-Me-A-Story) Manual.* Los Angeles: Western Psychological Services.

Cooper, P., and Stein, A. (2006). *Childhood Feeding Problems and Adolescent Eating Disorders.* New York: Routledge.

Coppolillo, H. P. (1987). *Psychodynamic Psychotherapy of Children.* Madison, CT: International Universities Press.

Corey, G., Corey, M. S., and Callanan, P. (2007). *Issues and Ethics in the Helping Professions* (7th ed.). Belmont, CA: Wadsworth.

Corning, A. F, Malofeeva, E. V., and Bucchianeri, M. M. (2007). Predicting termination type from client-therapist agreement on the severity of the presenting problem. *Psychotherapy: Theory, Research, Practice, Training, 44,* 193–204

Courtney, J. A. (2007). Assessing practitioner experiences of developmental play therapy. *Dissertation Abstracts International, 67(9-A),* 3590.

Crary, E., Katayama, M., and Steelsmith, S. (1996). *When You're Happy and You Know It.* Seattle: Parenting Press.

Creadick, T. A. (1985). The role of the expressive arts in therapy. *Journal of Reading, Writing, and Learning Disabilities International, 1,* 55–60.

Cross, W. E., Jr. (1971). The Negro-to-Black conversion experience: Toward a psychology of Black liberation. *Black World, 20,* 13–17.

Crosson-Tower, C. (2008). Understanding Child Abuse and Neglect (7th ed.). Boston: Allyn & Bacon.

Dana, R. H. (1993). *Multicultural Assessment Perspectives for Professional Psychology.* Needham Heights, MA: Allyn & Bacon.

Dana, R. H. (1996). Thematic Apperception Test (TAT). In C. S. Newmark (Ed.), *Major Psychological Assessment Instruments* (2nd ed., pp. 166–205). Boston: Allyn & Bacon.

DasGupta, S., Meyer, D., Calero-Breckheimer, A., Costley, A. W., and Guillen, S. (2006). Teaching cultural competency through narrative medicine: Intersections of classroom and community. *Teaching & Learning in Medicine, 2006, 18,* 14–17

Davis, C. (2006). Difference. In White, K. (Ed.), *Unmasking Race, Culture, and Attachment in the Psychoanalytic Space: Why Do We See? What Do We Think? What Do We Feel?* (pp. 46–53). London: Karnac.

Dewey, D., and Tupper, D. E. (2004). *Developmental Motor Disorders: A Neuropsychological Perspective.* New York: Guilford.

Dinnel, D. L, Kleinknecht, R. A., and Tanaka-Matsumi, J. (2002). A cross-cultural comparison of social phobia symptoms. *Journal of Psychopathology & Behavioral Assessment, 24,* 75–84.

Dishion, T. J., and Stormshak, E. A. (2007). Ethical and professional standards in child and family interventions. In T. J. Dishion and E. A. Stormshak (Eds.), *Intervening in Children's Lives: An Ecological, Family-Centered Approach to Mental Health* (pp. 241–264). Washington, DC: American Psychological Association.

Dodds, J. B. (1985). A *Child Psychotherapy Primer.* New York: Human Sciences.

Doll, B., and Doll, C. A. (1997). *Bibliotherapy with Young People: Librarians and Mental Health Professionals Working Together.* Englewood, CO: Libraries Unlimited.

Doll, E. A. (1953). *The measurement of social competence.* Circle Pines, MN: American Guidance Service.

Donaldson, M. (1987). *Children's Minds.* London: Fontana.

Donohue, B., Romero, V., and Devore, G. (2006). Cognitive and behavioral contributions. In R. T. Ammerman (Ed.), *Comprehensive Handbook of Personality and Psychopathology* (Vol. 3; pp. 38–46). Hoboken, NJ: Wiley.

Dougherty, E. H., and Schinka, J. A. (1989). *Mental Status Checklist for Children.* Odessa, FL: Psychological Assessment Resources.

Dowrick, P. W. (1986). *Social Survival for Children: A Trainer's Resource Book.* New York: Routledge.

Dowrick, P. W. (1991). *Practical Guide to Using Video in the Behavioral Sciences.* Hoboken, NJ: Wiley.

Dowrick, P. W., Kim-Rupnow, W. S., and Power, T. J. (2006). Video feedforward for reading. *Journal of Special Education, 39,* 194–207.

Draguns, J., and Tanaka-Matsumi, J. (2003). Assessment of psychopathology across and within cultures: Issues and findings. *Behavior Research & Therapy, 41,* 755–766.

Dreikurs, R., and Grey, L. (1990). *Logical Consequences: A New Approach to Discipline.* New York: Dutton/Plume.

Dundes, A. (1980). *Interpreting Folklore.* Bloomington: Indiana University Press.

Dunn, L. M., and Dunn, L. M. (2006). PPVT-IV: *Peabody Picture Vocabulary Test-Fourth Edition.* Bloomington, MN: Pearson Assessments.

Duran, E. (2006). *Healing the Soul Wound: Counseling with American Indians and Other Native Peoples.* New York: Teachers College.

Durfee, M. B. (1998). Use of ordinary office equipment. In C. Schaefer (Ed.), *The Therapeutic Use of Child's Play* (pp. 401–411). Lanham, MD: Jason Aronson.

Edgeson, T. L. (2007). Therapists' experience of vicarious traumatization: A phenomenological study. *Dissertation Abstracts International, 67 (10-B),* 6051.

Eliot, L. (1999). *What's Going on in There? How the Brain and Mind Develop in the First Five Years of Life.* New York: Bantam.

Ellis, A., and Bernard, M. E. (Eds.). (2006). *Rational Emotive Behavioral Approaches to Childhood Disorders: Theory, Practice, and Research.* New York: Springer.

Engel, S. (1999). *The Stories Children Tell: Making Sense of the Narratives of Childhood.* New York: W. H. Freeman.

Engel, S. (2005). The narrative worlds of what is and what if. *Cognitive Development, 20,* 514–525.

Erikson, E. (1950). *Childhood and Society.* New York: Norton.

Exner, J. E. (1994). *The Rorschach: A Comprehensive System: Vol. 3. Assessment of Children and Adolescents* (2nd ed.). Hoboken, NJ: Wiley.

Exner, J. E. (2002). *The Rorschach: A Comprehensive System: Vol. I. Basic Foundations and Principles of Interpretation* (4th ed.). Hoboken, NJ: Wiley.

Exner, J. E., and Erdberg, P. (2005). *The Rorschach: A Comprehensive System: Vol. 2. Advanced Interpretation* (3rd ed.). Hoboken, NJ: Wiley.

Fine, M. J., and Gardner, P. A. (1991). Counseling and education services for families: An empowerment perspective. *Elementary School Guidance and Counseling, 26,* 33–44.

Firestone, R. W. (2006). Suicide and the inner voice. In T. E. Ellis (Ed.), *Cognition and Suicide: Theory, Research, and Therapy* (pp. 119–147. Washington, DC: American Psychological Association.

Flavell, J. H., Shipstead, S. G., and Croft, K. (1978). Young children's knowledge about visual perception: Hiding objects from others. *Child Development, 49,* 1208–1211.

Fong, R. (2003). *Children of Neglect: When No One Cares.* New York: Routledge.

Foreman, D. M. (1999). The family rule: A framework for obtaining ethical consent for medical interventions from children. *Journal of Medical Ethics, 25,* 491–496.

Fouad, N. A., and Arrendondo, P. (2007b). Evaluating cultural identity and biases. In N. A. Fouad and P. Arrendondo (Eds.), *Becoming Culturally Oriented: Practical Advice for Psychologists and Educators* (pp. 15–34). Washington, DC: American Psychological Association.

Fouad, N. A., and Arrendondo, P. (Eds.). (2007a). *Becoming Culturally Oriented: Practical Advice for Psychologists and Educators* (pp. 15–34). Washington, DC: American Psychological Association.

Frances, A., and Ross, R. (2001). *DSM-IV-TR Case Studies.* Washington, DC: American Psychiatric Publishing.

Franklin, M. E., March, J. S., and Garcia, A. (2007). Treating obsessive-compulsive disorder in children and adolescents. In C. Purdon and L. J. Summerfeldt (Eds.), *Psychological Treatment of Obsessive-Compulsive Disorder: Fundamentals and Beyond* (pp. 253–266). Washington, DC: American Psychological Association.

Freeman, J., Epston, D., and Lobovits, D. (1997). *Playful Approaches to Serious Problems: Narrative Therapy with Children and Their Families.* New York: Norton.

French, L. (2002). *Counseling American Indians.* Lanham, MD: Rowman & Littlefield.

Freud, A. (1928). *Introduction to the Technique of Child Analysis.* New York: Ayer.

Freud, A. (1946). *The Ego and the Mechanisms of Defense.* New York: International Universities Press.

Freud, S. (1952). A *General Introduction to Psychoanalysis.* New York: Pocket Books.

Freud, S. (1959). The future prospects of psychoanalytic therapy. In E. Jones (Ed.), *Collected Papers* (Vol. 2, pp. 285–296). New York: Basic.

Friedrich, M, and Leiper, R. (2006). Countertransference reactions in therapeutic work with incestuous sexual abusers. *Journal of Child Sexual Abuse, 15,* 87–103.

Gabel, S. (1984). The Draw-a-Story game: An aid in understanding and working with children. *Arts in Psychotherapy, 11,* 187–196.

Gabel, S., Oster, G., and Pfeffer, C. R., (1993). *Difficult Moments in Child Psychotherapy.* Lanham, MD: Jason Aronson.

Gallahue, D. L., and Ozmun, J. C. (2005). *Understanding Motor Development: Infants, Children, Adolescents* (6th ed.). McGraw-Hill.

Gardner, R. A. (1971). *Therapeutic Communication with Children: The Mutual Storytelling Technique.* Lanham, MD: Jason Aronson.

Gardner, R. A. (1973). *The Talking, Feeling, Doing Game.* Cresskill, NJ: Creative Therapeutics.

Gardner, R. A. (1993a). *Child Psychotherapy: The Initial Screening and the Intensive Diagnostic Evaluation.* Lanham, MD: Jason Aronson.

Gardner, R. A. (1993b). *Storytelling in Psychotherapy with Children.* Lanham, MD: Jason Aronson.

Gardner, R. A. (1994). *Understanding Children.* Lanham, MD: Jason Aronson.

Gardner, R. A. (2002). Mutual storytelling. In C. E. Schaefer and D. Cangelosi (Eds.), *Play Therapy Techniques* (2nd ed., pp. 258–267). Lanham, MD: Jason Aronson.

Garner, D. M., and Garfinkel, P. E. (Eds.). (1997). *Handbook of Treatment for Eating Disorders* (2nd ed.). New York: Guilford.

Gasta, C. (1976). *Assertive Training in a High School Setting.* University of Alaska, Unpublished Master's Thesis.

Geisinger, K. F. (2003). Testing and assessment in cross-cultural psychology. In J. R. Graham and J. A. Naglieri (Eds.), *Handbook of Psychology: Assessment Psychology, Vol. 10* (pp. 95–117). Hoboken, NJ: Wiley.

Gelfand, D. M., and Hartmann, D. P. (1992). *Child Behavior Analysis and Therapy* (2nd ed.). Boston: Allyn & Bacon.

Gibbs, J. T., and Huang, L. N. (Eds.). (2003). *Children of Color: Psychological Interventions with Culturally Diverse Youth* (2nd ed.). San Francisco: Jossey-Bass.

Gil, E., and Drewes, A. A. (2005). *Cultural Issues in Play Therapy.* New York: Guilford.

Gil, E., and Rubin, L. (2005). Countertransference play: Informing and enhancing therapist self-awareness through play. *International Journal of Play Therapy, 14,* 87–102

Ginott, H. G. (1960). A rationale for selecting toys in play therapy. *Journal of Consulting and Clinical Psychology 24,* 243–246.

Ginott, H. G. (1964). Problems in the playroom. In M. R. Haworth (Ed.), *Child Psychotherapy* (pp. 125–130). New York: Basic.

Ginott, H. G. (1999). Play group therapy: A theoretical framework. In D. Sweeney and L. Homeyer (Eds.), *The Handbook of Group Play Therapy: Whom It's Best For, How It Works, How To Do It* (pp. 15–23). San Francisco: Jossey-Bass.

Gitlin-Weiner, K., Sandgrund, A., and Schaefer, C. (Eds.). (2000). *Play Diagnosis and Assessment* (2nd ed.). Hoboken, NJ: Wiley.

Godbole, A. Y. (1982). Dyad as a technique of behavioral change. *Psycho Lingua, 12,* 95–110.

Goldberg, C. (2003). Folktale research and the Pantheon fairy tale and folklore library. *Journal of American Folklore, 116,* 217–218.

Goodenough, F. L. (1926). *Measurement of Intelligence by Drawings.* New York: World Book.

Goodman, J. D. (1994). *The Child Mental Status Examination.* Lanham, MD: Jason Aronson.

Goodman, R. F. (2005). Art as a component of grief work with children. In N. B. Webb (Ed.), *Helping Bereaved Children: A Handbook for Practitioners* (2nd ed., pp. 297–322). New York: Guilford.

Gordon, R.A. (2000). *Eating Disorders: Anatomy of a Social Epidemic* (2nd. Ed.). Malden, MA: Blackwell.

Green, W. H. (2006). *Child and Adolescent Clinical Psychopharmacology* (4th ed.). New York: Lippincott Williams & Wilkins.

Greenbaum, L., and Holmes, I. H. (1983). The use of folktales in social work practice. *Social Casework, 64,* 414–418.

Greenspan, S. I., and Greenspan, N. T. (2003). *The Clinical Interview of the Child* (3rd. ed.). Washington, DC: American Psychiatric Press.

Grinder, R., and Bandler, J. (1975). *The Structure of Magic* (Vols. 1 and 2). Palo Alto, CA: Science Behavior Books.

Grotstein, J. S. (2000). *Splitting & Projective Identification.* Lanham, MD: Jason Aronson.

Gulley, P. A. (2005). Learning and communications disorders. In W. M. Klykylo and J. L. Kay (Eds.), *Clinical Child Psychiatry* (2nd ed., pp. 361–369). Hoboken, NJ: Wiley.

Gunn, W. B., Haley, J., and Lyness, A. M. P. (2007). Systemic approaches: Family therapy. In H. T. Prout and D. T. Brown (Eds.), *Counseling and Psychotherapy with Children and Adolescents: Theory and Practice for School and Clinical Settings* (4th ed., pp. 388–418). Hoboken, NJ: Wiley.

Hambridge, G. (1955). Structured play therapy. *American Journal of Orthopsychiatry, 25,* 601–617.

Hambridge, G. (2002). Structured play therapy. In C. E. Schaefer and D. Cangelosi (Eds.), *Play Therapy Techniques* (pp. 75–91). Lanham, MD: Jason Aronson.

Hammer, E. F. (1997). *Advances in Projective Drawing Interpretation* Springfield, IL: Charles C. Thomas.

Handen, B. L., and Gilchrist, R. H. (2006). Mental retardation. In E. J. Mash and R. A. Barkley (Eds.), *Treatment of Childhood Disorders* (3rd ed., pp. 411–454). New York: Guilford.

Handler, L. (1996). The clinical use of figure drawings. In C. S. Newmark (Ed.), *Major Psychological Assessment Instruments* (2nd ed., pp. 206–293). Boston: Allyn & Bacon.

Hart, B. M., and Risley, T. R. (1995). *Meaningful Differences in the Everyday Experience of Young American Children.* Baltimore: Brookes.

Hart, B. M., and Risley, T. R. (1999). *The Social World of Children Learning to Talk.* Baltimore: Brookes.

Hart, S. N. (1991). From property status to person status: Historical perspective on children's rights. *American Psychologist, 46,* 53–59.

Haworth, M. R., and Keller, M. J. (2002). The use of food in therapy. In C. E. Schaefer and D. Cangelosi (Eds.), *Play Therapy Techniques.* Lanham, MD: Jason Aronson.

Hays, P. A. (2001). Making meaningful connections: Establishing respect and rapport. *Addressing Cultural Complexities in Practice: A Framework for Clinicians and Counselors* (pp. 71–85). Washington, DC: American Psychological Association.

Haywood, K., and Getchell, N. (2005). *Life Span Motor Development* (4th ed.). Champaign, IL: Human Kinetics.

Hecker, L. L., and Sori, C. F. (2007). Therapy intake form. In L. L. Hecker and C. F. Sori (Eds.), *The Therapist's Notebook, Vol. 2: More Homework, Handouts, and Activities for Use in Psychotherapy.* Binghamton, NY: Haworth.

Helms, J. E., and Carter, R. T. (1993). Development of the White Racial Identity Inventory. In J. E. Helms (Ed.), *Black and White Racial Identity: Theory, Research, and Practice* (pp. 67–80). New York: Greenwood.

Henley, D. R. (1991). Facilitating the development of object relations through the use of clay in art therapy. *Journal of Art Therapy, 29,* 69–84.

Hickey, D. A. (2001). The nightmare box: Empowering children through dreamwork. In H. G. Kaduson and C. E. Schaefer (Eds.), *101 More Favorite Play Therapy Techniques* (Vol. 2; pp. 141–145). Lanham, MD: Jason Aronson.

Hill, P. (2006). Adjustment disorders. In C. Gillberg, R. Harrington, and H-C. Steinhausen (Eds.), *A Clinician's Handbook of Child and Adolescent Psychiatry* (pp. 207–220). New York: Cambridge University.

Hinman, C. (2003). Multicultural considerations in the delivery of *play* therapy services. *International Journal of Play Therapy, 12,* 107–122.

Hodgkinson, H. L. (1985). *All One System: Demographics of Education, Kindergarten through Graduate School.* Washington, DC: Institute for Educational Leadership.

Hogan, M. (2007). *Four Skills of Cultural Diversity Competence: A Process for Understanding and Practice* (3rd ed.). Belmont, CA: Wadsworth.

Holowiak-Urquhart, C., and Taylor, E. R. (2005). When theory collides with practice: One day in the life of a middle school counselor. *Professional School Counseling, 9,* 88–92.

Homeyer, L. E., and DeFrance, E. (2005). Play therapy. In C. A. Malchiodi (Ed.), *Expressive Therapies* (pp. 141–161). New York: Guilford.

Homeyer, L. E., and Sweeney, D. S. (2005). Sandtray therapy. In C. A. Malchiodi (Ed.), *Expressive Therapies* (pp. 162–181). New York: Guilford.

Horney, K. (1939). *New Ways in Psychoanalysis.* New York: W. W. Norton.

Horton, C., and Cruise, T. K. (2001). *Child Abuse and Neglect.* New York: Guilford.

Hosford, R. E. (1980). Self-as-a-model: A cognitive social learning technique. *The Counseling Psychologist, 9,* 45–62.

Hutchins, D. E., and Vaught, C. C. (1997). *Helping Relationships and Strategies* (3rd ed.). Belmont, CA: Wadsworth.

Iijima Hall, C. C. (1997). Cultural malpractice: The growing obsolescence of psychology with the changing U.S. population. *American Psychologist, 52,* 642–651.

International Union of Psychological Science (2005). *Universal Declaration of Ethical Principles for Psychologists.* Retrieved July 4, 2007, from http://www.am.org/iupsys/ethdraft.pdf.

Jackson, B. (1975). Black identity development. ME-FORM. *Journal of Educational Diversity and Innovation, 2,* 19–25.

James, O. O. (1997). *Play Therapy: A Comprehensive Guide.* Lanham, MD: Jason Aronson.

Jany, K. C. (2005). Überlegungen zum Behandlungsabbruch in der analytischen Kinder- und Jugendlichen-Psychotherapie. *Analytische Kinder- und Jugendlichenpsychotherapie, 36,* 181–211.

Jensen, P. S., Knapp, P., and Mrazek, D. A. (2006). *Toward a New Diagnostic System for Child Psychopathology: Moving Beyond the DSM.* New York: Guilford.

Johnson, J. H., Rasbury, W. C., and Siegel, L. J. (1997). *Approaches to Child Treatment* (2nd ed.). Boston: Allyn & Bacon.

Joshi, P. T., Daniolos, P. T., and Salpekar, J. A., (2004). Physical abuse of children. In J. M. Weiner and M. K. Doulcun (Eds.), *Textbook of Child and Adolescent Psychiatry* (3rd ed., pp. 837–852). Washington, DC: American Psychiatric Publishing.

Joyce, A. S., Piper, W. E., Ogrodniczuk, J. S., and Klein, R. H. (2006). *Termination in Psychotherapy: A Psychodynamic Model of Processes and Outcomes.* Washington, DC: American Psychological Association.

Kaduson, H. G., and Schaefer, C. E. (1997). *101 Favorite Play Therapy Techniques.* Lanham, MD: Jason Aronson.

Kaduson, H. G., and Schaefer, C. E. (Eds.). (2001). *101 More Favorite Play Therapy Techniques* Vol. 2. Lanham, MD: Jason Aronson.

Kaduson, H. G., and Schaefer, C. E. (Eds.). (2006). *Short-Term Play Therapy for Children* (2nd ed.). New York: Guilford.

Kagan, J., and Lamb, S. (1990). *The Emergence of Morality in Young Children.* Chicago: University of Chicago Press.

Kail, R. V. (2007). *Children and their Development* (4th ed.). New York: Prentice-Hall.

Kalichman, S. C., Craig, M. E., and Follingstad, D. R. (1990). Professionals' adherence to mandatory child abuse reporting laws: Effects of responsibility attribution, confidence ratings and situational factors. *Child Abuse and Neglect, 14,* 69–77.

Kaslow, N. J., Kaslow, F. W., Celano, M., and Farber, E. W. (2001). *Textbook of Family Theory and Therapy.* Hoboken, NJ: Wiley.

Kaufman, A. S., and Kaufman, N. L. (2004a). *KTEA-II: Kaufman Test of Educational Achievement* (2nd ed.). Bloomington, MN: Pearson Assessments.

Kaufman, A. S., and Kaufman, N. L. (2004b). *KABC-II: Kaufman Assessment Battery for Children* (2nd ed.).Bloomington, MN: Pearson Assessments.

Kaufman, A. S., and Kaufman, N. L. (2004c). *KBIT-2: Kaufman Brief Intelligence Test* (2nd ed.). Bloomington, MN: Pearson Assessments.

Kazdin, A. E. (1977). *The Token Economy: A Review and Evaluation.* New York: Plenum.

Kazdin, A. E. (2001). *Behavior Modification in Applied Settings* (6th ed.). Belmont, CA: Wadsworth.

Kehle, T. J., Bray, M. A., and Theodore, L. A. (2006). Selective mutism. In G. G. Bear, and K. M. Minke (Eds.), *Children's Needs III: Development, Prevention, and Intervention* (pp. 293–302). Washington, DC: National Association of School Psychologists.

Kendall, P. C. (Ed.). (2005). *Child and Adolescent Therapy: Cognitive-Behavioral Procedures* (3rd ed.). New York: Guilford.

Kenny, M. C. (2001). Child abuse reporting: Teachers' perceived deterrents. *Child Abuse and Neglect, 25,* 81–92.

Killen, M., and Hart, D. (Eds.). (2000). *Morality in Everyday Life: Developmental Perspectives.* Cambridge, England: Cambridge University Press.

Killen, M., and Smetana, J. (2006). *Handbook of Moral Development.* Mahwah, NJ: Lawrence Erlbaum Associates.

Kinzie, D. (2001). Cross-cultural treatment of PTSD. In J. Wilson, E. Friedman, and J. Mathew (Eds.), *Treating Psychological Trauma and PTSD* (pp. 255–277). New York: Guildford.

Kirmayer, L. and Groleau, D. (2003). Affective disorders in cultural context. *Psychiatric Clinics of North America, 24,* 465–478.

Klein, M. (1955). On identification. In M. Klein, *Envy and Gratitude and Other Works, 1946–1963* (pp. 141–175). New York: Delacorte Press/Seymour Laurence.

Klein, M. (1975). *The Psychoanalysis of Children* (A. Strachey, Trans.). New York: Delacorte.

Knobel, M. (1990). Significance and importance of the psychotherapist's personality and experience. *Psychotherapy and Psychosomatics, 53,* 58–63.

Knoff, H. M. (2003). Evaluation of projective drawings. In C. R. Reynolds and R. W. Kamphaus (Eds.), *Handbook of Psychological and Educational Assessment of Children: Personality, Behavior, and Context* (pp. 91–158). New York: Guilford.

Koeppen, A. S. (2002). Relaxation training for children. In C. E. Schaefer and D. Cangelosi (Eds.), *Play Therapy Techniques* (2nd ed., pp. 295–302). Lanham, MD: Jason Aronson.

Kohut, H. (1966). Forms and transformations of narcissism. *Journal of the American Psychoanalytic Association, 14,* 243–272.

Kohut, H. (1982). Introspection, empathy, and the semicircle of mental health. *International Journal of Psychoanalysis, 63,* 359–407.

Kohut, H. (1984). *How Does Analysis Cure?* Chicago: International Universities Press.

Kohut, H., and Wolf, E. (1978). Disorders of the self and their treatment. *International Journal of Psychoanalysis, 59,* 413–425.

Koplow, L. (1991) *Tanya and the Tobo Man / Tanya y el Hombre Tobo: A Story for Children Entering Therapy.* New York: Magination.

Kottman, T. (2002). *Partners in Play: An Adlerian Approach to Play Therapy* (2nd ed.). Alexandria, VA: American Counseling Association.

Kottman, T., and Ashby, J. (2002). Metaphoric stories. In C. E. Schaefer and D. M. Cangelosi (Eds.), *Play Therapy Techniques* (2nd ed., pp. 133–142). Lanham, MD: Jason Aronson.

Kottman, T., and Stiles, K. (1990). The mutual storytelling technique: An Adlerian application in child therapy. *Individual Psychology Journal of Adlerian Theory: Research and Practice, 46,* 148–156.

Kovacs, M. (1992). *CDI: Children's Depression Inventory.* North Tonawanda, NY: Multi-Health Systems.

Kramer, E. (1998). *Childhood and Art Therapy* (2nd ed.). Chicago: Magnolia Street.

Kratochwill, T. R., and Morris, R. J. (1998). *Treating Children's Fears and Phobias* (2nd ed.). New York: Prentice-Hall.

Kronenberger, W. G., and Meyer, R. G. (2001). *The Child Clinician's Handbook* (2nd ed.). Boston: Allyn & Bacon.

Kübler-Ross, E. (1971). The five stages of dying. *Encyclopedia Science Supplement,* 92–97. New York: Grolier.

Kübler-Ross, E. (1975). *Death: The Final Stage of Growth.* Englewood Cliffs, NJ: Prentice-Hall.

Kurlan, R. (Ed.). (2004). *Handbook of Tourette's Syndrome and Related Tic and Behavioral Disorders* (2nd ed.). New York: Marcel Dekker.

Lachar, D. (1982). *Personality Inventory for Children (PIC): Revised Format Manual Supplement.* Los Angeles: Western Psychological Services.

Lachar, D., and Gruber, C. P. (1995). *Manual for the Personality Inventory for Youth.* Los Angeles: Western Psychological Services.

Lachar, D., and Gruber, C. P. (2001). *Manual for the Personality Inventory for Children-Second Edition.* Los Angeles: Western Psychological Services.

Lachar, D., Wingenfeld, S. A., Kline, R. B., and Gruber, P. (2000). *Manual for the Student Behavior Survey.* Los Angeles: Western Psychological Services.

Landgarten, H. B. (1987). *Clinical Art Therapy: A Comprehensive Guide.* New York: Routledge.

Landreth, G. L. (2000). *Innovations in Play Therapy: Issues, Process, and Special Populations.* New York: Routledge.

Landreth, G. L. (2001). *Innovations in Play Therapy: Issues, Processes, and Special Populations.* New York: Routledge.

Landreth, G. L. (2002a). *Play Therapy: The Art of the Relationship* (2nd ed.). New York: Routledge.

Landreth, G. L. (2002b). Therapeutic limit setting in the play therapy relationship. *Professional Psychology: Research and Practice, 33,* 529–535.

Landreth, G. L., Sweeney, D. S., Ray, D. C., Homeyer, L., and Glover, G., (2005). *Play Therapy Interventions with Children's Problems: Case Studies with DSM-IV-TR Diagnoses* (2nd ed.). Lanham, MD: Jason Aronson.

Lane, R. D., and Schwartz, G. E. (1987). Levels of emotional awareness: A cognitive-developmental theory and its applications to psychopathology. *American Journal of Psychiatry, 144,* 133–143.

Lanyado, M. (1989). Variations on the theme of transference and countertransference in the treatment of a ten year old boy. *Journal of Child Psychotherapy, 15,* 85–101.

Lasch, C. (1979). *Culture of Narcissism.* New York: Warner Books.

Laughlin, H. P. (1983). *The Ego and Its Defenses* (rev. ed.). Lanham, MD: Jason Aronson.

Lebo, D. (1998). Toys for non-directive play therapy. In C. Schaefer (Ed.), *The Therapeutic Use of Child's Play.* Lanham, MD: Jason Aronson.

Lee, C. C. (2006). *Counseling for Social Justice.* Alexandria, VA: American Counseling Association.

Lee, C. C. (Ed.). (2005). *Multicultural Issues in Counseling: New Approaches to Diversity* (3rd ed.). Alexandria, VA: American Counseling Association.

Leong, F. T. L., Ebreo, A., Kinoshita, L., Inman, A. G., and Yang, L. H. (2007). *Handbook of Asian American Psychology* (2nd ed.). Thousand Oaks, CA: Sage.

Lerner, R. M., Skinner, E. A., and Sorrell, G. T. (1980). Methodological implications of contextual/dialectic theories of development. *Human Development, 23,* 225–235.

Levick, M. (1998). *See What I'm Saying: What Children Tell Us through Their Art.* Dubuque, IA: Islewest.

Levy, D. (1939). Release therapy. *American Journal of Orthopsychiatry, 9,* 713–736.

Levy, D. (1998). Release therapy. In C. E. Schaefer, *The Therapeutic Use of Child's Play.* Lanham, MD: Jason Aronson.

Lezak, M. D., Howieson, D. B., Loring, D. W., and Hannay, H. J. (2004). *Neuropsychological Assessment* (4th ed.). New York: Oxford University Press.

Lichtenberg, J. D. (1990). Einige Parallelen zwischen den Ergebnissen der Saeuglingsbeobachtung und klinischen Beobachtungen an Erwachsenen, besonders Borderline-Patienten und Patienten mit narzisstischer Persoenlichkeitsstoerung. *Psyche, 10,* 871–901.

Lichtenberg, J. D. (1991). *Psychoanalysis and Infant Research.* Hillsdale, NJ: Analytic Press.

Lodhi, S., and Greer, D. (1989). The speaker as listener. *Journal of the Experimental Analysis of Behavior, 51,* 353–359.

Lopez-Ibor, J. J. (2003). Cultural adaptations of current psychiatric classifications: Are they the solution? *Psychopathology 36,* 114–119.

Lovinger, S. L. (1998). *Child Psychotherapy: From Initial Therapeutic Contact to Termination.* Lanham, MD: Jason Aronson.

Lum, D. (2007). *Culturally Competent Practice: A Framework for Understanding Diverse Groups and Justice Issues* (3rd ed.). Belmont, CA: Wadsworth.

Luria, A. R. (1973). *The Working Brain: An Introduction to Neuropsychology.* New York: Basic.

Luria, A.R. (1976). *Cognitive Development: Its Cultural and Social Foundations.* Cambridge, MA: Harvard University Press.

Machover, K. (1952). *Personality Projection in the Drawing of the Human Figure.* Springfield, IL: Charles C. Thomas.

Malchiodi, C. A. (1997). *Breaking the Silence: Art Therapy with Children from Violent Homes.* New York: Routledge.

Malchiodi, C. A. (1998). *Understanding Children's Drawings.* New York: Guilford.

Malchiodi, C. A. (2003). *Handbook of Art Therapy.* New York: Guildford.

Malchiodi, C. A. (2005a). The impact of culture on art therapy with children. In E. Gil and A. A. Drewes (Eds.), *Cultural Issues in Play Therapy* (pp. 96–111). New York: Guilford.

Malchiodi, C. A. (2005b). Art therapy. In C. A. Malchiodi (Ed.), *Expressive Therapies* (pp. 16–45). New York: Guilford.

Mannarino, A. P., and Cohen, J. A. (2006). Child sexual abuse. In R. T. Ammerman, *Comprehensive Handbook of Personality and Psychopathology, Vol. 3* (pp. 388–402). Hoboken, NJ: Wiley.

Manson, S. (2004). *Meeting the Mental Health Needs of American Indians and Alaska Natives.* Washington, DC: U.S. Department of Health and Human Services, National Technical Assistance Center.

Marcus, I. W., and Marcus, P. (1990). *Scary Night Visitors: A Story for Children with Bedtime Fears.* New York: Magination.

Markwardt, F. C. (1997). *Manual for the Peabody Individual Achievement Test-Revised/Normative Update (PIAT-R/NU).* Bloomington, MN: Pearson Assessments.

Marsella, A., and Kaplan, A., (2003). Cultural considerations for understanding, assessing, and treating depressive experience and disorders. In M. A. Reinecke and M. R. Davison (Eds.), *Comparative Treatment of Depression* (pp. 47–78). New York: Springer.

Marsh, J. S. (1997). *MASC: Multidimensional Anxiety Scale for Children.* North Tonawanda, NY: Multi-Health Systems.

Martin, G., and Pear, J. (2007). *Behavior Modification: What It Is and How to Do It* (8th ed.). Englewood Cliffs, NJ: Prentice-Hall.

Mash, E. J., and Barkley, R. A. (Ed.). (2002). *Child psychopathology* (2nd ed.). New York: Guilford.

Mash, E. J., and Barkley, R. A. (Eds.) (2006). *Treatment of Childhood Disorders* (3rd ed.). New York: Guilford.

Masterson, J. F. (1985). *The Real Self: A Developmental, Self and Object Relations Approach.* New York: Routledge.

Matsumoto, D. (2000). *Cultural Influences on Research Methods and Statistics.* Long Grove, IL: Waveland Press.

McCabe, K. M. (2002). Factors that predict premature termination among Mexican-American children in outpatient psychotherapy. *Journal of Child and Family Studies, 11,* 347–359.

McConaughy, S. H. (2005). *Clinical Interviews for Children and Adolescents: Assessment to Intervention.* New York: Guilford.

McConaughy, S. H., and Achenbach, T. M. (2001). *Manual for the Semistructured Clinical Interview for Children and Adolescents* (2nd ed.). Burlington: University of Vermont, Research Center for Children, Youth, & Families.

McConaughy, S. H., and Achenbach, T. M. (2004). *Manual for the Test Observation Form for Ages 2–18.* Burlington: University of Vermont, Center for Children, Youth, & Families.

McElroy, L. P., and McElroy, R. A. (1991). Countertransference issues in the treatment of incest families. *Psychotherapy, 21,* 48–54.

McGoldrick, M., and Gerson, R. (1999). *Genograms: Assessment and Intervention* (2nd ed.). New York: W. W. Norton.

McGoldrick, M., Giordano, J., and Pearce, J. K. (Eds.). (2005). *Ethnicity and Family Therapy* (3rd ed.). New York: Guilford.

McGrew, K. S. (2005). The Cattell-Horn-Carroll theory of cognitive abilities: Past, present, and future. In D. Flanagan and P. L. Harrison (Eds.), *Contemporary Intellectual Assessment: Theories, Tests, and Issues* (2nd ed., pp. 136–181). New York: Guilford.

Melton, G. B. (1991). Socialization in the global community: Respect for the dignity of children. *American Psychologist, 46,* 66–71.

Melton, G. B., Ehrenreich, N. S., and Lyons, P. M. (2001). Ethical and legal issues in mental health services for children. In C. E. Walker and M. C. Roberts (Eds.), *Handbook of Clinical Child Psychology* (3rd ed., pp. 1074–1093). Hoboken, NJ: Wiley.

Metcalf, L. M. (2002). Countertransference among child therapists: Implications for therapist development and supervision. *Dissertation Abstracts International, 63(6-B),* 3016.

Meyer, Robert G., and Weaver, Christopher M. (2007). *The Clinician's Handbook: Integrated Diagnostics, Assessment, and Intervention in Adult and Adolescent Psychopathology* (5th ed.). Long Grove, IL: Waveland Press.

Miller, C., and Boe, J. (1990). Tears into diamonds: Transformation of child psychic trauma through sandplay and storytelling. *Arts in Psychotherapy, 17,* 247–257.

Miller, P. J., and Moore, B. B. (1989). Narrative conjunction of caregiver and child: A comparative perspective in socialization through stories. *Ethos, 17,* 429–449.

Miller-Perrin, C. L., and Perrin, R. D. (2007). *Child Maltreatment: An Introduction* (2nd ed.). Thousand Oaks, CA: Sage.

Mills, J. C., and Crowley, R. J. (2001). *Therapeutic Metaphors for Children and the Child Within.* New York: Routledge.

Minuchin, S., Lee, W-Y., and Simon, G. M. (2006). *Mastering Family Therapy: Journeys of Growth and Transformation* (2nd ed.). Hoboken, NJ: Wiley.

Miranda, A., and Fraser, L (2002). Culture-bound syndromes: Initial perspectives from individual psychology. *Journal of Individual Psychology 58,* 422–433.

Mishler, C., and Simeone, W. E. (2004). *Hän hwëch'in / Han: People of the River.* Fairbanks: University of Alaska Press.

Monges, M. M. (1998). Beyond the melting pot: A values clarification exercise for teachers and human service professionals. In T. M. Singelis (Ed.), *Teaching about Culture, Ethnicity, and Diversity: Exercises and Planned Activities* (pp. 3–8). Thousand Oaks, CA: Sage.

Moore, L., Sager, D., Keopraseuth, K., Chao, L. H., Riley, C., and Robinson, E. (2001). Rheumatological disorders and somatization in U.S. Mien and Lao refugees with depression and posttraumatic stress disorder: A cross-cultural comparison. *Transcultural Psychiatry 38,* 481–505.

Morris, R. J. and Kratochwill, T. R. (Eds.). (1998). *The Practice of Child Therapy* (3rd ed.). Boston: Allyn & Bacon.

Morris, T. L., and March, J. S. (Ed.). (2004). *Anxiety Disorders in Children and Adolescents* (2nd ed.). New York: Guilford.

Morrison, J., and Anders, T. F. (1999). *Interviewing Children and Adolescents: Skills and Strategies for Effective DSM-IV-TR Diagnosis.* New York: Guilford.

Mueller, E., and Tingley, E. (1990). The Bear's Picnic: Children's representations of themselves and their families. *New Directions for Child Development, 48,* 47–65.

Muro, J., Ray, D., and Schottelkorb, A. (2006). Quantitative analysis of long-term child-centered play therapy. *International Journal of Play Therapy, 15,* 35–58

Murphy, J. (2001). *Art Therapy with Young Survivors of Sexual Abuse: Lost for Words.* New York: Routledge.

Myers, J. E. B. (2005). Legal issues for mental health professionals treating victims of child sexual abuse. In P. F. Talley (Ed.), *Handbook for the Treatment of Abused and Neglected Children* (pp. 359–396). Binghamton, NY: Haworth.

Myers, J. E. B., Berliner, L., Briere, J., Jenny, C., Hendrix, C. T., and Reid, T. (2002). *The APSAC Handbook on Child Maltreatment* (2nd ed.). Thousand Oaks, CA: Sage.

Namyniuk, L. (1996, November). *Cultural considerations in substance abuse treatment.* Paper presented at the 3rd Biennial Conference of the Alaska Psychological Association, Anchorage, AK.

Namyniuk, L., Brems, C., and Clarson, S. (1997). Dena A Coy: A model program for the treatment of pregnant substance-abusing women. *Journal of Substance Abuse Treatment, 14,* 285–298.

National Association of School Psychologists. (2000). *Professional Conduct Manual for School Psychologists.* Bethesda, MD: Author.

National Association of Social Workers. (2000). *Code of Ethics of the National Association of Social Workers.* Washington, DC: Author.

National Center on Child Abuse and Neglect (1985). *Review of child abuse and neglect research.* Washington, DC: U.S. Department of Education.

Naumberg, M. (1966). *Dynamically Oriented Art Therapy: Its Principles and Practice.* New York: Grune and Stratton.

Neimeyer, R. A. Fortner, B., and Melby, D. (2001) Personal and professional factors and suicide intervention skills. *Suicide and Life-Threatening Behavior, 31,* 71–82

Nemiroff, M. A., and Annunziata, J. (1990). *A Child's First Book about Play Therapy.* Washington, DC: American Psychological Association.

Newman, B. M., and Newman, P. R. (2006). *Development Through Life: A Psychosocial Approach* (9th ed.). Belmont, CA: Wadsworth.

Nichols, M. P., and Schwartz, R. C., (2006). *Family Therapy: Concepts & Methods* (7th ed.). Boston: Allyn & Bacon.

Nicholson, B. C., Janz, P. C., and Fox, R. A. (1998). Evaluating a brief parental-education program for parents of young children. *Psychological Reports, 82,* 1107–1113.

Nock, M. K., and Kazdin, A. E. (2001). Parent expectancies for child therapy: Assessment and relation to participation in treatment. *Journal of Child and Family Studies, 10,* 155–180.

Norton, C. C., and Norton, B. E. (2006). Experiential play therapy. In C. E. Schaefer and H. G. Kaduson (Eds.), *Contemporary Play Therapy: Theory, Research, and Practice* (pp. 28–54). New York: Guilford.

O'Conner, K. J. (2000). *The Play Therapy Primer* (2nd ed.). Hoboken, NJ: Wiley.

Oates, R. K. (1996). *The Spectrum of Child Abuse: Assessment, Treatment, and Prevention.* New York: Routledge.

Ogden, D. (2001). *Psychodiagnostics and Personality Assessment: A Handbook* (3rd ed.). Los Angeles: Western Psychological Corporation.

Ogden, T. H. (1993). *Projective Identification and Psychotherapeutic Technique.* (2nd ed.). Lanham, MD: Jason Aronson.

Ogden, T. H. (2004). The analytic third: Implications for psychoanalytic theory and technique. *The Psychoanalytic Quarterly, 73,* 167–95.

Ollendick, T. H., King, N. J., and Chorpita, B. F. (2005). Empirically supported treatments for children and adolescents. In. P. C. Kendall (Ed.), *Child and Adolescent Therapy: Cognitive-Behavioral Procedures* (3rd ed., pp. 492–520). New York: Guilford.

Olness, K., and Kohen, D. P. (1996). *Hypnosis and Hypnotherapy with Children* (3rd ed.). New York: Guilford.

Oster, G. D., and Crone, P. G. (2004). *Using Drawings in Assessment and Therapy: A Guide for Mental Health Professionals* (2nd ed.). New York: Routledge.

Owens. R. E., Jr. (2008). *Language Development: An Introduction* (7th ed.). Boston: Allyn & Bacon.

Patterson, G. R. (1977). *Living with Children: New Methods for Parents and Teachers* (rev. ed.). Champaign, IL: Research Press.

Paul, M., Foreman, D. M., and Kent, L. (2000). Out-patient clinic attendance consent from children and young people: Ethical aspects and practical considerations. *Clinical Child Psychology and Psychiatry, 5,* 203–211.

Pavlov, I. P. (1927). *Conditioned Reflexes.* London: Oxford University Press.

Pearce, S. S. (1995). *Flash of Insight: Metaphor and Narrative in Therapy.* Boston: Allyn & Bacon.

Pearson, M. (1998). *Emotional Healing and Self-Esteem: Inner-Life Skills of Relaxation, Visualisation and Meditation for Children and Adolescents.* Sterling, VA: Stylus.

Pedersen, P. B. (2000). A *Handbook for Developing Multicultural Awareness* (3rd ed.). Alexandria, VA: American Counseling Association.

Pedersen, P. B. (2008). Ethics, competence, and other professional issues in cross cultural-centered counseling. In P. B. Pedersen, J. G. Draguns, W. J. Lonner, and J. E. Trimble (Eds.), *Counseling Across Cultures* (6th ed., pp. 3–28). Thousand Oaks, CA: Sage.

Pedersen, P. B., Draguns, J. G., Lonner, W. J., and Trimble, J. E. (Eds.). (2008). *Counseling Across Cultures* (6th ed.). Thousand Oaks, CA: Sage.

Pellowski, A. (1990). *The World of Storytelling.* Bronx: H. W. Wilson.

Philips, B. (2007). Ideas of cure as a predictor of premature termination, early alliance and outcome in psychoanalytic psychotherapy. *Psychology and Psychotherapy, 80,* 229–245.

Phinney, J. S. (1990). Ethnic identity in adolescents and adults: Review of research. *Psychological Bulletin, 108,* 499–514.

Phinney, J. S. (1996). When we talk about American ethnic groups, what do we mean? *American Psychologist, 51,* 918–927.

Piaget, J. (1967). Genesis and structure in the psychology of intelligence. *Six Psychological Studies by Piaget.* Chicago: Random House.

Piers, E. V., Harris, D. B., and Herzberg, D. S. (2002). *Piers-Harris Children's Self-Concept Scale, Second Edition.* Los Angeles, CA: Western Psychological Services.

Pomerantz, K. A. (2007). Helping children explore their emotional and social worlds through therapeutic stories. *Educational and Child Psychology, 24,* 46–55.

Ponterotto, J. G., Casas, J. M., Suzuki, L. A., and Alexander, C. M. (2001). *Handbook of Multicultural Counseling* (2nd ed.). Thousand Oaks, CA: Sage.

Ponterotto, J. G., Utsey, S. O., and Pedersen, P. B. (2006). *Preventing Prejudice: A Guide for Counselors, Educators, and Parents* (2nd ed.). Thousand Oaks, CA: Sage.

Pope, K. S., and Vasquez, M. J. T. (2007). *Ethics in Psychotherapy and Counseling: A Practical Guide* (3rd ed.). New York: Jossey-Bass.

Powell, L. (2006). A thin line between love and hate: An exploration of countertransference in psychoanalytic psychotherapy with children and adolescents served in a community clinic. *Dissertation Abstracts International, 66 (10-B),* 5692.

Powers, S. W. (2001). Behavior therapy with children. In C. E. Walker and M. C. Roberts (Eds.), *Handbook of Clinical Child Psychology* (3rd ed., pp. 825–839). Hoboken, NJ: Wiley.

Pratt, M. W., and Fiese, B. H. (Eds.) (2004). *Family Stories and the Life Course: Across Time and Generations.* Mahwah, NJ: Lawrence Erlbaum Associates.

Prout, S. M., and Prout, H. T. (2007). Ethical and legal issues in psychological interventions with children and adolescents. In H. T. Prout and D. T. Brown (Eds.), *Theory and Practice for School and Clinical Settings* (pp. 32–63). Hoboken, NJ: Wiley.

Putnam, F. W. (1996). Posttraumatic stress disorder in children and adolescents. *American Psychiatric Press Review of Psychiatry, 15,* 447–467.

Rabin, A. I. (1974). *Assessment with Projective Techniques.* New York: Springer.

Rambert, M. L. (1964). The use of drawings as a method of child psychoanalysis. In M. R. Haworth (Ed.), *Child Psychotherapy* (pp. 340–349). New York: Basic.

Rashkin, R. (2005). *Feeling Better: A Kid's Book about Therapy.* New York: Magination.

Reamer, F G. (2003). *Social work malpractice and liability: Strategies for prevention* (2nd ed.). New York: Columbia University Press.

Reamer, F. G. (2005). Update on confidentiality issues in practice with children: Ethics risk management. *Children & Schools, 27,* 117–120.

Reinherz, H. Z., Giaconia, R. M., Paradis, A. D., Wasserman, M. S., and Hauf, A. M. C. (2000). General and specific childhood risk factors for depression and drug disorders by early adulthood. *Journal of the American Academy of Child & Adolescent Psychiatry, 39,* 223–231.

Renner, C. (2006). Gods and heroes. *School Library Journal, 52,* 59.

Renninger, S. M., Veach, P. M., and Bagdade, P. (2002). Psychologists' knowledge, opinions, and decision-making processes regarding child abuse and neglect reporting laws. *Professional Psychology: Research and Practice, 33,* 19–23.

Reynolds, C. R., and Kamphaus, R. W. (2002). *A Clinician's Guide to the Behavior Assessment System for Children.* New York: Guildford.

Reynolds, C. R., and Kamphaus, R. W. (2004). *Manual for the Behavior Assessment System for Children* (2nd ed.). Bloomington, MN: Pearson Assessments.

Reynolds-Mejia, P., and Levitan, S. (1990). Countertransference issues in the in-home treatment of child sexual abuse. *Child Welfare, 69,* 53–61.

Riley, S. (1987). The advantages of art therapy in an outpatient clinic. *American Journal of Art Therapy, 26,* 21–29.

Roberts, L.W., and Dyer, A. R. (2004). *Concise Guide to Ethics in Mental Health Care.* Washington, DC: American Psychiatric Publishing.

Roberts, M. C., and Walker, C. E. (1997). *Casebook of Child and Pediatric Psychology.* New York: Guilford.

Robertson, G. S., Hori, S. E., and Powell, K. J. (2006). Schizophrenia: An integrative approach to modelling a complex disorder. *Journal of Psychiatry & Neuroscience, 31,* 157–167.

Robertson, M., and Barford, F. (1998). Story making in the psychotherapy with a chronically ill child. In C. Schaefer (Ed.), *The Therapeutic Use of Child's Play.* Lanham, MD: Jason Aronson.

Roid, G. H. (2003a). *Stanford-Binet Intelligence Scales, Fifth Edition.* Itasca, IL: Riverside.

Roid, G. H. (2003b). *Stanford-Binet Intelligence Scales, Fifth Edition: Technical Manual.* Itasca, IL: Riverside.

Rorschach, H. (1942). *Psychodiagnostics: A Diagnostic Test Based on Perception.* Bern: Huber, 1942 (1st German Edition, 1921; U. S. distributor: Grime and Strutton).

Rowan, J., and Jacobs, M. (2002). *The Therapist's Use of Self.* Buckingham: Open University Press.

Roysircar, G., Sandhu, D. S., and Bibbins, V. E. (2003). *Multicultural Competencies: A Guidebook of Practices.* Alexandria, VA: Association for Multicultural Counseling & Development.

Rubin, J. A. (1998). *Art Therapy: An Introduction.* Philadelphia: Taylor & Francis.

Rubin, J. A. (2001). *Approaches to Art Therapy: Theory and Technique.* Philadelphia: Psychology Press.

Rubin, J. A. (2005). *Artful Therapy.* Hoboken, NJ: Wiley.

Rubin, L. C. (Ed.). (2006). *Using Superheroes in Counseling and Play Therapy.* New York: Springer.

Rubin, R. (1978). *Bibliotherapy Sourcebook.* Phoenix: Oryz.

Russ, S. R., and Freedheim, D. K. (2001). Psychotherapy with children. In C. E. Walker and M. C. Roberts (Eds.), *Handbook of Clinical Child Psychology* (3rd ed., 840–859.). Hoboken, NJ: Wiley.

Sable, J., and Hoffman, L. (2005). *Characteristics of the 100 Largest Elementary and Secondary School Districts in the United States: 2002–2003.* Retrieved August 3, 2007, from http://nces.ed.gov/pubs2005/2005312.pdf.

Sameroff, A. J., Lewis, M., and Miller, S. M. (Eds.). (2000). *Handbook of Developmental Psychopathology* (2nd ed.). New York: Plenum.

Samuda, R. J. (1998). *Psychological Testing of American Minorities* (2nd ed.). Thousand Oaks, CA: Sage.

Santostefano, S. (2004). *Child Therapy in the Great Outdoors: A Relational View.* Hillsdale, NJ: Analytic.

Sanville, J. (1987). Creativity and the constructing of the self. *Psychoanalytic Review, 74,* 263–279.

Satir, V. (1967). *Conjoint Family Therapy: A Guide to Theory and Technique.* Palo Alto, CA: Science and Behavior Books.

Sattler, J. M. (2001). *Assessment of Children: Cognitive applications* (4th ed.). La Mesa, CA: Author.

Sattler, J. M. (2004). *Assessment of Children: WISC-IV and WPPSI-III Supplement.* La Mesa, CA: Author.

Sattler, J. M. (2005). *Assessment of Children: Behavioral, Social, and Clinical Foundations* (5th ed.). La Mesa, CA: Author.

Scarf, M. (1987). *Intimate Partners.* New York: Random House.

Schaefer, C. E. (2000). *The Therapeutic Use of Child's Play.* Lanham, MD: Jason Aronson.

Schaefer, C. E., and Kaduson, H. G. (2006). *Contemporary Play Therapy: Theory, Research, and Practice.* New York: Guilford.

Schaefer, C. E., and Reid, S. E. (2000). *Game Play: Therapeutic Use of Childhood Games.* Hoboken, NJ: Wiley.

Schickedanz, J. A., Schickedanz, D. I., Forsyth, P. D., and Forsyth, G. A. (2001). *Understanding Children and Adolescents.* Boston: Allyn & Bacon.

Schowalter, J. E. (1985). Countertransference in work with children: Review of a neglected concept. *Journal of the American Academy of Child Psychiatry, 25,* 40–45.

Schroeder, C. S., and Gordon, B. N. (2002). *Assessment and Treatment of Childhood Problems: A Clinician's Guide* (2nd ed.). New York: Guilford.

Schwartz, E. K. (1964). A psychoanalytic study of the fairy tale. In M. R. Haworth (Ed.), *Child Psychotherapy* (pp. 383–395). New York: Basic.

Schwartz, M. S., and Andrasik, F. (2003). *Biofeedback: A Practitioner's Guide* (3rd ed.) New York: Guilford.

Seifer, R. (2000). Temperament and goodness of fit: Implications for developmental psychopathology. In A. J. Sameroff, M. Lewis, and S. M. Miller (Eds.), *Handbook of Developmental Psychopathology* (2nd ed., pp. 257–276). New York: Plenum.

Shadle, C., and Graham, J. (1981). *The Talking/Listening Game.* San Luis Obispo, CA: Dandy Lion.

Shaffer, D. R. (2005). *Social and Personality Development* (5th ed.). Belmont, CA: Wadsworth.

Shapiro, E. S., and Clemens, N. H. (2005). Systematic direct classroom observation to define school-related problems. In R. Brown-Chidsey (Ed.), *Assessment for Intervention: A Problem-Solving Approach.* New York: Guildford.

Shapiro, E. S., and Kratochwill, T. R. (Eds.). (2000). *Conducting School-Based Assessments of Child and Adolescent Behavior.* New York: Guilford.

Sharma, P., and Lucero-Miller. D. (1998). Beyond political correctness. In T. M. Singelis (Ed.), *Teaching about Culture, Ethnicity, and Diversity: Exercises and Planned Activities* (pp. 191–194). Thousand Oaks, CA: Sage.

Shelef, K. (2005). Adolescent and parent alliance and treatment outcome in multidimensional family therapy. *Journal of Consulting and Clinical Psychology, 73,* 689–698.

Sherman, M. H. (1990). Family narratives: Internal representations of family relationships and affective themes. *Infant Mental Health Journal, 11,* 253–258.

Siegel, H. B. (1990). Working with abrasive patients. *Issues in Ego-Psychology, 13,* 48–53.

Silva, R. R. (Ed.). (2004). *Posttraumatic Stress Disorder in Children and Adolescents.* New York: W. W. Norton.

Simmons, J. E. (1987). *Psychiatric Examination of Children* (4th ed.). Philadelphia: Lea and Febinger.

Sinason, V. (1988). Dolls and bears: From symbolic equation to symbol. *British Journal of Psychotherapy, 4,* 349–363.

Skinner, B. F. (1971). *Beyond Freedom and Dignity.* New York: Knopf.

Skinner, B. F. (1976). *About Behaviorism.* New York: Random House.

Smith, C. A. (1989). *From Wonder to Wisdom: Using Stories to Help Children Grow.* New York: New American Library.

Smith, S. R., and Handler, L. (Eds.). (2007). *The Clinical Assessment of Children and Adolescents: A Practitioner's Handbook.* Mahwah, NJ: Lawrence Erlbaum Associates.

Sokol, R. J., Delaney-Black, V., and Nordstrom, B. (2003). Fetal alcohol spectrum disorder. *JAMA: Journal of the American Medical Association, 290,* 2996–2999.

Sparrow, S. S., Cicchetti, D. V., and Balla, D. A. (2005). *Vineland Adaptive Behavior Scales, Second Edition (Vineland-II).* Bloomington, MN: Pearson Assessments.

Spero, M. H. (2002). Use of the telephone in play therapy. In C. E. Schaefer and D. M. Cangelosi (Eds.), *Play Therapy Techniques* (2nd ed., pp. 143–152). Lanham, MD: Jason Aronson.

Spiegel, S. (1989). *An Interpersonal Approach to Child Therapy.* New York: Columbia University Press.

Spiegel, S. (1996). *An Interpersonal Approach to Child & Adolescent Psychotherapy.* Lanham, MD: Jason Aronson.

Spiegler, M. D., and Guevremont, D. C. (2003). *Contemporary Behavior Therapy* (4th ed.). Belmont, CA: Wadsworth.

Spitzer, R. L., Gibbon, M., Skodol, A. E., Williams, J. B. W. and First, M. B. (2002). *DSM-IV-TR Casebook, Vol 1: A Learning Companion to the Diagnostic and Statistical Manual of Mental Disorders.* Washington, DC: American Psychiatric Publishing.

Spitzer, R. L., Gibbon, M., Skodol, A. E., Williams, J. B. W. and First, M. B. (2006). *DSM-IV-TR Casebook, Vol 2: Experts Tell How They Treated Their Own Patients.* Washington, DC: American Psychiatric Publishing.

Stafford, B. S., and Zeanah, C. H. (2006). Attachment disorders. In J. L. Luby (Ed.), *Handbook of Preschool Mental Health: Development, Disorders, and Treatment.* New York: Guilford.

Stark, K. D., Sander, J., Hauser, M., Simpson, J., Schnoebelen, S., Glenn, R., and Molnar, J. (2006). Depressive disorders during childhood and adolescence. In E. J. Mash and R. A. Barkley (Eds.), *Treatment of Childhood Disorders* (3rd ed., pp. 336–410). New York: Guilford.

Stein, M. A., Barrueco, S. L., and Halperin, J. M. (2004). Psychological and neuropsychological testing. In J. M. Wiener and M. K. Dulcan (Eds.), *The American Psychiatric Publishing Textbook of Child and Adolescent Psychiatry* (3rd ed.) Washington, DC: American Psychiatric Publishing.

Stern, D. N. (1977). *The First Relationship: Infant and Mother.* Cambridge, MA: Harvard University Press.

Stern, D. N. (1985). *The Interpersonal World of the Infant.* New York: Basic.

Stern, D. N. (1989). The representation of relational patterns. In A. J. Sameroff and R. N. Emde (Eds.), *Relationships and Relationship Disorders.* New York: Basic.

Stern, R., Hyman, L., and Martin, C. E. (2006). The importance of self-awareness for school counselors. In J. Pellitteri, R. Stern, C. Shelton, and B. Muller-Ackerman (Eds.), *Emotionally Intelligent School Counseling* (pp. 49–62). Mahwah, NJ: Lawrence Erlbaum Associates.

Stevenson, S. R., and Kitchener, K. S. (2001). Ethical issues in the practice of psychology with clients with HIV/AIDS. In J. R. Anderson and R. L. Barret (Eds.), *Ethics in HIV-Related Psychotherapy: Clinical Decision Making in Complex Cases* (pp. 19–42). Washington, DC: American Psychological Association.

Stiles, K., and Kottman, T. (1990). Mutual storytelling: An intervention for depressed and suicidal children. *School Counselor, 37,* 337–342.

Stine, J. J. (2005). The use of metaphors in the service of the therapeutic alliance and therapeutic communication. *The Journal of the American Academy of Psychoanalysis and Dynamic Psychiatry 33*, 531–545.

Stores, G. (2006). Sleep disorders. In C. Gillberg, R. Harrington, and H-C. Steinhausen (Eds.), *A Clinician's Handbook of Child and Adolescent Psychiatry* (pp. 304–338). New York: Cambridge University.

Straus, M. B. (1999). *No-Talk Therapy for Children and Adolescents.* New York: Norton.

Sue, D. W., and Sue, D. (2007). *Counseling the Culturally Different: Theory and Practice* (5th ed.). New York Wiley.

Sullivan, A., and Brems, C. (1997). The psychological repercussions of the sociocultural oppression of Alaska Native peoples. *Genetic, Social, and General Psychology Monographs, 123,* 411–440.

Suzuki, L. A., Meller, P. J., and Ponterotto, J. G. (2007). *Handbook of Multicultural Assessment: Clinical, Psychological, and Educational Applications* (3rd ed.). New York: Jossey-Bass.

Swanson, D. P., Spencer, M. B., Hapalani, V, Dupree, D., Noll, E., Ginzburg, S., and Seaton, G. (2003). Psychosocial development in racially and ethnically diverse youth: Conceptual and methodological challenges in the 21st century. *Development and Psychopathology, 15,* 743–771.

Swenson, L. C. (1997). *Psychology and the Law* (2nd ed.). Belmont, CA: Wadsworth.

Tan, J., and Fegert, J. (2004). Capacity and competence in child and adolescent psychiatry. *Health Care Analysis, 12,* 285–294.

Tansey, M. J., and Burke, W. F. (1995). *Understanding Countertransference: From Projective Identification to Empathy.* Hillsdale, NJ: Analytic Press.

Tataki, R. T. (1993). *A Different Mirror: A History of Multicultural America.* Boston: Little, Brown.

Terr, L.C. (2006). Children's turn-arounds in psychotherapy: The doctor's gesture. *The Psychoanalytic Study of The Child, 61,* 56–81.

Teyber, E. (2006). *Interpersonal Process in Therapy: An Integrative Model* (5th ed.). Belmont, CA: Wadsworth.

Thomas, R. M. (2005). *Comparing Theories of Child Development* (6th ed.). Belmont, CA: Wadsworth.

Thompson, C. L., and Kennedy, P. (1987). Healing the betrayed: Issues in psychotherapy with child victims of trauma. *Journal of Contemporary Psychotherapy, 17,* 195–202.

Thompson, C. L. and Rudolf, L. B. (2007). *Counseling Children* (7th ed.). Belmont, CA: Wadsworth.

Todd, J. and Bohart, A. C. (2006). *Foundations of Clinical and Counseling Psychology* (4th ed.). Long Grove, IL: Waveland Press.

Tsai, L. Y., and Champine, D. J. (2006). Schizophrenia and other psychotic disorders. In M. K. Dulcan and J. Wiener (Eds.), *Essentials of child and adolescent psychiatry* (pp. 235–265). Washington, DC: American Psychiatric Publishing.

U. S. Census Bureau. (1980). *Population Profile of the United Stales: 1980. Population Characteristics* (Series P-25, No. 952). Washington, DC: U.S. Government Printing Office.

U.S. Census Bureau. (2001). *Census 2000 Redistricting Data (P.L. 94–171).* Washington, DC: U.S. Government Printing Office.

United Nations General Assembly. (1989). *Adoption of a Convention on the Rights of the Child.* New York: Author.

van Beekum, S. (2005). The therapist as a new object. *Transactional Analysis Journal, 35,* 187–191.

VandeCreek, L., and Knapp, S. (2001). *Tarasoff and Beyond: Legal and Clinical Considerations in the Treatment of Life-Endangering Patients* (3rd ed.). Sarasota, FL: Professional Resource.

Volkmar, F. R., Paul, R., Klin, A., and Cohen, D. J. (Eds.). (2005a). *Handbook of Autism and Pervasive Developmental Disorders, Vol. 1: Diagnosis, Neurobiology, and Behavior* (3rd ed.). Hoboken, NJ: Wiley.

Volkmar, F. R., Paul, R., Klin, A., and Cohen, D. J. (Eds.). (2005b). *Handbook of Autism and Pervasive Developmental Disorders, Vol. 2: Assessment, Interventions, and Policy* (3rd ed.). Hoboken, NJ: Wiley.

Von Gontard, A. (2006). Elimination disorders: Enuresis and encopresis. In C. Gillberg, R. Harrington, and H-C. Steinhausen (Eds.), *A Clinician's Handbook of Child and Adolescent Psychiatry* (pp. 625–654). New York: Cambridge University.

Waldram, J. B. (2004). *Revenge of the Windigo: The Construction of the Mind and Mental Health of North American Aboriginal Peoples.* Toronto: University of Toronto Press.

Walker, C. E. (2003). Elimination disorders: Enuresis and encopresis. In M. C. Roberts (Ed.), *Handbook of Pediatric Psychology* (3rd ed., pp. 544–560). New York: Guilford.

Walker, C. E., Bonner, B. L., and Kaufman, K. L. (1988). *The Physically and Sexually Abused Child: Evaluation and Treatment.* New York: Pergamon.

Walker, N. E., Brooks, C. M., and Wrightsman, L. S. (1999). *Children's Rights in the United States: In Search of a National Policy.* Thousand Oaks, CA: Sage.

Walkup, N. (2006). What's the story? *School Arts, 105,* 4.

Walsh, J. (2007). *Endings in Clinical Practice: Effective Closure in Diverse Settings* (2nd ed.). Chicago: Lyceum.

Watson, T. S., and Gresham, F. M. (Eds.). (1998). *Handbook of Child Behavior Therapy.* New York: Basic.

Webb, N. B. (1989). Supervision of child therapy: Analyzing therapeutic impasses and monitoring countertransference. *The Clinical Supervisor, 7,* 61–76.

Webb, N. B. (Ed.) (2007). *Play Therapy with Children in Crisis: Individual, Group, and Family Treatment* (3rd ed.). New York: Guilford.

Wechsler, D. (1999). *Manual for the Wechsler Abbreviated Scale of Intelligence.* San Antonio, TX: Psychological Corporation.

Wechsler, D. (2001). *Manual for the Wechsler Individual Achievement Test* (2nd ed.). San Antonio, TX: Psychological Corporation.

Wechsler, D. (2002) *Manual for the Wechsler Preschool and Primary School Scale of Intelligence* (3rd ed.). San Antonio, TX: Psychological Corporation.

Wechsler, D. (2003) *Manual for the Wechsler Intelligence Scale for Children* (4th ed.). San Antonio, TX: Psychological Corporation.

Wenar, C. (1982). Developmental psychopathology: Its nature and models. *Journal of Clinical Child Psychology, 11,* 192–201.

Wenar, C., and Kerig, P. (2005). *Developmental Psychopathology* (5th ed.). New York: McGraw-Hill.

Westen, D., Klepser, J., Ruffins, S. A., Silverman, M., Lifton, N., and Boekamp, J. (1991). Object relations in childhood and adolescence: The development of working representations. *Journal of Consulting and Clinical Psychology, 59,* 400–409.

Wester, J., and Sugarman, L. I. (Eds.). (2007). *Therapeutic Hypnosis with Children and Adolescents.* Norwalk, CT: Crown House

Whitehurst, G. J. (1982). Language development. In B. B. Wolman (Ed.), *Handbook of Developmental Psychology* (pp. 367–386). Englewood Cliffs, NJ: Prentice-Hall.

Whitmore, K., Willems, G., and Hart, H. (2000). *A Neurodevelopmental Approach to Specific Learning Disorders.* Cambridge, England: Cambridge University Press.

Wicks-Nelson, R., and Israel, A. C. (2006). *Behavior Disorders of Childhood* (6th ed.). New York: Prentice-Hall.

Wiger, D. E. (2005). *The Clinical Documentation Sourcebook: The Complete Paperwork Resource for your Mental Health Practice* (3rd ed.). Hoboken, NJ: Wiley.

Wilcox, B. L., and Naimark, H. (1991). The Rights of the Child: Progress toward human dignity. *American Psychologist, 46,* 49–52.

Wilkinson, G. S., and Robertson, G. J. (2006). *Manual for the Wide Range Achievement Test-Fourth Edition.* Lutz, FL: Psychological Assessment Resources.

Wilmshurst, W. (2005). *Essentials of Child Psychopathology.* Hoboken, NJ: Wiley.

Wimbarti, S., and Self, P. A. (1992). Developmental psychology for the clinical child psychologist. In C. E. Walker and M. C. Roberts (Eds.), *Handbook of Clinical Child Psychology* (2nd ed., pp. 33–46). New York: John Wiley.

Wirt, R. D., Lachar, D., Klinedinst, J. K., and Seat, P. D. (1977). *Multidimensional Description of Child Personality: A Manual for the Personality Inventory for Children.* Los Angeles: Western Psychological Services.

Wirth, L. (1945). The problem of minority groups. In R. Linton (Ed.), *The Science of Man in the World Crisis* (pp. 347–372). New York: Columbia University Press.

Wise, D. (2006). Child abuse assessment. In M. Hersen (Ed.), *Clinician's Handbook of Child Behavioral Assessment* (pp. 549–568). San Diego: Elsevier Academic.

Wodrich, D. L., and Schmitt, A. J. (2006). *Patterns of Learning Disorders: Working Systematically from Assessment to Intervention.* New York: Guilford.

Wolpe, J. (1958). *Psychotherapy by Reciprocal Inhibition.* Stanford, CA: Stanford University Press.

Woltman, A. G. (1964). Concepts of play therapy techniques. In M. R. Haworth (Ed.), *Child Psychotherapy.* New York: Basic.

Woodcock, R. W., and Johnson, M. B. (1989). *Woodcock-Johnson Psycho-Educational Battery-Revised.* Allen, TX: DLM Teaching Resources.

Woodcock, R. W., McGrew, K. S., and Mather, N. (2007). WJ-III NU: *Manual for the Woodcock Johnson III Normative Update Complete.* Itasca, IL: Riverside.

Wustinger, L. (2006). Aspekte der unbewussten Beziehungsdynamik zwischen Therapeut und Patient im Zuge der diagnostischen Arbeit mit Kindern und Jugendlichen. *Zeitschrift für Individualpsychologie, 31,* 289–304.

Youngstrom, E. A., Findling, R. L., and Feeny, N. (2004). Assessment of bipolar spectrum disorders in children and adolescents. In S. L. Johnson and R. L. Leahy (Eds.), *Psychological Treatment of Bipolar Disorder.* New York: Guilford.

Zakich, R. (1975). *The Ungame.* Placentia, CA: The Ungame Company.

Zakich, R., and Monroe, S. (1979). *Reunion.* Placentia, CA: The Ungame Company.

Zalsman, G., Oquendo, M. A., Greenhill, L., Goldberg, P. H., Kamali, M., Martin, A., and Mann, J. J. (2006). Neurobiology of depression in children and adolescents. *Child and Adolescent Psychiatric Clinics of North America, 15,* 843–868.

Zeanah, C. H., Anders, T. F., Seifer, R., and Stern, D. N. (1991). Implications of research on infant development for psychodynamic theory and practice. In S. Chess and M. E. Hertzig (Eds.). *Annual Progress in Child Psychiatry and Child Development* (pp. 5–34). New York: Routledge.

Zeckhausen, D. (2007). *Full Mouse, Empty Mouse: A Tale of Food and Feelings.* New York: Magination.

Zellman, G. L. (1990). Child abuse reporting and failure to report among mandated reporters. *Journal of Interpersonal Violence, 5,* 3–22.

Zinn, H. (2003). A *People's History of the United States.* New York: Harper.

Zucker, K. J. (2006). Gender identity disorder. In D. A. Wolfe and E. J. Mash (Eds.), *Behavioral and Emotional Disorders in Adolescents: Nature, Assessment, and Treatment* (pp. 535–562). New York: Guilford.

Zuckerman, E. L. (2003). *The Paper Office: Forms, Guidelines, and Resources to Make your Practice Work Ethically, Legally, and Profitably* (3rd ed.). New York: Guilford.

Zwiers, M. L., and Morrissette, P. J. (1999). *Effective Interviewing of Children: A Comprehensive Guide for Counselors and Human Service Workers.* Philadelphia: Accelerated Development.

Name Index

Abela, J. R. Z., 224
Ablon, S. L., 380
Aboff, M., 88
Achenbach, T. M., 49, 185, 187, 214, 222
Adams, P. L., 23, 156
Akullian, J., 364
Alcantara, C., 223
Alexander, C. M., 38, 39, 45, 49
Allen, J., 53
Altman, N., 4, 8, 17
Anastasi, A., 190
Anders, T. F., 64, 177, 214
Anderson, B. S., 111
Anderson, M. J., 108
Andrasik, F., 275
Änggård, E., 303
Annunziata, J., 88, 142
Armour-Thomas, E., 46
Arrendondo, P., 39, 44, 51
Ashby, J., 305
Atkinson, D. R., 43, 45
Autti-Raemoe, I., 224
Axline, V., 13, 249, 276, 282

Bagdade, P., 28
Bakur Weiner, M., 88
Baldwin, M., 14
Balla, D. A., 189
Bandler, J., 146
Bandura, A., 285, 347, 363
Barford, F., 303
Barker, P., 13
Barkley, R. A., 214, 222, 227, 275, 354
Barnett, O. W., 117, 120
Barrett-Lennard, G., 256

Barrueco, S. L., 206
Baumrind, D., 153
Baxter, S., 14
Beck, A. T., 198
Beck, J. S., 198
Becvar, D. S., 143, 169
Becvar, R. J., 143, 169
Beidel, D. C., 224
Beirne-Smith, M., 214, 224
Bellak, L., 204
Bellak, S. S., 204
Bellini, S., 364
Bellinson, J., 93
Berk, L. E., 63, 64
Bernard, M. E., 164, 275
Bernstein, I., 15, 17, 18, 19
Bersoff, D. N., 113, 116, 117, 122
Bibbins, V. E., 39
Billick, S. B., 112
Bion, W. R., 262
Birmaher, B., 224
Bjorklund, D. F., 4, 67
Blom, R., 12
Blomquist, G. M., 88
Blomquist, P. B., 88
Boe, J., 310
Bohart, A. C., 227
Boik, B. L., 275
Bonner, B. L., 117, 118
Bornstein, B., 32
Bourg, W., 131
Bowlby, J., 218, 223
Bradley, J. D. D., 224
Brandell, J. R., 4, 304
Bratton, S. C., 85
Brave Heart-Yellowhorse, M., 44

Bray, M. A., 218
Brems, C., 4, 8, 11, 14, 18, 47, 51, 64, 114, 117, 119, 121, 122, 146, 147, 157, 164, 203, 222, 223, 224, 240, 241, 256, 262, 264
Broadhurst, D., 117
Brooks, C. M., 109
Brooks, J. B., 64, 153
Brown, C. D., 328
Browne, K, D., 118
Buber, M., 324
Bucchianeri, M. M., 378
Buck, J. N., 329
Buck, J. W., 202
Burke, W. F., 262
Burks, H. F., 106
Burns, R. C., 202, 329, 333, 335

Cain, J., 88
Cain, W. J., 311
Callanan, P., 112, 117, 122
Cangelosi, D. M., 378, 380
Canino, I. A., 39, 49, 54
Carroll, J. B., 89, 194
Carter, R. T., 43
Casas, J. M., 38, 39, 45, 49
Casat, C. D., 177
Cattanach, A., 302, 303, 305
Cautela, J., 355
Celano, M., 275
Champine, D. J., 218
Chang, C. Y., 101, 103
Chazan, S. E., 92, 277
Chenneville, T., 117
Chess, S., 64
Chethik, M., 168, 249, 266

Cheung, M., 275, 277, 355
Chorpita, B. F., 219, 346
Christophersen, E. R., 217
Christy, V. F., 378
Chused, J. F., 12, 14
Cicchetti, D. V., 189
Clark, L. A., 88
Clarson, S., 51
Clemens, N. H., 175
Close, H. T., 305
Cohen, C. P., 109
Cohen, D. J., 216, 224
Cohen, J. A., 120
Conners, C. K., 189
Constantino, G., 205
Cooper, P., 64, 216
Coppolillo, H. P., 10, 85, 93, 97,
    380
Corey, G., 112, 117, 122
Corey, M. S., 112, 117, 122
Corning, A. F., 378
Courtney, J. A., 6
Craig, M. E., 28
Crary, E., 88
Creadick, T. A., 325
Croft, K., 67
Crone, P. G., 330, 336
Cross, W. E., Jr., 43
Crosson-Tower, C., 14, 23, 118,
    119, 120
Crowley, R. J., 275
Cruise, T. K., 28

Dana, R. H., 46, 204, 205
Daniolos, P. T., 20
DasGupta, S., 301, 302
Davis, C., 39
DeFrance, E., 277
Delaney-Black, V., 224
Devore, G., 346
Dewey, D., 215
Dinnel, D. L., 47
Dishion, T. J., 114
Dodds, J. B., 97, 272, 387
Doll, B., 275
Doll, C. A., 275
Doll, E. A., 189
Donohue, B., 346
Dougherty, E. H., 177
Dowrick, P. W., 275, 364
Draguns, J. G., 43, 45, 46
Dreikurs, R., 270
Drewes, A. A., 92

Dundes, A., 301
Dunn, L. M., 195
Duran, E., 44, 45
Durfee, M. B., 106
Dyer, A. R., 111, 113

Ebreo, A., 46
Edgeson, T. L., 18
Ehrenreich, N. S., 113, 114
Ellis, A., 164, 275
Engel, S., 301, 303
Epston, D., 302
Erdberg, P., 203
Erikson, E., 4, 63, 241, 276
Erikson, M., 305

Farber, E. W., 275
Feeny, N., 219
Fegert, J., 112
Fiese, B. H., 301, 302
Findling, R. L., 219
Fine, M. J., 168
First, M. B., 211
Flavell, J. H., 67
Follingstad, D. R., 28
Fong, R., 120
Foreman, D. M., 112
Forsyth, G. A., 66, 67, 73
Forsyth, P. D., 66, 67, 73
Fortner, B., 117
Fouad, N. A., 39, 44, 51
Frances, A., 211
Franklin, M. E., 220
Fraser, L., 46
Freedheim, D. K., 60, 240, 257,
    259, 265
Freeman, J., 302
French, L., 46
Freud, A., 183, 282
Freud, S., 4, 15, 63, 277, 378,
    380
Friedrich, M., 23
Friman, P. C., 217

Gabel, S., 274, 311, 338
Gallahue, D. L., 63
Garcia, A., 220
Gardner, R. A., 106, 159, 168,
    268, 300, 304, 305, 307,
    310, 311, 312, 313, 314,
    322
Gasta, C., 138
Geisinger, K. F., 45

Gelfand, D. M., 364
Gerson, R., 135
Getchell, N., 63
Giaconia, R. M., 223
Gibbon, N., 211
Gibbs, J. T., 9, 44, 54
Gil, E., 14
Gilchrist, R. H., 214
Ginott, H. G., 13, 93, 106, 268
Giordano, J., 45
Gitlin-Weiner, K., 159
Glenn, J., 15, 17, 18, 19
Glover, G., 275
Godbole, A. Y., 302
Goldberg, C., 301
Golden, C. J., 224
Gone, J. P., 223
Goodenough, F. L., 159, 201
Goodman, J. D., 177
Goodman, R. F., 328
Goodwin, E. A., 275
Gopaul-McNicol, S. A., 46
Gordon, B. N., 60
Gordon, R. A., 223
Graham, J., 106
Green, W. H., 275
Greenbaum, L., 301, 304
Greenspan, N. T., 131, 147, 151,
    163, 164
Greenspan, S. I., 131, 147, 151,
    163, 164
Gresham, F. M., 346
Grey, L., 270
Grinder, R., 146
Groden, J., 355
Groleau, D., 47
Grotstein, J. S., 262
Gruber, C. P., 199
Gruber, P., 199, 200
Guevremont, D. C., 355
Gulley, P. A., 215
Gunn, W. B., 143, 169

Haley, J., 143, 169
Halperin, J. M., 206
Hambridge, G., 285
Hamilton, C., 118
Hammer, E. F., 201, 202
Handen, B. L., 214
Handler, L., 200, 201
Hanking, B. L., 224
Hanks, H., 118
Hannay, H. J., 206

Hart, B. M., 66
Hart, D., 63
Hart, H., 215
Hartmann, D. P., 364
Hauf, A. M. C., 223
Haworth, M. R., 101
Hays, D. G., 101, 103
Hays, P. A., 49
Haywood, K., 63
Hecker, L. L., 132
Helms, J. E., 43
Henley, D. R., 338
Hertzig, M. E., 64
Hickey, D. A., 328
Hill, P., 221
Hinman, C., 37, 44
Hoffman, L., 37
Hogan, M., 39, 52
Holmes, I. H., 301, 304
Holowiak-Urquhart, C., 9
Homeyer, L. E., 103, 275, 277
Hori, S. E., 224
Horney, K., 380
Horton, C., 28
Howieson, D. B., 206
Huang, L. N., 9, 44, 45
Hutchins, D. E., 380
Hyman, L., 8

Iijima Hall, C. C., 46, 47
Inman, A. G., 46
Israel, A. C., 214

Jackson, B., 43
Jacobs, M., 12
James, O. O., 282, 286
Jany, K. C., 378, 379
Jensen, P. S., 210
Johnson, J. H., 65
Johnson, M. B., 193
Johnson, M. E., 34
Jolly, J., 198
Joshi, P. T., 20
Joyce, A. S., 380
Jung, C. G., 380

Kaduson, H. G., 97, 160, 164,
    249, 252, 276, 286, 288
Kagan, J., 4
Kail, R. V., 60, 63
Kalichman, S. C., 28
Kamphaus, R. W., 188
Kaplan, A., 47

Kaslow, F. W., 275
Kaslow, N. J., 275
Katayama, M., 88
Kaufman, A. S., 190, 191, 194
Kaufman, K. L., 117, 118
Kaufman, N. L., 190, 191, 194
Kaufman, S. H., 202, 329
Kazdin, A. E., 346, 351, 353,
    354, 357, 360, 365, 378
Kehle, T. J., 218
Keller, M. J., 101
Kendall, P. C., 275, 346
Kennedy, P., 21
Kenny, M. C., 28
Kent, L., 112
Kerig, P., 64
Killen, M., 63
Kim, S. H., 214, 224
Kim-Rupnow, W. S., 364
King, N. J., 346
Kinoshita, L., 46
Kinzie, D., 46
Kirmayer, L., 47
Kitchener, K. S., 117
Klein, M., 17, 262, 282
Klein, R. H., 380
Kleinknecht, R. A., 47
Klin, A., 216, 224
Kline, R. B., 199, 200
Klinedinst, J. K., 199
Knapp, P., 210
Knapp, S., 116
Knobel, M., 12
Knoff, H. M., 159
Koeppen, A. S., 275, 355, 367
Kohen, D. P., 275
Kohut, H., 10, 12, 147, 183,
    255, 260, 261, 264, 324,
    326, 380
Koplow, L., 88
Kottman, T., 141, 168, 305, 311
Kovacs, M., 198
Kramer, E., 324, 325, 328, 329,
    336, 337
Kratochwill, T. R., 175, 275,
    355
Kronenberger, W. G., 64
Kübler-Ross, E., 387, 388
Kurlan, R., 217

Lachar, D., 199, 200
Lamb, S., 4
Landgarten, H. B., 330, 336, 339

Landreth, G. L., 85, 89, 92, 93,
    97, 249, 257, 266, 267, 272,
    273, 275, 276, 277, 283,
    284, 286, 380, 382, 384,
    387
Lanyado, M., 16, 18
Lasch, C., 324
Laughlin, H., 183
Lebo, D., 97
Lee, C. C., 38, 39, 45
Lee, W-Y., 143, 147, 148, 149,
    275
Leiper, R., 23
Leong, F. T. L., 46
Lerner, R. M., 61
Levick, M., 333
Levitan, S., 23
Levy, D., 285
Lewis, M., 64
Lezak, M. D., 206
Lichtenberg, J. D., 64
Lilleskov, R., 15
Lobovits, D., 302
Lonner, W. J., 43, 45
Lopez-Ibor, J. J., 47
Loring, D. W., 206
Lovinger, S. L., 157
Lum, D., 46, 48
Luria, A. R., 194
Lyness, A. M. P., 143, 169
Lyons, P. M., 113, 114

Machover, K., 329
Malchiodi, C. A., 159, 328, 329,
    332, 335
Malgady, R. G., 205
Malofeeva, E. V., 378
Mannarino, A. P., 120
Manson, S., 47, 51
March, J. S., 220
Marcus, I. W., 88
Marcus, P., 88
Markwardt, F. C., 191
Marsella, A., 47
Marsh, J. S., 198
Martin, C. E., 8
Martin, G., 346, 353, 357
Mash, E. J., 214, 222, 227, 275,
    354
Masterson, J. F., 324
Mather, N., 193
Matsumoto, D., 45, 47
McCabe, K. M., 378

McConaughy, S. H., 131, 185, 187
McElroy, L. P., 22, 23
McElroy, R. A., 22, 23
McGoldrick, M., 45, 135
McGrew, K. S., 193, 194
Melby, D., 117
Meller, P. J., 45, 47
Melton, G. B., 109, 110, 113, 114
Metcalf, L. M., 8
Meyer, R. G., 64, 211
Miller, C., 310
Miller, P. J., 302
Miller, S. M., 64
Miller-Perrin, C. L., 117, 118, 120
Mills, J. C., 275
Minuchin, S., 143, 147, 148, 149, 275
Miranda, A., 46
Mishler, C., 47
Monges, M. M., 52
Monroe, S., 106
Moore, B. B., 302
Moore, L., 47
Morris, R. J., 275, 355
Morris, T. L., 220
Morrison, J., 177, 214
Morrissette, P. J., 131
Morten, G., 43, 45
Mrazek, D. A., 210
Mueller, E., 304
Muro, J., 85
Murphy, J., 328
Myers, J. E. B., 118, 119, 120

Naimark, H., 109
Namyniuk, L., 39, 44, 51
Naumberg, M., 336
Neimark, J., 88
Neimeyer, R. A., 117
Nemiroff, M. A., 88, 142
Newman, B. M., 60, 63
Newman, P. R., 60, 63
Nichols, M. P., 143, 147, 148, 149
Nock, M. K., 378
Nordstrom, B., 224
Norton, B. E., 93, 94, 380, 394
Norton, C. C., 93, 94, 380, 394

O'Conner, K. J., 249, 253, 257, 259, 260, 267, 276, 286, 378, 380, 384, 386

Ogden, T. H., 18, 262, 332, 333, 335
Ogrodniczuk, J. S., 380
Ollendick, T. H., 346
Olness, K., 275
Oster, G. D., 274, 330, 336
Owens, R. E., Jr., 4, 63
Ozmun, J. C., 63

Paradis, A. D., 223
Patterson, G. R., 285
Patton, J. M., 214, 224
Paul, M., 112, 216
Paul, R., 216, 224
Pavlov, I., 347
Pear, J., 346, 353, 357
Pearce, J. K., 45
Pearce, S. S., 305
Pearson, D. A., 177
Pearson, M., 275
Pedersen, P. B., 39, 43, 44, 45, 47, 52
Pellowski, A., 300, 301
Perrin, R. D., 117, 118, 120
Pfeffer, C. R., 274
Philips, B., 378
Phinney, J. S., 35
Piaget, J., 4, 63, 67, 74
Piper, W. E., 380
Pomerantz, K. A., 300, 302
Ponterotto, J. G., 38, 39, 43, 45, 47, 49, 52
Pope, K. S., 113, 114, 116, 117, 119
Powell, K. J., 224
Powell, L., 23
Power, T. J., 364
Powers, S. W., 355, 363
Pratt, M. W., 301, 302
Prout, H. T., 112, 113
Prout, S. M., 112, 113
Putnam, F. W., 223

Rabin, A. I., 201
Rambert, M. L., 325
Rasbury, W. C., 65
Rashkin, R., 88
Ray, D. C., 85, 275
Reamer, F. G., 113
Reid, S. E., 106
Reinherz, H. Z., 223
Renner, C., 300, 301
Renninger, S. M., 28

Rescorla, L. A., 49, 185, 187, 214, 222
Reynolds, C. R., 188
Reynolds-Mejia, P., 23
Rhine, T., 85
Riley, S., 337
Ringel, S., 4
Risley, T. R., 66
Ritter, K. B., 101, 103
Roberts, L. W., 111, 113
Roberts, M. C., 275
Robertson, G. J., 192
Robertson, G. S., 224
Robertson, M., 303
Rogler, L., 205
Roid, G. H., 195
Romero, V., 346
Rorschach, H., 202, 203
Ross, R., 211
Rowan, J., 12
Roysircar, G., 39
Rubin, J. A., 325, 326, 328, 329, 334, 336, 337, 338, 339
Rubin, L. C., 14, 92
Rudolph, L. B., 275
Russ, S. R., 60, 240, 257, 259, 265

Sable, J., 37
Salpekar, J. A., 20
Sameroff, A. J., 64
Samuda, R. J., 45
Sandgrun, A., 159
Sandhu, D. S., 39
Sandler, J., 15
Santostefano, S., 89
Satir, V., 275
Sattler, J. M., 175, 190, 194, 197
Scarf, M., 135
Schaefer, C. E., 97, 106, 160, 164, 249, 252, 276, 286, 288
Schickedanz, D. I., 66, 67, 73
Schickedanz, J. A., 66, 67, 73
Schinka, J. A., 177
Schmitt, A. J., 215
Schottelkorb, A., 85
Schowalter, J. E., 15
Schroeder, C. S., 60
Schwartz, E. K., 302
Schwartz, M. S., 275
Schwartz, R. C., 143, 147, 148, 149

Seat, P. D., 199
Sedlak, A., 117
Seifer, R., 64, 224
Self, P. A., 4, 61, 63
Shadle, C., 106
Shaffer, D. R., 63
Shapiro, E. S., 175
Shelef, K., 378
Sherman, M. H., 302, 304
Shipstead, S. G., 67
Siegel, H. B., 8
Siegel, L. J., 65
Silva, R. R., 223
Simeone, W. E., 47
Simmons, J. E., 85
Simon, G. M., 143, 147, 148, 149, 275
Sinason, V., 96
Skinner, B. F., 285, 347, 353
Skinner, E. A., 61
Skodol, A. E., 211
Smetana, J., 63
Smith, S. R., 200
Sokol, R. J., 224
Sori, C. F., 132
Sorrell, G. T., 61
Southam-Gerow, M. A., 219
Sparrow, S. S., 189
Spero, M. H., 104
Spiegel, S., 85, 100, 241, 268, 274, 380, 384, 386, 394
Spiegler, M. D., 355
Spitzer, R. L., 211
Spurlock, J., 39, 49, 54
Stafford, B. S., 218, 224
Stark, K. D., 219
Steelsmith, S., 88
Stein, A., 64, 216
Stein, M. A., 206
Stern, D. N., 4, 11, 63, 64, 68, 146, 241, 256
Stern, R., 8
Stevenson, S. R., 117
Stiles, K., 305, 311

Stine, J. J., 275
Stores, G., 220
Stormshak, E. A., 114
Stratton, P., 118
Straus, M. B., 101
Sue, D., 45, 49
Sue, D. W., 43, 45, 49
Sugarman, L. I., 275
Sullivan, A., 223
Suzuki, L. A., 38, 39, 45, 47, 49
Swanson, D. P., 46
Sweeney, D. S., 103, 275
Swenson, L. C., 116, 118

Tan, J., 112
Tanaka-Matsumi, J., 46, 47
Tansey, M. J., 262
Tataki, R. T., 44
Taylor, E. R., 9
Terr, L. C., 275
Teyber, E., 380
Theodore, L. A., 218
Thomas, R. M., 63, 64
Thompson, C. L., 21, 275
Tingley, E., 304
Todd, J., 227
Trimble, J. E., 43, 45
Tsai, L. Y., 218
Tupper, D. E., 215
Turner, S. M., 224

Utsey, S. O., 43, 52

van Beekum, S., 17
VandeCreek, L., 116
Vasquez, M. J. T., 113, 114, 116, 117, 119
Vaught, C. C., 380
Veach, P. M., 28
Volkmar, F. R., 216, 224
Von Gontard, A., 217

Waldram, J. B., 47
Walker, C. E., 117, 118, 275, 355

Walker, N. E., 109
Walkup, N., 301
Walsh, J., 380
Wasserman, M. S., 223
Watson, T. S., 346
Weaver, C. M., 211
Webb, N. B., 21, 22, 286
Wechsler, D., 196, 197
Wenar, C., 64
Westen, D., 64
Wester, J., 275
Whitmore, K., 215
Wicks-Nelson, R., 214
Wiger, D. E., 132
Wilkinson, G. S., 192
Willems, G., 215
Williams, J. B. W., 211
Wilmshurst, W., 214
Wimbarti, S., 4, 61, 63
Wingenfeld, S. A., 199, 200
Wirt, R. D., 199
Wirth, L., 35
Wise, D., 117
Wodrich, D. L., 215
Wolf, E., 255
Wolpe, J., 347
Woltman, A. G., 276
Woodcock, R. W., 193
Wrightsman, L. S., 109
Wustinger, L., 10

Yang, L. H., 46
Youngstrom, E. A., 219

Zakich, R., 106
Zalsman, G., 224
Zeanah, C. H., 64, 218, 224
Zeckhausen, D., 88
Zellman, G. L., 117
Zinn, H., 44
Zucker, K. J., 220
Zuckerman, E. L., 132
Zwiers, M. L., 131

Subject Index

Abreaction, 285–286
Abstracting ability, 180
Abuse. *See* Child abuse/neglect
Academic achievement/performance, 171–172, 180, 209, 222
Accident proneness, 210
Acculturation, 43–44, 138, 222. *See also* Culture; Ethnicity
Achenbach System of Empirically Based Assessment (ASEBA), 185, 187
Achievement testing, 186, 190–193
Achievement vs. aptitude, 190
Acting out behaviors, 180, 184, 225, 251, 270–271
Active listening, 152
Acute stress disorder, 219
Adjustment disorders, 221–222
Adolescence, diagnosing disorders of, 217–218. *See also* Late childhood
Adult clients/interventions, training for, 3–4
Affect
    acceptance and metabolization of, 263
    child's fluctuations in, 32–33
    expression through play, 277–278
    mood and, 177–178
    projection and reintrojection of, 262
Age-normed developmental expectations, 62
Aggression management, limit-setting skills for, 270–271

Agoraphobia, 219
Ambiguity, tolerance of, 12
Anorexia nervosa, 174, 217
Antisocial behavior, 222
Anxiety disorders, 219–220
Appearance vs. reality, early childhood differentiation of, 68
Apperception testing, 204
Aptitude vs. achievement, 190
Art
    application to child therapy/counseling, 328–336
    art therapists vs. general clinicians, 337
    assessment through, 328–329
    for cathartic purposes, 329
    conceptual background of, 325–328
    content interpretation of, 333–336
    criteria for selecting materials, 338
    developmental phases of, 326–328
    form interpretation of, 332–333
    formal assessment procedures using, 336
    as growth-promoting medium, 329–330
    implementation, case example of, 339–344
    play vs., 325
    precursors to production of, 324–325
    process interpretation of, 332
    purposes of, 325–326, 330

    skill development through, 326
    techniques, practical implementation of, 337–339
    therapeutic interpretation of, 330–336
    variations on the therapeutic technique, 336–337
As-if explanations, 259–260
Asperger's disorder, 216
Assessment
    art as tool for, 328–329, 336
    instruments, list of, 186
    intake interview, 131–168
    materials used in, 105–106
    neuropsychological, 205–206
    personality, 197–200
    psychological, 175–206
    storytelling used in, 305
    supplementary strategies for, 170–206
Attachment, 18–19
Attention-deficit/hyperactivity disorder, 174, 214–215, 224
Attunement, 256, 261
Authenticity, 12–13
Authoritarian/authoritative parents, 153
Autistic disorder, 215–216
Aversive conditioning, 357
Avoidance, 183–184
Awareness and orientation, 179
Awareness, cultural, 39–44

Babysitter countertransference, 25
Beck Youth Inventories, Second Edition, 198

Behavior
    children's responsibility for,
        251
    fluctuations in, 32–33
    incompatible, reinforcement
        of, 358, 369–370
    nonpathological, as normal
        child development, 64–65
    observation and data gather-
        ing about, 140, 180–181
    rating scales/forms, 137,
        185–190
Behavior Assessment System for
    Children-2, 188
Behavioral techniques/interven-
    tions
    case example of, 366–370
    cognitive-behavioral perspec-
        tives, 347
    conceptual background of,
        346–353
    learning theory and,
        347–353
    practical implementation of,
        364–366
Behavioral theories of play,
    284–285
Bereavement, 222
Best friends, exploring relation-
    ships with, 137
Bias, cultural
    countertransference and, 57
    developing awareness of,
        41–43
    in minority assessment tools,
        45–46
    See also Discrimination; Prej-
        udice
Big sibling countertransference,
    25
Bingeing and purging, 217
Biological factors affecting
    development, 62, 224
Bipolar disorders, 219
Biracial children, cultural iden-
    tity confusion in, 58
Body language, 31
Borderline intellectual function-
    ing, 222
Breathing-related sleep disor-
    der, 221
Brief psychotic disorder, 218
Bulimia nervosa, 174, 217

Caregiver-teacher report forms,
    185, 187
Caretaker
    desire to be, 21
    stance, 8
Case conceptualization. See
    Conceptualization
Case dynamics, understanding
    in treatment planning,
        222–230
Catalysts for change
    art as, 329
    creation of a therapeutic
        environment, 247–251
    creation of a therapeutic
        relationship, 251–255
    defenses, symptoms, and
        resistance, 264–266. See
        also Counseling process,
        challenges to
    expressing empathy and
        understanding, 255–256
    internalization, 260–262
    methods and levels of
        explaining, 256–260
    projective identification,
        262–264
Catatonia, 218–219
Catharsis, 259, 277, 281, 286,
    329
Certification/licensure, 4
Challenges of child therapy
    children's invitations to
        guessing games, 273
    dealing with theft, 273–274
    food or drink in the play-
        room, 271
    giving and receiving gifts, 272
    questions loaded with
        unmentioned values,
        affects, and needs,
        272–273
    reluctance/refusal to end the
        session, 267–268
    reluctance/refusal to enter
        the playroom, 266–267
    request for early termination
        of a session, 268–269
    requests to use the restroom,
        ulterior motives for,
        269–270
    taking objects home from the
        playroom, 271–272

threats of physical aggres-
    sion, 270–271
understanding questions
    with transferential mean-
    ing, 269
Change, catalysts for, 247–266
Chaotic discharge, definition of,
    324
Character traits, expression of,
    15
Child abuse/neglect
    common symptoms of,
        119–120
    disorders resulting from, 222
    duty to report, 28, 117–118,
        121
    emotional, 118–120
    medical evidence of, 139–140
    parental, 28
    physical, 117, 119–120, 139,
        222
    sexual. See Sexual abuse
Child behavior checklists, 185,
    187
Child clinicians
    challenges in working with
        parents, 26–29
    common reactions of, 14–19
    common vulnerabilities of,
        19–22
    cultivating cultural sensitiv-
        ity, 38–53
    development made relevant
        to, 63–75
    educational needs and back-
        grounds of, 3–6
    effective, markers of, 3–33
    parental relationship issues,
        22, 26
    positive personal traits of,
        6–14
    reassurance and comfort
        from, 251–252
    training qualifications/rec-
        ommended coursework
        for, 4–5
    See also Child-clinician rela-
        tionship; Therapists
Child focus, in creating thera-
    peutic relationships, 251
Child therapy/counseling
    behavior techniques in,
        346–373

challenges to process of, 266–275
cultural sensitivity in, 34–58
developmental context for, 60–82
environments and materials for, 32, 84–106
framework for, 239–275. See also Counseling process
graphic and sculpting art in, 324–345
legal and ethical issues in, 108–128
storytelling in, 300–323
use of play in, 276–299
Child/children
as identified client(s), 27
developmental needs/milestones of, 63–83
expectations about treatment, 27–28
friendship patterns of, 137–138
identification with, 16–17
nonpathologizing developmentally appropriate behaviors of, 64–65
respect for, 10
right to privacy of, 109
sensitivity to developmental level of, 31–32
working with special needs of, 29–33
Child-clinician relationship
facilitating through play, 280, 284, 288
transference in, 253–255, 283
Children's Depression Inventory, 198
Child-specific countertransference, 16
Chronic motor disorder, 217
Circadian rhythm sleep disorder, 221
Civil law/mental health statutes, 110
Clarifying questions, 257–258
Classical conditioning model of learning, 347–348
Classroom observation, 174–175
Clinic design and furnishings, 85–86, 89, 91, 97

Clinical syndromes, 211
Clinicians. See Child clinicians; Therapists
Clinics
first impressions of, 84–85
physical layout, design and furnishings of, 85–91
playroom features, 91–97
unconventional therapy spaces in, 89–91
waiting area, 88–89
Clothing choice, and therapeutic style, 13–14
Codes of ethics, 110–111
Cognitive abilities, testing, 193
Cognitive development
in early childhood, 66–67
in late childhood, 74
in middle childhood, 71–72
norms, 63
Piaget's model of, 76
Cognitive functioning, 179–180
Cognitive-behavioral perspectives, 347
Comfort, in therapeutic relationships, 251–252
Communication
addressing the ethnic child client, 54
autistic disorder and, 216
culturally preferred modes of, 49–50
diagnosis of disorders in, 215
expression of counselors' availability for, 252
expressive art as, 325
family session, 146
metaphoric. See Metaphor
nonverbal, through play, 276, 278–279
projective identification as, 262
simple language in, 157
storytelling as, 301–303
symbolic, during creative play, 92–93, 256
See also Language
Compulsions, 219–220
Conceptualization
choice of therapeutic approach to, 226–227
diagnosis and, 208–222. See also Diagnosis

as direct precursor to treatment planning, 230
family dynamics and, 228–229
interpersonal matrix dynamics and, 229–230
intrapsychic dynamics and, 226–228
mental status exams and, 184
perpetuating factors of, 225–226
precipitating factors of, 224–226
predisposing factors of, 222–224, 226
of presenting problem, 165–166
understanding case dynamics, 222–230
Conduct disorders, 214–215, 224
Confidentiality
clinic design and, 86–87
informed consents and, 119
intake interview, 145
legal/ethical aspects of, 113–114
limits to, 115–121
practical considerations of, 114–115
respect for, 10
Conflict model of pathology, 282–283
Conflict resolution
abandoning metaphor in, 299
art as means of, 329
Conners Third Edition ratings scales, 189
Consciousness, 179
Consequences, logical and natural, 152
Conservation, 67, 71
Construction materials, 102–103
Content interpretation of art, 333–336
Contingency setting, following through on, 270
Convention on the Rights of the Child (CRC), 108–110
Cop countertransference, 26

Coping strategies, 182–183, 265
Counseling process
    challenges to, 266–275
    phases of, 241–247
    provider-induced problems
        in, 234–235
Counseling. *See* Child therapy/
    counseling; Therapy
Counselors. *See* Child clinicians;
    Therapists
Counteridentification, projec-
    tive, 17
Countertransference, 15–16
    babysitter, 25
    big sibling, 25
    cop, 26
    cross-cultural, 57
    good-enough parent, 24–25
    me adult/you child, 24
    negative, toward parents, 14
    teacher, 25–26
Coursework, recommended,
    4–5
Covert discrimination, 38
Covert prejudice, 39
Creativity, materials/toys to
    promote, 94, 101–102
Cross-cultural therapy, 45, 53,
    56–57
Cross-gender identification, 220
Cultural awareness, 39–44
Cultural identity development,
    35, 43–44, 58
Cultural sensitivity
    acquiring as a clinician,
        38–59
    through cultural awareness,
        39–44
    through cultural knowledge,
        39, 44–48
    through cultural skills, 48–52
    positive personal trait of,
        9–10
    process issues in working
        with children, 53–58
    through self-monitoring,
        52–53
Cultural skills, 39, 48–52
Cultural storytelling, 302–304
Cultural transference/counter-
    transference, 57
Cultural/ethnic diversity in the
    United States, 36–38

Culture
    achievement testing bias
        and, 190
    definition of, 35
    factors affecting develop-
        ment, 62
    problems associated with,
        208–209
    rejection of cultural heri-
        tage, 57
    value differences between
        therapist and client,
        56–57
Curiosity, in early childhood,
    68
Cyclothymic disorder, 219

Defense mechanisms, 262, 282
    as catalyst for change,
        264–266
Delusional disorder, 180,
    218–219
Denial, 184
Depressive disorders, 219
Desensitization programs, 285,
    288, 355–357, 366,
    368–369
Development
    art as tool for facilitating,
        326
    deficits and delays in, 209
    definition of, 61
    dialectic model of, 61–63
    disorders, pervasive,
        215–216
    goals, 241
    influences on, 61–62
    relevance to child clinicians,
        63–75
    theories, course work in, 4
    types of, 62
Developmental stages
    early childhood, 65–69
    form interpretations of art
        and, 333
    late childhood, 73–75
    middle childhood, 69–73
    sensitivity of clinician to,
        31–32
Developmental trajectory of the
    child, goals relating to, 241
Developmental/health-related
    information, 139–140

Diagnosis
    of adjustment disorders,
        221–222
    of anxiety disorders,
        219–220
    of attention-deficit/disrup-
        tive behavior disorders,
        214–215
    of communication disor-
        ders, 215
    differential, 214
    of elimination disorders, 217
    of feeding/eating disorders
        in infancy/early child-
        hood, 216–217
    of learning disorders, 215
    of mental retardation, 214
    of mood disorders, 219
    of motor skills disorders, 215
    multiaxial system of,
        211–214
    of other disorders in
        infancy/childhood/ado-
        lescence, 217–218
    of pervasive developmental
        disorders, 215–216
    problem lists and, 208–210
    of schizophrenia and other
        psychotic disorders,
        218–219
    of sexual/gender identity
        disorders, 220
    of sleep disorders, 220–221
    of tic disorders, 217
    V-code, 222
*Diagnostic and Statistical Manual
    of Mental Disorders*, 210–214
Dialectic model of develop-
    ment, 61–63
Differential diagnosis, 214
Direct observation form, 187
Discipline strategies, determin-
    ing, 152–154
Disclosure function of play,
    280–281
Discrimination
    clinician advocacy against, 52
    covert, 38
    minority, abuse by peers, 35,
        58
    See also Bias, cultural; Preju-
        dice
Disorders, culture-bound, 46–47

Disruptive behavior disorder, 214–215
Dissociations, 179
Diversion, 183–184
Dolls and dollhouses, 95, 99–100, 201–202, 329, 338, 340
Draw-A-Person Test, 201–202, 329, 340
Draw-a-Story Game, 338
Drawing, associative/manifest/ latent content of, 159, 311, 333–334. *See also* Art
Dress, awareness of, 13–14
Dual relationships, 122
Duty to protect, 167
Duty to report, 117–121, 167
Duty to warn, 116–117, 167
Dynamics
    family, 228–229
    interpersonal matrix, 229–230
    intrapsychic, 226–228
Dyssomnias, 220
Dysthymic disorder, 219

Early childhood
    development, 65–69
    feeding and eating disorders of, 216–217
    motor development in, 81–82
    reactive attachment disorder of, 217–218
    social development in, 66–67
Eating disorders, 174, 216–217, 223
Eclectic integrative model of play therapy, 287
Education
    child clinician, needs and backgrounds of, 3–5
    ongoing, of seasoned child clinicians, 122
    parental, 116, 317, 366–367
    See also Training
Egocentric perspective, 68
Elimination disorders, 174, 217
Emotional abuse/neglect, 118–120
Emotional adjustment, 208
Emotional development
    in early childhood, 68
    in late childhood, 74

in middle childhood, 72
    norms, 63, 77
Emotional differentiation, 31–32
Emotions
    identification of sources of, 258–259
    in relation to the perpetrator, 23
    in relation to the victim, 23
    therapist's, evoked, 33
Empathy
    between parents, 155
    importance in the therapeutic relationship, 255–256
    positive personal trait of, 10–12
    sympathy vs., 23
Entertainment, storytelling as, 301
Enuresis/encopresis, 134, 174, 217, 225
Environment
    developmental consideration of, 32
    influence on behavior, 353
    limit setting in, 160–161, 249, 270–271
    of office, 32
    of playroom, 91–92
    predisposing factors, 223
    problems in, 208, 212
    safety of, 85–87, 89, 92, 95
    therapeutic, creation of, 36, 247–251
    of therapy/treatment room, 87–88
Epistemological feeling, 12
Equipment, developmental consideration of, 32
Ethical training, 5
Ethical/legal issues, miscellaneous, 122–123
Ethical violations, reporting, 122–123
Ethics codes, 110–111
Ethnic identity, 43, 58, 100
Ethnic sensitivity, 9–10, 99–100. *See also* Cultural sensitivity
Ethnic/cultural diversity in the United States, 36–38
Ethnicity
    doll families of ethnic variety, 99–100

impact on counseling process, 54
    impact on family life, 138–139
    minority status and, 35–36
    race vs., 34–35
    sociocultural factors relating to, 138
Eurocentric nature of personality theories, 46
Evasion, 183
Experience, practical, 6
Explaining strategies
    asking clarifying questions, 257–258
    methods and levels of, 256–260
    pointing out patterns, 257
Exploring strategies
    as-if explanations, 259–260
    catharsis, 259
    identification of sources of feelings, 258–259
    interpretation, 260
Expressive art, definition of, 325
Expressive language disorder, 215
Extinction, 152, 351
Eye contact, cultural differences in, 56

Familial predisposing factors, 224
Familial problems, 209
Family
    competence, 149
    cultural backgrounds and attitudes of, 138
    dynamics, 228–229
    future plans, fantasies, daydreams, 140
    impact of culture/ethnicity on, 138–139
    intake interview of, 134–135, 145–150
    interventions, training in, 5
    process, 149–150
    recreation, interests and hobbies of, 139
    relating, 150
    relationships, questions about, 134–135
    religiosity/spirituality in, 139

sociocultural factors defining, 138–139
spousal relationship within, 155–156
storytelling/narratives, 302–303
structure, 148–149
values, respect for, 9
Fantasy, differentiating from reality, 179
Feedback session, assessment vs. counseling in, 164
Feeding and eating disorders of infancy/early childhood, 216–217
Feelings. *See* Emotions
Fetal alcohol spectrum disorder (FASD), 180, 224
Flexibility, 12, 24, 157, 231
Food, 101, 272
Form interpretation of art, 332–333
Free play vs. structured play, 286

Games, therapeutic use of, 106
Gender
    identity disorders, 220
    role socialization, 73–74
    sensitivity, 9–10, 99–100
    stereotyping, 100
Generalized anxiety disorder, 219–220
Genograms, 135–136
Gift giving and receiving, 272
Global Assessment of Functioning Scale (GAF), 212–213
Goals, setting in counseling/therapy process, 145, 167, 239–241
Good-enough parent countertransference, 24–25
Grammar, 66, 70
Growth model of pathology, 284
Growth, art as a medium promoting, 329–330

Habitual modes of relating, 15
Hallucinations, 179, 218–219
Halstead-Reitan Neuropsychological Test Battery for Children, 205

Harm, personal, wish to undo, 20
Healing function of play, 281–282
Health and development, 180
Health issues, 139–140
Hearing deficits, 174
Hierarchy of feared stimuli, 356, 368–369
Holons, definition of, 143
Hospitalization, trauma of, 173
House-tree-person drawing, 329
Hypersomnia, 221
Hypomania, 219

Iatrogenesis, 12
Identifications
    with the child, 16–17
    with the parents, 18
    projective, 17–18
    reactive, 18
Identified client interview
    limit setting for, 160–162
    outline of, 162–163
    rapport-building strategies for, 157, 159–160
Identity development, cultural, 43
Identity problems, 222
Idioms, in child communication, 158
Imagine! game, 106
Imitation, internalization through, 260–261
Impulse control, artistic manifestation of, 332
In loco parentis countertransference, 16
In vivo desensitization program, 356, 366, 368–369
Incompatible behaviors, reinforcement of, 358, 369–370
Individuals with Disabilities Education Act (IDEA), 192
Infants
    eating/feeding disorders in, 216–217
    shifts in social presence of, 64
Informed consent, 111–113
Initiative, early childhood development of, 68–69
Inkblot testing, 202–204

Insomnia, 221
Intake forms, 132
Intake interview
    behavioral observations during, 140
    client background information for, 151–152
    components of, 131
    developmental/health issues, questions about, 139–140
    family relationships, questions about134–135
    feedback and recommendations section of, 144, 164–168
    format of, 143–144
    future plans, fantasies, and daydreams, questions about, 140
    goal setting in, 145, 167
    with the identified child, 157–163
    information to be derived from, 133–134
    interests, hobbies and recreational activities, questions about, 139
    interviewer(s), 144
    joint family interviews, 145–150
    outline and order of, 145
    with parents, 151–156
    preliminary data collection for, 132
    preparation for treatment, 141–143, 167–168
    purpose of, 131
    recreation, interests and hobbies, questions about, 139
    school/preschool issues, questions about, 135, 137
    sharing conceptualization of presenting problem, 165–166
    sharing recommendations, 166–167
    with siblings, 156
    social/peer relationships, questions about137–138
    sociocultural factors, questions about, 138–139
    structure of, 140

Integrative play therapy, 286–289
Intelligence tests, 186, 193–197
Internalization, 184, 246, 260–262
Internship, child-focused, 6
Interpersonal adjustment, 208
Interpersonal matrix, 225, 228–230
Interpersonal relations, 181
Interpretation, 260
Intervention techniques, culturally sensitive, 49
Intrapsychic adjustment, 208
Intrapsychic dynamics, 226–228
Issue-specific countertransference, 15

Kaufman Assessment Battery for Children, Second Edition, 194
Kaufman Brief Intelligence Test, Second Edition, 194–195
Kaufman Test of Educational Achievement-II, 190–191
Kinetic family drawing, 329, 340
Kinetic house-tree-person drawing, 329, 340–342
Kinetic house-tree-person drawing test, 202
Knowledge, cultural, 44–48

Language
    adapting to differences between cultures through, 47, 49
    development norms, 63
    development survey, 185
    early childhood development of, 66
    expressive language disorder, 215
    late childhood development of, 74
    middle childhood development of, 70, 72
    prejudicial, 38
    and reasoning, adjusting to child's capabilities, 31
    Rett's Disorder and, 216
Late childhood development, 73–75

Learning
    disorders, 215
    operant conditioning model of, 348–352
    respondent (classical) conditioning model of, 347–348
    social (observational) theory of, 351–353
Legal/ethical issues, 5, 122–123
Licensure/certification, 4
Limit-setting for acting out behaviors, 249, 160–161, 270–271
Linguistic prejudice, 38
Listening, importance of, 10–12
Live modeling, 363
Logic, development of, 71–74

Major depressive disorder, 219
Mathematics disorder, 215
Maturation function of play, 279
Me adult/you child countertransference, 24
Media-induced societal values, 223
Medical records/referrals, 173–174, 180
Medical/physiological problems, 209
Memory and recall, 179
Mental health centers. See Clinics
Mental health laws/statutes, 110–111
Mental health services, cultural stigma associated with, 47
Mental retardation, 211–212, 214
Mental status examination, 176–184
Metacommunication, storytelling as, 305
Metaphor
    abandoning in conflict resolution, 299
    communication through, 256
    little house/monster animal example, 12
    reexperience through, 245–246
    storytelling and, 305, 312
    understanding and responding to, 30–31, 158

Middle childhood development, 69–73
Minorities
    barriers to utilization of mental health services, 47, 51
    discrimination/abuse by peers, 35, 58
    history of mental health treatment for, 45
    negative view of mental health services, 47
    status of, impact on counseling process, 35–36, 54
Mixed receptive-expressive language disorder, 215
Model Act for State Licensure of Psychologists, 115–116
Modeling
    internalization through, 260–261
    learning new behaviors through, 351–352
    strategies based on social learning, 363–364
Mood and affect, 177–178
Mood disorders, 218–219, 224
Moral attitudes, 223
Moral development, 63, 73
Motor skills
    development, adjusting to children's needs, 31
    development norms, 63, 81–82
    disorders, 215
    early childhood development of, 65–66
    late childhood development of, 74
    middle childhood development of, 69–70
Multiaxial system of diagnosis, 211–214
Multidimensional Anxiety Scale for Children, 198–199
Multigroup/multicultural sensitivity, 35. See also Cultural sensitivity
Mutism, selective, 217–218
Mutual storytelling technique
    case example of, 317–322
    child's story, 313–314
    clinician's story, 315–317

delays between stories,
314–315
instructions for, 312–313
mechanics of, 316

Narcissistic extension, 18
Narcolepsy, 221
Negative reinforcement, 350
Neglect, definition of, 118. *See
also* Child abuse/neglect
Neurological/neuropsychologi-
cal problems, 209
Neuropsychological assessment,
205–206
Nightmares/night terrors, 179,
221, 290, 297
Nonpathologizing developmentally appropriate behav-
iors, 64–65
Nonverbal communication
cultural differences in, 55–56
cultural emphasis on, 49
through play, 276, 278–279
unique to each individual
child, 31
Nurturance materials, 101

Objective personality assessment, 186, 197–200
Observational learning theory,
351–353
Obsessions, 180, 220
Obsessive-compulsive disorder,
219–220
Office environment and equipment, 32
Open-mindedness, 9
Operant conditioning model of
learning, 348–352
extinction and, 351
negative reinforcement and,
350
positive reinforcement and,
349–350
punishment and, 350–351
strategies based on, 357–363
Oppositional defiant disorder,
214–215
Orientation and awareness, 179
Originator instinct, 324
Ostracism, 209, 223, 279
Outerphysical factors affecting
development, 62

Overanxious disorder, 220
Overeating, 174

Panic attack, 219
Parasomnias, 221
Parent rating scales/relationship
questionnaire, 188
Parental storytelling, 302
Parent-child relational problem,
222
Parenting styles, determining,
152–154
Parents
authoritative/authoritarian,
153
challenges in working with,
26–29
child abuse/neglect by. *See*
Child abuse/neglect
child's idealization of, 22
competing with, 22
consultation about a child's
treatment, 28–29
cooperation of, in treating
their child, 29
coordinating multiple sets of,
29
education and consultation
training, 5
empowerment of, 169
expectations about treat-
ment, 27–28
idealization of, 22
identification with, 18
intake interview with,
151–156
parental abuse or neglect, 28
permissive, 153
respect for, 14
session updates with, 168
Participant modeling, 364
Patterns, pointing out, 257
Peabody Individual Achievement Test-Revised/Nor-
mative Update, 191
Peabody Picture Vocabulary
Test, Fourth Edition, 195
*Peck v. Counseling Services of Addi-
son County, Inc.*, 116
Peer relationships, 35, 38,
137–138, 156
Perception and sensorium, 179
Permissiveness, 53, 157

Perpetrator, emotions relating
to, 23
Perpetuating factors, 225–226
Perreira v. Colorado, 116
Personal harm, wish to undo, 20
Personal predisposing factors,
224
Personal space, cultural differences in, 56
Personal traits, positive
being true to one's self,
12–13
cultural/gender sensitivity,
9–10
empathy/willingness to listen, 10–12
flexibility/tolerance of ambiguity, 12
open-mindedness, 9
respect for the child, 10
self-awareness, 8
self-respect and self-esteem, 7
Personality
assessment, objective, 4,
197–200
authenticity of, 12–13
disorders, 211–212
theories, Eurocentric nature
of, 46
traits, counterproductive, 13
Personality Inventory for Children Family of Tests,
199–200
Perspective, early childhood
development of, 67–68
Pervasive developmental disorders, 215–216
Phobias, specific/social,
219–220
Phonological disorder, 215
Physical abuse/neglect, 117,
119–120, 139, 222
Physical activity, appearance/
level of, 177
Physical aggression, threats of,
270–271
Physical disorders, 212
Physical restraint, 270–271
Physical safety. *See* Environ-
ment
Physical touch, 252–253
Physiological/medical prob-
lems, 209

Pica, 216
Pictographs, definition of, 325
Piers-Harris Children's Self-
    Concept Scale, Second
    Edition, 200
Play
    art vs., 325
    behavioral theories of,
        284–285
    cathartic function of,
        285–286
    conceptual background of,
        276–277
    conflict resolution through,
        280
    disclosure function of, 280
    eclectic integrative model of
        play therapy, 286–288
    exploratory function of, 279
    free vs. structured, 286
    healing function of, 281–282
    interpretive use of, 159–160
    mastery function of, 277
    maturation function of, 279
    nonverbal communication
        through, 276, 278–279
    practical implementation of,
        287–289
    problem-solving function of,
        281–282
    psychoanalytic/psychody-
        namic theories of,
        282–283
    recollection through, 243
    reconstruction through,
        243–244
    reexperience through,
        245–246
    relationship function of,
        279–280
    relationship theories of,
        283–284
    release and structure theories
        of, 285–286
    sand play, storytelling in
        conjunction with, 311.
        See also Sandtrays/sand-
        boxes
    self-development function
        of, 277–279
    stimulation through,
        278–279
    symbolic value of toys, 94, 96

symbolism of, 277, 280, 289
therapeutic. See Play therapy
unconscious purposefulness
    of, 277
Play therapy
    case example of, 289–299
    eclectic integrative model of,
        286–289
    manifesting protective mech-
        anisms through, 265
    research demonstrating
        effectiveness of, 85
    safety issues concerning, 86
Playroom
    cleanup arrangements for,
        90–91
    environment of, 91–92
    food or drink in, 271
    guidelines for materials
        selection for, 92–97
    taking objects home from,
        271–272
    toys/materials to support
        work in, 97–106
    use for intake interviews,
        144
Popularity, importance in mid-
    dle childhood, 73
Positive reinforcement,
    349–350, 369
Posttraumatic stress disorder,
    219–220, 223
Power issues, 26
Practical experience, 6
Practicum, child-focused, 6
Precipitating factors, 224–225
Predisposing factors, 222–224
Prejudice
    alienating children from
        their parents, 58
    covert, 38–39
    developing awareness of,
        41–43
    predisposing factor of, 223
    See also Bias, cultural; Dis-
        crimination; Minorities
Preoccupations, 180
Presenting problems, 133–134,
    165, 240, 246–247, 328
Pretend play materials, 104–105
Previous treatment records, 173
Primary hypersomnia, 221
Primary insomnia, 221

Privacy
    children's right to, 109
    clinic design and, 86–87
    respect for, 10
    of waiting parents, 88
Problem lists
    academic problems, 209
    psychological problems, 208
    social and cultural prob-
        lems, 208–209
Problems
    familial, 209
    psychological, 208
Problem-solving
    function of play, 281–282
    learning alternative strate-
        gies for, 265
Process interpretation of art,
    332
Process phases of therapy/coun-
    seling, 241–247
Professionalism, and adequacy
    of training, 122, 176
Projection, 184
Projective counteridentifica-
    tion, 17, 263–264
Projective drawings, 159
Projective identification, 16–18,
    184, 262–264
Projective personality assess-
    ment instruments, 186
Projective questions, 158
Projective testing, 200–205
Protective mechanisms,
    264–265
Protector, desire to be, 21
Psychoanalytic/conflict model
    of psychopathology, 283
Psychoanalytic/psychody-
    namic theories of play,
    282–283
Psychological adjustment goals,
    240–241
Psychological assessment,
    175–176
Psychological defenses, 182–183
Psychological factors affecting
    development, 62
Psychological safety. See Envi-
    ronment
Psychopathology conflict model
    of, 283
Psychopathology, training in, 4

Psychoses, 174
Psychosexual/psychosocial development norms, 63, 78–79
Psychosocial problems, 212
Psychotic disorders, 218–219
Punishment, 350–351
Puppets, 98–99, 258

Questioning strategies, 158
Questions, clarifying vs. information gathering, 257–258

Race, 34–35. *See also* Ethnicity; Minorities
Racism, knowledge about societal role of, 44–45
Rapport-building strategies, 158, 252–253
Rationalization, 184
Reactive Attachment Disorder of Infancy or Early Childhood, 217–218
Reactive attachment disorders, 224
Reactive identification, 16, 18
Reading disorder, 215
Reality
    contact, 179
    differentiating from fantasy, 179
    vs. appearance, early childhood differentiation of, 68
Reassurance, in therapeutic relationships, 251–252
Recollection phase, 242–243
Reconstruction phase, 243–244
Reexperience phase, 244–246
Referral sources and consultation, 137, 173–175
Reflection, 257
Reinforcement, positive and negative, 349–350
Reintrojection, 17, 263
Reitan-Indiana Neuropsychological Test Battery for Children, 206
Relating, habitual modes of, 15
Relational patterns, common, 23–26
Relationship
    function of play, 279
    problems in, 222

theories of play, 283–284
See also Therapeutic relationships
Relaxation programs/techniques, 285, 288, 355
Release and structure theories of play, 285–286
Religiosity/spirituality, 139
Religious problems, 208
Rescuer role, vulnerability of, 21–22
Resistance as catalyst for change, 264–266
Respect
    for the child, 10
    for confidentiality and privacy, 10
    of the identified client, 158
    for parents, 14
    in therapeutic relationships, 252
Respondent (classical) conditioning model of learning, 347–348
    strategies based on, 355–357
Response cost procedures, 358–360
Restrooms, 87, 269–270
Rett's disorder, 215–216
Reunion game, 106
Rights, children's, 108–110
Rigidity, avoidance of, 24
Rorschach Inkblot Test, 202–204
Rules and regulations, internalization of, 261–262
Rumination disorder, 174, 216
Running commentary, 257

Safety
    creating a therapeutic environment, 247–251
    of playroom equipment, 92
    prioritizing in clinic design, 85–87, 89
    of toys in the playroom, 95
Sandtrays/sandboxes, 91–92, 103–104, 311
Schizophreniform/schizoaffective disorder, 218–219, 224
School figures/records, 100–101, 170–172

School/preschool performance and related behaviors, 135, 137
Sculpting, formal assessment procedures using, 336–337. *See also* Art
Search and seizure, 122
Seizure disorders, 179
Selective mutism disorder, 217–218, 223
Self modeling, 364
Self, being true to, 12–13
Self-appraisal, realistic, 181
Self-awareness, 8
Self-concept, 181
Self-development function of play, 277–279
Self-development norms, 63, 80
Self-esteem/self-confidence, 7, 181, 261
Self-expression
    internalization of, 261
    safety in expressing, 249
    toys to promote, 93–94
Self-identity, 181
Self-monitoring, 52–53
Self-Report of Personality, 188
Semistructured Clinical Interview for Children and Adolescents, 185, 187
Sensitivity. *See* Cultural sensitivity; Gender sensitivity
Sensorium and perception, 179
Sensory modalities, 146
Separation anxiety disorder, 217–218, 223, 266
Session updates, 168
Sexual abuse
    anatomically correct dolls to diagnose, 100
    art as vehicle for revealing, 341–343
    definition of, 118
    DSM-IV-TR diagnosis of, 222
    symptoms of, 120
Sexual disorders, 220
Shaping, 357–358
Shared psychotic disorder, 218–219
Sibling relationships, 135, 156, 222
Silence, respect communicated by, 252

Skills, cultural, 48–52
Sleep disorders, 220–221
Social (observational) learning
    theory, 351–353
Social development
    in late childhood, 74
    in middle childhood, 72–73
Social learning
    model of pathology, 285
    strategies based on, 363–364
Social phobia, 219
Social problems, 208–209
Social relationships, 137–138
Societal consensus, toys that
    reflect, 94
Societal/social predisposing fac-
    tors, 223
Sociograms, 137
Somatization, 184
Soothing materials, 105
Specific phobia, 219
Speech deficits, 174
Speech and verbalizations,
    exploration of, 180
Splitting defense, 22, 334
Spousal relationship, examina-
    tion of, 155–156
Stereotype activity, definition
    of, 325
Stereotypes/stereotyping
    avoiding ethnic categoriza-
        tion, 51
    countertransference and, 57
    identification/awareness of,
        41–42
Stereotypic movement disorder,
    218, 224
Stimulus-specific countertrans-
    ference, 15
Storytelling
    application to child therapy/
        counseling, 303–310
    communication about the
        self through, 302–303
    conceptual background of,
        300–303
    cultural beliefs, values, and
        knowledge transmitted
        through, 301–302
    family lore, values and wis-
        dom transmitted through,
        302
    during intake session, 159

mutual technique of. *See*
    Mutual storytelling tech-
    nique
    nonintrusive/nonobvious
        nature of, 304–305
    personal purposes of, 302–303
    practical implementation of,
        312–317
    projective testing and, 205
    technique variations for,
        310–312
    themes, 304–311
    therapy stories, 305–310
Stress disorders, 219–220
Structure and release theories of
    play, 285–286
Structure, lack of, 153
Structured developmental his-
    tory, 188
Student observation system, 188
Stuttering, 215
Substance-induced anxiety/
    sleep disorders, 219–220
Suicidal ideation, 117, 210, 219,
    223
Symbolic modeling, 363–364
Symbols/symbolism
    in art, 325, 334–335
    in child communication, 30,
        158
    in play, 277, 280, 289
    in toys, 94, 96
Sympathy vs. empathy, 23
Symptoms
    as catalyst for change,
        264–266
    in conflict model of pathol-
        ogy, 282–283
    reinforcing/perpetuating,
        225–226
    understanding vs. confronta-
        tion of, 265
Syntax rules, childhood devel-
    opment of, 70
Systematic desensitization pro-
    grams, 355–357, 368

Talking, Feeling, Doing Game,
    106, 159
Talking/Listening Game, 106
Tape recorders, 106
*Tarasoff v. Regents of the University
    of California*, 116

Teachers
    communicating with, 172
    countertransference, 25–26
    rating scales, 188
    report form, 187
    stance, 8
Tell-Me-A-Story (TEMAS), 205
Termination, 29, 309–310, 322,
    339
Tests/testing
    achievement, 190–193
    of cognitive abilities, 193
    intelligence, 186, 193–197
    mental status examinations,
        178
    projective, 200–205
    See also Assessment
Theft, dealing with, 273–275
Thematic Apperception Test,
    Children's Apperception
    Test-Animal, and Chil-
    dren's Apperception Test-
    Human, 204
Therapeutic by-products, 266
Therapeutic environment. *See*
    Environment
Therapeutic modalities, cultural
    differences in choice of, 49
Therapeutic play. *See* Play; Play
    therapy
Therapeutic relationships
    child focus in, 251
    creation of, 251–255
    empathy and understanding
        in, 255–256
    methods and levels of
        explaining in, 256–260
    physical touch in, 252–253
    reassurance and comfort in,
        251–252
    respect in, 252
    transference in, 253–255
Therapeutic style, and choice of
    clothing, 13–14
Therapists
    evoked feelings of, 33
    reassurance and comfort
        from, 251–252
    self-disclosure issues, 269
    See also Child clinicians
Therapy
    disclosure function of play
        in, 280

healing function of play in, 281–282
phases of, 241–247
setting limits in, 160–161, 249
stories, nature and themes of, 305–310
unconventional spaces for, 89–90
See also Counseling process; Child therapy/counseling
Therapy room
    checklist of toys and materials for, 97
    location of, 86–87
    placement/location of, 86–87
    safety in design of, 86
Tic disorders, 174, 217
Time, sense of, 32
Time-out, 3152, 58–360
Token economies, 360–363, 369
Tools for change, 247–266. *See also* Catalysts for change
Touch, physical, 56, 252–253
Tourette's disorder, 217
Toys
    choosing for the client's benefit, 96–97
    construction-related, 102–103
    creative, 101–102
    culturally appropriate, 93–94
    dolls/dollhouses, ethnic doll families, 99–100
    essential, checklist of, 97–98
    extras unique to individuals, 105–106
    games, therapeutic use of, 106
    meaningful selection of, 92–93
    multiple-use, 94–95
    nurturing, 101
    pretend play materials, 104–105
    promoting creativity, 94
    promoting self-expression, 93–94
    puppets, 98–99, 258
    safety of, 95
    school figures, 100–101
    societal consensus about, 94
    symbolic value of, 94, 96
    therapeutic value of, 93, 95

Training
    adequate, ethical issue of, 122
    in apperception testing, 204
    continuing education of child clinicians, 122
    culturally sensitive, 37 41, 48
    ethical, 5
    in family interventions, 5
    generalist, for adult clients/ interventions, 3–4
    in intelligence testing, 194, 196–197
    in legal issues, 5
    in neuropsychological assessment, 205–206
    professional, adequacy of, 122
    in projective testing, 201–202
    for psychological assessment, 175–176
    in psychopathology, 4
    qualifications, 4–5
    in Rorschach testing, 203
    See also Education
Trait-specific countertransference, 15–16
Transference
    cross-cultural, 57
    in psychoanalytic model of psychopathology, 283
    during the reexperience phase of counseling/therapy, 244–245
    in the therapeutic relationship, 253–255
Transient tic disorder, 217
Trauma, 20–21, 220
Treatment
    adaptability of strategies, 12
    alternative settings for, 89–90
    art reflecting progress in, 328
    behavior techniques/interventions in, 353–354
    children's and parents' expectations about, 27–28
    expected hindrances to, 234–235
    facilitated by strengths of child and family, 235
    factors affecting completion/ retention of, 378–379
    goals, 230–232

informed consent and, 111–112
    parent consultation about, 28–29
    phases of, 241–247
    planning, 222–235
    preparation for, 167–168
    records, previous, 173
    relationship function of play in, 280
    resistance to, 234–235, 265
    storytelling technique applied to. *See* Storytelling
    strategies of, 231–233
    termination of, 298–299
Treatment room, environment/ floor plan of, 87–88
Triangulation, 209–210
True-faith healer, relational pattern of, 24

UN Convention on the Rights of the Child (CRC), 108–110
Understanding, expression of, 255–256
Undoing, defensive, 184, 332
Unidentifiable but foreseeable standard, 116
United States, ethic/cultural diversity of, 36–38

Values
    family, respect for, 9
    open-mindedness about, 9
    societal, media-induced, 223
    storytelling as transmission method for, 302
    therapist's, inappropriate imposition on client, 56–57
    unmentioned, questions loaded with, 272–273
V-code diagnoses, 222
Verbal intelligence/ability, measurement of, 195
Vicarious introspection, 255
Victim, emotions relating to, 23
Vineland Adaptive Behavior Scales-II, 189–190
Vineland Social Maturity Scale, 189
Vocabulary, 195
Vocal tic disorder, 217

Vulnerabilities
    being the rescuer, 21–22
    desire to be a child again, 19
    fear of being a child again, 20
    reemergence of personal
        trauma, 20–21
    wish to caretake and protect,
        21
    wish to undo personal harm,
        20

Waiting area, design and fur-
    nishing of, 86–89

Wechsler Abbreviated Scale of
    Intelligence, 196
Wechsler Individual Achieve-
    ment Test, Second Edi-
    tion, 191–192
Wechsler Intelligence Scale for
    Children, Fourth Edition,
    196–197
Wechsler Preschool and Pri-
    mary Scale of Intelligence,
    Third Edition, 197
"Why" questions, avoidance of,
    158

Wide Range Achievement Test,
    Fourth Edition, 192–193
Withdrawal, 184
Woodcock-Johnson III Norma-
    tive Update Complete, 193
Woodcock-Johnson Psycho-
    Educational Battery, 193
Written expression disorder, 215

Youth self-report, 185

Zeckhausen, D., 88
Zeitgeist, 223